Textbook on Administrative Law

Textbook on
Administrative Law

....

Eighth Edition

Peter Leyland

Professor of Law, SOAS, University of London

Gordon Anthony

Professor of Public Law, Queen's University, Belfast; Barrister-at-Law

OXFORD

UNIVERSITY PRESS

OXFORD

UNIVERSITY PRESS

Great Clarendon Street, Oxford, OX2 6DP,
United Kingdom

Oxford University Press is a department of the University of Oxford.
It furthers the University's objective of excellence in research, scholarship,
and education by publishing worldwide. Oxford is a registered trade mark of
Oxford University Press in the UK and in certain other countries

© Peter Leyland & Gordon Anthony 2016

The moral rights of the authors have been asserted

Fifth edition 2005
Sixth edition 2008
Seventh edition 2012

Impression: 1

Public sector information reproduced under Open Government Licence v3.0
(http://www.nationalarchives.gov.uk/doc/open-government-licence/open-government-licence.htm)

Published in the United States of America by Oxford University Press
198 Madison Avenue, New York, NY 10016, United States of America

British Library Cataloguing in Publication Data
Data available

Library of Congress Control Number: 2016940663

ISBN 978–0–19–871305–0

Printed in Great Britain by
Bell & Bain Ltd., Glasgow

OUTLINE CONTENTS

DETAILED CONTENTS

6   The ombudsman principle   132

7   Dispute resolution: tribunals and inquiries   163

8   Introduction to judicial review   186

9   Extending the reach of judicial review: the public–private divide and the Royal prerogative   221

Online Resource Centre

This book is accompanied by an Online Resource Centre containing a wealth of resources designed to support your study of public law. These resources will help you to keep up-to-date with what is happening in the law and politics, as well as introducing you to key debates and providing a host of links to further material to help you direct your online study.

The following resources are all available on the site free of charge:

- **Regular updates** ensure that you are aware of key legal and political developments, and their significance to the public lawyer
- An extensive **library of web links** is an invaluable resource that directs you to further sources of information on each of the core topics usually taught as part of a public law course, including websites, audio and video clips, blogs, and journal articles
- A **timeline of key dates** in British political history provides a fascinating insight into the events that have influenced the development of constitutional and administrative law in the UK
- **'Oxford NewsNow'** RSS feeds provide constantly refreshed links to the latest relevant news stories from sources such as the Guardian and BBC News websites

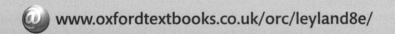

www.oxfordtextbooks.co.uk/orc/leyland8e/

PREFACE

This edition appears just over one year after the Conservative Government was formed following the 2015 general election. As with previous editions, we have sought to look back at changes that pre-dated the election as well as at those that have since been made and may yet have an impact on administrative law. The effects of cutbacks across public services remain a key matter for the administrative state, but the upcoming referendum on EU membership, coupled with debates about the Human Rights Act 1998, means that much of administrative law may be about to undergo radical transformation. This is in addition to changes that have resulted from the Scottish independence referendum of 2014, including the controversial EVEL reform of legislative procedure at Westminster and the staggered introduction of a layer of Mayors and citywide government in some parts of England.

As with earlier editions, a substantial proportion of the book is devoted to analysing the pivotal area of judicial review. The case law here has continued to change rapidly and there have been many important judgments. Those that we analyse include: *Imperial Tobacco v Lord Advocate*[1] (on the legislative powers of the Scottish Parliament); *Pham v Home Secretary*[2] (on the legal basis of EU membership); *R (Nicklinson) v Ministry of Justice*[3] (on declarations of incompatibility under the Human Rights Act 1998); *Bank Mellat v HM Treasury (No 2)*[4] (on proportionality, and procedural fairness); *Michael v Chief Constable of South Wales Police*[5] (on the negligence liability of the police); *Keyu v Foreign Secretary*[6] (on the retrospective effect of the Human Rights Act 1998, and the relationship between *Wednesbury* and proportionality); and *Sandiford v Foreign Secretary*[7] (on the Royal prerogative).

Readers familiar with our book will see that the sequence of chapters for this edition is the same as that which we used in the seventh edition. After a general introduction and consideration of the constitutional context, attention is devoted to supranational questions relating to EU law in an administrative law context and human rights law, before we discuss the nature of the modern administrative state.

The text then turns more specifically to the crucial issue of the different levels of legal accountability by reference to what we continue to term a 'grievance chain'. The remedies provided to citizens by the various ombudsmen and tribunals and inquiries are assessed, before the focus turns to detailed consideration of judicial review and the wider role of the courts. We begin by considering both procedural issues and the reach of judicial review (and some factors that tend to limit its availability) before moving on to cover the grounds of judicial review. The heads of illegality, irrationality, and procedural impropriety elaborated by Lord Diplock in

---

[1] [2012] UKSC 61, 2013 SC (UKSC) 153.
[2] [2015] UKSC 19, [2015] 1 WLR 1591.
[3] [2014] UKSC 38, [2015] AC 657.
[4] [2013] UKSC 39, [2014] AC 700.
[5] [2015] UKSC 2, [2015] AC 1732.
[6] [2015] UKSC 69, [2015] 3 WLR 1665.
[7] [2014] UKSC 44, [2014] 1 WLR 2697.

the *GCHQ* case, together now with proportionality, continue to be a useful method of organising the discussion of the established grounds of review, while the chapters on equality and legitimate expectation reflect the increased prominence of these grounds of review. Procedural impropriety is then examined in two chapters on, respectively, statutory requirements and the common law rules of fairness. The remainder of the book covers remedies and the contractual and tortious liability of public bodies. Our final chapter seeks to draw together the strands in the light of current debates and come to some general conclusions relating to the current state of administrative law.

Terry Woods conceived the idea of this textbook on administrative law with Peter back in 1992 but decided that he did not wish to continue his involvement as co-author following completion of the fourth edition. We would like to acknowledge his enormous contribution to this project over the years. At OUP, we extend many thanks to Tom Young, Janine Fisher, Anna Foning, and Fiona Tatham for their hard work and support in the preparation of this edition.

Peter would like to thank Nicholas Bamforth, Andrew Harding, Sebastian Payne, Nicola Lupo, Paul O'Connell, and Alison Riley for general discussion, help and advice on legal issues.

Peter would like to thank his wife Putachad for her fantastic support and encouragement during the preparation of all editions of the book.

Gordon would like to thank friends and colleagues in the School of Law at Queen's: Jack Anderson, Brice Dickson, Natasa Mavronicola, Chris McCrudden, Kieran McEvoy, John Morison, and Sal Wheeler. He dedicates the book to Jill, Emily, Louis, Ben, and Toby.

The law is stated as on 4 May 2016.

Peter Leyland and Gordon Anthony

TABLE OF CASES

TABLE OF LEGISLATION

Other National Legislation

GLOSSARY OF TERMS

This glossary contains some of the important terminology which is central to understanding the subject and which appears in the pages that follow, particularly in the chapters dealing with judicial review. It should be noted that the Civil Procedure Rules (CPR), introduced in England and Wales in 2000, renamed certain central elements, including the designation of the Administrative Court and the names of the prerogative remedies.

Administrative Court Office (ACO) The name under the Civil Procedure Rules (CPR) for the old **Crown Office List**. The Administrative Court is the specialist court dealing with judicial review, located within the Queen's Bench Division of the High Court.

applicant Under the old Order 53 procedure the party who applied for judicial review (now known under CPR as the claimant).

audi alteram partem (hear the other side) One of the rules of natural justice/fairness. At its height, means that individuals should have an opportunity to be heard in relation to decisions that are going to affect them.

certiorari Originally a writ directed at an inferior court commanding it to certify some judicial matter, now used under the judicial review procedure to review and quash the decisions of inferior courts, tribunals, and other public decision-makers. (Now known as a **quashing order**—see below).

claim An action in the courts for judicial review is now defined as: 'claim to review the lawfulness of: (i) an enactment; or (ii) a decision, action or failure to act in relation to the exercise of a public function'.

claimant This is the party under CPR who makes a claim for judicial review, formerly known as the applicant (and see defendant below).

declarations of incompatibility These may be made under section 4 of the Human Rights Act 1998 where a court is unable to read an Act of the Westminister Parliament, or certain forms of *subordinate legislation*, in a way that is compatible with the European Convention on Human Rights. In order not to interfere with the doctrine of Parliamentary sovereignty the contested measure remains in force after the declaration of incompatibility has been issued.

defendant The party against whom a claim for judicial review is made (see claimant above).

delegatus non potest delegare (a delegate cannot delegate) A legal principle in some areas of public law whereby a minister/official/person on whom a power has been conferred may not inappropriately delegate the exercise of that power. See, most famously, *Carltona Ltd v Commissioner of Works* [1943] 2 All ER 560.

discovery This is now termed disclosure. It is the procedure that allows a party to discover the evidence held by the other side.

estoppel This is a rule of evidence that prevents a person denying the truth of a statement he has made previously. A form of promissory estoppel had historically been applied in some public law cases where there had been a clear statement of fact or assurance by a public authority that a person had acted upon which had subsequently been withdrawn. Such cases are now dealt with under the doctrine of legitimate expectation.

ex parte (on behalf of) It is now termed under CPR 'without notice'. It can mean either a claim/application (i) by a person who is not an interested party, or (ii) in the absence of the other side.

injunction (interim relief) This remedy allows the court, in judicial review proceedings, to require the defendant authority to refrain from some action, or to undertake some action.

interim injunction (interlocutory injunction) Not final, granted to preserve the status quo until the case is heard on its merits. See *American Cyanamid Co v Ethicon Ltd* [1975] AC 396.

intra vires Within its powers/within its jurisdiction.

jurisdiction The power that a court has to decide cases or entertain matters.

jurisdictional error Can be a ground for intervention in judicial review, i.e., when a body purports to exercise a jurisdiction it does not have, or fails to exercise a jurisdiction it does possess. Now almost wholly displaced by the *ultra vires* doctrine (below).

justiciable Suited to determination by a court of law.

leave Judicial review is a two-stage process. An applicant under Order 53 was originally required to obtain leave from a High Court judge before a full hearing. This initial stage, under the CPR, is now called 'permission'. (See also permission.)

mandatory order (*mandamus*) A remedy under the judicial review procedure which compels a public decision-maker to perform a public duty.

nemo judex in causa sua potest (no man shall be a judge in his own cause) A rule of natural justice/fairness which prevents a person who is, or may reasonably be thought to be, biased from determining a matter.

nullity Invalid; having no force or effect.

Order 53 An application/claim for judicial review was made under the old Order 53 of the Rules of the Supreme Court, subsequently enacted as the Supreme Court Act 1981, section 31 (now Senior Courts Act 1981). This was replaced in 2000 by

Part 54 of the Civil Procedure Rules, which is almost identical in its practical effects to the old Order 53.

permission The first stage in making a claim for judicial review under the Civil Procedure Rules. See also 'leave' above.

prerogative writs This term refers to the remedies of quashing order (*certiorari*), mandatory order (*mandamus*), prohibiting order (prohibition), and habeas corpus.

prohibiting order (formerly prohibition) A remedy available under the judicial review procedure which serves to prevent a body undertaking any action which is beyond its power.

quashing order Originally the writ of *certiorari*, the new terminology was introduced in the CPR. However its function remains the same. It can thus be directed at an inferior court commanding it to certify some judicial matter, or be based under the judicial review procedure to review and quash the decisions of inferior courts, tribunals, and other public decision-makers (see also *certiorari*).

severance This can arise when there is question of partial invalidity, e.g., with regard to delegated legislation. The court may be required to decide if the invalid part can be separated (severed) from the valid part, which can be allowed to stand. See *DPP v Hutchinson* [1990] 2 AC 783.

standing (*locus standi*) Senior Courts Act 1981, section 31(3) provides that 'No application for judicial review shall be made unless the [permission] of the High Court has been obtained in accordance with the rules of the court; and the court shall not grant [permission] to make such an application unless it considers that the [claimant] has a sufficient interest in the matter to which the application relates.' Note that, under section 7 of the Human Rights Act 1998 the test for standing is somewhat narrower in that 'sufficient interest' becomes that of 'victim' in line with the Strasbourg jurisprudence.

ultra vires (beyond the power) The principle of *ultra vires* is central to judicial review; it means that if an authority acts beyond the powers legally conferred upon it, its action will be unlawful and that a remedy may issue.

void Having no legal effect and incapable of being valid.

void ab initio Void from the beginning; as if it never existed.

voidable Capable of being declared void. This arises where there is a right to challenge a rule, act, decision, etc., but until this is done it will continue to have full effect. A term that is more of historical, than contemporary, relevance.

without notice Formerly *ex parte*. See above.

1

···

Introduction: theory and history

1.1 **Introduction**

In the late Victorian era, AV Dicey, whom some continue to regard as the foremost authority on English constitutional law of his time, believed that administrative law (as he conceived it to be on the Continent) should have no place in the British Constitution. Indeed, M Barthelemy, Dean of the Law Faculty of Paris University, recounts that, while spending a weekend with Dicey, he asked him about the status of administrative law in England. Dicey retorted: 'In England we know nothing of administrative law; and we wish to know nothing.' To the contrary, today it is generally acknowledged that administrative law not only exists—some say that it has, in fact, existed for centuries[1]—but that it has grown enormously in scope and significance. Textbooks and articles are regularly published and widely disseminated. Judges are assigned specifically to the Administrative Court to hear judicial review cases, in effect becoming specialists in the field. Why has this area of law emerged from the shadows of obscurity? A first clue to answering this question must lie in the topicality of the issues with which it is so often concerned. Significant cases come before the courts on a regular basis and are assigned a prominent place in newspapers and on television. The focus of publicity is in large measure because these cases often involve clarifying the relationship between the state (however measured and defined) and the individual in important areas of our lives, regarding matters of concern to us all. Other, and more important, answers to this question will emerge during the course of our discussion below.

1.2 **Definition**

First we must ask another question: What is administrative law? Normally, it is regarded as the area of law concerned with the control of governmental powers. In real terms, these refer to powers derived from, or duties imposed by, statute law (primary and subordinate/delegated); the Royal prerogative; and legislation of various forms emanating from the European Union (EU). One key function of administrative law is thus to control decision-making on the basis of these powers,

---

1 e.g., P Craig, *UK, EU and Global Administrative Law: Foundations and Challenges* (Cambridge: Cambridge University Press, 2015), ch 1.

whether at the level of central government, at the level of devolved government, at the level of local government, or where other bodies such as the police make decisions in relation to individuals. It embodies general principles which can be applied to the exercise of the powers and duties of authorities in order to ensure that the myriad of rules and discretionary powers available to the executive and other public decision-makers conform to basic standards of legality and fairness. The ostensible purpose of these principles is to ensure that, as well as observance of the rule of law, there is accountability, transparency, and effectiveness in the exercise of power in the public domain.

By now it will already be apparent that this is a very large arena. Unfortunately, there is no universally accepted method of dividing it up, of objectively segregating one area of concern from another. Nevertheless, for convenience sake, we can list those activities that it conventionally concerns as including social security, health, housing, planning, education, immigration, the exercise of powers by central and local government and the police, and tribunals and inquiries. You will also notice that these roughly correspond to the main activities of the modern state. Insofar as it is possible to identify a common body of principles and procedures that apply in these areas, such principles, taken together, form the basis of what we call administrative law.

1.2.1 **Functions and characteristics**

Certain functions and characteristics of administrative law flow from the above, broad, definition:

(a) It has a control function, acting in a negative sense as a brake or check in respect of the unlawful exercise or abuse of governmental/administrative power.

(b) It can have a command function by making public bodies perform their public duties, including the exercise of discretion under a statute.

(c) It embodies positive principles to facilitate good administrative practice, for example in ensuring that the rules of natural justice or fairness are adhered to.

(d) It operates to provide for accountability and transparency, including participation by interested individuals and parties in the process of government (individuals may either participate on their own—that is, as the person to be affected by a decision—or through membership of a pressure or interest group such as Greenpeace where some broader matter of public interest is involved).

(e) It may provide a remedy for grievances occasioned at the hands of public authorities.

Some of these matters will be dealt with informally through a *non-legal* remedy, for example, by an MP, a local councillor, an ombudsman, or an internal grievance procedure (such as in the NHS). But otherwise the resolution of such grievances will be by means of a *legal* remedy. The most high-profile of these is judicial review, although legal remedies may also be found in tribunal proceedings in areas that include immigration and social security. It is well worth keeping this distinction between non-legal and legal remedies in mind even though it will become apparent that, in some instances, an individual can pursue a legal remedy only after he or she has first exhausted a non-legal remedy.

1.2.2 **Examples**

The precise role of such functions as are noted in 1.2.1 can be readily illustrated by examples coming from the varied areas of public activity that will be discussed in more detail in later chapters. For the present, here are a number of questions that will give some insight into the nature of the issues that can arise:

- Was the Greater London Council (the then elected authority responsible for London-wide government) acting lawfully when it cut fares on London Transport, or was this contrary to the wider interests of ratepayers?[2]

- Can a taxi driver be deprived of his licence to operate at Heathrow because of alleged misconduct without first being given a chance to put his side of the case?[3]

- Should an elderly citizen who has been in receipt of a particular form of social care, but has had the care withdrawn, be allowed to challenge the decision?[4]

- Can parents force a local authority to keep its local schools open during a strike of ancillary workers?[5]

- What does an individual do when he or she has suffered injustice as a result of maladministration by a public body? Can an ombudsman be petitioned?[6]

- Are there any limits to the powers of the Home Office in determining who can enter the country and who can be expelled?[7]

- Can the Home Secretary, when ordering the deportation of an asylum seeker, ignore the authority of the High Court with impunity?[8]

- Is a prisoner serving a life sentence entitled to know the reasons why the penal element of his sentence has been set at a particular level?[9]

- Is a local authority entitled to ban deer hunting on moral grounds?[10]

- Could a woman use the frozen semen of her husband for the purpose of conceiving a child, despite the fact that he had not given written consent before he died?[11]

- Was a former military dictator and Head of State immune from prosecution for crimes against humanity?[12]

---

2 *Bromley London Borough Council v GLC* [1983] 1 AC 768, at 11.5.2.

3 *Cinnamond v British Airports Authority* [1980] 1 WLR 582.

4 *R (McDonald) v Royal Borough of Kensington and Chelsea* [2011] UKSC 33, [2011] 4 All ER 881, at 11.5.1.

5 *Meade v Haringey London Borough Council* [1979] 2 All ER 1016, at 11.4.1.1.

6 Ch 6.

7 *R (WL) v Home Secretary* [2011] UKSC 12; [2012] 1 AC 245.

8 *M v Home Office* [1994] 1 AC 377, at chs 3 and 18.

9 *R v Secretary of State for the Home Department, ex p Doody* [1993] 3 All ER 92, at 17.3.5.

10 *R v Somerset County Council, ex p Fewings* [1994] 3 All ER 20, at 11.4.1.1.

11 *R v Human Fertilisation and Embryology Authority, ex p Blood* [1997] 2 All ER 687.

12 *R v Bow Street Metropolitan Stipendiary Magistrates, ex p Pinochet Ugarte (No 3)* [1999] 2 WLR 827, at 17.4.2.2.

- Could a British woman who had been sentenced to death in Indonesia for drugs offences challenge the government's policy whereby it did not provide funding for legal representation in overseas trials?[13]

- Is there an absolute right to the assumed confidentiality of privileged legal correspondence?[14]

- Could a newspaper use the Freedom of Information Act 2000 to gain access to letters that Prince Charles had written to government ministers?[15]

- Were the provisions of the Anti-Terrorism, Crime and Security Act 2001 that provided for the indefinite detention of foreign nationals suspected of terrorism compatible with the European Convention on Human Rights (ECHR)?[16]

- Was a school's admission policy unlawful because it favoured applications from pupils who were either the blood descendants of Jewish mothers or who had undertaken a qualifying course of Orthodox conversion?[17]

- Was the uniform policy of a school which prevented a Muslim girl from wearing her preferred form of religious dress an unlawful violation of her right to manifest her religious beliefs under Article 9 of the ECHR?[18]

The legal implications of all these matters have been the concern of administrative law. In each case it has been necessary to adjudicate between competing interests in the community and to determine questions about the reach of legal rules, principles, and discretion. As will become apparent in later chapters, the answers to these questions reveal much about the workings of the modern administrative state, whether as regards housing, prison discipline, social security, access to information, and so on.

1.3 **Law and context**

It is sometimes asserted that 'Behind every theory of administrative law lies a theory of the state'.[19] We would strongly endorse this view. In fact, this is another reason why we believe that a broad definition of the subject is most helpful to the student. Any implicit background assumption that society or the public interest can be conceived of as a non-contentious, unified, and homogeneous whole is not acceptable. Rather, when assessing the role of administrative law it is of crucial importance to recognise whose standpoint is being adopted. Through whose eyes are we surveying the terrain? To resolve this, it is necessary to attempt to answer certain fundamental questions: What is administrative law being required to do? What specific tasks is it capable of performing? Whose interests is it really serving?

---

13 *R (Sandiford) v Secretary of State for Foreign and Commonwealth Affairs* [2014] UKSC 44, [2014] 1 WLR 2697, at 9.3.2.2.

14 *R (Daly) v Secretary of State for the Home Department* [2001] 2 WLR 1622, at 13.6.1.

15 *R (Evans) v Attorney General* [2015] UKSC 21, [2015] AC 1787.

16 *A v Home Secretary* [2005] 2 AC 68, at 4.4.3 and 13.6.3.1.

17 *R (E) v Governing Body and the Admissions Appeal Panel of JFS* [2009] UKSC 15; [2010] 2 AC 728, at 14.5.

18 *R (SB) v Headteacher and Governors of Denbigh High School* [2007] 1 AC 100, at 13.6.1.

19 C Harlow and R Rawlings, *Law and Administration*, 3rd edn (Cambridge: Cambridge University Press, 2009), 1.

In providing answers to these questions, we start by recognising that *any* system of law operates in a pluralistic society, one comprised of a multitude of public bodies, institutions, and interests. It is made up of individuals who have interests associated with their profession or occupation, their class or ethnicity; individuals who hold varied political and social opinions. These include politicians, public servants, and judges, as well as citizens (satisfied or aggrieved) who end up on the receiving end of the decision-making process. Each belongs to the same society, composed of many (sometimes antagonistic) sectional interests. If we accept this, it follows that there can be no single, coherent perspective which underpins public law, in either theory or practice. As we proceed, it will become increasingly evident to the attentive reader that these varied perspectives colour both the formulation of the law and the decisions that emanate from the courts and other public bodies.

Administrative law, then, has developed against this background; and it is not to be regarded as an autonomous discipline which can be satisfactorily studied as a set of self-contained rules on its own black letter terms, as some might argue. As a practice, law (including administrative law) is part of the prevailing and constantly changing and developing currents of thought and life which at any one time contribute to the formation and maintenance of society.

1.4 Red and green light perspectives

The role of law in the modern state is evidently a complex one. So, how can a student approaching it for the first time make sense of it all? For our purposes it is helpful to consider how current legal thought and practice crystallises around two contrasting models that have been labelled by Harlow and Rawlings as the 'red light' and 'green light' theories of administrative law.[20] Although the theories do not exist in isolation from another, the former theory is generally regarded as conservative in thrust and focused upon the judicial control of public power, while the latter is seen as more liberal/social democratic in orientation and facilitative in nature. Each theory has developed in tandem with the emergence of the modern state and they serve to describe what administrative law *is* and also to tell us what law's role in society *ought* to be (a normative dimension concerned with political morality). However, in using the terms we should emphasise that this is how *we* view the red light and green light theories and that it should not be supposed that Harlow and Rawlings use them in exactly the same way as we do or, indeed, that they would necessarily share our approach. We therefore use the theories not to provide definitive statements about what happens in any circumstances where lawyers and judges make decisions but rather to describe what, in the real world of everyday legal activity, is a continuum of assumptions ranging from red light at one end of the spectrum to green light at the other.

1.4.1 Red light theory

The red light theory can be seen to originate from the *laissez-faire* political tradition of the nineteenth century. It embodied a deep-rooted suspicion of governmental

---

20 Ibid, ch 1.

power and sought to minimise the encroachment of the state on the rights (especially property rights) of individuals. Dicey, writing at around the turn of the twentieth century, believed that the visibly gathering momentum of 'collectivist' social legislation had a tendency to destroy the moral fibre of the nation, sapping individual initiative and enterprise. To see why this was so we must step back a little.

Dicey maintained that the concept of *legal* sovereignty (the ground rule of our constitution) favours the supremacy of law. Parliament establishes a framework of general rules in society, the executive should govern according to these rules, and, should it not do so, the courts can control the executive to ensure that it acts lawfully. Such a view is closely allied to the idea of a 'self-correcting democracy' in which all law (including administrative law, which, remember, did not exist separately from constitutional law for Dicey) is regarded as an autonomous and coherent discipline, which performs an important control function (a part of the constitutional system of 'checks and balances'). The rule of law remains the key concept, ensuring that all public and private bodies, as well as individuals, act only according to the law. The law will operate to contain illegality and abuse, but without necessarily having, or needing, an explicit moral and political foundation. There are no such special guiding principles for law in general (or administrative law in particular) as the philosophy underpinning the common law is entirely one of pragmatism, that is, of adjustment to changing circumstances. At its most basic level, then, what we have termed the Diceyan view, which is still influential in a modified form in many judicial and academic circles today, sanctions judicial intervention when, and only when, public bodies (or any other body or individual) exceed their legal powers (i.e., act *ultra vires* or abuse their powers). The corresponding assumption is that the bureaucratic and executive power of the state and its institutions would, if unchecked, threaten the liberty of us all.

There is a further problem that the red light approach seeks to overcome. In terms of the philosophy emanating from this view, we find that law is considered as having an essentially adjudicative and control function. There is an obvious reluctance to deal directly with questions of policy or merits.

The modern state, and with it all the attendant baggage of administrative procedures, guidance, and discretion was established at the same time as the emergence of party government, and obviously there have often been quite pronounced differences in ideological perspective between the main political parties as it evolved. For red light adherents the judiciary is regarded as being autonomous and impartial. It is imbued with its own standards of independence and fairness, and can be relied upon as a kind of referee to adjudicate, not on the political or even the practical validity of any decision, but simply on the legality of executive action. This has led over time to the formation and development of principles which serve to keep law out of politics, most notably '*Wednesbury* unreasonableness'/'irrationality'.[21] However, this only works on the strongly contested assumption that the law *can* stand aside from politics and morality, a matter that was discussed by the courts when rejecting an attempt by a local authority to ban deer hunting.[22] It is also worth pointing out that such an approach

---

21 See ch 13.
22 *R v Somerset County Council, ex p Fewings* [1995] 3 All ER 20.

starts from a premise of seemingly endorsing a narrow caste of judicial mind. The main function of the judiciary is perceived as interpreting and applying the strict letter of the law. This, it is argued, serves the needs of the legal profession well by perpetuating a separation of law from policy issues, with the emphasis being placed on the strict construction of statutes or rules in isolation from their broader contextual framework.

However, today even those lawyers and academics holding a broadly red light perspective would not accept Dicey's view in its purest form, that is, that the liberty of the citizen is threatened by a developing system of administrative law, evolving co-terminously with the conferment of certain special powers on ministers and officials. This is not least because it is self-evident that the evolution of such a system has occurred during the twentieth century without apparent erosion of liberty or justice. Rather, the danger is now more accurately perceived as being that ministers and officials might tend to shelter behind a body of rules and delegated powers which have been created to facilitate the tasks of administration. Thus it is that, in a negative sense, judicial intervention becomes possible as a kind of safety net, by taking up the democratic slack in those areas where Parliamentary control is manifestly found wanting, or by being activated during those periods when Parliamentary opposition is regarded as being weak and ineffective. Red light assumptions can be identified in decisions displaying a natural resistance to executive discretion, whenever or wherever this appears to fall outside the law as enacted by Parliament. This view, which regards administrative law as having emerged as a system of independent legal principles evolved through the common law, fractured alike from political theory and social context, is an attitude which has left us without a proper *tradition* of administrative law. The unfortunate result, at least until recent decades, of this reluctance to accept the need for change was a lack of response to the growing evidence of abuse of power in both central and local government. On the other hand, in comparable nations we have seen administrative law being developed and systematically applied as a set of principles on a general basis, most notably in France.[23]

1.4.2 **Green light theory**

The green light perspective (also referred to as functionalism) starts from the standpoint of a more positive, largely social democratic, view of the state, one which impliedly introduces a political and sociological context into law. It is a position which in essence derives from the utilitarian tradition (usually associated with Bentham and Mill and the Fabian Society founded in 1884), the moral imperative being to promote the greatest good for the greatest number, in this case by means of egalitarian and ameliorative social reform. A priority in achieving this objective is to encourage the contribution of the state, regarded as an effective means of facilitating the delivery of communitarian goals. It does this by assuming responsibility for at least basic minimum standards of provision, including housing, education, health, social security, and local services. The emergence of

---

23 See N Brown and J Bell, *French Administrative Law*, 5th edn (Oxford: Oxford University Press, 1998).

administrative law as we know it today not only coincides with the political and economic changes that have witnessed the development of the modern state, but is inseparably linked to these changes. The expansion of the state has given rise to the centralisation of powers in some areas, for instance central government, the civil service, agencies (such as the UK Border Agency), and quasi-government bodies; and the broad territorial diffusion of power in others, for example, the emergence of local government in the nineteenth and twentieth centuries, and the creation of devolved legislatures in Northern Ireland, Scotland, and Wales. In sum, power that is exercised by public bodies has greatly expanded; accordingly, the mechanisms for accountability have assumed a new importance, particularly since the 1960s.

The liberal and democratic socialist theorists coming from the green light stable, for example, Jennings, Griffiths, Robson, and Laski, broadly supported the introduction of policies aiming to develop public service provision.[24] It has been an equally important objective to establish organised institutions which are properly accountable but at the same time capable of delivering these services effectively. Law is perceived as a useful weapon, an enabling tool. In particular, legislation is something very concrete and it can provide, in principle at least, the proper authority and framework with which to govern consensually. There is the acknowledgment that it is very much more difficult to achieve an adequate and sustainable provision of services without having the law on your side. Law, in the form of legislation, thus comes to embody, in equal measure, both political legitimacy and moral persuasiveness.

However, while there has been a growth of service provision and of bureaucracy in the public domain, and with it a proliferation of delegated legislation, administrative rules, codes, and circulars, many argue that the emergence of strong party government (or 'elective dictatorship') has meant, at the same time, that Parliament no longer operates as anything like an adequate forum of accountability. This is largely because it has generally failed to provide effective mechanisms for scrutiny of the executive.[25] As citizens, what rights do we have in the face of omnipresent central and local government powers or, indeed, the powers exercised by bodies now in the private sector, for example privatised utilities? One response has been to build into the decision-making process certain rights, and a degree of participation by the citizen. We can see a reflection of this in the growth of administrative tribunals and, perhaps to a lesser extent, in proposals centring upon freedom of information and informal dispute resolution mechanisms such as Citizens' Charters, Tenants' Charters, etc. Here the central concern has been the conferral of social welfare rights and a general empowerment of individuals in regard to the exercise of powers by public bodies.[26] Equally, green light advocates might wish to see the grounds of review in the courts developed to be more precisely focused on the detailed workings of particular administrative structures, for example in the areas of social security or immigration control. Additional rights and powers to work through tribunals might be advocated, as these bodies can act as decision-makers/facilitators, as well as encouraging

---

24 See further Harlow and Rawlings, n 19.
25 See ch 2.
26 See generally M Adler (ed), *Administrative Justice in Context* (Oxford: Hart Publishing, 2010).

internal dispute resolution. We can see that this view implicitly challenges and corrects some of the misconceptions that may arise from the red light view. It does this by adopting an instrumental approach (i.e., it concentrates on effectiveness) as opposed to a pragmatic one. Administrative law becomes accepted as part of the total apparatus of government, not something largely distinct from it. It can be made to act as a regulator and facilitator to enable social policy to be implemented effectively and fairly.

Despite this apparent coherence of objectives, it is clear that establishing such mechanisms does not necessarily overcome problems in administration. Thus where tribunals exist they may be too formal, result in excessive delay, and provide inadequate representation. Many of the same criticisms can be levelled at judicial review where this is available. Indeed, the courts are regarded as being far from ideally suited or equipped to perform a role as overseer and regulator. In general the judges have no training or knowledge of public administration, and yet they are still frequently called upon to make decisions which may have far-reaching implications in the public sphere. Perhaps even more crucially, the judiciary is not in any sense accountable. Not only is it unelected, but the consequences of judgments can serve to undermine the legitimacy of decisions made by democratically elected politicians.[27] The procedural training of lawyers can easily come into conflict with the policy choices of politicians. The result of this disquiet at the role of the judiciary, in particular, is that green light theorists usually prefer to endorse democratic, political control over judicial control. They might well see such dangers as supporting the case for modification, or more far-reaching reform, of the present system of administrative law. In some areas this could lead to a more limited role for the courts; nevertheless, any changes should not be an excuse for neglecting the provision of both formal and informal means of redress that are available to the citizen, for instance the option of a complaint to the ombudsman.[28]

Yet another matter for those concerned about accountability is that of ensuring that a full range of interests is being represented in the process of administration. This brings us back to our complex and pluralistic society, comprised of many 'lobby' or interest groups which are specifically organised to bend the ears of officialdom. How does one avoid establishing a system which, while encouraging participation in general, in practice favours narrow vested interests? The question for the green light approach here essentially becomes one of which groups of citizens are going to be regarded as part of the community, as it is defined at any one time. For example, one issue that has previously given rise to much controversy is the work of the Child Support Agency. This is because it can be unclear whether children, male parents, or female parents benefit most from such a scheme. Indeed, from a different viewpoint, one might wonder whether it is middle class parents as opposed to parents receiving state benefits who gain most from such initiatives. The positions of the Child Poverty Action Group, women's groups, and men's groups may all have been canvassed in drawing up the rules, but inevitably some of the groups felt aggrieved at the outcome, notwithstanding the consultation attendant on the process. There is, in truth, no ideal (balanced) outcome waiting to

27 See ch 13.
28 See ch 6.

be discovered. The attainable objective, in an imperfect world, would be for legal principles to be developed as part of administrative law so that any rules that are formed act as a facilitator for good, democratic decision-making and not as a potentially over-intrusive obstructor to it.

Lastly, it will be clear that the green light position has historically been based on the assumption that large scale government is a permanent feature of modern society. But is this still true given current governmental policies on the reduction of public debt and the size of the state? Indeed, even before the great government cut-backs that began after the election of 2010, there had already been a fundamental challenge to this assumption, with a widespread tendency towards promoting agency status for many central government functions through what was called the 'Next Steps' initiative, the privatisation of many services that were once in the public sector, and the development of public–private partnerships. That said, the question of ownership and the precise status of any public body might be considered to be a matter of subsidiary importance. A green light theorist might still be concerned to enquire whether any of these changes have lessened the need for accountability and for participation by interested parties. Moreover, it may be that recent trends will only increase the pressure for new mechanisms of control or adjudication and that it will be appropriate to consider alternative ways of protecting the public from the decisions taken by nominally private bodies. Should we seek to increase the role of courts and tribunals, or should we elevate the dispute resolution role played by ombudsmen and other alternative dispute resolution mechanisms?[29]

1.4.3 A meeting point at amber?

Today there has perhaps been something of a convergence of the two basic positions, with a new balance being sought between external and internal checks on administration and leaving public administrators to do their job. This position is sometimes referred to as the *amber* light perspective, a synthesis which combines the necessity for some control over the myriad of administrative decisions with concern for setting good standards of administrative conduct, effective decision-taking, accountability, and human rights. Despite this attempt at unification there is, nevertheless, a need for some simplified criteria of rational decision-making. It remains pedagogically useful to continue to think of the process in terms of two models: the first placing the emphasis on adjudication and control; the second accepting the role of the modern administrative state as regulator and facilitator of good practice, as well as ensuring participation by interested parties. But we stress, once again, that such models are useful not as actual empirical descriptions of reality, but rather as a method of highlighting certain differences of viewpoint and assumptions underpinning legal activity and judicial decision-making. Bearing this clearly in mind as you read this book will help you to understand some of the issues and controversies which are inseparable from the study of administrative law in an era of 'reinvented government'.[30]

---

29 See chs 6 and 7.
30 On which see ch 5.

1.5 Administrative law and the origins of the modern state

We now turn, in the second part of this chapter, from debates about the theoretical or conceptual foundations of administrative law, to focus on its historical, political, and social origins. Just how did the modern administrative state emerge?

One of the first things that any student of our domestic constitutional law is taught is that the UK is a nation with an unwritten, or uncodified, constitution. For our purposes, discussing administrative law, this means that, in more senses than in almost any other country, it is possible to identify a continuum with the past. Ancient institutions and practices have become etched into the system as the foundations of the state have evolved naturally and in parallel with the common law tradition. In fact, it soon becomes very apparent to the student of the subject that contemporary administrative law can trace something of an unbroken history from the seventeenth century to the present day.[31] Indeed, certain important aspects of the current system can boast a genealogy stretching back even further, to medieval times. One might think here of the writ system that has its origins in that period and, moreover, of the rules of natural justice that emerged at that time.

We must look (albeit very selectively) at some of these developments. First of all, it is important to remember that medieval monarchs were absolute (or near absolute) rulers, primarily concerned with raising taxation and dealing with the administration of affairs of state. Early parliaments had a very limited role in approving the raising of revenue and in responding to grievances from citizens submitted in the form of petitions, the precursors of modern legislation. In order to discharge routine matters, such as the raising of revenue and the administration of justice, a splitting of the King's Council occurred around 1200 which led to the delegation of responsibilities away from this royal council to the Exchequer. It also represented a division of functions, with certain important matters being left to judicial members of the Council, which later became the King's Bench. One task that it assumed became the supervisory (i.e., inherent common law, not statutory) jurisdiction of inferior courts and tribunals. Here also lie the origins of the prerogative writs which operated in order to issue commands and to compel attendance of subjects before the King. These were the direct precursors of the remedies of *certiorari*, *prohibition*, and *mandamus* (now renamed as a quashing order, a prohibiting order, and a mandatory order respectively), which later became more widely employed to review decisions of inferior (subordinate) courts.

How was government and administration, insofar as it existed, put into practice? Justices of the peace emerged in medieval times as the executive agents of the monarch throughout the country. They were given statutory power to maintain law and order by the Justices of the Peace Act 1361. But in addition to this better-known criminal jurisdiction, they acquired many administrative and governmental responsibilities. In the allocation of these powers, it is noticeable that, even at this early period, there was a significant overlap of judicial and administrative functions. The justices effectively acted as courts as well as administrators. Further centralisation of the state took place as Tudor monarchs, such as Henry VIII, set about strengthening their position as rulers. To achieve this effectively, a means of

---

31 See further Craig, n 1.

enforcement was required to ensure that policies were properly implemented on a nationwide basis, and wider control of the justices was exercised by the King's Bench using the writ system.

The next steps of which we need to take account are the challenges to the absolute executive authority of the monarch. In fact, the concentration of power in the hands of the monarchy that occurred during the Tudor and Stuart periods had been reined in before the close of the seventeenth century. Indeed, even before the Civil War of the 1640s the courts were already signalling their concerns about the untrammelled exercise of the prerogative power. The case of *Prohibitions del Roy*[32] asserted that personal adjudication by the King was no longer possible, while the *Case of Proclamations*[33] restricted the right of the King to create new offences. Although these cases are cited as evidence of the limitation of Royal prerogative powers, for a time James I, and later Charles I, operated by alternative means of dubious legality. One such vehicle was the Court of Star Chamber, which gained a particularly controversial reputation through its inquisitorial procedures and its politically charged judgments. The rise of the Court of Star Chamber also saw the temporary disappearance of much of the executive power that had previously been in the hands of the Privy Council. A backlash was not long in coming. By the time the Court of Star Chamber was abolished in 1640, the constitution and the nation were already deep in crisis. Within a single generation, the defeat of Charles I in the Civil War of 1642, the subsequent establishment of the Protectorate of Oliver Cromwell, the overthrow of James II followed by the 'Glorious Revolution' of 1688, had led to what was to prove an irrevocable shift of power away from monarchical government. By the enactment of the Bill of Rights in 1688/89, Parliament gradually gained supreme, sovereign legislative authority. Ministers now had to account to Parliament for their actions, and this led to the development of a recognisable form of individual ministerial responsibility. In sum, we have seen a transition from an era when absolute monarchs sought to assert their authority on a nationwide basis by means of mechanisms which had been put in place to facilitate the exercise of executive and administrative power; at the same time, we have observed the emergence of a supervisory jurisdiction of the courts, capable of acting as a modest, but real, counterbalance to the use of these powers. The outcome of these events also resulted in the eventual victory of nascent parliamentary government.

1.5.1 Law and the reality of the modern administrative state

As we consider the steps that were taken towards the development of a recognisably modern system of central and local government, it will be apparent that the courts have consistently responded, after some delay, by modifying the remedies available to them to deal with changes in administrative practice that were already underway. The justices of the peace retained an important role in the eighteenth century as the predecessors of modern local government. Indeed, at the commencement of the nineteenth century the power to discharge governmental

---

32 (1607) 12 Co Rep 63.
33 (1611) 12 Co Rep 74.

functions, insofar as they had developed, was still mainly in their hands. But by the end of the nineteenth century the justices had been largely replaced by elected authorities. The Municipal Corporations Act 1835 was one early step in establishing a system of reformed local authorities which gradually acquired the responsibilities of their modern counterparts. The reorganisations that occurred later were to lead to a progressively wider range of powers and functions being delegated to local authorities and to statutory boards, for example, school boards.

How accountable were these bodies? First, appellate procedures were sometimes provided for under statute. This meant that it was possible, in recognised circumstances, to challenge decisions before a higher authority, which could retake the decision or grant a remedy to the individual (as appropriate). In other words, a decision of the justices, and later of local authorities, could be subject to control on the basis provided for in the relevant statute. The Quarter Sessions (a jurisdiction which now lies with the Crown Court) dealt with many of these appeals (the Crown Court still does in some cases, a good example being in regard to licensing functions). Secondly, where a right of appeal was not granted, the Court of King's Bench could be called upon to decide on the extent of any powers that had been conferred on the justices (and later the boards and local authorities). It was able to do this by the use of its supervisory jurisdiction. By the end of the seventeenth century, after the disintegration of the old system, the King's Bench once again assumed an important role as the old prerogative writs were further adapted to perform a supervisory function. In fact, it was already recognisable as something akin to a court of judicial review, having exclusive power to grant the prerogative remedies of *certiorari*, *prohibition*, and *mandamus*, and to award damages. The writs were a useful device that could be employed in order to dispute administrative acts in two ways: on a narrow basis, to correct an error of law on the face of the record; and much more generally, to quash convictions or orders when a body exceeded its jurisdiction (*certiorari*) or to compel the performance of a public duty (*mandamus*; *prohibition*). It was in this way that the *ultra vires* principle developed by adaptation not revolution under the aegis of the common law.

During the nineteenth century, parallel with the emergence of local government, there were steps towards the growth of a central government bureaucracy, with increased executive authority being placed in the hands of officials. The potential need for judicial intervention increased in tandem with these developments, especially in the eyes of those we have labelled as being of red light persuasion, such as Dicey, and those seeking to defend their property rights.[34] This expansion of bureaucracy became even more true as the building blocks of the modern welfare state were put into place after the end of the Second World War in 1945. At the beginning of the nineteenth century, it is striking just how limited the size of central government was by contemporary standards. In 1832, when the Great Reform Act extended the franchise and redistributed parliamentary seats, the entire civil service accounted for something like 21,000 civilians. The implementation of a stream of legislative measures, originating in the nineteenth century, led to a steady increase in the size and range of activities performed by existing government departments. It also saw the formation of several

---

34 See 1.4.1.

new departments as the old board system declined, for example the Poor Law Commission was replaced in 1847 by a ministry, while the old Board of Education was replaced by the Ministry of Education in 1944. In turn, the importance of the civil service increased, as did the sophistication of the techniques that were employed to implement complex policy measures, one example being the growth of delegated legislation. Following the Northcote-Trevelyan report of 1854, the civil service was reorganised on a professional footing with officials being recruited by professional examinations. The trend towards large-scale government gathered momentum even more rapidly during the twentieth century. For example, old age pensions were introduced in 1908 and, following the publication of the Beveridge Report in 1942, a universal system of healthcare and social security became a reality. At the same time, different types of tribunals were introduced in some areas to assist in the implementation of policy. A measure of the expansion of central government was that the number of civil servants had risen to 50,000 by 1900; by 1980 the figure had reached well over half a million. More recently, this trend has been reversed, a change that has gained pace since the introduction of large-scale public spending cuts since 2010. Historically, the size of government coincided with a large increase in the size of public expenditure's share of the total gross national product (GNP). In the late nineteenth century it was only around 10 per cent of GNP; by 2002 it was not far from 50 per cent. The amount of legislation passing through Parliament each year has also increased: from hundreds of pages to thousands of pages today.

1.5.2 Accountability and the administrative state

The upshot of this very brief survey of the development of the modern administrative state is to emphasise that it is now widely recognised by public lawyers that the concentration of power represented by these changes should be viewed with some concern because it is at one with the reality that modern governments, once elected, can usually manipulate parliamentary majorities to guarantee the passage of their main legislative proposals. Measures passed by majority vote are those for which governments seem to be barely accountable. This sometimes appears to be the case regardless of how unpopular these turn out to be, for example, the introduction and repeal of the community charge (or 'poll tax') during the 1980s, or the privatisation of the railways in the 1990s. On the other hand, there was a moment of particular constitutional controversy in October 2015 when the House of Lords voted to reject government proposals for tax credit cuts which were projected to have most damaging implications for low income families. This stood out almost as an exception that proved the rule about the extent of the government's powers. Indeed, the government argued that the vote of the unelected House of Lords to withhold approval for such financial measures clashed with a long established constitutional convention reinforced by the provisions of the Parliament Act 1911. In their defence, opposition parties contended that the Tax Credit Act 2002 which introduced these measures had not been certified as a money Bill by the Speaker and was therefore not covered by the convention.[35]

---

35 M Russell, 'The Lords, Politics and Finance' UK Const L Blog, 2 November 2015.

This trend towards party government was famously referred to by Lord Hailsham as 'elective dictatorship'.[36] It is a trend that makes it all the more necessary to evaluate the adequacy of the mechanisms that have been established to check the exercise of such potentially awesome governmental power. This is not least because statutes (frequently 'open textured' in nature), once enacted, often confer wide discretionary powers of decision-making on ministers and officials. The role of the courts in being able and willing to intervene in these decisions is one of the central themes of our book. Further, the administration of massive schemes under wide-ranging legislation has not only involved many more decisions being taken by officials, but officials have also been left with much more discretion as a result when implementing policy initiatives. Accordingly, the supervisory jurisdiction of the courts has become as relevant to decision-making by central government as it was (and is) in the sphere of local government. The courts can be called upon to consider whether a central government department is acting lawfully and not abusing its powers. But how can we get a bearing on the courts' reaction to these changes? What is it that the courts are seeking to achieve, and is it legitimate for them to do so?

1.6 Conclusion: towards a grievance chain in administrative justice?

In our discussion in 1.4, we briefly considered two broad underlying theoretical approaches to such questions. These are associated with distinct ideas about the role of the state and have been characterised as 'red light' and 'green light' perspectives. At the same time, the views of the judiciary when they are involved in deciding cases will undoubtedly be influenced by their own attitudes. In our view, these can usefully be measured along a continuum, from red light to green light positions, with some bias today towards the 'middle ground' of amber. (Notice again, we are *not* saying that any particular judge, or any particular judgment, can be so measured and quantified and that examples often bring a blend of different perspectives.) This allows us to ask to what extent the court is applying the strict letter of the law, or has in mind the underlying purpose of the legislation, and whether it is thereby facilitating fairer and more efficacious administration. We have noted that the judicial oversight function has emerged as a response, and a potential counterbalance, to the vesting of powers in the modern state. Indeed, by the early years of the twentieth century the *ultra vires* principle had in one sense already been firmly established as a means of judicial intervention in the administrative process. For example, in *R v Electricity Commissioners*, Atkin LJ stated that: 'Whenever any body of persons having legal authority to determine questions affecting the rights of subjects, and having the duty to act judicially, act in excess of their legal authority, they are subject to the controlling jurisdiction of the King's Bench Division exercised in [the] writs of [*certiorari*] and [prohibition]'.[37]

---

36 See Lord Hailsham, *The Dilemma of Democracy* (London: Fontana, 1978), p 126.
37 *R v Electricity Commissioners, ex p London Electricity Joint Committee* [1924] 1 KB 171, 205.

However, we will also see in later chapters that the record of the courts in applying these principles has not always been consistent. There were phases in the twentieth century when the judiciary generally retreated from applying the *ultra vires* doctrine, save on narrowly defined grounds. These phases have been referred to as 'judicial quietism', where *Local Government Board v Arlidge* and *Nakkuda Ali v Jayaratne*, on natural justice, are two well-known examples of such a judicial approach.[38] Why is it that these quietist periods have followed periods when the courts appeared more ready to intervene? Part of the explanation can be linked to the discretionary nature of the public law remedies, and part to the questions that had to be answered before an applicant could seek a public law remedy (was the decision under challenge administrative rather than judicial; was a matter one of public law or private law, etc?).[39] It can also be attributed in part to the fear, often expressed by judges, that the courts were in danger of being unwittingly dragged into the political arena, especially in times of war or social conflict. Another aspect of the explanation lies in a certain deference by the courts to the perceived interests of the government following the victory of Labour in 1945 and the post-war consensus on the Keynesian welfare state.

Despite these oscillations of mood, in more recent times, most notably since the 1960s, a more generally sustained attitude of judicial activism has become a reality. This has occurred in two clearly identifiable stages. First, a series of influential judgments by the House of Lords during the 1960s signalled a new willingness to sweep aside some of the more technical impediments. These included the following landmark judgments: *Ridge v Baldwin*,[40] where the court insisted on basic standards of natural justice being observed; *Padfield v Minister of Agriculture*,[41] where the court intervened to insist on the exercise of ministerial discretion for a proper purpose; *Anisminic v Foreign Compensation Commission*,[42] where the House of Lords reasserted the supervisory role of the courts; and *Conway v Rimmer*,[43] which resulted in a number of significant qualifications to the doctrine of public interest immunity. These decisions, and others discussed later, significantly widened the scope for intervention by the courts. The second, and equally crucial stage in opening up judicial review was the streamlining of procedures under Order 53 of (what were then) the Rules of the Supreme Court (RSC Ord 53) (later enacted in the Senior Courts Act 1981, section 31; formerly the Supreme Court Act 1981). This established a single procedure for applications for judicial review, the exclusivity of which was acknowledged in the decision in *O'Reilly v Mackman*.[44] The number of cases coming before the courts has increased significantly since these innovations.[45] By the mid-1980s senior civil servants were being issued with an internal government leaflet entitled 'The Judge Over Your Shoulder', which outlined the nature of administrative law and the grounds of review. This was in order to reduce the growing risk of legal challenges to executive/administrative action in the

---

38 [1915] AC 120 and [1951] AC 66, respectively. See further ch 17.
39 See ch 8.
40 [1964] AC 40.
41 [1968] AC 997.
42 [1969] 2 AC 147.
43 [1968] AC 910.
44 [1983] 2 AC 237.
45 See ch 8 *et seq.*

courts. Applications for judicial review have continued to increase ever since. In fact, judicial review gained further momentum following the enactment of the Human Rights Act 1998. When it came into force in 2000 this important constitutional measure created another avenue for claimants wishing to assert their rights before the domestic courts under the ECHR.[46]

However, despite the substantial growth of judicial review, it must be stressed that relatively few of the seemingly innumerable decisions taken by public bodies each year that are challenged actually give rise to proceedings in the courts. In fact, there is, what we will term throughout this book, 'a grievance chain'. This grievance chain has two aspects, which have already been mentioned above: non-legal remedies and legal remedies. The first of these comprises the less formal mechanisms for the resolution of grievances, including recourse to an MP[47] or to an ombudsman, or some means for internal review within the body that took the decision under challenge.[48] The second comprises appeals to tribunals under the terms of relevant statutes,[49] or a claim for judicial review, something that is regarded very much as a remedy of last resort.[50] Our task in this book will be to consider and evaluate these various aspects of the grievance chain in turn, before we are in a position to offer our conclusions on the adequacy of the system as a whole in chapter 21.

FURTHER READING

Adler, M (ed) (2010) *Administrative Justice in Context* (Oxford: Hart Publishing).

Allison, JWF (1997) 'Theoretical and Institutional Underpinnings of a Separate Administrative Law', in Taggart, M (ed), *The Province of Administrative Law* (Oxford: Hart Publishing).

Allan, TRS (1993) *Law, Liberty and Justice: The Legal Foundations of British Constitutionalism* (Oxford: Clarendon Press).

Bingham, T (2010) *The Rule of Law* (London: Allen Lane).

Craig, PP (1991) 'Dicey: Unitary, Self-Correcting Democracy and Public Law' 106 *Law Quarterly Review* 105.

Craig, PP (2012) *Administrative Law*, 7th edn (London: Sweet & Maxwell), chapter 1.

Craig, PP (2015) *UK, EU and Global Administrative Law* (Cambridge: Cambridge University Press).

Griffith, JAG (1979) 'The Political Constitution' 42 *Modern Law Review* 1.

Griffith, JAG (1997) *The Politics of the Judiciary*, 5th edn (London: Fontana), chapters 1, 8, and 9.

Hailsham, Lord (1978) *The Dilemma of Democracy* (London: Fontana).

Harlow, C [2000] 'Export, Import: The Ebb and Flow of English Public Law' *Public Law* 240.

Harlow, C and Rawlings, R (2009) *Law and Administration*, 3rd edn (Cambridge: Cambridge University Press), chapters 1 and 2.

---

46 See ch 4.
47 Ch 2.
48 Adler, n 26; ch 6.
49 Ch 7.
50 Ch 8 *et seq.*

Leyland, P and Woods, T (1997) 'Public Law History and Theory: Some Notes Towards a New Foundationalism', in Leyland, P and Woods, T (eds), *Administrative Law Facing the Future: Old Constraints and New Horizons* (London: Blackstone Press).

Loughlin, M (1992) *Public Law and Political Theory* (Oxford: Clarendon Press), chapter 2.

Nolan, Lord and Sedley, Sir Stephen (1997) *The Making and Remaking of the British Constitution* (London: Blackstone Press), especially chapter 2, 'The Common Law and the Constitution' by Sir Stephen Sedley.

Sugarman, D (1983) 'The Legal Boundaries of Liberty: Dicey, Liberalism and Legal Science' 46 *Modern Law Review* 102.

Wade, HWR and Forsyth, CF (2014) *Administrative Law*, 11th edn (Oxford: Oxford University Press), chapter 1.

Willis, J (1935) 'Three Approaches to Administrative Law: The Judicial, the Conceptual and the Functional' 1 *University of Toronto Law Journal* 53.

2

....

Constitutional context

2.1 Introduction

In chapter 1 we sketched in the theoretical and historical backdrop to administrative law. Here we will consider the wider constitutional context by outlining those centrally important constitutional concepts, originating for the most part in the nineteenth century,[1] which frame and lend explanatory significance to any analysis of the workings of the contemporary system of administrative law. At another level, it will be important to ask just how well these background conceptual concepts, operating at the heart of government and administration, serve individual citizens or groups when they are in need of defending their rights or safeguarding their interests (e.g., in respect of remedying an injustice or attempting to achieve legislative change from outside, or from within, the framework offered by the established British political parties). Bearing this question in mind, it will already be apparent to the student of constitutional law that in the UK there is no single constitutional code or document which sets out the parameters within which the system is constrained.[2] Nevertheless, there are a number of ways in which power exercised by the executive, executive agencies, and other administrative bodies, can be challenged from within Parliament itself.[3] In sum, we concentrate on the conceptual background and then the role of Parliament both as characteristic features of this 'uncodified' constitution, and in order to assess their impact on administrative law and, more generally, the workings of the entire political and legal system.

It will become apparent in the chapter that many of the defining concepts of UK constitutionalism are increasingly under strain as a result of changing understandings of where power is located. Some of this strain is as a result of developments that are 'internal' to the UK; that is, changes in terms of the allocation of power that have been brought about as a result of deliberate choices on the part of successive governments starting with the Labour Government that was elected to power in 1997. However, we will also see that there are challenges from 'external' sources too. The activities of the European Union (EU), the Council of Europe, and other

---

1 See W Bagehot, *The English Constitution* (Glasgow: Fontana, 1963), introduction by RS Crossman; and AV Dicey, *An Introduction to the Study of the Law of the Constitution*, 10th edn (London: Macmillan, 1959).

2 But for a recent proposal see R Gordon, *Repairing British Politics: A Blueprint for Constitutional Change* (Oxford: Hart Publishing, 2010).

3 See 2.4.

international organisations—these all have a direct and indirect impact on UK constitutional processes. While it might be argued that any direct impact follows from an internal decision to, for instance, join the EU (though see 3.1 on the referendum on membership that is upcoming at the time of writing), the indirect consequences depend much less upon the specific preferences of our governments. Such implications follow instead from international processes that affect UK policy choices simply by virtue of linkages and overlap in a globalising world.[4] Much of what defines UK constitutionalism therefore originates from a particular model of state sovereignty that is increasingly being strained by contemporary legal and political realities.[5]

2.2 **Parliamentary sovereignty**

The first and most important of the constitution's concepts is the doctrine of the legal sovereignty of Parliament. Under this doctrine no other body is higher than Parliament, which has an unqualified legal capacity to enact new legislation. The doctrine thereby also entails that no Parliament can bind its successor and, where there is a conflict between two statutes, the courts will always give effect to the most recent statement of Parliament's intentions under the doctrine of implied repeal.[6] Moreover, where there is a conflict between statute law and the common law, statute law will prevail.

This sovereign nature of Parliament's law-making powers leaves enormous scope for flexibility, since the constitution is not constrained by codified rules such as might be found in an entrenched bill of rights (as opposed to a broad background of common law rights and constitutional conventions laid down to preserve fundamental principles).[7] Parliament can, in constitutional theory, legislate on any matter whatever, and the courts, theoretically, will also give effect to the latest statement of Parliament's intentions. As Lord Reid famously stated in *Madzimbamuto v Lardner-Burke*:

It is often said that it would be unconstitutional for the UK Parliament to do certain things, meaning that the moral, political and other reasons against doing them are so strong that most people would regard it as highly improper if Parliament did these things. But that does not mean that it is beyond the power of Parliament to do so such things. If Parliament chose to do any of them the courts would not hold the Act of Parliament invalid.[8]

This core proposition can, however, now be seen as challenged in a number of ways. Most obvious is the impact of membership of the EU. When a state joins the EU it is bound by the constitutional principles of that organisation, the most important of which is the doctrine of the supremacy of EU law.[9] This doctrine means

---

4 See G Anthony et al, *Values in Global Administrative Law* (Oxford: Hart Publishing, 2011).

5 See further N Bamforth and P Leyland (eds), *Public Law in a Multi-layered Constitution* (Oxford: Hart Publishing, 2003).

6 *Ellen Street Estates Ltd v Minister of Health* [1934] 1 KB 590 and *Vauxhall Estates Ltd v Liverpool Corporation* [1932] 1 KB 733.

7 See 4.2.

8 [1969] 1 AC 645, 723.

9 See 3.2.1.2.

that, where there is a conflict between EU law and any piece of national legislation (*whenever* enacted), EU law is to prevail. There are then two supremacies—that of EU law and that of the UK constitutional order—and UK courts have had to modify the content of the doctrine of parliamentary sovereignty to ensure that membership remains problem free. In other words, the courts now give prior effect to EU law even where legislation passed after the UK became a member is inconsistent with European obligations.[10]

Tensions can also be seen in respect of the devolution of power to Scotland, Northern Ireland, and Wales, and in respect of incorporation of the European Convention on Human Rights (devolution and incorporation were central to a post-1997 reform programme introduced by the then Labour Government). Although the devolution Acts and the Human Rights Act 1998 are couched in terms that reassert the sovereignty of Parliament, the political reality is that it would now be difficult for Parliament to, for instance, legislate to abolish the Scottish Parliament in the absence of Scottish support for such a development.[11] Given the point, the courts have recently described the devolution legislation and Human Rights Act (among others) as common law 'constitutional statutes'.[12] While this does not mean that the Acts cannot be repealed by Parliament, it does impose 'formal' limitations on Parliament's powers, as the courts require that the Westminster Parliament use express words to repeal or amend a constitutional statute, or words that achieve that result by necessary implication.[13] That said, the Supreme Court has also stated that the Scottish Parliament—and, by analogy, the Northern Ireland Assembly and the National Assembly for Wales (NAW)—is not legally sovereign in the sense that the Westminster Parliament is.[14] Nevertheless, the Supreme Court emphasised in the *AXA* case that, given that the Scottish Parliament is a democratically elected body, the courts should be reluctant to intervene in its legislative choices and that they would do so in only exceptional circumstances (for instance, if the Parliament purported to abolish access to justice).[15] The Supreme Court in *Imperial Tobacco v Lord Advocate*[16] unanimously rejected another challenge to Scottish legislation but, by stating that the question of competence was always one for the courts to decide, perhaps Lord Hope left open the possibility of challenges to legislation of devolved bodies, albeit within closely defined limits set out in the judgment. Subsequently, a legislative choice of the NAW was challenged successfully in *Recovery of Medical Costs for Asbestos Diseases (Wales) Bill: Reference by the Counsel General for Wales.*[17] The Supreme Court held that the provisions of the Welsh private members' Bill which would have made insurers liable for charges payable to the Welsh Government

---

10 On the constitutional implications of this conundrum see further 3.3.2 ('Sovereignty and Supremacy: from *Factortame* to *Pham*').

11 For in depth analysis of the current constitutional position see M Elliott, 'The Principle of Parliamentary Sovereignty in Legal, Constitutional, and Political Perspective' in J Jowell, D Oliver, and C O'Cinneide (eds), *The Changing Constitution*, 8th edn (Oxford: Oxford University Press, 2015), ch 2. See now also section 1 of the Scotland Act 2016.

12 *Thoburn v Sunderland City Council* [2003] QB 151 and, e.g., *R (Brynmawr Foundation School Governors) v Welsh Ministers* [2011] EWHC 519, para 73.

13 M Elliott, 'Embracing "Constitutional" Legislation: Towards Fundamental Law?' (2003) 54 *Northern Ireland Legal Quarterly* 25.

14 *Axa General Insurance Limited and others v Lord Advocate* [2011] UKSC 46, [2012] 2 AC 868. The case is discussed further at 13.6.3.1.

15 But compare *Salvesen v Riddell* [2013] UKSC 22, 2013 SC (UKSC) 236.

16 [2012] UKSC 61, 2013 SC (UKSC) 153.

17 [2015] UKSC 3, [2015] AC 1016.

were not concerned with the 'organisation and funding' of the National Health Service and, in consequence, that they fell outwith the devolved competence of the Welsh Assembly under section 108 of the Government of Wales Act (GOWA) 2006. Notwithstanding that the above Scottish cases are distinguishable as they concerned the Scotland Act 1998, it is significant that Lord Mance's judgment for the majority sees 'the court's function, under the GOWA, [as being] to evaluate the relevant considerations and to form its own judgment, on the issue both of legislative competence and of consistency with Convention rights'.[18] In other words, without any special justification for the retrospectivity involved under this Bill the emphasis is placed on a narrower interpretation of what is undoubtedly a 'constitutional' statute. On the other hand, Lord Thomas in an important dissenting opinion echoes the approach of Lord Hope in the Scottish cases by attaching much greater weight to the judgment of the Welsh Assembly as a democratically elected body. Against a background of political change in Scotland and Wales in the wake of the 2014 Scottish independence referendum, the ground rules for applying the law in devolution cases appear to be evolving, but it seems clear that, in the absence of formal limitations, the Westminster Parliament continues to rank above the other democratically elected legislatures in the UK in terms of enjoying final sovereign authority.

2.3 The Westminster and Whitehall models

Academic commentators have frequently used these two concepts to enhance our understanding of contemporary constitutional arrangements. The first is the orthodox, or 'Westminster', model, which has its origins in the late nineteenth century. It suggested that government was both 'representative and responsible'. It is representative in that the people as a whole elect a Parliament (here the House of Commons, as opposed to the still unelected House of Lords), and it is responsible in that it holds to account the executive government which largely emanates from within it. It follows, in turn, that both Parliament and government are politically accountable to the electorate at the next general election. As Craig put it, another aspect of sovereignty recognises that:

[A]ll government power should be channelled through Parliament for legitimation and oversight by the Commons. Dicey believed that the Commons controlled the executive, and that all public power should be subject to legislative oversight. This democratic system was also 'self-correcting,' in that Dicey believed that the Commons accurately reflected the will of the people and controlled the executive. The all-powerful parliament would not therefore be likely to pass legislation which was contrary to the wishes of the electorate.[19]

However, twentieth-century developments have accelerated tendencies which were already discernible in Dicey's time and which have been referred to as the executive dominance, or 'Whitehall', model of governance. In broad terms, a party with majority support in the House of Commons and backed by the Whitehall

---

machine forms a government and can ultimately insist upon the enactment of almost all of its legislative proposals until it loses its majority, or until the next general election. This near dominance of Parliament by the government is possible without majority electoral support (in terms of the popular vote) due to party loyalty and the power and patronage exercised by the Prime Minister and the party machine. While the former Coalition Government marked a departure from the more typical experience of single party dominance, support for the Coalition's own legislative programme was nevertheless virtually guaranteed because defeat in Parliament on a vote of No Confidence would have led to an early election and possible humiliation of the governing parties at the polls. Given this, it is often said that the majority of the population can be disenfranchised and disempowered by the quirks of our electoral system which allow this situation to arise. Indeed, there have been repeated demands for electoral reform in recent decades by various pressure groups that include Charter 88 (now a part of 'Unlock Democracy'). Moreover, the Liberal Democrats have long campaigned in favour of electoral reform and, on forming a coalition government with the Conservatives in 2010, they insisted upon a referendum on the introduction of the so-called 'alternative vote' electoral system. However, the referendum was lost and many of the weaknesses within the Whitehall model remain. Despite the fact that a wide range of interest groups may be consulted at the stage when legislation is being drafted, certain sections of the population are therefore vulnerable to profound changes in policy, which may, for instance, redefine the role of local government or the nature of public service provision. It is also the case that, once the basic rules have been re-cast by legislation, groups such as the homeless, those suffering changes to their benefits entitlement, or environmental protestors have only limited practical alternatives beyond awaiting the hoped-for change of policy with the election of another government.

2.4 Individual ministerial responsibility and the role of Parliament and MPs

As part of what we have termed a 'grievance chain', the central concept of accountability needs to be considered in the light of important non-legal mechanisms of dispute resolution as they work in practice. Parliament seeks to make the executive accountable for its actions, and is the focus of discussion here because so much executive action now has its origins in Acts of Parliament that enable the executive by statute to make law by means of delegated legislation. The convention of individual ministerial responsibility serves as the point of reconciliation between the concept of executive accountability to Parliament and the rule of law. Vile explains that this idea allowed the integration of the two theories:

The 'executive' must act according to the law, the 'government' must exercise leadership in the development of policy; but if the government was subject to the control of parliament, and the executive to control of the courts, then a harmony could be established between the two roles of the ministers of the Crown. Ministerial responsibility, legal and political, was thus the crux of the English system of government. Whilst it remained a reality the whole edifice of constitutionalism could be maintained; should it cease to be a workable concept the process of disintegration between the legal basis and the operation of the government would begin.[20]

This 'classic' (perhaps mythical) doctrine of individual ministerial responsibility can be summarised in its essence as 'the minister takes the praise and the blame', thereby identifying the minister as the source of all decisions, with the ultimate sanction being resignation. In other words, ministers inside or outside the cabinet are largely responsible for policy issues, for their personal behaviour as relates to their office, and for any mistakes, or alleged mistakes, in their departments; and this is still recognised by the government.[21] It should also be noted that these categories frequently overlap in practice. Indeed, a major justification for the government being formed exclusively from members of the House of Commons and the House of Lords is so that ministers can be held accountable to Parliament or at least answerable to Parliament for their own conduct and for the activities of their officials. In consequence, ministers have a conspicuous public profile as heads of their departments, which is evident in their parliamentary role at Question Time, before select committees, during general debates, and outside Parliament through appearances in the media. By contrast, in theory at least, civil servants are anonymous, merely carrying out policy once it has been decided by the minister. They are thereby more insulated from day-to-day political controversy. The doctrine is also used to underpin the culture of secrecy that pervades Whitehall, despite the introduction of the Freedom of Information Act 2000, by preventing the spotlight from being directed too closely at individuals working within the executive.

We have outlined individual ministerial responsibility as being one of the basic features of the 'Westminster model', but it is important to note that there are certain qualifications that need to be made to the classic doctrine. First, the complexity of modern administration requires that many decisions are delegated so that in practice they are taken by officials in the *name* of the minister.[22] Secondly, it should be pointed out that many caveats can be made to the orthodox doctrine of individual responsibility, in particular the limited accountability to Parliament (as opposed to the executive) of local government, the very few remaining nationalised industries, executive agencies, regulators of the privatised utilities, and other bodies known as quangos.[23] Thirdly, the very definition of what accountability might entail has been evolving against a background of changes to the nature of government. There are precedents which suggested that resignation might be expected in situations where the minister is involved in, or aware of, serious departmental fault. The *Crichel Down* case, discussed in chapter 6, and Lord Carrington's resignation as Foreign Secretary over the inadequate steps taken to prevent the Argentinian invasion of the Falkland Islands in 1982 can be cited as two such examples.[24] However,

---

20 M Vile, *Constitutionalism and the Separation of Powers* (Oxford: Clarendon Press, 1967), 231.

21 Ministerial Code, Cabinet Office October 2015, s 1.2(b): 'Ministers have a duty to Parliament to account, and be held to account, for the policies, decisions and actions of their departments and agencies . . . '

22 This is recognised by the courts as the '*Carltona* principle', following the case of *Carltona Ltd v Commissioner of Works* [1943] 2 All ER 560. And see 12.5.2.

23 See 5.5.2.

24 D Woodhouse, 'Ministerial Responsibility' in V Bogdanor (ed), *The British Constitution in the Twentieth Century* (Oxford: Oxford University Press, 2003), 310.

in practice, it is almost unknown for ministers to sacrifice themselves on behalf of their officials, making the very idea of full political accountability remote from the reality of contemporary application to the workings of departments. Furthermore, the problem is that the traditional concept of ministerial responsibility no longer accords with the structure of the modern civil service which, as we shall see in chapter 5, has now been broken down into agencies. 'Cracks and gaps appear and serious accountability issues flow from the division of functions between agency chief executives appointed by ministers and the minister, notionally accountable to Parliament.'[25] The failure of Michael Howard (the Home Secretary) to resign over the Whitemoor prison escape in 1995, despite a very critical report on the escape, clearly illustrated this point. Rather than falling on his own sword, the head of the prison service (Derek Lewis) was sacked by the minister, who relied on a much-disputed distinction between policy matters falling within the minister's responsibility and operational matters (including the escape) falling under the head of the service and therefore an operational matter.[26] The upshot is that ministers are still supposed to be accountable to Parliament, but their senior officials may now find themselves open to criticism.[27] Given that they frequently appear before select committees, any claim to anonymity is difficult to sustain.

2.4.1 Parliamentary oversight mechanisms

MPs have an important role in redressing the grievances of their constituents and holding the executive to account. The routine practical exercise of ministerial responsibility can be observed through a number of procedures that allow MPs to perform this function. Individuals and groups can contact their MP through constituency surgeries, by post or email, and at occasional meetings where they can pursue an issue on their own behalf. It is important to note that the intervention of an MP at this early stage can be conducive to an *informal* settlement of a dispute, for example, by a word in the minister's ear. However, if such informal methods prove inadequate, there remains a range of *formal* opportunities where MPs can raise matters, including early day motions, sponsorship of a bill under the 10-minute rule, adjournment debates, general debates, emergency debates, and the tabling of parliamentary questions. All these devices can help to gauge the strength of opinion and, incidentally, provide free publicity through press releases, although they are limited by the sometimes anachronistic way Parliament organises itself. The respective role of parliamentary questions, departmental select committees, and the public accounts committee need to be mentioned further.

2.4.1.1 Parliamentary questions

The capacity to table questions for oral or written answer is an important weapon in the hands of the individual member, not least because, since the advent of the televising of Parliament, the occasion of Question Time, always the highlight of

---

25 C Harlow and R Rawlings, *Law and Administration* (Cambridge: Cambridge University Press, 2009), 63.

26 A Tomkins, *The Constitution After Scott: Government Unwrapped* (Oxford: Clarendon Press, 1998), 45ff.

27 A King, *The British Constitution* (Oxford: Oxford University Press, 2007), 351.

the parliamentary day, has been brought to the attention of the wider public. Backbenchers have a chance to interrogate the executive by framing questions that are directed towards ministers of the Crown or which are designed to obtain information from within departments. From a different standpoint, the response to parliamentary questions might also demonstrate executive control over the flow of information, as ministers have been in a position to mislead MPs by the selective release of information, thus illustrating the unequal struggle MPs have in genuinely exercising their oversight function.[28]

2.4.1.2 Departmental select committees

It is recognised that Parliament exercises a supervisory function by way of its select committees.[29] In fact, they should be regarded as an important extension of ministerial responsibility, helping to keep track of what ministers do with their responsibility for their departments and other agencies, in an era when change is very rapid. The election of 1979 led to significant changes to the system then in place in the House of Commons. Instead of the limited number of select committees and the various *ad hoc* committees that had previously sought to investigate particular areas of executive activity, 14 departmental select committees were established. Currently 21 such committees oversee the executive and policy-making by government.[30] Unlike the courts, which deal with *ultra vires* executive action or the abuse of power, the committees are at an advantage in that they can have an informal influence on the formative stage of policy-making, examining at their discretion political, social, and economic issues as they arise, but they can also initiate investigations into policy areas at any time in response to public concern.

These departmental select committees have been compared to those within the American system. However, there are substantial differences in their structure and effectiveness. With regard to structure, a central characteristic of the separation of powers in the US Constitution is the way the legislature keeps check on the executive by means of Congressional committees. Although their wider reputation has been based on a number of scandals that have been revealed by special investigations (most notable of all being Watergate in 1973/4), the committees undertake on a day-to-day basis the more routine tasks of initiating policy and scrutinising the executive, with their specific terms of reference being administration, policy, and expenditure. In fact, the Congressional committees are powerful bodies which are generously funded and equipped with full-time staff. Nevertheless the departmental select committees have formidable powers to summon before them papers or persons, including Secretaries of State (ministers) and top civil service officials and

---

28 This was one of the key findings of the Scott Report: *Report of the Inquiry into Exports of Defence Equipment and Dual-Use Goods to Iraq and Related Prosecutions*, HC 115 1995–96 vol 1.

29 R Kelly, 'Select Committees: Powers and Functions' in A Horne, G Drewry, and D Oliver (eds), *Parliament and the Law* (Oxford: Hart Publishing, 2013).

30 The Departmental Select Committees post 2015 are: Business, Innovation and Skills; Communities and Local Government; Culture, Media and Sport; Defence; Education; Energy and Climate Change; Environment Food and Rural Affairs; Foreign Affairs; Health; Home Affairs; International Development; Justice; Northern Ireland Affairs; Petitions, Public Administration and Constitutional Affairs; Science and Technology; Scottish Affairs; Transport; Treasury; Welsh Affairs; Women and Equalities, Work and Pensions.

advisers. They conduct routine investigations, but also investigate issues of topical public concern.[31]

In line with the recommendations of the Wright Committee[32] some significant changes were introduced following the 2010 election to minimise the control by the Government of the Commons' agenda. This objective was achieved through the formation of a Backbench Business Committee. The revision of standing orders for the election of committee chairs was another important change designed to increase the independence of the departmental select committees by insulating them from the influence of the party whips. These reforms have also resulted in the main parties introducing an internal procedure for electing their quota of select committee members. Russell was correct in concluding that: 'This should give them a greater sense of legitimacy and more confidence to speak for the chamber as a whole. It may also give them an enhanced media profile with which to do so.'[33]

2.4.1.3 Public Accounts Committee and National Audit Office

The Public Accounts Committee (PAC) is the main device through which the House of Commons exercises some degree of control over government finances, now running at over £400 billion per annum. It operates in a non-partisan, non party-political way, and consists of not more than 16 MPs, the chair being a senior member of the Opposition, usually with experience as a Treasury minister. Ministers and departmental accounting officers (usually permanent secretaries) appear before the PAC to be questioned, even interrogated, on issues arising from the annual audit of departmental accounts. Further, the advent of television cameras in the House of Commons has introduced these proceedings, and the important issues examined, to the wider public.

The PAC, unlike the other select committees, enjoys the backing and support of the National Audit Office (NAO) headed by the Comptroller and Auditor General (C & AG).[34] Until 1983 the C & AG was appointed by the government of the day, but the National Audit Act of that year established the post as an officer of the House of Commons. The method of appointment now consists of a commission, of which the Prime Minister and the chair of the PAC are members. This reinforces the element of independence in the system of accountability. The NAO works with a staff of more than 1,000 in close accord with the PAC, examining the effectiveness with which governmental bodies implement their assigned policy goals and carrying out Value for Money (VFM) audits to eliminate waste. The reports by the NAO, consequential on the annual audit of all government departments, to which the remit of the committee is limited, are passed to the PAC where the evidence

---

31 There have been many high-profile investigations, e.g., the salmonella in eggs affair (1988); Marking the Millennium in the UK (2000); the decision to go to war in Iraq (2003); and recently the News of the World phone hacking scandal by the Culture, Media and Sport Select Committee, Phone Hacking, 19 July 2011, HC 903 ii, and Home Affairs Committee, Unauthorised tapping into or hacking of mobile communications, Thirteenth Report of Session 2010–12, HC 907.

32 Select Committee on Reform of the House of Commons, chaired by Tony Wright MP.

33 M Russell, '"Never Allow a Crisis Go To Waste": The Wright Committee Reforms to Strengthen the House of Commons' (2011) 64 (4) *Parliamentary Affairs*, 612–33, 628.

34 P Dunleavy, C Gilson, S Bastow, and J Tinkler, *The National Audit Office, the Public Accounts Committee and the Risk Landscape in UK Public Policy*, Risk and Regulation Advisory Council, October 2009.

contained therein can be used effectively as a tool with which to probe into the details of expenditure, and this gives the reports of the PAC added authority. In recent years concern has been expressed over the capacity of the NAO to oversee over 900 Private Finance Initiative (PFI) projects, and the financial crisis of recent years has exposed the limitations of the ex post scrutiny of the PAC and other select committees. Nevertheless, one influential commentator states that: 'It is possible to see financial controls as a model of what can be achieved with systemic change over 40 years through the appropriate combination of external expertise in the form of the NAO and the internal scrutiny performed by select committees [including the PAC].'[35]

We conclude this section by noting that the public image of Parliament was seriously tarnished by the scandal concerning MPs' expenses which was revealed in 2009.[36] This has prompted the introduction of more rigorous rules governing disclosure of interests and the general conduct of MPs.[37] The restoration of the reputation of Parliament is of great importance because MPs perform a vital executive oversight function. Moreover, the effectiveness of these mechanisms at the disposal of ordinary members must be assessed against the tendency for the government to dominate Parliament through the party whips.[38] Recent reforms to the scheduling of House of Commons business and to the select committee system will go some way towards redrawing the balance in favour of MPs by making existing parliamentary mechanisms more independent of the party or parties exercising political power.

2.5 Parliamentary sovereignty and the assertion of judicial authority

Returning now to the legal nature of Parliament's power, we find ourselves in the situation where the sovereign legislature—the Crown, the Commons, and the Lords—has historically been able to legislate at will and without concern for the possibility of legislation being challenged as unconstitutional. The situation is, however, in the process of changing. In the first place the Constitutional Reform Act 2005 engineered significant constitutional changes which were introduced to consolidate a separation of powers between Parliament and the judiciary. The Act not only transformed the ancient role of the Lord Chancellor so that he or she can no longer combine parliamentary, executive, and judicial functions, but it also put the system of judicial appointments on a statutory footing and replaced the Appellate Committee of the House of Lords with a Supreme Court that is housed separately from Parliament (we discuss this further later). Although the composition and powers of the Supreme Court are largely the same

35 J McEldowney, 'Public Expenditure and the Control of Public Finance' in Jowell, Oliver, and O'Cinneide, n 11, 368ff.

36 P Leyland, *The Constitution of the United Kingdom: A Contextual Analysis*, 2nd edn (Oxford: Hart Publishing, 2012), 122ff.

37 See Parliamentary Commissioner for Standards, Annual Report 2014–15, July 2015, HC 329; and R Kelly and M Hamlyn, 'The Law and Conduct of Members of Parliament' in Horne, Drewry, and Oliver, n 29.

38 See Lord Hailsham, *The Dilemma of Democracy* (London: Fontana, 1978), who coined the phrase 'elective dictatorship'.

as those enjoyed by the Appellate Committee, the creation of the new court provided a symbolic, and important, confirmation of a separation of powers between Parliament and the courts.

In the second place, there has been an increasing assertion of judicial authority which many commentators regard as shifting the balance between Parliament and the courts. In the hunting case, *R (Jackson) v Attorney General*,[39] the House of Lords was prepared to entertain arguments concerning the validity of an Act of Parliament which had been passed under the procedure introduced under the Parliament Acts of 1911 and 1949 (the legislation in question—the Hunting Act 2004—had made unlawful the hunting of wild animals with dogs). Although their Lordships did not attempt to set aside the statute, simply by considering the case before them they neglected to follow the 'enrolled Act' rule, which arguably made the matter non-justiciable. However, perhaps even more significantly, three of the judges were prepared to make *obiter* statements to the effect that they could envisage exceptional circumstances, such as parliamentary attempts to abolish judicial review or to threaten the rights of the individual, where the courts might declare a statute to be invalid. While there have since been some judicial statements that have arguably diluted the importance of *Jackson*,[40] the *obiter* comments made in it remain influential. Jeffrey Jowell summarises their implications as follows:

It may take some time, provocative legislation and considerable judicial courage for the courts to assert the primacy of the Rule of Law over Parliamentary sovereignty, but it is no longer self evident, or generally accepted, that a legislature in a modern democracy should be able with impunity to violate the strictures of the rule of law.[41]

In the third place, the Human Rights Act 1998 has led to the courts acquiring a much more prominent role in defending human rights and fundamental freedoms.[42] In particular, they have been empowered to interpret legislation widely to achieve compliance with the European Convention on Human Rights (ECHR), and, if this is not possible, to make declarations of incompatibility between the relevant legislation and the ECHR.[43] While such declarations do not invalidate the legislation in respect of which they are made, thereby preserving the sovereignty of Parliament, they usually have the effect of prompting Parliament to amend the offending legislation. The significant increase in judicial profile that this has entailed, most notably where it has involved the importation of 'European' human rights values into domestic law, has proved highly controversial and the government has frequently been critical of UK and European Court rulings. However, while this is suggestive of a struggle for primacy between the judges and the executive and legislature, some judges have described the relationship more in terms of 'relative institutional competence'. As Lord Bingham put it:

The more purely political (in a broad or narrow sense) a question is, the more appropriate it will be for political resolution and the less likely it is to be an appropriate matter for judicial decision. The smaller, therefore, will be the potential role of the court. It is the *function of*

---

39 [2005] UKHL 56, [2006] 1 AC 262.

40 *Axa General Insurance Limited and others v Lord Advocate* [2011] UKSC 46, [2012] 2 AC 868.

41 J Jowell, 'The Rule of Law', in Jowell, Oliver, and O'Cinneide, n 11, 34. See also Lord Hodge's comments in *Re Moohan* [2015] AC 901, 925, para 35.

42 See ch 4.

43 Human Rights Act 1998, ss 3 and 4.

political and not judicial bodies to resolve political questions. Conversely, the greater the legal content of any issue, the greater the potential role of the court, because under our constitution and subject to the sovereign power of Parliament it is the function of the courts and not of political bodies to resolve legal questions.[44]

Such comments make clear that the courts will typically give effect to Parliamentary choices in the political realm, although there are some important qualifications to their willingness to do so. Principal among these is the requirement that Parliament should use *express terms* where it wishes to achieve a particular outcome, or words that achieve that outcome by way of necessary implication. The courts have used this requirement—which is essentially a rule of statutory interpretation—to considerable effect when common law fundamental rights have been in issue, and it has become synonymous with an increased constitutional responsibility alongside that associated with the Human Rights Act 1998.[45] The interpretive approach has also been central to the courts' accommodation of the demands of EU law, where they have long held that they will give effect to legislation that is contrary to EU law only where Parliament expressly states that a conflict is deliberate.[46]

Another manifestation of judicial authority has been through the recognition of a category of common law 'constitutional statutes', noted earlier. In the celebrated *Thoburn* case,[47] Laws LJ explained that there are now certain statutes that are no longer subject to the ordinary domestic rules of implied repeal. Such statutes— which include the devolution Acts, the European Communities Act 1972, and the Human Rights Act 1998—can instead be repealed only where there are 'express words in the later statute, or . . . words so specific that the inference of an actual determination to effect the result contended for (is) irresistible'.[48] Such a view regards constitutional statutes as beyond the reach of implied repeal and it places the courts in an even more influential position, as it is they—through the use of the common law—who become responsible for identifying constitutional statutes (Laws LJ's list was by no means exhaustive).[49]

We will see, in subsequent chapters, that such developments are not without controversy and they can raise difficult questions about judicial activism. But are they, in any event, to be welcomed? At one level, the answer must be 'yes', as they suggest the placing of some limitations upon far-reaching governmental power that often takes form behind the workings of the core constitutional doctrine of parliamentary sovereignty. On the other hand, it is important to note of the nature of the concerns about judicial activism.[50] One of the strengths of the UK's system of democratic balance is that unelected judges have historically been unable to trump the preferences of the legislature elected by the people. If the formal limitations in *Thoburn* were to be developed into substantive

---

   44 *A v Home Secretary* [2005] 2 AC 68, 102, para 29; emphasis added.

   45 See *R v Home Secretary, ex p Leech (No 2)* [1993] 4 All ER 539, discussed at 4.2.2; and, e.g., *HM Treasury v Ahmed* [2010] 2 AC 534.

   46 For the genesis of the point see *Macarthys Ltd v Smith* [1979] 3 All ER 325, 329, Lord Denning.

   47 *Thoburn v Sunderland City Council* [2003] QB 151.

   48 Ibid, 187.

   49 The existence of constitutional statutes (as explained by Laws LJ) has since been recognised by the Supreme Court in *R (HS2 Action Alliance Ltd) v SS for Transport* [2014] UKSC 3, [2014] 1 WLR 324, 383, para 208, Lords Neuberger and Mance.

   50 For an older but still leading collection see C Forsyth (ed), *Judicial Review and the Constitution* (Oxford: Hart Publishing, 2000).

limitations (in the sense that the courts would strike down primary legislation) this may in turn give rise to issues of legitimacy. As we will discuss in the following section, the idea of the separation of powers—that is, the legislative, executive, and judicial—is of central importance to democratic systems of governance. When thinking about the role of the courts, we should therefore also think about the nature of the constitutional role that we wish to ascribe to the legislature and the executive.

2.6 Separation of powers: nature and implications

One of the most famous statements about the separation of powers was made by Montesquieu in his *De L'Esprit des Lois*, published in 1748. In his work he said that:

When the legislative and executive powers are united in the same person, or in the same body of magistrates, there can be no liberty . . . Again, there is no liberty, if the judicial power be not separated from the legislative and executive. Were it joined with the legislative, the life and liberty of the subject would be exposed to arbitrary control; for the judge would then be the legislator. Were it joined to the executive, however, the judge might behave with violence and oppression. There would be an end to everything, were the same man, or the same body . . . to exercise those three powers . . . [51]

This doctrine of the 'separation of powers' developed as a political theory to prescribe what *ought* to happen in relation to the distribution of powers within a constitution. Essentially, it suggests that the abuse of power will be limited by distributing different functions—legislative, executive, and judicial—between state institutions to prevent any one of them from predominating, thus preventing power from being concentrated in a single person or body. The separation of powers has remained an influential idea since it was first proposed in the eighteenth century, with the concept being most clearly acknowledged in both the post-revolutionary French and US constitutions drafted over 200 years ago. The judiciary in this country frequently reasserts its validity, always mindful of its desire to separate the legality of executive action from its merits, or substantive policy implications. For instance, in *Duport Steels Ltd v Sirs*, Lord Diplock commented that: 'it cannot be too strongly emphasised that the British constitution, though largely unwritten, is firmly based upon the separation of powers; Parliament makes the laws, the judiciary interpret them'.[52] Related comments about the relationship between the separation of powers and the rule of law have been made in many other cases too.[53]

Notwithstanding such comments, how far has this theoretical ideal been incorporated in practice under the British Constitution? And what has been the comparative experience of the United States, noted above?

---

51 Book XI, ch 6, quoted in MJC Vile, *Constitutionalism and the Separation of Powers* (Oxford: Oxford University Press, 1967).

52 [1980] 1 All ER 529, 541.

53 See, among other rulings, *M v Home Office* [1994] 1 AC 377, discussed at 18.3.4 and *R v Home Secretary, ex p Fire Brigades Union* [1995] 2 AC 513, at 9.3.2.3.

2.6.1 **The British Constitution**

It is perhaps surprising that the concept of the separation of powers has ever even been considered to be significant to the British Constitution, given that the most influential version of it, propagated by Montesquieu, emerged after the fundamentals of our constitutional arrangements were set in place in the late seventeenth century. As Loughlin has pointed out, this may be because the separation of powers helped mould Dicey's belief that parliamentary sovereignty favours the supremacy of law:

The idea here is that Parliament will set the framework of general rules for society, the executive will govern within those rules and an independent judiciary will resolve disputes over the meaning of those rules, and will, in particular, keep the executive within the boundaries of the law.[54]

Certainly, as we have already seen, judicial pronouncements have long lent support to the continuing recognition of the doctrine, with another example being given by Sir John Donaldson MR in *R v HM Treasury, ex p Smedley*:

Although the UK has no written constitution, it is a constitutional convention of the highest importance that the legislature and the judicature are separate and independent of one another, subject to certain ultimate rights of Parliament . . . It therefore behoves the courts to be ever sensitive to the paramount need to refrain from trespassing on the province of Parliament or, so far as this can be avoided, even appearing to do so.[55]

Despite such emphasis being placed on the concept at the most senior levels of the judiciary, there was a long-held scepticism about how far aspects of the role of the UK judiciary truly complied with a separation of powers. This scepticism was one of the reasons for the Constitutional Reform Act 2005. For instance, prior to the Act the Lord Chancellor was not only head of the judiciary and responsible for recommending most judicial appointments; he was also a cabinet minister with his own executive department, and a prominent member of the House of Lords. The Lord Chancellor could moreover sit as a judge,[56] an option that was criticised by a working party of the law reform group, 'JUSTICE', on the grounds that it was 'inherently flawed' and created an appearance of bias. The problem of bias more generally—both at common law and under Article 6 of the ECHR—also presented itself in relation to the potential for Law Lords to debate a Bill as it passed through Parliament and then to hear a case in which the Act was in issue.[57] According to the Labour Government that introduced the corresponding Bill in Parliament, the Constitutional Reform Act 2005 was enacted in response to such criticisms. The Act thus specifically eliminated the Lord Chancellor's judicial role, established mechanisms which limit his contribution to the most senior judicial appointments, and required that he relinquish the Speakership of the House of Lords. In addition, and, as was mentioned earlier, the Act also created the UK Supreme Court whose members are not allowed to participate in the work of the House of Lords as a Parliamentary legislature.

---

54 M Loughlin, *Public Law and Political Theory* (Oxford: Clarendon Press, 1992), 145.
55 [1985] 1 All ER 589, 593.
56 See, e.g., *DPP v Jones* [1999] 2 WLR 625.
57 See further *Davidson v Scottish Ministers* [2004] HRLR 34.

Another problem with the idea of the separation of powers in the UK is that the executive branch itself emanates from *within* Parliament. Indeed, it is a convention of the constitution that all ministers *must* come from either the Commons or the Lords. Many commentators have doubted whether such arrangements can underpin a true separation of powers. For example, Vile pointed out that rules are made by legislators, civil servants, and judges; that they are applied by the courts as well as by the executive; and that judgements—in the sense of value judgements—are made by civil servants and ministers as well as by judges.[58] We have already argued that rather than government being responsible *to* Parliament, it is in practice the governing party that exercises political power through being able to secure a majority for its legislative proposals *in* Parliament. There are only rare occasions when government policy is abandoned or trimmed. This is more likely to result from strong and coordinated opposition from within the governing party, in the circumstances of a small majority, than more generally from within Parliament itself. A good illustration is a proposal which appeared in the autumn of 1992 and which would have resulted in a drastic reduction in coal mines (31 overall) and manpower in the coal industry. This was eventually modified following strong opposition from within the ruling party itself and an adverse court judgment in *R v Secretary of State for Trade, ex p Vardy*.[59] However, this very example also reveals the limits of such opposition, for, after a lapse of some months while the proposal was delayed, the closures resumed at much the same pace with no comparable opposition from government supporters.

Despite such instances of rebellion, the prevailing superiority of the executive over Parliament is possible not simply because the executive branch, including the Prime Minister, cabinet, and all other ministers, are members of the legislature, but, above all, because the survival of the government depends on the maintenance of its parliamentary majority. MPs supporting the government are made well aware, by the party whips, of the consequences of taking action that might lead to defeat in the House of Commons. Where such a defeat is a realistic prospect, would MPs really go so far as to risk the fall of government and a general election which would be fought under adverse conditions of division and demoralisation? The answer will almost always be 'no', and this dominance of Parliament by the executive has famously been described by an ex-Lord Chancellor, Lord Hailsham, as 'elective dictatorship'.[60]

2.6.2 The US Constitution

By comparison, in the United States, the eighteenth-century ideal of the separation of powers has come nearer to full realisation.[61] A system of 'balanced' (or limited) government was conceived as part of a codified constitution which ensured a clear distinction between legislative, executive, and judicial powers. A number of safeguards were included in this approach. The President and his administration

---

58 MJC Vile, *Constitutionalism and the Separation of Powers* (Oxford: Oxford University Press, 1967).

59 [1993] ICR 720.

60 N 38 above.

61 On the US system see M Tushnet, *The Constitution of the United States of America: A Contextual Analysis*, 2nd edn (Oxford: Hart Publishing, 2015).

(government) wield enormous power by being vested with a predominantly executive function. He or she is the Commander-in-Chief of the armed forces and is responsible for the formation of foreign policy. The President personally proposes appointments to government posts, and the government, once appointed, is responsible for implementing policy by being able to introduce legislative measures in Congress. The Secretaries of State (the equivalent of ministers) are not members of Congress and are unable to vote themselves.

On the other hand, Congress is a legislature set apart from the administration of policy. Not only are no members of Congress part of the government, but Congress also has the power to vote down legislation. Even with a popular mandate and with a favourable partisan majority in the Senate and the House of Representatives (the two Houses of Congress), the President cannot rely on legislative programmes being approved. In fact, Congress often rejects important presidential proposals. While this may reduce the effectiveness of the government, it does not result in the President or the government falling from power. It has been remarked that while 'the President proposes, Congress disposes'. In addition, as part of its 'oversight function' of administrative action, Congress assumes a crucial role in scrutinising the executive branch through its powerful committee systems.

Lastly, the Supreme Court, as the final appellate court, has an important formal role in adjudicating controversial constitutional issues, such as desegregation;[62] abortion rights;[63] rights for same-sex partners;[64] and gay marriage.[65] However, it is important to note that the Supreme Court is often viewed as an intensely political and activist institution. It is, moreover, wrong to suppose that the US Constitution succeeds entirely in eliminating the overlap and duplication of functions. For example, the President is responsible for the appointment of judges to the Supreme Court, subject to the approval of Congress. Once in place judges cannot be dismissed by presidential action, even though the conservative or liberal leanings of appointees can and do have a major impact on the interpretation of the constitution, and hence of the policies of the executive branch of government. The policy areas cited above are good examples of this.

2.6.3 Do UK judges observe the separation of powers in practice?

Of course, the above points about the UK and US constitutions go to the normative framework within which power is allocated among the branches of the state. But do UK courts actually observe the separation of powers *in practice*? We have already seen that they cannot review the constitutionality of legislation, so they are in that sense precluded from interfering in the legislature's choices. But what is the significance of judicial approaches to the interpretation of legislation discussed earlier at 2.5? Does this not potentially involve the courts in a process of legislating? And what of judicial control of government departments and other public bodies which Parliament entrusts with statutory powers and duties (a control which is central to judicial review)?

---

62 *Brown v Board of Education* (1954) 347 US 483.
63 *Roe v Wade* 93 S Ct 705 (1973).
64 *Lawrence v Texas* 123 S Ct 2472 (2003).
65 *Obergefell v Hodges*, judgment of 26 June 2015 (576 US_(2015)).

These questions are answered in much more detail in the following chapters. However, there are a few points that are relevant here. The first concerns statutory interpretation. Interpretive techniques—particularly the purposive approach—have long been understood to offer courts the opportunity to engage in a process that can amount to legislating. It might be suggested that there were earlier generations of judges who preferred to interpret legislation literally, precisely because such an approach was understood to avoid the perils of judicial activism.[66] However, the courts have become increasingly inventive in recent years and this has corresponded with more pervasive arguments about activism.[67] Moreover, we have noted above the potential for significant judicial activism through interpretation under the terms of the Human Rights Act 1998. Section 3 of the Act requires courts 'so far as it is possible to do so' to interpret all legislation in a manner that is ECHR compliant. This is a very strong obligation and there have been several controversial decisions.[68]

In relation to the judicial review of decisions of government departments and other public bodies, the case law has ebbed and flowed between activism and restraint. In the first place the courts have a wide discretion in deciding whether to intervene at all.[69] Secondly, the see-saw between activism and restraint has been influenced by the judicial development of the general principles of law that form the grounds for review.[70] Some of these grounds (e.g., proportionality) allow the courts—at least potentially—to take a decision in the place of the recipient of a power.[71] This possibility goes to the very heart of the idea of the separation of powers, and the challenge for the courts is how to separate policy issues from legal issues. As Griffith noted, 'Democracy requires that some group of persons acts as an arbiter not only between individuals but also between governmental power and the individual'.[72] However, when judges hear politically contentious cases this potential conflict of roles has the capacity to undermine their authority in the eyes of important sections of the wider community. Should the courts therefore always emphasise that they wish to remain at the outer reaches of the process of administrative decision-making? Or should they take a more activist approach where an individual's fundamental rights are affected? We will see that there are no easy answers to such questions and that the courts try continually to strike a balance between competing constitutional imperatives such as the separation of powers and the protection of individuals.

A particularly good example of the difficulties that courts face when delimiting their role is provided by the controversial case of *R (Corner House Research) v Director of the Serious Fraud Office*.[73] This was a case in which the claimant, a public interest group, challenged a decision of the Director of the Serious Fraud Office to end an investigation into allegations of bribery in the context of arms contracts between BAE and the Kingdom of Saudi Arabia (the Director's power of investigation was

---

66 See, e.g., R Bellamy, *Political Constitutionalism* (Cambridge: Cambridge University Press, 2007).

67 See Forsyth, n 50.

68 See D Nicol, 'Statutory Interpretation and Human Rights after *Anderson*' [2004] *Public Law* 274.

69 See T Bingham, 'Should Public Law Remedies be Discretionary?' [1991] *Public Law* 64, and ch 18.

70 P Craig, *UK, EU and Global Administrative Law: Foundations and Challenges* (Cambridge: Cambridge University Press, 2015), 236ff.

71 See ch 13.

72 J Griffith, *The Politics of the Judiciary*, 5th edn (London: Fontana, 1997), 291.

73 [2009] 1 AC 756.

sourced in section 1 of the Criminal Justice Act 1987). The decision, which was said to have been taken for reasons of 'public interest', was made against a back-drop of Saudi threats to the effect that close intelligence and diplomatic contacts between Saudi Arabia and the UK would cease in the event that the Serious Fraud Office's investigation continued. Holding that the Director of the Serious Fraud Office had acted unlawfully in bringing the investigation to a close, the Divisional Court stated that the separation of powers doctrine entails that the courts should consider what steps are needed to preserve the integrity of the criminal justice system. While the Divisional Court accepted that the judicial branch of the state should not trespass on a decision affecting foreign policy, it considered that this was not such a decision but rather one concerned with the rule of law and the administration of justice. However, the House of Lords disagreed with the finding of the Divisional Court and held that the Director had acted lawfully when making the impugned decision. Although their Lordships recognised that there is a 'public interest' in upholding the rule of law, they equally noted the 'public interest' in protecting members of the public from the peril of terrorist violence. Noting that these two 'public interests' may not always be complementary, the House of Lords asked whether the Director had been entitled to weigh the competing interests in the way that he had. Holding that he had been so entitled, the House of Lords emphasised that its role as a reviewing court was not to ask whether there was an alternative course of action open to the Director, but rather whether he had law-fully exercised the discretion that Parliament had given to him. Approached in that way, it could not be said that the Director had acted outside his powers.[74]

2.7 The rule of law

2.7.1 Definition

The Donoughmore Committee stated in 1932 that 'The . . . rule of law . . . is a rec-ognised principle of the English Constitution, a conventional obligation. But it is a term open to a wide variety of interpretations'.[75] To understand the idea of the rule of law in the context of administrative law, it is therefore helpful to refer to the 'red' and 'green' light theories which were discussed in chapter 1. A widely held view in the legal profession and elsewhere would lean towards the red light per-spective, namely, that the rule of law at its broadest is a framework that constrains arbitrary use of power. Indeed, it is for that reason that it is frequently linked to the separation of powers and the idea that public power, where exercised, should always be subject to the principle of accountability before the law. In other words, it sets parameters within which, for example, private citizens should be allowed to lead their lives without undue interference from the state and its representatives. However, when the intervention of the state becomes inevitable or desirable, it should always follow that public authorities are accountable for any actions that they might take.

---

74 For critical analysis see J Jowell, 'Caving in: Threats and the Rule of Law' (2008) 13 *Judicial Review* 273. On the separation of powers see also *Evans v Attorney-General* [2015] UKSC 21, at 5.10.
75 *Minister's Powers*, Cmnd 4060, p 71.

2.7.2 **Dicey's theory**

For our purposes in analysing the nature of administrative law, the most influential definition for lawyers since the late nineteenth century has been that provided by AV Dicey.[76] In broad terms, there are generally said to be three elements to his theory:

(a) 'It means in the first place, the absolute supremacy or predominance of regular law as opposed to the influence of arbitrary power, and excludes the existence of arbitrariness, of prerogative, or even wide discretionary authority on the part of the government. . . . '[77]

(b) It means 'equality before the law, or the equal subjection of all classes to the ordinary law of the land administered by the ordinary law courts'.[78]

(c) It means the constitution is the result of the ordinary law as developed by the courts through the common law tradition and provides for the legal protection of the individual not via a Bill of Rights, but through the development of the common law.[79]

How have these elements stood the test of time? In relation to (a) there is little doubt that government and other public authorities have often enjoyed far-reaching power—for instance, police powers under the Police and Criminal Evidence Act 1984—and the statement is to that extent undermined. We will also see, in other chapters, how legislation has previously been introduced which has given the Home Secretary wide-ranging powers to detain foreign nationals.[80] So does this mean that the ordinary law no longer dominates as Dicey envisaged? Or are more extreme measures the 'exception', set in place to ensure that the prevalence of the ordinary law is the 'rule'? More controversially, is the fact that such laws can be introduced at all a basis for challenging element (c)?; that is, is there a need for a form of constitutional control of the legislature, at which stage the ordinary law would become subordinate to higher norms?

Element (b)—equality before the law—has also been overtaken in one sense, although it remains in a problematic form too. The aspect that has been superseded concerns the idea that there should be no distinction between public and private persons ('equal subjection of all classes'). Dicey rejected the French system of administrative law known as *droit administratif* because of his emphasis on the ordinary law courts and of equality before them (in France and other systems there were specialised administrative tribunals to deal with disputes involving the state). However, as we will see in the following chapters, the modern administrative state and the legal order is now characterised by a public–private divide that results in different legal rules, principles, and procedures depending on the parties involved.[81] Indeed, England and Wales now has its own Administrative Court as a division of the High Court.[82]

---

76 AV Dicey, *An Introduction to the Study of the Law of the Constitution* 10th edn (London: Macmillan, 1959).

77 See, e.g., *Entick v Carrington* (1765) 19 St Tr 1030, Lord Camden.

78 See, e.g., *Conway v Rimmer* [1968] AC 910.

79 See, e.g., *Ridge v Baldwin* [1964] AC 40.

80 Anti-terrorism, Crime and Security Act 2001, s 23, repealed in the light of *A v Home Secretary* [2005] 2 AC 68. And see 4.4.4.3 and 13.6.3.1.

81 See JWF Allison, *A Continental Distinction in the Common Law: A Historical and Comparative Perspective on English Public Law* (Oxford: Oxford University Press, 2000).

82 See ch 8.

The problematic aspect of element (b) concerns discrimination, notwithstanding the emphasis on equality. When the rule of law concept is wedded to the doctrine of parliamentary sovereignty, it in effect allows for the introduction of discriminatory legislation (the legislation is beyond constitutional review and is applied 'equally' to all affected by it). The outstanding example in recent times remains the Anti-terrorism, Crime and Security Act 2001, as the Secretary of State's powers of detention under the Act were used only in respect of non-UK nationals. The relevant provision of the Act—contained in section 23—was subsequently made the subject of a declaration of incompatibility with Article 14 of the ECHR and legislative change followed (albeit that the later legislation itself has given rise to much litigation).[83]

Element (c) has undoubtedly survived the passage of time best, although it, too, is starting to come under strain. For Dicey, the statement that the constitution is the result of the ordinary law, as developed by the courts through the common law tradition, meant an emphasis on judge-made law as opposed to powers that emanate from statute, or which were embodied in a codified constitutional framework. He believed that the courts, by means of developing case law, would prevent the unrestricted use of power by executive authorities and thereby protect the liberties of the citizen. In essence, the wielding of such authority in an excessive manner would be curbed precisely because it violated the spirit of our constitution. The case of *Entick v Carrington*[84] was an early classic example of such judicial intervention to curb executive power, and it was said that the courts could be relied upon in comparable situations to act as guarantors of liberty for the subject. In his judgment, Lord Camden stated that 'by the laws of England every invasion of private property, be it ever so minute, is a trespass'. While the record of the common law in protecting citizens in the centuries after *Entick v Carrington* was inconsistent, the courts have, as we have seen earlier, more recently adopted a reinvigorated approach to developing the common law and judicial review (a process that is usually taken to have started in the late 1960s and which represents much of the body of law that now challenges Dicey's understanding that there should be no distinction between public law and private law). A question for the future, however, is whether the emergence of common law 'constitutional statutes' and the impact of European fundamental rights standards will result in the perception of the ordinary common law as protecting individuals being lost.

2.8 **Conclusion**

In this chapter we have considered certain central concepts, viewed against the background of the largely uncodified constitutional framework of the UK. However, as we stated at the outset, it should be borne in mind that we have not been discussing developments with sole reference to precepts of constitutional law. Rather, we have concentrated our attention on assessing the adequacy of this conceptual framework as a means of understanding administrative law. While Dicey stressed

---

83 See further 17.3.2.
84 (1765) 19 St Tr 1030.

the essentially 'self-correcting' nature of the orthodox 'Westminster model' of accountability, current thinking has analysed the enormous expansion of the state since the late nineteenth century from the perspective of the executive's dominance over Parliament, through the 'Whitehall model'. This demonstrates the undoubted inadequacy of earlier conceptions and, taken together, party dominance and the Whitehall machine undermine adequate parliamentary accountability. If this view is accepted, it follows that the 'efficient' element of the constitution which Dicey considered to lie in the hands of a sovereign Parliament that could 'make and unmake any law', is today to a very considerable degree under the control of the executive.

If we accept this, it will by now be evident that the application of the concept of the separation of powers, already limited in the UK, has been further eroded by the domination of the executive. Nevertheless, Parliament should still have a significant role to play in making government accountable, and the question is, has it sufficient tools to allow the undertaking of such a crucial task? At the same time, we have also addressed the role that the judiciary can play in bringing balance to the constitution. Although there is no formal power to review the constitutionality of legislation, the emergence of revised interpretive techniques and the development of the grounds of judicial review have given an added weight to the judicial role. As against that, we have also discussed how too much judicial activism can, in itself, be problematic in terms of the separation of powers. Judges have therefore often been reluctant to become involved in policy/political matters, a point that will frequently be highlighted when we discuss judicial review in chapters 8 to 18.

Finally, this chapter has drawn attention to the impact of supranational and international law—particularly EU law and the ECHR—on our core constitutional concepts. In the discussion that follows in subsequent chapters it will be apparent that this body of jurisprudence has had an important and growing influence on the evolving grounds of judicial review. There are, in the result, many aspects to the constitutional structures that condition contemporary administrative law.

FURTHER READING

Allan, TRS (2001) *Constitutional Justice: A Liberal Theory of the Rule of Law* (Oxford: Oxford University Press).

Allison, JWF (2000) *A Continental Distinction in the Common Law*, 2nd edn (Oxford: Oxford University Press).

Allison, JWF (2013) 'The Spirits of the Constitution' in Bamforth N and P Leyland (eds), *Accountability in the Contemporary Constitution* (Oxford: Oxford University Press).

Anthony, G, Auby, J-B., Morison, J, and Zwart, T (2011) *Values in Global Administrative Law* (Oxford:Hart Publishing).

Bagehot, W (1963) *The English Constitution* (Glasgow: Fontana), introduction by RS Crossman.

Bamforth, N and Leyland, P (eds) (2003) *Public Law in a Multi-Layered Constitution* (Oxford: Hart Publishing).

Cole, DH (2001) '"An Unqualified Human Good"; E. P. Thompson and the Rule of Law' 28 *Journal of Law and Society* 177.

Craig, P (2015) *UK, EU and Global Administrative Law: Foundations and Challenges* (Cambridge: Cambridge University Press).

Dicey, AV (1959) *An Introduction to the Study of the Law of the Constitution*, 10th edn (London: Macmillan).

Elliott, M (2003) 'Embracing "Constitutional" Legislation: Towards Fundamental Law?' 54 *Northern Ireland Legal Quarterly* 25.

Elliott, M (2015) 'The Principle of Parliamentary Sovereignty in Legal, Constitutional and Political Perspective' in Jowell, J, Oliver, D, and O'Cinneide, C (eds), *The Changing Constitution*, 8th edn (Oxford: Oxford University Press).

Forsyth, C (ed) (2000) *Judicial Review and the Constitution* (Oxford: Hart Publishing).

Gordon, R (2010) *Repairing British Politics: A Blueprint for Constitutional Change* (Hart Publishing, Oxford).

Griffith, JAG (1997) *The Politics of the Judiciary* (London: Fontana).

Horne, A, Drewry, G, and Oliver D (eds) (2013) *Parliament and the Law* (Oxford: Hart Publishing).

Jennings, WI (1959) *The Law and the Constitution*, 5th edn (London: University of London Press).

Jowell, J [2006] 'Parliamentary Sovereignty Under the New Constitutional Hypothesis' *Public Law* 562.

Jowell, J (2015) 'The Rule of Law', in Jowell, J, Oliver, D, and O'Cinneide, C (eds), *The Changing Constitution*, 8th edn (Oxford: Oxford University Press).

Laws, Sir John [1995] 'Law and Democracy' *Public Law* 57.

Lazare, D (2001) *The Velvet Coup: The Constitution, The Supreme Court, and the Decline of American Democracy* (London: Verso Press).

Leyland, P (2016) *The Constitution of the United Kingdom: A Contextual Analysis*, 3rd edn (Oxford: Hart Publishing), chapters 3 and 5.

Loughlin, M (1992) *Public Law* and *Political Theory* (Oxford: Clarendon Press).

Peele, G (2002) 'The US Supreme Court: Politicians in Disguise?' *Politics Review* 8 April.

Tomkins, A (1998) *The Constitution after Scott: Government Unwrapped* (Oxford: Oxford University Press).

Tushnet, M (2015) *The Constitution of the United States of America: A Contextual Analysis*, 2nd edn (Oxford: Hart Publishing).

Williams, Sir D [2000] 'Bias; the Judges and the Separation of Powers' *Public Law* 45.

Young, A [2006] 'Hunting Sovereignty' *Public Law* 187.

3

....

European Union law and administrative law

3.1 Introduction

This chapter considers the implications that membership of the European Union (EU) has for UK administrative law. Its principal focus is the demands that EU law makes of the Member State legal systems and the impact that those demands have had within the specific context of the UK. For instance, we have already noted in the previous chapter that EU membership has challenged the fundamental precepts of the UK constitution and that this challenge is consonant with other pressures for constitutional realignment that are both internal and external to the UK legal order (devolution, globalisation, etc). In developing that point more fully, this chapter considers the key doctrines and general principles of EU law that have defined the challenge for the UK and how the courts, in particular, have reacted to that challenge. The chapter also considers the deeper impact that EU law can have in the domestic system—while EU law has its most immediate impact when it is directly in issue in proceedings, the courts sometimes draw upon EU jurisprudence when developing the common law in cases in which no point of EU law arises.[1]

The chapter divides into two main sections. The first considers the various demands of EU membership, for instance the requirement that directly effective EU law should enjoy supremacy over domestic law of whatever form and whenever enacted. On this basis, the second section examines the manner in which the UK legislature and courts have provided for the reception of EU law into the domestic system, and the resulting impact that EU law has had on legal principle and practice. The conclusion offers some more general, evaluative comments about the interface between the domestic and supranational orders.

There are two further points that should be made by way of introduction. The first is that this chapter does not purport to provide an account of the history, evolution, and objectives of the EU, *viz* from its beginnings as an essentially economic Community through to a Union which enjoys competence in areas that include a common foreign and security policy.[2] This is because such analysis would not be possible in a single chapter and also because it would move analysis too far beyond issues of relevance to the workings of UK administrative law. What the current chapter provides, therefore, is an overview of the features of EU administrative

---

1 See generally G Anthony, *UK Public Law and European Law: The Dynamics of Legal Integration* (Oxford: Hart Publishing, 2002).

2 For an excellent account *pre*-Lisbon see W van Gerven, *The European Union: A Polity of States and Peoples* (Oxford: Hart Publishing, 2005). And on Lisbon see P Craig, *The Lisbon Treaty: Law, Politics and Treaty Reform* (Oxford: Oxford University Press, 2010).

law that apply to the decision-making processes of Member State authorities and, so far as is relevant for our purposes, the workings of the EU institutions. The reader who desires a more detailed account of the nature of EU law and its concomitant processes should consult one or more of the many excellent textbooks on the subject.[3]

The second point is that there is, at the time of writing this edition, an upcoming referendum on continued UK membership of the EU.[4] While a vote to remain within the EU would mean that EU law's various doctrines etc would continue to apply in UK law, a vote to leave the EU need not mean that EU law would thereafter be irrelevant to the UK legal system. This is essentially a point about the general principles of EU law, which we discuss later in this chapter and mention again in subsequent chapters. Those general principles have influenced common law approaches to the grounds for judicial review in particular, and UK courts will still use the common law principles that have evolved over the years. When reading this chapter, and those that follow, we would therefore encourage the reader to think laterally about how our principles of law develop and about how they overlap with other systems of law.

3.2 EU law and national legal systems: the obligations of membership

The obligations that EU law imposes upon national legal systems are very far-reaching and have sparked wide-ranging constitutional debates about the nature and implications of membership.[5] From the perspective of EU law itself, the obligations have been deemed necessary to ensure that the EU can achieve its objective of social, economic, and political integration by requiring national legal orders to adhere to common legal standards and principles. However, from the perspective of national legal orders, adherence to those standards and principles can sometimes prove difficult, as there are differences in legal cultures within Europe, most notably between the common law and the civilian legal traditions. Even leaving the controversial question of sovereignty to one side, the obligations of membership can present other challenges by requiring courts to assimilate 'external' legal concepts into domestic law. Indeed, it is the UK courts' experience of having done just that which means that EU law may still have an influence on UK law even if the UK votes to leave the EU.

There are perhaps four key obligations associated with membership, and these concern: (1) the direct effect and supremacy of EU law; (2) the general principles of EU law; (3) fundamental rights; and (4) remedies.

3 See, among others, e.g., P Craig and G de Búrca, *EU Law: Text Cases and Materials*, 6th edn (Oxford: Oxford University Press, 2015) and D Chalmers, G Davies, and G Monti, *European Union Law: Cases and Materials*, 3rd edn (Cambridge: Cambridge University Press, 2014).

4 See European Union Referendum Act 2015. For some possible implications see A Biondi and P Birkinshaw (eds), *Britain Alone!: The Implications and Consequences of UK Exit from the EU* (The Netherlands: Kluwer, 2016).

5 For some perspectives see, e.g., K Jaklic, *Constitutional Pluralism in the EU* (Oxford: Oxford University Press, 2014).

3.2.1 **Direct effect and supremacy**

The doctrines of the direct effect and supremacy of EU law are at the very heart of the EU legal order. The doctrines, which were introduced by the Court of Justice of the European Union (CJEU) early in the integration process,[6] have served to define the EU legal order in terms that were without parallel in the history of international law and relations. For instance, before those judgments were delivered it was axiomatic that individuals could rely upon norms of international law only where the relevant international Treaty expressly gave them the right to do so. However, in *Van Gend en Loos* the CJEU described the EU as a 'new legal order' in which international law orthodoxy was displaced and said that individuals could rely upon certain provisions of EU law in national courts notwithstanding that the Treaties were silent on the point (direct effect).[7] The CJEU built upon this understanding in the famous *Costa* case when ruling that directly effective provisions of EU law should enjoy primacy over any conflicting provision of national law (the supremacy doctrine).[8]

3.2.1.1 **Direct effect**

The direct effect doctrine allows individuals to rely upon a provision of EU law in domestic courts where the provision is: (1) clear and unambiguous; (2) unconditional; and (3) not dependent on further action being taken by EU or national authorities. Quite clearly, the doctrine does not entail that every provision of EU law can have direct effect, but only those that may be said to be 'self-executing' (a provision, for these purposes, may be a Treaty Article, a regulation, a directive, or a decision).[9] Nevertheless, the doctrine has resulted in the conferral upon individuals of a very significant range of rights that are, when read with the supremacy doctrine, enforceable at the national level. Such enforcement, in turn, has been central to the success of the European project.[10]

One problem with the doctrine, however, has been that concerned with the distinction between 'vertical' effect (whereby measures are enforced against state authorities) and 'horizontal' effect (whereby measures are enforced against private parties). While it has long been established that Treaty Articles, regulations, and decisions are potentially capable of having either form of effect,[11] the CJEU has consistently held that directives are capable of having only vertical effect because they are addressed specifically to Member States.[12] In one sense, this is not a point that has any great relevance for the workings of administrative law in the UK, as individuals will still be able to enforce directives against public authorities once the

---

6 Case 26/62, *Van Gend en Loos* [1963] ECR 1 and Case 6/64, *Costa v ENEL* [1964] ECR 585.

7 Case 26/62, *Van Gend en Loos* [1963] ECR 1.

8 Case 6/64, *Costa v ENEL* [1964] ECR 585.

9 On the different types of EU measures, and the hierarchy between them, see Craig and de Búrca, n 3, ch 4.

10 But note also the role and importance of enforcement proceedings that the European Commission can take in the CJEU against Member States under Art 258 TFEU.

11 On the direct effect of these, and other sources of law, including the EU Charter of Fundamental Rights and international agreements, see Craig and de Búrca, n 3, ch 7.

12 See, most famously, Case 152/84, *Marshall v Southampton and South-West Hampshire Area Health Authority* [1986] ECR 723.

time limit for their implementation has passed.[13] However, the CJEU's approach has also been much criticised for the reason that it potentially leaves individuals without the full protection of the law,[14] and the CJEU has since introduced a number of other obligations that have a general importance to the workings of domestic public law.[15] The most significant of these are the 'indirect effect' and 'state liability' doctrines under which, respectively, national courts must: (1) attempt to interpret national legislation, so far as possible, in conformity with a non-directly effective directive that is relevant to proceedings between two parties;[16] and (2) make an award of damages to an individual who has suffered loss as a result of non-implementation of a directive because, among other things, he or she could not enforce horizontally the directive.[17] As we will see below, the workings of the doctrines in UK law have introduced the courts to new techniques and remedies that have raised questions about how far those techniques and remedies should be allowed to 'spill-over' into domestic administrative law more generally.

3.2.1.2 Supremacy

The supremacy doctrine entails at its most simple that directly effective EU law is to be regarded as superior to all norms of national law and that, where there is a conflict between the two, EU law is to prevail.[18] The point was first established in *Costa v ENEL*, where the CJEU, having noted that the Member States had created a Community (now Union) of unlimited duration, stated that the Member States had thereby limited their sovereign rights and that the corresponding body of EU law 'could not, because of its special and original nature, be overridden by domestic legal provisions, however framed, without being deprived of its character as [EU] law and with the legal basis of the [EU] itself being called into question'.[19] Subsequent case law also established that the doctrine applies to each and every national legal norm, whether adopted/enacted prior or subsequent to the EU rule in question. For the CJEU, any other eventuality would 'impair the effectiveness' of EU law.[20]

Cast in these terms, the supremacy doctrine defines the challenge that EU membership presents to constitutional orthodoxy in the UK, as it in effect means that the doctrine of parliamentary sovereignty must cede to the demands of EU law.[21] However, it is important to note that the above formulation is *that of the CJEU* rather than that of the national courts of the Member States. Thus, even though EU law enjoys primacy throughout the Member States as a matter of practice, there

---

13 Case 41/74, *Van Duyn v Home Office* [1974] ECR 1337. Note too that CJEU case law adopts a broad understanding of the state for these purposes, *viz* that it includes any body 'which has been made responsible, pursuant to a measure adopted by the State, for providing a public service under the control of the State and has for that purpose special powers beyond those which result from the normal rules applicable in relations between individuals'—Case C-188/89, *Foster v British Gas* [1990] ECR I-3313, 3348–9, para 20.

14 For a notable account see J Coppel, 'Rights, Duties and the End of Marshall' (1994) 57 *Modern Law Review* 859.

15 Craig and de Búrca, n 3, ch 7.

16 Case 14/83, *Von Colson and Kamann v Land Nordrhein-Westfalen* [1984] ECR 1891 and Case C-106/89, *Marleasing SA v La Comercial Internacional de Alimentacion SA* [1990] ECR I-4135.

17 Cases C-6 & 9/90, *Francovich and Bonifaci v Italy* [1991] ECR I-5357.

18 See Declaration 17 to the Treaty of Lisbon.

19 Case 6/64, [1964] ECR 585, 593.

20 Case 106/77, *Amministrazione delle Finanze dello Stato v Simmenthal SpA* [1978] ECR 629, para 22.

21 See ch 2.

have been a number of well-documented instances of national court resistance to the CJEU's demand that EU law should enjoy supremacy.[22] That resistance has followed from the fact that national courts define their own role with reference to their domestic constitutions, which, in their view, are normatively superior to EU law. In other words, national courts may emphasise that EU membership is contingent upon national constitutional legitimation of such membership and that EU law is in that sense subject to the prior force of the domestic constitution. This is an important point to bear in mind when examining the justification that UK courts have offered for the ascription of supremacy to EU law, considered later.[23]

3.2.2 General principles of law

A correlate of the doctrine of the supremacy of EU law is the requirement that national courts give effect to the general principles of EU law in cases which raise issues about directly effective provisions of the Treaty and acts such as directives, regulations, and so on. The general principles that apply here are the same as those that the CJEU uses when reviewing the legality of EU acts under Article 263 of the Treaty on the Functioning of the European Union (TFEU), and they include principles drawn from national legal traditions that may be different to that of the common law. Of the principles, those of proportionality, equality, and legitimate expectation are of particular note, as they envisage a role for courts that is, in some significant respects, different from historical understandings of the role of the courts in the UK.[24] Also of note are the general principles that have been developed with reference to fundamental rights standards such as those found in the European Convention on Human Rights (ECHR). However, the story of fundamental rights in the EU is about much more than simply the elaboration of general principles of law, and we consider the significance of those principles under a separate heading below.

3.2.2.1 Proportionality

The proportionality principle requires balance in decision-making processes; that is, it entails that a decision or other measure that pursues a particular objective and which interferes with an individual's rights should interfere with those rights no more than is necessary to achieve the objective. The principle, which has its origins in German law,[25] may become operative in the EU context where, for instance, national legislation prohibits the sale of particular goods for reasons of morality, or where an administrator refuses to grant a licence to a non-UK national who wishes to provide a particular economic service in the UK.[26] Under such circumstances, the affected individual may challenge the legislation or decision in court, and the judge must enquire: (a) whether the limitation is suitable for the attainment of a public interest objective expressly prescribed in the Treaty or found in CJEU case

---

22 Craig and de Búrca, n 3, ch 9.

23 For further comparative analysis see A Dyevre, 'European Integration and National Courts: Defending Sovereignty Under Institutional Constraints?' (2013) 9 *European Constitutional Law Review* 139.

24 See further chs 13–15.

25 See G Nolte, 'General Principles of German and European Administrative Law—A Comparison in Historical Perspective' (1994) 57 *Modern Law Review* 191.

26 Decisions of this kind would fall under, respectively, Arts 34–36 TFEU and Arts 56–62 TFEU.

law; (b) whether the measure adopted or decision taken was necessary to achieve the objective (*viz* the objective cannot be achieved by less restrictive means); and (c) whether the measure imposed an excessive burden on the individual *vis-à-vis* the objective pursued.[27] In the event that the measure or decision is found to be disproportionate, the individual is entitled to a remedy that will ensure effective protection of his or her EU law rights. Depending on circumstance, that remedy may take form in an award of damages (considered later).

The principle clearly envisages close judicial review of national measures that fall within the scope of EU law, and its reception by UK courts has not been without difficulty.[28] This is because judicial review in the UK has historically centred on the ground of *Wednesbury* unreasonableness,[29] which posits judicial self-restraint in the face of administrative and secondary legislative choices (on the [non]-review of Acts of the Westminster Parliament legislation see chapter 2). On the other hand, it is true that the proportionality principle is context sensitive and that it can be applied variably by the CJEU and, by association, national courts.[30] Hence where an administrative decision has an adverse impact upon an individual's fundamental rights, there is authority to say that courts should look closely at the impugned measure, as 'courts regard it as a natural and proper part of their legitimate function to adjudicate on the boundary lines between state action and individual rights'.[31] However, where a decision is one of social or economic policy and has been taken in a field in which the decision-maker has a wide discretion, there is long-established CJEU authority to suggest that use of the proportionality principle should be moderated by appropriate judicial restraint.[32] At the national level, such restraint may then be particularly apparent when the choice in question is that of the legislature, although it is accepted that administrative decision-makers may also enjoy a 'margin of appreciation'.[33]

3.2.2.2 Equality

Equality—or non-discrimination—exists in the EU order both as a general principle of law and as a substantive requirement of various provisions of the TFEU.[34] As a general principle of law, it requires decision-makers to treat like situations alike and different situations differently, unless there is good reason for them not to do so. For instance, the principle might be said to be breached where a government compensation scheme distinguishes between different sectors in an industry that is affected by a production ban introduced for reasons of public health.[35] Under such circumstances, the equality principle would require that the decision-maker

---

27 Case C-331/88, *R v Minister for Agriculture, Fisheries and Food, ex p Fedesa* [1990] ECR I-4023.

28 See ch 13.

29 *Associated Provincial Picture Houses v Wednesbury Corporation* [1948] 1 KB 223.

30 The leading account remains G de Búrca, 'Proportionality in EC Law' (1993) 13 *Yearbook of European Law* 105; and for recent judicial consideration of the nature of the test see *R (Lumsdon) v Legal Services Board* [2015] UKSC 41, [2015] 3 WLR 121.

31 Case 44/79, *Hauer v Land Rheinland-Pflaz* [1979] ECR 3727.

32 See, e.g., Case C-331/88, *R v Minister for Agriculture, Fisheries and Food, ex p Fedesa* [1990] ECR 4023, where the issue before the CJEU was the legality of a directive in the field of the Common Agricultural Policy.

33 See, e.g, *R v Secretary of State, ex p Eastside Cheese Company* [1999] 3 CMLR 123.

34 See further 14.3.

35 As in, e.g., *R v Ministry of Agriculture, Fisheries and Food, ex p First City Trading Ltd* [1997] 1 CMLR 250—although note that the High Court refused to give effect to the principle in this case.

treat comparable sectors the same unless there is a justification for not doing so. In the event that there is no such justification, the scheme or other measure will be unlawful.

The central question for a court that is tasked with assessing whether a measure has breached the equality principle is, again, how closely it should look at the justification for differential treatment.[36] Here, the proportionality principle would, in its purest form, require that the court examine in detail the justification for differential treatment when determining whether there had been lawful discrimination. However, we have already seen that the proportionality principle can also be applied variably, and the context of a case may lead a reviewing court to exercise restraint when considering a measure's lawfulness. This latter approach is certainly one that would fit more easily with common law orthodoxy, as UK courts have traditionally asked whether any differential treatment was *Wednesbury* unreasonable.[37]

3.2.2.3 Legitimate expectation

The EU law general principle of legitimate expectation has been developed on the basis of the doctrine of legal certainty (which doctrine also precludes measures from having, among other things, retroactive effect).[38] Its basic premise is that a public authority which has made a representation to an individual that the authority will act in a particular manner cannot subsequently resile from that representation unless there is an overriding reason of public interest for doing so. The link to legal certainty in EU law thus lies in the need for individuals to be able to arrange their affairs in the light of legal representations made to them, or to rely on the policies or practices of an authority.[39] At common law, the courts may also speak of the need for legal certainty, albeit that the origins of the domestic principle lie in common law fairness.[40]

It is important to note that the principle of legitimate expectation may be procedural and/or substantive in form. The procedural dimension goes to the manner in which a decision is taken, and can require that an individual who will be affected by a decision or other measure be consulted in advance of the decision being finalised. On the other hand, the substantive dimension can require that an individual who has been promised a particular benefit receive that benefit (for instance, a licence), save where there are compelling reasons of public interest for denying it.[41] The leading example in EU law remains *Mulder v Minister van Landbouw en Visserij*,[42] which illustrates how far the general principles of EU law can involve courts in the close review of administrative and other choices. The facts of the case were that the applicant, a farmer, had undertaken to cease producing milk for five years in return for a premium. When he subsequently sought to resume production on

---

36 See, e.g., *R (Rotherham MBC) v Secretary of State for Business, Innovation and Skills* [2015] UKSC 6, [2015] 3 CMLR 20, discussed at 14.3.

37 See, e.g., *Matadeen v Pointu* [1999] 1 AC 98, 109, Lord Hoffmann; and on *Wednesbury* see ch 13.

38 See P Craig, *European Administrative Law*, 2nd edn (Oxford University Press, 2012), ch 18.

39 See S Schønberg, *Legitimate Expectations in Administrative Law* (Oxford: Oxford University Press, 2000), ch 1.

40 See ch 15.

41 See, e.g., Case C-152/88, *Sofrimport v Commission* [1990] ECR I-2477.

42 Case 120/86, [1988] ECR 2321.

the expiry of the five-year period, he was refused a quota on the grounds that he had to have produced milk the preceding year in order to be eligible for a quota for the forthcoming year. This provision had, however, been introduced during the said five-year period, and Mulder argued that it frustrated his expectation of re-entering the milk market. Given this, the CJEU proceeded to balance the general policy objective the EU was pursuing against Mulder's stated interests (here using the proportionality principle). While noting that the applicant could not expect to re-enter the market under exactly the same conditions as he 'left' it, the CJEU nevertheless concluded that he 'may legitimately expect not to be subject, upon the expiry of his undertaking, to restrictions which specifically affect him precisely because he availed himself of the possibilities offered by the (EU) provisions'. Moreover, when the EU institutions subsequently revised their position to allow Mulder to resume production with a quota of 60 per cent of his previous production, the CJEU decided on a further action by Mulder that the 60 per cent quota was too low. The result was that the revised position had to be reconsidered.

3.2.3 **Fundamental rights**

The development of EU law's general principles with reference to fundamental rights standards is, as we have noted earlier, part of a much longer story about the place of fundamental rights in the EU legal order. That story is essentially about how the EU has changed from the historical position of having no formal bill of rights that bound the institutions and the Member States when implementing EU law, through to the position where it now has just such a bill in the form of the EU Charter of Fundamental Rights.[43] The impetus for the change is often said to have been provided by the German Federal Constitutional Court's judgment in *Internationale Handelsgesellschaft* (*'Solange I'*),[44] where the court said that it would not accept unquestioningly the primacy of EU law so long as that body of law did not meet the democratic controls and standards of protection of human rights afforded by the German Basic Law (note that comparable issues also arose in other systems).[45] This represented a clear challenge to the doctrine of the supremacy of EU law, discussed earlier, and the EU institutions moved to address the concerns underlying the German court's ruling in an attempt to re-establish supremacy as a workable doctrine. For instance, the European Parliament, the Council, and the Commission adopted a Declaration that reaffirmed the importance of fundamental rights within the EU process;[46] and the CJEU began to develop the general principles of law with increased reference to fundamental rights standards found in the national constitutional traditions and in international instruments such as the ECHR and the International Covenant on Civil and Political Rights.[47] The effect of this latter development was for EU and national measures to be reviewed with reference to fundamental rights standards as 'rules of law' that relate to the interpretation of the Treaty, for instance where a national administrative measure impacted upon rights to freedom of movement.[48] Through

---

43 The Charter has the force of Treaty law by virtue of Art 6 TEU.
44 [1974] 2 CMLR 540.
45 See TC Hartley, *Constitutional Problems of the European Union* (Oxford: Hart Publishing, 1999).
46 OJ 1977 C 103/1.
47 See, e.g., Case 374/87, *Orkem v Commission* [1989] ECR 3283.
48 e.g., *R v Secretary of State for the Home Department, ex p McQuillan* [1995] 4 All ER 400.

time, the German Federal Constitutional Court thus accepted that fundamental rights received sufficient protection under EU law and it has therefore not exercised its 'reserve power' to review EU law in the light of Germany's national fundamental rights standards (although the Court has since noted other limits to the EU's powers).[49] The CJEU, for its part, has since also held that fundamental rights standards are so central to EU law that it reserves the right to review the legality of EU measures that have been adopted to give effect to Resolutions of the UN Security Council.[50] This has been so notwithstanding that the UN Charter that provides the basis for Resolutions supposedly sits at the apex of the international legal order.[51]

The binding force of the EU Charter of Fundamental Rights—it now governs the actions of the EU institutions and the Member States when they are implementing EU law—is a consequence of the entry into force of the Treaty of Lisbon. In general terms, this is highly significant, as it has concretised long-standing developments in EU law and, moreover, progressed the protection of rights by giving legal effect to more modern standards such as those related to data protection, the environment, and good administration (the Charter sub-divides into six main sections on 'dignity', 'freedoms', 'equality', 'solidarity', 'citizen's rights', and 'justice').[52] On the other hand, this general point must be read beside a more specific one about the Charter and its application in the UK (and Poland). In short, a Protocol appended to the Treaty of Lisbon states that, 'The Charter does not extend the ability of the [CJEU], or any court or tribunal of [the UK], to find that the laws, regulations, or administrative provisions, practices or action of [the UK] are inconsistent with the fundamental rights, freedoms and principles it reaffirms'.[53] Initially, it was thought that this meant that the Charter would not be directly arguable in respect of the UK either in its own courts or in enforcement proceedings brought against the UK by the European Commission (albeit that it was recognised that the Charter could still have an indirect impact through the general principles of EU law and that UK courts may make voluntary references to it when developing the common law).[54] However, the nature of the wording in the Protocol was such that it led some to argue that most of the provisions of the Charter could be read as binding on the UK when acting in areas of EU competence, and the CJEU has now held that it does have that effect, save, it would seem, for the section headed 'solidarity'.[55]

One further point concerns the relationship between the EU and the ECHR. Here, the Lisbon Treaty again marked a significant change by providing that the EU may accede to the ECHR. This, previously, was something that the CJEU considered could not occur under the Treaties, as there was no Article that provided either expressly or impliedly for accession.[56] By making express provision to that effect, the Lisbon Treaty thus created the very real possibility that the legality of

---

49 On rights see *Re Wünsche HandelsGesellschaft 'Solange II'* [1987] 3 CMLR 225; and on the fuller picture see Craig and de Búrca, n 3, 279–90.

50 See, most famously, Cases C-402 and 415/05, *Kadi v Council and Commission* [2008] ECR I-6351.

51 On the contemporary nature of EU law's regime see further the CJEU's *Opinion pursuant to Article 218(11) TFEU (2/13)* [2015] 2 CMLR 21 (re accession to the ECHR).

52 On the Charter see further K Beal and T Hickman, 'Beano No More: The Charter of Rights After Lisbon' [2011] 16 *Judicial Review* 113.

53 Protocol 30.

54 As in, e.g., *A and others v East Sussex County Council* [2003] All ER (D) 233, at para 73 Munby J.

55 Case C-411/10, *NS v Secretary of State for the Home Department* [2012] 2 CMLR 9, discussed at 4.5.

56 See Opinion 2/94 on *Accession by the Community to the ECHR* [1996] ECR I-1759.

EU measures would come to be challenged before the European Court of Human Rights.[57] However, the CJEU has since noted very real difficulties with the possibility of any accession agreement that would affect the internal autonomy of the EU legal order, and a formal coming together of the two orders may yet be some time away.[58]

3.2.4 Remedies and the effective protection of the individual

The final obligation of EU membership to consider is that concerned with remedies in national courts for breaches of EU law. In this context, the CJEU has drawn upon the supremacy and direct effect doctrines, as well as more general ideas of Member State fidelity to the integration project. Although the CJEU has long emphasised that EU law rights are to be protected through national procedures and practices (subject to the requirement that the protection is effective and equivalent to that given to rights under national law),[59] it has since also introduced a number of specific remedies requirements that exist beyond those provided by national systems.[60] The case law has thus seen the CJEU develop much more fully its understanding of what 'effective protection' of the individual requires, with the corresponding objective being the attainment of uniform protection throughout the EU irrespective of disparities in national legal practice.

The shift in the CJEU's case law can be illustrated with reference to two remedies, which have emerged in case law involving, among other courts, those of the UK. The first is interim protection of the individual, which is associated with the seminal *Factortame* case.[61] The facts were that a group of Spanish fishing boat operators sought an injunction in UK courts to prevent the Secretary of State for Transport enforcing the terms of the Merchant Shipping Act 1988, which the operators challenged as contrary to the nationality, establishment, and capital provisions of the (then) EC Treaty. An Article 177 EC (now Article 267 TFEU) reference to the CJEU had in turn been made, as the House of Lords considered that it could not grant the injunction because of the domestic rule that prevents the grant of injunctions against ministers of the Crown in civil proceedings (*viz* section 21 of the Crown Proceedings Act 1947).[62] However, the CJEU stated in its ruling that 'the full effectiveness of EU law would be . . . impaired if a rule of national law could prevent a court . . . granting interim relief in order to ensure the full effectiveness of the judgment to be given on the existence of the rights claimed under EU law. It follows that if a court which, in those circumstances would grant interim relief, if it were not for a rule of national law, is obliged to set aside that rule'.[63] The House of Lords subsequently granted the injunction in the light of the CJEU's ruling, with the result that the Act of 1988 was disapplied. This led some commentators to speak of a constitutional 'revolution' in the UK, as the Parliament that had enacted the European Communities Act 1972 had in effect bound its successor.[64]

---

57 Art 6.2 TEU, as read with Protocol 8.

58 See *Opinion pursuant to Article 218(11) TFEU (2/13)* [2015] 2 CMLR 21 (re accession to the ECHR).

59 See, e.g., Case 33/76, *Rewe-Zentralfinanz eG and Rewe-Zentral AG v Landwirtschaftskammer für das Saarland* [1976] ECR 1989.

60 See generally Craig and de Búrca, n 3, ch 8.

61 *R v Secretary of State for Transport, ex p Factortame Ltd (No 2)* [1991] 1 AC 603.

62 *Factortame Ltd v Secretary of State for Transport* [1990] 2 AC 85.

63 Case C-213/89, *Factortame* [1990] ECR I-2433, 2465, para 21.

64 HWR Wade, 'Sovereignty—Revolution or Evolution?' (1996) 112 *Law Quarterly Review* 56. On the case see further ch 18.

The second remedy is damages, which an individual may seek where the state acts or fails to act in breach of the individual's EU law rights. This doctrine of 'state liability' was originally of application only where the individual suffered loss as a result of a state's failure to implement a directive in domestic law,[65] but it has since been developed to cover any 'sufficiently serious' breach of an individual's EU law rights by any of the branches of the state.[66] Case law has thus established that a state may be liable at the behest of an individual where its legislature has enacted legislation that is contrary to EU law rights;[67] where it has failed to repeal legislation that is contrary to EU law;[68] or, per the origins of the doctrine, where it has failed to introduce legislation to implement a directive.[69] The case law has likewise established that liability may sound where administrative discretion is exercised contrary to EU law rights or where those rights are breached by a judicial act or omission.[70]

The corresponding EU law test for liability has three elements, namely: (1) is there an EU law provision that confers enforceable rights upon individuals?; (2) has there been a 'sufficiently serious' breach of the provision by the state?; and (3) has the individual suffered loss as a direct result of the breach? Of these elements the most important in many cases is that concerned with 'sufficient seriousness', as the CJEU has emphasised that the question of liability must be resolved with reference to the context of any state action or inaction. Hence, where a Member State authority has a wide discretion in a particular area, for example the national legislature introducing national legislation, liability will rest only where the state 'manifestly and gravely disregards the limits of its discretion'.[71] By contrast, where a Member State has only very limited or no discretion, for example making an administrative decision in a policy area closely regulated by EU law, the 'mere infringement' of an EU provision may be enough to occasion liability.[72] Cases between these two examples, for instance where a national legislature is introducing legislation to implement an EU directive, must then be resolved with reference to the CJEU's suggested list of criteria for identifying a sufficiently serious breach: was the EU law provision that was breached clear? Was the breach/damage intentional? Was any error of law on the part of the state excusable? Had the Member State been adopting or retaining practices contrary to EU law?[73]

---

65 Cases C-6/90, *Francovich and Bonifaci v Italy* [1991] ECR I-5357.

66 Cases C-46 and 48/93, *Brasserie du Pêcheur SA v Germany, R v Secretary of State for Transport, ex p Factortame Ltd* [1996] I-ECR 1029.

67 *R v Secretary of State for Transport, ex p Factortame* [2000] 1 AC 524.

68 Cases C-46 and 48/93, *Brasserie du Pêcheur SA v Germany, R v Secretary of State for Transport, ex p Factortame Ltd* [1996] 1 ECR 1029.

69 Cases C-178–9/94, 188–190/94, *Dillenkofer v Federal Republic of Germany* [1996] ECR I-4845.

70 See, respectively, Case C-5/94, *R v Ministry of Agriculture, Fisheries and Food, ex p Hedley Lomas (Ireland) Ltd* [1996] ECR I-2553, and Case C-224/01, *Köbler v Austria* [2003] ECR I-10239.

71 Cases C-46 and 48/93, *Brasserie du Pêcheur SA v Germany, R v Secretary of State for Transport, ex p Factortame Ltd* [1996] ECR I-1029, para 55—'manifest disregard' is also the threshold for liability in the context of judicial acts and omissions: Case C-224/01, *Köbler v Austria* [2003] ECR I-10239.

72 Case C-5/94, *R v Ministry of Agriculture, Fisheries and Food, ex p Hedley Lomas (Ireland) Ltd* [1996] ECR I-2553, para 28.

73 Joined Cases C-46 and 48/93, *Brasserie du Pêcheur SA v Germany, R v Secretary of State for Transport, ex p Factortame Ltd* [1996] ECR I-1029, para 56. And for further guidance from the CJEU see, e.g., Case C-118/00, *Larsy v INASTI* [2001] ECR I-5063 and Case C-150/99, *Stockholm Lindöpark Aktiebolag v Sweden* [2001] ECR I-493.

3.3 **EU law in the UK**

We turn now to consider more closely the manner in which EU law has been received into the specific context of the UK legal order. Our aim here is to bring together some of the above references to the UK experience with EU law, and to develop a more complete picture of how EU norms have been accommodated within the common law system. At its heart this is an enquiry into the workings of the direct effect and supremacy doctrines (considered at 3.2.1.1 and 3.2.1.2), as it is those doctrines that have shaped most other aspects of the EU order that make demands of national courts. However, EU law can also have a broader impact, for instance where national courts draw upon it when developing the common law in domestic cases in which EU law is not directly in issue. We term this indirect impact as 'spill-over'.

3.3.1 **The European Communities Act 1972**

Because the UK has a dualist constitutional tradition—on which see chapter 2—it was self-evident that an Act of Parliament would be required before rights and obligations under EU law could be enforced in the domestic courts. At the same time, it was acknowledged that the enactment of legislation for that purpose would need to address the apparently irreconcilable conflict between the domestic doctrine of parliamentary sovereignty and the doctrine of the supremacy of EU law. Indeed, the scope for such conflict had already been acknowledged well in advance of EU membership,[74] and it was suggested during parliamentary debates that the legislation should include a statement to the effect that no Parliament would legislate contrary to EU law. However, the government of the day declined to insert such a clause for the reason that a future Parliament could disregard any supremacy provision. The implication, therefore, was that future legislation that conflicted with EU law would prevail in accordance with domestic orthodoxy.

The central provisions of the resulting legislation—the European Communities Act 1972—are sections 2 and 3. Section 2(1) provides for the direct effect of EU law in the UK domestic system by stating:

All such rights, powers, liabilities, obligations, and restrictions from time to time created or arising by or under the Treaties, and all such remedies and procedures from time to time provided for by or under the Treaties, as in accordance with the Treaties are without further enactment to be given legal effect or used in the United Kingdom shall be recognised and available in law, and be enforced, allowed and followed accordingly; and the expression 'enforceable EU right' and similar expressions shall be read as referring to one to which this subsection applies.

Section 2(2) then enables Her Majesty by Order in Council and designated ministers or departments (which may include ministers and departments in the devolved institutions) to make regulations for the purpose of implementing EU law in some areas;[75] and section 2(4) imposes an interpretive obligation whereby all

---

74 See PB Keenan, 'Some Legal Consequences of Britain's Entry into the European Common Market' [1962] *Public Law* 327.
75 See further Sch 2 to the Act.

past and future legislation is to be read and given effect subject to the provisions of the European Communities Act 1972. This sub-section is thus the closest that the Act has to a supremacy clause—although we can compare now section 18 of the European Union Act 2011, discussed at 3.3.3—as it requires the courts to interpret all past and future legislation in the light of EU law. That interpretive duty is moreover to be guided by section 3, which reads: 'For the purposes of all legal proceedings any question as to the meaning or effect of any of the Treaties . . . or . . . any EU instrument, shall be treated as a question of law (and, if not referred to the European Court, be for determination as such in accordance with the . . . relevant decision of the European Court).'

3.3.2 Sovereignty and supremacy: from *Factortame* to *Pham*

The corresponding body of case law under the Act is complex, and fuller analyses are provided elsewhere.[76] For present purposes, however, there are four cases that are key to understanding how the UK courts have approached the sovereignty and supremacy problem. The first is *R v Secretary of State for Transport, ex p Factortame Ltd*.[77] As we have already seen at 3.2.4, this case resulted with the House of Lords granting an interim injunction to prevent the Secretary of State for Transport enforcing the terms of the Merchant Shipping Act 1988. In real terms, this meant that the 1972 Act had prevailed over the 1988 Act, and some commentators considered that this could only be viewed as 'revolutionary' in terms of the UK constitution.[78] But the House of Lords was notably less sensationalist when justifying its decision, stating that 'whatever limitation of its sovereignty Parliament accepted when it enacted the European Communities Act 1972 it has always been clear that it was the duty of a United Kingdom court, when delivering final judgment, to override any rule of national law found to be in conflict with any directly enforceable rule' of EU law.[79] The supremacy of EU law was thereby accepted by the House of Lords as a consequence of legislative choice, with subsequent judgments giving further indications of the far-reaching implications of that outcome. Hence in *R v Secretary of State for Employment, ex p Equal Opportunities Commission*[80] the House of Lords made a declaration that various provisions of the Employment Protection Consolidation Act 1978 were contrary to EU law's equal pay guarantees for men and women; and in *Webb v EMO Air Cargo (No 2)*, the House accepted the obligation to interpret domestic legislation, whenever enacted, in the light of non-directly effective directives that were relevant to a dispute between two private parties (on indirect effect see 3.2.1.1).[81]

---

76 e.g., P Craig, 'Britain in the European Union' in J Jowell, D Oliver, and C O'Cinneide (eds), *The Changing Constitution*, 8th edn (Oxford: Oxford University Press, 2011), ch 4; and G Anthony, *UK Public Law and European Law: The Dynamics of Legal Integration* (Oxford: Hart Publishing, 2002), ch 4.

77 [1991] 1 AC 603.

78 HWR Wade, 'Sovereignty—Revolution or Evolution?' (1996) 112 *Law Quarterly Review* 56. But compare TRS Allan, 'Parliamentary Sovereignty: Law, Politics and Revolution' (1997) 113 *Law Quarterly Review* 443.

79 *Factortame* (No 2) [1991] 1 AC 603, 658, Lord Bridge.

80 [1995] 1 AC 1.

81 [1995] 4 All ER 577. And on the interpretation of national law in the light of EU law see further, e.g., *Assange v Swedish Prosecution Authority* [2012] UKSC 22, [2012] 2 AC 471.

The justification for the ascription of supremacy to EU law in *Factortame* was, however, essentially contractarian in form (i.e., the UK has joined a club with certain rules),[82] and it was only with the Divisional Court's judgment in our second case, *Thoburn v Sunderland City Council*,[83] that a more elaborate line of reasoning started to emerge. In *Thoburn*, the issue was whether regulations made under the 1972 Act could be used to modify the Weights and Measures Act 1985, or whether this was not possible because the 1985 Act had impliedly repealed the earlier statute.[84] Although Laws LJ ultimately considered that the implied repeal doctrine was not engaged by the statutes, he explained how the 1985 legislation could not, in any event, impliedly repeal the Act of 1972.[85] This was because the common law now recognised the Act of 1972 as one of a number of 'constitutional statutes', which were no longer subject to the ordinary rules of implied repeal. Such statutes, which were said to be those that (a) condition the legal relationship between citizen and state in some general, overarching manner and/or (b) enlarge or diminish the scope of fundamental constitutional rights, can instead be repealed only where there are 'express words in the later statute, or . . . words so specific that the inference of an actual determination to effect the result contended for [is] irresistible'.[86] It was against this backdrop that the outcome in *Factortame* was to be understood: while the subsequent legislation in that case was inconsistent with the earlier Act, there was no express repeal of the former, and the former Act—a constitutional statute—thereby prevailed.

It is important to be clear precisely what *Thoburn* sought to establish. In short, it accepted that EU law enjoys supremacy in domestic law, but that that supremacy is contingent upon both the European Communities Act 1972 and the common law's reading of the Act. This, in turn, is an approach that brings the UK reception of EU law more immediately into line with that of other Member States. For instance, we noted above that constitutional courts in other Member States have emphasised the primacy of their domestic constitutions in the sense that it is those constitutions, rather than the demands of the CJEU, that legitimise EU law's place in the domestic order (3.2.1.2). While *Thoburn* is not, of course, founded upon a written constitutional document, it is premised upon comparable ideas of the normative superiority of the UK constitution. As Laws LJ put it:

(1) All the specific rights and obligations which EU law creates are by the 1972 Act incorporated into our domestic law and rank supreme . . . This is true even where the inconsistent municipal provision is contained in primary legislation. (2) The 1972 Act is a constitutional statute: that is, it cannot be impliedly repealed. (3) The truth of (2) is derived, not from EU law, but purely from the law of [the UK]: the common law recognises a category of constitutional statutes. (4) The fundamental legal basis of [the UK's] relationship with the EU rests with the domestic, not the European legal powers.[87]

---

82 For commentary to this effect see P Craig, 'Britain in the European Union' in Jowell, Oliver, and O'Cinneide, n 76, ch 4.

83 [2003] QB 151.

84 On implied repeal see 2.2 and 2.5.

85 See also Sir John Laws, *The Common Law Constitution* (Cambridge: Cambridge University Press, 2014), 64–71.

86 [2003] QB 151, 187.

87 [2003] QB 151, 189.

Our third case is *R (Buckinghamshire CC) v Secretary of State for Transport* or, as it is more commonly known, '*HS2*'.[88] This was a complex environmental law case that was concerned with two main questions: (1) whether a government paper that announced the development of a high speed rail initiative ('HS2') should have been preceded by an assessment under the Strategic Environmental Assessment Directive; and (2) whether use of hybrid Bills in Parliament as the means to obtain planning permission would comply with the procedural requirements of EU law's directive on environmental impact assessment. While those two questions were answered in a manner that led the Court to conclude that there had not been any illegality in the case, legal arguments about Parliament's internal choice as to the form of Bill engaged the Court in some discussion of constitutional fundamentals, not least the status of Article 9 of the Bill of Rights. The precise judicial comments that were made on that point need not concern us here, although we would note that some of their Lordships looked towards *Thoburn* as having shed light on how to resolve the constitutional challenge of EU membership. Lords Neuberger and Mance, delivering a joint opinion, stated that *Thoburn* gave 'important insights into potential issues in this area' and said that Laws LJ had provided a 'penetrating discussion'.[89] Lord Reed, to like effect, reasoned that conflicts between EU law and UK law 'cannot be resolved simply by applying the doctrine developed by the Court of Justice of the supremacy of EU law, since the application of that doctrine in our law itself depends upon the 1972 Act. If there is a conflict between a constitutional principle, such as that embodied in Article 9 of the Bill of Rights, and EU law, that conflict has to be resolved by our courts as an issue arising under the constitutional law of the United Kingdom'.[90]

The fourth case—*Pham*—embedded much of the logic of the above comments and confirmed that EU law's place in the UK legal order is wholly contingent upon the domestic constitution.[91] The relevant issue in *Pham* concerned the reach of EU law's citizenship requirements when the UK Government wished to deprive a dual British and Vietnamese national of his British citizenship for reasons of his alleged involvement in terrorism. In a wide-ranging judgment that touched upon the nature of EU Treaties and the jurisdiction of the CJEU, some of the Justices emphasised that EU law enjoys primacy only because Parliament has willed that outcome. To quote once more from Lord Mance:[92]

For a domestic court, the starting point is, in any event, to identify the ultimate legislative authority in its jurisdiction according to the relevant rule of recognition. The search is simple in a country like the United Kingdom with an explicitly dualist approach to obligations undertaken at a supranational level. European law is certainly special and represents a remarkable development in the world's legal history. But, unless and until the rule of recognition by which we shape our decisions is altered, we must view the United Kingdom as independent, Parliament as sovereign and European law as part of domestic law because Parliament has so willed. The question how far Parliament has so willed is thus determined by construing the 1972 Act.

---

88 [2014] UKSC 3, [2014] 1 WLR 324.
89 Ibid, 383, para 208.
90 [2014] UKSC 3, [2014] 1 WLR 324, 349, para 79.
91 *Pham v Secretary of State for the Home Department* [2015] UKSC 19, [2015] 1 WLR 1591.
92 [2015] UKSC 19, [2015] 1 WLR 1591, 1617, para 80.

3.3.3 **The European Union Act 2011**

The significance of the above cases must also be seen in the light of the European Union Act 2011, which includes a so-called 'sovereignty' clause in section 18. This reads:

Directly applicable or directly effective EU law (. . . as referred to in section 2(1) of the European Communities Act 1972) falls to be recognised and available in law in the United Kingdom only by virtue of that Act or where it is required to be recognised and available in law by virtue of any other Act.

When introducing this provision in Parliament, the government of the day was of the view that section 18 would place the common law position that had been outlined in *Thoburn* on a statutory footing and that this would negate any argument that EU law can entrench itself as supreme within the UK constitutional order.[93] Corresponding analysis of the section has, however, doubted that it has anything like that effect. For instance, Paul Craig has drawn a distinction between 'sovereignty as dualism' and 'sovereignty as primacy', and argued that section 18 merely reaffirms the constitution's dualist basis for the reception of EU law.[94] By this, Craig means that section 18 reflects the fact that provisions within international treaties can have an impact in UK courts only where Parliament enacts legislation to achieve that effect—a function that is of course performed by the European Communities Act 1972. However, on the matter of 'sovereignty as primacy', Craig states that the Act of 2011 'tells us nothing about the relation between EU law and national law in the event of a clash between the two'.[95] We can therefore conclude that any analysis of the primacy/supremacy issue should continue to start with *Thoburn* and the model of common law constitutionalism that has apparently also informed *HS2* and *Pham*.[96]

Before leaving the Act of 2011, we should also note that it changed fundamentally the structures that govern UK participation in the EU's broader political processes, notably on the question of amending the Treaties.[97] Here, the Act provides, in certain circumstances, for referenda on further transfers of competence to the EU, something that is intended to lend greater democratic legitimacy to UK participation in any deepening of the integration project. However, it should also be noted, again, that there is an upcoming referendum on the very issue of membership and that a vote in favour of Brexit would mean that legislation such as the Act of 2011 would become superfluous. Of course, should Brexit not occur, it will remain to be seen what will happen with the Act of 2011 and its preferred model of popular decision-making.

---

93 For debate about s 18—then in the form of 'clause 18'—see *The EU Bill and Parliamentary Sovereignty*, European Scrutiny Committee, Tenth Report of Session 2010–2011, Vols I and II, available at <http://www.parliament.uk/business/committees/committees-a-z/commons-select/european-scrutiny-committee/publications/>.

94 P Craig, 'The European Union Act 2011: Locks, Limits, and Legality' (2011) 48 *Common Market Law Review* 1915, 1937ff.

95 (2011) 48 *Common Market Law Review* 1915, 1938.

96 On common law constitutionalism see further ch 2. And for further analysis of the Act of 2011 see M Gordon and M Dougan, 'The United Kingdom's European Union Act 2011: "Who Won the Bloody War Anyway?"' (2012) 37 *European Law Review* 1.

97 See Part I of the Act.

3.3.4 **Influence of EU law or 'spill-over'**

We turn, in this final part, to consider the influence that EU law can have on administrative law in cases that do not fall under the European Communities Act 1972. The point here is about the 'spill-over' of EU norms or, put differently, the Europeanisation of UK law.[98] Spill-over occurs when a court that is hearing a case which does not raise any issue of EU law draws upon prior experience with the supranational standard by way of resolving the domestic law dispute. Such recourse to EU law is thus entirely voluntary, as the domestic court allows EU law principle and practice to have an impact beyond its immediate sphere of influence. Nevertheless, the indirect influence of EU law can result in very significant changes to domestic principle and practice and, indeed, to the balance of power between the judiciary and executive and administrative decision-makers.

The leading example of spill-over is *M v Home Office*.[99] This case arose when the government deported an asylum seeker in contravention of an earlier commitment to the court that it would not deport the individual pending an application for judicial review which challenged the government's refusal of asylum. When the matter came before the House of Lords, the central question was whether interim and final injunctions could be issued against ministers of the Crown in judicial review proceedings notwithstanding that section 21 of the Crown Proceedings Act 1947 prohibits such relief in civil proceedings. In ruling that they could be issued, the House of Lords held not only that section 21 did not apply to the instant case because judicial review proceedings are not 'civil proceedings' for the purposes of the 1947 Act; it also noted that injunctions were already available in proceedings under the European Communities Act 1972 as a result of the *Factortame* litigation.[100] This, it was said, gave rise to an 'unhappy' situation whereby rights could be protected by injunction where they were rights under EU law but not where they were domestic in origin. To correct this, the House of Lords thus borrowed from the EU standard when establishing the new domestic rule.[101]

Spill-over—or certainly consideration of its desirability—has also characterised the development of the grounds for judicial review. For instance, prior to the Human Rights Act 1998 there was a long-standing debate about whether the proportionality principle—considered at 3.2.2.1—should be developed as a free-standing ground for review in domestic law.[102] Although the greater weight of judicial opinion opposed further development of the ground for the reason that it could involve courts more closely in the review of administrative choices, some judges pointed towards its emergence as almost an inevitability.[103] Academic commentators also highlighted the perceived merits of the principle, arguing

---

98 G Anthony, *UK Public Law and European Law: The Dynamics of Legal Integration* (Oxford: Hart Publishing, 2002).

99 [1994] 1 AC 377; and 18.3.4.

100 *R v Secretary of State for Transport, ex p Factortame Ltd* [1991] 1 AC 603.

101 For analysis of the analogous value of other aspects of EU law's remedies regime—in particular the state liability doctrine—see P Craig, 'Once More onto the Breach: The Community, the State and Damages Liability' (1997) 105 *Law Quarterly Review* 67; and, e.g., *Cullen v Chief Constable of the RUC* [2003] 1 WLR 1763, Lords Bingham and Steyn.

102 On the position since the Human Rights Act came into force see ch 13.

103 See, most famously, *Council of Civil Service Unions v Minister for Civil Service* [1985] AC 374, 410–11, Lord Diplock.

that its emergence would give greater structure and coherence to the workings of judicial review.[104] Similar arguments were made about the insights that might be drawn from the EU law approach to the protection of substantive legitimate expectations.[105]

The imagery of spill-over can likewise be used in relation to fundamental rights standards, where it has both past and (potential) future dimensions. In terms of past instances of borrowing, there have been cases in which the courts have drawn upon EU law's general principles when developing common law fundamental rights standards. For instance, in *R v Secretary of State for the Home Department, ex p McQuillan*[106]—a case that involved a challenge to the lawfulness of an exclusion order whereby an Irish citizen was not allowed to enter Great Britain—Sedley J (as he then was) spoke of the common law 'marching together' with the general principles of EU law and with those of the ECHR. This was remarkable not just because it emphasised a high degree of overlap between EU law and the common law, but also because it linked that relationship to guarantees found in the ECHR. Aside from the point of spill-over, *McQuillan* thus stands as one of a limited number of cases in which the ECHR had an impact on the common law even before the enactment of the Human Rights Act 1998.

The future dimension concerns the relevance of the Charter of Fundamental Rights of the European Union. As we have seen above, it is now accepted that the Charter is, with the apparent exception of its 'solidarity' section, binding on UK public authorities when they are taking decisions and so on in areas of EU competence.[107] This of course means that the UK courts will increasingly develop a direct experience with the Charter in cases under the European Communities Act 1972, where one judge has described it as a 'a dynamic, revolutionary and directly effective measure of EU law'.[108] However, even outside the European Communities Act 1972, it may be that the courts will also refer to the Charter as a source of inspiration when developing the common law more generally. This is certainly something that the courts have long been willing to do in respect of other sources of fundamental rights standards,[109] and some limited references had already been made to the Charter even before it was accorded binding force.[110] Should such references become more commonplace, this will allow the Charter to have an indirect influence that may result in a further modernisation of common law approaches to the protection of rights. An indirect influence might likewise result from the ECHR, as the European Court of Human Rights has sometimes also referred to the Charter in its case law and, as we will see in the next chapter, UK courts must take that case law 'into account' in proceedings under the Human Rights Act 1998.[111]

---

104 e.g., J Jowell and A Lester, 'Beyond *Wednesbury*: Substantive Principles of Administrative Law' [1987] *Public Law* 368.

105 See *R v Ministry of Agriculture, Fisheries and Food, ex p Hamble (Offshore) Fisheries Ltd* [1995] 2 All ER 714; and 15.3.2.

106 [1995] 4 All ER 400.

107 Case C-411/10, *NS v Secretary of State for the Home Department* [2012] 2 CMLR 9.

108 *AB & Ors v Facebook Ireland Ltd* [2013] NIQB 14, para 14, McCloskey J.

109 See 4.2.3.

110 As in, e.g., *A and others v East Sussex County Council* [2003] All ER (D) 233, at para 73 Munby J.

111 Section 2. For an example of the ECtHR referring to the Charter see *Goodwin v UK* (2002) 35 EHRR 447.

3.4 **Conclusion**

In this chapter we have provided a short overview of the demands of EU member-ship and the corresponding implications that these have for UK administrative law. We have seen that much within the EU legal order is the result of the activism of the CJEU, which has introduced the range of core doctrines that can have a profound impact on Member States. We have also seen how UK courts have, in general, been receptive to those doctrines and that they have modified principle and practice to ensure that the obligations of membership are met. It has lastly been noted that EU law has had an impact beyond its immediate areas of influence when the courts have permitted doctrines, principles, and remedies to 'spill-over' into domestic law in non-EU law cases.

Two further points remain to be made by way of conclusion. The first concerns the limits to the process of spill-over and any assumption that UK law should always be open to the deeper reception of European norms. Although we have seen that domestic law can benefit when the courts borrow from their experience with EU law, it is to be remembered that EU law brings together a range of different legal traditions and that its corresponding principles and so on may not always complement those of the common law. For instance, we will see in chapter 8 that the provisions of the judicial review procedure that govern time limits have been criticised by the CJEU for the reason that they lack in legal certainty and thereby undermine the effective protection of the individual.[112] However, while this may be apparent from the perspective of the CJEU, the procedure within the UK has been designed to ensure that there is a degree of flexibility that can accommodate the respective needs of individuals and the wider public on a case-by-case basis. Given that objective, is this one area where it might legitimately be said that the common law tradition should remain undisturbed?

The second point concerns current judicial approaches to the constitutional basis for EU membership and whether that is suited to the contemporary context surrounding administrative law. For instance, this chapter has described how *Thoburn*, *HS2*, and *Pham* have situated the reception of EU law within a framework that renders the supremacy of EU law contingent upon domestic legal forces and the principle of conferred powers. While this approach is very much in keeping with that adopted by the courts in other Member States, it might be queried whether a domestic law-centred justification for the reception of EU law is consonant with today's post-modern constitutional structures. In short, it has been said that the EU is one manifestation of a much wider process of globalisation and that that wider process renders anachronistic any traditional understandings of states as sovereign.[113] So, should the current UK approach to the sovereignty and supremacy problem be criticised, or is it misleading to suggest that national courts should, or can, reason with reference to anything other than national values? We will return to these—and other questions—in our next chapter on 'Human rights and administrative law'.

---

112 Case C-406/08, *Uniplex (UK) Ltd v NHS Business Services Authority* [2010] 2 CMLR 47; and 8.11.
113 See ch 2.

FURTHER READING

Anthony, G (2002) *UK Public Law and European Law: The Dynamics of Legal Integration* (Oxford: Hart Publishing).

Biondi, A and Birkinshaw, P (eds) (2016) *Britain Alone!: The Implications and Consequences of UK Exit from the EU* (The Netherlands: Kluwer).

Birkinshaw, P (2014) *European Public Law*, 2nd edn (London: Butterworths).

Craig, P (2011) 'The European Union Act 2011: Locks, Limits, and Legality' 48 *Common Market Law Review* 1915.

Craig, P (2012) *EU Administrative Law* (Oxford: Oxford University Press).

Craig, P (2015) *UK, EU and Global Administrative Law: Foundations and Challenges* (Cambridge: Cambridge University Press).

Craig, P (2015) 'Britain in the European Union' in J Jowell, D Oliver, and C O'Cinneide (eds), *The Changing Constitution*, 8th edn (Oxford: Oxford University Press), chapter 4.

Craig, P and de Búrca, G (2015) *EU Law: Text, Cases and Materials*, 6th edn (Oxford: Oxford University Press).

de Búrca, G (1993) 'Proportionality in EC Law' 13 *Yearbook of European Law* 105.

Dyevre, A (2013) 'European Integration and National Courts: Defending Sovereignty Under Institutional Constraints?' 9 *European Constitutional Law Review* 139.

Gordon, M and Dougan, M (2012) 'The United Kingdom's European Union Act 2011: "Who Won the Bloody War Anyway?"' 37 *European Law Review* 1.

Hartley, TC (1999) *Constitutional Problems of the European Union* (Oxford: Hart Publishing).

Jaklic, K (2014) *Constitutional Pluralism in the EU* (Oxford: Oxford University Press).

Jowell, J and Lester, A [1987] 'Beyond *Wednesbury*: Substantive Principles of Administrative Law' *Public Law* 368.

Keenan, PB [1962] 'Some Legal Consequences of Britain's Entry into the European Common Market' *Public Law* 327.

van Gerven, W (2005) *The European Union: A Polity of States and Peoples* (Oxford: Hart Publishing).

Wade, HWR (1996) 'Sovereignty—Revolution or Evolution?' 112 *Law Quarterly Review* 56.

4

....

Human rights and administrative law

4.1 Introduction

The purpose of this chapter is to describe the ways in which human rights law limits the actions of government and public authorities. Human rights, as we shall see, have long received some protection from the common law, and they have become increasingly important since the Human Rights Act 1998 came into force on 2 October 2000 (on the constitutional positioning of which—a 'constitutional statute' as recognised by the common law—see chapter 2).[1] The Human Rights Act 1998 gives effect in domestic law to most of the European Convention on Human Rights (ECHR) and it has had an impact upon the decision-making processes of courts, legislatures, and a wide range of executive and administrative bodies. This chapter thus identifies the features of the Act that have allowed it to have such a wide-ranging influence. It also notes the overlap that the Act now has with the EU Charter of Fundamental Rights, which is, for the most part, binding on public bodies when they are acting in the field of EU law.[2]

The chapter begins with a brief historical and contemporary overview of some of the ways in which the common law has been used to protect human rights. The objective here is to introduce not only a range of juridical techniques that have been developed by the courts, but also to identify a number of legislative and judicial shortcomings that existed in the human rights field pre-Human Rights Act 1998. Although the common law had made some significant developments in terms of protecting human rights, the UK's unwritten constitutional tradition contained many problem areas, and there was a steady stream of cases to Strasbourg in which aspects of UK law were found to be in violation of ECHR standards. It is against this backdrop that the chapter considers the significance of the Human Rights Act 1998, as seen in its developing body of case law. While the case law is continuing to evolve (notwithstanding that the Act has been in force for more than 15 years), there have been a number of landmark developments and the chapter chronicles these by way of contextualising discussion in subsequent chapters.[3] In doing so, the chapter also highlights a number of constitutional themes that accompany the workings of human rights law, in particular as relate to the role of the courts.

Three further points remain to be made by way of introduction. The first is that human rights standards do not as yet provide a basis for a full review of the

---

1 On the Act see also M Amos, *Human Rights Law*, 2nd edn (Oxford: Hart Publishing, 2014).
2 Case C-411/10, *NS v Secretary of State for the Home Department* [2013] QB 102; and 3.2.3.
3 Principally in chs 9–19.

constitutionality of Acts of the Westminster Parliament (the position with regard to primary Acts of the devolved legislatures is different).[4] Although we will see that constitutional practice has moved steadily towards such a system of review,[5] Diceyan notions of the sovereignty of Parliament still retain a high degree of influence and Acts of Parliament remain sovereign. Human rights standards—in both the common law and the Human Rights Act—will therefore be seen to have had their principal impact at the levels of judicial approaches to statutory interpretation and to the review of administrative and executive action (approaches which have, in turn, led to questions about the limits to the constitutional role of the courts). However, full-blown review of the kind discussed in chapter 2 remains absent, save for those cases where EU law rights are in issue.[6]

The second point concerns the meaning given to the term 'human rights'. Because the UK has an unwritten constitution, the content and scope of human rights remained, certainly until the enactment of the Human Rights Act 1998, largely undefined. Human rights in UK law were instead those that the courts developed with reference to the common law and, while the law sometimes developed through the drawing of comparisons with rights under the (then) unincorporated ECHR or other common law systems,[7] judicial development of the law was essentially piecemeal (e.g., there were unresolved questions about whether UK law embraced concepts of socio-economic rights—housing, employment, medical treatment, etc—in addition to civil and political rights such as the right to life, privacy, expression, etc).[8] In using the term human rights, this chapter therefore takes as its starting point the historical lack of definition in the UK system and it does not attempt to forward a comprehensive definition of what human rights are, or what they should contain. Discussion instead takes its lead from case law that has used the terms 'human rights' and 'fundamental rights', while attaching a corresponding importance to cases that have arisen under the Human Rights Act 1998.[9]

The third point is that there is, at the time of writing, an ongoing political debate about whether the Human Rights Act 1998 should be amended, repealed, and/ or replaced by a specially tailored UK Bill of Rights (and responsibilities).[10] While the full repeal of the Act is perhaps a remote possibility, it should be noted that not only is the language of rights contested but also that court rulings have been subjected to criticism by politicians and the press.[11] When reading this chapter, it should thus be remembered that human rights are not always accepted unquestioningly and that judicial recourse to them can result in arguments that courts are acquiring too much power on matters that would better be left to the political

---

4 Government of Wales Act 2006, ss 94 and 108; Northern Ireland Act 1998, s 6; and Scotland Act 1998, s 29. And see *Axa General Insurance v Lord Advocate* [2011] UKSC 46; [2012] 2 AC 868.

5 For recent judicial consideration of the possibility of such review see *Re Moohan* [2014] UKSC 67, [2015] AC 901, 925, para 35, Lord Hodge.

6 *R v Secretary of State for Transport, ex p Factortame (No 2)* [1991] 1 AC 603.

7 See, e.g., *R v Secretary of State for the Home Department, ex p Simms* [2000] 2 AC 115.

8 But on the problematic nature of the distinction between groups of rights see *R v Cambridge Health Authority, ex p Child B* [1995] 2 All ER 129.

9 For discussion of the meaning of human rights etc see D Feldman, *Civil Liberties and Human Rights in England and Wales*, 2nd edn (Oxford: Oxford University Press, 2002), ch 1.

10 See S Greer and R Slowe, 'The Conservatives' Proposals for a British Bill of Rights' [2015] EHRLR 372.

11 See *Hirst*, n 82, in relation to the ban on prisoner voting rights; and S Dimelow and A Young, *'Common Sense' or Confusion? The Human Rights Act and the Conservative Party* (London: The Constitution Society, 2015).

realm. On the other hand, it should also be remembered that such criticisms are not always valid as the courts regard the protection of human rights as central to the doctrine of the rule of law. That doctrine, in turn, is synonymous with the judicial role in contemporary law and politics.[12]

4.2 Human rights and the common law pre-Human Rights Act

4.2.1 General principles of law

One of the best-known historical examples of the common law's protection of human rights is *Bagg's Case*.[13] This case arose when Bagg, a chief burgess of Plymouth, was removed from office for unseemly behaviour that ranged from calling the mayor 'a cozening knave' through to the turning of 'the hinder part of his body in an inhuman and uncivil manner towards the aforesaid Thomas Fowens, scoffingly, contemptuously, and uncivilly, with a loud voice, [saying] . . . "Come and kiss"'. However repulsive Bagg's behaviour may have been, an order of *mandamus* was subsequently issued against Plymouth because Bagg had been deprived of his office without a hearing. This principle—the right to a hearing—grew to become a central aspect of the common law's rules of natural justice/fairness,[14] and it now also finds expression in the procedural protections contained in Article 6 of the ECHR. The core objective of the principle is to ensure that, where a decision that is to be taken will affect an individual's interests or rights, the individual should be allowed to make representations on their behalf, and also to question evidence and representations made against them. Although it will be seen in later chapters that not every decision of a public authority need be preceded by such a hearing, the basic position is that, the more vital the interest or right that is to be affected, the greater is the assumption that a hearing should be given.[15] The common law here thus works to fill gaps that may be left where legislative protections are absent, or where legislation remains silent on the issue of whether a hearing is needed.[16]

In addition to the rules of natural justice/fairness, there are many other general principles of law that have evolved from within the common law to protect an individual's interests and rights (e.g., reasonableness, legitimate expectations, the duty to give reasons). The content of these principles and their field of application—they are not only used when human rights are in issue, but also act as general constraints on the exercise of public power by public bodies—are examined in much greater detail in subsequent chapters on the workings of judicial review.[17] However, one overarching point that can be made at this stage concerns the fact that the general principles of law are judge-made principles that have been developed with a

---

12 See generally T Bingham, *The Rule of Law* (London: Penguin, 2010). And on the wider debate see H Fenwick, 'The Human Rights Act or a British Bill of Rights' [2012] *Public Law* 468.

13 (1615) 11 Co Rep 93b.

14 See also, e.g., *Dr Bonham's Case* (1610) 8 Co Rep 113a; *City of London v Wood* (1701) 12 Mod 669; *Cooper v Wandsworth Board of Works* (1863) 14 CB(NS) 180; and ch 17.

15 *McInnes v Onslow Fane* [1978] 3 All ER 211.

16 On statute law and fairness see ch 16.

17 See chs 16 and 17.

particular vigour by the courts in more recent decades.[18] As these judge-made principles have served to limit in ever more far-reaching ways the exercise of power by
recipients of delegated power (local authorities, central government departments,
etc), they have long prompted debate about how far it is legitimate for courts to
intervene in the exercise of public power.[19] The debate has, as we have already seen
in chapters 1 and 2, focused on the question of whether the development of the
principles has amounted to an unwarranted judicial activism, or whether it has
been required to meet the challenge of an apparent lack of political accountability
and control. And while there are those who consider that the courts have inevitably gone too far in constitutional terms, others have viewed the developments as
less problematic and have asked whether the principles should be developed even
more aggressively. Others have gone further still, and suggested that the principles
should now be developed beyond the control of delegated power and towards the
control of the legislative powers of the Westminster Parliament.[20]

The nature of the debate can be illustrated with reference to the principle of legality that the courts used, pre-Human Rights Act 1998, to found the 'anxious scrutiny' of administrative decisions that infringed an individual's human rights.[21]
'Anxious scrutiny' was shorthand for the courts' willingness to look more closely
at the merits of a decision on an application for judicial review, something that the
courts were ordinarily reluctant to do.[22] By indicating a willingness to examine
more closely the basis for some decisions, the courts were therefore signalling that
common law notions of legality and the rule of law demanded that constitutional
norms might need to be modified if a decision is argued to affect an individual's
human rights. The case that is most often taken to have established the point is
Bugdaycay v Secretary of State for the Home Department.[23] In this case a challenge was
made to, among other things, a decision of the Home Secretary which ordered
that an asylum seeker be returned to the safe country from which he had come
(Kenya—the applicant was a Ugandan refugee). The Home Secretary had made his
decision without examining the applicant's claim, first, that he would likely be
refused entry to Kenya (a point confirmed by a Kenyan diplomat) and, secondly,
that his life would be in danger should he be returned to Uganda. Given this failure on the part of the Home Secretary, the House of Lords overturned the decision
at hand. While the House acknowledged that the courts perform only a limited
review function with regard to exercises of administrative discretion, Lord Bridge
stated that, under circumstances such as those in the instant case, the courts must
nevertheless be alert to the need fully to protect the individual's rights:

(W)ithin those limitations the court must . . . be entitled to subject an administrative decision to the more rigorous examination, to ensure that it is in no way flawed, according to
the gravity of the issue which the decision determines. The most fundamental of all human

---

18 S Sedley, 'The Sound of Silence: Constitutional Law Without a Constitution' (1994) 110 *Law
Quarterly Review* 270.

19 See generally CF Forsyth (ed), *Judicial Review and the Constitution* (Oxford: Hart Publishing, 2000);
and Sir John Laws, *The Common Law Constitution* (Cambridge: Cambridge University Press, 2014).

20 See the various contributions to [2004] (2) *Judicial Review*; and for recent judicial consideration of
the possibility see Lord Hodge, n 5.

21 For recent consideration of the common law approach see *Pham v Secretary of State for the Home
Department* [2015] UKSC 19, [2015] 1 WLR 1591, 1625ff, Lord Sumption.

22 *Associated Provincial Picture Houses v Wednesbury Corporation* [1948] 1 KB 223, considered in ch 13.

23 [1987] AC 514.

rights is the individual's right to life and when an administrative decision under challenge is said to be one which may put the applicant's life at risk, the basis of the decision must surely call for the most anxious scrutiny.[24]

This approach was subsequently followed by the courts in a number of other common law human rights cases that involved, among other things, medical treatment, sexual orientation, and the right to life.[25] While the approach adopted did not mean that every application to the courts was successful, it did start to push public law debate and discourse in new directions. One of the most prominent changes of direction was in respect of the role that the European proportionality principle should play in domestic law. Proportionality is central to the workings of both EU law and the ECHR, and it requires, in its purest form, that courts balance the reasons for a public authority's decision against the extent of the interference with an individual's human rights. Given that the anxious scrutiny test was likewise concerned with 'closer look' review, this led some commentators and judges to suggest that the European proportionality principle should be developed as a free-standing ground of review in domestic law too.[26] However, while the argument appeared persuasive to some, the fact that the ECHR had not been given effect in domestic law ultimately led the House of Lords to rule that proportionality could not be developed as a separate ground of review.[27] The result was for formal recognition of the principle to be put on hold until the Human Rights Act 1998 came into force, albeit that it was quickly recognised in domestic law and is now even said to be almost at one with anxious scrutiny.[28] We return to the significance of this development and the relevant case law in chapter 13.

4.2.2 Statutory interpretation and human rights

A further way in which the courts protected human rights was through the interpretation of primary legislation. What the courts did here was interpret primary legislation in a way that limited the extent to which secondary legislation or administrative acts could infringe an individual's human rights as recognised by the common law. Secondary legislation and administrative acts are almost always sourced in empowering provisions within primary legislation and the courts emphasised that, where secondary legislation or an act infringed an individual's rights, the corresponding primary legislation had to authorise that infringement either in express terms or by necessary implication.[29] This approach was to assume a particular importance in the prison context, where the House of Lords emphasised that convicted prisoners retained 'all civil rights which (had not been) taken away expressly or by necessary implication'.[30] For example, in *R v Home Secretary,*

---

24 [1987] AC 514, 531.

25 See, respectively, *R v Cambridge Health Authority, ex p B* [1995] 25 BMLR 5 and [1995] 2 All ER 129 (compare and contrast the High Court and Court of Appeal); *R v Ministry of Defence, ex p Smith* [1995] 4 All ER 427; and *R v Lord Saville of Newdigate, ex p A* [2000] 1 WLR 1855.

26 e.g., M Hunt, *Using Human Rights Law in English Courts* (Oxford: Hart Publishing, 1997).

27 *R v Secretary of State for the Home Department, ex p Brind* [1991] 1 AC 696.

28 *R v Home Secretary, ex p Daly* [2001] 2 AC 532 and *Pham v Secretary of State for the Home Department* [2015] UKSC 19, [2015] 1 WLR 1591.

29 Note that some types of secondary legislation and administrative acts may be made pursuant to the Royal prerogative: see further 5.2 and 9.3.

30 *Raymond v Honey* [1983] 1 AC 1, 10.

ex p Leech (No 2),[31] the issue for the Court of Appeal was the legality of a Prison Rule that allowed prisoner governors to intercept correspondence between prisoners and their lawyers. The only exception to the Rule was in respect of correspondence concerning ongoing legal proceedings, and the court thereby considered that the Rule interfered with common law rights of access to courts, as prisoners were denied unimpeded access to their lawyers for purposes of considering whether to initiate proceedings. Having concluded that the interference was not expressly provided for on the face of the primary legislation (the Prison Act 1952, section 47), the court also held that the power could not be read into the primary legislation by way of necessary implication. Although the court accepted that there might be a need for some screening of correspondence, it nevertheless considered that the current power was too broad and intrusive of the human right to be justified. The Rule, as it affected correspondence between prisoners and lawyers, was, in consequence, *ultra vires*.[32]

The interpretive technique was also used in cases outside the prison context. For instance, in *R v Lord Chancellor, ex p Witham*,[33] a challenge was made to the Lord Chancellor's decision to change a policy that exempted individuals on income support from having to pay court fees. The Lord Chancellor had introduced the change—contained in the Supreme Court Fees (Amendment) Order 1996—on the basis of section 130 of the (then) Supreme Court Act 1981 (the provision gave the Lord Chancellor a general power to prescribe court fees).[34] When the challenge was made Laws J ruled that section 130 did not expressly provide for measures which interfere with rights of access to the courts and that the Order was, as such, *ultra vires* the Act. As the judge said: 'Access to the courts is a constitutional right; it can only be denied by the government if it persuades Parliament to pass legislation which specifically—in effect by express provision—permits the executive to turn people away from the court door. That has not been done in this case.'[35]

Of course, with the coming into force of the Human Rights Act 1998, there has been much less need for the courts to have recourse to the common law interpretive presumption (see, in particular, the significance of the interpretive obligation in section 3 of the Human Rights Act, considered at 4.4.2).[36] Nevertheless, it should be noted that common law constitutional rights can still be of more general importance to the resolution of disputes as the courts may consider them in tandem with those in the ECHR and, in some instances, even consider common law rights before turning to those in the ECHR.[37] Indeed, to the extent that 'common law constitutionalism' may appear less influential, it has been suggested that it may still lead the courts towards a system of the review of the constitutionality of Acts of the Westminster Parliament.[38] Thus, although such review is presently prohibited

---

31 [1993] 4 All ER 539.

32 See also, e.g., *R v Secretary of State for the Home Department, ex p Simms* [2000] 2 AC 115.

33 [1998] QB 575.

34 The Act is now known as the Senior Courts Act 1981; and note that s 130 was repealed by the Courts Act 2003.

35 [1998] QB 575, 586.

36 Although see, e.g., *HM Treasury v Ahmed* [2010] 2 AC 534 as read in the light of the Terrorist Asset Freezing (Temporary Provisions) Act 2010; and 18.3.1.

37 See, e.g., *In Re Officer L* [2007] 1 WLR 2135, considering the common law right to life in tandem with Art 2 ECHR, and *Re Reilly's Application* [2013] UKSC 61, [2014] AC 1115, considering the common law right to a hearing in advance of that under the ECHR.

38 See n 5.

by constitutional orthodoxy and under the Human Rights Act 1998, it has been noted that the common law has already taken some tentative steps towards such review and that the Supreme Court may at some stage take review to that next level.[39] Should that happen, the common law presumption will have provided the foundation for something that is altogether more significant.

4.2.3 Human rights, the common law, and the ECHR pre-Human Rights Act

Another point of importance about the protection of rights prior to the Human Rights Act 1998 concerns the relationship that the common law had with the ECHR. While it has already been seen above that the courts refused to recognise the European proportionality principle as a free standing ground of review in domestic law, it is important to note that the ECHR still had some impact on the domestic order. While this impact was essentially sporadic—constitutional dualism entailed that ECHR case law could not be argued directly in the courts[40]—the ECHR did have what might be termed an indirect impact on domestic developments. One means of impact, for instance, was through the courts making comparisons with ECHR standards when developing the content of common law human rights.[41] And another means of impact was through a further rule of statutory interpretation. This rule, which applies generally in respect of the relationship between domestic law and international law, holds that, where Parliament introduces legislation on a matter that touches international obligations, it is to be assumed that the legislation is not intended to be contrary to those obligations.[42] While this of course left it open to Parliament expressly to legislate in contravention of international standards, it did allow the courts to emphasise how the ECHR was not entirely without relevance. The ECHR was thus considered by the courts in cases in a number of highly significant policy areas, such as immigration.[43]

The ECHR also had some impact through the medium of EU law. Its impact here followed from the fact that the ECHR has long influenced the development of the general principles of EU law that national courts must give effect to when EU law provisions are in issue in domestic proceedings.[44] Although there were only very few cases in which the courts openly acknowledged that fact, judicial consideration of the relationship between EU law and the ECHR nevertheless led to some strong statements of the potential for developing the common law in the light of its European equivalents.[45] Such statements contrasted with more orthodox understandings of the relationship between domestic law and international law, and it would be misleading to suggest that they came to subsume a dualist orthodoxy

---

39 M Elliott, 'Embracing "Constitutional" Legislation: Towards Fundamental Law?' (2003) 54 *Northern Ireland Legal Quarterly* 25; and M Fordham, 'Judicial Review: The Future' [2008] *Judicial Review* 66.

40 On dualism see G Anthony, *UK Public Law and European Law: The Dynamics of Legal Integration* (Oxford: Hart Publishing, 2002).

41 e.g., *Attorney General v Guardian Newspapers Ltd (No 2)* [1988] 3 All ER 545; and *R v Secretary of State for the Home Department, ex p Al-Hasan* [2005] HRLR 421, 423, Lord Rodger.

42 *Garland v British Rail Engineering Ltd* [1983] 2 AC 751.

43 See, e.g., *R v Chief Immigration Officer, Heathrow Airport, ex p Salamat Bibi* [1976] 3 All ER 843.

44 On the relationship between EU law and the ECHR see ch 3.

45 See, most notably, *R v Secretary of State for the Home Department, ex p McQuillan* [1995] 4 All ER 400.

than has been reasserted even in the era of the Human Rights Act 1998.[46] Yet, whatever the limiting influence of such orthodoxy, the *communitaire* comments in some earlier case law still remain as interesting departures within the wider body of jurisprudence. Some authors have for that reason cited the comments in support of the argument that globalisation and Europeanisation present far-reaching challenges for contemporary public law and that the non-'orthodox' judicial approach is merited.[47]

4.3 Why give effect to the ECHR?

The decision to give effect to the ECHR in domestic law—thereby bringing to an end the period of sporadic and indirect impact—was prompted by a number of considerations. First, there was the political concern, commonly expressed from the early 1980s, that certain individual rights and other freedoms were being eroded, especially by legislation that tended to give greater power to the executive.[48] Although the common law had gone some way towards achieving fuller protection, the normative underpinnings of rights guarantees in the UK were unsatisfactory. The doctrine of parliamentary sovereignty in particular meant that any rights were ultimately subject to the preferences of the government which was largely able to dominate the legislature. It was often said, for example, that everyone in the UK was 'free to do anything, subject only to the provisions of the law'.[49] While this suggested an emphasis on the liberty of the individual, it also belied the fact that Parliament could interfere with that liberty, or expressly authorise others to do so (the point was, after all, at the heart of *Leech (No 2)* etc, considered earlier). By introducing the ECHR into domestic law under the terms of the Human Rights Act, the Labour Government of the day thus hoped to enter safeguards in the face of potentially overweening legislative and executive power. As Lord Irvine, the then Lord Chancellor, commented, the Human Rights Act was intended to mark a shift towards a rights based system that would provide a positive statement of guarantees, as accompanied by clear guidance on the limits of governmental power *vis-à-vis* those rights.[50]

Another factor—and one closely related to the above—was the fact of individuals bringing cases before the European Court of Human Rights (ECtHR) in Strasbourg (an option that still remains open, notwithstanding the passage of the Act).[51] The UK ratified the ECHR on 8 March 1951 (the ECHR came into force on 3 September 1953), and it accepted the right of individual petition to the Court in

---

46 e.g., *Re McKerr* [2004] 1 WLR 807. But see now, on its facts, *Re McCaughey's Application* [2011] 2 WLR 1279, considered at 4.4.6 alongside *Keyu* [2015] UKSC 69, [2015] 3 WLR 1665.

47 See ch 2 and, e.g., Hunt, n 26, chs 1–3.

48 See K Ewing and C Gearty, *Freedom Under Thatcher* (Oxford: Clarendon Press, 1990).

49 *Attorney General v Guardian Newspapers Ltd (No 2)* [1988] 3 All ER 545, 660, Lord Goff.

50 Lord Irvine of Lairg, 'The Development of Human Rights in Britain under an Incorporated European Convention on Human Rights [1998] *Public Law* 221.

51 See, e.g., *Al-Jedda v UK* (2011) 53 EHRR 23 (UK had violated the applicant's Art 5 ECHR right to liberty by detaining him in Iraq pursuant to a UN Resolution) and *Ali v United Kingdom*, judgment of 20 October 2015, noted at 17.4.5 (no violation of Art 6 ECHR when applicant challenged housing allocation decision before the County Court on ordinary judicial review principles).

January 1966. The right to petition, which can be both costly and time-consuming for the individual, resulted in many of the shortcomings of the domestic order being 'laid bare' in Strasbourg. These shortcomings included not only the fact that domestic law did not appreciate or accommodate to the full some of the nuances of rights;[52] they also included the fact that some of the courts' common law jurisprudence did not go far enough to satisfy European standards.[53] In consequence, it was envisaged that the Human Rights Act 1998 would serve to remedy these and a number of other problems: it would 'bring rights home' and thereby allow individuals to raise arguments in domestic courts without having to invest time and money going to Strasbourg; it would allow more problems to be addressed at the national level; and it would afford the courts the chance finally to develop common law standards in a manner that better corresponds with European norms.

By deciding to give effect to the ECHR, the government of the day was, however, faced with a number of fundamental constitutional questions. Most obvious among these was the question of how to reconcile positive statements of human rights guarantees with the doctrine of parliamentary sovereignty. Under many other national constitutions, rights can be used to trump primary legislation introduced by the legislature; in other words, they can provide a basis for a full review of the constitutionality of legislation. As such review is historically anathema to the UK system (subject to the exception generated by EU law), the government was left with the question of how to make rights meaningful in UK law without disturbing core constitutional principles. Should the Act permit individuals to rely upon the ECHR to trump legislative initiatives? Or could the existing constitutional equilibrium be maintained, while at the same time giving rights an enhanced value?

A related difficulty concerned the extent to which ECHR standards should be regarded as binding upon domestic authorities (most notably courts). The substantive and procedural guarantees contained in the ECHR are complemented by a number of important general principles of law that do not always correspond with those of national legal systems (the principles include legality, effectiveness, proportionality, and the margin of appreciation).[54] The question for the government was thus how far these principles should be taken to enjoy precedence over existing domestic principle and practice. We have already seen above, for example, that the UK courts had approached the European proportionality principle with caution and that they had been reluctant to develop the principle in domestic law in the absence of national legislation to give effect to the ECHR. Did the decision to give domestic effect to the ECHR then mean that the ECHR's proportionality principle should be applied without modification in domestic proceedings? Or could the ECHR have effect in such a way that would reduce the scope for violations of ECHR standards, while at the same time accommodating the fact that there are differences between the ECHR (international law) and UK human rights standards (national law)?

---

52 e.g., the right to privacy in *Malone v UK* (1984) EHRR A 82, as followed by the Interception of Communications Act 1985. And see now also the Regulation of Investigatory Powers Act 2000.

53 See, e.g., the criticism of 'anxious scrutiny' in *Smith and Grady v UK* [2000] 29 EHRR 493.

54 See generally J Simor and B Emmerson, *Human Rights Practice* (London: Sweet and Maxwell, 2014).

4.4 **The Human Rights Act, the ECHR, and constitutional principle**

The Human Rights Act that was enacted in the light of these considerations strikes a sophisticated balance between maintaining the sovereignty of Parliament, furthering the protection of rights, and ensuring that the reception of ECHR principles is sensitive to the national context.[55] The ECHR guarantees that have effect in domestic law are contained in Schedule 1 to the Act and include the Article 2 right to life; the Article 3 guarantee of freedom from torture, inhuman or degrading treatment; the Article 5 right to liberty; the Article 6 right to a fair trial; the Article 8 right to privacy; the Article 10 guarantee of freedom of expression; the Article 14 prohibition of discrimination; and the Article 1, Protocol 1 right to property.[56] In terms of balancing each of the competing constitutional considerations, the most important provisions of the Act—when read together and/or in the light of others—are sections 2–4 and 6–8.

4.4.1 **Section 2: the requirement that courts 'take into account' ECHR jurisprudence**

Section 2 of the Human Rights Act addresses the matter of how far courts and tribunals should give effect to ECHR jurisprudence when the ECHR is in issue. It states that courts and tribunals are to 'take into account' ECHR jurisprudence, 'whenever (that jurisprudence) was made or given, so far as, in the opinion of the court or tribunal, it is relevant to the proceedings in which that question has arisen'. The section's use of the terms 'take into account' and 'in the opinion of the court and tribunal' thus makes clear that ECHR jurisprudence is not formally binding on courts and tribunals. However, while it has since been emphasised that the courts may thereby distinguish between the principles of domestic law and those of the ECHR—the Supreme Court has, for instance, refused to allow ECHR case law to prevail over the domestic law approach to hearsay evidence in criminal trials[57]—it has been recognised that it would be highly problematic were the courts to ignore relevant ECHR authority or to erect unnecessary barriers to the reception of general principles of law. In *Ullah*, the House of Lords thus said that, even though the domestic courts need do no more than 'keep pace with the Strasbourg jurisprudence as it evolves over time', they should ordinarily follow the 'clear and constant jurisprudence' of the Strasbourg Court.[58] Although the Supreme Court has since emphasised that ECHR case law should not become a 'straitjacket' in domestic proceedings, the case law has made clear that rulings of the ECtHR should be followed save in the circumstance where it is inconsistent with some fundamental

---

55 See further A Young, *Parliamentary Sovereignty and the Human Rights Act* (Oxford: Hart Publishing, 2009).

56 On the rights given effect to—the principal exceptions are Arts 1 and 13 and those Protocols that the UK has not ratified—see J Wadham et al, *Blackstone's Guide to the Human Rights Act 1998*, 6th edn (Oxford: Oxford University Press, 2011).

57 *R v Horncastle* [2010] 2 AC 373. And see the ECtHR's ruling in *Al-Khawaja v UK* (2012) 54 EHRR 23, accommodating the domestic law approach to hearsay evidence.

58 *R (Ullah) v Special Adjudicator* [2004] 2 AC 323, 350, para 20, Lord Bingham. See, to like effect, Lord Slynn's comments in *R (Alconbury) v Environment Secretary* [2003] 2 AC 295, 313, para 26.

principle of our domestic law.[59] The practical reason for this is, of course, that a failure to follow any clear authority would be likely to lead to a subsequent petition to Strasbourg for final resolution, where the outcome would almost certainly be in line with the Strasbourg Court's established case law. To the extent that the Act thus envisages that there will be circumstances in which it will be appropriate to limit the impact of ECHR principle, the courts have equally been aware that limitations should be the exception rather than the rule. The result has been for many aspects of domestic principle and practice to be modified, albeit in such manner that is often sensitive to the national legal context (e.g., the manner in which the courts have wedded recognition of the proportionality principle to a corresponding doctrine of the 'discretionary area of judgement' of decision-makers).[60]

An interesting example of the courts taking ECHR case law into account while ultimately rejecting the arguments before them is provided by *N v Secretary of State for the Home Department*.[61] The appellant, an asylum seeker, had arrived in the UK from Uganda in 1998 and shortly after was diagnosed as HIV positive with an AIDS-related illness. She thereafter received medical treatment and her condition improved to the point that she was told that she could live for several decades if such treatment continued. However, in 2001 her claim for asylum was rejected and she was told that she was to be returned to Uganda. Challenging the decision, she argued that she should be allowed to stay in the UK on the authority of *D v UK*,[62] which had established that the UK would be acting in contravention of the Article 3 ECHR prohibition of inhuman and degrading treatment by returning a chronically ill AIDS sufferer to St Kitts. Rejecting the claimant's argument, the House of Lords considered that *D v UK* applied only in exceptional circumstances—*viz* where the individual's condition is critical—and that no such circumstances were established here. This was because the appellant was fit to travel; would remain fit should she continue to receive treatment; could receive that treatment in Uganda (albeit at considerable expense); and, in contrast to the individual in *D*, had relatives in her country of origin (albeit that she claimed that they were unwilling to take care of her). There would therefore be no violation of Article 3 of the ECHR were she to be removed to Uganda.

4.4.2 Section 3: the interpretation of legislation

The need to 'take into account' ECHR jurisprudence in turn underpins section 3, the arguable lynchpin of the Act (see also the importance of section 6 of the Act, at 4.4.4). Section 3 reads: 'So far as it is possible to do so, primary legislation and subordinate legislation, must be read and given effect in a way which is compatible with the Convention rights' (primary and subordinate legislation for these purposes are defined in section 21 of the Act). This in effect means that, where possible, all legislation—including past legislation—must be read and given effect by the courts in a way that is ECHR compliant. This would, on its face, appear to go far beyond pre-existing approaches to statutory interpretation ('express' and

---

59 *Re Moohan* [2014] UKSC 67, [2015] AC 901, 942–4, para 104, Lord Wilson, and cases noted therein.
60 See 13.6.2.
61 [2005] 2 AC 296.
62 (1997) 24 EHRR 423.

'necessary implication' etc—see 4.2.2) as, rather than reading an Act to determine whether it actively permits the limiting of rights, the courts are now required to read legislation in such a way as might remove those very limitations. This would appear to be so even if it means distorting the literal meaning of the statutory language by adopting a purposive construction.

Section 3 therefore introduces a very strong interpretative obligation; a powerful tool placed in the hands of the judges and one which has already been put to use in some significant decisions. For example, in *R v A*,[63] one of the very first, and best known, cases on the interpretative obligation, section 41 of the Youth Justice and Criminal Evidence Act 1999 was challenged as contrary to Article 6 of the ECHR for the reason that the section restricted the right to cross-examination in rape cases and introduced a test of admissibility which prevented evidence of previous sexual relations between the accused and the complainant from being brought before the trial court. The House of Lords had to consider: (a) whether to read section 41 in a way that was compatible with the guarantee of a fair trial under Article 6 of the ECHR; or (b) whether to make a declaration of incompatibility (on which mechanism see below). Their Lordships followed the first course of action, with Lord Steyn stating:

> In my view section 3 requires the court to subordinate the niceties of the language of section 41(3)(c), and in particular the touchstone of coincidence, to broader considerations of relevance judged by logical and common sense criteria of time and circumstances. After all, it is realistic to proceed on the basis that the legislature would not, if alerted to the problem, have wished to deny the right of an accused to put forward a full and complete defence by advancing truly probative material. It is therefore possible under section 3 [Human Rights Act 1998] to read section 41, and in particular section 41(3)(c), as subject to the implied provision that evidence or questioning which is required to ensure a fair trial under article 6 of the Convention should not be treated as inadmissible. The result of such a reading would be that sometimes logically relevant sexual experiences between a complainant and an accused may be admitted under section 41(3)(c).[64]

In a similar vein, Lord Slynn acknowledged that the wording of the section was very restrictive but held that, nevertheless, it could be read in a way that is compatible with the ECHR. He stated:

> It seems to me that your Lordships cannot say that it is not possible to read section 41(3)(c) together with Article 6 of the Convention rights in a way which will result in a fair hearing. In my view section 41(3)(c) is to be read as permitting the admission of evidence or questioning which relates to a relevant issue in the case and which the trial judge considers is necessary to make the trial a fair one.[65]

Such expansive interpretative approaches have prompted far-ranging debates about the limits of the judicial role, both among academics and among members of the judiciary.[66] Indeed, case law has brought forward sharply diverging opinions about what it is constitutionally permissible for the courts to do in the light of the interpretative obligation, and it appears that there will never be

---

63 [2002] 1 AC 45.
64 [2002] 1 AC 45, 68, para 45.
65 [2002] 1 AC 45, 56, para 13.
66 See generally A Kavanagh, *Constitutional Review under the UK Human Rights Act* (Cambridge: Cambridge University Press, 2009), chs 2–5.

judicial unanimity on how section 3 should be used. The key point of division is on the question of when 'interpreting' becomes 'legislating', and one of the best examples of judicial disagreement remains that found in the House of Lords ruling in *Ghaidan v Godin-Mendoza*.[67] The case, which concerned the tenancy rights of same-sex couples living together in stable relationships, saw a majority of the House adopt an expansive approach to the interpretation of the meaning of 'spouse' for the purposes of paragraph 2(2) of Schedule 1 to the Rent Act 1977. The approach, which allowed a surviving same-sex partner to enjoy the same tenancy rights as a spouse or long-term partner in a heterosexual relationship, had significant social implications, something that led Lord Millett, dissenting, to conclude that the House had strayed over the line that separates the judicial and legislative functions. But the majority disagreed and emphasised how, in their opinion, the approach adopted was entirely consistent with the scheme laid down by Parliament in section 3 of the Human Rights Act. The case is thus a paradigm example both of how far the section 3 obligation can effect practical change, and also of how far such change can engender disagreement at the very highest judicial levels.

One further point about the interpretative obligation relates to the doctrine of 'implied repeal'. Under this doctrine, the courts give effect to the most recent expression of Parliament's will; that is, any conflict between two statutes is re-solved by giving effect to the more recent Act. Section 3 would on its face appear to contradict this doctrine, as the interpretative obligation 'applies to primary legislation . . . whenever enacted' (i.e., an Act passed in, for instance, 2012 should insofar as possible be interpreted in a manner that it is consistent with the ECHR, even if there is a clear conflict on a literal reading). This problem is one that the courts have had experience with in respect of EU law, where the doctrine of implied repeal has been overtaken by a requirement that Parliament expressly state in subsequent legislation that a measure is intended to be contrary to EU law (as given effect by the European Communities Act 1972).[68] However, in respect of section 3, it is likely that the problem can now be resolved with reference to the fact that the Human Rights Act is recognised as one of the common law 'constitutional statutes' that are no longer subject to implied repeal (the European Communities Act falls into this category too). The provisions of such statutes can instead be repealed only where the legislature uses express words in the later statute or 'words so specific that the inference of an actual determination to effect the result contended for (is) irresistible '.[69] This point should, however, also be read in the light of the fact that, where words in a statute cannot be read in a manner that is compliant with the ECHR, the courts can only make a declaration of incompatibility *vis-à-vis* the offending Act. The courts are therefore not able to strike down an Act that cannot be read compatibly with the ECHR, even if the Act does not contain an express provision of incompatibility (a position that differs in comparison with EU law). We develop the significance of this point at 4.4.3.

---

67 [2004] 2 AC 557.
68 See *Macarthys Ltd v Smith* [1979] 3 All ER 325, 329, Lord Denning.
69 *Thoburn v Sunderland City Council* [2003] QB 151, 187, Laws LJ.

4.4.3 **Section 4: declarations of incompatibility and the sovereignty of Parliament**

The Act's emphasis on the sovereignty of Parliament is reflected most clearly in section 4, which provides that the courts *may* make a 'declaration of incompatibility' where primary legislation—defined in section 21 to include Acts of the Westminster Parliament—cannot be read in a manner that is compatible with the ECHR[70] (a prominent example of a declaration is given by the *'Belmarsh detainees'* case, discussed later).[71] The word 'may' has here been emphasised, as the courts have a discretion whether to make a declaration of incompatibility and they may (albeit exceptionally) decide that the fuller context to a case means that they should not use the section 4 power.[72] For instance, in the tragic case of *R (Nicklinson) v Ministry of Justice*,[73] one issue was whether the Supreme Court should make a declaration of incompatibility as between section 2(1) of the Suicide Act 1961—which makes it an offence to assist a person to commit suicide—and Article 8 of the ECHR. The issue had arisen because the claimant in the case wished to end his life but was unable to do so because of his physical condition, and he argued that the blanket nature of section 2(1) was disproportionate in its effects on his right to private and family life. While there was detailed discussion within the case about whether Article 8 of the ECHR was breached by the legislation—Lady Hale and Lord Kerr, dissenting, agreed that the legislation was disproportionate and that a declaration of incompatibility should be made—the other members of the Court were concerned about the limits to their powers in an area of religious and moral complexity. As Lord Neuberger expressed the point:

There is a number of reasons which, when taken together, persuade me that it would be institutionally inappropriate at this juncture for a court to declare that section 2 is incompatible with article 8, as opposed to giving Parliament the opportunity to consider the position without a declaration. First, the question whether the provisions of section 2 should be modified raises a difficult, controversial and sensitive issue, with moral and religious dimensions, which undoubtedly justifies a relatively cautious approach from the courts. Secondly, this is not a case . . . where the incompatibility is simple to identify and simple to cure: whether, and if so how, to amend section 2 would require much anxious consideration from the legislature; this also suggests that the courts should, as it were, take matters relatively slowly. Thirdly, section 2 has . . . been considered on a number of occasions in Parliament, and it is currently due to be debated in the House of Lords in the near future; so this is a case where the legislature is and has been actively considering the issue. Fourthly, less than 13 years ago, the House of Lords in *R (Pretty) v Director of Public Prosecutions* [2002] 1 AC 800 gave Parliament to understand that a declaration of incompatibility in relation to section 2 would be inappropriate, a view reinforced by the conclusions reached by the Divisional Court and the Court of Appeal in this case: a declaration of incompatibility on this appeal would represent an unheralded volte-face.[74]

---

70 Note that the power to declare is limited to those courts listed in s 4(5), which are essentially the High Court and above.

71 *A v Home Secretary* [2005] 2 AC 68. For another interesting example see *R (F) v Home Secretary* [2011] 1 AC 331, discussed at 13.6.3.1 (notification requirements in the Sexual Offences Act 2003, ss 82–86, whereby sex offenders must notify the police of certain personal details, incompatible with Art 8 ECHR).

72 See *R (Chester) v Secretary of State for Justice* [2013] UKSC 63, [2014] AC 271, 303, para 39, Lord Mance.

73 [2014] UKSC 38, [2015] AC 657.

74 [2014] UKSC 38, [2015] AC 657, 793, para 116. Note that a subsequent petition to the ECtHR was deemed inadmissible: *Nicklinson v UK* (2015) 61 EHRR SE7.

In cases in which a declaration of incompatibility is made—and it should be noted, again, that *Nicklinson* is very much an exception rather than a rule—the sovereignty of Parliament is safeguarded because a declaration 'does not affect the validity, continuing operation or enforcement of the provision in respect of which it is given'.[75] Although Parliament's sovereignty may, in a practical sense, be affected by an expansive judicial reading of the interpretative obligation under section 3 (*viz* the debate about 'interpreting' and 'legislating'), section 4 limits the powers of the courts in the sense that they cannot strike down primary legislation. For example, in the celebrated *Alconbury* litigation, the Divisional Court found a structural incompatibility between Article 6 of the ECHR and the system of planning appeals contained in sections 77–79 of the Town and Country Planning Act 1999, and made a declaration of incompatibility.[76] When the matter came before the House of Lords on appeal, their Lordships disagreed with the conclusions of the Divisional Court and overturned the decision. However, even if the House of Lords had supported the decision of the lower court, the system of planning appeals would have remained in operation, as declarations do not affect the validity of the law in question. The position in respect of the Human Rights Act 1998 is thus different to that under the European Communities Act 1972, which latter Act is now read as permitting the courts to disapply Acts of Parliament that are contrary to EU law.[77]

Once declarations have been made—whether in respect of primary or subordinate legislation—section 10 of, and Schedule 2 to, the Human Rights Act 1998 provide for a special legislative means for amending the incompatible legislation. This fast-track procedure, which is led by the government in the event that Parliament does not elect to introduce a wholly new legislative scheme, provides for 'remedial orders' to be made under the supervision of Parliament (the fast-track procedure may also be used in respect of subordinate legislation that is deemed *ultra vires*).[78] Use of the remedial procedure is not automatic, as the responsible minister is not obliged to introduce amending legislation following a declaration of incompatibility and may do so only if there are compelling reasons (a declaration of incompatibility will not, in itself, amount to a compelling reason). However, where declarations have been made, remedial orders will ordinarily follow. For example, in *H v Mental Health Review Tribunal, N & E London Region*,[79] a declaration of incompatibility was issued in respect of section 73 of the Mental Health Act 1983, as read with Article 5 of the ECHR (the section was considered to have reversed the burden of proof on the question of whether to continue with the detention of a mental health patient, i.e., it placed the burden on the patient rather than the authorities). The government responded with its first remedial order, something that gave an early insight into the workings of the Act and how it could impact upon the legislative process.[80] In contrast, successive governments have so far refused to take

---

75 Section 4(6). Although note that the position is different in relation to subordinate legislation—also defined in s 21—as such legislation may be quashed for the reason that it is incompatible with the ECHR, save where primary legislation 'prevents removal of the incompatibility': s 4(4).

76 *Alconbury Developments Ltd v Secretary of State for the Environment, Transport and the Regions* [2003] 2 AC 295.

77 *R v Secretary of State for Transport, ex p Factortame Ltd (No 2)* [1991] 1 AC 603; and ch 3.

78 Section 10(3), (4), (5) and Sch 2.

79 [2001] 3 WLR 512.

80 Mental Health Act 1983 (Remedial) Order 2001, SI 2001/3712.

remedial action in the face of a declaration of incompatibility made in respect of sections 3–4 of the Representation of the People Act 1983. Those provisions disenfranchise all serving prisoners, and the Court of Session in Scotland made a declaration of incompatibility between the sections and the election rights of some prisoners under Article 3 of Protocol 1 of the ECHR.[81] The Court of Session's ruling had, in turn, been influenced by the Strasbourg case of *Hirst v UK (No 2)*,[82] which held that the blanket nature of the provisions in sections 3–4 rendered them disproportionate in their interference with the rights in question. However, *Hirst* has since been highly controversial in political terms, and it has come to define much of the political debate about the utility of rights that was noted in the introduction to this chapter. Against that backdrop, no remedial action has been taken, even though this has resulted in the UK being placed in ongoing breach of its obligations under international law.

Two further points should be made under this heading. The first relates to a procedure that is used at the drafting stage and which seeks to ensure compliance with the ECHR. The relevant provision of the Act is section 19, which requires a minister in charge of a Bill to make a 'statement of compatibility' with the ECHR or to make a statement that he or she is unable to do so (this is made before the second reading of the Bill in Parliament). The key point to note about statements of compatibility, where made, is that they do not protect the legislation from subsequent scrutiny by the courts, as the question of compatibility with the ECHR is ultimately a question of law. As Lord Hope emphasised in *R v A*,[83] a statement of compatibility attached to a Bill (in this case the Bill that preceded the Youth Justice and Criminal Evidence Act 1999) is no more than an expression of opinion that is not even persuasive authority in court. Acts that government ministers have previously identified as compatible with the ECHR can therefore be examined by the courts and, if necessary, be made the subject of a declaration of incompatibility.

The second point is that declarations of incompatibility may issue in respect of legislation even where the legislation purports to derogate from rights under the ECHR. The point can be illustrated with reference to the Anti-Terrorism, Crime and Security Act 2001 that was enacted shortly after the 11 September 2001 attacks on the USA. Sections 23–32 of the Act gave the Home Secretary wide-ranging powers that included a power to detain indefinitely without trial non-British citizens who were suspected of involvement in international terrorism (the power conflicted with the right to liberty guarantee contained in Article 5 of the ECHR). Such measures are permissible under Article 15(1) of the ECHR when a government considers that they are being taken 'in time of war or other public emergency threatening the life of the nation', and the government entered a derogation at Strasbourg and made the corresponding Human Rights Act 1998 (Designated Derogation) Order 2001.[84] However, the Act and Order were subsequently challenged in the courts, where the House of Lords held that the legislative scheme was both lacking in proportion and discriminatory.[85]

---

81 *Smith v Scott* (2007) CSIH 9. For subsequent consideration of *Smith* see *Chester* [2013] UKSC, [2014] AC 271.

82 (2006) 42 EHRR 41.

83 [2002] 1 AC 45.

84 SI 2001/3644.

85 *A v Home Secretary* [2005] 2 AC 68.

Their Lordships thus made a declaration of incompatibility in respect of the relevant provisions of the Act and quashed the Order, and, while the provisions of the Act of 2001 remained in force, the government came under increasing pressure to introduce in Parliament a new legislative scheme that would be more in keeping with human rights principles in an era of counter-terrorism. The result was the Prevention of Terrorism Act 2005, albeit that parts of that Act were also challenged in court and subsequently repealed and replaced by the Terrorism Prevention and Investigation Measures Act 2011.[86]

4.4.4 Section 6: the ECHR as a bind on public authorities

The provision of the Act that is most relevant to public authorities is section 6. Under sub-section 1 of this section, it is unlawful 'for a public authority to act in a way which is incompatible with a Convention right' (and note that the Act is capable of having extra-territorial effect and can therefore potentially apply to UK public authorities when they are making decisions within other countries, e.g., the army engaged in overseas military operations).[87] Section 6 thus acts as a bind on the activities of public authorities; that is, the actions or inactions of public authorities that are contrary to the ECHR will be *ultra vires* (subordinate legislation is also embraced by the section, as read in the light of sections 3 and 4). Section 6 does, however, also recognise that public authorities should have a defence to any argument of illegality where: '(a) as the result of one or more provisions of primary legislation, the authority could not have acted differently; or (b) in the case of one of more provisions of, or made under, primary legislation which cannot be read or given effect in a way which is compatible with the Convention rights, the authority was acting so as to give effect to or enforce those provisions'.[88] Consistent with the Act's more general emphasis on parliamentary sovereignty, a public authority will therefore not act unlawfully if its actions or inactions are specifically mandated or permitted by, most obviously, an Act of Parliament.[89]

Section 6 is key to the design of the Act, and there have been many cases under it that have served to redefine the workings of administrative law. At the same time, there have been other cases that have cast doubt on how far the courts are truly using section 6 to create a new human rights culture in public decision-making. For instance, one question for the courts has been whether public authorities are to be taken to have acted unlawfully where they fail to give express consideration to human rights law during the decision-making process. Although there have been some lower court judgments to the effect that such a failure should ordinarily render a decision unlawful because the authority could not have satisfied itself that its decision was ECHR compliant, the House of Lords held in a number of cases involving qualified rights that a failure to have regard for human rights

---

86 For the leading case in relation to the Act of 2005 see *Home Secretary v AF* [2010] 2 AC 269. See also 17.3.2 on Art 6 ECHR and the use of 'closed material' when imposing 'control orders' on terror suspects.

87 See, in respect of the war in Iraq, *Al-Skeini v Secretary of State for Defence* [2008] 1 AC 153, as read in the light of *Al-Skeini v UK* (2011) 53 EHRR 18.

88 Section 6(2), considered in *R (Hooper) v Secretary of State for Work and Pensions* [2005] 1 WLR 1681 and *Manchester City Council v Pinnock (Nos 1 & 2)* [2011] 2 AC 104. See also *R (GC) v Metropolitan Police Commissioner* [2011] 1 WLR 1230, 1249–50, paras 67–8, Baroness Hale.

89 Although note that s 21 also defines primary legislation to include, among other things, prerogative Orders in Council.

considerations need not have that effect.[90] For the Lords, the central question in all cases is whether the final decision of the authority violates a right and, in the event that it does not, it is said that there is no anterior requirement that the process leading to the decision should have been informed by human rights considerations. This thus means that human rights law need not be foremost in the decision-maker's mind, albeit that a failure to consider rights may have implications for any subsequent role to be played by a reviewing court. In other words, it has been said that, should a decision-maker not give consideration to rights during the decision-making process, it may be that the court would have to subject the final decision to close scrutiny to ensure that the decision-maker has struck the appropriate balance between all affected rights and is in that way compliant with the ECHR.[91] The courts may therefore have to engage in the type of 'closer look' review that we referred to above and which is now synonymous with the proportionality principle.[92]

The second aspect of the case law that casts doubt on the impact of the Act is the interpretation that has been given to the term 'public authority'. Section 6(3)(b) states that the term is to include courts and tribunals and 'any person certain of whose functions are functions of a public nature' (but note that the term excludes 'either House of Parliament or a person exercising functions in connection with proceedings in Parliament'). This 'public function' formulation was widely understood to have been used to ensure that human rights protections would extend beyond obvious public bodies such as the police and government departments, to cover other *de facto* public decision-makers such as regulatory bodies, privatised utilities, and companies performing contracted-out public functions.[93] However, case law has since established that section 6(3)(b) is to be given a narrow reading, at least in cases involving contracted-out functions. The leading authority on the point remains *YL v Birmingham City Council*,[94] which concerned the question whether a privately owned, profit-earning care home that provided accommodation for publicly funded residents fell within the meaning of 'public authority' (the issue had arisen when an individual who had been placed with the care home under the terms of a contract between the home and a local authority that had a statutory duty to make arrangements for accommodation for the individual sought to rely upon the ECHR when challenging the care home's decision to move her from the home). In finding that the care home was not embraced by section 6, the majority of the House of Lords held that there was an important distinction to be drawn between the act of the local authority in making arrangements for the accommodation of the individual (which corresponded with the performance of

---

90 See *Belfast City Council v Miss Behavin' Ltd* [2007] 1 WLR 1420, regarding Art 10 freedom of expression and Art 1, Protocol 1 property rights; and *R (SB) v Governors of Denbigh High School* [2007] 1 AC 1000, regarding Art 9 manifestations of religious belief. But compare *Manchester City Council v Pinnock (Nos 1 & 2)* [2011] 2 AC 104, 134, where Lord Neuberger noted that it was 'common ground' that the housing authority 'must take into account a demoted tenant's article 8 rights when taking possession proceedings under' the Housing Act 1996. And for criticism of the *Belfast* and *Denbigh* cases see D Mead, 'Outcomes Aren't All' [2012] *Public Law* 61.

91 *Belfast City Council v Miss Behavin' Ltd* [2007] 1 WLR 1420, 1432, para 37, Baroness Hale.

92 *R v Home Secretary, ex p Daly* [2001] 3 All ER 433; and see ch 13.

93 See, for instance, the White Paper that preceded the Human Rights Bill and Act, *Rights Brought Home: The Human Rights Bill* Cm 3782 (1997), para 2.2—although note that the Act does not apply to s 6(3)(b) bodies when the nature of the act is private: s 6(5).

94 [2008] 1 AC 95, followed in, e.g., *R (Weaver) v London & Quadrant Housing Trust* [2010] 1 WLR 363.

a public function under the Act) and the subsequent actions of the care home in providing the accommodation under the terms of the contract (which had a commercial basis and thereby fell outwith section 6(3)(b)). Thus, even though the minority in the House felt that the existence of public funding and the wider public interest in the provision of care services meant that the care home was performing a public function, the majority placed the activities of the care home squarely on the private law side of the public–private divide.[95] Any further protection for individuals was said to be a matter for the legislature, not the courts.

The correctness of this narrow approach has been much contested, and Parliament soon intervened to reverse the effect of the ruling in context of social care.[96] For instance, prior to Parliament's intervention Mark Elliott argued that the minority's approach was to be preferred as it built 'upon the insight advanced by the parliamentary Joint Committee on Human Rights that few functions are inherently public or inherently private . . . [questions of the public–private divide] . . . must instead be identified by reference to empirical criteria which recognise that it is a manifestation—and so a function—of whatever is the prevailing political philosophy concerning the proper role of government'.[97] Moreover, Landau rejected the majority's suggestion that one of the purposes of contracting out was to avoid 'some of the legal restraints' which apply to pure public bodies but not to private bodies. He argued that this was inconsistent with Parliament's intention when enacting the Human Rights Act 1998, which was to have the effect of extending human rights protection in UK law. The result in terms of rights protection in the contemporary state was thus anomalous in the sense that citizens cared for in homes or hospitals run directly by local authorities were covered under the Act, while those whose care was arranged and payrolled by the state but provided under a private law contract by a private company were not. It was to avoid such discrepancies in the protection of individuals that Parliament legislated to remove the anomaly in respect of care homes.

4.4.5 Section 7: who can use the Act?—the 'victim' requirement

The Human Rights Act 1998 also creates a freestanding cause of action against public authorities. Section 7 provides that, in regard to any action which is made unlawful under section 6(1), a person can: '(a) bring proceedings against the authority in an appropriate court or tribunal; or (b) rely on the Convention right or rights in any legal proceedings, but only if he is (or would be) a victim of the unlawful act'. The word 'victim' is borrowed from the ECHR system itself (*viz* Article 34 of the ECHR), and it essentially means that anyone who wishes to bring an action under the Act has been, or will be, directly affected by the action complained about.[98] However, depending on the circumstances of a case, the action may alternatively be taken by a relative of the affected party, for example where someone has been

---

95 On which concept see further 9.2.3.

96 Health and Social Care Act 2008, s 145, considered in *R (Broadway Care Centre) v Caerphilly CBC* [2012] EWHC 37. Note that s 145 has since been repealed by para 90 of Sch 1 to SI 2015/914 but that substantially the same provision has been enacted in s 73 of the Care Act 2014.

97 M Elliott, '"Public" and "Private": Defining the Scope of the Human Rights Act' (2007) 66 *Cambridge Law Journal* 485, 487.

98 For consideration see *Axa General Insurance v Lord Advocate* [2011] UKSC 46, [2012] 1 AC 868.

killed by state agents.[99] It is now also clear that the close relatives of a deceased person can be 'victims' in their own right and that they can sue under Article 2 of the ECHR for their bereavement.[100]

The government's decision to include the victim requirement in the Act was not without controversy. This is because the requirement was taken to be considerably more narrow than the standing requirement that is applied by the courts in judicial review proceedings.[101] The courts had, in short, adopted a very liberal approach to the interpretation of the standing requirement under the judicial review procedure, and this was something that had allowed pressure groups and other representative organisations to have access to the courts for purposes of challenging government actions.[102] By preferring the victim requirement for Human Rights Act cases, the government was criticised as having removed the potential for representative groups such as the Joint Council for the Welfare of Immigrants to bring proceedings that would vindicate the rights of, for instance, asylum seekers.[103] However, the force of such arguments has perhaps since been mediated by the realisation that representative groups may instead provide financial support for a named individual who can then 'front' the action. There is also the point that human rights arguments often arise in tandem with other issues and that, where arguments based on the ECHR are not open, it may be possible to raise parallel arguments about common law rights.[104] Lastly, it is possible for discrete pieces of legislation to enable organisations to bring proceedings under the Human Rights Act 1998 even though the organisations would not themselves come within the original section 7 definition of victims.[105]

4.4.6 Section 7: time limits and retrospectivity

An individual wishing to bring proceedings under section 7 must normally do so within a time limit of one year (this can be extended at the discretion of the court).[106] This appears on its face to be much longer than the time limit for bringing judicial review proceedings ('promptly, and in any event not later than three months'), although it is important to note that section 7(5) stipulates that the one-year limit is 'subject to any rule imposing a stricter limit in relation to

---

99 e.g., *Re McCaughey's Application* [2011] 2 WLR 1279.

100 *Rabone v Pennine Care NHS Trust* [2012] 2 AC 72.

101 See 8.10.

102 See, e.g., *R v Secretary of State for Foreign Affairs, ex p World Development Movement* [1995] 1 WLR 386; but for a robust criticism of the courts' willingness to accept such applications see C Harlow, 'Public Law and Popular Justice' (2002) 65 *Modern Law Review* 1.

103 For such an action under the judicial review procedure see, e.g., *R v Secretary of State for Social Security, ex p The Joint Council for the Welfare of Immigrants* [1997] 1 WLR 275.

104 For an apparently more generous approach to s 7 see, e.g., *R (Rusbridger) v Attorney General* [2004] 1 AC 357, where it was said by Lord Steyn that a newspaper that could in theory be subject to criminal proceedings for publishing a story that advocates Republicanism could potentially rely on the ECHR. But for an example of the section being used to prevent argument on the ECHR, see *Re Committee for the Administration of Justice's Application* [2005] NIQB 25: human rights NGO not allowed to rely on Art 2 ECHR when seeking information on the ongoing police investigation into the murder of one of its members.

105 e.g., s 71 of the Northern Ireland Act 1998 as relates to the powers of the Northern Ireland Human Rights Commission. And see *Re Northern Ireland Human Rights Commission's Application* [2014] NI 263.

106 As in, e.g., *Rabone v Pennine Care NHS Trust* [2012] 2 AC 72—parents of a suicide victim allowed to bring proceedings nearly four months after the one-year period as the state had owed their daughter a duty under Art 2 ECHR and the parents were also victims on account of their bereavement (and see 20.5).

the procedure in question'. This will therefore typically mean that judicial review proceedings under the Act must still be brought within the promptly/three-month period.[107]

Another highly important aspect of section 7 concerns retrospective effect. Section 7 is here to be read with section 22, the clear purpose of which is to limit retrospective effect by preventing proceedings against public authorities in respect of conduct that took place prior to the Act's coming into force on 2 October 2000. Case law and argument on the combined effect of sections 7 and 22 (and other provisions of the Act) has become very detailed and complex, and it is sufficient for our purposes to note that the courts have consistently stated that the Act is not intended to have retrospective effect.[108] Indeed, the only inroad into this rule has been made in relation to the Article 2 ECHR right to life and the investigation of deaths that occurred at the hands of state agents before the Act came into force on 2 October 2000 but which fall to be investigated after that date. Under Article 2 of the ECHR, states are required to hold independent and effective investigations into such deaths[109] and, while the courts initially held that the Act did not apply where deaths had pre-dated the Act's coming into force,[110] they have since modified their approach in the light of the ECtHR ruling in *Šilih v Slovenia*.[111] In that case, the ECtHR held that Article 2 of the ECHR could apply to the investigation of a death that had occurred before a state formally acceded to the ECHR so long as the death was being investigated *after* accession had been taken place. While this represented something of a departure from previous ECtHR case law, it was justified by the fact that 'the procedural obligation to carry out an effective investigation under article 2 has evolved into a separate and autonomous duty . . . it can be considered to be a detachable obligation arising out of article 2 capable of binding the state'.[112] In *McCaughey*,[113] the Supreme Court thus adopted this logic when holding that Article 2 of the ECHR applies to the investigation of a small number of deaths that occurred during the Northern Ireland conflict and which are the subject of ongoing investigation by a coroner.

McCaughey is now to be read in the light of the Supreme Court's ruling in *Keyu*, which was a case concerning the lawfulness of the UK government's refusal to hold an inquiry into shootings in colonial Malaya in 1948 in which British soldiers killed 24 civilians.[114] Much of the Court's ruling centred on the question whether the facts of the case came within the temporal reach of the ECHR itself or whether Article 2 of the ECHR did not apply because the shootings pre-dated both the moment when the UK was bound by the ECHR in international law (1953) and when the UK accepted the right of individual petition to the Strasbourg Court (1966). On this point, the Justices of the Supreme Court held (albeit for different reasons) that Article 2 of the ECHR did not apply and that any duty to hold an inquiry could

---

107 On the judicial review time limit see 8.11.

108 See, e.g., *R v Lambert* [2002] 2 AC 545, as read in the light of *R v Kansal* [2002] 1 All ER 257; *Wilson v First County Trust (No 2)* [2004] 1 AC 816; and *Wainwright v Home Office* [2004] 2 AC 406.

109 On the requirements of Art 2 ECHR see *R (Amin) v Home Secretary* [2004] 1 AC 653.

110 *R (Hurst) v London Northern District Coroner* [2007] 2 AC 189; *Jordan v Lord Chancellor* [2007] 2 AC 226; and *In Re McKerr* [2004] 1 WLR 807.

111 (2009) 49 EHRR 996; and see also *Janowiec v Russia* (2014) 58 EHRR 30.

112 (2009) 49 EHRR 996, para 159.

113 [2011] 2 WLR 1279.

114 *Keyu v Secretary of State for Foreign and Commonwealth Affairs* [2015] UKSC 69, [2015] 3 WLR 1665.

not be grounded in the ECHR (only Lady Hale thought that the government was acting unlawfully, *viz* because its refusal to hold an inquiry was *Wednesbury* unreasonable).[115] However, the point in the case as related to *McCaughey* was whether the alternative finding—that the shootings had come within the temporal reach of the ECHR—would have meant that they would thereby have to be examined in domestic law under the terms of the Human Rights Act 1998. This was a matter that the Court did not need to decide given its findings in relation to the temporal reach of the ECHR, but Lord Kerr and Lady Hale did note some of the complexities surrounding the question of the reach of the Human Rights Act 1998 and the case law of the ECtHR. It is to be expected that this issue will soon require the further attention of the Supreme Court.

4.4.7 Section 8: remedies

Where arguments based on the ECHR are made successfully, section 8(1) provides: 'In relation to any act (or proposed act) of a public authority which the court finds is (or would be) unlawful, it may grant such relief or remedy, or make such order, within its powers as it considers just and appropriate'. In the context of judicial review proceedings under the Human Rights Act, this means that each of the remedies available under the Senior Courts Act 1981 and the Civil Procedure Rules are at the disposal of the courts.[116] Depending on context, a court may therefore quash an administrative decision as having been taken in breach of the ECHR, or order an authority to act in a particular way where that is deemed necessary to ensure compliance with the authority's obligations under section 6 of the Act.[117]

Section 8(3) also provides for awards of damages where the court is satisfied that this is necessary to afford 'just satisfaction' to the person in whose favour the award is to be made (note that the term 'just satisfaction' corresponds directly with the language of Article 41 of the ECHR; note too that damages are not available in respect of judicial acts done in good faith otherwise than to compensate a person to the extent required by Article 5(5) of the ECHR, that is, where someone has been denied their liberty on account of an unlawful arrest or detention).[118] We consider the issue of damages actions against public authorities in more detail in chapter 20, although one point to be made here is that the courts can be reluctant to award damages against public authorities. In the context of the Human Rights Act, the courts have thus emphasised that damages should not be awarded too readily, even in cases involving argued breaches of an individual's so-called absolute rights.[119] The leading authority on the restrictive approach remains *R (Greenfield) v Home Secretary*,[120] which concerned the question whether a prisoner whose Article

---

115 On this ground for review see ch 13.

116 The corresponding legislation in Northern Ireland is the Judicature (Northern Ireland) Act 1978 and the Rules of the Court of Judicature; and in Scotland see Chapter 58 of the Rules of the Court of Session.

117 On remedies see ch 18.

118 Section 9(3).

119 See, e.g., *Van Colle v Chief Constable of Hertfordshire* [2009] 1 AC 225: police not liable under Art 2 ECHR for death of witness who was killed by the person against whom he was due to give evidence and from whom he had been receiving threats (see also *Van Colle v United Kingdom* (2013) 56 EHRR 23: no violation of Art 2 ECHR). But compare *Rabone v Pennine Care NHS Trust* [2012] 2 AC 72. And see further 20.5.

120 [2005] 1 WLR 673, applied in, e.g., *R (Sturnham) v Parole Board* [2013] UKSC 23, [2013] 2 AC 254.

6 ECHR rights had been violated by a prison disciplinary procedure should receive damages in addition to a declaration that the respondent had acted unlawfully. In holding that a declaration was sufficient in the context of the case, the House of Lords emphasised that the ECtHR itself frequently does not make awards of damages in Article 6 ECHR cases and that it tends to do so only where it finds a causal connection between the violation of Article 6 of the ECHR and any monetary loss for which the individual claims compensation (awards for anxiety and frustration attributable to violations of Article 6 of the ECHR would, moreover, be made very sparingly and for modest sums). The House of Lords also emphasised that the Human Rights Act 1998 should not, in any event, be regarded as a tort statute that automatically gives rise to a remedy in damages, as the Act's objectives of ensuring compliance with human rights standards can in many cases be met simply through the finding of a violation. In addition, it was said that the Act is not intended to give individuals access to better remedies than they would have were they to go to Strasbourg, but rather to incorporate in domestic law the ECtHR's case-by-case approach and to require domestic courts to have regard to that approach. On the facts of the *Greenfield* case as read with the Strasbourg jurisprudence, there were thus no special features that warranted an award of damages.

4.5 The EU Charter of Fundamental Rights

The last issue to be considered in this chapter is the role that the EU Charter of Fundamental Rights plays in protecting rights in the UK. As we saw in chapter 3 on EU law, the Charter provides an important statement of contemporary rights standards that sub-divides into six main sections on 'dignity', 'freedoms', 'equality', 'solidarity', 'citizen's rights', and 'justice'. While the Charter was originally proclaimed as only a non-binding statement of rights *vis-à-vis* the EU institutions and its Member States, it was given the full force of treaty law under the Lisbon Treaty of 2007. The Charter is thus an important part of the overall constitutional framework of the EU and it has had a significant impact on the case law of the Court of Justice of the European Union (CJEU) and the General Court.[121]

The corresponding point about the Charter's role in UK law concerns its enforceability in the domestic courts. Although the Lisbon Treaty included a Protocol that was initially thought to limit the Charter's applicability in the courts of the UK and Poland (Protocol 30), it is now clear that the great majority of the Charter rights are enforceable in the UK courts when EU law is in issue. This is the result of the CJEU's ruling in *R (NS) v Secretary of State for the Home Department*,[122] which concerned questions about the workings of the Common European Asylum System. The case arose when an Afghan asylum seeker who had arrived in the UK via, among other countries, Greece, challenged a decision to remove him to Greece so that his claim for asylum could be processed in accordance with the Asylum System's rules (rules that require that applications for asylum be processed by the EU Member State in

---

121 See generally S Peers et al (eds), *The EU Charter of Fundamental Rights: A Commentary* (Oxford: Hart Publishing, 2014).
122 Case C-411/10, [2012] 2 CMLR 9.

which an asylum seeker first arrives). NS argued that his removal to Greece would result in a violation of, among other things, the prohibition on torture and inhuman or degrading treatment under Article 4 of the EU Charter, and the Court of Appeal referred to the CJEU the question whether the applicant could rely upon the Charter in UK courts. Having noted Advocate General Trstenjak's textual analysis of Protocol 30—which distinguished the Charter rights in the instant case from the Charter's social rights grouped under the heading of 'solidarity'—the Court held that he could rely upon the rights to challenge the removal decision. This therefore means that Protocol 30 does not amount to an 'opt-out' from the Charter and that, with the exception of 'solidarity' rights (about which nothing more was said by the CJEU), its provisions can be pleaded in UK courts.[123]

There are two points to note about the implications of NS. The first is that UK courts are now legally obliged to protect Charter rights only in those proceedings that concern the implementation of EU law (albeit that the Charter may also have an indirect influence on case law through the 'spill-over' of norms).[124] This, in turn, is something that might give rise to difficult questions about the reach of the Charter, as there are more or less expansive understandings of what 'implementation' entails and the Charter's reach could of course vary accordingly.[125] However, for our purposes, it is sufficient to note that questions about rights under the Charter will be most likely to arise where an individual can point to some other provision of EU law that is being affected by a public authority's actions or inactions. In that instance, the doctrine of the supremacy of EU law would require courts to give prior effect to the relevant provisions of the Charter and the case law of the CJEU.

The second point concerns the relationship between the rights in the Charter and those provisions of the ECHR that have effect under the terms of the Human Rights Act 1998. In some—perhaps many—cases it will be possible for an individual to rely upon essentially equivalent rights under both the Charter and the ECHR (for instance, Article 4 of the EU Charter, above, parallels Article 3 of the ECHR). While this may appear potentially confusing, it is to be noted that the Charter provides, in Article 52(3), that: 'In so far as this Charter contains rights which correspond to rights guaranteed by the [ECHR] . . . the meaning and scope of those rights shall be the same as those laid down by [the ECHR]. This provision shall not prevent Union law providing more extensive protection.' This therefore means that rights under the EU Charter should be interpreted consistently with those under the ECHR and that a different interpretation should be given only where that would provide for a higher standard of protection for the individual. UK courts might consequently expect that the settled case law of the Human Rights Act 1998 will remain largely unaffected by that emerging under the Charter and that 'new standards' will emerge only where the courts hear arguments about rights not previously embraced by the ECHR. A revised approach may also be required should the CJEU be asked, at some later date, for further guidance on the precise place of 'solidarity' rights under the Charter and Protocol 30.

---

123 On its enforceability see further *R (EM) v Secretary of State for the Home Department* [2014] 1321, 1342, para 62, Lord Kerr.

124 See 3.3.4.

125 For analysis see K Beal and T Hickman, 'Beano No More: The Charter of Rights After Lisbon' [2011] 16 *Judicial Review* 113. For the CJEU's (expansive) view see Case C-617/10, *Aklagaren v Fransson* [2013] 2 CMLR 46.

4.6 **Conclusion**

In this chapter, we have tried to provide an overview of some of the key themes in the workings of human rights law, and to introduce some of the ways in which the Human Rights Act is impacting upon those themes. In doing so, we have made many cross-references to other chapters that both precede and follow this one. Such cross-referencing simply reflects the fact that human rights law is, principally because of the Human Rights Act but now also because of the EU Charter of Fundamental Rights, becoming ever more significant in an increasing number of areas. While it is of course important not to overstate the relevance of one particular piece of legislation such as the Human Rights Act, it is clear that human rights law is changing the workings of public law in many fundamental ways. Practical support, perhaps, for Laws LJ's normative description of the Act as 'constitutional' in form.[126]

In later chapters, we will take up many of the points made here. For example, in chapter 13 we will discuss the relationship between *Wednesbury* review and proportionality as principles that are central to administrative law and the protection of human rights. It will also become apparent that Human Rights Act issues have arisen in numerous other cases alongside the other grounds of judicial review, namely illegality and procedural impropriety. Each of the chapters on those grounds for review (chapters 11–12 and 16–17) will therefore analyse more closely how the Human Rights Act has impacted upon the grounds of review. We will finally see, in chapter 20, how the courts have modified their approach to public authority liability in tort in the light of the emerging rights jurisprudence.

FURTHER READING

Amos, M (2014) *Human Rights Law*, 2nd edn (Oxford: Hart Publishing).

Anthony, G (2002) *UK Public Law and European Law: The Dynamics of Legal Integration* (Oxford: Hart Publishing).

Chandrachud, C [2014] 'Reconfiguring the Discourse on Political Responses to Declarations of Incompatibility' *Public Law* 625.

Clayton, R [2015] 'The Empire Strikes Back: Common Law Rights and the Human Rights Act' *Public Law* 3.

Craig, P (2002) 'Contracting out, the Human Rights Act, and the Scope of Judicial Review' 118 *Law Quarterly Review* 551.

Elliott, M (2007) '"Public" and "Private": Defining the Scope of the Human Rights Act' 66 (3) *CLJ*, 485–7.

Ewing, K and Gearty, C (1990) *Freedom Under Thatcher* (Oxford: Clarendon Press).

Feldman, D (2002) *Civil Liberties and Human Rights in England and Wales*, 2nd edn (Oxford: Oxford University Press).

Fenwick, H (2004) 'Clashing Rights, the Welfare of the Child and the Human Rights Act' 67 *Modern Law Review* 889.

Forsyth, C (ed) (2000) *Judicial Review and the Constitution* (Oxford: Hart Publishing).

---

126 See *Thoburn v Sunderland City Council* [2003] QB 151.

Greer, S and Slowe, R [2015] 'The Conservatives' Proposals for a British Bill of Rights' *European Human Rights Law Review* 372.

Harlow, C (2002) 'Public Law and Popular Justice' 65 *Modern Law Review* 1.

Hunt, M (1997) *Using Human Rights Law in English Courts* (Oxford: Hart Publishing).

Laws, J (2014) *The Common Law Constitution* (Cambridge: Cambridge University Press).

O'Cinneide, C (2013) 'Legal Accountability and Social Justice' in N Bamforth and P Leyland (eds), *Accountability in the Contemporary Constitution* (Oxford: Oxford University Press).

O'Cinneide, C (2105) 'Human Rights and the UK Constitution' in Jowell, J, Oliver, D and O'Cinneide, C (eds), *The Changing Constitution*, 8th edn (Oxford: Oxford University Press).

Oliver, D [2004] 'Functions of a Public Nature under the Human Rights Act' *Public Law* 476.

Wadham, J, Mountfield, H, Edmundson, A, and Gallagher, C (2011) *Blackstone's Guide to the Human Rights Act 1998*, 6th edn (Oxford: Oxford University Press).

Young, A (2009) *Parliamentary Sovereignty and the Human Rights Act* (Oxford: Hart Publishing).

Young, A (2013) 'Accountability, Human Rights Adjudication and the Human Rights Act 1998' in N Bamforth and P Leyland (eds), *Accountability in the Contemporary Constitution* (Oxford: Oxford University Press).

5

....

The modern administrative state

5.1 Introduction

While our survey of administrative law is primarily concerned with the mechanisms of accountability and the remedies available to the citizen when confronted
with a potential *ultra vires* excess or abuse of power, it is also important to be able
to identify the distribution of power within the institutional and legal framework of the UK. This is because administrative law is essentially bounded by what
government does and how public authorities directly, or through the agency of
private companies, exercise these powers and fulfil a variety of duties. We need
to inquire—where do their powers come from and what are these institutions?
Answering these questions is not an entirely straightforward task, in part because
the British Constitution is 'uncodified' and does not provide anything resembling a strict separation of legislative and executive functions, and in part because
Britain has never had a recognisably tidy and coherently organised body of administrative institutions. In this chapter, therefore, we briefly identify the sources of
legal power and then proceed to map not only the principal state institutions but
the other public bodies and private organisations which are responsible for delivering and/or overseeing the delivery of services both at a national and at a local level.

5.1.1 The state, the Crown, and the government

At the outset it is useful to be clear about the rather confusing terminology which
is applied to the institution of central government itself. The state is usually identified as a primarily political entity, historically defined as the defender of territorial
integrity and law and order. Today it is involved in a very extensive range of activities, reaching into every aspect of life. However, it does not exist as a strict legal
entity in the UK and is hardly ever mentioned in statutes or case law; but it was referred to in *Chandler v DPP*[1] by Lord Reid, who argued that 'Perhaps the country or
the realm are as good synonyms as one can find and I would be prepared to accept
the organised community as coming as near to a definition as one can get'; while
Lord Devlin expressed the view that the term is used 'to denote the organs of government of a national community. In the United Kingdom . . . , that organ is the
Crown.' The term 'the Crown' is commonly used in statutes when referring to the
government acting in its official executive capacity. Central government is carried

---

1 [1964] AC 763.

on in the name of the Crown; and ministers, civil servants, and members of the armed forces are all servants of the Crown. This term can also be used to represent the sum total of the powers of central government, whether these be derived from primary or secondary (delegated) legislation, or the Royal prerogative.

There are occasions when it will be important to ascertain whether the term 'Crown' is describing a function, a service, an institution, or a servant. This is because the Crown is afforded certain immunities and privileges at law (regulated by the Crown Immunities Act 1947) and is bound by a statute only when the Act expressly provides that it is. For example, no planning permission will be required for the Crown in many circumstances. In *Chandler v DPP*[2] Lord Diplock argued that when referring to the executive acts of government that it would be more accurate to use 'the government' rather than 'the Crown'. The latter term would be reserved for actions relating to the armed forces and the defence of the realm. But this is a controversial view because of the fact that Crown servants *do* enjoy certain immunities. If these were to apply to ministers it might have the effect of reducing their susceptibility to legal challenge, for example, when exercising the prerogative powers, while, when acting on statutory authority, they are potentially open to the full range of judicial review remedies. This is why powers are conferred on ministers personally and not on the Crown. Therefore, despite the fact that the term 'government' can clearly be conventionally employed to encompass the executive organs of the state, the civil service, and the armed forces, it should not be regarded as a legal entity and confused with the Crown. On the other hand, the terms 'the state' and 'the government' can reasonably, in the United Kingdom, be regarded as meaning much the same thing.[3]

5.1.2 **The contracting state**

Since 1979, successive governments have transformed the role of what we term the 'administrative state' (including, e.g., the civil service, local authorities, non-departmental public bodies, and nationalised industries) by means of a series of policy initiatives which have fundamentally revised ideas and expectations about the application of different forms of contracting in the public sector. This was originally linked to an ideological crusade to provide market orientated solutions and to tackle what has been claimed to be endemic problems of welfare-bureaucracy and large-scale government. A range of strategies have been employed, ostensibly designed to reduce the role of the state by streamlining the executive branch through improvements in efficiency, privatisation, reduction of red tape, etc.[4] The Deregulation and Contracting Out Act 1994 (discussed below and now superseded by the Regulatory Reform Act 2001, the Legislative and Regulatory Reform Act 2006, and the Deregulation Act 2015) was one notable attempt at furthering this aim. These policies have cumulatively resulted in many significant changes in the discharge of governmental responsibilities. While in most cases overall responsibility for policy-making functions has remained with central or local government,

---

2 Ibid.

3 See *M v Home Office* [1994] 1 AC 377.

4 See generally R Austin, 'Administrative Law's Reaction to the Changing Concept of Public Services' in P Leyland and T Woods (eds), *Administrative Law Facing the Future* (London: Blackstone Press, 1997), ch 1.

part of the administrative structure has had agency status conferred on it, for example, this is the approach adopted for the Prison Service and the social security system (the Benefits Agency). However, in other areas, many functions, ranging from prisoner escort services to street cleaning, are now provided by means of contract through private companies which are entirely independent of central government or local authorities. Whatever the virtues of such policies in terms of the effective delivery of services, these developments pose many challenging questions for public lawyers. The Labour Government of 1997–2010 and the Conservative Liberal Coalition Government of 2010–15 continued with and refined many of these policy initiatives.

This has meant that many functions that were carried out by government departments and local government are now performed by independent, privately owned, companies. For example, these include prisoner escort services, court shorthand reporting, refuse collection, road repairs, maintenance and repair of council housing, and highway construction to name but a very few. This tendency has significant legal consequences because of the continued application of privity of contract, which means that when a private outside body enters into a contract to provide such a service an enforceable agreement will be negotiated only between the service provider and the department, agency, or local authority. On the other hand, the consumer, who is not party to the agreement, cannot sue, and is therefore deprived of a legal remedy.[5] For example, the council taxpayer cannot take an action in regard to any alleged failings in contracted-out refuse services. In another area, the Prisons Agency enters into formal contracts with security firms to provide escort services to and from the courts. It follows that any dispute that arises in respect of such a contract will normally be settled in the civil courts between the department/agency and service provider. However, there may be issues that demand public accountability and public law remedies. These could well involve situations where the consumer of the service has no private law rights at all, for example, if prisoners claim that the conditions in which they are forced to travel are unsafe or unhygienic, or that guards have treated them inhumanely. What options are available? As we shall see when considering Next Steps agencies (at 5.3), the contracting-out procedure has resulted in the established avenues of responsibility, through MPs to the minister, being a stage further removed from parliamentary oversight. But, more seriously, if the agency or department has negotiated a contract with a private firm that is defective, in that it fails to provide a remedy in regard to such crucial questions, should such a contract be allowed to continue without modification?

5.2 **Powers**

It will be readily apparent that the institutions which will be outlined in the latter part of this chapter have a variety of powers vested in them. We must now discuss the nature of these powers. The government in the guise of the Crown acts under

---

5 See G Drewry, 'The Executive: Towards Accountable Government and Effective Governance' in J Jowell and D Oliver (eds), *The Changing Constitution*, 7th edn (Oxford: Oxford University Press, 2011).

the prerogative, as well as being able to initiate legislation, but many other bodies have direct legislative authority or depend on powers delegated to them from central government. Before proceeding further it is important to remember that the legal sovereignty of the UK is, in effect, limited through its membership of the European Union (EU) (European Communities Act 1972) and that EU law is a very important source of domestic law in areas covered by the treaties, but European institutions and law are considered in more detail in chapter 3.

5.2.1 **The Royal prerogative**

The term 'Royal prerogative' reflects the fact that, up until the seventeenth century, certain exceptional powers and privileges, for instance the power to make war or to sign treaties, were vested in the sovereign personally. These non-statutory, residual common law powers cover a range of important rights, immunities, and privileges that are (arguably) required by the Crown in order to perform its constitutional duties and carry on the government of the country. Today, these powers are invariably exercised by the Prime Minister, other ministers of the Crown, or ministers in the devolved institutions.

In the eighteenth century Blackstone had defined the term prerogative as referring only to those rights which the Crown alone enjoys.[6] Essentially, these were the traditional powers of the monarch. They included, among others, the declaring of war, the making of peace, the granting of honours, and the Royal assent to bills, that is, not those powers that were enjoyed in common with the monarch's subjects, such as conveying land. In short, they were—and are—legal attributes of the Crown which are significantly different from those enjoyed by private persons. Of course, the trend away from absolute monarchy was reinforced in the eighteenth century with the Hanoverian succession to the throne, when ministers became directly responsible for the day-to-day running of government, and culminated in the nineteenth and twentieth centuries with the doctrine of the sovereignty of Parliament. Equally, while in the eighteenth century the scope of government activity was much smaller, with only a few key Whitehall departments (such as the Treasury or Foreign Office), the foundation of the contemporary administrative state in the twentieth century saw the role of government being greatly expanded and the monarch becoming peripheral to the central activities of the executive. Given these developments, it is not surprising that for Dicey, writing when the transition to constitutional monarchy was almost complete, the prerogative included much more than powers that are exclusive to the monarch and was viewed, instead, as 'the residue of discretionary or arbitrary authority left in the hands of the Crown'. On this definition, it came to embrace any act that government can lawfully perform without the authority of Parliament.[7]

Today, the prerogative retains a considerable importance to the workings of the modern administrative state. For instance, a parliamentary paper published in 2009 said that, while 'it is difficult to provide a comprehensive catalogue of the prerogative powers', the areas in which the powers operate include the legislature;

---

6 W Blackstone, *Commentaries on the Laws of England*, Vol 1 (London: Sweet and Maxwell, 1836), 239.

7 A Dicey, *An Introduction to the Study of the Law of the Constitution*, 10th edn (Basingstoke: Macmillan, 1959), 425.

aspects of the judicial system; powers relating to foreign affairs; powers relating to the armed forces; appointments and honours; immunities and privileges; powers in times of emergency; and miscellaneous powers in respect of, among other things, metal, coinage, treasure trove, and printing.[8] This makes clear that use of the prerogative powers can range across matters that are relatively trivial through to those concerned with the sovereign existence of the state. At the same time, the powers are not immutable, and the parliamentary paper of 2009 was produced in advance of anticipated reform of aspects of the prerogative. In the event, the Constitutional Reform and Governance Act 2010 placed prerogative powers concerning the management of the civil service and the ratification of international treaties on a statutory footing.

It is also to be emphasised that there are two important constraints on the prerogative. The first is that provided by Parliament, which can hold ministers to account for decisions that they take on the basis of the prerogative through, for instance, parliamentary questions and/or the workings of parliamentary committees.[9] Parliament can alternatively enact legislation, as happened with the Act of 2010. This has the effect of extinguishing prerogative powers insofar as they overlap with the area governed by statute,[10] something that corresponds with the understanding that the Westminster Parliament is legally sovereign.

The other constraint is that imposed by the courts through judicial review. We deal more fully with the emergence of that constraint in chapter 9, and we need only note here that the courts have been increasingly concerned by the potential for the prerogative powers to be used in a manner that is essentially anti-democratic.[11] To guard against this danger, the courts have thus held that an increasing number of prerogative powers are subject to judicial control and that remedies should issue where there has been an abuse of power.[12] That said, the courts accept that some prerogative powers are non-justiciable and that it would be constitutionally inappropriate for them to supervise decisions taken in areas of 'high policy'.[13] The courts also accept that, even if the subject matter of a decision may be justiciable, the decision in question may have been taken in circumstances where the courts should exercise restraint (for instance, where national security was in issue).[14]

5.2.2 Legislation

There are different kinds of legislation, and there are different procedures in place to deal with them.

5.2.2.1 Parliamentary legislation

The central government is the focus of power in the UK. Indeed, until very recently, with the restrictions placed on local authorities and the increasing concentration

---

8 L Maer and O Gay, 'The Royal Prerogative', SN/PC/03861, s 2, referring to A Bradley, K Ewing, and C Knight, *Constitutional and Administrative Law*, 16th edn (Harlow: Longmans, 2014), 250–67.

9 See ch 2.

10 *A-G v De Keyser's Royal Hotel Ltd* [1920] AC 508, discussed in ch 9.

11 *R v Home Secretary, ex p Fire Brigade's Union* [1995] 2 AC 513.

12 Ibid.

13 *R v Secretary of State for Foreign and Commonwealth Affairs, ex p Everett* [1989] 1 All ER 655, 668.

14 *Council of Civil Service Unions v Minister for the Civil Service* [1985] AC 374.

of power in government hands, it is arguable that this feature of our constitution has been significantly enhanced. This is because, in theory at least, under the doctrine of unlimited sovereignty, Parliament enjoys enormous capacity to make and repeal any legislation. It does this by passing Acts of Parliament or 'statutes'. Central government legislation is largely concerned with the implementation of policy, often originating from manifesto commitments or departmental needs, and then approved by the cabinet. For the most part, Parliament is dominated by the government, able on all but a few occasions, usually following some consultation (but not always), to direct its majority towards guaranteeing the enactment of its legislative proposals. These proposals are introduced in the form of public bills which pass through the same distinct stages of debate and discussion in both Houses of Parliament. Assuming a bill is properly enacted, the legislative power of Parliament cannot be challenged in the courts,[15] unless it is contrary to EU law.[16]

In the context of administrative law, it is not simply the acknowledgement of this legislative authority that interests us, but the manner in which the power is exercised. In many cases Acts of Parliament will vest discretionary powers in the hands of ministers by making provision for delegated legislation. This tendency has greatly increased over the last 35 years in both quantity and scope. These provisions will frequently only come into force when the Secretary of State makes a commencement order (see 5.2.3).

5.2.2.2 **Private Bills**

Parliament also provides a mechanism for the legitimation of legislation required by other bodies. Private Bills are introduced by local authorities, nationalised industries, and even by individuals, rather than the government. A good example was the Channel Tunnel Rail Link Act 1996 which enables the railway connections for the Channel Tunnel link to be completed. A range of additional powers was needed here to see to fruition an ambitious enterprise, for example, one involving the acquisition of land and the execution of large-scale construction works. More recently, the Humber Bridge Act 2013 conferred revised powers for the setting of tolls and financial management to the board responsible for running the Humber Bridge. Private Bills have the same legislative force as other Bills when they are passed by Parliament, but they undergo a different passage through Parliament before receiving the Royal Assent. This is directed at establishing the general merits of the proposals. From the procedural point of view, this is most pronounced at the committee stage. If the Bill is opposed in committee, it will undergo a quasi-judicial process before the committee where the promoters and challengers, represented by counsel, are able to present their case. Opposers must have standing, that is, an interest that is affected by the Bill. Having surmounted the hurdle of the committee stage the Bill will proceed to become law in the normal way.

The procedures for making private legislation were reviewed in 1988 by a special joint committee of both Houses of Parliament. The recommendations which followed these deliberations have largely been implemented. Additionally, the Transport and Works Act 1992 has introduced an extra-parliamentary system for

---

15 See *Pickin v British Railways Board* [1974] AC 765.
16 See *R v Secretary of State for Transport, ex p Factortame Ltd (No 2)* [1991] 1 AC 603.

approving building and development projects with regard to railways, tramways, and harbours. The Secretary of State now makes an Order without parliamentary approval being required, unless the project is one which is of 'national significance' where parliamentary approval is required from both Houses. The result of these changes is that, by 1999, the number of Private Bills had dropped to insignificant levels (to around three to four Bills each year, compared to between 30 and 40 in previous years).

5.2.2.3 Private Member's Bills

Private Member's Bills may also be introduced in Parliament. But although MPs do have the capacity to initiate legislative proposals, the significance of these Bills is marginal. This is not only because parliamentary time is limited, but also because it is very difficult to secure a parliamentary majority for such proposals, especially if a Bill conflicts with the government's legislative programme or priorities. The point to note is that there is little scope for MPs to gain backing for even popular legislation without the support of the government. Nevertheless, it should be said that, once enacted, some of these measures may be of considerable importance in social terms, for example, the legislation in the 1960s on abortion, the abolition of the death penalty, and reform of the laws on divorce and homosexuality have had wide repercussions in subsequent decades.

5.2.2.4 Scotland, Northern Ireland, and Wales

The Scottish Parliament, the Northern Ireland Assembly, and the Welsh Assembly are empowered to pass primary legislation within limits set respectively by the Scotland Act 1998, the Northern Ireland Act 1998, and the Government of Wales Act 2006 (although note that this is subordinate legislation for the purposes of section 21 of the Human Rights Act 1998). For example, see the Scotland Act, section 29(1) which states that 'An Act of the Scottish Parliament is not law so far as any provision of the Act is outside the legislative competence of the Scottish Parliament' and Schedule 5. The Northern Ireland Act 1998, section 5 states that the Assembly may make laws, to be known as Acts, while section 6 states that 'a provision of an Act is not law if it is outside the legislative competence of the Assembly'.

5.2.3 Delegated legislation

Towards the beginning of the twentieth century the expansion of subordinate (or 'delegated') legislation was regarded by Lord Hewart CJ in *The New Despotism* (1929) as an abdication by Parliament of its principal constitutional, legislative role. But although it would appear that a trend towards delegation confirms that there has been a significant shift of power to the executive organs of the state, at the same time it should be recognised that delegation can in most cases be justified because of the greatly enlarged role of governmental activities in this century, and the obvious constraints that this expansion places on parliamentary time. In fact, delegated legislation is essential because Parliament is incapable of making all law, and even when it does pass statutes there are obvious limits to the amount of detail that can be contained therein. The complexity and detail involved in making administrative rules requires that primary legislation is supported by delegated powers which also allow for greater flexibility, especially in times of emergency.

Indeed, legislation in the UK is usually detailed and tightly drafted, leaving only a residue of power to the executive, compared to the continental tradition where it is common for statutes to be very broad statements of policy, leaving it to the executive to implement the policy by delegated legislation. (But legislation in the area of government administration is often more skeletal. For example, the Child Support Act 1991 was in skeleton form. This meant that details of the Child Support Agency, set up under the Act, were filled in by regulations introduced at a later stage.)

Additionally, delegated legislation permits powers to be conferred by Parliament on other bodies. This is achieved by various means, including ministerial orders, by-laws, departmental circulars, guidelines, and codes of conduct.[17]

5.2.3.1 Statutory instruments

These are rules and orders made by ministers that are governed by provisions which are defined in the Statutory Instruments Act 1946, section 1. In fact, the term 'statutory instrument' is a wide-ranging expression which covers all forms of legislation embraced by this Act.

The Statutory Instruments Act 1946, section 1(1), provides:

Where by this Act or any Act passed after the commencement of this Act power to make, confirm or approve orders, rules, regulations or other subordinate legislation, is conferred on His Majesty in Council or on any Minister of the Crown then, if the power is expressed

(a) in the case of a power conferred on His Majesty, to be exercisable by Order in Council;

(b) in the case of a power conferred in a Minister of the Crown, to be exercisable by statutory instrument,

any document by which that power is exercised shall be known as a 'statutory instrument' and the provision of this Act shall apply thereto accordingly . . .

Statutory instruments are generally laid before Parliament for approval. Following publication, statutory instruments normally come into effect when they are signed by the minister, but there may be a requirement for pre-publication consultation. For example, the Social Security Act 1980, sections 9 and 10, provide that social security regulations have to be submitted in draft form to the Social Security Advisory Committee. Its report must be laid before Parliament together with the regulations.

The requirement for publication is important. The basic issue of continuing debate is whether a statutory instrument can come into effect without those who are affected by it being notified.[18]

Under the 1946 Act either:

(a) an enabling statute may specify the procedure that has to be used for publicising the instrument in advance, or

(b) the enabling Act may state that the procedures laid down in the 1946 Act are followed. This involves sending the instrument to the Stationery Office where the date of printing will be conclusive evidence of when the instrument was first issued.

---

17 e.g., the Highway Code discussed later.
18 See *Johnson v Sargant & Sons Ltd* [1918] 1 KB 101.

Some instruments are altogether exempted from publication under section 8 of the 1946 Act and under the Statutory Instruments Regulations 1948.[19] Some Orders in Council can be made under the Royal prerogative.[20]

The House of Lords used its power of veto over secondary legislation controversially in October 2015 to prevent the implementation of government changes to a flagship policy on tax credits. It did this in respect of a matter of financial management, under constitutional convention normally regarded as the province of the lower house, and did so within months of the May 2015 election.[21] In response, following the Strathclyde Review, the government has announced its intention to legislate to replace this absolute veto power over statutory instruments with a lesser power, for example, giving the Lords the option of referring the statutory instrument back to the Commons so that it can be considered again.[22] Such a change would not only alter the balance within Parliament in favour of the elected House of Commons, but it would also strengthen the position of the government which often uses delegated legislation as a vehicle for implementing policy changes.[23]

5.2.3.2 **By-laws**

In common with other types of delegated legislation, by-laws can be made by local authorities and other administrative agencies under powers conferred by statute. For example, these include local laws needed for regulation in particular situations existing or arising in any locality; but they also include rules made by, or on behalf of, any authority, for example, rail authorities for the regulation or administration of a district, property, or undertaking. Section 235 of the Local Government Act 1972 allows local authorities to make by-laws covering a wide variety of matters, such as the fouling of pavements by dogs, litter in public places, the riding of bicycles on footpaths, and the sale of contraceptives. There are also model sets of by-laws which can be and often are adopted by authorities, but at the same time by-laws prepared by central government can be modified for a specific purpose thus providing considerable scope for flexibility.

As with other forms of delegated legislation, the validity of by-laws can be challenged in the courts. This can be either directly, as being *ultra vires*; or indirectly, when there is a prosecution under the by-law. In *Boddington* it was argued that a conviction should be void because the by-law itself was invalid. The House of Lords held that by way of a defence a challenge to the validity of a by-law is permitted unless Parliament has expressly provided to the contrary in the primary legislation.[24]

5.2.3.3 **Compulsory purchase orders**

Local authorities generally are empowered by the Acquisition of Land Act 1981 to issue compulsory purchase orders to acquire land for development purposes. These orders are, in the view of many, a form of delegated legislation.

---

19 SI 1948/1.

20 See *Council of Civil Service Unions v Minister for the Civil Service* [1985] AC 374.

21 See M Russell, 'The Lords, Politics and Finance' UK Const L Blog, 2 November 2015; and 1.5.2.

22 Hansard, col 1740, 17 December 2015.

23 A Tucker, 'Tax Credits, Delegated Legislation, and Executive Power' UK Const L Blog, 5 November 2015.

24 See *Boddington v British Transport Police* [1999] 2 AC 143 (HL).

5.2.3.4 **Administrative rules**

Codes of practice, circulars, and guidelines play an important part in the administration of government. Indeed, there has been an increasing trend in recent years
towards adopting these various forms of what has been termed 'quasi legislation'
across a broad spectrum of policy-making, for example, planning, health, safety
at work, race relations, animal welfare, police powers, and pollution control. There
are obvious advantages in adopting such rules. For example, they are likely to be
more flexible and may well indicate how any discretion in the application of a rule
will be exercised. Also, they will tend to be drawn up in less precise legal language.
In many cases a code of practice issued by an official body may be highly desirable
in performing an informational function, but the question for us to consider is
whether such provisions are legally enforceable.

Take the Highway Code, familiar to most citizens. It sets out some of the measures that are contained in the Road Traffic Acts, but it also goes beyond this and
provides 'directions for the guidance' of road users, suggesting how they should
conduct themselves in a wide variety of situations. Failure to observe the provisions
of the Highway Code will not in itself render a person liable to criminal proceedings, but where failure to abide by the Highway Code coincides with some other
breach of the legislation then the road user may be liable to prosecution. Similarly,
the Codes of Practice that accompany the Police and Criminal Evidence Act 1984
are not strictly enforceable. However, if the police do not follow the codes when
arresting a suspect this can lead to the court deeming the arrest to be unlawful, although this will not necessarily be the case. Further, members of the public cannot
take proceedings against officers solely on the basis of non-compliance with the
code(s) through criminal or civil proceedings, but an officer breaking the code(s)
may be liable to disciplinary proceedings as a result of his action. In some cases the
relevant legislation is supported by rules that are issued by the Secretary of State.

5.3 **Central government**

The term 'central government' refers to diverse types of official and quasi-official
bodies which all have varying degrees of power vested in them. This list includes:
government departments, governmental agencies, public corporations, and
quangos (quasi-autonomous non-governmental bodies).

5.3.1 **Central government departments**

Central government departments are responsible for carrying out the core duties of
government. The majority of departmental functions and powers are established
by statute, but certain powers remain under the prerogative to be exercised by ministers. Each department is headed by a minister or Secretary of State and funded
directly by the Treasury. The senior civil servants are the permanent officials who
assist ministers in the formulation and administration of policy, while (see chapter
2) the convention of individual ministerial responsibility, in theory at least, holds
the minister politically accountable to Parliament for the actions of the department

and its officials. At the same time, the PO (Parliamentary Ombudsman) can investigate complaints referred by MPs concerning maladministration within departments (see chapter 6). The previous Coalition Government, as part of a strategy of reducing public expenditure, was strongly committed to cutting the number of civil servants by 23 per cent under its Civil Service Reform Plan[25] and by 2014 the total had shrunk to 410,000.[26]

Alongside full-time officials, since the 1960s there has been an increasingly widespread appointment of various types of special advisers by ministers (including press secretaries, academics subject specialists, economists, political advisers, etc). This has elements in common with a spoils system, since these advisers can wield considerable power within 10 Downing Street, the Cabinet Office, and other departments of state. Their tenure of office is strictly dependent on the survival of the government, however, 'special advisers' make up a relatively small part of the government machine and, on the whole, it could be argued that they perform a useful function. Only recently under the Constitutional Reform and Governance Act 2010 have they been made constitutionally accountable for their actions.

Some ministries at the heart of government, such as the Treasury and the Lord Chancellor's Department, have evolved from medieval offices of state. Others, including the Foreign Office and the Home Office, rose to their current prominence during the nineteenth century. In fact, the Home Office has steadily acquired many varied responsibilities in relation to domestic policy-making including, for example, prisons, the police, immigration, and broadcasting. However, during the twentieth century, especially after 1945, important departments have been established to cope with the greatly expanded post-war role of government. The Ministers of the Crown Act 1975 allows the reorganisation and transfer of departmental responsibilities by Order in Council (a form of delegated legislation, see 5.2.3). Several of these departments have been reorganised on a number of occasions to accommodate shifting trends in policy, through what might be referred to as a process of fission and fusion. Take, for example, the Ministry of Health; it was considered unwieldy after the Second World War and some of its functions were distributed between the Ministry of Housing and Local Government and the Ministry of Social Security. A subsequent reorganisation in 1970 combined Health and Social Security into one giant ministry with responsibility for coordinating this area of policy formulation, but still with only a single representative at the cabinet table. However, in 1988 Health and Social Security were once again separated into distinct departments, each with their own cabinet minister. The main functions of the Department of Social Security were transferred to a new Department of Works and Pensions in 2001. Similarly, Trade and Industry have been split and joined on a number of occasions, and the department is now called Business, Innovation and Skills. However, despite these changes there has been an inevitable tendency for policy initiatives to fall outside strict departmental boundaries, leading to overlap of functions and endemic interdepartmental rivalries. Consider the demarcation of responsibility for environmental issues, which led to ongoing rivalry between

25 G Freeguard, 'Counting Down: The Latest Civil Service Staff Numbers, *Institute for Government*, 11 June 2014.
26 Office for National Statistics: Statistical Bulletin, Civil Service Statistics 2014.

the Ministry of Transport and the Department of the Environment (these were amalgamated in 1997 to form the Department of the Environment, Transport and the Regions). In May 2002, following a cabinet reshuffle, the department was abolished, with Transport once more becoming a government department in its own right, while responsibility for local government and the regions was moved to the office of the Deputy Prime Minister. Another change was the renaming of the Department of National Heritage, which became the Department for Culture, Media and Sport. The Department of Constitutional Affairs was restyled as the Ministry of Justice (2007) when it took over responsibility for the Prison Service which previously lay with the Home Office. The Department of Education and Skills was divided between a department of Children, Schools and Families and a separate Department of Innovation, Universities and Skills (2007). Responsibility for universities and further education has since moved to the Department of Business, Innovation and Skills, while education until the age of 19 falls under the Department of Education.

In view of the fact that it is usual for government legislation to be initiated by departments, it is not surprising that policy considerations at the drafting stage will very often determine the nature and scope of the powers conferred and the degree of discretion available to ministers and civil servants. Furthermore, it is worthwhile mentioning that it is not uncommon for statutes to combine law-making and adjudicatory functions as part of the same Act. For example, the Town and Country Planning Act 1990 enables local authorities and the Secretary of State for the Environment to oversee most uses of land, but the relationship between the two bodies is significant in this context. The relevant local authority is required to have a planning policy and outline structure plan for the area, which has to be submitted to the local planning authority for approval. Also, the Act requires anyone wishing to develop or change the use of land to apply to an authority for planning permission. If permission is refused there is a statutory right of appeal to the minister.

5.3.2 Next Steps agencies: formation and scope

At the beginning of this chapter (5.1.2) it was pointed out that initiatives in public service provision over the past two decades have been employed as a means of delivering public services more efficiently, competitively, and at a lower cost base to the taxpayer. In some cases the shift towards contracting and market principles has taken the form of outright privatisation or a transfer of functions to private sector organisations (see 5.9). Broadly speaking, the strategy has been to leave central policy-making powers in the hands of a small coterie of ministers and senior civil servants, while making the agency responsible for the detailed day-to-day implementation of policy. Next Steps agencies originated in the 1988 report, published by the PM's efficiency unit, entitled 'Improving Management in Government: The Next Steps'; and it will become clear that this initiative has proved particularly significant with regard to redefining the relationship between the government and public officials. Indeed they might be regarded as creating a new type of public service organisation. This has had a very significant impact on civil service organisation. By 1999 out of a total of 466,000 civil servants 362,000 were assigned to 138 Next Steps agencies. In the case of the Home Office the UK

Border Agency retains its original designation but many of the original Next Steps agencies across government have since been reconstituted with new titles or they have had responsibilities re-assigned.

Some important elements of the report were taken from the Swedish agency model. However, in contrast to the UK experience, Swedish executive agencies are independent of government. Not only do they report directly to Parliament and are made subject to external audits, but they have also been established in a country where freedom of information legislation applies to all public bodies.

Unlike the majority of quangos, which are set up by statute, Next Steps agencies have been formed by framework agreements and do not have full corporate identity. An agency is expected to undertake market testing to ascertain whether service delivery can be achieved more efficiently, involving specifying the service and then obtaining bids in the form of business plans. Such information is fed into the drafting of a framework document (FD) which is used to define 'the functions and goals of the agency'. The FD sets out status, aims, and objectives, the relationship between the department and the agency, and performance targets and accounts. It also provides for a regular review of the performance of the agency. Next Steps, then, has introduced corporate responsibility and corporate identity for the executive agencies, but without giving them corporate legal personality. It is worth mentioning that the Government Trading Act 1990 and the Civil Service (Management Functions) Act 1992 were passed to help facilitate these changes. The former deals with questions of funding; the latter with the management of employment within the agencies. In addition to the FD, the agency will enter into annual performance agreements. However, these are not the precise equivalent of private law contracts. Rather, the position is that the contract specifies in detail the service to be provided by 'defining goals, setting targets and monitoring performance'.

The essential features were that:

Each agency has defined responsibilities, and clear aims and objectives, set out in a Ministerially-approved Framework Document. It operates within, and gives effect to, policies laid down by Ministers. It is set annual performance targets approved by Ministers. The Chief Executive of the agency is personally responsible for the agency's performance in relation to these objectives and targets. The agency's performance is monitored by its department, and full details of the tasks the agency has been given, and its performance against them, are published in its annual report and accounts.[27]

It will be immediately apparent that this places great emphasis on financial efficiency as the main measure of accountability. In fact, one drawback of these modified arrangements is that agency staff spend a significant amount of time and resources in setting targets and devising new mechanisms of standardisation and control, an exercise that can be highly bureaucratic.

A further characteristic of Next Steps agencies has been exposure to revised approaches to staffing and management. Not only does the FD establish something akin to a contractual relationship between the minister and chief executive, but the doctrine of New Public Management (NPM) seeks to promote an ethos of a more professional management style in the public sector, with agency recruitment and industrial relations placed firmly in the hands of the chief executive. In

27 Next Steps Agencies in Government, Review 1993, Cm 2430.

general, staff have remained civil servants, but the changes within agencies may well affect the uniformity of the civil service in order 'to give Agencies the specific tools and facilities they need to carry out their own immensely varied tasks.'[28]

The conferment of agency status raised important questions of accountability in respect of decision-making. The classic position between ministers and civil servants is that, on the one hand, discretion under a statute must not be 'surrendered, abdicated or permitted to be the subject of dictation or fettering by over-rigid rules which pre-empt its meaningful exercise'.[29] On the other hand, the *'Carltona* principle' qualifies the rule against delegation and allows 'powers or discretions to be exercised in accordance with the dictates of good administrative practice'.[30] This principle extends to officials working in all executive agencies. At the same time, the Civil Service Management Functions Act 1992 allows management functions to be delegated from central government departments to executive agencies, so that Next Steps agencies frequently exercised a primary decision-making function and the cloak of civil service anonymity was removed from the chief executive.

5.3.2.1 Next Steps: wider implications

A number of problems arose with the new agencies and these can be illustrated by briefly considering the relationship between the Prison Service as an executive 'Next Steps' agency and the Home Office (responsibility for the Prison Service has since shifted to the Ministry of Justice, created in 2007). It became ever more apparent as time passed that the 'Next Steps' initiative introduced some questions regarding the impartiality and general accountability of public service employees. In part this is because, as we have just noted, the established line of command between ministers and civil servants is called into question. The Prison Service is a critical area which helps to illustrate the difficulties in trying to clarify the relative duties and responsibilities of civil servants and ministers following the changeover to agency status.

Following the breakouts at Parkhurst and Whitemoor Prisons, the Learmont Report,[31] commissioned by the Home Secretary, made wide-ranging criticisms of the Prison Service. It is true that resignations by Home Secretaries have not been the norm, even after the most spectacular escapes from prison; however, the minister in this instance not only refused to take ultimate responsibility for the many failures identified by Learmont, but also took the unprecedented step of dismissing the Director-General of the Prison Service. No disciplinary reasons were given and this action was in clear breach of the Civil Service Management Code. An action for wrongful dismissal was settled out of court, with the Home Office paying in full the compensation that had been claimed. (It was somewhat ironic that the incumbent was an outsider to the civil service introduced from the business sector by a previous Home Secretary to run the service on a more businesslike footing.)

How far was this ministerial action defensible? If all the failures identified by Learmont had in fact been at an operational level the dismissal could conceivably

28 P Kemp, House of Commons, Treasury and Civil Service, *Progress in the Next Steps Initiative*, 8th Report, HC 481 (1989–90).

29 M Freedland, 'The Rule Against Delegation and the Carltona Doctrine in Agency Context [1996] *Public Law* 19, 22–3.

30 See *Carltona v Commissioner of Works* [1943] 2 All ER 560.

31 1995, London, HMSO, Cm 3020.

have been justified because of the revised status of the Director-General of the service. As chief executive he was employed on a fixed-term contract which included incentives such as performance-related pay, the objective being to introduce equivalent competitive pressures to those experienced in the private sector for tight and efficient financial and general management of an organisation. It would seem reasonable that any chief executive who manifestly failed to reach targets and/or discharge his or her responsibilities could expect at least reductions in remuneration, or at worst outright dismissal. However, subsequently, in contesting his dismissal, the former Director-General pointed to evidence that the Home Secretary regularly interfered with matters that fell into the category of the day-to-day running of the service.[32] Such a dispute was significant, for it highlighted the problem of the blurring of boundaries in the allocation of functions. In fact, commentators had already anticipated the danger that 'The lack of a clear dividing line between policy and operational matters can result in "policy" being incrementally defined to suit ministers, department headquarters and, to a lesser extent, agencies . . . Flexibility can therefore only progress if the watch-dogs are called off or marginalised'.[33]

The prison escapes mentioned above led to a debate over where responsibility lies, but it is a matter of central importance that accountability is clearly established so that the public at large can have confidence in the running of the Prison Service. This is not only because imprisonment deprives individuals of their liberty and subjects them to rules and procedures that may have profound effects on their lives, but also because breaches in security will have an impact on local communities. Further, if things do go seriously wrong—as they did with the riots at Strangeways and other prisons in 1990 and with the escapes from Whitemoor Prison in 1994 and Parkhurst Prison in 1995—this will adversely affect the government and the career prospects of the minister in charge. Bearing this in mind, it is hardly credible that an astute politician would desist from interfering with day-to-day issues when these are likely to have such profound implications. The evidence that emerged during the Whitemoor affair indicated that criticisms could not all be placed at the door of the chief executive; and in the light of such evidence of ministerial interference the summary dismissal of Derek Lewis set a dubious precedent, one that suggested that ministers might all too easily sacrifice a chief executive or other officials rather than personally shoulder the blame for their own failings. Indeed, despite the fact that the Labour Opposition demanded the Home Secretary's immediate resignation, he was shielded from further criticism by maintaining the support of his party and the PM.

In essence, it appeared that Next Steps was undermining ministerial responsibility. This change suggested that matters of day-to-day supervision now fell under the chief executive while the Secretary of State and parent department were left with responsibility for general policy and budgeting.[34] Any gains in efficiency were being obtained at a price in the form of a loss of democratic control over the

---

32 'Minutes of Evidence Taken Before the Public Services Committee', 22 May 1996, HC 313.

33 P Greer, 'The Next Steps Initiative: An Examination of the Agency Framework Documents' in D Galligan (ed), *A Reader in Administrative Law* (Oxford: Oxford University Press, 1996), 127.

34 C Harlow and R Rawlings, *Law and Administration*, 3rd edn (Cambridge: Cambridge University Press, 2009), 65.

exercise of power at the heart of government. Although the situation was partially rectified under the Labour Government in 1997 with a re-assertion of ministerial responsibility in regard to Next Steps there remains a plethora of arm's length public bodies and the accountability for these bodies is confused, overlapping, and neglected, with blurred boundaries and responsibilities. Adopting a clearer taxonomy for such bodies might simplify and rationalise the structure of the state while at the same time improving channels of accountability.[35]

5.3.3 Privatisation of central government services

Government departments have been free to privatise the performance of many of their functions without statutory authority, largely because of the open-ended nature of their residual power to enter into private contracts. A further issue that has arisen in regard to the awarding of private contracts is that this has led to circumstances in which information (including relevant financial details of contracts) has been suppressed on grounds of commercial confidentiality necessary for the contract. The official position under the Thatcher/Major governments was that the established line of accountability through ministerial responsibility to Parliament remained intact and that the mechanisms did appear to work: more information is available for public scrutiny in regard to agencies, with the publication of framework documents; chief executives of agencies appear regularly before select committees; and agencies are subject to investigations by the Public Accounts Committee and the Parliamentary Ombudsman. The question, then, is how well the general public interest has been served by these developments, given that the initiative leaves unresolved critical issues concerning the determination of broader questions of public policy and the introduction of democratic mechanisms of accountability. Indeed, it has been argued in the light of the developments in new public management highlighted above that working out a proper working relationship between Parliament and the various extra-parliamentary means of control, including the role of the Ombudsman, National Audit Office, and judicial review, is a central constitutional issue that needs to be fully addressed.[36]

5.3.4 Value for money and standards in public life

In both central and local government a concern to obtain value for money, coupled with a desire to improve the competitiveness of suppliers, has greatly influenced the manner in which departmental operations have been conducted in recent years. When it comes to the matter of tendering, the private sector has to be kept at arm's length, since there is obvious potential for abuse if particular companies manage to gain a privileged status. But in certain areas, for example, defence, where there is only a handful of domestic manufacturers and suppliers, a close, almost symbiotic, relationship can develop as large-scale, highly classified projects are worked on over long periods. Several critical reports in the 1960s by the Public

---

35 'Who's Accountable? Relationships between Government and Arm's Length Bodies' *Public Administration Select Committee*, First Report of Session 2014–15, HC 110, 10.

36 See, e.g., P Barberis, 'The New Public Management and A New Accountability' (1998) 76 *Public Administration*, 451–70, 462ff.

Accounts Committee exposed excessive profits by certain companies at the public's expense. Parliament first responded by establishing an advisory committee in 1969 between the Treasury and the Confederation of British Industry (CBI) to investigate excessive profits in the public sector. But reports by the Public Accounts Committee have continued to identify contract overspends of this nature. One such example was the Nimrod project to develop early warning radar for the RAF.[37] More recently, the Public Accounts Committee has been critical of the value for money of PFI projects. The report recommends more transparent comparison with alternative forms of funding, with a recommendation that the Treasury should issue new guidance on more rigorous methods of assessing the value for money of such projects.[38] Generally, the process of government contracting is overseen by the Public Accounts Committee in close partnership with the Comptroller and Auditor General and the Audit Commission.

A tendency for senior politicians to be elevated directly to the boards of major companies on their retirement from office has attracted criticism.[39] For example, Lord Tebbit, largely responsible for the privatisation of British Telecom, retired from being Secretary of State for Trade and Industry and received a non-executive directorship of the newly privatised British Telecom. Lord Lawson, following his resignation as Chancellor of the Exchequer in 1989, was appointed in February 1990 as a non-executive director of Barclays Bank. Lord Walker, who held many cabinet positions, including Secretary of State for Trade and Industry, became a non-executive director of British Gas, another newly privatised utility, in 1991. Senior civil servants have been equally ready to exchange their jobs in the public sector for prestigious appointments in large companies. For example, following retirement as head of the Diplomatic Service in 1991, Lord Wright of Richmond accepted appointment to the boards of British Petroleum, Barclays Bank, and the British Airports Authority. This issue has caused some raised eyebrows in recent years since such individuals might continue to have influential contacts with ex-colleagues and with their former departments. A possible duality of interests could arise if their company tendered for contracts with central government, or if their company proposed a takeover that might be referred to the Competition Commission. Equally, the revelation of donations to the Labour Party from Bernie Ecclestone after the 1997 election and subsequently the Hinduja brothers and Lakshmi Mittal led to serious concern over possible links between substantial sums of financial support and the modification of government policy decisions. Senior civil servants should take responsibility for identifying potential conflicts of interest.[40]

5.3.4.1 European Union law and competitive tendering

European Union law has had an important impact in this area, largely because provisions to create a single market after 1986 have implications for contracting in the public sector. For example, government procurement contracts for public supply

---

37 PAC 16th Report, 'MoD Major Projects Statement 1983–84', HC 273, 1984/85; NAO Production Costs of Defence Equipment in Non-competitive Contracts, HC 505 1984/85.

38 44th report—Lessons from PFI and other projects, HC 1201, 19 August 2011.

39 The Committee on Standards in Public Life (the 'Nolan Report') Cm 2859.

40 See Cabinet Office Guidance of Civil Servants: Contact with Lobbyists, May 2010.

and works that are set above a stipulated level of expenditure (generally €200,000) must conform to certain procedures. This is in order to ensure equal opportunities for nationals anywhere in the Community to bid to provide contracts and services. But the main thrust of the EU directives is to insist upon common advertising and common award criteria to allow for genuine competitive tendering to take place. Contracts should be awarded either to the lowest tender or to 'the most economically advantageous tender'. Further, the authority is required to provide reasons for its decisions. To this end EU directives on public procurement are incorporated as part of domestic delegated legislation (see chapter 19).[41]

The European Commission is responsible for enforcement of these directives by bringing an action in the European Court under Article 258 of the Treaty on the Functioning of the European Union (TFEU) against a Member State (but see also the state liability doctrine discussed in chapter 3: this also allows individuals to sue governments for failure to give full effect to a directive). One example is that cases have arisen in respect of tendering for contracts involving discrimination by Member States against citizens from other Member States. In *Commission v Ireland*,[42] it was found that a water company was in breach of the Treaty when it set out an Irish standard for pipes which could be met by only a single Irish firm.[43] Opening up competition in services that are contracted out becomes, then, a general legal requirement, and these measures apply to ministers of the Crown, to government departments, to local authorities, and to fire and police authorities.[44]

5.4 The National Health Service

The NHS was established by the Health Service Act of 1946, which imposes a duty on the minister to provide a comprehensive health service, including hospital accommodation and nursing services. The service consumes a significant proportion of government expenditure, which makes the question of accountability an important one. Health authorities are Crown bodies and hospitals are Crown property. In light of the increasing sums spent on health there have been a number of government initiatives to contain the spiralling costs of healthcare.

Since 2000 the service has run on three main tiers. The Secretary of State is at the apex and may direct the next tier, that being the Strategic Health Authorities (SHAs) which have been responsible for overseeing all NHS operations. NHS Primary Care Trusts were the main fundholders and they commissioned healthcare from hospitals and GPs. Funding has been granted to them according to guidelines set out by the Department of Health. Although the NHS is a publicly funded body, since the 1980s 'pseudo-contracts' have been employed internally between purchaser and

---

41 See, e.g., Public Contracts Regulations 2006 (SI 2006/5) and Utilities Contracts Regulations 2006 (SI 2006/6); Directive 2014/24/EU of the European Parliament and of the Council of 26 February 2014 on public procurement and repealing Directive 2004/18/EC; Directive 2014/25/EU of the European Parliament and the Council of 26 February 2014 on procurement by entities operating in the water, energy, transport and postal services sectors repealing Directive 2004/17/EC; Directive 2014/23/EU of the European Parliament and of the Council of 26 February 2014 on the award of concession contracts.

42 Case 45/87, [1988] ECR 4929.

43 P Craig, *Administrative Law*, 7th edn (London: Sweet and Maxwell, 2012), 128.

44 I Harden, *The Contracting State* (Buckingham: Open University Press, 1992), 55ff.

provider to create an internal market. The system was strongly criticised and the basic structure was subsequently modified.[45] The previous approach to reducing costs by promoting competition between health providers was replaced by encouraging partnership. The revised system provided for payments relating to past performance and sought to reward efficient health authorities and primary care trusts that demonstrated progress in meeting plans for improving healthcare by achieving their targets. This approach retained the new public management (NPM) methodology which encouraged efficiency while seeking to eliminate waste, but a new duty of quality, which was measured in terms of the overall standards of clinical care required throughout the service, and a Commission for Health Improvement accountable to Parliament monitor performance (Health Act 1999, section 17). The number of NHS Primary Care Trusts was reduced from 303 to 152 as from 1 October 2006.

As part of the most recent NHS reorganisation the Health and Social Care Act 2012 abolished Strategic Health Authorities and Primary Care Trusts. National and regional specialist services are now commissioned by a new NHS commissioning body taking over many of the functions of the Strategic Health Authorities. The bottom-up emphasis of the new legislation means that consortia of General Practitioners (GPs) bid for the major part of the NHS budget which is used to fund hospital services. Consortia of GPs assume control of 80 per cent of the NHS budget, buying services from providers in the public, private, and charity sectors. Private healthcare providers and family doctors compete for patients who are able to choose the treatment and care. At the same time NHS hospitals offer treatment to private patients. From 2013 GPs have been responsible for buying in patient care with a new NHS commissioning board overseeing the process.[46]

The central questions for a publicly funded service remain. How can efficiency be gauged in the provision of services which are based upon care? Are private sector management strategies appropriate for public sector organisations? The changes introduced by government in recent years have sought to restructure the bureaucratic framework to achieve better value and now better quality of clinical service. However, headline figures publicising the length of NHS waiting lists tend to obscure genuine underlying problems of resource allocation and service rationing. It should be remembered that health treatment is expensive, resources are limited by the funding parameters set by central government, and these are subject to political influence.

5.4.1 The PFI and the NHS

The Private Finance Initiative (PFI) is a form of public–private partnership, which has been regarded by successive governments as an important method for improving the quality and cost-effectiveness of public services. It enlists the skills and expertise of the private sector in providing public services and facilities. In regard to the NHS these PFI schemes seek to create mutually beneficial partnerships in situations where capital investment is required, typically to build new large hospitals. The facilities are designed based on the requirements specified by the NHS.

---

45 See White Paper in 1997, *The New NHS*, Cm 3807 and Health Act 1999.

46 A Davies, 'Beyond New Public Management: Problems of Accountability in the Modern Administrative State' in N Bamforth and P Leyland (eds), *Accountability in the Contemporary Constitution* (Oxford: Oxford University Press, 2013), 341ff.

The private sector builds the hospital to time and at fixed cost, and then manages the facilities and support services. The private sector finances the capital cost but recovers this expenditure over a period of years through continuing to make the facilities available to meet NHS's requirements. According to figures from the Department of Health, partnerships totalling over £2 billion had been negotiated by the end of 2001. Such schemes must demonstrate value for money (VFM) and have the obvious advantage of saving the government from finding large capital sums, but there has been some criticism of these arrangements, particularly concerning the overall financial burden for the Treasury and thus whether they serve the longer term interests of taxpayers.[47]

5.5 Non-departmental public bodies

5.5.1 Public corporations and nationalised industries

Public corporations are non-departmental public bodies that have been set up by statute to run industries or services. They are a form of hybrid institution with a semi-autonomous status, but they are not part of the Crown with attendant Crown immunities or privileges, nor are their employees Crown servants. In many cases the government retains powers of regulation and funding but a board is charged with, and responsible for, the routine day-to-day management and operation of the body.

The ITC (Independent Television Commission), before it was replaced by the Office of Communications (Ofcom) in 2003, was a good example of a public corporation. It was set up to regulate television within the private sector, replacing the Independent Broadcasting Authority in performing this role. The ITC was responsible for ensuring that the independent television companies worked within the provisions of the Broadcasting Acts 1990 and 1996. The board of the ITC was appointed by the government. Under this legislation, which deregulated and relaxed controls on broadcasting, there were financial penalties that could be imposed by the ITC on companies that failed to meet the standards and quotas for programmes across the country. In contrast, it is worth noting that the arrangements for the BBC are different. It was formed by Royal Charter under the prerogative, the current Charter dating from 2006. The BBC is mainly funded by a licence fee set by a licence agreement with the Home Secretary, who is also responsible for appointing members of the BBC's board of governors. Once in place, the board decides the long-term strategic as well as the day-to-day policy of the organisation. Editorial control in broadcasting has been a controversial issue and the political nature of some appointments (as well as the overall direction of the medium) has sometimes raised questions about the independence and status of the main broadcasting organisations. See, now, the Communications Act 2003 for the government's policy towards the communications industry.

Nationalised industries (very few now remain) are a form of public corporation; but this category refers more specifically to a number of bodies and enterprises that

---

47 See Harlow and Rawlings, n 34, 422.

for political and/or economic reasons were taken into public ownership, mainly after 1945, for example, coal, gas, electricity supply, and the railways. They share the same semi-autonomous status as public corporations, and in each case they have been formed by statutory enactment. Therefore, in order to determine the nature of these industries, it is necessary to turn to the legislation which gave them their individual status, and which sets out the functions, duties, and powers of the body. In every example, the day-to-day running will be undertaken by a board that has a similar role to the board of directors of a private sector company, but appointments to the board are within the gift of the minister. The separation of functions between the minister and the board means that the minister is not considered to be responsible to Parliament for the routine day-to-day operation of the industry. Nevertheless, ministers often have power under the enabling legislation to issue directives setting out long-term strategy and they can greatly influence the commercial viability of these industries by the allocation of subsidies, the imposition of price and wage controls, by the setting of financial targets, and by placing a bar on commercial expansion. The debates about the future of the coal industry following the publication of British Coal's pit closure proposals in 1992 and subsequent events following the privatisation of the industry under the Coal Industry Act 1994 illustrate this clearly. Arguments in 1994 and subsequently regarding the wish of the Post Office to compete in the private commercial sector provide another such example. The government decided in 1998 that the Post Office will remain in the public sector, but with much more commercial freedom as an independent plc within the framework of state ownership. Also, the Transport Act 2000 has led to the partial privatisation of air traffic control services, despite concerns over the implications for safety of such a change. The financial crash in 2007 exposed the vulnerability of UK banks and resulted in the passage of the Banking (Special Provisions) Act 2008 which provided for Northern Rock to be nationalised.

Virtually the only nationalised industries and services of any size in 2008 are the remaining public sector energy suppliers (the nuclear industry), the Post Office, and London Passenger Transport (now part privatised). This is because the number of nationalised industries was drastically reduced during the 1980s as a result of privatisation, that is, shares in these enterprises were offered for sale to commercial and individual private investors. However, in the case of many of the newly privatised industries, there was an attempt to retain residual powers of regulation over aspects of the business and at the same time protect the interests of the consumer by means of statutory regulation (see further 5.8).

5.5.2 Quangos and the 'bonfire of the quangos'

There are numerous organisations set up by statute which are not part of any government department, but which perform important executive, regulatory, or advisory functions. Such organisations are often referred to as 'quangos' or as 'non-departmental public bodies'. Common characteristics of these bodies are that they are formed by statute and are at least partly funded by the government. The government often retains powers to make appointments to the boards of management, but at the same time the activities of these semi-official bodies (in theory, at least) are placed outside the mainstream of political controversy. The employees of these organisations are not civil servants and they are generally not protected by Crown immunity.

A list of important quangos might include:

- Arts Council England
- Atomic Energy Authority
- British Library
- Civil Aviation Authority
- Competition Commission
- English Tourist Board
- Equality and Human Rights Commission
- Food Standards Agency
- Health and Safety Executive
- Homes and Communities Agency
- Natural England
- Parole Board
- Research Councils UK.

The Public Bodies Act 2011 was intended to substantially reduce the number of quangos by allowing ministers, by order, to abolish, merge, or transfer the functions of listed public bodies. This initiative was presented by the Coalition Government as not just a cost-cutting exercise but an attempt to improve public sector efficiency while maintaining the level of service to the citizen. Headline figures in October 2010 suggested that 192 out of 901 would be scrapped, but closer examination suggests that in many cases the functions have been transferred to other quangos or to central government departments.[48] As will be apparent in chapter 7, the Administrative Justice and Tribunals Council which performed a useful role in improving the standard of grievance resolution was among the bodies axed as part of this reorganisation.

5.6 Devolution and local government

The devolution arrangements which came into effect in 1999 following elections in Scotland, Wales, and Northern Ireland have resulted in a significant redistribution of power under the provisions contained in the Scotland Act 1998, the Government of Wales Act 1998, and the Northern Ireland Act 1998. In addition, a new layer of local government for London has been introduced with an elected Mayor and Assembly.

However, throughout the United Kingdom local authorities operate beneath central government within a framework laid down by statute and these bodies have a wide range of statutory duties which they are required to fulfil. They also possess an even wider range of discretionary powers enabling them to undertake defined activities if they wish to do so.

---

48 R Rawlings, 'A Coalition Government in Westminster' in J Jowell, D Oliver, and C O'Cinneide (eds), *The Changing Constitution*, 8th edn (Oxford: Oxford University Press, 2015), 208ff.

5.6.1 Devolution: Scotland, Wales, and Northern Ireland

The United Kingdom now has an asymmetrical system of devolved government that has been tailored to suit the individual needs of Scotland, Wales, and Northern Ireland. Scotland has a Parliament of 129 members elected by an additional member system every four years. Each elector has two votes, one for a constituency member and one for the party of his or her choice. 'Additional Members' are elected from party lists drawn up for each of the current European Parliament constituencies. Apart from having the power to pass primary legislation, the Parliament has a system of subject committees that combine the functions of the Westminster standing committees which scrutinise legislation and select committees which oversee the work of the executive. Part II of the Act provides for a Scottish Executive and administration, including a First Minister, and other ministers, which have taken over responsibility for many of the competences which were formerly the responsibility of the Secretary of State for Scotland and the Scottish Office.[49] The major areas of policy over which the Scottish Parliament has legislative powers are: education, law, courts, prisons, judicial appointments, economic development, agriculture, fisheries, local government, the environment, housing, passenger and road transport, forestry, and the arts. Although devolution is mainly funded by way of a block grant from Westminster calculated according to spending levels for equivalent policy areas in England referred to as the Barnett Formula, the Scotland Act 1998 granted the Scottish Parliament powers to raise income tax by up to three pence in the pound. However, these arrangements are set to change. Following the 2014 independence referendum in Scotland, the recommendations of the Smith Commission for the introduction of a locally raised Scottish income tax and for the Scottish Executive to retain a proportion of local VAT receipts have been included in the Scotland Act 2016.[50] The allocation to Scotland under the Barnett Formula is adjusted to allow for the revenues raised in Scotland. In addition, a number of other important functions are placed in the hands of the Scottish Government, including welfare benefits, employment support, and broadcasting regulation.[51]

The Government of Wales Act 1998, as now largely replaced by the Government of Wales Act 2006, set up a National Assembly of 60 members for Wales, which first met in 1999. Originally, the Welsh Assembly had very limited making powers, but the Secretary of State for Wales was under a duty to consult with the Assembly about the Westminster Parliament's legislative programme to allow necessary legislative measures to be introduced at Westminster. However, the Welsh Assembly now has its own law-making capacity within its areas of competence.[52] The Government of Wales Act 2006 provided for a referendum to be held in Wales on the grant of legislative powers which would be triggered by a vote in favour by two-thirds or more of Assembly members. Following approval at such a referendum held in March 2011, the Assembly elected in May 2011 was the first to have its own legislative programme. In light of the recommendations by the Silk Commission further

---

49 Scotland Act 1998, ss 44–63.

50 The Calman Commission Report (Serving Scotland Better: Scotland and the United Kingdom in the 21st century: Final Report, 2009) previously recommended more modest proposals for financial reform, including locally raised income tax included in the Scotland Act 2012.

51 See the Scotland Act 2016, Parts II and III.

52 See further 2.2.

reform for Wales is on the horizon. This is likely to be based on changing to a reserved, as opposed to the current conferred, powers model of devolution and the introduction in Wales of local tax raising powers comparable to those adopted in Scotland.[53]

The Northern Ireland Act 1998 provides for a directly elected Northern Ireland Assembly, with law-making powers, consisting of 108 members, elected every four years. They are elected by single transferable vote (STV) from 18 six-member constituencies. The Assembly is given competence to exercise legislative authority in respect of those matters that have been 'transferred' to it, and the corresponding policy areas include: agriculture; culture and arts; economic development; education; environment; finance; health and social services; and justice. Executive authority is placed in the hands of an executive committee, which is headed by the joint office of the First and Deputy First Minister. Although this 'cabinet style' arrangement is somewhat similar to the one adopted in Scotland and Wales, certain safeguards are built into its method of formation to guarantee power sharing between Unionists and Nationalists. Other features have been introduced to accommodate Nationalist aspirations for a united Ireland (the system of government is linked to that of the Republic of Ireland through the North–South Ministerial Council) and to allay Unionist fears that the union could be severed without consent (the Act also confirms links with the United Kingdom through the British–Irish Council). While devolution in Northern Ireland has been problematic, with the operation of the Assembly and the Executive having been suspended on a number of occasions, there are now clear signs that the institutions have bedded-down and that there is a stable system of government. This is largely as a result of the St Andrews Agreement 2006, the Hillsborough Agreement of 2010, and the Stormont House Agreement of 2014.

Finally, it should be noted that devolution remains primarily associated with Scotland, Northern Ireland, and Wales. However, at the same time there have been discussions about the need for devolution in England by introducing new forms of enhanced local government and more locally devolved powers.

5.6.2 Local government

It is important to emphasise the position of local government as local authorities are the elected bodies which perform the majority of essential everyday governmental functions. For example, education provision is for the most part in the hands of local government, as is refuse collection and the provision and upkeep of social housing. It will already be apparent that Parliament, subject to certain exceptions where European law is concerned, is considered to enjoy absolute law-making powers. Local authorities share with Parliament the characteristic of being elected, and in this sense they are representative bodies of the communities for which they administer services. By contrast, however, the powers of local government are defined by statute (primary legislation) that emanates from Parliament. The nature of the institutions of local government can be radically transformed by statute, see e.g., the Local Government Act 2000 (discussed at 5.6.2.3). For

---

53 See 'Powers for a Purpose: Towards a Lasting Devolution Settlement for Wales', Cm 9020, February 2015; and the Wales Act 2014.

example, a layer of local government, including the Greater London Council and the Metropolitan Authorities, was dissolved by the Local Government Act 1985. Local authorities consist of a council of elected members. The composition of the authority changes with elections, but the Local Government Act 1972 lays down that each authority is a body corporate that exists in perpetuity. This means that authorities are distinct legal entities able to acquire property, enter contracts, and be party to private legal proceedings.

5.6.2.1 The framework of local government

The framework of local government was established in outline by the Local Government Act 1972, which came into force in April 1974, aspects of which have been revised by the Localism Act 2011 discussed at 5.6.2.4. This framework has been subject to ongoing review since 1997, for example, regarding the introduction of an elected mayor and assembly for London.

(1) In rural areas the 1972 Act provides a two-tier division of the main powers between county councils and district councils. Parish councils have responsibility for minor matters.

(2) The Act originally created 39 county councils, responsible for education, strategic planning, personal social services, major highways, public transport, consumer protection, fire, and police services (fire and police services may spread over more than one authority). The county areas were subdivided into 296 non-metropolitan district councils, with responsibility for housing, environmental health, public health and sanitation, and refuse collection. Responsibility for town and country planning is shared with district councils.

(3) The situation for London and the main cities was somewhat different, and the position was modified significantly by the Local Government Act 1985 which abolished the Greater London Council and the six Metropolitan Area Councils. This left the 32 London boroughs and 36 metropolitan district councils as a single tier of local government in urban areas. These councils are now typically responsible for providing education (with the exception of those schools opting out), personal social services, highways and transportation, refuse disposal, town and country planning, consumer protection, parks and recreation, and libraries.

5.6.2.2 Mayor and Assembly for London

Following the disappearance of the Greater London Council, London lacked a layer of government which many commentators considered necessary to provide democratic accountability and to coordinate strategic aspects of administration that cut across the role of the inner and outer London boroughs. The Greater London Authority Act 1999 introduced a Mayor and Assembly for London. This was after a referendum approving the principle was held and then elections by an additional member system of PR. The Mayor and Assembly are responsible for spending approximately £13 billion each year. The main areas of competence include: transport (an integrated strategy for London and traffic management and regulation); economic development (responsibility for London Development Agency); police, fire, and emergency services (the Act creates a new Metropolitan Police Authority);

planning (requirement to develop a land use strategy for London); environment (air quality and waste management); and culture (museums, library services, and the arts). The Mayor is placed at the head of the executive and is directly responsible for the strategies the Greater London Assembly adopts to achieve its objectives and for the quality and effectiveness of the services which it delivers. On the other hand, to ensure a separation of powers, the Assembly is responsible for holding the Mayor to account by being able to question the Mayor and the Mayor's staff and by holding public hearings on issues of importance.

5.6.2.3 City regions and Mayors

An attempt to revitalise English regions is one response by government to the constitutional asymmetry caused by the consolidation of devolution in Scotland, Northern Ireland, and Wales discussed above. The previous Coalition Government initiated this process by launching a directly elected Mayor of Greater Manchester.[54] The office holder will have a strategic role in some respects comparable to that of the London Mayor, mainly with responsibility for a devolved consolidated transport budget. Additional powers will include responsibility for devolved support budgets and control of apprenticeship grants. Once elected, political oversight will be provided by a scrutiny committee of a combined authority which will be empowered to reject spending plans by a two-thirds majority. The Manchester city region mayoral election will take place in early 2017.[55] The enabling legislation will allow the Secretary of State to approve directly elected metropolitan mayors for other city regions in England.[56]

5.6.2.4 A revised role for local government?

The Localism Act 2011 is designed as part of the 'Big Society' idea to devolve more powers to local authorities, communities, and third-sector organisations. One commentator has observed that 'The Big Society idea speaks to a Tory tradition of public duty and the social responsibility of the well off to the disadvantaged. It sits within the idea of welfare being provided by an organic civil society rather than the state . . . '[57] According to the government this is to be achieved by creating more opportunities for citizen involvement and by diversifying the supply of public services. While it may be desirable for decisions to be taken closer to the community during the passage of the legislation through Parliament, there is still a lack of clarity over what this enhanced community involvement will mean in practice.[58]

Against a background of voter apathy with turnouts in many parts of the country falling well below 30 per cent in the last 20 years or so, central government has been keen to overhaul local government.[59] The Localism Act 2011 serves as a good example. The stated objective is to lighten the burden of bureaucracy by

---

[54] Consisting of: Bolton, Bury, Manchester, Oldham, Rochdale, Salford, Tameside, Trafford, and Wigan.

[55] 'Devo Manc: What Powers Will the New Greater Manchester Mayor Have?' *The Guardian*, 3 November 2014.

[56] See the Cities and Local Government Devolution Act 2015.

[57] M Smith, 'From Big Government to Big Society: Changing the State–Society Balance' (2010) 63 (4) *Parliamentary Affairs*, 818, 830.

[58] Communities and Local Government Committee, *Localism*, Third Report 2010–12, HC 547, at paras 22, 23.

[59] See, e.g., White Paper, *Modern Local Government: In Touch with the People* 1998 (Cm 4014).

removing the cost and control of unnecessary red tape and regulation which is regarded by the Coalition Government as an impediment to local action, while, at the same time, empowering citizens by encouraging their greater involvement in local affairs.

In terms of the type of elected local authority the Localism Act follows on from the Local Government Act 2000 which provided three choices.[60] Councils could be based upon: a directly elected mayor and cabinet; a directly elected executive; and an indirectly elected leader and cabinet. The executive arrangements under the 2011 Act must consist of either a directly elected mayor and two or more councillors appointed to the executive by the mayor, or a councillor elected as leader of the executive by the authority and two or more councillors of the authority appointed to the executive by the council leader.[61] The intention has been to create a new decision-making framework in which there is a separation of decision-making, concentrated in one of the above forms of executive. Decisions of the executive must be referred to an overview and scrutiny committee which has the power to review decisions and make reports and recommendations.[62] The executive is placed under a statutory duty to respond to the committee.

Notwithstanding the stated intention to devolve powers to communities, the Localism Act 2011 is a centralising measure in the way it grants formidable new powers to the Westminster government.[63] In the first place the Secretary of State is able to determine what functions should fall under the responsibility of the authority. Second, in a positive sense s/he has a wide discretion to override any statutory provision which prevents or restricts a local authority from exercising its power, but also in a negative sense the Secretary of State may make an order preventing a local authority from exercising a general power.[64] Third, s/he is able to direct a local authority to hold a referendum on changing its governance arrangements, for example, from council leader to directly elected mayor. This will permit the government to require the 12 largest cities to hold referenda on having elected mayors.[65] Fourth, after receiving a petition supported by 5 per cent of the local electorate, the Act grants the Secretary of State the power to direct a local authority to hold a referendum on whether spending that is considered excessive should be contained.[66]

5.6.2.5 Powers of local authorities

It has already been stated that the main powers of local authorities are defined by legislation, and section 101 of the Local Government Act 1972 provides that many decision-making powers can be delegated by an authority to council committees, subcommittees, or officers of the authority. However, delegation to individual council members, including committee chairpersons, is unlawful. The title of these committees will correspond to the nature of the functions for which each is responsible. These committees used to draw up and discuss the more detailed

---

60 Local Government Act 2000, s 21.
61 Localism Act 2011, Sch 2, 9C.
62 Localism Act 2011, Sch 2, 9F.
63 <http://blogs.lse.ac.uk/politicsandpolicy/2011/03/11/localism-bill-and-centralism/>.
64 Localism Act 2011, s 5 and Sch 2.
65 Localism Act 2011, Sch 2, 9ME.
66 Localism Act 2011, Sch 2, 9MC.

questions of policy formation and their recommendations were usually presented to the main body of the council for ratification, but now decision-making is in the hands of the leader/mayor and cabinet. Once policy is formed the power to implement it at a local level by officers of the council will then usually not be by direct means, but rather through other forms of statutory provision, including by-laws and compulsory purchase orders.

Certain statutes provide wide powers for local authorities to use contracts in furtherance of policy. For example, this applies in the area of planning under the Town and Country Planning Act 1971. Local authorities may reach agreements under their planning powers to restrict development. It is not uncommon for local authorities to attach conditions in regard to the development and use of land. These may be inserted as a *quid pro quo* for the grant of planning permission. Moreover, it should be stressed that if any local authority steps beyond the scope of these powers judicial review may be available as a method of control. An example is *Hazell v Hammersmith and Fulham London Borough Council*,[67] where a series of interest rate swapping transactions by local authorities were held to be unlawful.[68] The effects of such agreements have since been mitigated by the Local Government (Contracts) Act 1997.

5.6.2.6 Local government tendering: from CCT to best value

It has been observed that obtaining value for money has been a basic pre-occupation for central government at all levels of operation and we find that, originating in the 1980s, there was a parallel concern to attain greater efficiency in local government that also led to market-oriented policies. Under the local government legislation introduced by the Conservative Governments of 1979–97,[69] an authority was required to offer the contract either to the lowest tender or to the one that is the most economically advantageous. This meant that local authorities were heavily constrained in the way in which they were allowed to exercise their contracting powers. Further, they were not entitled to refuse to grant a contract because of any views they might have about the employment practices of a sub-contractor; this would include the fact that the contractor pays low wages or favours the employment of non-union labour. The 1988 Act offered a special remedy to contractors who consider that they have been treated unfairly by not having been awarded a contract if they have met the criteria specified by the authority.

The Labour Government also strongly supported market-driven policies in the public sector but it abolished compulsory competitive tendering (CCT) for local authorities in favour of a new system. The Local Government Act 1999 requires local authorities to make arrangements for 'best value' in the performance of their functions. This is defined in section 3 as 'securing continuous improvement in the exercise of all functions undertaken by the authority, whether statutory or not, having regard to a combination of economy, efficiency and effectiveness'. A number of performance indicators are to be applied and the relevant standards can be set by the Secretary of State having regard to any recommendations made to him by the Audit Commission. Local authorities are further required to provide 'best value' performance plans for each financial year under section 6. The new

---

67 [1992] 2 AC 1.

68 See also *Credit Suisse v Allerdale Borough Council* [1997] QB 306; Craig, n 43, 143ff.

69 See, e.g., Local Government Act 1988, s 2, which introduced compulsory competitive tendering (CCT).

legislation is intended to allow improved efficiency and effectiveness in the use of resources, but also to achieve significant improvements in service quality. This means that for contracted services a local authority is able to consider the appropriateness of contracting for that service and it also provides greater flexibility in the negotiation of different forms of contract and contractual relationship. At the same time the legislation proposes to increase local financial accountability by reference to new performance indicators and standards.

5.6.2.7 Relationship with central government

In constitutional theory Parliament, but in reality central government, has the power to completely abolish local government. This, of course, would be most unlikely to occur, but it has imposed important statutory duties and limitations on local authorities. For example, the Education Act 1944 requires the appropriate authority to ensure that there are sufficient schools in its locality; the Housing Act 1985 imposes a duty on local authorities to maintain council housing in their areas, while the Housing Act 1985, Part III imposes a duty to accommodate certain limited categories of homeless persons.

A significant area of involvement for central government has been in respect of the financing of local authorities. The community charge (or 'poll tax'), which was introduced by the Local Government Finance Act 1988, turned out to be an unpopular attempt to reform local government finance by imposing on all residents in a locality a flat rate tax, instead of a property-based tax, like the old rating system. (The council tax replaced the community charge under the provisions of the Local Government Finance Act 1992.) Similarly, there have been repeated efforts since the early 1980s to impose strict cash limits by 'capping' local government spending. The Treasury has always supplemented the budgets of councils by making up a fixed proportion of the requirements of the authority that were not met by taxation raised at a local level. This now represents the larger part of local authority revenue, to the extent that by 2002 the amount raised by local taxes (council tax) has fallen to 20 per cent of the total. The rest comes from central government, which obviously has considerable implications for councils' political and administrative independence. (This position should be compared with that existing in many European countries, e.g., Germany, where a much higher percentage of local revenue is raised locally.) Rate-capping measures, first introduced in the 1980s, were a new departure and meant that financial penalties were imposed on councils that failed to operate within the limits set by the government. The expenditure guidance for 1984–85 was challenged unsuccessfully on the ground that following it would be *ultra vires* in regard to the Local Government and Planning Act 1980, section 59, by interfering with the authority's capacity to comply with its statutory duties.[70] Subsequently, central government has attempted to exclude authorities from applying to the courts for judicial review in respect of such rate capping provisions (see the Local Government Finance Act 1987, section 4(1)). These measures were the product of bitter political controversy between central government and the local authorities (often in different political hands) during the 1980s. It has been widely recognised by commentators that the imposition of such rigid financial constraints has reduced direct accountability to the local electorate, since

---

70 See *R v Secretary of State for the Environment, ex p Hackney London Borough Council* [1984] 1 All ER 956.

many councils have found it necessary to cut their services to meet government financial targets without regard to electoral commitments to continue with them or expand them, for example, library services, social services, or sports facilities. Central government is currently able to regulate increases in council tax under Part II of the Local Government Act 1999. This repeals the previous 'rate-capping' measures which have been replaced by a somewhat more flexible system, but tight financial control is retained over expenditure and over the power to raise revenue.

5.6.2.8 **Accountability mechanisms**

In order to improve the public perception of local government and local councillors Part III of the Local Government Act 2000 establishes a new ethical framework which includes the introduction of statutory codes of conduct, with a requirement for every council to adopt a code covering the behaviour of elected members and of officers, and the creation of a standards committee for each authority. This approach has many characteristics in common with the Westminster regime for parliamentary standards. The improvement of ethical standards and greater transparency are also important themes of the Localism Act 2011. This includes a duty to promote high standards of conduct, clearer guidelines on the disclosure of personal interests by office holders, and provisions for the publication of the remuneration of chief officers and other staff employed by local authorities.[71] However, the external Standards Board with responsibility for maintaining standards of conduct is abolished by the Act.[72]

In addition, the Local Government Act 1972, section 151, provides that councils must ensure the proper administration of their financial affairs, and the Local Government Finance Act 1982 sets in place the mechanism for external audits by an Audit Commission for local authorities in England and Wales. This introduced commercial accounting methods to the local government sector. (For the auditors' current powers see the Audit Commission Act 1998.) The district auditor has the duty to see that public money is spent according to the law. If it is found that there has been unlawful expenditure by the authority in the discharge of its public duties, the auditor has the power to enforce financial penalties against named councillors or officials. The most notorious case in recent years concerned allegations made against Westminster London Borough Council that it ran a 'homes for votes' policy. The result was that the auditor imposed massive surcharges against a number of councillors, including the leader of the council. In *Porter v Magill*[73] the House of Lords overturned an earlier ruling by the Court of Appeal and upheld the original decision of the auditor and the Divisional Court which found that Lady Porter, David Weeks, and Westminster Council had disposed of land in the form of council properties in marginal wards during the mid-1980s. This was because the policy had been knowingly and corruptly pursued in the expectation that purchasers in marginal wards were likely to support the ruling Conservative party. A surcharge of £31 million was later re-imposed. Finally, the Local Government Act 1974, Part III, allows a local government ombudsman to investigate complaints concerning questions of local maladministration. These matters are referred directly or through a local councillor (see Ombudsman, chapter 6).

---

71 Localism Act, ss 27, 28, and 38.
72 Localism Act, Sch 4.
73 [2001] UKHL 67, [2002] 1 All ER 465.

5.6.2.9 *Ultra vires*, general competence, and judicial control

In general, judicial control is exercised under the *ultra vires* principle or that of abuse of power, that is, the local authority may be challenged if it appears to exceed the express or implied limits of its statutory authority, or it may be challenged for not properly exercising discretionary powers.[74] However, section 1 of the Localism Act 2011 has changed the nature of the legal basis for local authority decision-making by providing that: 'a local authority has power to do anything that individuals generally may do'. In principle, granting this enhanced competence extends the scope for decision-making by local authorities, subject only to certain exclusions in the Act, such as the power to raise taxes or provide services that local authorities are not obliged to provide, and other legislation such as the Human Rights Act 1998.[75] We return to the nature of this change in chapter 8 as it impacts on the *ultra vires* principle forming the basis of judicial review.[76]

Nevertheless, there had already been some judicial discussion of whether the rigid application of the *ultra vires* principle was suited to section 111 of the Local Government Act 1972. This section empowers authorities 'to do any thing (whether or not involving the expenditure, borrowing or lending of money or the acquisition or disposal of property or rights) which is calculated to facilitate, or is conducive or incidental to, the discharge of any of their functions'. For instance, in *McCarthy & Stone (Developments) Ltd v Richmond upon Thames London Borough Council*,[77] the House of Lords held that the section did not authorise, either expressly or by necessary implication, the imposition of a charge of £25 for dealing with speculative development proposals. It remains a basic rule that councils cannot make or be bound by a contract which is *ultra vires*. In a case with far wider political implications than *Richmond London Borough Council*, the House of Lords found in *Hazell v Hammersmith and Fulham London Borough Council*[78] that interest rate swap agreements were *ultra vires* the authority's powers and could not be validated by reference to section 111.

It is also worth noting that if there is a disputed question of law, a local authority may obtain a declaration from the High Court to establish the scope of its rights, duties, and powers. And specific statutory remedies and appeals may be available to persons aggrieved by a council's decision; for example, such a procedure is available against demolition orders.

5.7 **Police authorities**

There are now 43 police authorities that have the task of maintaining an 'adequate and efficient' police force. A new structure was formalised in the Police and Magistrates' Courts Act 1994 as part of the search by the government for more effective policing. This was consolidated in the Police Act 1996, which replaces the

---

74 See further 8.1.
75 P Craig, *Administrative Law*, 7th edn (London: Sweet and Maxwell, 2012), 154.
76 See further I Leigh, 'The Changing Nature of Local Government' in Jowell, Oliver, and O'Cinneide, n 48, 288ff.
77 [1991] 4 All ER 897.
78 [1992] 2 AC 1.

Police Act 1964. In addition to the Metropolitan Police and the City of London Police there are 41 police areas, with one police force for each area. The police authorities consist of 17 appointed members, comprising eight 'independents', at least one of whom must be a local magistrate, and nine members from local councils. The chair is appointed from among the members. The duty of the police authority is to achieve 'efficient and effective' policing of its area. There is also a role for the Home Secretary and Chief Constables, for example, the Home Secretary may be involved in the procedure for the selection of lay members, she has the power to set objectives for police authorities and to direct the authorities to meet performance targets which will fulfil these objectives. The London Metropolitan Police force was directly accountable to the Home Secretary who also appointed the Metropolitan Police Commissioner. The Commissioner was then responsible for the day-to-day running of the force. A pressing matter in recent years has been the question of police accountability, particularly in London. In response to this problem a Metropolitan Police Authority (MPA) was established in July 2000 to provide a much greater degree of democratic control over London's policing. This authority consists of 23 members, 12 drawn from the Greater London Assembly, four magistrates, and seven independent members. The Mayor of London has been made responsible for policing and crime reduction in London. Under the Police Reform and Social Responsibility Act 2011 s/he is responsible for setting the annual budget, establishing priorities, and the overall performance of the Metropolitan Police. It is important to note that operational matters remain under the control of the Metropolitan Police Commissioner. The Mayor is assisted by a new advisory body which will replace the MPA and s/he is responsible to the London Assembly through a committee called the Police and Crime Panel.

It should also be noted that, under the Police Reform Act of 2002, an Independent Police Complaints Commission (IPCC) was set up in 2004 to investigate serious allegations of misconduct against the police. In response to persistent dissatisfaction with the fact that the police were previously responsible for conducting investigations when complaints were made, the IPCC can now use its own investigators to conduct independent investigations. Also, where appropriate, investigations can be carried out by police professional standards departments under the direction and control of the IPCC.[79] The latest initiative designed to make the police more accountable has been the introduction of elected police and crime commissioners.[80] These new posts and bodies are meant to oversee the running of the police force and ensure that the police are answerable to the local community.[81]

The Race Relations (Amendment) Act 2000 was another significant reform which makes discrimination on racial grounds in any public authority functions, not previously covered by the Race Relations Act 1976, unlawful. 'Public authority' is now defined widely for this purpose. This means that *law enforcement*, whether by the police, local authorities, or tax inspectors, is for the *first time* subject to the laws governing racial discrimination. The Act also places a general duty on

---

79 <https://www.ipcc.gov.uk.>.
80 See the Police Reform and Social Responsibility Act 2011, s 157(1).
81 In the first elections for 41 posts in England and Wales held in November 2012 there was a derisory turnout of 15 per cent.

public authorities to work towards the elimination of unlawful discrimination and promote equality of opportunity and good relations between persons of different racial groups.[82]

5.8 Privatisation and regulation

Another important aspect in which there has been a blurring of distinctions between public and private law has arisen through the privatisation initiatives of the 1980s and 1990s. It should be remembered that the policies of the post-war Labour governments between 1945 and 1951 involved nationalising a string of strategically important and often monopolistic industries, including the public utilities. Following public ownership, these industries operated under a statutory framework that allowed them to function, in theory at least, at arm's length from government control, while enjoying state-regulated funding or subsidy. Each year the broad financial parameters were set out by the government, while the chairman and the board of the industry were responsible for the day-to-day management of the organisation.

The drive towards privatisation of nationalised industries and governmental functions initiated by the Thatcher and Major governments in past decades was an ideologically motivated reversal of this policy. To engineer the change, shares in many of the utilities were offered to the public at very favourable prices. The list of state-owned industries that have been privatised include: British Telecom, British Airways, British Aerospace, British Airports Authority, British Steel, British Rail, the water industry, the electricity industry, power generation, and gas. Thus privatisation proved, in the short term at least, a substantial source of additional public revenue, with highly publicised 'sell offs' being trumpeted as the first step in the quest for a share-owning democracy. A further aim of successive governments has been to achieve more efficient performance from these industries by introducing them to competitive market pressures.

A rationale for the privatisation of some industries was not hard to find. However, many aspects of privatisation have, from the outset, been a source of political and economic controversy. For example, certain of these public utilities retain monopolistic characteristics and they continue to dominate particular markets. There is only a single set of telephone cables, gas pipes, power generators, or railway lines. Promoting competition in such circumstances has often proved to be problematic and not self-evident in the public interest. The enthusiasts for it have maintained that freeing up markets would deliver long-term benefits of efficiency, economy, and consumer choice; but privatisation has given rise to a raft of fresh problems. The introduction of full market pricing for the installation of power supplies, sewerage services, and telephones was one possible outcome of privatisation and without regulation this could have adversely affected vulnerable groups in society living in remote areas. In some of the utilities, such as water and gas, the workforce was greatly reduced in order to save money, yet there was a failure to invest at levels

---

[82] This was one of many recommendations flowing from the publication of the Macpherson Report into the killing of Stephen Lawrence in 1993. See *Stephen Lawrence Inquiry* (1999) Cm 4262.

necessary to maintain the quality of services. For example, Yorkshire Water was able to pay healthy additional dividends to its shareholders while many customers suffered severe water shortages during the summer drought in 1995. Indeed, the scheme of water regulation has been modified by the Water Industry Act 1999. This Act changes the emphasis by sanctioning an approach that gives the minister powers to make regulations, but also empowers the minister to issue detailed guidance to the regulator. The Secretary of State has the power to make regulations in regard to charging schemes and the Director General of Water Services has been given power to approve charging schemes. This guidance addresses some of the problems to do with reaching an accommodation between the conflicting considerations and marks a shift in emphasis from the previous Water Industry Act of 1991. Another matter of particular controversy has been the way certain senior executives have increased their own salaries in line with those of other private sector companies and the sums paid to them on retirement or redundancy (e.g., the chief executive of British Gas who retired in 1996 and Railtrack executives who resigned in 2000–01 following the disastrous performance of the company).

The mechanism provided by the government to safeguard the quality of delivery of the privatised industries and protect the interests of consumers were statutory regulators responsible for overseeing the process of transition from the public sector to the private sector, and to act as oversight agencies for the foreseeable future. From the standpoint of administrative law we must assess how effectively the new systems of regulation have provided an adequate framework of accountability. A central objective of regulation includes controlling the level of profit and seeing that the pricing of goods and services takes account of the wider public interests.[83] The Littlechild Report, commissioned by the government in the 1980s to look into this issue, was strongly in favour of promoting competition and envisaged regulation as merely a holding operation until competition, with its supposed benefits, could be more generally achieved. The process of enforcement and regulation adopted in the USA incorporates accountable decision-making procedures and this might have served as a model. For example, American practice includes elements of participation, with formal hearings for affected interests, while regulators are under a duty to give reasons for their decisions. In the UK the Competition and Service Utilities Act 1992, sections 1, 5(1), 6(1), and 7(1), imposed a duty on the regulator to provide reasons for certain decisions, but the US blueprint was rejected because it was perceived as being overly formal, complex, and legalistic.

But how should the process of regulation be managed? The regulators are called upon to make very difficult and, at times, controversial judgements, always working within the parameters of the relevant Act. The enabling legislation has attempted, with only limited success, to minimise the discretionary element for the regulators by reference to a detailed pricing formula, and the fixing of pricing levels has been the subject of much political and academic debate. (Claims that the regulator has been provided with incomplete access to certain types of information e.g. from British Gas concerning the details of its internal financial affairs, has been another matter of concern.) However, the overriding issue for regulators under the original legislation was to promote competition. For example in the case

---

83 See the Littlechild Report (Regulation of British Telecommunications Profitability, London: HMSO, 1983).

of British Gas the regulator was responsible for creating a climate of competitive pressures, and thus was acting as a form of 'surrogate competition'.

Following privatisation, the regulators have been 'distanced' from the ambit of ministerial responsibility by being given the status of 'non ministerial government departments'. The effect of this is that the rules under which they operate are not subject to parliamentary approval and there is no form of direct democratic accountability as ministerial responsibility does not apply to the privatised industries themselves. Nevertheless, ministers still retain powers to appoint the regulators and to determine the extent of competition by being able to at least partly determine licences which are essential to permit each industry to do business.[84]

The regulatory agencies which have been set up include: the Office of Telecommunications (OFTEL) (under the Telecommunications Act 1984); and the Office of Water Services (OFWAT) (under the Water Industry Act 1991). Each of these regulatory bodies is headed by a Director-General in whom the powers are personally invested, although the exact scope of these powers varies for each regulator.

5.8.1 Utilities Act 2000

While overall regulation has achieved greater openness than often prevailed under public ownership, one serious drawback that has emerged from each utility having its own regulator is that this provides little scope for intervening strategically across the range to promote policies that are in the public interest. This Utilities Act 2000 combines the Office of Gas Supply (OFGAS), formed under the Gas Act 1986, and the Office of Electricity Regulation (OFFER) formed under the Electricity Act 1989, into a single regulator for gas and electricity (OFGEM). The result is that, to some extent, the lack of uniformity in the approach to the regulation of gas and electricity is addressed by the new Act which applies to England, Wales, and Scotland. It provides a single regulatory authority rather than an individual regulator for each industry, and, in setting out to promote effective competition, it is intended to reflect increasing convergence between the two sectors. This is already very evident from the interpenetration of utility companies with interests in gas, electricity, and water in various combinations. However, the role of OFGEM reaches beyond a purely economic agenda, and the Utilities Act differs from previous legislation by placing much greater emphasis on protecting the interests of consumers and particularly disadvantaged groups. For example, it stipulates that the interests of those on low incomes and the chronically sick and disabled must be taken into account. The Act contains provisions to enable the gas and electricity sectors to make an appropriate contribution to the government's social and environmental objectives.[85]

A common criticism of the initial regimes of regulation was that too much discretion was left in the hands of regulators who were able to adopt an individual and highly pragmatic approach to their task. Indeed, this sometimes involved undignified haggling between the industry and the regulator over such central matters as pricing levels or competition policy. Prosser advocates a more coherent system of procedural requirements based on developing sound criteria for regulation.[86]

---

84 For further critical discussion see J Black, 'Calling Regulators to Account: Challenges, Capacities and Prospects' in Bamforth and Leyland, n 46, 362ff.

85 Utilities Act 2000, ss 67–95.

86 T Prosser, 'Regulation and Legitimacy' in Jowell, Oliver, and O'Cinneide, n 48, 335, 347.

Such substantive principles are essential in his view, because the idea of an open market emerging by itself has proved illusory. At the same time, registration and licensing systems are costly to administer and tend to interfere with the process of competition. However, the liberalisation of the British gas and electricity supply markets has been an important step towards allowing greater competition in some areas. For example, consumers are increasingly able to choose between energy suppliers, with the emergence of multi-utilities (gas and electricity companies) offering to provide both gas and electricity. Also, there is some evidence to suggest that competition contributed in the short term at least to a reduction in energy prices.

5.8.2 Railway privatisation and regulation: back to government?

The regulation of the railways has been problematic with the standard of service delivery on most routes declining markedly following the privatisation of the industry in the mid-1990s. In regard to rail it is worth noting that in response to changing conditions the role of government has been transformed and the intensity of regulation has been recalibrated on more than one occasion. Privatisation was achieved by forming a separate company called Railtrack which inherited all track, signalling, stations, and property from British Rail. Railtrack was then made responsible for leasing its track to a series of 25 separate regional train operating companies (TOCs) that took over from British Rail franchises for operating specific routes. Under the Railways Act 1993 a Franchising Director (Office of Passenger Rail Franchising) was given a regulatory responsibility for overseeing the bidding process. The rolling stock leasing companies (ROSCOs) were formed to control the rolling stock originating from British Rail, which they leased to the TOCs. Crucially, the legislation specified that TOCs were to continue to provide a comparable service on routes that they bid for. A second regulator, the Office of the Rail Regulator (ORR), was originally granted responsibility under the Railways Act 1993 for overseeing the standard of service delivery and was given certain powers to set targets and impose fines on companies that failed to meet them. However, the division of functions between Railtrack, TOCs, and ROSCOs created a complex interaction of 'players' whose contribution needed to be coordinated to provide efficiency, reliability, and safety. In practice, the fragmentation of the structure led to an alarming decline in the reliability of services without clearly delineating responsibility for problems that arose.

Under the original privatisation scheme the rail network depended on Railtrack to maintain and improve the infrastructure from revenues received from leasing the track to operators, and from a substantial government subsidy, but the condition of the railway network was not independently monitored by any of the regulators and the privatisation measures did not require Railtrack to divert profits away from shareholders into upgrading the system. The situation reached crisis point following the fatal accident at Hatfield in 2000. This crash was caused by defective track and inadequate maintenance. Serious safety concerns were raised immediately over the condition of the entire railway. While urgent remedial work was carried out great inconvenience was caused to all passengers over many months. Moreover, the cost of this extensive unscheduled maintenance programme led to Railtrack becoming insolvent. The company was put into administration by the

Minister for Transport, Local Government and the Regions in October 2001. To oversee the operation of the rail infrastructure, the minister subsequently established a not-for-profit company, Network Rail, which took over the running of the railway from the administrators in March 2002.

In response to continued poor performance the government also intervened to modify the regulatory framework. In place of the Office of Passenger Franchising it introduced a Strategic Rail Authority (SRA) under the Transport Act 2000 (sections 201–222). The new authority was designed to work alongside ORR with a different, more strategic, remit, related to overall transport policy. The SRA was given powers, subject to the direction and guidance of the Secretary of State, to impose conditions on train operating companies. However, the SRA was not effective since it was required to set targets, determine outputs, grow and lead the industry as a whole without having any control over the rail infrastructure. In July 2004, following further consultation, the government announced new plans to transform the regulatory framework.[87] First, without resorting to re-nationalisation, the Department of Transport as financial underwriter accountable to Parliament is much more directly involved. For example, it has assumed responsibility for establishing the overall strategy for the railways, and in consultation with the ORR, it sets the amount of public funding by considering the levels of capacity and reliability that are required. Secondly, under the revised structure Network Rail was made clearly responsible for ensuring that the rail network delivers a reliable service by means of an agreement with the Department of Transport. Thirdly, the Office of Rail Regulation was reformulated as the sole industry regulator. It determines the precise amount of income which Network Rail needs in order to deliver its performance objectives, oversees its operations, and has taken over responsibility for rail safety from the Health and Safety Executive. The Railways and Transport Safety Act 2003 brought the railways into line with other regulated industries by replacing an individual regulator with a regulatory board responsible for protecting the legitimate interest of customers. Fourthly, the majority of functions of the SRA, for example in relation to passenger rail franchising, have reverted to the Secretary of State for Transport. The increased degree of government involvement in the running of the railways introduces much clearer political accountability but arguably this is achieved at the price of regulatory independence.

5.8.3 Judicial review and rail regulation

In principle, judicial review offers a means of overseeing the process of regulation. However, *R v Director of Passenger Rail Franchising, ex p Save Our Railways*[88] serves as a useful illustration of the limits of this remedy in challenging the actions of regulators. The grounds for seeking judicial review were that the rail franchising director had failed to take proper account of published ministerial guidance, issued as part of the Railway Act 1993. This set out minimum service levels to be maintained when franchises were awarded. The court was prepared to accept that the pressure group Save Our Railways had standing to apply for judicial review on behalf of rail

---

87 See White Paper: *The Future of Rail* 2004; and the Railways Act 2005.
88 *The Times*, 18 December 1995.

users. Furthermore, it intervened to the extent of holding that, in respect of many of the franchises, the franchise director had not properly understood ministerial instructions. However, no mandatory remedy was granted by the court.

The question was referred back for consideration by the franchising director. At this point, he was under a (moral) obligation to ensure the guidelines were followed. Alternatively, the minister responsible for instigating the policy in the first place was in a position to amend the guidelines to conform with the director's interpretation. Such challenges, even when they are possible, do not necessarily lead to a change in outcome. It should also be noted that in most cases the main service provisions will be contained in private law contracts between the regulator and privatised operator and the discretion exercised in drawing up such contracts will generally be beyond the scope of judicial review.[89] Another problem is that monitoring the process of regulation depends on full access to relevant information and it has been suggested that the prospect of judicial review may sometimes deter regulators from revealing the full reasons for their decisions.

5.8.4 **The failure of financial regulation**

The intensity of the financial crisis, which first came to light in the UK with the failure of Northern Rock in 2007, exposed glaring inadequacies in the regulatory regime in the banking and financial sector. The Financial Services and Markets Act 2000 had established a Financial Services Authority (as a private company) with a brief which ranged from maintaining market confidence to the reduction of financial crime and the protection of consumers. As Harlow and Rawlings observe, its shortcomings were manifest: 'The FSA's own audit confirmed a catalogue of error: no detailed financial analysis; lengthened periods between risk assessments; no risk mitigation programmes [and] failure to re-assess as market conditions worsened . . . '[90] The Coalition Government, elected in 2010, decided to scrap the FSA and partly return regulatory authority to the Bank of England. From 2013 a Prudential Regulation Authority as a subsidiary of the Bank of England has assumed responsibility for promoting stable and prudent operation of the financial system, while a Financial Conduct Authority has been established to take over responsibility for consumer protection.[91]

5.8.5 **Deregulation**

In recent years, with the backing of British Chambers of Commerce, the Federation of Small Businesses, and the CBI, successive governments have been concerned to reduce the burden of 'red tape' imposed on industry and commerce by state regulations. Under the present government the task of reducing regulation has been approached at the highest levels of policy formation with the establishment

---

89 See *R v Director-General of Gas Supply, ex p Smith* CRO/1398/88 QBD, 31 July 1989, and *R v Director General of Telecommunications, ex p Let's Talk (UK) Ltd* CO/77/92 QBD, 6 April 1992 for further examples of challenges to the decisions of regulators by way of judicial review. Although applications for judicial review were granted in both cases, the courts were reluctant to overturn the regulator's decision given the wide discretion that he had been given.

90 Harlow and Rawlings, n 34, 275.

91 See the Financial Services Act 2012.

within the Cabinet Office of the Regulatory Impact Unit, which operates in conjunction with the independent Better Regulation Taskforce to assess the impact of regulation on an on-going basis. In addition, the statutory mechanisms to reduce regulation have been significantly modified. The Conservative Government introduced the Deregulation and Contracting Out Act 1994, which, as well as allowing departmental and local government services to be performed wherever possible by private contractors, conferred significant powers on ministers to reduce regulation. To achieve this, it was felt necessary to circumvent the need for primary legislation in every case that was likely to arise. This meant that the original Act conferred very wide delegated powers on the minister and operated as an all-embracing 'Henry VIII clause' (a clause allowing the minister to repeal or alter existing primary legislation without obtaining further approval from Parliament). Despite limited safeguards the extent of delegated power this placed in the hands of a minister was regarded as a significant erosion of parliamentary sovereignty.[92]

The 1994 Act has now been largely superseded by the Regulatory Reform Act 2001 and the Legislative and Regulatory Reform Act 2006. The 2006 Act also allows ministers to use the device of statutory instruments widely to reduce the burden of regulation and in a greater range of circumstances. To this end regulatory reform orders can: make and re-enact statutory provisions; impose proportionate additional burdens provided this reduces other burdens; remove inconsistencies and anomalies; change burdensome situations caused by a lack of statutory provisions to do something; relieve burdens from anyone, including ministers and government departments, but not where only they would benefit; and permit administrative and minor detail to be further amended by delegated legislation.

The main purpose of the Deregulation and Contracting Out Act 1994 was to facilitate the contracting out of central and local government functions on a more widespread basis. Section 59(1) provided that the functions of a minister, office holder, or local authority could be contracted out subject to specified conditions and normally for a time limit of 10 years. It is worth noting that, in principle, the chain of accountability was left unaffected by the new legislation, for example, section 72 of the Act provided that contracted services were to be treated as if done by the minister. This suggests that ministerial responsibility continued to apply and that the activities that were contracted out remained within the ambit of investigation by the Parliamentary Ombudsman. In practice, however, it has been much more difficult to get ministers to account for such activities, as the Act also made provision for preventing the disclosure of information in respect of the exercise of a particular function which is to be contracted out. This was justified because of the potential commercial sensitivity of any such financial information. In the latest attempts to minimise regulation on individuals and small businesses the Coalition Government declared that it would support growth and enterprise by ensuring that vital public protections are delivered in proportionate, risk-based, and consistent ways.[93] The legislation is designed to ensure that the need for regulation is kept under review and it enables the removal of regulation

---

92 G Ganz, 'Delegated Legislation: A Necessary Evil or A Constitutional Outrage' in P Leyland and T Woods (eds), *Administrative Law Facing the Future* (London: Blackstone Press, 1997), 65ff.

93 See the Enterprise and Regulatory Reform Act 2013 and the Deregulation Act 2015.

which the public feel is no longer required. The legislation also seeks to achieve greater consistency in enforcement by local authorities through the provision of assured advice in regulatory compliance.[94]

5.9 Citizen's Charter to Customer Service Excellence

The Citizen's Charter introduced originally by the Conservative Government in the early 1990s developed in parallel with Next Steps agencies. This innovation sought to prioritise customer satisfaction in public sector services. Hence one hall-mark of service provision has been the emphasis placed on quality and perfor-mance. The Charter introduced the idea of objective standards of performance, coupled with redress and complaints mechanisms. A central concern is to set meas-urable standards for service delivery and then assess actual annual performance against those standards. In essence, the consumer is not only offered a degree of openness, consultation, and, where possible, choice in respect of the service itself, but, in addition, has recourse to some kind of remedy if the service falls below an agreed threshold of acceptability.

An initiative directed at improving the quality of public services by setting out expectations and remedies for the citizen has enormous potential and the idea was developed not only for government (200 national charters by 2002) and local gov-ernment (10,000 local charters) but extended to the privatised utilities. For exam-ple, charters have been introduced for patients in the NHS, students at schools and universities, passengers on public transport, taxpayers, citizens receiving benefits, litigants in the courts, the Police Service, and the Prison Service. Some charters set out rights and responsibilities in considerable detail and resemble contracts, for example, The Council Tenants Charter, while others are much more general, for example, London Bus Passengers Charter. A more general awareness of the stand-ards of service delivery is achieved by the publication of performance league tables (e.g., in health and education).

Following the publication of the Modernising Government White Paper in 1999 the Labour Government placed an increasingly high emphasis on the delivery of consumer services which it presented in terms of 'the battle for world class public services'. To encourage the spread of good practice throughout the public sector a special unit was formed within the Cabinet Office. The result of this quest for sus-tained improvement involved relaunching and rebranding the Citizens' Charter as 'Service First: the New Charter Programme'. This places greater emphasis on achieving higher quality and more responsive public services by increasing citizen involvement through partnership and by auditing the quality of service delivery through benchmarking. The objective was to thoroughly integrate nine principles of public service delivery. Accordingly, each public service should: set standards of service; be open and provide full information; consult and involve; encourage access and the promotion of choice; treat all fairly; put things right when they go wrong; use resources effectively; innovate and improve; and work with other

94 Enterprise and Regulatory Reform Act 2013, Policy Paper, Department for Business, Innovation and Skills, June 2013.

providers. Following the 2001 general election the 'Service First' unit was renamed the *Office of Public Services Reform* and became part of the Prime Minister's Office at 10 Downing Street. The initiative continued to modernise by promoting the new four key principles of 'standards, delegation, flexibility, expanding choice' but is driven by the Prime Minister's own department at the heart of government.[95]

The public sector modernisation programme has been repeatedly relaunched as 'Service First', 'Public Service Reform', 'Charter Mark', and 'Customer Service Excellence'. The customer focus engendered by these initiatives has contributed to some improvement in the delivery of many, but by no means all, services. Citizen expectations can be raised, only to be disappointed, by inadequate delivery on promises; and questions have been raised concerning the methods of compilation and presentation of statistics showing performance which seems at variance with the actual experience of consumers. Moreover, any redress that is available tends to be limited to what a Charter provides. In many situations this is likely to be inadequate, for instance, a promise that a patient will receive attention within a given time but no provision for compensation if this proves impossible, or a flat rate refund of several pounds/ticket voucher for a train that arrives more than an hour late. The result of these deficiencies has been that these charters have a marginal effect on service delivery. Moreover, it should be recognised that the ones introduced so far are no substitute for a genuine legal remedy capable of providing full compensation for any inconvenience or loss that may have been caused by the failure of a service.

5.10 Freedom of information

The accountability of governmental institutions is linked to their transparency. Citizens need to have access to information relating to the functioning of public bodies in many different contexts. For example, how decisions have been taken, the reasons for decisions, and how money has been spent. However, the civil service in the United Kingdom had a reputation for secrecy, and could rely upon wide-ranging official secrets legislation (e.g., the Official Secrets Act 1989). Indeed, one of the important criticisms contained in the Scott Report into the Matrix Churchill Affair related to unnecessary government secrecy.[96] The Freedom of Information Act 2000 (FOI) which was introduced in response to such criticisms made very significant changes,[97] although the Act failed to go as far as the proposals in the White Paper that preceded it.[98]

Part I of the Act, which came fully into force in 2005, imposes a duty on public authorities to provide information in response to requests in writing, meaning there is a general obligation on public authorities to disclose exempt information unless the public interest in maintaining exemption outweighs the public interest

---

95 See *Reforming Public Services: Principles into Practice*, March 2002.

96 *Report of the Inquiry into the Export of Defence Equipment and Dual-Use Goods to Iraq and Related Prosecutions* HC (1995–96), 115.

97 See P Birkinshaw, *Freedom of Information*, 4th edn (Cambridge: Cambridge University Press, 2010).

98 *Your Right to Know*, 1997, Cm 3818.

in disclosure. However, Part II establishes a lengthy list of areas where information is exempted from disclosure. These include, for example, all work done by the security forces; defence; communications with the Royal family; all political advice; international relations; relations between the parliaments and assemblies of the UK, Scotland, Wales, and Northern Ireland; the economy; investigations by the police and customs and excise; court records; commercial information; health and safety; and all personal information and information provided to government in confidence. These categories constitute catch-all exemptions allowing information to be refused without real evidence of any harm. The public will not normally be allowed information that could 'prejudice' government unless Whitehall bodies or other public authorities decide to release it under discretionary powers. In order to justify refusal to disclose, there is only a requirement to show 'prejudice' or 'likely prejudice' rather than a 'substantial harm' test that had been recommended in the 1997 White Paper. This would have placed a much greater burden on the executive before being able to claim an exemption. Another positive feature of the FOI is that it requires many public bodies to adopt publication schemes which are overseen by the Information Commissioner.

The Information Commissioner has powers to recommend publication in the public interest in those areas where government departments have a discretion to release information, with the caveat that the Commissioner can be overruled by a minister or the Attorney-General. This means that considerable discretion is left in the hands of ministers and officials in deciding what information is actually released into the public domain. The recent *Evans* decision suggests that, in practice, this ministerial discretion may be limited if the matter has already been fully considered by the Upper Tribunal. The case concerned correspondence between Prince Charles and various government departments which were made subject to an information request by a *Guardian* journalist. There was a strong implication that Charles had been seeking to influence government policy behind the scenes in a personal capacity by writing letters on environmental and other matters without publishing them. A veto to prevent disclosure was issued by the Attorney General after the Upper Tribunal had overruled the Information Commissioner and ordered disclosure of the letters. It is important to note that the Attorney General, by exercising this veto, had, in effect, set aside a judicial determination in a manner that raised questions about the separation of powers. The veto was first challenged unsuccessfully by way of judicial review. But finally the Supreme Court ruled that the Attorney General had acted unlawfully in overruling the decision of the Upper Tribunal. For the majority, Lord Neuberger held that the Attorney General does not have the right to override the Tribunal merely because he takes a different view. From a constitutional standpoint the decision of a court is binding and cannot simply be set aside. The dissenting judgment of Lord Mance recognised that it would be possible to issue a certificate if he disagreed but only if he did so with the clearest possible justification.[99]

The exclusions and ministerial veto raised serious doubts about the government's commitment to public law values of openness, accountability, participation, and democracy. However, notwithstanding such criticism, the Act, which

---

[99] *Evans v Attorney-General* [2015] UKSC 21, [2015] AC 1787. See A Young, 'R (Evans) v Attorney General—The Anisminic of the 21st Century?' UK Const L Blog, 31 March 2015.

came fully into force on 1 January 2005, provides citizens with a general right to be provided with information held by central government, local authorities, and a very wide range of public bodies.[100] Moreover, the legislation is resulting in changes of practice by government and public bodies. Much more information than was previously the case is placed in the public domain. For example, the disclosure of details of MPs expenses in 2009 was perhaps the most prominent issue to be exposed as a result of FOI requests. The national scandal that resulted from these revelations not only led to the prosecution of some MPs and the resignation of others, but also to a revision of the system by which MPs claim expenses.[101] This trend towards FOI must be welcomed, since access to such information is an integral aspect of accountable government.

5.11 Conclusion

This chapter has outlined the powers of government and has provided a map of the multifarious public bodies, hybrid organisations, and private bodies that comprise the modern administrative state. A central theme has been the promotion of 'choice', 'effectiveness', and 'efficiency' by the introduction of market-led solutions for the delivery of many services. Indeed, the trends towards privatisation, Next Steps developments, and contracting out of services by public bodies gathered momentum during the 1980s and 1990s, but also continued into the new century under both Labour and the Conservative–Liberal Democrat Coalition governments. The public law mechanisms of accountability and control (Parliament, regulators, and courts) have struggled to keep pace with these rapid changes in the institutional landscape. In particular, we have noted evidence of further erosion in the doctrine of ministerial responsibility. The uneven performance and limited effectiveness of the regulators in discharging their statutory duty in regard to the privatised utilities has been another prominent issue. On another (related) front, the extent of the supervisory role of the courts has been difficult to resolve because of continuing problems in reaching a clear distinction between the public and private law spheres (see chapter 8).

The election of Labour in 1997 not only led to a recasting at a political level but also to a raft of new legislation, which included the introduction of devolved government, a new Mayor and Assembly for London, and further reform to the health service, local government, and to regimes of regulation. In response to the prevailing economic crisis, the priority for the Conservative–Liberal Democrat Coalition Government, which was formed in 2010, was to tackle the deficit by cutting public expenditure. Not only is the size of administrative state being reduced by slimming down central and local government and by dispensing with quangos, but also the language has changed from 'Modernising Government' under Blair to the 'Big Society' under Cameron. As a response to the marked increase in devolution for

---

100 But for some of the limits to the Act see *Kennedy v Information Commissioner* [2014] UKSC 20, [2015] AC 455.

101 P Leyland, 'Freedom of Information and the 2009 Parliamentary Expenses Scandal' [2009] *Public Law* 675.

Scotland and Wales following the 2014 Scottish referendum, further devolution of power to English local government in the form of city-wide mayors and increased financial autonomy is emerging as a policy innovation under the Conservative Government elected in May 2015.[102] The Cities and Local Government Devolution Act 2016 and the Localism Act 2011 serve as instruments for delivering this policy. The emphasis is shifting towards a less centralised state, greater community involvement in decision-making, and a greater role for voluntary activity. Nevertheless, the dominance of market-led initiatives for public sector delivery of services continues. Despite more inclusive language and additional accountability mechanisms (e.g., new parliaments, assemblies, reform of local government), there is limited evidence (perhaps with the exception of devolution) that the concentration of power at the top, which left much less discretion in the hands of local government and other public institutions, has been substantially re-distributed downwards.

FURTHER READING

General

Bamforth, N and Leyland, P (2013) 'Introduction: Accountability in the Contemporary Constitution' in Bamforth, N and Leyland, P (eds), *Accountability in the Contemporary Constitution* (Oxford: Oxford University Press).

Foster, C (2005) *British Government in Crisis* (Oxford: Hart Publishing).

Painter, C (1999) 'Public Service Reform from Thatcher to Blair: A Third Way' *Parliamentary Affairs* 94–112.

Pattie, C and Johnston, R (2011) 'How Big is the Big Society' 64 (3) *Parliamentary Affairs*, 403–424.

Smith, MJ (2010) 'From Big Government to Big Society: Changing the State-Society Balance' 63 (4) *Parliamentary Affairs*, 818–833.

Central government and civil service

Barberis, P (1998) 'The New Public Management and a New Accountability' 76 *Public Administration* 451–70.

Davies, A (2013) 'Beyond New Public Management: Problems of Accountability in the Modern Adminstrative State' in Bamforth, N and Leyland, P (eds), *Accountability in the Contemporary Constitution* (Oxford: Oxford University Press).

Drewry, G [2002] 'Whatever Happened to the Citizen's Charter' *Public Law* 9.

Drewry, G (2011) 'The Executive: Towards Accountable Government and Effective Governance' in Jowell, J and Oliver, D (eds), *The Changing Constitution*, 7th edn (Oxford: Clarendon Press).

Freedland, M (1999) 'The Crown and the Changing Nature of Government' in Sunkin, M and Payne, S, *The Nature of the Crown* (Oxford: Oxford University Press).

Harden, I (1992) *The Contracting State* (Buckingham: Open University Press), chapter 3 'The Contractual Approach to Public Services: Three Examples'. Also in Galligan, DJ (ed), *A Reader on Administrative Law* (Oxford: Oxford University Press, 1996).

Rawlings, R (2015) 'A Coalition Government at Westminster' in Jowell, J, Oliver, D, and O'Cinneide, C (eds), *The Changing Constitution*, 8th edn (Oxford: Oxford University Press).

---

102 Devolution in England: The Case for Local Government, Communities and Local Government Committee, First Report of Session 2014–15, HC 503, 3.

Local government and devolution

Brooks, J (2000) 'Labour's Modernization of Local Government' 78 (3) *Public Administration*, 593–612.

Hazell, R and Rawlings, R (2005) *Devolution, Law-Making and the Constitution* (Exeter: Imprint Academic).

Leigh, I (2015) 'The Changing Nature of the Local State' in Jowell, J, Oliver, D, and O'Cinneide C (eds), *The Changing Constitution*, 8th edn (Oxford: Oxford University Press).

Leyland, P (2011) 'The Multifaceted Constitutional Dynamics of UK Devolution' 9 (1) *ICON*, 252–273.

Rawlings, R (2003) *Delineating Wales: Constitutional, Legal and Administrative Aspects of National Devolution* (Cardiff: Cardiff University Press).

Regulation and deregulation

Black, J (2013) 'Calling Regulators to Account: Challenges, Capacities and Prospects' in Bamforth, N and Leyland, P (eds), *Accountability in the Contemporary Constitution* (Oxford: Oxford University Press).

Graham, C (2000) *Regulating Public Utilities: A Constitutional Approach* (Oxford: Hart Publishing).

Leyland, P (2003) 'UK Utility Regulation in an Age of Governance' in Bamforth, N and Leyland, P, *Public Law in a Multi-Layered Constitution* (Oxford: Hart Publishing).

Oliver, D, Prosser, T, and Rawlings R (eds) (2010) *The Regulatory State: Constitutional Implications* (Oxford: Oxford University Press).

Prosser, T (2015) 'Regulation and Legitimacy' in Jowell, J, Oliver, D, and O'Cinneide, C (eds), *The Changing Constitution*, 8th edn (Oxford: Oxford University Press).

Freedom of information

Birkinshaw, P (2015) 'Regulating Information' in Jowell, J, Oliver, D, and O'Cinneide, C (eds), *The Changing Constitution*, 8th edn (Oxford: Oxford University Press).

Birkinshaw, P (2010) *Freedom of Information*, 4th edn (Cambridge: Cambridge University Press).

Coppel, P (2014) *Information Rights: Law and Practice*, 4th edn (Oxford: Hart Publishing).

Hazell, R, Worthy, B, and Glover, M (2010) *The Impact of the Freedom of Information Act on Central Government in the UK: Does FOI Work?* (Basingstoke: Palgrave Macmillan).

Palmer, S (2003) 'Freedom of Information: A New Constitutional Landscape' in Bamforth, N and Leyland, P, *Public Law in a Multi-Layered Constitution* (Oxford: Hart Publishing).

6

The ombudsman principle

6.1 Introduction

The ombudsman concept is based on the idea that citizens should be entitled to complain against specific acts of their rulers, and that their complaints should be independently investigated.[1]

This chapter mainly discusses the role of the Parliamentary and Health Service Ombudsman (hereinafter PO), but it also provides an outline of the other specialist ombudsmen which have been created to oversee many aspects of public administration. There are now a series of public sector ombudsmen, each with their own jurisdiction. The efficacy of this method of grievance handling has to be considered alongside the role of MPs in Parliament, the availability of administrative tribunals, and recourse to the courts via judicial review. Indeed, a Parliamentary Ombudsman was first introduced under the Parliamentary Commissioner Act of 1967 (hereafter referred to as the PCA) to address the shortcomings in parliamentary oversight mechanisms. However, as the former Parliamentary Ombudsman points out:

The original purpose of providing an aid to Parliament in its constitutional scrutiny of the Executive has evolved alongside the increasing sophistication of administrative law in the intervening period. Whilst the office would not expressly espouse a role as 'people's champion' in emulation of some overseas models, it has certainly carved for itself a distinctive niche in the judicial landscape, as a source of dispute resolution, as a guardian of good public administration, and as a systematic check upon departmental effectiveness.[2]

The primary role of the Parliamentary Ombudsman as an officer of the House of Commons is to thoroughly investigate complaints referred by Westminster MPs which relate to the workings of central government and other non-departmental governmental bodies. As a complaint investigator the ombudsman is vested with formidable investigative powers which includes the capacity to scrutinise the internal workings of departments, which might mean requiring officials to provide evidence and produce documents, but unlike tribunals or courts the PO is not able to take remedial action directly. Rather, after completing an investigation, the PO reports back. If the complaint of maladministration is sustained, recommendations

---

1 M Seneviratne, *Ombudsmen: Public Services and Administrative Justice* (London: Butterworths, 2002), 2.
2 Ann Abraham, Preface to R Kirkham, *Parliamentary Ombudsman: Withstanding the Test of Time*, 4th Report Session 2006–2007, HC 421, Stationery Office, 2007.

will usually be made, including the payment of compensation if this is deemed appropriate. In general, the PO's recommendations are followed. However, there is no legal requirement for civil service departments or other public bodies to comply with such recommendations. Should the recommendations be ignored, there is one final option, which is to lay a report before Parliament. The publicity which will be caused by so doing might exert additional pressure on ministers and/or officials to comply. One of the issues which will be raised in the discussion that follows is whether the PO should be granted additional powers.

It will soon be apparent that the contribution of ombudsmen has been transformed in recent years. On the one hand, this is because there has been an introduction of private law values in the public sector which has placed a strong emphasis on customer satisfaction. There is now increasing recognition of good administration and the elimination of systemic shortcomings. On the other hand, the various ombudsman office holders have been committed to increased accessibility. In the contemporary environment, very widespread access to the internet now allows citizens to visit the websites of complaints handlers from their homes, and in many cases to initiate the process of complaining online. While the major part of this chapter is concerned with the role of the PO in relation to the workings of central government, it should be emphasised that ombudsmen are ubiquitous as grievance handlers across both the public and private sector.

Finally, a note on terminology, the Parliamentary Commissioner Act of 1967 officially introduced a Parliamentary Commissioner for Administration. Later, the full title has changed to the Parliamentary and Health Service Ombudsman but in the remainder of this chapter we will simply refer to the Parliamentary Ombudsman as the PO.

6.2 Constitutional context

The Crichel Down Affair in 1954 exposed a manifest gap in the available grievance mechanisms. In particular it demonstrated the inadequacy of any proper procedure to deal either politically or legally with the consequences of what we would now term maladministration. The facts were that farmland in Dorset had been acquired by the Air Ministry in 1938 under a compulsory purchase order to be used as bombing range. After the war the land was transferred to the Ministry of Agriculture which no longer required it. The family of Lieutenant-Commander Marten, the previous owner, wanted the land back. As Prime Minister in 1941, Winston Churchill had stated in Parliament that the land would be returned. Subsequently, misleading replies and false assurances were given to the family and its request to repurchase the land was refused. After some delay, an inaccurate report was prepared by a junior civil servant which led to a scheme whereby the land was to be let to a single tenant. Conservative MPs took up the matter on behalf of the Marten family in the House of Commons. This resulted in a public inquiry which published a report that was highly critical of individual officials and the civil service. The parliamentary debate on this report was the catalyst which prompted the minister to resign. It is significant, however, that despite the criticism of named officials in the report, no serving civil servant was dismissed or seriously reprimanded for his or her actions. The crisis for the government followed the disclosure of wide-ranging incompetence by officials some 10 years after the original incident occurred, by which time the original minister, and many senior officials involved at the time, had retired.

One immediate outcome was the Franks Report on Administrative Tribunals and Inquiries.[3] There was also an obvious need for a new, effective, and cheap non-legal remedy to be made available in the face of deficiencies revealed in the role of MPs in holding ministers to account through the then available parliamentary procedures. For example, without the departmental select committee system introduced after the 1979 general election, MPs had no ready means of accessing/investigating departments of state. On the other hand, at the end of the grievance chain, judicial review before the courts as a means of remedying unlawful (*ultra vires*) action by public bodies was and is limited by cost, time, and a number of procedural requirements.[4] In any event, this procedure tends to emphasise adversarial dispute resolution rather than the more inquisitorial, investigatory approach found in the new select committees, and firmly embodied in the institution of the Parliamentary Ombudsman and other ombudsmen.

An ombudsman-based approach to plugging this gap in the grievance chain was recognised by Parliament with the passage of the Parliamentary Commissioner Act 1967. The legislation was a follow-up to a report published by the organisation, JUSTICE in 1961 entitled 'The Citizen and the Administration: the Redress of Grievances', commonly referred to as the Whyatt Report. This recommended that a commissioner for complaints should be appointed. Offices of this type were not a recent innovation. Sweden appointed the first parliamentary ombudsman (*Justitieombudsmannen*) in 1809 to achieve a balance between the potentially overwhelming power of the state and the perceived weakness of the individual citizen in securing justice. Denmark followed in 1954, and it was the obvious effectiveness with which the mechanism appeared to work there that encouraged its emulation elsewhere. In 1962, New Zealand introduced an ombudsman (the first one in a common law country); the British Parliamentary Commissioner for Administration (referred to here as the PO) followed in 1967. France established the equivalent office of *médiateur* in 1973[5] (the only other commissioner with an indirect method of receiving complaints, although with a much wider jurisdiction).[6] The French ombudsman was renamed *défenseur des droits* (defender of rights) and the office partly remodelled on its Spanish counterpart, the *defensor del pueblo*, which had been established in 1981.[7] Two relatively recent additions have been the South African Ombudsman, termed the 'Public Protector' under section 14 of the 1996 Constitution, and the Ombudsman for the EU institutions, introduced in 1995. Ombudsmen have proliferated around the world in both public and private sectors, and now exist in more than 90 countries.

The basic idea of an ombudsman (a 'grievance person') can be stated simply: a complaint of maladministration from a relevant source is investigated by an

---

3 See ch 7.
4 See chs 8–18.
5 N Brown and J Bell, *French Administrative Law* (Oxford: Oxford University Press, 1998), 34.
6 S Boyron, *The Constitution of France: A Contextual Analysis* (Oxford: Hart Publishing, 2013), 203ff.
7 V Comella, *The Constitution of Spain: A Contextual Analysis* (Oxford: Hart Publishing, 2013), 152ff.

official with appropriate powers, clearly independent of the administrative authorities which are subject to scrutiny. This principle is incorporated in the Parliamentary Commissioner Act 1967 and subsequent statutes. As an officer of the House of Commons the PO is formally appointed by the Crown on the advice of the Prime Minister, but the appointment is made with the approval of the Leader of the Opposition and following consultation with the chairman of the Public Administration Select Committee. In setting out the provisions for appointment, tenure, salary, and administration of the office the emphasis was on establishing an independent official, appointed for a renewable or fixed term whose salary is charged on the Consolidated Fund (sections 1–3 of the Act). As in the case of judges, removal from office can only be by address of both Houses of Parliament or through medical incapacity. The latest office holder, Dame Julie Mellor, became the Parliamentary and Health Service Ombudsman in January 2012 for what has recently been established as a seven-year term.

6.3 Parliamentary Ombudsman: 'MP filter' or direct access

From the inception of the institution all complaints to the PO had to be routed through an MP. The effect that an independent official as omubudsman would have on the traditional role of MPs and the accountability of ministers to Parliament under the convention of individual ministerial responsibility was an initial concern voiced in Parliament which has not been borne out in practice. The involvement of MPs in the ombudsman process was defended in some quarters by pointing out that the role of UK MPs in dealing with complaints differed from most continental parliamentary systems, that is, that there has been an individual link to their constituencies, making MPs (in effect) ombudsmen for their own constituents. Open access to the general public would potentially usurp, or at least undermine, the focal role of MPs as investigators for complaints. Complaint handling, so it was argued, was a task MPs have always performed, dealing collectively with a *very* much greater case load than an ombudsman. Rather than acting as a competitor, it will be apparent that the PO should be regarded as an adjunct to the existing system, providing redress at a different level and in a different way.[8]

A fear that the office would be swamped, and therefore unable to cope with the workload, was another objection to direct access. Initially, it was thought that the potential for referrals from a large population (by comparison with, for instance, Sweden, Denmark, and New Zealand) would overwhelm the PO. In turn, this burden would require a considerable staff, placing an additional expense on the taxpayer. This also contributed to the rationale for a more limited UK institution, despite the suggestion from some quarters that more references would increase the authority and visibility of the office. Accordingly, when it came to drafting the legislation many MPs argued that they wished to retain their investigative role; and, indeed, that this would have the incidental advantage at an early stage of weeding out many complaints that would inevitably fall outside the statutory provision,

---

8 H Wade and C Forsyth, *Administrative Law*, 11th edn (Oxford: Oxford University Press, 2009), 68ff.

thus imposing a similar requirement to that of *locus standi* (standing) in applications for judicial review. However, in the current situation, with a proliferation of public sector ombudsmen already operating with their specialist jurisdictions, there is little prospect that the PO would become flooded with complaints by allowing direct access.

Next, when we come to examine the take up of the institution, the actual position is that MPs have an uneven record in referring matters to the PO, with many of them not using the PO at all. In one study only 19 per cent of MPs found the PO very useful, with 67 per cent considering the office to be of only marginal relevance to them and 11 per cent taking the view that the PO was of no use to them.[9] Such surveys suggest that access of constituents to the PO may depend on the view towards the office of their individual MP. To partly address the problem of indirect referral through MPs, since 1978 a form of 'direct access by the back door' has been accepted by the PO.[10] Any complaint sent directly which is considered worthy of investigation will be forwarded to an MP who can then sanction an inquiry. The mood of MPs has changed and a more recent survey suggests that a majority of MPs support direct access (Public Administration Select Committee 2004). Furthermore, it will be apparent from this discussion that the argument for direct access has prevailed with the extension of ombudsmen to local and devolved government and to other public and private sector institutions.

With the advent of the internet and the design of user friendly websites aimed at aggrieved citizens, great strides have been taken towards publicising the role of the PO. In general citizens today expect to have direct access to complaints' mechanisms with a telephone hotline or a form available online. While an end to the MP filter has already been introduced in regard to Health Service complaints, it remains a barrier for other complaints despite abolition being widely canvassed within Parliament[11] and supported by all recent office holders.[12] The problem has been that such a change is dependent on the allocation of parliamentary time to pass the necessary legislation. Virtually all commentators agree that the MP filter mechanism has contributed to the under-utilisation of the office and the diversion of complaints to other channels of grievance resolution, to some extent at least, has impeded the development of the PO as a citizen's champion.[13]

6.4 What is maladministration?

Given that the PO is responsible for investigating cases of maladministration it is of crucial importance to reach an understanding of what comprises 'maladministration'. The word can be found in section 5(1)(a) and section 10(3) of the PCA 1967

9 See G Drewry and C Harlow, 'A "Cutting Edge"? The Parliamentary Commissioner and MPs' (1990) 53 *Modern Law Review* 745, 761.

10 Report of PO for 1978, HC 205, 1978–79.

11 See 'Time for a People's Ombudsman Service' *Public Administration Select Committee*, Fourteenth Report of Session 2013–14, 28 April 2014, HC 655.

12 A Abraham, 'The Parliamentary Ombudsman and Administrative Justice: Shaping the Next 50 Years', Tom Sargant memorial lecture (London: Justice, 2011), 28.

13 For further discussion of this issue see, e.g., M Elliott, 'Asymmetric Devolution and Ombudsman Reform in England' [2006] *Public Law* 84, 90ff.

but no statutory definition is provided. The government of the day thought it was inappropriate to elaborate on the meaning of the concept because any definition would inevitably work to limit the potential for development inherent in this term. However, Richard Crossman, the Minister of Housing and Local Government, who was instrumental in securing the passing of the 1967 legislation, attempted a definition in the second reading debate on the Bill. This is usually referred to as the 'Crossman catalogue'. He said that it included, 'bias, neglect, inattention, delay, incompetence, ineptitude, perversity, turpitude, arbitrariness and so on'.[14] This is usually understood as meaning injustice, hardship which should not have arisen, something that is wider than legally redressable damage. The term 'injustice' is also undefined but it may be understood as the anger and frustration that may arise from a given case of maladministration and will be taken into account in the PO's findings.

'Maladministration' was further elaborated and updated by the PO in 1993.[15] For the first time a 15-point list of behaviour which constitutes maladministration was produced. This includes: rudeness; unwillingness to treat the complainant as a person with rights; refusal to answer reasonable questions; neglecting to inform a complainant on request of his or her rights or entitlement; knowingly giving misleading or inadequate advice; ignoring valid advice or overruling considerations which would produce an uncomfortable result for the overruler; offering no redress; showing bias; omission to notify those who thereby lose a right of appeal; refusal to inform adequately of the right of appeal; faulty procedures; failure by management to monitor compliance with adequate procedures; cavalier disregard of guidance which is intended to be followed in the interest of equitable treatment of those who use a service; partiality; and failure to mitigate the effects of rigid adherence to the letter of the law where that produces manifestly inequitable treatment.

While Lord Donaldson MR in *R v Local Commissioner for Administration, ex p Eastleigh Borough Council*[16] defined it as having 'nothing to do with the nature, quality or reasonableness of the decision itself', Sir Alan Marre, a former PO, in his 1973 report to the Select Committee, proposed that maladministration might encompass 'any administrative short-comings'. This has all the virtue of succinctness; nevertheless, it remains simply one more proposed gloss on what, as we have said, is nowhere defined in the statute itself. A more recent description by the current PO mentions poor administration or the wrong application of rules. In truth, both 'maladministration' and 'injustice' have had to be worked out in the practice of the PO as the office has developed over time, and all of these definitions are considerably more restrictive than those found in almost any other jurisdiction. For example, in *R v Local Commissioner for Administration in the North and North East England, ex p Liverpool City Council*,[17] a failure by city councillors to observe the requirement to declare financial interests when taking part in the determination of a planning decision was declared by the Court of Appeal to amount to maladministration. JUSTICE (1977) recommended that the term 'maladministration' should be expanded to include a power to investigate 'unreasonable, unjust or oppressive

---

14 734 HC Deb (5th Series), col 51.
15 See Annual Report, 1993, para 7.
16 [1988] QB 855.
17 *The Times*, 3 March 2000.

action' by government departments, as in New Zealand and Denmark.[18] Rather than a concern with a further definition of maladministration with the present ombudsman, the emphasis has shifted towards developing positive principles of good administration (see 6.11).

It has been confirmed in an important decision *R (on the application of Bradley) v Secretary of State for Works and Pensions*[19] that a minister cannot simply reject findings of maladministration (also discussed below). The PO had published a highly critical report *Trusting in the pensions promise: Government bodies and the security of final salary occupational pensions*[20] in which it was found that the department had committed maladministration in respect to the publication of misleading information (which was not clear, complete, consistent, or always accurate) and in respect to changes in the minimum funding requirements (MFR) for pensions. Injustice and loss had resulted from this maladministration. It was held by Sir John Chadwick, giving the lead judgment, that: 'It is not enough that the Secretary of State has reached his own view on rational grounds: it is necessary that his decision to reject the Ombudsman's findings in favour of his own view is, itself, not irrational having regard to the legislative intention which underlies 1967 Act: he must have a reason (other than simply a preference for his own view) for rejecting a finding which the Ombudsman has made after an investigation under the powers conferred by the Act.' The quashing order handed out in the Administrative Court[21] invalidating the Secretary of State's refusal to accept the PO's first finding of maladministration was upheld. Nevertheless, the Court of Appeal expressly rejected the contention that *R v Local Commissioner for Administration, ex p Eastleigh Borough Council*[22] was authority for the view that a minister is bound by the PO's findings unless they are quashed in judicial review proceedings. The Secretary of State is not precluded from rejecting findings of maladministration provided there are sound reasons for doing so. In rejecting the third finding of maladministration, relating to the decision to change the basis of the MFR for pensions, Sir John Chadwick, emphasised that it was not being held that the ombudsman had not been entitled to reach a conclusion on this matter, but rather that the Secretary of State had not acted irrationally by rejecting the PO's findings.

6.4.1 Procedural and substantive maladministration: question of 'merits' or 'quality'

Whatever the purpose of the government in not defining 'maladministration', it was clearly the intention of those who drafted the PCA that the PO was to be mainly concerned with procedural matters rather than substantive (merits and policy) issues. For example, take the wording of section 12(3):

nothing in this Act authorises or requires the Commissioner to question the merits of a decision taken without maladministration by a government department or other authority in the exercise of a discretion vested in that department or authority . . .

18 D Widdicombe, *Our Fettered Ombudsman: A Report* (London: Justice, 1977).
19 [2008] EWCA 36.
20 (HC 984), 15 March 2006.
21 [2007] EWHC 242.
22 [1988] 1 QB 855.

The complainant will tend to place emphasis (understandably) on the injustice they believe they have suffered, rather than on the actual causes of the maladministration which led to this injustice. However, to fall under the PO's remit any injustice suffered must be linked to maladministration. Section 12(3) can be taken to mean that where a discretionary decision is taken and errors have been made in the administrative procedures leading to such a decision, the PO is on sure ground in finding maladministration. In other words, there is an implication that where a decision is taken with maladministration then the PO can legally consider the merits of the decision.[23]

At this point, the distinction between procedural and substantive maladministration needs to be clarified further. To do so, we take an example of procedural maladministration. In a recent case reported by the PO an asylum seeker had been given exceptional leave to remain by the Immigration and Nationality Directorate (IND). After inquiring about the progress of his application for permanent leave to remain in the UK, he was later interviewed but his asylum application was refused on the same day. The letter setting out the full reasons was never sent by IND. His file was moved from one office to another within the directorate, but no action was taken in regard to the application itself, despite further letters from the claimant's solicitor and MP. He later received a letter removing his permission to work which was later rescinded. Following an investigation, the PO found what we might term procedural maladministration relating to the clearly incompetent handling of the case which included the failure to send the letter with reasons and the unacceptable delay in processing the application and subsequent inquiries. Following the PO's intervention the IND agreed to give the claimant another interview, to offer an apology for the shoddy treatment and a payment of £250 in recognition of the distress caused. However, the PO's intervention was not in respect of the substantive question of whether the claimant was given indefinite leave to remain in the UK. In other words, the substantive decision remained with the IND.[24]

Looking more closely at substantive maladministration and considering its status under section 12(3), it might appear to have more than one aspect to it. The first suggests that the PO should not look into the *quality* of the rules and regulations themselves which are being called into question. The second is that the PO should not question 'the *merits* of a decision taken without maladministration' (emphasis added). These are known, respectively, as the 'bad rule' and the 'bad decision'. To illustrate this, we can take a common sense example of a student who is called before a disciplinary hearing. Let us suppose, the rules of the board stipulate that students must prepare their case within 48 hours of being notified of a hearing. The student duly complies with this rule and due to inadequate preparation time presents an inadequate case in his/her defence. The board decide to exclude the student from the course being taken at the university. Such a decision might well be an example of both aspects of substantive maladministration. It is 'bad rule' because of the manifest absurdity revealed in expecting the student to prepare material pertaining to the accusations within the 48 hours allowed. It is a 'bad decision' because we can infer from it that the effect on the student concerned is so unjust

23 R Kirkham, *Parliamentary Ombudsman: Withstanding the Test of Time*, 4th Report Session 2006–2007, HC 421, Stationery Office, 2007, 7.
24 Parliamentary and Health Service Ombudsman, Annual Report 2006–07, p 15.

and disproportionate in its impact that the quality of the decision itself must be questionable. In turn, there is a suggestion that there has been maladministration in the decision-making process attributable to the application of this bad rule.

6.5 Investigatory procedures and powers established under the Parliamentary Commissioner Act 1967

The original statute establishes the MP filter system providing that every complaint investigated by the PO must be channelled through an MP[25] (this rule does not apply to NHS complaints or to other ombudsmen). Furthermore, the procedure followed is investigatory in the sense of being inquisitorial rather than adversarial. The process of investigation is designed to examine the evidence and it is conducted on behalf of the complainant by the PO. Once a case is referred to the PO she has a wide discretion in deciding whether or not to take the matter further. In order to streamline the process complaint handling is considered in three stages. There is an initial assessment to see if it falls within the jurisdiction of the office. If it does not, advice will be given on alternative remedies or courses of action that are available. The second stage involves an assessment of the complaint to consider whether an investigation should be made and the third stage is the decision and report following the completion of the investigation.

The PO is precluded from conducting an investigation where the complainant already has a remedy available (e.g., right of appeal or reference to a tribunal) which has not been exhausted.[26] However, an investigation is possible where the complainant could not reasonably have been expected to have resorted to an existing remedy of this kind.[27] This provision was included to avoid overlap with the jurisdiction of tribunals and courts.[28]

In addition, the PCA set a time limit for complaints.[29] A complaint must be made to an MP within 12 months from the time that the complainant had notice of the matter that is the subject of the complaint unless there are special circumstances that might dictate otherwise. When the office receives a complaint four questions are asked: (i) Is the complaint about a body and a matter within the ombudsman's jurisdiction?; (ii) Is there evidence of administrative failure?; (iii) Did that failure cause personal injustice which has not been put right?; (iv) Is it likely that the ombudsman's intervention will secure a worthwhile remedy?

It has already been observed that the PO has a wide discretion, within the remit, whether or not to pursue a complaint, and to select the main issues to be investigated. If she declines to do so, there is no legal means to compel the PO to investigate.[30] This was confirmed by the House of Lords in *Re Fletcher's Application*.[31]

---

25 PCA, s 5(1).

26 PCA, s 5(2).

27 PCA, s 5(3).

28 See *R v Commissioner for Local Administration, ex p Croydon London Borough Council* [1989] 1 All ER 1033.

29 PCA, s 6(3).

30 PCA, s 5(5).

31 [1970] 2 All ER 527.

Further, the PO has wide discretion as to how the investigation is conducted once it is initiated.[32] It is not possible to draw a rigid distinction between cases which are and cases which are not accepted for investigation. Rather, the approach has increasingly been to take each case as far as is necessary for a just resolution to be reached. The result is that far more cases (some hundreds per year) are now settled in this way, by informal enquiries, with the investigator concentrating on settling the dispute for the individual rather than on finding maladministration. These do not constitute full investigations in the old sense of the term. The PCA provides that the subject of the complaint must have an opportunity to comment on the allegations made by the complainant.[33] Investigations must be carried out in private and without any attendant publicity.

Once the PO has decided to investigate a matter the courts are reluctant to assess how the office exercises its discretion, or to overturn its findings. For instance, in *R v Parliamentary Commissioner for Administration, ex p Dyer*[34] there was an application to have a decision of the PO in respect of a complaint against the Department of Social Security overturned. Simon Brown LJ held that 'It does not follow that this Court will readily be persuaded to interfere with the exercise of the PO's discretion. Quite the contrary. The intended breadth of these discretions is made strikingly clear by the legislature'. The facts were that Mrs Dyer had alleged maladministration by the Department of Social Security in regard to a number of claims she had made for invalidity benefit, supplementary benefit, and income support. The PO found her complaint to be justified, and the Department made her an *ex gratia* payment of £500 to cover any costs she had incurred while making her claim. In addition, she received an apology for any injustice suffered. However, Mrs Dyer believed the PO to have been mistaken in not investigating all of her complaints, with the result that the outcome had been less satisfactory for her than it otherwise might have been. Her application for judicial review was dismissed and, given the wide discretion resting with the PO which was recognised by Simon Brown LJ, the implications were that only the most unusual circumstances would justify the court overturning a finding of the PO.

Just such a case was *R v Parliamentary Commissioner for Administration, ex p Balchin*,[35] which provides a rare example of decisions by the PO being quashed in the courts. The Department of Transport had made certain road orders that had an adverse affect on the Balchins' property by causing planning blight. When the case was referred to the PO for investigation it was contended that the Department had failed to offer correct advice on what the council's powers might be regarding a discretion they had to purchase property which was subject to planning blight. The PO found that no injustice had been suffered and he failed to press the intransigent local authority into purchasing the property which had been rendered worthless. However, it was held by Sedley J that the PO had failed to recognise the defective guidance/advice by the local authority. This advice was a relevant consideration which led to maladministration, and, in consequence, the PO had not properly exercised his jurisdiction. The matter was referred back to the ombudsman to find

---

32 PCA, s 7(2).
33 PCA, s 7(1).
34 [1994] 1 All ER 375.
35 [1998] 1 PLR 1.

(or not) maladministration on the facts. Unprecedentedly, the PO's fresh (second) determination of the Balchins' case, following the 1997 judgment of the court, was also overturned in the High Court by Dyson J in *R v Parliamentary Commissioner for Administration, ex p Balchin (No 2)*,[36] on the basis that the ombudsman's reasoning in arriving at his decision was flawed. The issue was later resolved amicably when Mr and Mrs Balchin were awarded £200,000 compensation, with the Department of Transport and Norfolk County Council each contributing half of this sum.

In practice then, the PO not only determines the procedure to be followed, but may also be personally involved in the conduct of the investigation. The staff representing the PO or in some cases the PO herself gains access to the material relating to the complaint and, if necessary, interviews the officials concerned. In comparison with MPs operating individually or collectively through the select committee system, the PO can be far more effective in 'looking behind the scenes' within a government department. The approach is inquisitorial and often involves looking into the operating practices of the department or administrative authority concerned. These enhanced investigatory powers have important implications. It means that accountability is extended, since the PO may not be satisfied with an answer provided by civil servants on behalf of the minister, as would normally be the case with an MP putting down a parliamentary question, or by a refusal of witnesses to respond to the questioning of a select committee. However, there is a degree of similarity with the select committee system in the capacity under section 8 to call for written and oral evidence and to examine departmental files pertinent to the case. Indeed, the PO regards one of her objectives as being akin to an external audit of organisations. Further, wilful obstruction of the PO is punishable in an equivalent way to contempt proceedings in the courts,[37] while the PO's reports are protected by absolute privilege.[38] Ministers are not in a position to veto investigations, nor can they or their officials hide behind public interest immunity. In fact, the PO has the power to call for information and documents from anyone, including ministers, except where they relate to the proceedings of the cabinet or its committees, as certified by the Secretary of the Cabinet with the approval of the Prime Minister.[39]

After a complaint has been investigated, a report is normally sent to the MP and to the head of the department/administrative body for comment.[40] In the vast majority of cases this is the end of the matter, because the complainant will obtain a satisfactory resolution of the issue. In the most common concerns relating to tax and social security there will simply be a refund, back payment of benefit, repayment of the claimant's costs, or, where appropriate, compensation may be forthcoming. However, if following the submission of the report, the PO believes that the injustice caused by maladministration has not been or will not be remedied, she has the power to lay a special report on the case before both Houses of Parliament for their consideration,[41] as distinguished from the annual report or

---

36 [2000] 2 LGLR 87.
37 PCA, s 9(1).
38 PCA, s 10(5).
39 PCA, s 8(4).
40 PCA, s 10(1) and (2).
41 PCA, s 10(3).

individual reports submitted to MPs (see Court Line case, the Channel Tunnel case, and the Pensions Promise case, all discussed later).

The PO may find maladministration and make recommendations, including the payment of financial compensation. However, the PO has no direct legal powers to compel public bodies to act in accordance with these recommendations. The reports compiled by the PO can be very effective in precipitating remedial action which may go beyond the individual complaint. For instance, officials in the Ministry of Agriculture and Fisheries were found to have mishandled numerous claims for compensation from farmers whose poultry stocks were compulsorily slaughtered.[42] Another case involved a couple who had received refunds of national insurance contributions, but without interest. The Contributions Agency agreed to pay 12 months' interest on the amounts refunded, and to examine a further 6,500 such cases with a view to extending the same treatment to others in the same situations.[43] After another prominent investigation the PO found serious maladministration in the Department of Social Security and the Benefits Agency regarding incomplete and misleading information concerning the rights of widows and widowers. This was in connection with prospective changes in the State Earnings-Related Pension Scheme (SERPS). Subsequently, the government set up a scheme to provide for those affected, and announced that certain persons would not now be affected at all by the changes.[44] In this instance the PO issued a further report welcoming the government's proposals as providing a 'global solution' to the problem of providing redress for past maladministration.[45] After a serious robbery causing extensive injuries the Criminal Injuries Compensation Authority took more than five years to act on evidence that the claimant would not be able to work again and would need special care. It was found that this delay had caused distress, frustration, and inconvenience. As well as the award for £500,000 in line with the PO's recommendations, the authority apologised and awarded a further £80,000 for poor complaint handling.[46]

In discussing the evolving role of the PO a distinction is made between the original conception of the role as a 'fire fighter' and a shift towards becoming a 'fire watcher'. As originally conceived, the 'fire fighter' ombudsman has the power and authority to deal with individual complaints as an adjunct to Parliament.[47] Relatively minor investigations as well as in-depth inquiries are conducted by an experienced investigator with the authority to search behind the scenes. The prospect of such thorough investigation acts as a deterrent thus minimising further maladministration. Despite not having the power to legally enforce a remedy where maladministration is identified, the ombudsman can, however, make recommendations. Indeed, the effectiveness of the office is because such recommendations are likely to have political implications and carry with them considerable

---

42 Fourth Report: Compensation to Farmers for Slaughtered Poultry, HC 519, 1992–93.

43 Annual Report, 5th Report, HC 845, 1997–98.

44 Annual Report to Parliament, HC 305, 1999–2000.

45 State earnings-related pension scheme (SERPS) inheritance provisions: redress for maladministration, 2nd report 2000–2001, HC 271.

46 Annual Report 2010–11, HC 1404, p 19.

47 C Harlow and R Rawlings, *Law and Administration* (Cambridge: Cambridge University Press, 2009), ch 12.

moral force.[48] In fact, it is established practice for officials to take remedial action in line with the findings of the PO to avoid the prospect of exposure to high profile criticism.[49] By way of contrast the 'fire watching' role goes further and would suggest a decisive change of emphasis towards own initiative investigations allowing the PO to oversee public bodies, identifying impending systemic problems that may have a wide impact on the public.[50]

The cases and the examples discussed at 6.10 illustrate not only the role of the Office in correcting injustice due to maladministration, but also the ombudsman's role in securing high administrative standards. Currently, there is a renewed commitment to an improved and more 'joined up' system of complaint handling under a five-year strategic plan running from 2013/14 to 2017/18, but no clear reference to assuming a wider role in seeking out systemic failings.[51]

6.6 Limits to the PO's jurisdiction

We have already noted that the PO (and this applies to most other ombudsmen) will not investigate a matter unless existing remedial mechanisms have already been exhausted. It has already been observed that the PCA provides that the Commissioner should not investigate cases where a remedy exists in a court of law or before a tribunal. An exception is when the PO is satisfied that it is unreasonable to expect the complainant to have resorted to a legal remedy. In *ex p Croydon London Borough Council*[52] the court found that the Local Commissioner had acted *ultra vires* (beyond the power) in investigating a matter, since the complainants ought to have pursued their grievance through the relevant tribunal because it was more appropriate in the circumstances. Moreover, the Local Commissioner could not investigate a matter which had been decided upon by the courts. A party who has already obtained a judicial review should not seek to avail him- or herself of an alternative right of complaint to an ombudsman.[53] However, despite the distinction made in the statute, there is sometimes an element of duplication with the courts. The case of *Congreve v Home Office*[54] is a very good example of such overlap. After the PO had looked into the matter and condemned the action in a special report, a complainant then had recourse to litigation in the courts. *R v Secretary of State for the Environment, ex p Ostler*[55] illustrates the opposite scenario, where the

---

48 M Elliott, 'Ombudsmen, Tribunals, Inquiries: Re-fashioning Accountability beyond the Courts' in N Bamforth and P Leyland (eds), *Accountability in the Contemporary Constitution* (Oxford: Oxford University Press, 2013), 246ff.

49 But see, by way of an exception, *R (on the application of Bradley) v Secretary of State for Works and Pensions* [2008] EWCA 36, discussed later.

50 Another possibility is the trend, as seen in Scotland, towards a one-stop shop to deal with grievances. See C Gill, 'The Evolving Role of the Ombudsman: A Conceptual and Constitutional Analysis of the "Scottish Solution" to Administrative Justice' [2014] *Public Law* 662.

51 Annual Report and Accounts 2014–15, 6, 7.

52 [1989] 1 All ER 1033.

53 See *R v Commissioner for Local Administration, ex p H (a Minor)*, *The Times*, 8 January, 1999.

54 [1976] 1 All ER 697. For further discussion of this case see 11.3.

55 [1977] QB 122.

applicants lost in court because they had exceeded the statutory time limit, but were able to gain some compensation from the PO at a later date.

6.6.1 Schedule 2

The PCA specifies under Schedule 2[56] and Schedule 3 what is included in and what is excluded from the Commissioner's jurisdiction. This list can be updated, because departments are both created and abolished with considerable frequency.[57] The Schedules cover most government and quasi-government bodies, as listed below. It is worth noting that this jurisdiction is similar to that of MPs in holding such bodies to account, in respect of their administrative function, through the convention of ministerial responsibility.

Schedule 2 originally embraced all the major government departments, and some other bodies subject to investigation. However, the 1987 Act, Schedule 1, amended and extended the remit of the ombudsmen from fewer than 50 to more than 100 departments and non-departmental government bodies, although not all non-departmental government bodies, or 'quangos' as they are frequently called, are covered (e.g., those coming under the control of the Council of Tribunals—see chapter 7). In 1999 there was another considerable expansion in the number of executive non-departmental public bodies and advisory non-departmental public bodies brought within the ombudsman's remit.[58] In 2010, nearly 400 governmental departments and other governmental bodies fell under the ombudsman's jurisdiction, but with the abolition and merger of quangos being undertaken during 2010–2012 the jurisdictional boundaries will be modified.

Quasi-governmental bodies listed include, among others: the Royal Mint; the Arts Council; the Charity Commission; the Crown Estate Office; the Horse Race Betting Levy Board; the Human Fertilisation and Embryology Authority; the British Library; the Equality and Human Rights Commission; the Criminal Injuries Compensation Board; the Industrial Training Boards; the Rail Regulator; the English Tourist Board; and the Director General of Water Services. Further additions included the Biotechnology and Biological Sciences Research Council and the Food Standards Agency. The PCA restricts bodies to government departments, bodies acting on behalf of the Crown, those established by the prerogative, or bodies which are at least 50 per cent financed by Parliament.

The Health Service Commissioners Act 1993 and the Deregulation and Contracting Out Act 1994 also extended the remit of the PO and the local ombudsman's jurisdiction to functions of central and local government which have been contracted out. The health ombudsman can investigate such services created as a result of the introduction of the internal market in the NHS.[59] This role continued under the Labour Government's measures further reforming the NHS. Note, too, that the courts have a similar public law function, albeit that the contracting-out of governmental functions apparently limits the reach of public law principles (see judicial review in chapters 8 *et seq.*).

---

56 See also Sch 1 to the Parliamentary and Health Service Commissioners Act 1987 Act.
57 The list in Sch 2 may be amended by Order in Council under s 4.
58 The Parliamentary Commissioner Order 1999 (SI 1999/277).
59 See the National Health Service and Community Care Act 1990, s 7(2).

6.6.2 **Schedule 3**

The PO is excluded under the PCA from investigating certain areas.[60] For example, matters relating to foreign relations or dealings with the UK by other governments and international organisations; action taken by officials outside the UK; action taken in connection with territory overseas forming part of HM dominions; investigation of crime; the commencement or conduct of criminal or civil proceedings before any UK court; and the exercise of the prerogative of mercy. Some of these exemptions might be expected, but the exclusions concerning commercial contracts between central government and the private sector and in respect of appointments, removals, and personnel matters relating to the civil service have been repeatedly criticised by the PO, academics, and other organisations.[61] This is a cause of concern since government departments frequently use their contractual powers to further what are, in essence, political (policy) goals and these powers are placed outside the remit of the PO. Despite having the power to revoke any of these restrictions under section 4 of the 1967 Act, government has continued to resist change in this area.

6.7 **Open government and freedom of information**

Prior to the enactment of the Freedom of Information Act 2000 disclosure of official information relied on a non-statutory Code of Practice on access to government information. The provisions were limited and unenforceable at law, but the PO was responsible for overseeing the code and conducted investigations into complaints, following referral by an MP, that the code has not been honoured. Indeed, the ombudsman found Whitehall in breach of its own Open Government code for the first time in 1994. The PO's 2003–04 report states that:

Our aim is to ensure that nobody who has been refused information to which they think they have a right is denied the opportunity to have their complaint considered by an appropriate body. We will continue to monitor adherence to the requirements of the Memorandum of Understanding (governing the release of official information) until January 2005.

The coming into force of the Freedom of Information Act 2000 (FOI) on 1 January 2005 opened a new chapter in this area for the PO. In particular, bodies within the jurisdiction of the Office were subject to the provisions of the Act (and its exclusions) which meant that the ombudsman ceased to investigate complaints which were wholly or mainly about access to official information. This task has passed to the Information Commissioner, established under the legislation (section 18), who has the power to investigate any complaint that an authority is not complying with the Act.[62] In regard to the PO there is an FOI publication scheme available on the website, but an emerging problem for the office is the burden of responding to more than 250 requests for information a year under the FOI from members of the public and from complainants.

---

60 PCA, s 5(3) and Sch 3.

61 See, e.g., the Annual Report for 1988, HC 301, the Select Committee (Fourth Report for 1979/80, 'The Jurisdiction of the Parliamentary Commissioner', HC 593).

62 See also Pts IV and V of the FOI Act 2000.

6.8 **The PO's workload**

The statistics in relation to complaints in 2015—available on the PO's website—provide us with an overall breakdown of the caseload and illustrate the general throughput of cases.[63]

During the year 2014–15 the PO handled 29,000 cases of which 6,815 were assessed for investigation under stage 2 of the procedure and 5,058 were resolved without needing further investigation.[64] Of those assessed for in-depth investigation, 5,531 related to the NHS in England and 1,271 concerned government departments and other public bodies. In other words, about 80 per cent of complaints concerned the Health Service where no MP filter applies, while the remainder of central government departments and organisations only accounted for around 20 per cent of cases investigated. More generally, the total of complaints to the PO has steadily increased over the years. In terms of first enquiries an examination of these figures highlights the fact that a small number of departments tend to generate a high proportion of complaints but it will be apparent that the cases assessed for investigation under stage 2 of the procedure, indicated by the second figure in brackets, is very much smaller. The largest number of enquiries received in 2014–15 relating to government departments (excluding the NHS) were: Department for Works and Pensions, 2,162 (201); Ministry of Justice, 1450 (467); HM Revenue and Customs, 1000 (163); Home Office, 851 (145); Department for Business, Innovation and Skills 403 (38); and the Department of Transport, 383 (57). The total number of cases reaching stage 3 across Whitehall, including the NHS, and taken forward for full investigation in 2014–15, was 4,280. This reflects a lowering of the threshold to include complaints where there is an indication that things have gone wrong and not been corrected rather than assessing whether the complaint is likely to be upheld. A change in approach has resulted in a very substantial increase from 2011–12 where the figure investigated was only 421. In investigations completed in 2014–15 the complaint was partly or fully upheld in 1,521 instances (37%) and not upheld in 2,279 instances (55%). A further 8 per cent were either resolved prior to investigation or later withdrawn.

In common with previous years, a significant number of complaints were rejected for being 'not properly made'. Most frequently the rejection of complaints is because existing procedures have not been used, no attempt has been made to resolve the complaint, the complaint has not been referred through the MP filter, or redress of some kind has already been offered.

It is not altogether surprising that the number of cases accepted for investigation tended to decline until recently since the jurisdiction of the PO has been partly taken over by other specialist ombudsmen, including those in Scotland, Wales, and Northern Ireland post devolution (in fact, Northern Ireland has had its own equivalent of the PO since 1969—see further 6.10). For example, there were 2,567 cases handled in 2002–03 and 2,319 cases in 2003–04. Also, it is worth noting that other ombudsmen from around the world appear to have a much greater case load. The French *défenseur des droits* and his team of deputies specialising in children's

---

63 Complaints about UK government departments and agencies, and some UK public organisations 2014–15, 31.

64 Annual Report and Accounts 2014–15.

rights, equality rights, and security ethics, received a total of 85,000 cases and, of this total, 72,000 complaints were investigated in 2014.[65] Complaints may now be made online but the *défenseur* shares a form of indirect access through 397 representatives spread thoughout France and its overseas dependencies. The figures are not strictly comparable, as the *défenseur des droits* enjoys a wider jurisdiction than the PO.[66] Nevertheless, even bearing this qualification in mind, if we take any year's statistics for the PO there is a relatively small throughput of completed cases.

Another obvious reason for this modest case load is that the PO performs a more in depth investigatory function which is ancillary to the complaint-handling role of MPs. To many MPs who are accustomed to receiving routine complaints, the utility of the ombudsman is perceived as being limited. This is because MPs working in a political climate will often wish to see rapid results when a matter is raised. Although the average turnaround time for cases investigated by the PO has been reduced to well under a year, the delay in achieving a result may still be regarded as too long with political events rapidly unfolding, for example, in the run up to elections, etc. Further, MPs are able to directly resolve the vast majority of complaints received by them via a parliamentary question, a letter to a minister, or an unofficial approach to the minister. As well as the obvious kudos derived from solving such problems personally, the majority of backbench MPs consider complaint handling as perhaps *the* central part of their job. The reports have drawn particular attention to cases where departments have given confusing guidance or inadequate information, where delays have caused injustice, and where there have been persistent errors and poor complaint handling.

6.9 Investigations by the PO

In regard to citizens wishing to use the ombudsman, there has been an increasing emphasis by the PO on customer service standards. An acknowledgment to inquiries in all cases is sent out between one and two working days, and an initial response to the complainant is made within five working days, but investigations tend to be more protracted. On average, they take several months and sometimes up to a year to complete. This throughput rate can be compared with the much more rapid turnaround time averaging four months which applies to the French *défenseur*. The term 'Rolls Royce method' has been used to denote the thoroughness and professionalism with which investigations have been conducted. But, as was noted earlier, the time taken to complete an investigation has been a major reason why some MPs have been reluctant to refer cases to the PO as they require a much more rapid response which might be achieved by writing directly to the minister or by an informal approach. A new 'fast track' procedure for complaints was introduced in 1996/97. For complaints falling within the PO's jurisdiction the 2003–04 Annual Report notes that the aim is to lodge a statement of complaint with the relevant body within five weeks. This target had only been reached in 53 per cent of

65 Rapport annuel d'activité 2014, published 27 January 2014.
66 <http://www.defenseurdesdroits.fr/en>.

cases, but in 96 per cent of cases a statement of complaint had been lodged within 13 weeks. The aim was to reach a conclusion within 41 weeks but the average time from beginning to final resolution was 48 weeks.

To deal with the workload of the office the PO is assisted by 200 staff, about half of whom are investigators. A substantial number are drawn from the civil service. Much of the time is spent on screening and investigation of complaints, after an initial scrutiny to check that a complaint was within the jurisdiction of the office. Following a full statutory investigation, the case worker will write a report. There are basically two kinds of report: the first is sent to the referring MP and the body concerned at the conclusion of an inquiry; the second is the PO's Annual Report to Parliament at the end of each year's work. (There are other kinds of report made to the Select Committee on Public Administration and Constitutional Affairs, but these are not discussed here.) We have already alluded to the fact that, by comparison to MPs, the PO is equipped with an extra dimension when conducting an inquiry. In the words of Ann Abrahams, the former PO, 'It is after all one of the unique selling points of any Ombudsman scheme, that unlike the courts, it has the inbuilt ability to get beyond the individual case, to spot patterns of deficiency and to make recommendations for systemic change that go much further than redressing the failings of a single individual's adverse encounter with an organ of the state'.[67]

The next question is: what does this extra dimension really amount to? To attempt to answer this question, we need to assess the impact of the office by referring to a number of case studies, some of which blur the distinction between procedural maladministration and policy issues. These reveal not only how the PO fulfils the task, but also how the findings contained in the reports are received by the relevant authorities, including MPs, the bodies under investigation, and ministers. Once again, it should be noted that if the PO finds maladministration she cannot order the department to quash its decision, rescind or alter its decision, or to halt, delay, or speed up action, or pay compensation. On the face of it, the reports would appear to be the extent of the power. But despite these apparent limitations, it is generally true to say that government departments have been willing to make reasonable amends by changing decisions or by paying compensation.

6.9.1 Examples of completed investigations

6.9.1.1 The Fleet Street Casuals case 1982

This case illustrates well the discretion of the PO in investigating a complaint. Here, the facts concerned the evasion of tax arrangements. The PO, Sir Cecil Clothier, declined to proceed on the ground that he would be drawn into political controversy. Further, he considered that the allegations of injustice in the administration of the tax system affected all taxpayers and, in a sense, the whole nation. This made it a subject outside his remit, confined as the office is to investigating individual cases. (Litigation was the outcome: see *Inland Revenue Commissioners v National Federation of Self-Employed and Small Businesses Ltd.*)[68] It is worth remembering that this right

---

67 Abraham, n 12.
68 [1982] AC 617. See the discussion of *locus standi* in 8.10.1.

to refuse to investigate matters can be exercised without having to give any reasons. This discretion has been questioned.

6.9.1.2 **The Sachsenhausen case 1967**

The Sachsenhausen case in the first year of its operation was the first occasion on which the office of the PO found departmental errors of a serious nature. It involved 12 victims of Nazi persecution during the Second World War who had been denied compensation by the Foreign Office. They fell outside rules for distribution of the moneys concerned which had been drawn up by a previous Foreign Secretary in 1964. After parliamentary pressure by MPs had failed to reverse the decision the matter was referred to the PO. It was found by the PO in a report (HC 54) that the Foreign Office was seriously in error. In particular, there were many defects in administrative procedure affecting the way the Foreign Office reached its decision and subsequently defended it. In turn, this had damaged the reputation of these claimants. The Foreign Secretary not only put up a vigorous defence of his officials but also contended that the principle of individual ministerial responsibility was being eroded by this process. Despite this, compensation was paid to the victims following the publication of the PO's report.

This payment of compensation by the government after initial refusal has almost obtained the status of a constitutional convention, as we will see from the case discussed below. The reaction of MPs on the Select Committee to this investigation was highly significant. In their report for 1967–68 (HC 258, paras 13–16) they expressed dissatisfaction at the evidence received from the Foreign Office and stressed that ministers were meant to be subject to examination and potential criticism. The final issue considered by the Select Committee concerned the reluctance of the PO to consider the 'merits' of the rules under which the compensation had been denied. They thought that he had interpreted his authority too narrowly in regard to this question. See 6.4.1 on this aspect.

6.9.1.3 **The Barlow Clowes affair 1989**

The background

This case is worthy of special consideration because it involved the then PO, Sir Anthony Barrowclough, in what he described as 'by far the longest and most detailed [report] produced by the office'.[69] During the course of this investigation he found substantial maladministration in five crucial areas, and these findings were in turn accorded the most publicity that the PO has ever received for any single report in its history. The scale of concern is indicated in that around a quarter of the total membership of the House of Commons had received complaints from 18,000 savers affected by the collapse of Barlow Clowes. Eventually, the matter was formally referred to the PO by 12 MPs. Of particular interest for us is the outcome, since this was an investigation that provided a remedy for the many victims of the collapse. Despite the fact that the government categorically rejected all the most serious criticisms by the Commissioner of the conduct of the Department of Trade and Industry, it awarded *ex gratia* payments to investors of the order of some £150 million, compensating them for 90 per cent of their losses. This represents the

---

69 Annual Report for 1989, HC 353, para 64.

largest financial award for investors ever to flow from an inquiry, although 60 to 70 of them had died, some in destitution, before the rescue plan was announced.

The facts

The Barlow Clowes companies collapsed in 1988, leaving in their wake much injustice and considerable financial loss to, amongst others, elderly savers who depended on investment funds for their retirement. Many had been attracted by what they had thought were government stocks and, therefore, a safe as well as tax-efficient form of investment. Why was this allowed to happen? Were the authorities in error?

Barlow Clowes had been set up in the mid-1970s. The Department of Trade and Industry (DTI) was required by the Prevention of Fraud (Investments) Act 1958 to perform a regulatory function in regard to such companies, which involved surveillance and issuing licences. Despite this fact, under its discretionary powers, the Department had allowed Barlow Clowes to operate for 10 years without such a licence. The existence of a separate Jersey partnership of Barlow Clowes, unknown to the Department, was to prove of great significance in the practice of fraud over the coming decade.

In 1984 Barlow Clowes applied for a licence, at which point the Department sought to bring the operations of the company within the regulatory framework provided for by the 1958 Act. Accordingly, the company received a licence in 1985 which was renewed for the next two years. Following the expression of considerable disquiet about financial irregularities, including alleged fraud, over the period from 1987, inspectors were appointed in late 1987 under the powers granted by the Financial Services Act 1986 to investigate the affairs of the company. This finally went into compulsory liquidation in 1988, shut down under the City of London's new regulatory system brought into existence by the 1986 Act. Further widespread anger following the collapse of Barlow Clowes led to a fact-finding inquiry being set up by the Secretary of State under Sir Godfray Le Quesne QC. His report was published in October 1988. Meanwhile, investors were claiming that their loss was at least partly due to departmental maladministration. They argued that if the Department had exercised its supervisory function adequately they would not have believed that they were investing in government stocks. Thus many investors would not have become involved in the first place, while others would have been alerted to the risks at an earlier stage and not have suffered losses on the scale that eventually occurred.

Following the publication of the Le Quesne report the matter was referred to the PO who agreed to conduct a formal investigation. This commenced in November of the same year, and he reported his findings 13 months later in December 1989. Sir Anthony Barrowclough commented that there had clearly been maladministration by the Department in its dealings with Barlow Clowes in five main areas.

The findings of the report

The PO's findings summarised below were contained in a 120,000 word report.[70]

    (a) In 1975–76 the DTI had given the wrong advice to Barlow Clowes which amounted to maladministration.

---

70 First Report—Session 1989–90 HC 76 and at para 64 of the Annual Report for 1989/1990, HC 353.

(b) The Department in late 1984 ought to have checked information already in its possession against that proffered to it by Barlow Clowes. Such action would have revealed irregularities and also brought to light the Jersey partnership. This turned out to be a centrally important error, in that the existence of a separate Jersey based operation from 1978 provided substantial latitude for financial abuse and fraud.

(c) The DTI granted a licence in March 1985, mainly to cover itself for allowing an unlicensed operation before that date. However, in taking this decision to legitimise the Barlow Clowes operation not enough attention was paid to the interests of investors.

(d) The Commissioner criticised the unsatisfactory nature of the auditing work carried out on behalf of the DTI on the group's accounts. This was not capable of providing the degree of reassurance necessary in respect of the genuine concerns raised.

(e) Lastly, adverse reference was made to delays incurred by the Department between July and October 1987 in acting and dealing with possible fraud. Its reaction in responding to worrying information about the company, and further errors in correctly identifying the options open to the Department, were unsatisfactory. At this stage had the viability of the schemes offered by Barlow Clowes been considered adequately in all probability licences would not have been granted and the company would have been wound up with losses being capped at £31 million.

The implications of Barlow Clowes

Having found maladministration, the PO submitted his findings to the Department in the normal way before publishing his wide-ranging report. The government strongly disagreed with his conclusions, and would later set out its views concurrently with the publication of the report (this illustrates the problems which can arise in making a distinction between maladministration and questions of merit). Nevertheless, the minister conceded, in the light of the considerable hardship suffered by the investors, generous *ex gratia* payments to investors. Despite disagreement with his findings, the PO took some satisfaction in the knowledge that the government was prepared to provide a remedy for injustice through maladministration. In 1995 the full DTI Inquiry was published, supporting the PO's findings.

The Barlow Clowes report could be said to demonstrate the potential of the office. It involved just the kind of detailed scrutiny, access to persons and papers which fully utilised the resources available to the PO. Indeed, it was a more formidable investigative exercise than MPs or the media acting alone could have brought to bear. And, as we have seen, it did bring substantial relief in the form of compensation to the complainants. But the central question remains: did it set any worthwhile precedent for the future? This is not necessarily the case, because, although Barlow Clowes could be regarded as the high watermark of the Commissioner's work since 1967, it guarantees no such resolution in any future case. In short, it is an individual remedy for an individual grievance.

6.9.1.4 **The Channel Tunnel rail link case 1996**

In 1993, the PO received the first complaints alleging exceptional hardship from three MPs holding constituencies in Kent. Home owners living next to the proposed route of the Channel Tunnel rail link were prevented from selling their properties because of planning blight. The PO accepted five complaints as warranting investigation, but he treated these as representative 'specimen' examples within the context of the Department of Transport's overall handling of the project. This was the largest single investigation during Sir William Reid's tenure of the office, one needing a great deal of time and involving the examination of thousands of documents. Following a finding of maladministration because the Department of Transport had taken no steps to provide redress for persons suffering considerable (or even extreme) hardship not covered by existing compensation schemes, the Department rejected the finding.[71] The PO then went on to lay a Special Report before Parliament, acting under section 10(3) of the 1967 Act for only the second time in the history of the body. This strong, assertive response by the PO was backed by the Select Committee, but the Department remained inflexible. Eventually it examined the possibility of compensation for those most seriously affected by the scheme, but without any direct admission of fault or liability. Following the 1997 General Election, the Labour Government offered up to £10,000 in compensation payment. The scheme was advertised and applications for compensations invited.[72]

6.9.1.5 Occupational Pension Cases and Debt of Honour Report

A number of pensioners claimed that they had lost pension rights as a result of inaccurate and misleading information supplied by the Department of Works and Pensions. A leaflet provided by the department had failed to inform workers that the minimum funding requirement for pension schemes set by the government meant that those who had yet to retire stood only a 50 per cent chance of receiving a full pension when the scheme came to an end. Many who reached retirement between 1997 and 2005 received less than half their expected pension, and in some cases nothing at all. It was recognised that between 75,000 and 125,000 people might be entitled to compensation which was likely to amount to at least £3.7 billion. In this instance despite a meticulous report which detailed departmental errors and pointed out the considerable injustice suffered as a result, the minister flatly rejected the PO's findings of maladministration and acted in defiance of the government's own rule book, *Government Accounting* which states (in paragraph 5 of Annex 18.1): 'In the light of the investigation of a case, the Parliamentary Ombudsman will decide whether complainants have suffered injustice because of maladministration; and whether any injustice has been, or will be, remedied. The Parliamentary Ombudsman's findings on maladministration are final; there is no established avenue of appeal.'

This unprecedented action by government first prompted the PO to use powers under section 10(3) of the Parliamentary Commissioner Act 1967 to place a report before Parliament and to raise the issue before the Public Administration Select Committee given the considerable constitutional implications.[73] Second, the courts were used to pursue the matter further. A group of pensioners challenged the decision to reject these findings on the grounds that the minister had

---

71 See the Twelfth Report of the PO, HC 193, 1994–1995.

72 For a good overview and analysis of this investigation, see D Longley and R James, *Administrative Justice: Central Issues in UK and European Administrative Law* (London: Cavendish, 1999), 51ff.

73 See Parliamentary and Health Service Ombudsman Annual Report 2005–2006, HC 1363, p 12.

acted unlawfully in doing so. In *R (on the application of Bradley) v Secretary of State for Works and Pensions*[74] (discussed earlier) it was held that the minister can refuse to accept the PO's findings if he has reasons for doing so, but the quashing order invalidating the decision to reject the PO's finding of maladministration was upheld by the Court of Appeal. This was in respect to inaccurate information in a departmental leaflet which gave the clear impression that pension scheme members could be reassured that their pensions would be safe whatever happens. The struggle to obtain compensation continued after the court cases. The PO reported in 2010 that once again: 'We took the exceptional step of laying before Parliament a special report to highlight that the then (Labour) government's proposals for an ex gratia scheme were inadequate as a means to remedy the injustice previously identified.'[75] The Labour Government accepted further findings of maladministration but only proposed a limited compensation scheme. Subsequently, the Coalition Government agreed to implement the ombudsman's recommendations to make fair and equitable payments to the Equitable Life policy holders. The Equitable Life (Payments) Act 2010 set aside £1.5 billion for the purpose of paying compensation. Although an improvement on the previous responses by government, this scheme stopped short of meeting compensation claims in full.[76]

6.10 **The complaints industry: a proliferation of ombudsmen**

Since the introduction of the PO in 1967 not only has the administrative state increased in complexity but there has been far reaching constitutional reform which has changed the constitutional landscape significantly. The PO was soon accepted as a useful addition to the grievance chain but the original legislation prevented the PO from inquiring into important areas, where comparable issues of maladministration aroused considerable public concern. The response has been to extend the remit of the PO and to introduce additional ombudsmen. The National Health Service Reorganisation Acts 1972 and 1973 (consolidated under Health Service Commissioners Act 1993) brought the Health Service within the scope of the existing ombudsman system (with a separate provision for Scotland) and the remit was extended to include clinical judgement of health professionals. The PO holds all these offices, but the Health Service aspect of her work has a different procedure that dispenses with the MP filter and Health Service complaints are reported to Parliament as a separate area. The Local Government Act 1974 set up a local government ombudsman (LGO). More recent additions to public sector ombudsmanry have been a Courts and Legal Services Ombudsman (1990), Pensions Ombudsman (1991), a Prison and Probation Service Ombudsman (1994), Financial Ombudsman Service (2001) working under the Financial Services and Markets Act 1999, and a Judicial Appointments Ombudsman created under section 61 and Schedule 13 of the Constitutional Reform Act 2005. Finally, there is a European Ombudsman within the EU to deal with complaints of maladministration concerning the EU

---

74 [2008] EWCA 36.
75 Annual Report 'Making an Impact' 2009–2010, HC 274, p 25.
76 Annual Report 'A service for everyone' 2010–2011, HC 1404, p 23.

institutions.[77] The burgeoning of the ombudsman principle into so many distinct jurisdictions means that a citizen seeking a remedy is faced with a remedial system of bewildering complexity rather than being able to depend on a single system. It has been suggested that one public sector ombudsman would not function as a lone mechanism but as a part of wider system for securing redress and promoting good administration.

All these ombudsmen act as complaint handlers and, like the PO, they all offer a free service which can be directly accessed by complainants, but otherwise they only share basic characteristics as investigators called upon after internal complaints mechanisms have been exhausted. In other respects their powers and style of operation vary markedly. The Financial Ombudsman Service (FOS) has been conceived as part of a statutory regime to regulate the banking, insurance and pensions sector, elements of which had been strongly criticised for mis-selling their products during the 1990s. The service dealt with 518,778 cases in the year 2013/14[78] many of which were settled informally, but under section 229 of the Financial Services and Markets Act 2000 the FOS is empowered to make a mandatory award compensation for financial loss or damage to a complainant against a private company of up to £150,000. Further, if any decision of this ombudsman is accepted by the parties to a dispute, it is legally binding on them.

We might contrast the relatively weak position in terms of formal powers of the Local Government Ombudsman who is also able to make recommendations. The local government ombudsman for England is based in London, Coventry, and York. The service employs 168 members of staff. Most local authorities investigated follow the LGO's recommendations, but non-compliance remains a problem with a hard core of recalcitrant authorities.[79] Another reason why the LGO service has somewhat less authority than the PO is because the system lacks a direct link into Parliament supported by a parliamentary select committee. The nature of the case work of the LGO provides an indication of why compliance is not always easy. For example, a substantial proportion of investigations concern entitlement to allocation of council housing. Local authorities have limited stocks of social housing. Even if a complainant is able to establish that she is entitled to accommodation, the authority may not have suitable housing stock available. The issue of the levels of compensation is also controversial when it comes to hard-pressed public authorities with finite budgets. Providing compensation for the complainant could have the effect of depriving others of a particular service. Investigations into systemic defects involving a crop of similar cases can have the most beneficial impact on the functioning of local authorities and in recent years there has been a trend towards conducting joint investigations with the PO. Direct access and the increased use of the website of the LGO that guides the citizen through the process of making a complaint has resulted in a steady volume of cases in recent years 11,094 in 2014–15 compared to 11,725 in 2013–14, with 4,780 passed on for investigation to be considered in more detail.[80]

---

77 See Art 228 TFEU and C Harlow and R Rawlings, *Process and Procedure in EU Administration* (Oxford: Hart Publishing, 2014), ch 3.

78 Financial Ombudsman Service: Annual report and account for the year ended 31 March 2014, HC 477.

79 M Seneviratne, Ombudsman: *Public Services and Administrative Justice* (London: Butterworths, 2002), 217ff.

80 Local Government Ombudsman: Annual Report and Accounts 2014–15, Quality Counts, Commission for Local Administration in England, 2015.

The Prison and Probation Service Ombudsman (PPO) reinforces the view that to a significant extent the nature of each office and the style of investigations and reporting varies with each ombudsman. This ombudsman originated from recommendations in the Woolf Report for an independent investigator to deal with complaints from prisoners.[81] The calls for an improvement in the internal grievance mechanisms came in the wake of a devastating series of riots which started in Strangeways prison. However, the PPO is not a creation of statute. The incumbent was made directly accountable to the Home Secretary, who was able to limit the ambit of his jurisdiction. The terms of reference were widened in 1997 and the office was extended further to include the probation service in 2001. However, the merits of ministerial decisions and matters of ministerial policy remain beyond PPO's remit. The PPO, who has an annual budget of £5.5 million, received 4,964 complaints in 2014–15 of which 92 per cent concerned the Prison Service.[82] As well as routine complaints, for example into the treatment of prisoners by staff, the PPO is responsible for investigating fatalities which occur in prison. In responding to complaints it may be possible to reach an informal resolution of the issues as part of a strategy of restorative justice. Alternatively, the PPO can uphold or reject a complaint and make formal recommendations which will be followed up by the office to encourage compliance. Following the departmental re-organisation in 2007, prisons and the probation service have been transferred from the Home Office to the Ministry of Justice presided over by the Lord Chancellor who is also the Secretary of State for Justice.

6.10.1 Ombudsmen and devolution

The introduction of devolution in 1998 launched a new set of governmental institutions in the form of the Scottish Parliament, Northern Ireland Assembly, and Welsh Assembly with varying degrees of law-making powers. Further, it resulted in the majority of the officials of the Scottish and Welsh offices being transferred to new departments in Scotland and Wales which reflect this conference of devolved functions. (The situation in Northern Ireland is somewhat different as officials were already mainly locally based.) Such changes also required revised arrangements for dispute resolution to mirror the redistribution of functions actuated by devolution. There is now a Scottish Public Services Ombudsman Parliamentary created under Schedules 2 and 3 of the Scottish Public Services Ombudsman Act 2002. The Public Services Ombudsman (Wales) Act 2005 has created an integrated ombudsman service for Wales (Welsh administration was very closely integrated with England prior to devolution). A Northern Ireland Ombudsman was first established in 1969. The office now combines the roles of Assembly Ombudsman and Northern Ireland Commissioner for Complaints and deals with maladministration at the hands of government departments and other public bodies, including healthcare and local authorities in Northern Ireland.[83] In each of these jurisdictions there is a 'one-stop shop' style of grievance handling in line with

---

81 Prison disturbances April 1990: report of an inquiry by the Lord Justice Woolf, (HMSO), 1991.

82 Prisons and Probation Ombudsman, Annual Report 2014–15, Cm 9127, September 2015.

83 See the Ombudsman (Northern Ireland) 1996 and the Commissioner for Complaints (Amendment) (Northern Ireland) Order 1997.

Collcutt recommendations,[84] where a principal recommendation was a unified system and for England this meant joining up the English Health Service and Local Government ombudsmen; in other words there would be a single public sector ombudsman who ranged over all policy areas. It has been suggested that in order to provide an equivalent English system to those in Scotland, Wales, and Northern Ireland there should be a one-stop local English ombudsman who would not only have a proactive remit and combine the roles of the Health Service and Local Government ombudsman but also be responsible for complaints relating to other areas of English domestic policy.[85] A further question concerns whether the PO should be integrated as part of such a reform or remain in place with jurisdiction over those matters of policy that continue to be dealt with at a national level, for example, taxation and pensions, defence, immigration, etc.[86]

6.10.2 Private sector

Although generally beyond the scope of this book, it is worth pointing out that some of the most innovative extensions of the principle have been in the private sector. These ombudsmen have normally been introduced by the industries or services themselves rather than by way of legislation, and there are now ombudsman schemes for insurance (1981), banking (1986), building societies (1986), investment (1989)—these now come under the new Financial Services Ombudsman), and corporate estate agents (1990). *R v Insurance Ombudsman Bureau, ex p Aegon Life Assurance Ltd*[87] confirmed that decisions by the insurance ombudsman were not reviewable by the Administrative Court because judicial review applied only to the public sector (see chapter 8 which discusses the 'exclusivity principle').

6.11 Citizen's Charter, Customer Service Excellence, and the quest for 'good administration'

A much more customer-focused approach to the delivery of public services has been evident in recent years. Part of the change that is involved has meant that the citizen as a customer has the right to expect not only improved levels of service, but often that a remedy of some kind should be available if the service level drops below an acceptable standard (e.g., at least an explanation or an apology from the body concerned, and in certain circumstances a right to compensation). This revised approach to the concept of public service referred to as 'Citizens Charter' originated from the government of John Major during the 1990s, but the idea has been relaunched and rebranded by the government in office on more than one occasion since 1997. For example, *Service First: The New Charter Programme* (1998), which was run initially from the Office of Public Service Reform inside the PM's office at 10 Downing Street and later as Customer Service Excellence run from the

---

84 See *Review of the Public Sector Ombudsmen in England* (2000).
85 Gill, n 50, 680.
86 M Elliot, 'Asymmetric Devolution and Ombudsman Reform in England' [2006] *Public Law* 84, 101.
87 [1994] CLC 88.

Cabinet Office. The aim of embedding national standards of excellence in public service has been followed up by the PO.

6.11.1 Principles of good administration

The idea that public services should set out in advance high performance standards to be expected and then strive to achieve these standards has been introduced widely throughout the public sector. The present ombudsman has taken this approach a stage further by developing: 'broad statements of what . . . public bodies within jurisdiction should be doing to deliver good administration and customer service'. Principles of Good Administration, Principles of Good Complaint Handling, and Principle for Remedy have been developed as a template for public bodies in their dealings with citizens. The principles of good administration are reproduced below. This list constitutes a comprehensive set of positive values or principles that relate to the practical task of policy implementation in many different contexts which ought to be generally applied.[88]

Good administration by a public body means:

1. *Getting it right*
   Acting in accordance with the law and with due regard for the rights of those concerned.
   Acting in accordance with the public body's policy and guidance (published or internal).
   Taking proper account of established good practice.
   Providing effective services, using appropriately trained and competent staff.
   Taking reasonable decisions, based on all relevant considerations.

2. *Being customer focused*
   Ensuring people can access services easily.
   Informing customers what they can expect and what the public body expects of them.
   Keeping to its commitments, including any published service standards.
   Dealing with people helpfully, promptly, and sensitively, bearing in mind their individual circumstances.
   Responding to customers' needs flexibly, including, where appropriate, coordinating a response with other service providers.

3. *Being open and accountable*
   Being open and clear about policies and procedures and ensuring that information, and any advice provided, is clear, accurate, and complete.
   Stating its criteria for decision-making and giving reasons for decisions.
   Handling information properly and appropriately.
   Keeping proper and appropriate records.
   Taking responsibility for its actions.

4. *Acting fairly and proportionately*
   Treating people impartially, with respect and courtesy.
   Treating people without unlawful discrimination or prejudice, and ensuring no conflict of interests.
   Dealing with people and issues objectively and consistently.
   Ensuring that decisions and actions are proportionate, appropriate, and fair.

---

88 See <http://www.ombudsman.org.uk/__data/assets/pdf_file/0013/1039/0188-Principles-of-Good-Administration-bookletweb.pdf>

5. *Putting things right*

   Acknowledging mistakes and apologising where appropriate.

   Putting mistakes right quickly and effectively.

   Providing clear and timely information on how and when to appeal or complain.

   Operating an effective complaints procedure, which includes offering a fair and appropriate remedy when a complaint is upheld.

6. *Seeking continuous improvement*

   Reviewing policies and procedures regularly to ensure they are effective.

   Asking for feedback and using it to improve services and performance.

   Ensuring that the public body learns lessons from complaints and uses these to improve services and performance.

There is a clear implication behind this initiative that a failure to reach these standards of performance might constitute maladministration with the possibility of remedial action being available at an appropriate level to tackle the inadequate service or injustice that might arise as a consequence.

The introduction of lay adjudicators in some areas is another innovation which has been introduced alongside the PO to speed up the grant of remedies. For example, in 1993 a Revenue Adjudicator was appointed and this has been followed with adjudicators for Customs and Excise Service and the Contributions Agency and a case examiner for the Child Support Agency (1997). The Adjudicator represented a new type of operationally autonomous complaints procedure for the taxpayer, introduced not by legislation, but by the administrative action of the department (with a small staff). Here the emphasis is on speed, cheapness, informality, and on the redress of grievances and improving customer service standards. The Revenue Adjudicator lacks any power to enforce a remedy, but in the first two years of the office there was 100 per cent compliance with the Adjudicator's findings. Overall, around half of the complaints heard annually have been upheld by the Adjudicator.

6.12 **Conclusion**

As the first ombudsman, the PO pioneered a new form of remedy which was specifically designed to tackle defects in public administration. Arguably the most potent feature of this office has been the capacity of an independent official to peer behind the scenes and thoroughly investigate instances of maladministration without there being cost implications for the complainant. Although no power was granted to impose a remedy, in general the findings of the PO have resulted in a positive response, with the complainant receiving at least an apology and often compensation. A very clear trend in the public sector has been towards creating specialist ombudsmen to cover the areas where complaints have tended to arise most often. However, there is an emerging view that this fragmentation into different jurisdictions causes problems for complainants in channelling their complaints down the appropriate avenue for effective redress. The proposed solution would be to create a single public services ombudsman for England embracing all of central and local government (covering NHS, housing, education, local councils, courts, prisons, etc) with branch offices spread across the country.[89] At the same time the long overdue abolition of the MP filter would open the way for a streamlined procedure accessible online or by telephone. With the advent of devolution as part of a multi-layered constitutional framework this division into many jurisdictions has become even more pronounced. Nevertheless, the evidence of collaborative working in Scotland appears to suggest that the Scottish Public Services Ombudsman could serve as a model for the one-stop shop approach to complaint handling.[90]

Another important effect is that the PO's intervention may result in a modification or reform of the administrative practice which has been subject to criticism. The trend here has been towards developing a test case strategy in order to root out systemic failure (see the Equitable Life and Channel Rail Link cases above). It might be argued that in common with Scandinavian models the PO and other ombudsman might be given the additional task of patrolling the territory on their own initiative on the lookout for administrative defects rather than wait for the referral of complaints. Rather the current emphasis has shifted towards promoting positive values of good administration. There has been an attempt to coordinate the investigatory remit of the main ombudsman offices. A Regulatory Reform (collaboration between ombudsmen) Order which came into effect in August 2007 means that, for the first time, the Parliamentary and Health Service Ombudsman and Local Government Ombudsmen can share information, carry out joint investigations, and issue joint reports on cases which are relevant to more than one of them.

It has been suggested that the ability to make mandatory awards of compensation, and the right to insist upon changes in administrative practices, would greatly increase the credibility of the office in the eyes of the public. In one area already the Financial Services Ombudsman operating under the Financial Services and Markets Act 2000 (as amended) is able to award compensation. However, if the PO were given such powers the possibility of review or appeal would be essential, and this would be likely to blur the distinction between ombudsmen, courts, and tribunals. Further, this might have the unintended effect of creating a reluctance to cooperate with investigations for fear of the consequences. In turn, this could lead to a degree of dissatisfaction with the conduct of investigations and ultimately the undermining of confidence in the role of the PO in a situation where the compliance rate for the PO is almost 100 per cent (although less so for local government). The constitutional framework of central government institutions has a Parliamentary Ombudsman which has been conceived mainly as a 'fire fighter' seeking to maintain and improve general standards of administrative conduct in response to citizen complaints, rather than a more proactive ombudsman model assuming a 'fire watching' role and prepared to intervene on her own initiative in order to control administrative shortcomings through systemic investigations.[91] To put it slightly differently, should a nominated official patrol the territory of officialdom and overturn the decisions of a democratically elected government, or indeed be able to interfere unduly in the legitimate decision-making powers of administrative bodies? Perhaps the greatest strength of ombudsmen in general is to be found in their ability to offer a means of adjudicating between disputants without the need to have recourse to costly legal remedies.

---

89 Time for a People's Ombudsman Service' Public Administration Select Committee, Fourteenth Report of Session 2013–14, HC 655, April 2014, para 29.

90 Gill, n 50, 681ff.

91 See Harlow and Rawlings, n 47, 537ff; Abraham, n 12, 28.

FURTHER READING

Abraham, A [2008] 'The Ombudsman and "Paths to Justice": A Just Alternative or Just an Alternative?' *Public Law* 1.

Abraham, A (2008) 'The Ombudsman as part of the UK Constitution: A Contested Role?' 61 (1) *Parliamentary Affairs*, 206–15.

Abraham, A (2008) 'The Ombudsman and Individual Rights' 61 (2) *Parliamentary Affairs*, 370–9.

Abraham, A (2011) 'The Parliamentary Ombudsman and Administrative Justice: Shaping the Next 50 Years' (Tom Sargant memorial lecture, Justice). <http://www.justice.org.uk/resources.php/304/the-parliamentary-ombudsman-and-administrative-justice>.

Buck, T, Kirkham, R, and Thompson, B (2011) *The Ombudsman Enterprise and Administrative Justice* (Farnham: Ashgate).

Drewry, G (1997) 'The Ombudsman: Parochial Stopgap or Global Panacea' in Leyland, P and Woods, T (eds), *Administrative Law Facing the Future: Old Constraints and New Horizons* (London: Blackstone Press).

Drewry, G [2002] 'Whatever Happened to the Citizen's Charter?' *Public Law* 9.

Elliot, M [2006] 'Asymmetric Devolution and Ombudsman Reform in England' *Public Law* 84.

Elliott, M (2013) 'Ombudsmen, Tribunals, Inquiries: Re-fashioning Accountability Beyond the Courts' in Bamforth, N and Leyland, P (eds), *Accountability in the Contemporary Constitution* (Oxford: Oxford University Press).

Giddings, P [2000] 'Ex p Baldwin: Findings of Maladministration and Injustice' *Public Law* 201.

Gill, C [2014] 'The Evolving Role of the Ombudsman: A Conceptual and Constitutional Analysis of the "Scottish Solution" to Administrative Justice' *Public Law* 662.

Gregory, R and Drewry, G [1991] 'Barlow Clowes and the Ombudsman' *Public Law* 192 and 408.

Harlow, C (1978) 'Ombudsmen in Search of a Role' 41 *Modern Law Review* 446.

Harlow, C and Rawlings, R (2009) *Law and Administration*, 3rd edn (Cambridge: Cambridge University Press), chapter 12.

Harlow, C and Rawlings, R (2014) *Process and Procedure in EU Administration* (Oxford: Hart Publishing).

James, R and Longley, D [1996] 'The Channel Tunnel Rail Link, the Ombudsman and the Select Committee' *Public Law* 38.

James, R and Morris, P [2002] 'The Financial Ombudsman Service: A Brave New World in "Ombudsmanry"?' *Public Law* 640.

Kirkham, R *Parliamentary Ombudsman: Withstanding the Test of Time*, 4th Report Session 2006–2007, HC 421, Stationery Office, 2007.

Kirkham, R, Thompson, B, and Buck, T [2008] 'When Putting Things Rights Goes Wrong: Enforcing the Recommendations of the Ombudsman' *Public Law* 510–30.

Kirkham, R (2009) 'Putting the Ombudsman into Constitutional Context' 62 *Parliamentary Affairs* 600.

Nobles, R [2001] 'Keeping Ombudsmen in their Place—The Courts and the Pensions Ombudsman' *Public Law* 308.

Nobles, R (2003) 'Rules, Principles and Ombudsmen' 66 *Modern Law Review* 781.

Scott, C [1999] 'Regulation inside Government: Re-badging the Citizen's Charter' *Public Law* 595.

Seneviratne, M (2002) *Ombudsmen: Public Services and Administrative Justice* (London: Butterworths).

Thompson, B (2001) 'Integrated Ombudsmanry: Joined-up to a Point' 64 *Modern Law Review* 459.

Websites

British and Irish Ombudsman Association: <http://www.bioa.org.uk/>

Cabinet Office (2000) 'Review of Public Sector Ombudsmen in England':
<http://webarchive.nationalarchives.gov.uk/+/http://www.cabinetoffice.gov.uk/media/cabinetoffice/propriety_and_ethics/assets/ombudsmenreview.pdf>

<http://www.ombudsman.org.uk/>

<http://www.lgo.org.uk/>

<http://www.policeombudsman.org/>

<http://www.spso.org.uk/>

<http://www.mediateur-republique.fr/>

7

··

Dispute resolution: tribunals and inquiries

7.1 **Introduction**

Tribunals might be regarded as a typical manifestation of the green light/functionalist approach to administrative justice.[1] Indeed, William Robson (1926–80), an influential Professor of Public Administrative Law at the London School of Economics, regarded the proliferation of tribunals, especially in the industrial field, as *the* major achievement of administrative law. For advocates of the green light view, law, in a positive sense, comes to be used as a facilitator for the delivery of policy by providing mechanisms through which it becomes possible to deliver the objectives of a modern social democracy. Statutory schemes are introduced for social security, housing, pensions, taxation, immigration, mental health, and special educational needs, which puts decision-making outside of private law and creates custom-designed mechanisms for the implementation of policy. The introduction of tribunals can be closely linked to the development of a coherent system of administrative justice on a scale comparable to *droit administratif* under the *Conseil d'Etat*. With the introduction of a National Tribunals Service in 2006 the UK now has established a system of dispute resolution which is in some respects comparable in its extent to its continental counterparts. In discussing tribunals and inquiries, this chapter deals with many of the bread-and-butter issues of administrative law and administrative justice, namely, citizen participation, appellate mechanisms, administrative law rights, reasons for decisions, and the availability of effective remedies. An important theme is the availability of a cheap, speedy, impartial, and relatively informal means of dispute resolution, often as part of the administrative process itself. The original idea behind many tribunals was to channel disputes away from courts, but the close resemblance of many tribunals to courts is one of the controversial questions that will be raised in the course of this discussion.

It should also be noted at the outset that there was strong resistance in some quarters to tribunals. Lord Hewart, a disciple of Dicey, viewed this trend as a negative development in *The New Despotism*.[2] For him the law was there to protect individual rights in cases brought before the courts. The introduction of statutory schemes that allowed the determination of outcomes outside of the normal courts threatened the fundamental concept of the rule of law. With the introduction of tribunals the routine decision-making of officialdom was placed beyond judicial oversight, except when a dispute arose over how a body interpreted the law. Predictably,

---

1 See ch 1.
2 G Hewart, *The New Despotism* (New York: Cosmopolitan Books, 1929).

the result was the setting up of a committee to investigate his various allegations of a 'bureaucratic conspiracy'. In 1932, the Donoughmore Committee on Ministers' Powers[3] decided that tribunals, as a feature of our legal system, were here to stay as a necessary component of the twentieth-century administrative state. But in the event the report actually made very few positive recommendations.

Twenty-five years later, as a result of the Crichel Down affair, the Franks Committee was set up and made its seminal report in 1957 (the irony being that the Crichel Down affair, discussed in chapter 6, had little or nothing to do with either tribunals or inquiries). The importance of the report was that, for the first time, a systematic look was taken at the whole area and an attempt was made to clarify the place of tribunals and inquiries as part of the scheme of administrative law. Many of the recommendations of Franks were accepted).[4] Some were enacted in the Tribunals and Inquiries Act 1958 (consolidating Acts followed in 1971 and 1992) and some by changes to the administrative rules. Tribunals became necessary for purely administrative reasons. It was important to ensure that the decisions that were to be taken by a tribunal were made independently of the department. Tribunals continue to be employed as an important instrument in policy implementation. To take some examples which also serve to illustrate the enormous diversity of tribunals: the School Standards and Framework Act 1998 established appeals panels for admission and expulsion from schools with an adjudicator to deal with disputes concerning school admissions; the National Minimum Wage Act 1998 allowed complaints in relation to the non-production of records to be referred to employment tribunals; the Financial Services and Markets Act 2000 established a Financial Services and Markets Tribunal. The Gender Recognition Act 2004 introduced the Gender Recognition Tribunal, which assesses and certificates transsexuals.

This chapter first discusses the main characteristics of tribunals before providing an overview of the National Tribunal Service which began its work in April 2006 as part of the wide-ranging reforms that followed the Leggatt Report. The later sections of this chapter consider the role and ground rules for inquiries, both in respect to their contribution to decision-making in the field of public law under statutory authority, and as *ad hoc* investigations into matters of importance set up by government but usually chaired by a senior judge.

7.2 **Courts and tribunals compared**

The special feature of tribunals in comparison to courts will be briefly considered under the following headings:

  (a) encouraging applicants: speed, economy, formality, representation;

  (b) flexibility of approach;

  (c) inquisitorial rather than adversarial procedure;

  (d) specialised jurisdictions.

---

3 Cmd 4060.
4 Report of the Committee on Administrative Tribunals and Enquiries, Cm 218 (1957).

7.2.1 **Encouraging applicants**

Accessible and expeditious justice has always been one of the main aims of tribunals. Increasing case loads in some areas have sometimes resulted in delays in tribunal throughput, and, as a result of such problems, the prompt disposal of cases remained one of the major concerns expressed in the annual reports of the Council on Tribunals. The recently launched Tribunals Service has adopted target setting as a means of circumventing delays relating to the various tribunals under its remit.

Equally, administrative justice at a relatively low cost has always been held out to be one of the major advantages of tribunals, certainly compared to courts. In many tribunals each side meets its own costs. An appeal to a tribunal usually costs nothing (unlike the issuing of a writ or a claim for judicial review which can be expensive). Costs are not generally awarded against the losing party, unless the claimant/appellant has acted unreasonably, in the sense of being frivolous or vexatious.[5] It is accepted in many tribunals that claimants should be in a position to conduct their own cases, without need of representation. However, in practice, the procedures for many tribunals are not simple and user-friendly. Any formal hearing may be a daunting prospect for many claimants.

The degree of formality which applies to a tribunal can vary with the subject matter it deals with. Tribunals may need formal rules of procedure to ensure that justice is done. When the Franks Committee considered the issue of whether it was possible to insist on one set of rules for all tribunals, it concluded that: 'Because of the great variety of the purposes for which tribunals are established . . . we do not think it would be appropriate to rely upon either a single code or a small number of codes.'[6] Nevertheless, the Franks criteria of openness, fairness, and impartiality were influential in recasting procedural rules of much greater consistency with the Council on Tribunals playing a major role in this development. The Tribunals and Inquiries Act 1992, section 8(1), specified that the Council must be consulted whenever procedural rules were being formulated.[7] In order for tribunals to be more user-friendly the rules of procedure may not be as strict as those which apply to courts. However, the rules applying to nearly all tribunals were revised following the enactment of the Human Rights Act 1998 to ensure that claimants enjoyed full protection under the European Convention on Human Rights (ECHR). Although, as noted above, the procedural rules vary according to the nature of the tribunal, the concern to protect convention rights has tended to increase rather than reduce the degree of formality. Many research projects have concentrated upon the value of representation which (though not necessarily legal representation) considerably aids the chance of success. The Free Representation Unit (FRU) is a charity which specialises in offering *pro bono* legal representation and advice, particularly at Employment Tribunals. This is usually provided by trainee legal professionals and law students. Other agencies, for example, trade unions, the

---

5 e.g., see the rules governing Employment Tribunals: Employment Tribunals (Constitution and Rules of Procedure) Regulations 2004 (SI 2004/1861).

6 Report of the Franks Committee on Tribunals and Enquiries, 1957, Cmnd 218, para 63.

7 Section 8(1).

Child Poverty Action Group, Shelter, etc, may also have special expertise and knowledge relating to their area of interest. However, the severe constraints on the availability of legal aid that continues to apply to nearly all tribunals remains controversial.

7.2.2 Flexible approach versus binding precedent

There are good reasons when setting up tribunals for avoiding a strict legal approach which is typical of a court of law (e.g., with respect to the conduct of the proceedings, rules of evidence, statutory interpretation, binding precedent, etc). For example, the rules of precedent might be deemed unsuitable, and a more flexible consideration of each case on its merits might be called for. On the other hand, consistency is equally important. This means that many tribunals have to walk a tightrope between legalism and informality. In other words, tribunals must have regard to a clear set of rules and, if possible, at the same time maintain a high measure of flexibility in their decisions, so that justice in individual cases prevails over mere consistency. The trend after the Franks Report was towards increased judicialisation of tribunals. Since the 2007 Act most tribunals have a uniform appellate procedure and decisions of the Upper Tribunal now bind first tier tribunals. The two tier system has been designed to provide 'authoritative guidance to those [first tier] tribunals, and to original decision-makers within government departments'.[8] Of course, the best way of avoiding formality is to encourage the parties to settle disputes before a hearing takes place. In response to the Leggatt proposals discussed below, there has been considerable emphasis on encouraging Proportional Dispute Resolution, with a formal hearing for certain types of tribunal viewed very much as a last resort. However, in fields such as immigration and mental health, a hearing will nearly always be necessary so that justice is seen to be done. There has been much criticism levelled at the over-judicialisation and increasing legalism of many tribunals.[9]

7.2.3 Inquisitorial rather than adversarial procedure

The conventional adversarial procedure is controversial in the tribunal context. Some commentators suggest that the issues confronted by certain tribunals should not always be viewed as a contest between two sides.[10] For example, with social security, pensions, and mental health, citizens are claiming rights from the state and it should not be seen as a battle between two sides. More tribunals could employ an inquisitorial approach, as is common in many continental European legal systems. An advantage of a procedure styled as an inquiry into the case is that it might be more likely to ensure that justice is done. The panel does not merely sit back and listen to a contest between opposing parties. This issue should be related to the treatment of unrepresented claimants who are common in tribunals, and who

---

8 C Radcliffe, 'The Tribunals Revolution' [2007] *Judicial Review* 197, 203.

9 See C Harlow and R Rawlings, *Law and Administration* (Cambridge: Cambridge University Press, 2009), 490ff.

10 P Cane, *Administrative Law*, 5th edn (Oxford: Oxford University Press, 2011), 393.

might well need help and guidance from the panel responsible for adjudication. In contrast, a more traditional view has always maintained that the adversarial principle is fundamental to any form of adjudication, including administrative justice, to ensure the impartiality of the process.[11]

7.2.4 Specialised (and thus expert) jurisdictions

One obvious advantage of having a specialised jurisdiction is that a tribunal will usually have experts as adjudicators, either chosen specifically for their expertise or because hearing similar cases will give them a familiarity with the law and the issues involved. The presence of a lawyer on the panel is also important, since all decisions have to be made against the background of the statutory scheme involved. The decision to create a professionally trained cadre of tribunal judges as part of the National Tribunal Service has introduced greater flexibility into the system, as tribunal chairs are no longer confined to one type of tribunal. The expertise of the other members of the panel is also crucial, as they may perform an important advisory role as part of the tribunal, and sometimes in a different capacity, as decision-maker. In some cases both functions are undertaken together. For example, the medical member of a mental health tribunal is required to carry out an examination prior to the hearing and also be party to the decision about the patient's detention following the hearing. In other tribunals experts may appear as witnesses before the tribunal.

7.3 Tribunal procedure and the Human Rights Act 1998

Under section 6 of the Human Rights Act statutory tribunals are regarded as public authorities and as such are required to act in a way which is compatible with the ECHR. In particular, 'the right to a fair trial' under Article 6(1) of the Convention comes into play and has certain obvious implications. Although this amounts to an open-ended, residual commitment to procedures that are fair, there are a number of specific safeguards that have been identified, and the model rules which act as guidelines for tribunals have been modified to emphasise the following:

(a) right of access to an impartial public hearing within a reasonable time. This will vary in accordance with the complexity of the case and what is at stake for the applicant;

(b) public pronouncement of a reasoned judgment;

(c) right of parties to be personally present;

(d) compliance with the principle of equality of arms which implies that each party must be afforded a reasonable opportunity to present their case; and

(e) rules of evidence must be fair, for example enable a party to have access to their opponent's evidence and to call and cross-examine witnesses.

---

11 W Wade and C Forsyth, *Administrative Law*, 11th edn (Oxford: Oxford University Press, 2014), ch 23.

Certain categories of tribunals make decisions which are concerned with fundamental rights, for instance the Mental Health Review Tribunal which has powers in relation to detention and compulsory treatment. In providing guidance after the Human Rights Act came into force, the Council on Tribunals made it clear that a right to a fair hearing does not simply consist of a number of set requirements and that the jurisprudence surrounding such issues is constantly developing (e.g., a case may require not only independent adjudication at an oral hearing but also appropriate representation). A judicial model of justice is encouraged by reference to ECHR standards, but it is a matter of debate whether a focus on oral hearings is always the best route to more efficient administration. It has been pointed out that the right to a full oral hearing might be waived if this is supplied at some stage during the decision-making process and that this oral hearing must be before an independent and impartial tribunal.[12] Nevertheless, public scrutiny of the decision-making process is extremely important in certain contexts. Oral hearings may not only expose evidence that would otherwise be concealed, but they can provide unrepresented claimants with poor literacy skills more chance to explain their case.

In any event, the procedure adopted must always be consistent with Article 6 ECHR's fair trial requirements.[13] Although there is no general duty to give reasons for decisions under the common law, there has been a strong trend towards giving reasons reflected in statutory provisions relating to tribunals. It is an essential element in promoting public confidence in the system that the parties affected by administrative decision-making should understand why they have won or lost. The Council of Tribunals in their guide to drafting rules (2003) emphasised that a statement of reasons should as a general rule be sent to each party (some exceptions have been recognised).

Tribunals are required under section 3 of the Human Rights Act 1998 to interpret primary and secondary legislation in a way that is compatible with Convention rights so far as it is possible to do so. However, the Upper Tribunal and lower tribunals are not empowered to issue a declaration of incompatibility if either consider that legislation is incompatible with the Convention, as it is only the courts listed in section 4(5) of the Human Rights Act that may do so.[14]

7.4 The Leggatt Report and the establishment of a unified and independent tribunal service

Sir Andrew Leggatt conducted a comprehensive review of tribunals on behalf of the government, which was published in August 2001.[15] The report made many important recommendations designed to improve the general performance of tribunals,

---

12 G Richardson and H Genn, 'Tribunals in Transition: Resolution or Adjudication?' [2007] *Public Law* 116, 127.

13 On which see chs 16 and 17.

14 See 4.4.3.

15 See Tribunals for Users One System, One Service: Report of the Review of Tribunals, The Stationery Office, 2001.

and this report led to fundamental changes. The most obvious innovation was the subsequent introduction of a National Tribunal Service (NTS) with a regional structure. This change resulted in the most important tribunals, previously falling under many different government departments, being fundamentally refashioned to create a single system with structural coherence, comprising first tier and an appellate second tier of tribunals. The citizen has access to a single, overarching structure, comprising all tribunals covered by the reform.

The introduction of the NTS reinforced an institutional separation of powers between executive and judicial branches of government. Certainly since the Franks Report there has been a continued emphasis on the independence of any tribunal from the executive body which takes the original decision. Leggatt argued for a clear separation between the ministers and other authorities whose policies and decisions are tested by tribunals, and the minister who appoints and supports them. To achieve this objective the Ministry of Justice (formerly the Department for Constitutional Affairs) has assumed responsibility for the administration of all tribunals as part of a unified Tribunals Service, with the Lord Chancellor/Secretary of State for Justice accountable to Parliament for its operation. Notwithstanding these changes to secure greater independence, the Ministry of Justice occupies a controversial position as it assumes a pivotal role in the administration of all courts and tribunals, the running of prisons, and in determining the ground rules for the availability of legal aid in civil and criminal cases.[16]

The day-to-day management of the service is the responsibility of a chief executive, while the Senior President of Tribunals, nominated by the Lord Chancellor, heads the tribunal judiciary. The Senior President has a multi-faceted role, which not only involves presiding over the First and Upper Tier tribunals, but also deciding with the Lord Chancellor how the chambers are organised in relation to the various jurisdictions. The Senior President has a liaising role which involves making written representations to Parliament on matters of importance to tribunal members and representing the views of tribunal members to Parliament, the Lord Chancellor, and other ministers.[17] Furthermore, the Senior President works together with the Lord Chief Justice in dealing with the training, guidance, and welfare of the tribunal judiciary.

The line of communication between each tribunal and the department responsible for administering the respective policy area has been severed by the move towards centralisation, and therefore communication between the tribunal and the department on contested issues related to policy implementation has arisen as an increasingly significant issue.

The NTS (launched in April 2006) is an executive agency responsible for the 25 tribunals falling under the Ministry of Justice. An impression of the scale of this post-Leggatt reorganisation is conveyed from the chart reproduced at Figure 7.1:

16 See A Le Sueur, 'The Foundations of Justice' in J Jowell, D Oliver, and C O'Cinneide (eds), *The Changing Constitution*, 8th edn (Oxford: Oxford University Press), esp. 237; and the Legal Aid, Sentencing and Punishment of Offenders Act 2012.

17 See Tribunals, Courts and Enforcement Act 2007, Sch 1.

Figure 7.1 First and Upper tier tribunal chambers (A Guide to Civil and Administrative Justice Statistics, Ministry of Justice, 13 August 2015, p 27)

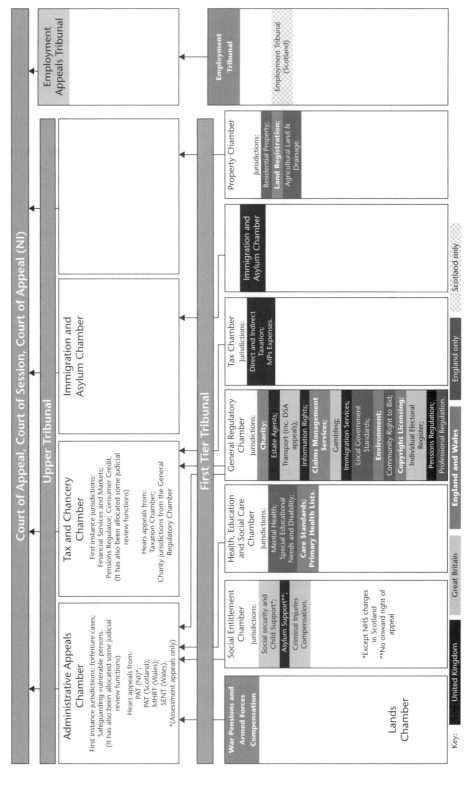

The Employment tribunal has not been integrated and the other tribunals which are not part of the NTS include: the Agricultural Land Tribunal; the Family Health Services Appeal Authority; the National Parking Adjudication Service; the Parking and Traffic Appeals Service; the Residential Property Tribunal Service; and the Valuation Tribunal Service.

A key objective of this major structural overhaul has been to create a single route of appeal to an appellate division for all tribunals, and a single route of appeal on a point of law which lies from first to second tier tribunals, then to the Court of Appeal. Judicial review of tribunal decisions is therefore often not necessary, as the individual has an effective alternative remedy under the relevant statute. Precedents are set by the President of each division of appellate tribunals and not by inferior tribunals.

7.4.1 Tribunal statistics

The published statistics provide a breakdown of the referrals and disposals before the main tribunals and give an indication of the throughput of cases. The total number of cases received in the year 2013–14 was 699,838 compared to the total of 848,990 for 2010–11. This represented a decrease of 150,000 cases. The largest fall over this period was in the number of immigration and asylum cases, which dropped from 172,649 to 104,996. However, the total number of disposals for 2013–14 was 876,775 cases.

Turning briefly to the main categories, 401,896 social security and child support cases were referred, and there were 543,609 disposals during the course of the year; of the 453,555 cleared at a hearing 40 per cent of claims were found in favour of the claimant. Employment tribunals received 105,803 claims, which represented a fall of 85,000 claims compared to the previous year. There were 148,387 disposals during 2013–14, of which 48 per cent were withdrawn, 21 per cent were ACAS conciliated, and 7 per cent were successful at hearing. The Immigration and Asylum tribunal received 104, 996 cases and there were 100,122 disposals. Sixty-seven per cent of these were determined and 20 per cent were withdrawn. The overall success rate at a hearing was 44 per cent while 56 per cent of cases determined on the papers without a hearing were dismissed or refused. The number of cases determined by the Upper Tribunal in this category was 7,407. There was a 37 per cent success rate at hearing and 63 per cent of determinations on the papers were dismissed or refused.

It is important to emphasise that access to tribunals always engages public expense and that the government has recently sought to limit some of the cost implications. Its attempts to do so were challenged in the case of *R (Unison) v Lord Chancellor*,[18] which was specifically concerned with the lawfulness of changes to the fees regime governing claims in employment tribunals.[19] The new regime required the payment of fees before claims and appeals could be brought in the tribunals, and the applicant, a public sector union, argued that the regime: (a) breached the EU law principle of effectiveness because many individuals would be unable to afford to bring proceedings; and (b) discriminated indirectly against women because a majority of claimants in employment cases are women. In dismissing the application

---

18 [2014] EWHC 4198 (Admin), [2015] 2 CMLR 4, 111.
19 The regime was contained in the Courts and Tribunals Fees Remission Order, SI 2013/2302.

for judicial review, the High Court noted that the EU law principle of effectiveness overlaps with the right of access to a court and that that right can be subject to limitation by way of fees so long as the fees do not make it virtually impossible to bring proceedings. While the Court accepted that there had been a drop in the number of tribunal claims since the introduction of the new regime, it considered that the applicant had not shown that this was because individuals were unable to bring proceedings as opposed to simply electing not to make claims. Moreover, on the matter of discrimination, the Court rejected the applicant's submissions as it found, on the evidence, that the fee structures were not indirectly discriminatory. The regime that had been put in place was therefore lawful: it pursued the legitimate objectives of seeking to transfer the costs of tribunals to those who used them whilst making the tribunals more efficient, and it did so through means that were proportionate to those objectives. The Court of Appeal upheld this finding.[20]

7.4.2 Administrative decision-making

A central theme for Leggatt and the White Paper that followed the report was how to improve the quality of administrative decision-making.[21] It should be recognised that the role of tribunals is very often to validate an earlier decision and that therefore the emphasis should always be on getting decisions right first time to minimise the work of the service.

When it comes to discussing the role of tribunals, there is some divergence of view on the amount of emphasis to place on the availability of an oral hearing. Recent reforms endorse an approach advocating Proportional Dispute Resolution (PDR) which is geared towards avoiding full oral hearings except for cases which cannot be otherwise resolved. There are obvious cost advantages in reaching a settlement at the earliest opportunity, but this trend has its drawbacks, too. However, a majority of users consulted in surveys express a preference for an oral hearing which gives them an opportunity to put their case and influence the outcome, even if they are ultimately unsuccessful. After a hearing they are more likely to understand the reasons for the decision. This perception is supported by some evidence that oral hearings actually deliver a higher success rate.[22]

In order to achieve a more user-focused tribunal system an emphasis has been placed upon developing best practice by removing procedural impediments. This has been tackled by providing all the information necessary in order to conduct a case effectively and by taking account of special needs. To this end, measures have been taken to make the service more customer-oriented. At the same time concern has been expressed relating to the general standard of initial decision-making by many governmental organisations against the backdrop that 'getting it right' has become widely recognised as one of the cardinal principles of 'good administration'. The high percentage of successful appeals to tribunals (e.g., 40% in the case of social security appeals) serves as testimony to the indifferent standard of initial decision-making. The suggestion here is that a cultural shift in practice

---

20 [2015] EWCA Civ 935.

21 See Transforming Public Services: Complaints, Redress and Tribunals, Cm 6243, The Stationery Office, London 2004.

22 G Richardson and H Genn, 'Tribunals in Transition: Resolution or Adjudication?' [2007] *Public Law* 116, 122.

by government agencies is required in order to address this problem and, in turn, reduce the workload of many tribunals.[23]

The NTS relies upon its own tribunal judiciary. Under the provisions of the Constitutional Reform Act 2005 the appointment of tribunal judges has been placed in the hands of the Judicial Appointments Commission, with the Lord Chancellor/Secretary of State for Justice formally approving recommendations made by the Commission after an open competition has been held.[24] Another significant change post-Leggatt has been to introduce a revised training regime. This is based upon the adoption of a competence-based approach to training, usually modelled on the Judicial Studies Board's competence framework, adapted for tribunals and the increasingly widespread use of appraisal and mentoring schemes. An important objective has been to achieve greater flexibility by training a cohort of tribunal judges capable of staffing different types of tribunal (rather than having adjudicators restricted to one type of tribunal, as was usually the case prior to these reforms).

The Leggatt Report made no general recommendations to introduce a system of legal aid for tribunals, but the extension of *pro bono* advice schemes was encouraged. It was further suggested that funding of legal representation should be delivered through grants to bodies which give advice, through the Community Legal Service. Such advice would be available according to criteria set out in advance and take into account the prospects of success. For Leggatt, the tribunal approach should be an enabling one, giving the parties confidence in their ability to participate, and in the tribunal's capacity to compensate for any lack of skills or knowledge. All the members of a tribunal should do all they can to understand the point of view, as well as the case, of the citizen. But it was recognised by Leggatt that there needed to be sufficient funding to support an efficient service and that the amounts contributed from government departments should be related to the case load of their respective tribunals.

7.4.3 Administrative justice and the Tribunals Council

Leggatt also recommended that an oversight body equivalent to the Council on Tribunals should be retained. The Tribunals Courts and Enforcement Act 2007 established the Administrative Justice and Tribunals Council (AJTC) as its replacement. The Council on Tribunals was set up following the Franks Report as a body reporting to Parliament which had a coordinating role and promoted good practice in most statutory tribunals by overseeing the drafting of procedural rules. The declared aim of its successor, the Administrative Justice and Tribunals Council, which has virtually identical membership, is to keep under review the whole administrative justice system 'with a view to making it accessible fair and efficient'. The Council has been keen to integrate the various remedies of courts, tribunals, and ombudsmen in order to provide the citizen with appropriate remedies. In the spending review following the 2010 General Election the AJTC was one of the quangos abolished as a cost-cutting measure.[25]

---

23 R Thomas 'Administrative Justice, Better Decisions, and Organizational Learning' [2015] *Public Law* 111, 115, 131.

24 See s 14.

25 See Public Bodies Act 2011, Sch 1; and see 21.1.

7.5 **Appeals, judicial review, and the *Cart* case**

The Franks Committee advocated a general right of appeal from tribunals of first instance to appellate tribunals, rather than to the courts, but this model was followed only for certain categories of tribunals. The Tribunals and Inquiries Act 1992 allowed appeals to the High Court on a point of law for tribunals covered by the Act.[26] As noted above, the standardisation of the system of appeals with a single appellate tier was one of the most important recommendations of the Leggatt Report. These proposals have now been implemented. For example, in the case of employment tribunals, appeals on a point of law will be directed to the Employment Appeal Tribunal. The appellate tribunal will consider legal reasoning but it will not normally re-examine the facts of the case. The Upper Tribunal as an appellate body is able to set precedents in order to facilitate clear and consistent decision-making, and the appellate level is reinforced with Circuit Judges and High Court Judges. Under the Tribunals, Courts and Enforcement Act 2007, appeals made on a point of law from the Upper Tribunal are directed to the Court of Appeal rather than to the High Court, as was previously the case.[27]

Another innovation is that the Tribunals Courts and Enforcement Act 2007 gives the Upper Tier tribunal a limited judicial review jurisdiction subject to certain conditions, one of which requires that a High Court or Appeal Court judge presides over the Upper Tier tribunal.[28] This change means that there is now increased scope to review the exercise of discretionary powers in the tribunals context. Certain tribunal decisions are also amenable to challenge by the claim for judicial review procedure. In practice (apart from immigration cases where judicial review is part of the procedure), this is relatively rare, as it should be remembered that judicial review will not be granted if an alternative remedy (e.g., an appeal from a tribunal) is available.

In *R (Cart) v Upper Tribunal*[29] the Supreme Court was required to consider the scope for judicial review of decisions by the Upper Tier tribunal where there is no further right to appeal. This includes cases where the Upper Tribunal refuses permission to hear an appeal where it is the final appellate body. The government argument that, as a superior court of record, the Upper Tribunal should be immune from review was firmly rejected. It was held that decisions by the Upper Tribunal should not be subject to routine judicial oversight but, in principle, they would be amenable to review. This was made subject to the proviso that a case raises important point(s) of principle or practice, or there is some other compelling reason for judicial review. In reaching this outcome their Lordships ruled out the re-introduction of a technical distinction between jurisdictional and non-jurisdictional error. Rather than establishing a doctrinal basis for intervention the outcome is that jurisdiction will be determined by practical concerns of 'proportionate dispute resolution'.[30] The decision to, in effect, ration the availability of judicial review

---

26 See s 11.
27 See ss 13 and 14.
28 See ss 15–21.
29 [2011] UKSC 28.
30 See M Elliott and R Thomas, 'Cart and Eba—The New Tribunals System and the Courts' Constitutional Law Group website 2011, at <http://ukconstitutionallaw.org/2011/10/05/mark-elliott-and-robert-thomas-cart-and-eba—the-new-tribunals-system-and-the-courts/>.

from the tribunal system on pragmatic grounds was clearly influenced by perceived limits to judicial resources.

In recent years there have been attempts by government to restrict the supervisory jurisdiction of the courts under the judicial review procedure which have been fiercely resisted both in Parliament and more widely. The inclusion of an ouster clause in the Asylum and Immigration (Treatment of Claimants etc) Bill 2004 to prevent cases from the Asylum and Immigration Tribunal from being challenged was eventually defeated and then dropped by the government. In cases where individual rights are at stake (immigration cases) the prospect of judicial review has been regarded as a crucial safeguard. Nevertheless there have been several initiatives to reinforce policy in order to make it increasingly difficult for asylum seekers.[31]

An equally strong trend requires that informal resolution under the existing complaints procedure is attempted before a claim to a tribunal can be made. For example, before appealing to a Social Security or Child Benefits Tribunal the applicant for benefits who has been refused must first write to the department that made the decision and request a mandatory reconsideration of that decision. Only after this process has taken place will a judge hear the argument from both sides before making a decision.[32] Similarly, alternative dispute resolution (ADR) must first be attempted where employment tribunals are called into play. Prior to a claim before an employment tribunal the claimant must contact the Advisory, Conciliation and Arbitration Service (ACAS) and ACAS will offer the prospect of resolving the claim informally by conciliation.[33]

7.6 Tribunals: conclusion

The new framework of tribunals now placed on a legislative footing under the Tribunals, Courts and Enforcement Act 2007 underscores the independence of tribunals and delivers a unified and comprehensible system. The upshot is that in the UK today there is an essentially self-contained tribunal service which bears more than a passing resemblance to the system of administrative courts found in continental systems.[34] The piloting of proportional dispute resolution allied to a case management approach might be regarded as part of a discernible trend towards channelling cases away from formal hearings and towards mediation and settlement. Feedback from users suggests that this move away from hearings is not always welcomed, particularly in certain policy areas. When there are hearings the degree of procedural protection needs to be related to the nature of adjudication which comes before the tribunal. The Asylum and Immigration Tribunal and the Mental Health Review Tribunal might be singled out because of the human rights implications which follow from their decisions. In these areas it is essential to provide strong procedural safeguards, namely, an oral hearing, full representation, and a right to appeal. With these reforms there is a danger that the specialist element of some tribunals will be watered down as the adjudication

---

31 See, e.g., R Rawlings, 'Review, Revenge and Retreat' (2005) 68 (3) *Modern Law Review* 378–410.
32 <https://www.gov.uk/social-security-child-support-tribunal/overview>.
33 See Making a claim to an Employment Tribunal, T420.
34 S Boyron, *The Constitution of France: A Contextual Analysis* (Oxford: Hart Publishing, 2013), 147ff.

process is performed by generic tribunal judges, not necessarily well versed in the particular field for which the statutory tribunal is set up. From the previous chapter it will be apparent that the Parliamentary Ombudsman is committed to achieving systemic change, with a strong emphasis now placed on embedding principles of good administration, rather than simply concentrating on curing individual cases of maladministration. The need for improved administration is widely acknowledged but this must come with enhanced coordination to utilise the full range of administrative law remedies which are available. Indeed, recent reports have stressed the importance of delivering a better service for users based on transparent justice with more modern access channels.[35] Any such revised procedures are increasingly likely to be combined with the pioneering of online dispute resolution which may be especially suitable for low status complaints and claims.[36]

7.7 **Inquiries**

7.7.1 **Introduction: distinguishing tribunals from inquiries**

Tribunals and inquiries usually have somewhat different functions within the administrative process. Tribunals are mainly adjudicative and act as court substitutes by hearing appeals against decisions; further, generally they have an important role in finding facts and applying legal rules derived from statutes and regulations. However, unlike the ordinary courts, the doctrine of binding precedent does not strictly apply to them. In contrast, while inquiries are often part of the original decision-making process, they are frequently activated only after an appeal has been lodged against the initial government decision. For certain types of inquiry (e.g., land and planning matters) the inspector also hears evidence and finds facts. The result of this kind of inquiry is usually a recommendation to the minister responsible, who may well have wider policy considerations to take into account before arriving at the final decision.

There are, however, many different forms of inquiry in administrative law. Inquiries are often held prior to certain types of administrative decision-making because the final outcome will inevitably have a profound impact on individuals and, indeed, sometimes on whole communities. In the planning field in particular enormous public controversy is frequently generated by proposals to proceed with major infrastructural projects such as nuclear power stations, new airport runways, and motorways. The Newbury by-pass and a third runway at Heathrow Airport are two prominent examples. The only way that projects on this scale can be realised is by displacing significant numbers of citizens, and causing disruption to thousands of others. The government, or the proposing authority, normally determines the appropriateness of objections to such schemes by holding public inquiries. For example, section 44 of the Planning and Compulsory Purchase Act 2004 allows the Secretary of State to decide which applications for major developments will be designated as major infra-structural projects.

---

35 HM Courts and Tribunal Service, Annual Report and Accounts 2014–15, HC 9, SG/2015/57, 12, 20.

36 'Online dispute resolution for Low Value Civil Claims', *Online Dispute Resolution Advisory Group, Civil Justice Council*, February 2015.

7.7.2 **Planning inquiries**

Planning provides a clear example of where the inquiry is part of the decision-making process. The inquiry is activated only if objections to the applicant's original plan are lodged, but once this has happened a clear procedure commences which, in effect, involves consultation with those involved.[37] An inspector is appointed who will hold a series of public meetings, listening to the arguments in favour of the proposal and objections from both individuals and pressure groups. Sometimes such inquiries extend over several months, or even years. The result may be only a recommendation to the minister, which is not always accepted. In this case, the inquiry is in danger of being seen as little more than a glorified public relations exercise. Nevertheless, objectors are often placated by feeling that their views have been heard, while the government can be seen to be consulting the public. The upshot is that, if the inspector recommends that the proposal should go ahead, the government has the backing of an independent inquiry. Equally, of course, if the inspector recommends rejection, the government is put under pressure and might suffer political embarrassment if it continues with the scheme. This is often referred to as the 'participatory democracy' model, giving the public at large a role to play in decision-making. However, it must also be remembered that inquiries might concern a much more limited issue, involving a very small geographical area—one street, one housing estate, or even one house. In such cases the inquiry is merely to ensure that the government, or other determining body, has all the facts before it in order to make a good and proper decision, having taken all the relevant considerations into account.

7.7.2.1 **The role of the inspector**

Inspectors are a specially trained group of civil servants appointed by the Secretary of State (Department of Communities and Local Government) to conduct hearings on his or her behalf. In certain inquiries the powers to make the final decision may be delegated to the inspector, as often occurs in practice for planning inquiries. About 95 per cent of planning appeals are dealt with in this way. Traditionally the notion of an inquiry is, as Lord Greene MR observed, 'merely a stage in the process of arriving at an administrative decision'.[38] Decisions are made by the Secretary of State after the full consultation process. However, now most decisions are delegated to the inspector for final decision and, in recent years, this has amounted to more than 95 per cent of the total. The public local inquiry really occurs only in a residue of cases where there is a controversial issue involved, and so an open, lengthy, and expensive process can be justified. The vast majority of inquiries take place on a routine basis and concern relatively straightforward decisions, particularly (as already noted) in the sphere of planning. Further, in less controversial cases it is likely that no public inquiry will be held at all. Just over 50 per cent of appeals dealt with by the Planning Inspectorate are by way of written representation, which saves time and money for the appellant, objectors, and the taxpayer alike.[39]

---

37 See the Town and Country Planning (Appeals) (Written Representation Procedure) (England) Regulations 2000, SI 2000/1628.

38 *B Johnson & Co (Builders) Ltd v Minister of Health* [1947] 2 All ER 395.

39 See Planning Inspectorate: Annual Report and Accounts 2006/07.

Legislative reform to streamline the planning system for major infrastructure projects was introduced under the Planning Act 2008. This sought to tackle the issue of multiple consent regimes and the delay this often caused in the planning process by adopting a plan-led system and by establishing an independent Infrastructure Planning Commission (IPC) to consider applications relating to nationally significant infrastructure projects. Harlow and Rawlings identify 'a seesaw progression towards judicialisation interrupted at regular intervals by government attempts to "de-judicialise"'.[40] Certainly, the idea behind the 2008 Act was to seek greater clarity and predictability through the publication of long-term national strategic policy statements for such projects. Under the Localism Act 2011, the IPC is subsumed as part of the Planning Inspectorate and is renamed the Major Infrastructure Projects Unit. Although it retains the same functions, the final decision will now be taken by the Secretary of State who is accountable to Parliament.

7.7.3 Reasons for decisions

For many types of inquiry the minister is required to provide reasons for the decision that is reached. It is important when it comes to making appeals to be able to have these reasons available. However, there has been some discussion in the case law about the adequacy of the reasons that are actually provided. In *South Buckinghamshire District Council v Porter* Lord Simon Brown provided an important summary of the requirements in a planning context:

The reasons for a decision must be intelligible and they must be adequate. They must enable the reader to understand why the matter was decided as it was and what conclusions were reached on the 'principal important controversial issues', disclosing how any issue of law or fact was resolved. Reasons can be briefly stated, the degree of particularity required depending entirely on the nature of the issues falling for decision. The reasoning must not give rise to a substantial doubt as to whether the decision-maker erred in law . . . The reasons need refer only to the main issues in the dispute, not to every material consideration. They should enable disappointed developers to assess their prospects of obtaining some alternative development permission, or, as the case may be, their unsuccessful opponents to understand how the policy or approach underlying the grant of permission may impact upon future such applications.[41]

In sum, a decision will only be quashed if the alleged deficiency in providing reasons has 'substantially prejudiced' the interests of the claimant, although the burden rests with her to prove not only that the reasons were inadequate, but also that she has suffered such prejudice as a result.

7.8 Public inquiries for special purposes

Apart from being part of the decision-making process, inquiries assume many forms and have very disparate functions and aims. The government may establish inquiries to investigate an issue considered to be of public importance. Such

---

40 Harlow and Rawlings, n 9, 588.
41 [2004] 1 WLR 1953, 1964.

inquiries may be a device to deflect criticism and thereby defuse a potential crisis by conveying the impression that the issue is under impartial investigation by a senior judge. There is a sense in which the matter is, at least temporarily, taken out of the hands of the executive branch, who have the power to set the terms of reference and provide the funding precisely because the inquiry is chaired by a judge and it is destined to publish its deliberations following the completion of a formal process.[42] For example, the Hutton Inquiry was set up in July 2003 by the Prime Minister following the apparent suicide of the Ministry of Defence scientist David Kelly. Kelly's death followed shortly after his cross-examination by members of the Parliamentary Foreign Affairs Select Committee, which itself was investigating the background to the government's controversial decision to invade Iraq. The terms of reference for Lord Hutton, as the judge conducting the investigation, were to investigate the circumstances surrounding Kelly's death. Despite the security implications and involvement of the security services, the government promised its fullest cooperation and all but the most obviously sensitive information appeared on a website set up expressly to keep public and press informed.[43] Another excellent example of an inquiry at the heart of politics was the investigation conducted by Scott LJ, following the collapse of the Matrix Churchill trial in 1993, to look into the export of arms to Iraq and, in the words outlining his remit, 'to examine and report on decisions taken by the prosecuting authority and those signing public interest immunity certificates in *R v Henderson*[44] and any other similar cases that he considers relevant to the inquiry'.[45] The report was finally published in February 1996.

Following revelations concerning phone hacking and the *News of the World* newspaper in July 2011, the Prime Minister announced a two-part inquiry under the Inquiries Act 2005 (discussed below) chaired by Leveson LJ into 'Culture, Practice and Ethics of the Press'. The hearings were open to members of the public and available live on TV from the website.[46] The comprehensive report made a series of recommendations relating to press regulation and governance consistent with maintaining freedom of the press and ensuring the highest ethical and professional standards in reporting.[47] In particular, it stated that the current regime of self-regulation should be abolished and replaced by a new independent self-organised regulatory system.[48]

In terms of their impact, the position is that public inquiries may exert influence but their recommendations have no effect until they are implemented by government or through the passage of legislation by Parliament. In consequence, the advice can simply be ignored by the politicians. Despite indications to the contrary

---

42 M Elliott, 'Ombudsment, Tribunals, Inquiries: Refashioning Accountability Beyond the Courts' in N Bamforth and P Leyland (eds), *Accountability in the Contemporary Constitution* (Oxford: Oxford University, Press, 2013), 252.

43 Lord Hutton, 'The Media Reaction to the Hutton Report' [2006] *Public Law* 807.

44 (1992) unreported, 5 October.

45 See ch 10 for further discussion of public interest immunity and the Scott Inquiry, and ch 2 in relation to parliamentary accountability of ministers.

46 <http://www.levesoninquiry.org.uk/>.

47 An Inquiry into the Culture, Practices and Ethics of the Press: Report (Leveson) vols I, II, III, IV, HC 780-1-IV, November 2012.

48 Leveson vol IV, ch 7, 'Conclusions and recommendations for future regulation of the press', para 7.4.

by the Prime Minister in the case of the Leveson recommendations, the obviously controversial aspects from the standpoint of the popular press have not been implemented by the government. Most notably, the government has not acted upon a recommendation that there should be a new press regulatory body supported by legislation to guarantee that the regulatory element is not only independent but also effective in terms of imposing remedies for the citizen.[49]

The above inquiries and several other examples cited in this chapter demonstrate that, while judges may be perceived as impartial, their presence does not neutralise the political element which underlies controversial subject matter. Indeed, it might even be claimed that the independence of the judiciary as a whole can be called into question by judicial involvement in such inquiries. Moreover, it is far from clear whether the management of adversarial legal procedures provides judges with appropriate experience and technical expertise for handling the investigative brief of a specialised public inquiry.[50]

As will already be apparent the subject matter of *ad hoc* inquiries, which may be established on the basis of the Royal prerogative or statute, has varied enormously. To take another example, the public inquiry conducted by Sir William Macpherson into the flawed police investigation following the brutal murder of the black teenager Stephen Lawrence addressed some of the same issues of institutional racism that had been identified by Lord Scarman's inquiry into the Brixton Disorders 17 years previously.[51] Although Lord Scarman's recommendations concerning policing methods, training, discipline, and recruitment were largely accepted by the then Conservative Government, only limited steps were taken to initiate changes. In the political climate following Macpherson there was a greater commitment to implementing many of the 70 recommendations made in the report. For example, in February 1999 the Home Secretary announced targets for ethnic recruitment into the Police Service. Other examples of *ad hoc* inquiries include the investigations into the Kings Cross underground fire in 1987, and into the Bradford City football stadium fire in 1985. Following the conviction of Harold Shipman for the murder of 15 of his patients, an inquiry was set up under Dame Janet Smith, a High Court Judge, to consider the extent of his unlawful activities (how many other patients he might have murdered) and to consider what steps might be taken to protect patients in the future. The Final Report of the Shipman Inquiry was published on 27 January 2005. In yet another context, following the fatal Ladbroke Grove train crash on 5 October 1999, a public inquiry was set up by the Health and Safety Executive, with the consent of the Secretary of State under section 14(2)(b) of the Health and Safety at Work etc Act 1974, chaired by Lord Cullen. The remit of this inquiry was to take account of the immediate causes of the accident, and then make recommendations for the future safety of the railways in the light of the current regulatory regime, and factors which affect the management of railway safety.

The recommendations that follow from such inquiries may result in legislation being introduced or being amended. More formal versions of such inquiries may be set up under the Inquiries Act 2005, which repealed the Tribunals of Inquiry

---

49 'One year on, UK press regulator criticised for lack of bite' *Financial Times*, 10 September 2015.

50 J Beatson, 'Should Judges Chair Public Inquiries?' (2005) *Law Quarterly Review* 221, 235.

51 See W Macpherson, 'The Stephen Lawrence Inquiry', Cm 4262, February 1999; Lord Scarman 'Report to the Rt Hon William Whitelaw, Sec of State for the Home Dept on the Brixton Disorders of 10–12 April 1981', Cm 8427, November 1981.

(Evidence) Act 1921. These are used only very rarely, where an event has caused particular political controversy or where a disaster has caused such public concern that it is felt appropriate to hold a searching investigation into the facts. Examples include the disclosure of budget secrets by the Chancellor of the Exchequer in 1936 and the Aberfan coal slippage disaster in 1967. It should be emphasised that this type of inquiry is very much an exceptional event.

7.8.1 Procedure for inquiries

From a procedural standpoint it is important to remember that in many respects such inquiries tend to be inquisitorial, assuming the role of 'detective, inquisitor, advocate and judge' (as Lord Denning put it in the Profumo Inquiry). The inquiry will be responsible for gathering the evidence and for determining the progress and direction of the proceedings. In order to do this effectively it may be given powers equivalent to those of the High Court to summon witnesses, send for documents, administer oaths, etc. And, of course, in many cases the reason that such inquiries have been established in the first place is to apportion blame for what has manifestly been seen to have gone wrong.

In 1966, a Royal Commission chaired by Salmon LJ (as he then was) was set up with a view to protecting the position of persons called to give evidence to inquiries of this kind. The Salmon Report made six cardinal recommendations which are set out below:

(1) Before any person becomes involved in an inquiry, the tribunal must be satisfied that there are circumstances which affect him and which the tribunal proposes to investigate.

(2) Before any person who is involved in an inquiry is called as a witness he should be informed of any allegations which are made against him and the substance of the evidence in support of them.

(3) Any person called to give evidence should be given an adequate opportunity to prepare his case and to be assisted by legal advisers. His legal expenses should be met out of public funds.

(4) Any person called should have the opportunity to be examined by his own solicitor or counsel and to state his case in public at the inquiry.

(5) Any material witnesses he wishes called at the inquiry should, if reasonably practicable, be heard.

(6) A witness should have the opportunity to test, by cross-examination conducted by his own solicitor or counsel, any evidence which may affect him.

7.8.1.1 Procedure at the Scott Inquiry, Hutton Inquiry, and Saville Inquiry

For his inquiry into the Matrix Churchill affair, Sir Richard Scott felt that the need to achieve fairness had to be balanced against considerations of speed, efficiency, and cost.[52] Accordingly, he substantially departed from the Salmon principles (above) and, in doing so, raised questions as to the conduct of future inquiries.

---

52 See Report of the Inquiry into the Export of Defence Equipment and Dual-Use Goods to Iraq and Related Prosecutions, HC (1995–96) 115.

It will be apparent that although the 'Salmon' safeguards are designed to protect fully the interests of any witness, they also introduce a substantial 'adversarial' element into the proceedings, with, for example, the rights to call and cross-examine witnesses. In a fact-finding inquiry Sir Richard Scott reasoned that there are no prior allegations, so that witnesses should be given notice only of potentially damaging evidence that emerges, and that they should be afforded assistance in preparing their own evidence and also in responding to any criticisms that emerge from the proceedings. In determining the approach to the inquiry into the circumstances surrounding the death of the civil servant Dr David Kelly, Lord Hutton, who presided over the inquiry, was concerned to meet the requirement of urgency contained in the terms of reference.[53] The first stage thus consisted of calling witnesses to be examined by counsel to the inquiry in a neutral way to elicit their knowledge and understanding of the facts. No examination by counsel representing them or cross-examination by counsel representing other parties was allowed at this stage. During a period of adjournment the solicitor to the inquiry wrote to witnesses, where possible criticisms arose from their evidence, informing them that if they wished to dispute these possible criticisms they would have the opportunity to submit written representations and to make oral submissions at the second stage of the inquiry. They were also informed that they might be subject to cross-examination by legal representatives for other interested parties and counsel to the inquiry. As already noted above, a particular innovation at the Hutton Inquiry was the use of a website to publish nearly all the evidence that came before the inquiry.

The relative speed of the Hutton Inquiry can be contrasted with the prolonged 'Bloody Sunday' Inquiry. This inquiry was set up under Lord Saville of Newdigate in 1998 to investigate the deaths of 14 civilians on 30 January 1972, when soldiers allegedly opened fire without warning on a crowd after a civil rights procession in Londonderry. 'Bloody Sunday' was an event of great controversy and this inquiry was established at a crucial time in the peace process in Northern Ireland, co-incidental in 1998 with the Good Friday Agreement, the Northern Ireland Act, and attempts to re-establish devolved power sharing between the communities. A particular problem was to ensure that all those associated with the incident felt able to present their evidence fully and frankly, each being adequately represented. Also, soldiers and former soldiers were concerned about possible reprisals and sought to give their evidence in secrecy and outside Londonderry, the main location of the inquiry.[54] Over 11 years the 'Bloody Sunday' Inquiry, costing £200 million, heard from more than 2,500 witnesses (900 orally) and then assessed a mountain of evidence in order to reveal what had happened on that day. Sir Louis Blom-Cooper has criticised the unnecessary cost and delay and questioned the adoption of an overly legalistic approach:

Far too much legalism has been injected into the process of public inquiries—the inevitable product of ingrained professional practices to see the 'truth' through independent investigation. Far too little attention, on the other hand, has been paid to the overriding purpose of public inquiries, which is to focus on failures in systems and services. Blameworthiness on

---

53 See Report of the Inquiry into the Circumstances Surrounding the Death of Dr David Kelly by Lord Hutton, 2004 HC 247.

54 See, e.g., *R v Lord Saville of Newdigate, ex p A* [1999] 4 All ER 860.

the part of individual actors in the public disaster or scandal under inquiry is often unnecessary and frequently distractive from the main thrust of the inquiry.[55]

The report by Lord Saville, published in June 2010, was heavily critical of the British army and found that paratroopers had not only lost control and opened fire on a crowd without warning, but that soldiers had made up false accounts in order to cover up their actions.[56] In a statement to the House of Commons to mark its publication, the Prime Minister on behalf of the British Government offered a profuse apology for the 'unjustified and unjustifiable' actions of the British soldiers involved. Although the inquiry on a symbolic level has had a cathartic effect, the question remains whether the impact would have been greater still if it had reported in a much more limited time frame. Another example of a non-statutory inquiry which has spent many years obtaining evidence before reporting was the Chilcott Inquiry into Iraq set up by Prime Minister Gordon Brown in 2009. Its terms of reference were to look into the run-up to the conflict in Iraq, the military action, and its aftermath in order to identify lessons that can be learned from the experience. Since the prospect of apportioning blame for an unsuccessful policy of intervention looms over such an inquiry, it was crucial that the proceedings conveyed the impression that the participants were treated fairly. In consequence, after taking evidence from many politicians and officials Chilcott still had not reached a conclusion approved by the main actors and no report had been forthcoming by the end of 2015.[57] Quite apart from the delay the inquiry has again been extremely expensive. To prevent the future repetition of such open ended investigations, Lord Chief Justice Thomas has recently proposed that, in the absence of exceptional factors, inquires should be time limited. He has also pointed out that, in contrast to the Saville and Chilcott inquiries, Leveson LJ was able to set himself a strict timetable which was then adhered to.[58]

7.9 The Inquiries Act 2005

The Inquiries Act 2005, mentioned above, seeks to consolidate previous legislation by providing a statutory framework for ministerial inquiries. It allows ministers to establish formal independent inquiries in response to events raising public concern and to set the terms of reference of any such inquiry. The minister is also granted powers to appoint a chairman and panel members.[59] There is a requirement of impartiality which prevents persons with a direct interest from involvement,[60] but individuals with special expertise may be appointed.[61] Once established, the Act confers powers on the chair of statutory inquiries to compel the appearance of witnesses or the production of evidence. Crucially, it is the chair who determines procedure, but in

---

55 Blom-Cooper Sir L, 'What Went Wrong on Bloody Sunday: A Critique of the Saville Inquiry' [2010] *Public Law* 61, 78.

56 <http://webarchive.nationalarchives.gov.uk/20101103103930/http://bloody-sunday-inquiry.org/>.

57 <http://www.iraqinquiry.org.uk>.

58 R Thomas, 'The Future of Public Inquiries' [2015] *Public Law* 225, 237.

59 Sections 1–6.

60 Section 9.

61 Section 8.

making any decisions relating to procedure s/he must act with fairness and with regard to the need to avoid any unnecessary cost.[62] Moreover, the chair is placed under a duty to report the finding to the minister who will lay the report before Parliament (or devolved Parliament/Assembly).[63] The Act provides that the inquiry must be held in public unless restrictions are justified according to specified grounds.[64]

7.10 Conclusion

The government maintained that the 2005 Act would codify best practice, as the respective roles of minister and chair of the inquiry are now clarified. On the other hand, the Act appears to increase ministerial control over statutory inquiries in a way that could compromise their independence leading to a loss of public confidence in the entire process. For example, the minister can set the terms of reference and is empowered to bring an inquiry to a conclusion before the publication of a report. Further, it gives the minister power to restrict attendance, disclosure, and publication of evidence. One consideration behind the Inquiries Act 2005 has been the spiralling costs of public inquiries. We have seen that under this Act there is a duty on an inquiry chair to have regard to the financial implications and the minister is granted some increased financial control over the remuneration which will be made available.[65] Dissatisfaction with the ministerial role under the new Act has been widely voiced by Amnesty and prominent judges in regard to the inquiry into the murder in 1989 of Belfast solicitor Patrick Finucane, in particular over the right of ministers to control public access and set the terms of reference.[66]

FURTHER READING

Adler, M (2006) 'Tribunal Reform: Proportionate Dispute Resolution and the Pursuit of Administrative Justice' 69 (6) *Modern Law Review* 958–85.

Adler, M (2010) *Administrative Justice in Context* (Oxford: Hart Publishing).

Beatson, Sir J (2005) 'Should Judges Conduct Public Inquiries?' 121 *Law Quarterly Review* 221.

Blom-Cooper, Sir L [2010] 'What Went Wrong on Bloody Sunday: A Critique of the Saville Inquiry' *Public Law* 61.

Cane, P (2009) *Administrative Tribunals and Adjudication* (Oxford: Hart Publishing).

Carnwath, R [2009] 'Tribunal Justice—A New Start' *Public Law* 48.

Elliott, M (2012) 'Tribunal Justice and Proportionate Dispute Resolution' *Cambridge Law Journal* 297–324.

Elliott, M (2013) 'Ombudsmen, Tribunals, Inquiries: Refashioning Accountability Beyond the Courts' in Bamforth, N and Leyland, P (eds), *Accountability in the Contemporary Constitution* (Oxford: Oxford University Press).

---

62 Section 17(3).
63 Sections 24 and 25.
64 Section 18.
65 Section 39(1).
66 On the Finucane case see, most recently, *Re Finucane's Application* [2015] NIQB 57.

Harlow, C and Rawlings, R (2009) *Law and Administration*, 3rd edn (Cambridge: Cambridge University Press).

Hutton, Lord, [2006] 'The Media Reaction to the Hutton Report' *Public Law* 807.

Laurie, R [2012] 'Assessing the Upper Tribunal's Potential to Deliver Administrative Justice' *Public Law* 288.

Radcliffe, C [2007] 'The Tribunals Revolution' *Judicial Review* 197.

Richardson, G (2004) 'Tribunals' in Feldman, F (ed), *English Public Law* (Oxford: Oxford University Press).

Richardson, G and Genn, H [2007] 'Tribunals in Transition: Resolution or Adjudication?' *Public Law* 116.

Thomas, (Lord) J [2015] 'The Future of Public Inquiries' *Public Law* 225.

Thomas, R (2011) *Administrative Justice and Asylum Appeals* (Oxford: Hart Publishing).

Thomas, R [2015] 'Administrative Justice, Better Decisions, and Organizational Learning' *Public Law* 111.

8

Introduction to judicial review

8.1 Introduction

Much of our focus so far has been on accountability. This has been discussed in the preceding chapters in terms of its doctrinal basis in the concepts and doctrines which underpin our constitution: the sovereignty of Parliament, the separation of powers, and the rule of law. It has also been discussed as a practical doctrine in everyday politics, concentrating on the role of MPs and select committees, and the Parliamentary Ombudsman.[1] Additionally, we have seen that tribunals play a fundamentally important part in the whole picture.[2] However, for many administrative lawyers, it is perhaps inevitable that judicial review of administrative and executive action should play a dominant role, despite the fact that, for a citizen with a grievance against the administration, a claim in the courts is normally something to be considered as the final remaining option, bearing in mind the considerable costs, and the time and effort involved.

The basic doctrine applied by the courts—the *ultra vires* doctrine—is, essentially, very easy to explain: an authority cannot act outside and/or abuse its powers, and it must also perform lawfully all public duties that are imposed upon it by statute. If an authority acts outside or abuses its powers, or fails to perform a public duty, it will thus act in a manner that is *ultra vires* the powers and duties that have been given to it and the courts may grant a remedy to the aggrieved citizen (although note that the remedies that are available on a claim for judicial review are discretionary).[3] On the other hand, if the authority acts in a way that is *intra vires* its powers or duties, the courts will not intervene on a claim for judicial review (the position may be different where an individual has a right of appeal against an act or decision). This is because Parliament will have entrusted the power of decision to the public authority and not to the courts, and it would thereby be contrary to the separation of powers doctrine for the courts to substitute their decisions for those of the original decision-maker. As we will see later, it is thus often said that the courts exercise a 'supervisory' jurisdiction on a claim for judicial review, in the sense that they are not concerned with the merits of a decision under challenge (i.e., whether a decision is 'good' or 'bad') but rather with its legality (the so-called 'review, not appeal' distinction).

Of course, the nature of judicial review is much more complex than this brief description of the *ultra vires* doctrine suggests, and the full extent of that complexity

---

1 Chs 2 and 6.
2 Ch 7.
3 See ch 18.

will become apparent on reading the subsequent chapters on the grounds for judicial review and the remedies. However, at this stage we need only introduce some of the more general features of judicial review and its constitutional significance. To that end, we have structured this chapter around five lines of enquiry, namely:

(a) where governmental 'power' comes from;

(b) why judicial review is 'supervisory' rather than 'appellate';

(c) the relationship between statutory powers, statutory duties, and discretion;

(d) how judicial review has evolved in UK public law (administrative law has, in fact, been recognised as a branch of law only relatively recently); and

(e) the nature of the judicial review procedure.

Before turning to those issues we should, however, make three further definitional points about our use of the term 'the *ultra vires* doctrine' both in this chapter and those that follow. The first is that the term is, essentially, a catch-all phrase that describes illegality in all its various forms, at least where the decision or other measure in question is taken within the framework of statute (we discuss non-statutory power in the next chapter). As will become apparent, a public authority may act unlawfully where it, among other things, takes into account irrelevant considerations, fetters its discretion, fails to observe the requirements of fairness, makes a decision that no reasonable decision-maker could make, acts disproportionately, and/or breaches an individual's legitimate expectations. While each of these grounds has, in turn, typically been placed under one or other of the broader headings of 'illegality', 'irrationality', and 'procedural impropriety' that were used by Lord Diplock in the *GCHQ* case,[4] it is important to note that such headings can run into one another and that it may be possible simultaneously to challenge a decision as illegal, irrational, and procedurally flawed.[5] It is also to be emphasised that the grounds for review continue to be developed by the courts—they are common law creations[6]—and that the content of the *ultra vires* doctrine does not stand still.

The second point is that we use the term *ultra vires* to refer only to illegality in the above sense and that we do not use it in the theoretical sense that is associated with a more general public law debate about the constitutional foundations of judicial review. That debate—sometimes called the *ultra vires* debate—centres on the question whether developments in judicial review are ultimately attributable to Parliament's intentions or whether the development of the grounds for review occurs with sole reference to the common law.[7] While the debate has been important it has, however, now largely produced a stalemate in the sense that the competing justifications for developments in judicial review appear to share much in common. We do not, in consequence, purport either to add to or to detract from that more general discussion.[8]

---

4 *Council of Civil Service Unions v Minister for Civil Service* [1985] AC 374, 410–11, Lord Diplock.

5 *Boddington v British Transport Police* [1999] 2 AC 143, 152, Lord Irvine LC.

6 See Sir John Laws, 'Law and Democracy' [1995] *Public Law* 72.

7 See generally CF Forsyth (ed), *Judicial Review and the Constitution* (Oxford: Hart Publishing, 2000). See also the discussion in P Craig, *UK, EU and Global Administrative Law: Foundations and Challenges* (Cambridge: Cambridge University Press, 2015), 125–53.

8 But for some related commentary see chs 1, 2, and, particularly, 21.

The third point is that the term *ultra vires* has become more prominent in the case law only in more recent years, and that earlier case law would often refer to ideas of jurisdictional error on the part of a decision-maker (e.g., in cases where the courts were hearing challenges to the decisions of the lower courts, tribunals and other quasi-judicial bodies). This jurisdictional theory of judicial review was premised upon a distinction between errors of law that went to the jurisdiction of the decision-maker (which were reviewable) and errors of law made within jurisdiction (which generally were not reviewable, save where there was error of law on the face of the record). However, starting with the seminal case of *Anisminic v Foreign Compensation Commission*,[9] the courts have steadily developed the understanding that any error of law is jurisdictional and that the courts should intervene to uphold the legislature's presumed preference for the rule of law. It is thus here that the language of the *ultra vires* doctrine has come to the fore and displaced old distinctions that were often regarded as unsatisfactory.

8.2 Governmental power

As we have already seen in chapter 5, central and local government typically acquires its power of decision from Acts of Parliament. Constitutionally speaking, the statute legitimises any action taken by government, whether that is a decision to compulsorily purchase property, to allow an asylum seeker to remain in the country, to award an educational grant, to give support to those on a low income, to house a homeless person, etc. In addition, the statute may lay down the parameters of the power to act, for example by specifying the purposes of the action, the considerations which must be taken into account, or the procedures which must be followed before the action is taken. At the same time, the courts, through statutory interpretation, may read powers into the statute ('by reasonable implication'), or impose constraints in the face of common law constitutional rights that are asserted by individuals. Either way, it is clear that the literal words in a statute cannot always be read as such and that legislation may be given a more or less expansive meaning depending on context.[10]

In addition to statute, central government also has a power to act on the basis of the Royal prerogative. We have already touched upon the nature of the prerogative powers in chapter 5 and, for present purposes, it suffices to say that these powers historically derive from the Crown's all-embracing authority in the early days of the English constitution, before the Civil War and the constitutional settlement of 1688/89. Since then, the powers have gradually been whittled away as Parliament has enacted statutes that encroach upon areas previously viewed as matters for the prerogative and displace it.[11] Nevertheless, it is still true to say that the government can operate in several important areas on the basis of the prerogative, rather than statute, with the result that central government does not necessarily need

---

9 [1969] 2 AC 147, considered in 10.2.2.

10 See further ch 11.

11 See *Attorney-General v De Keyser's Hotel Ltd* [1920] AC 508; and, e.g., *R (Munir) v Secretary of State for the Home Department* [2012] 1 WLR 2192, 2203, para 33, Lord Dyson.

parliamentary support for its decision(s). This, in turn, has raised important questions about how far the courts should intervene to control the prerogative by way of judicial review, and case law here continues to evolve and to lay down important constitutional markers. We return to that case law in the next chapter on the expanding reach of judicial review.

Central government also has the power to act under, what one commentator has called, the 'third source' of authority.[12] This refers to a power of decision that is not dependent upon 'positive law', which may here be said to comprise those legal rules that are adopted and endorsed by the state. Harris writes that 'thousands of government actions take place each day' on the basis of the third authority, in areas that include contract law, making pensions available to widowers, the making of *ex gratia* payments, and making information leaflets available to the community. In constitutional terms, the problem with this source of power is that it does not enjoy the legitimacy of statutory power, as Parliament has played no role in determining whether a particular decision should be taken (although there may be *post facto* Parliamentary control through, for instance, the work of Committees). This has led to questions about how best to regulate such power, albeit that no agreed approach has been adopted. In the absence of an agreed approach, this would thus appear to be one area in which judicial review offers some means of control.

The position in relation to local government is more complex, and has recently changed. Here, the historical approach posited that such authorities are purely statutory creations and that they can only ever do that which Parliament has sanctioned. While some of the corresponding legislation included broadly drafted provisions—for instance, section 111 of the Local Government Act 1972 provides that local authorities can 'do anything . . . which is calculated to facilitate, or is conducive or incidental to, the discharge of any of their functions'[13]—the starting point was that the powers of local authorities were limited to those contained within their empowering statutes (whether as expressly stated or as could be read into the statutes by reasonable implication). However, section 1 of the Localism Act 2011 now provides that 'A local authority has power to do anything that individuals generally may do'. Although this must be read in the light of restrictions within the Localism Act 2011 itself[14] and other statutory limitations on the powers of local authorities—most obviously under the Human Rights Act 1998—it would appear that local authorities now have an increased scope for decision-making.[15] That said, any such decision-making must still accord with the various grounds for judicial review and, depending on context, a local authority's decisions must not be disproportionate, unreasonable, unfair, and/or taken in breach of legitimate expectations (among other things). To the extent that there may be increased scope for local authority decision-making, there might also be an increase in the number of challenges to decisions by way of claims for judicial review.

---

12 BV Harris, 'The Third Source of Authority for Government Action Revisited' (2007) 123 *Law Quarterly Review* 225; and, e.g., *R (Shrewsbury & Atcham Borough Council) v Secretary of State for Communities and Local Government* [2008] EWCA Civ 148.

13 For some of the limits to the power see, e.g., *Crédit Suisse v Allerdale Borough Council* [1997] QB 306; although see, too, the Local Government (Contracts) Act 1997. See further 19.5.

14 e.g., local authorities are not permitted to raise taxes or trade in services they are already required to provide: see Localism Act 2011, s 5(1).

15 But compare A Bowes and J Stanton, 'The Localism Act 2011 and the General Power of Competence' [2014] *Public Law* 392.

These, then, are the various powers under which governmental authorities may act. Let us move to consider the basic doctrines and principles that guide the courts as they control them.

8.3 The supervisory/appellate distinction

It was stated in chapter 2 that Dicey's doctrine of the rule of law operates on the tripartite assumption that government should be under the law, that no one should be subject to arbitrary power, and that all should be equal before the law. The obvious consequence of this is that the courts should have the jurisdiction to rule upon the legality of government action, albeit that they cannot review the constitutionality of primary legislation (subject to the exceptions in respect of EU law and, to the limited extent provided by 'declarations of incompatibility', the European Convention on Human Rights (ECHR)).[16] That said, the doctrine of the separation of powers entails that each of the three principal organs of the state should be allowed to fulfil their allocated function, that is, the government should be allowed to govern and the courts should adjudicate if (and only if) the government has acted outside, or abused, the powers allocated to it by Parliament. In other words—and as we have indicated above—this means that the courts should not be allowed to make decisions which are more appropriately allocated to government and public bodies: the courts should exercise restraint in the face of executive and administrative action. Take, for example, the issue of the award of a discretionary grant to individuals. If a grant awarding body has made its final decision within legal parameters, which essentially means within the terms of the underlying statute, following the correct procedures and not acting irrationally, then it is not for the court to say that a particular person deserves a grant, however worthy the particular person may appear to be. In law there may be no appeal from such a decision; that is, Parliament may have decided that the grant awarding body should have primary decision-making powers. It will have an overall budget which it has to allocate appropriately according to its own priorities, which may derive from internally generated policies, imposed spending limits, or the influence of central government departments expressed in circulars.[17]

On the other hand, Parliament often provides for appeals from administrative decisions on matters of fact, law, or merits (or a combination of them, depending on the statute). As we have seen in chapter 7, many such appeals are heard by tribunals, with statute often also conferring a further right of appeal to, for instance, the Court of Appeal. Clearly, this is not an inherent right but depends solely upon whether the relevant statute has granted such a right. So, for example, a person dissatisfied with a decision in the immigration context has a right of appeal under the Nationality, Immigration and Asylum Act 2002, as read with the Immigration Act 2014. However, if a statute does not provide for an appeal, theory and justice alike demand that some remedy should still be available for an aggrieved citizen. Thus, over the centuries, the courts have felt it appropriate to develop a supervisory

---

16 Chs 3 and 4.

17 On the question of when available resources are a relevant consideration for decision-makers see 11.5.1.

jurisdiction whereby governmental power is controlled by ensuring that public authorities act within the legal powers granted to them. This has allowed them, where necessary, to protect individuals in the face of illegality and/or the arbitrary use of power.

Inevitably, the kind of remedy available under the supervisory jurisdiction is a limited one. The original decision by the authority may be held to be void, since there was no legal authority to make the decision, but it is not for the courts to make the final determination on the issue. Parliament has not provided an appeal, and therefore all the supervisory court can do is to decide whether the original decision is *intra* or *ultra vires*. If it is *ultra vires* then it may be quashed as void *ab initio*—that is, there was no power to make the decision and therefore, in law, it does not exist and never has existed. On the other hand, if no one challenges what might be an *ultra vires* decision then it will, invariably, be implemented and take effect as a perfectly valid decision, despite the possible invalidity. In addition, and as will be explained in chapter 18, the various remedies in this area of law are discretionary and the courts may therefore decide not to grant one, even though a decision may be tainted by illegality. Moreover, the time limit for seeking relief from the courts is quite short—generally it is 'promptly, and in any event within three months'—and therefore for this, and many other reasons, many possibly void decisions are never actually challenged.[18]

One related point concerns the question whether unlawful decisions are void, or merely voidable. This is a distinction that is often associated with the (outdated) jurisdictional theory of judicial review that we referred to above, which recognises that errors of law may go to the jurisdiction of the decision-maker or, alternatively, be made within jurisdiction. While it was axiomatic that an error of law that went to the jurisdiction of a decision-maker would render a decision void—a misunderstanding as to the legal basis of the power to decide could otherwise allow the decision-maker to expand their power beyond that specified by statute—it was sometimes said that errors of law within jurisdiction were voidable. However, the distinction has come under increasing strain in recent decades as the courts have referred to the ideal of the rule of law when developing an ever-more demanding *ultra vires* doctrine. In the words of Lord Irvine, case law starting with *Anisminic*:[19]

made obsolete the historic distinction between errors of law on the face of the record and other errors of law. It did so by extending the doctrine of *ultra vires*, so that any misdirection in law would render the relevant decision *ultra vires* and a nullity . . . Thus, today, the old distinction between void and voidable acts . . . no longer applies.[20]

Judicial review is therefore available as a means of challenging the legality of decisions of all governmental authorities, albeit that it is to be regarded as a procedure of last resort which should be used only where the individual has no alternative remedy such as a right of appeal (a procedural requirement that every judicial review claimant must satisfy). Moreover, where an appeal is available, it is usually preferable for an aggrieved citizen to pursue that option, since the appellate body may be able to substitute its decision for the decision of the original authority and to grant a remedy. An appeal may well involve a reconsideration of the merits of the case, not merely its legality, although this depends on the wording of the

---

18 On time limits see 8.11.
19 *Anisminic Ltd v Foreign Compensation Commission* [1969] 2 AC 147, discussed in ch 10.
20 *Boddington v British Transport Police* [1999] 2 AC 143, 154.

empowering statute, which might limit the appeal to a point of law only. On the other hand, a successful judicial review, which is always limited to legality, might merely prolong disappointment and expense for the individual with no realistic possibility of a successful outcome at the end of the day.[21] The original decision might be invalidated, but that is no guarantee of a favourable outcome when, for example, a new application for a grant is made. The administrative authority will have to reconsider the application, and this time it will abide by all the legal requirements, including the appropriate procedures, but may still refuse to award the grant. Assuming the second refusal is *intra vires*, the disappointed applicant now has no legal redress. Nevertheless, there is no doubt that judicial review, both in theory and in practice, can be a very efficacious tool in combating an abuse of power by government. The law will insist that authorities act legally, reasonably, proportionately, and fairly; and an authority might well be persuaded to change its mind, once it has fully appreciated the legal boundaries of its decision-making process.

Returning to, and summarising, some of the points made above, it is to be emphasised that, when considering a claim, a judge has a wide discretion as to whether or not to intervene in judicial review cases. The grounds and principles of review have been created almost entirely by the courts under the common law with no significant intervention from Parliament. They are very broadly conceived, overlap considerably, and are constantly developing. In addition, all the remedies are discretionary, which means that, although the decision might appear to be *ultra vires* or an abuse of power, a remedy can, in the discretion of the court, be refused. Equally, it must be borne in mind that in administrative law cases the judiciary is involved, unavoidably, in 'political' decisions, either between individuals and the state, or, occasionally, between two branches of the state (e.g., local and central government). The inevitable result can be a tension between the executive and judiciary, albeit that it should always be remembered that, in theory at least, the core role of the courts is to apply and interpret the law that emanates from Parliament, using the basic principles of statutory interpretation which are applied in *all* areas of law.[22]

8.4 Statutory powers, statutory duties, and discretion

Before we turn to consider in more detail the nature of the judicial review procedure, one further issue that we need to address is that of the relationship between statutory powers, statutory duties, and discretion in public decision-making (discretion can for these purposes be taken to connote the ability lawfully to choose between more than one outcome). As we have already mentioned above, a public decision-maker will often make decisions within the framework of a statute that will have either delegated a power to it or imposed a duty to act. However, this by

---

21 For judicial consideration of appeals on a point of law as compared to judicial review of the legality of a decision see *E v Secretary of State for the Home Department* [2004] 2 WLR 1351.

22 For some discussion of these issues see *R v Secretary of State for the Home Department, ex p Fire Brigades Union* [1995] 2 AC 513; and 9.3.2.3.

itself tells us little about the nature of statutory powers and statutory duties and, indeed, where the line between the two is to be drawn. For instance, are statutory powers always synonymous with discretion, and duties synonymous with an absence of discretion? Or how far can, and do, the courts read statutory language so as to modify the element of discretion that is, or is not, apparent from the literal language of an Act?

8.4.1 **Powers and duties**

We might start by observing that legislation will ordinarily be read as granting a decision-maker a statutory power to do something, or not to do something, where it uses permissive terms such as 'may' or 'as the [decision-maker] considers appropriate' (the permissive is to be contrasted with the mandatory 'shall' or 'must'). Where permissive terms are interpreted as giving the decision-maker discretionary powers, this will have a corresponding impact on the role of the courts in the sense that they should exercise restraint because of the separation of powers doctrine. That doctrine—noted above—entails that, where Parliament delegates a power of decision to a particular body, it is that body, and not the courts, that enjoys the primary decision-making function. Hence, where there is a wide discretion, the courts will typically emphasise that they are constitutionally forbidden from looking closely at the substance of a decision.[23] This may be all the more so where there is a pronounced 'political' context to a dispute, where the courts may consider that the imperative of restraint is even more pressing. An example here would be the case of *R v Secretary of State for the Environment, ex p Nottinghamshire County Council*,[24] where the court emphasised the need for restraint in the context of a challenge to economic directions issued by central government.

Permissive terms can, however, also be read more narrowly and the courts may, for instance, require that a power is exercised reasonably and that all relevant considerations are taken into account.[25] Furthermore, where fundamental rights are in issue, the courts may subject an exercise of power to a test of 'anxious scrutiny' and/or a test of proportionality.[26] In other circumstances, the courts may even read permissive terms as not importing discretion but rather as imposing a duty to act. Whether permissive terms will be read in this way will, however, depend on context and, in particular, on whether the 'power' is to be exercised for the benefit of particular individuals and/or the wider public. As Earl Cairns LC stated in *Julius v Bishop of Oxford*:

[T]here may be something in the nature of the thing empowered to be done, something in the object for which it is to be done, something in the conditions in which it is to be done, something in the title of the person or persons for whose benefit the power is to be exercised, which may couple the power with a duty, and make it the duty of the person on whom the power is reposed, to exercise that power when called upon to do so.[27]

---

23 See ch 13 on *Wednesbury* unreasonableness.
24 [1986] AC 240.
25 See ch 11.
26 See chs 4 and 13.
27 (1880) 5 App Cas 214, 222; considered in, e.g., *M v Scottish Ministers* [2012] UKSC 58, [2012] 1 WLR 3386.

The courts may finally say that recipients of statutory power are under a number of common law duties in respect of the exercise of discretion (these duties continue to develop both independently and in the light of the ECHR). Here, the recipient of statutory powers thus continues to have discretion but must exercise it in the light of common law/ECHR obligations. Depending on the context, these can include:

(a) the duty to consider whether to exercise the power;[28]

(b) the duty to act reasonably;[29]

(c) the duty to act in good faith;[30]

(d) the duty to act fairly;[31]

(e) the duty to act in the public interest;[32]

(f) the duty to avoid undue delay in decision-making;[33]

(g) the duty to communicate a decision;[34]

(h) the duty to give reasons;[35] and

(i) the duty to act in a manner that is consistent with the purpose of the legislation.[36]

8.4.2 **Duties and discretion**

The existence of a statutory duty is then typically signified by the use of mandatory language in a statute, for instance, the word 'shall'. The basic distinction between a statutory power and a statutory duty lies in enforceability: while a statutory power need not be exercised should the recipient of the power decide not to exercise it (subject to arguments about its nature and context), a statutory duty must be performed. Should a public authority expressly refuse to discharge its duty and/or act in a manner that suggests non-compliance with its duties, a claimant should therefore typically seek a mandatory order as the remedy most suited to ensuring that the decision-maker's obligations are met.[37] Depending on context, the claimant may also seek damages for any loss he or she has suffered in consequence of the non-performance of the duty.[38]

Legislation can, however, also be read as including discretion as to how a duty is to be performed, and this can complicate the question of what, if anything, a court should do. Such an interpretation is most often given to legislation that imposes so-called 'target duties' in relation to the provision of public services like policing,

---

28 *R v Secretary of State for the Home Department, ex p Fire Brigades Union* [1995] 2 AC 513.

29 *Secretary of State for Education and Science v Tameside Metropolitan Borough Council* [1977] AC 1014, 1047, Lord Wilberforce.

30 *Board of Education v Rice* [1911] AC 179.

31 Ibid.

32 *R v Tower Hamlets London Borough Council, ex p Chetnik Developments* [1988] AC 858, 872, Lord Bridge.

33 *R v Home Secretary, ex p Phansopkar* [1976] QB 606.

34 *R (Anufrijeva) v Secretary of State for the Home Department* [2004] 1 AC 604.

35 *R v Secretary of State for the Home Department, ex p Doody* [1994] 1 AC 531.

36 *Padfield v Minister for Agriculture, Fisheries and Food* [1968] AC 997.

37 See 18.3.3.

38 On damages actions see ch 20.

healthcare, housing, child protection, road safety, etc.[39] While the use of mandatory language in such legislation reflects the social imperative of providing services to members of society, the courts are aware that public authorities may here have to make value judgements about how to meet the target and that the courts should, for reasons of relative expertise, be slow to intervene in the decision-making process. This may be particularly so where a decision is concerned with spending priorities, as the courts accept that limited financial resources may mean that difficult discretionary choices may have to be taken in the performance of a statutory duty. That said, all will depend on context, and arguments about spending priorities may not always be decisive (albeit that the leading case law would suggest that they frequently will be).[40]

8.5 The emergence of judicial review

We have already considered in chapter 1 how administrative law came to exist as a discrete area of law in the UK. Without revisiting that discussion in any detail, three points can be addressed to help us understand both how the current judicial review procedure came into being and why it is so important. These relate to: (a) the historical role of the courts and of Parliament; (b) misapprehensions about the nature of administrative law; and (c) the challenge of the welfare state. On this basis we can make some comments about the incidence of judicial review in the modern era and the corresponding procedure that governs it.

8.5.1 The historical role of the courts and of Parliament

To comprehend the role that the courts and Parliament played in controlling public decision-makers, one needs to think of how the balance of power in England has shifted over the centuries. Certainly, in the medieval and Tudor periods, before the Civil War in the seventeenth century, government was in the hands of the monarch, and we can still see relics of that monarchical power today in the Royal prerogative as a source of governmental authority.[41] However, English history thereafter is a story of the steady accretion of parliamentary power and of the emergence of the Westminster Parliament as legally sovereign. In terms of controlling the executive, Parliament thus came to perform a key role, which, again, we can still see today in features such as Prime Minister's questions and the workings of Parliamentary committees.[42] In other words, Parliament was regarded as the supreme legal and political forum and it was only right that the executive should be held to account there.[43]

At the same time, the courts began to play an ever-more important role in controlling subordinate decision-makers such as justices of the peace and local

---

39 See, e.g., *R v Inner London Education Authority, ex p Ali* (1990) 2 Admin LR 822, referring to 'target duties' in the context of educational provision.

40 See ch 11; see also *R (McDonald) v Kensington and Chelsea RLBC* [2011] 4 All ER 881 (as read in the light of *McDonald v UK* (2015) 60 EHRR 1) and *R v Gloucestershire County Council, ex p Barry* [1997] AC 584. Compare *R v East Sussex County Council, ex p Tandy* [1998] AC 714.

41 Chs 5 and 9.

42 See further P Leyland, *The Constitution of the United Kingdom: A Contextual Analysis*, 3rd edn (Oxford: Hart Publishing, 2016), ch 5.

43 For an excellent—if provocative— account see A Tomkins, *English Public Law* (Oxford: Clarendon Press, 2003).

officials. However, this control of public decision-makers did not occur in specialist courts but rather in the ordinary courts, and it is here that the historical absence of a body of administrative law can be seen most clearly. In short, while administrative law envisages specialist tribunals for resolving disputes involving public decision-makers, the ordinary common law courts came to enjoy unchallenged superiority in the administration of justice between all parties (albeit that their work was supplemented by the Courts of Equity). For some, this reliance on the common law courts was a reaction to the history and practice of the Star Chamber that was abolished in 1640 and which had acted to centralise power. The result was that the ordinary courts came to resolve disputes involving public authorities on the basis of old principles that were often taken from private law and adapted to the needs of the (then) administrative state. Indeed, the sole distinction that could be drawn was in respect of remedies, as there was a range of prerogative orders that could be issued only in respect of courts and non-royal decision-makers.

One final point to be made under this sub-heading concerns the relationship between the courts and Parliament. In sum, Parliament's supreme position in the constitution resulted in an understanding that no other controller of executive power was necessary, and this was something that the courts occasionally colluded in to the detriment of accountability. Although parliamentary control of executive action was not—and is not—a complete myth, it came to be used as an excuse for refusing judicial intervention when an authority had arguably acted unlawfully. One of the best known examples came with the case of *Liversidge v Anderson*,[44] which concerned an unsuccessful challenge to the Home Secretary's decision to detain the plaintiff 'as a person of hostile associations' during the Second World War (the power of detention was contained in regulation 18B of the Defence (General) Regulations 1939). While the fact that the case involved use of emergency powers during the Second World War was a factor which inevitably influenced the courts in their exercise of restraint, legal opinion, even then, was divided as to whether the decision of the House of Lords was a correct one. The latter day view, expressed by Lord Diplock, is that it was not:

For my part I think the time has come to acknowledge openly that the majority of this House in *Liversidge v Anderson* were expediently and, at that time, perhaps, excusably wrong.[45]

8.5.2 Misapprehensions about the nature of administrative law

The starting point here is AV Dicey's rule of law principle as outlined in his *Introduction to the Law of the Constitution*.[46] In this work he emphasised how the rule of law entails that all public and private figures should be equally subject to the ordinary law of the land, as this removes the scope for arbitrary discretionary power. At the same time, Dicey was generally dismissive of the French administrative law system as, in his view, the French administrative court, the *Conseil d'Etat*, was part of the administration and therefore could not provide the necessary *independent* check on government. For Dicey, the emphasis throughout was thus on the advantages of the ordinary law applied and enforced in the ordinary courts of law.

---

44 [1942] AC 206; and see 17.2.6.

45 *R v Inland Revenue Commissioners, ex p Rossminster Ltd* [1980] AC 952, 1011.

46 AV Dicey, *Introduction to the Law of the Constitution*, 10th edn (London: Macmillan, 1959). And see ch 2.

There was an element of truth in his assertion. The result of the influence of the French philosopher Montesquieu, who promoted one popular idea of the doctrine of separation of powers in his seminal work *L'Esprit des Lois*, was that the French judiciary were not allowed to interfere or intervene in any way in the executive sphere of government—it would thus be possible to have only an 'in-house' body to supervise executive activity. Strictly speaking, therefore, the *Conseil d'Etat* is a part of the executive, rather than the judiciary, for this purpose, although no one doubts today its true independence. However, the unfortunate result of Dicey's strictures was a general assumption, which prevailed for nearly a century, that *droit administratif* (administrative law) was something to be avoided. For instance, Lord Hewart, writing in the 1930s, famously described administrative law as 'Continental jargon',[47] while Salmon LJ stated in *Re Grosvenor Hotel, London (No 2)* that: 'I do not believe that the court would be obliged to accept the *ipse dixit* [i.e., an assertion made but not proved] of the minister just because he is a member of the executive. There is no *droit administratif* in England.'[48] Clearly this was a misunderstanding of the notion of administrative law and its aims, but it does help to explain the prejudices that had been built up against the development of appropriate procedures for the supervision, regulation, and control of executive action.

8.5.3 The challenge of the welfare state

In terms of the development of administrative law, additional problems were caused by the two World Wars, particularly the second (1939–45). For instance, we have already referred above to *Liversidge v Anderson*, and it was perhaps inevitable that the executive had to be given exceptional powers to combat the emergency and, moreover, that the courts would take a fairly lenient view when asked to supervise the exercise of those powers. Frequently, the subject matter of the decision involved in a judicial review affects the court's attitude towards its willingness to intervene. This is even more pronounced when issues of national security are involved, as these matters have been continually problematic, both in terms of the evidence available and the court's view of the appropriate role it should play in respect to them. It was arguably unfortunate that this judicial self-restraint continued into the 1950s and that a culture of non-intervention was generated.

However, the years immediately after the Second World War were years of great change in the UK, where the welfare state was consolidated in the light of, most notably, the Beveridge Report of 1942. Although there had been some state intervention and provision in the earlier part of the twentieth century (and before), the post-Second World War era redefined the state both in terms of its size and its responsibilities. Government grew, and so too did the administrative challenges for wider society, and the 1950s and 1960s became a period of profound change in administrative law. Hence, major modifications were made to the tribunal system as a result of the Franks Report in 1957 and the Tribunals and Inquiries Act 1958;[49] and a variety of pressures, including the influential JUSTICE report, *The Citizen and the Administration: the Redress of Grievances* in 1961, led to the creation of the office of Parliamentary Commissioner for Administration (Parliamentary Ombudsman) in 1967 (this was followed by a wide range of other commissioners in various areas,

---

47 Lord Hewart, *Not Without Prejudice* (London: Hutchinson, 1937), 96.
48 [1965] Ch 1210, 1261.
49 See ch 7.

both public and private).[50] At around the same time, the role of select committees was gradually being developed by both Houses of Parliament, which led to the introduction of a revised departmental committee system in 1979.[51]

This impetus was maintained by the courts in a series of landmark decisions of the House of Lords, which transformed attitudes to administrative law and laid the basis for a body of judicial review that would be more suited to the challenge of controlling governmental power in the late twentieth century. Four decisions from the 1960s—each of which are considered in later chapters—are regarded as of seminal importance:

(a) *Ridge v Baldwin*, which extended the scope of natural justice/fairness;[52]

(b) *Padfield v Minister for Agriculture, Fisheries and Food*, which considered the exercise of ministerial discretion in subjectively worded clauses;[53]

(c) *Conway v Rimmer*, which set out new parameters with regard to discovery of documents and claims for public interest immunity;[54] and

(d) *Anisminic v Foreign Compensation Commission*, which addressed 'ouster clauses' and the reach of the jurisdictional theory of judicial review.[55]

8.5.4 The incidence and importance of judicial review

Since the 1960s applications for judicial review have increased dramatically. But this is difficult to express in purely statistical terms, because, before the introduction of procedural reforms in the late 1970s/early 1980s, only cases in which a prerogative remedy was sought were listed for the Divisional Court of the Queen's Bench Division. Further, not all of these cases involved applications for judicial review: some concerned the supervisory jurisdiction exercised by the Queen's Bench Division over inferior courts (cases involving private law applications for injunctions and declarations were heard in the Chancery Division). However, the initial numbers were strikingly small. For example, there were only 95 applications for prerogative orders in 1968. By 1978, this figure had risen to 364.

The following figures indicate (on the face of it) a huge increase in judicial review cases in England and Wales over recent decades:

Applications for permission to apply (now 'claims') for judicial review

1982	685
1992	2,439
1994	3,208
1996	3,901
2001	5,298
2004	5,498
2006	6,456
2010	10,600[56]

50 See ch 6.
51 On parliamentary oversight, see ch 2.
52 [1964] AC 40, considered in 17.2.3.
53 [1968] AC 997, considered in 11.4.1.
54 [1968] AC 910, considered in 10.5.3.3.
55 [1969] 2 AC 147, considered in 10.2.2.
56 Judicial and Court Statistics 2010, available at <https://www.gov.uk/government/organisations/ministry-of-justice/about/statistics>.

In fact there has been a spectacular increase between 1981 and the present day. That said, while the number of claims has steadily risen—albeit that many immigration cases are now heard by the Upper Tribunal rather than by way of judicial review—these raw statistics can be misleading, since the number of claims to reach the final determination stage is only a small proportion of the original actions. More than 50 per cent may be refused at first consideration; and of the remaining, many do not go to a full hearing because the claimant withdraws or the matter is resolved. In addition, a large percentage of applications are concerned with limited areas of governmental activity, for instance, prisons, policing, and housing and homelessness. Another myth is that central government departments are the sole focus of judicial review. In fact, local authorities are often the respondents in judicial review cases.[57]

These qualifications to the statistics for claims must raise doubts about access to judicial review and about the centrality of its impact on governmental administration as a whole. Nevertheless—and although judicial review may be a remedy of last resort—it remains true to say that more and more aggrieved citizens are turning to it.

8.6 The judicial review procedure

The corresponding procedure that governs claims for judicial review has relatively recent origins. Certainly, it is true that historically there has been no separate administrative court structure as in (for instance) France,[58] and that it has only been since 1977 that there has been a formalised procedure under which many administrative law cases have been heard in the Queen's Bench Division of the High Court (claims for judicial review in England and Wales have, in fact, been heard by an 'Administrative Court' since the Civil Procedure Rules entered into force in 2000; 'applications' in Northern Ireland continue to be heard in the Queen's Bench Division of the High Court; while 'petitions' in Scotland are made to the Court of Session).[59] However, to understand more fully the significance of the 1977 procedure,[60] it is important to know some points of detail about the procedure and practice that predominated before the reforms were introduced. We will thus begin our analysis with some comments about the availability of remedies in proceedings against public authorities before 1977.

8.6.1 The old procedure

Prior to the reforms, judicial review was obtainable either from the Divisional Court using the prerogative remedies of *certiorari*, *mandamus*, or *prohibition* (now,

---

57 See further M Sunkin, 'Mapping the Use of Judicial Review to Challenge Local Authorities in England and Wales' [2007] *Public Law* 545.

58 See JWF Allison, *A Continental Distinction in the Common Law* (Oxford: Oxford University Press, 1996).

59 On Northern Ireland see G Anthony, *Judicial Review in Northern Ireland*, 2nd edn (Oxford: Hart Publishing, 2014); and on Scottish law see C Himsworth, 'Judicial Review in Scotland' in M Supperstone, J Goudie, and P Walker (eds), *Judicial Review*, 5th edn (London: Butterworths, LexisNexis, 2014), ch 22.

60 Rules of the Supreme Court (Amendment No 3) (SI 1977/1955)—the reforms came into effect on 11 January 1978.

respectively, a quashing order, a mandatory order, or a prohibiting order), or from the Chancery Division using the equitable remedies of injunction or declaration. All these remedies will be dealt with in more detail in chapter 18, but an outline of their various uses is needed here. In short, an order of *certiorari* had the effect of quashing an *ultra vires* decision or other measure; an order of *mandamus* instructed (mandated) an authority to perform its statutory duty, which might include the common law duty to consider properly the question of whether to exercise a statutory power; and prohibition served to prevent the authority from acting unlawfully in the future. These three ancient remedies, historically known as 'prerogative' writs, were thus the traditional means of controlling public authorities. Indeed, while originally available only to the Crown—that is where the word 'prerogative' comes from—they were, by the end of the sixteenth century, also available, at least in principle, to any aggrieved citizen.

The main function of these remedies, until well into the nineteenth century, was to supervise the activities of local justices of the peace who exercised wide-ranging administrative as well as judicial functions. However, many administrative functions were later transferred to an enormous variety of special purpose boards such as the Poor Law Commissioners, Boards of Health, etc, while local authorities were created in a series of statutes, culminating in the Local Government Act 1888. These bodies were given the task of administering many aspects of the ever-increasing intervention by government (the late nineteenth-century administrative state) in people's lives. The courts, faced with the problem of controlling local government activities, utilised the established procedures of the prerogative writs, since Parliament had failed to provide any new mechanism to contain these developing powers.

Proceedings for the prerogative orders were nominally taken in the name of the Crown, which is why some administrative law cases are cited as, for example, *R v Secretary of State for the Environment, ex p Ostler*.[61] However, where the applicant sought an equitable remedy, proceedings were brought in the ordinary way and listed accordingly, for instance as *Boyce v Paddington Borough Council*.[62] Cases today in England and Wales are now listed under Part 54 of the Civil Procedure Rules as *R (on the application of the claimant) v the public body against which proceedings are brought* (i.e., the respondent).

It should also be added that there is a fourth prerogative remedy which still retains the name of a writ: that of *habeas corpus*. This tests the legality of a detention by, for example, the police, immigration authorities, mental health hospitals, etc. *Habeas corpus* is, however, governed by its own special procedures, recognising what is usually an emergency situation, and access to it has not been affected by procedural reforms in the field of judicial review.

Finally, it should be noted that the equitable remedies of the injunction and declaration have a relatively recent history in public law terms. Indeed, it was not until the prerogative remedies were well established in the late nineteenth century that it was appreciated that the injunction and declaration might be useful in proceedings against public bodies. The injunction was used mainly as an alternative to prohibition, as it was thought to be freer from procedural technicalities

---

61 [1976] 3 All ER 90.
62 [1903] 1 Ch 109.

and therefore, in some cases, easier to obtain. In turn, the use of the declaration in public law cases dates back to *Dyson v Attorney General*.[63] Despite parliamentary encouragement in various statutes, the Courts of Chancery had previously been unwilling to grant a declaration by itself, rather than as an adjunct to another remedy. However, the willingness of the court in this case to grant a declaration against the Inland Revenue Commissioners paved the way for the future, and the declaration has since proved to be one of the most useful remedies in public law. Its great advantage is generally understood to be its flexibility, as its declaratory nature does not change the legal position between the parties but merely confirms respective rights and responsibilities and/or states whether a particular measure is *intra* or *ultra vires*. Hence, where there is a challenge to, for instance, secondary legislation that has since provided the basis for a range of other administrative decisions, the courts may refuse to quash the legislation in the event that is *ultra vires* and instead make a declaration as to its illegality.[64] This is because a quashing order would remove the legal basis for decisions taken with reference to the legislation (something that could greatly complicate the workings of the administration), and the court may therefore wish simply to declare that the legislation is unlawful and allow the government voluntarily to make the necessary amendments in the light of the judgment of the court. That said, it is important to note that declarations are non-coercive remedies and that failure to comply with a declaratory order will not amount to contempt of court, albeit that a coercive order may later be granted by the court where there is a failure to comply with a declaration.[65]

8.6.2 The post-1977 procedure

Until 1977, therefore, there were various remedies available to an aggrieved citizen. The difficulty, however, was that the decision whether to seek a prerogative remedy from the Divisional Court, or an equitable remedy from the Courts of Chancery, was not at all an easy one. Entirely different procedures, time limits, and rules of *locus standi* applied, and even the conduct of the actual hearing itself could vary. In 1969, the Law Commission thus recommended to the Lord Chancellor that a Royal Commission be set up to undertake a wide-ranging review of administrative law covering both the grounds of review and the available remedies. However, the Lord Chancellor assigned to the Law Commission the task of reviewing only remedies, with a view to evolving a simpler and more effective procedure.

The result of the Law Commission's recommendations was initially, in 1977, a change in Order 53 of (what were then) the Rules of the Supreme Court, which was subsequently paralleled by the enactment of section 31 of the (then) Supreme Court Act 1981 (now Senior Courts Act 1981). The essential nature of the reform was that there should be one single procedure for administrative law cases, to be known as the application for judicial review. However, applicants would still have to specify which particular remedy or remedies they were seeking from the old list of five. A novelty was the possibility of adding a claim for damages to one of the five, but only if an ordinary claim for damages, for instance in tort or contract,

---

63 [1911] 1 KB 410.
64 But compare *HM Treasury v Ahmed* [2010] 2 AC 534, considered at 18.3.1.
65 See, e.g., *Webster v Southwark London Borough Council* [1983] QB 698.

could be established. No new head of damages was introduced. Thus, in this respect, the principal advantage was to avoid the duplication of proceedings in seeking a judicial review from one court and damages from another.

The upshot of the Law Commission's recommendations was therefore a procedure that was essentially based on that of the old prerogative remedies. Indeed, while the procedure introduced in England and Wales in 1977 has since been modified by Part 54 of the Civil Procedure Rules, many of its key features remain the same and there has in that sense been continuity since 1977.[66] The procedure thus involves two stages, the first of which is an application for permission (formerly 'leave'). This stage acts as a 'filter' that allows the courts to consider, among other things, whether the judicial review procedure is the appropriate procedure given the remedy that is sought; whether the claimant has an effective, alternative remedy; whether the claimant has an arguable case; whether the claimant has standing; and whether the claim was delayed. Only where permission/leave is granted will the case then progress to the second stage, which is the full hearing. It is usually—though not always—at that stage that the court receives detailed arguments about legal doctrine and the grounds for judicial review.

We will return to the grounds for review in chapters 11 to 17 and, in the remainder of this chapter, we propose to examine more closely the matters that the courts consider at the permission/leave stage. How do those matters serve to determine which cases can proceed to a substantive hearing? And have the courts approached such matters rigidly, or has the case law been characterised by flexibility?

8.7 Public law and private law remedies: which procedure?

One of the key questions for any claimant is the nature of the remedial order that he or she wishes to obtain from the court and the procedure that he or she should thereby use. Of course, in many cases it will be obvious that the matters arising are matters of 'public law'; that the individual will want one or more of the prerogative orders as a remedy; and that the judicial review procedure should be followed (we discuss the idea and reach of 'public law' in chapter 9). However, what is the position in cases that also affect the 'private law' rights of the individual, or in which the individual wishes to obtain only a declaration and/or an injunction from the court? Should the judicial review procedure always be used in such cases, or can the (historically) private law remedies also be sought outside of the judicial review procedure?

The law on these questions is now fairly clear, but it was not always so and certainly was not in the initial years after the introduction of the new procedure in 1977. Part of the problem stemmed from the wording of the relevant rules of court. These stated that an application for one of the prerogative remedies 'shall be made by way of an application for judicial review'. Equally, however, they provided that an application for a declaration or an injunction might be made by way of an application for judicial review if the court was satisfied of certain conditions, namely that, having

---

[66] On the 1977 procedure and that under Part 54 of the Civil Procedure Rules see T Griffiths, 'The Procedural Impact of Bowman and Part 54 of the CPR' [2000] 5 *Judicial Review* 209.

regard to the matters in respect of which the relief may be granted, the nature of the persons and bodies against whom the relief may be granted, and all the circumstances of the case, it would be just and convenient for the remedy to be granted.[67] Some confusion remained as to whether this meant that there was still a choice as to procedure if an injunction or declaration was sought, and conflicting judicial decisions were made between 1978 and 1982. The result was an uncertainty in the law that had the obvious potential to work to the disadvantage of individuals.

8.7.1 The significance of *O'Reilly v Mackman*

In *O'Reilly v Mackman*[68] the House of Lords attempted to clear up the confusion, although the case arguably resulted in even more procedural problems. In *O'Reilly*, several prisoners alleged that a prison Board of Visitors had acted outside its disciplinary powers and, in particular, in breach of the rules of natural justice when it had reached a decision to impose penalties (loss of remission) on prisoners involved in prison riots. The four prisoners all sought declarations, but did not use the new judicial review procedure, and the House of Lords unanimously decided that this was an abuse of the process of the court. The application for judicial review procedure, then under Order 53 of the Rules of the Supreme Court, had been set up specifically to deal with public law issues and to impose, in the public interest, safeguards against 'groundless, unmeritorious or tardy attacks upon the validity of decisions made by public authorities in the field of public law'.[69] The public interest was therefore given priority over the interests of the private individuals (prisoners), and it was emphasised that the normal route would in future be by way of Order 53, with only a number of limited exceptions being made to this general rule. These would be, first, where the invalidity of a decision arises as a collateral issue in proceedings concerning the private law rights of the individual; secondly, where none of the parties objected to a remedy being sought otherwise than in proceedings for judicial review; and thirdly, where a further exception could be established on the facts of an individual case. It was also noted that none of the prisoners had any private law right which he could have pursued, since remission of sentence was not a right but an 'indulgence'. All that they had was a legitimate expectation that the decision of the Board of Visitors would be taken lawfully. Therefore, by pursuing a private law remedy they were attempting to circumvent the special protection which had been provided by Parliament for statutory authorities, especially the need for leave and short time limits (considered later). Furthermore, as Lord Diplock stated, many of the previous procedural disadvantages of using the Divisional Court procedure had, in theory at least, been removed, for example the old discovery procedure which had been replaced by the use of affidavit evidence.

    O'Reilly v Mackman was said to have ushered in a rule of 'procedural exclusivity' and it was criticised as overly rigid and as generating even greater procedural uncertainty.[70] For instance, the scope for uncertainty was apparent in *Cocks v Thanet*

---

67 See, too, the wording of s 31 of the Supreme Court (now Senior Courts) Act 1981.

68 [1983] 2 AC 237.

69 Ibid, 282, Lord Diplock.

70 See, e.g., C Harlow, '"Public" and "Private Law": Definition without Distinction' (1980) *Modern Law Review* 241 and S Fredman and G Morris, 'The Cost of Exclusivity: Public–Private Re-examined' [1994] *Public Law* 69.

District Council,[71] where private law proceedings had been brought in the County Court. The issue involved in that case was the nature of the duty that the Housing (Homeless Person) Act 1977 imposed upon local authorities, which the House of Lords held divided into two. The first was a public law duty to act lawfully and to apply the provisions of the relevant statute properly to the individual case, including through following the correct procedures, making inquiries, and taking all relevant considerations into account. Once an authority had done this, and had decided that it had a statutory duty to house the individual, the second private law duty arose, which was to be enforced by way of private law proceedings. On the facts, it was thus held that the applicant should have brought judicial review proceedings as he was seeking to challenge decisions in respect of the first part of the duty. To allow the issue to be raised by way of private law would be contrary to public policy and an abuse of process.[72]

In contrast, *Davy v Spelthorne Borough Council* appeared as something of an exception to the exclusivity principle.[73] The facts were that in 1979 the plaintiff reached agreement with the council that he would not oppose an enforcement notice terminating his right to use his premises, but this was on the condition that the council agreed not to enforce the notice for three years. However, the council subsequently served a notice which required the removal of buildings belonging to the plaintiff, and the plaintiff commenced a private law action seeking an injunction to prevent the notice from being implemented, an order to have it set aside, and damages for the negligent advice given by the council. The local authority sought to have all the claims struck out on the basis that these were rights that should enjoy protection exclusively under public law, and the first two claims were dealt with in that way. However, on appeal to the House of Lords it was held that the claim for damages did not fall within the realm of public law (no decision of the council was being impugned) but rather came within the ordinary principles of tort law. Lord Fraser thus pointed out that the cause of action centred on the fact that the plaintiff had followed the negligent advice of the council and thereby lost the opportunity to appeal against the notice. Damages were being sought for compensation as a result of the council's negligent advice and not primarily to enforce a public law right. This judgment therefore appeared to indicate that an action against a public authority in contract or tort for damages that did not involve a 'live' public law dimension did not have to be taken under the judicial review procedure. In other words, the public law element was here regarded as peripheral, with Lord Wilberforce emphasising that English law 'fastens not on principles but on remedies' and calling for a pragmatic, flexible approach to deciding such questions in order to avoid 'rigidity and procedural hardship for plaintiffs'. In other words, his Lordships favoured a case-by-case, common law approach that would offset the limitations of a rigid demarcation between 'public' and 'private' law.[74]

In an area of increasing complexity, one of the most important judgments was *Roy v Kensington and Chelsea and Westminster Family Practitioner Committee*.[75] Dr Roy

---

71 [1983] 2 AC 286.

72 See, too, *Mohram Ali v Tower Hamlets London Borough Council* [1993] QB 407 and *O'Rourke v Camden London Borough Council* [1998] AC 188.

73 [1984] AC 262. See, too, *Wandsworth London Borough Council v Winder* [1985] AC 461.

74 [1984] AC 262, 276.

75 [1992] 1 AC 624.

was a GP who, under the relevant regulations, had to devote a substantial amount of time to the NHS in order to qualify for the full rate of financial allowance from the local Family Practice Committee. However, the Committee decided that he had not fulfilled this requirement and, when it reduced his allowance by 20 per cent, he sought a declaration in the Chancery Division. The first instance judge, holding that the decision in question was of a public law nature, struck out the claim as an abuse of process, but both the Court of Appeal and the House of Lords considered that Dr Roy had private law rights (the right to be paid for the work that he had done) which could be asserted in a private action. Although public law issues were clearly pertinent to the case, the House of Lords appeared to recognise that the plaintiff should have some procedural options. For instance, Lord Lowry marked the retreat from an over-rigid application of the *O'Reilly* exclusivity principle by distinguishing between two approaches. The first, which he described as the 'broad approach', demanded recourse to judicial review to challenge an act or decision of a public body only where *no* private law rights were at issue. The second 'narrow approach'—that of Lord Diplock in *O'Reilly v Mackman*—demanded that all challenges to public law matters should be by way of application for judicial review, save for some limited exceptions. For his part, Lord Lowry stressed that he preferred the broad approach (although he managed to decide the issue before him by use of the 'narrow approach'), and that not the smallest reason for doing so was the sense that it would help to eliminate the procedural wrangles which had arisen since *O'Reilly* and the introduction of the exclusivity principle. As his Lordship expressed it: ' . . even if I treat it [the *O'Reilly* principle] as a general rule, there are many indications in favour of a liberal attitude towards the exceptions contemplated but not spelt out by Lord Diplock.'[76]

8.7.2 **An end to the procedural wrangling?**

The case law after *Roy* further sought to end the procedural difficulties of *O'Reilly*. For instance, in *Trustees of the Dennis Rye Pension Fund v Sheffield City Council*[77] Lord Woolf made three 'pragmatic suggestions' about how procedural issues might be resolved. The dispute here had arisen when the plaintiffs had been served with repair notices in respect of properties but were subsequently refused improvement grants for the work done because the council did not consider that the work had been completed to its satisfaction (grants were applied for and made under the Local Government and Housing Act 1989, section 117(3)). The plaintiffs commenced an action in private law for recovery of the money due. The council in turn contended that the proceedings should be struck out as an abuse of process because, first, there were no grounds for the action and, secondly, because, even if there were grounds, the action should have been brought by way of judicial review. However, Lord Woolf MR held that the plaintiff's action was not an abuse of process and that, once an application for a grant had been approved and the applicant had fulfilled the statutory conditions, the individual could enforce the resulting duty to pay the money by way of private law proceedings. Applying *Roy*,

---

76 Ibid, 654. And for development of the broad approach see *Mercury Communications Ltd v Director-General of Telecommunications* [1996] 1 WLR 48.

77 [1998] 1 WLR 840.

Lord Woolf remarked that 'largely tactical issues' regarding procedure had once again led to a situation where the costs incurred and the time spent in litigation had been 'to little or no purpose'. Following a review of the persisting problems arising from *O'Reilly v Mackman*, he said that, rather than the court immersing itself in technical distinctions between public and private rights, it should focus on the *practical* consequences of pursuing different courses of action. In other words, the court should exercise its judgment in each case rather than be bound over by presumptions about procedural rigidity.

Turning to the need for pragmatism, Lord Woolf's suggestions were:

(1) If it is not clear whether judicial review or an ordinary action is the correct procedure it will be safer to make an application for judicial review than commence an ordinary action since there should be no question of it being treated as an abuse of process by avoiding the protection provided by judicial review.

(2) If a case is brought by ordinary action and there is an application to strike out the case, the court should, at least if it is unclear whether the case should have been brought by judicial review, ask itself whether, if the case had been brought by judicial review when the action was commenced, it is clear leave would have been granted. If it would, then that is at least an indication that there has been no harm to the interests judicial review is designed to protect.

(3) Finally, in cases where it is unclear whether proceedings have been correctly brought by an ordinary action it should be remembered that after consulting the Crown Office a case can always be transferred to the Crown Office List as an alternative to being struck out. (See [1998] 1 WLR 840, 848–9).

Another case that developed the flexible (broad) approach was *Steed v Secretary of State for the Home Department*.[78] The issue here concerned a delay over compensation due to the plaintiff for the surrender of handguns. Steed made a claim by means of a summons in the County Court, but the Home Office contended, *inter alia*, that the complaint should have been decided by means of an application for judicial review. Lord Slynn, reviewing the case law discussed above, held that, if the challenge had been to the *vires* of the entire scheme of compensation, an application for judicial review would have been the appropriate course. But here it was convenient to begin by ordinary summons and to deal with a particular claim on its merits.

In addition to the changing emphasis in the case law, the rules that now govern the judicial review procedure in England and Wales—contained in Part 54 of the Civil Procedure Rules—have likewise sought to encourage flexibility. That this was to be their effect was clear from the Court of Appeal's judgment in *Clark v University of Lincolnshire and Humberside*.[79] A student had failed a coursework-based module after allegations of plagiarism by the university. Following a dispute over the university's appeals procedures, she sued the university in contract. However, the university argued that the student should have proceeded by way of a claim for judicial review because the institution did not possess a visitor (a form of internal disputes resolution mechanism). Although the matter was open to judicial review, the court allowed the student to proceed by means of a private law claim

---

78 [2000] 1 WLR 1169.
79 [2000] 1 WLR 1988.

in contract. This was because the Court considered that it would be wrong in the instant case to prevent the claim as an abuse of process, albeit that the courts can still intervene for that reason in other cases. As Lord Woolf MR put it:

Where a student has, as here, a claim in contract, the court will not strike out a claim which could more appropriately be made [by way of judicial review] solely because of the procedure which has been adopted. It may however do so, if it comes to the conclusion that in all the circumstances, including the delay in initiating the proceedings, there has been an abuse of the process of the court under the CPR . . . What is likely to be important . . . will not be whether the right procedure has been adopted but whether the protection provided by Order 53 has been flouted in circumstances which are inconsistent with the proceedings being able to be conducted justly in accordance with the general principles in CPR Part 1.[80]

The emphasis on the need for flexibility has continued in subsequent case law, and it is now accepted that arguments of form should not frustrate the resolution of genuine disputes.[81] Indeed, Michael Fordham QC has previously gone so far as to say that the earlier authorities on exclusivity are now 'increasingly irrelevant having been overtaken by the CPR and the fully matured version of the principle, where raising public law issues outside CPR 54(I) is impermissible only if an abuse of process'.[82] It might therefore be said that the true value of the above case law lies not in what it reveals about current practice, but more in what reveals about how judicial reasoning can both create and then remedy problems within the legal system.[83]

8.8 Effective alternative remedies

The above analysis of when public law proceedings should be brought by way of judicial review is, however, subject to one important qualification. Put simply, recourse to the judicial review procedure is always subject to the requirement that the claimant has already exhausted, or has had no access to, an alternative, effective remedy. A requirement to this effect has a sound logic to it. First, there is an obvious danger that, if the matter goes first to the court on a claim for judicial review, the distinction between an appellate and review function will become blurred. Secondly, by directing the claimant/litigant towards whatever body might finally resolve the dispute, the court may be giving effect to a statutory provision which may well lay down that this other body or tribunal has jurisdiction in the matter. At the same time, the alternative path (other than judicial review) might be advantageous by being cheaper, with a more expeditious procedure and having the incidental benefit of relieving the High Court from having to deal with the case.

There are numerous examples of judicial review being denied because of the availability of appeals or other remedies. For instance, in *R v Peterkin, ex p Soni*,[84] an

---

80 Ibid, 1998. Note that, in accordance with the Higher Education Act 2004, student complaints are now heard by the Office of the Independent Adjudicator.

81 Authorities include *R (Cowl) v Plymouth City Council* [2001] EWCA Civ 193, [2002] 1 WLR 803, CA and *R (on the application of Heather) v Leonard Cheshire Foundation* [2002] 2 All ER 936.

82 *Judicial Review Handbook*, 4th edn (Oxford: Hart Publishing, 2004), 571.

83 For recognition of the need for flexibility see also *Ruddy v Chief Constable of, Strathclyde Police* [2012] UKSC 57, 2013 SC (UKSC) 126.

84 [1972] Imm AR 253.

immigration case, *certiorari* was refused because there was an appeal mechanism from the Immigration Adjudicator to the Immigration Appeals Tribunal. Similarly, *R v Hillingdon London Borough Council, ex p Royco Homes Ltd*[85] was a planning case with a statutory appeals procedure available to the Secretary of State. Lord Widgery stated that, if there is a system of appeals available, this will be considered more effective and therefore more appropriate than *certiorari* because a minister will, in one hearing, have 'jurisdiction to deal with [all the issues], whereas of course an application for *certiorari* is limited to cases where the issue is a matter of law'.[86]

That said, the requirement that other remedies have to be exhausted first is by no means absolute. For example, in *R v Chief Constable of Merseyside Police, ex p Calveley*,[87] it was held that, if the appellate procedure itself contained possible breaches of natural justice, the court would exercise its discretion to grant judicial review (albeit that it was further stated that this would be in exceptional cases only). Moreover, in *R v Leeds City Council, ex p Hendry*,[88] it was stated by Latham J that the existence of a statutory appeal procedure to challenge a decision did not automatically mean that the alternative route should be followed. The question was not whether there was an alternative avenue of statutory appeal, but whether, in the context of that procedure, the real issue could be determined by that means. In fact, it appears that there is a clear element of pragmatism—discernible in the case law—albeit that the starting point remains the presumption that alternative remedies must be exhausted before an applicant can have resort to judicial review.

8.9 **An arguable case**

We can deal with this point in very short form. Basically, the onus of proof throughout judicial review proceedings is on the applicant—save where there is a *prima facie* case of illegality[89]—and he or she must demonstrate at the permission stage that he or she has an 'arguable case'. This is sometimes alternatively formulated as an arguable case with a 'realistic prospect of success',[90] although all will depend on the context to the case and whether the judge, in his or her discretion, considers that the case should go forward. As Lord Diplock said in *R v Inland Revenue Commissioners, ex p National Federation of Self-employed and Small Businesses Ltd*:

The whole purpose of requiring that [permission] should first be obtained to make the application for judicial review would be defeated if the court were to go into the matter in any depth at that stage. If, on a quick perusal of the material then available, the court thinks that it discloses what might on further consideration turn out to be an arguable case in favour of granting to the applicant the relief claimed, it ought, in the exercise of judicial discretion, to give him [permission] to apply for that relief.[91]

---

85 [1974] QB 720.
86 Ibid, 729.
87 [1986] 1 QB 424.
88 (1994) 6 Admin LR 439.
89 *R v Home Secretary, ex p Khawaja* [1984] AC 74.
90 *Sharma v Brown-Antoine* [2007] 1 WLR 780, 787.
91 [1982] AC 617, 643–4. But see now also s 31(3C)–(3F) of the Senior Courts Act 1981, whereby the court must, save in a case of 'exceptional public interest', refuse to grant permission where it forms the view that it is 'highly likely' that the outcome for the applicant would not have been 'substantially different' if the conduct complained of had not occurred.

The very fact that individual judges must decide whether a case is arguable inevitably means that there can be differences of opinion about whether a particular case should proceed. For instance, in *Re Morrow and Campbell's Application for Leave*,[92] Kerr J considered that two Democratic Unionist Party (DUP) Ministers of the Executive Committee of the Northern Ireland Assembly had failed to demonstrate that they had an arguable case in respect of a decision of the First and Deputy First Ministers to withhold certain Committee documents from them in advance of Committee meetings (the decision to withhold documents had been taken in the face the DUP's refusal to be bound by confidentiality in respect of Committee deliberations). However, the Court of Appeal disagreed with this conclusion and considered that the substantive issues should be heard. The substantive issues were thus argued before the High Court, where Coghlin J granted the application for judicial review in the light of the unlawful frustration of the applicants' substantive legitimate expectation that they would be provided with some of the documents at issue.[93]

8.10 Standing

The rules on standing—or *locus standi*—essentially require that a claimant demonstrate to the court that there is some reason why he or she is entitled to challenge a decision or other measure by way of judicial review. It might appear at first sight that such rules are necessary to prevent the frivolous or vexatious claimant from troubling the already overburdened courts or disrupting unduly the administrative process. However, it is just as undesirable for such rules to be construed too narrowly, having the effect of providing yet another obstacle to obtaining relief, and excluding from a remedy all but the most directly affected of applicants. Take, for example, the decision to close a hospital. This may have profound consequences for hundreds of people, but can ordinary citizens opposing the policy take a public law action to oppose the decision? Should the right be confined to one or more of the interested groups, for example, health service managers, doctors, nurses, ancillary workers, patients, or trade unions whose members are affected? How does one determine which of these groups has standing to mount a challenge? In many situations where there has been *ultra vires* action by a public authority an adversely affected section of the community will be in need of a champion for its cause.

Before the reforms of the judicial review procedure in 1977, each remedy had its own standing requirements and these varied according to the remedy that was sought (for *certiorari* and *prohibition*, the person concerned had to be directly affected in some way; the rules were narrower still for *mandamus* because the applicant had to show, in addition, the infringement of a right). The test is now laid down in section 31(3) of the Senior Courts Act 1981, which provides:

No application for judicial review shall be made unless [permission] of the High Court has been obtained in accordance with the rules of court; and the court shall not grant [permission] to make such an application unless it considers that the [claimant] has a sufficient interest in the matter to which the application relates.

---

92 [2001] NI 261.
93 *Re Morrow and Campbell's Application* [2002] NIQB 4. On legitimate expectations see ch 15.

8.10.1 **The Fleet Street Casuals case**

R v Inland Revenue Commissioners, ex parte National Federation of Self-Employed and Small Businesses Ltd,[94] commonly referred to as the Fleet Street Casuals case, provided the first comprehensive discussion of the new standing rules. Briefly, the facts were that over a number of years there had been evidence of malpractice by workers in the newspaper industry. Many employees had been in the habit of presenting false claims for casual work under fictitious names (e.g., 'Mickey Mouse'). After they had been alerted to the practice, the Inland Revenue struck a deal regarding collection of future taxes whereby it agreed not to pursue any claims for previously unpaid tax. This decision infuriated the National Federation, a body broadly representative of the self-employed and small businesses, whose interest in this case was as ordinary taxpayers. The National Federation applied for a declaration that the agreement was unlawful and for an order of *mandamus* to compel the Revenue to collect the tax due.

The House of Lords began by considering the stage at which the matter of standing was to be resolved in proceedings. Under section 31 of (what was then) the Supreme Court Act 1981 an application (now claim) for judicial review is in the two stages we discussed above: the application for leave (now permission), followed by the full hearing of the case itself. The solution, which was accepted unanimously, was that standing should not be looked at in any detail as a preliminary matter, and that the filter provided by leave should be used only to weed out frivolous applications that are entirely without merit or brought by busy-bodies.[95] In so finding, the House of Lords emphasised that standing cannot be divorced from the merits of an application and that sufficiency of interest can only be gauged properly in the light of the full legal and factual circumstances (Lord Roskill, for instance, stated that standing 'is not simply a point of law to be determined in the abstract or upon assumed facts—but upon a due appraisal of many different factors revealed by the evidence presented by the parties, few if any of which will be able to be wholly isolated from the others').[96] The result of this more generous approach was that very few cases would fail at the leave stage because of a lack of standing even though it may quickly become apparent at the full hearing that the application is unlikely to succeed.

Their Lordships next turned to the question of the standard that would determine whether applicants have a sufficient interest for the purposes of obtaining a remedy. The approach adopted marked a significant liberalisation of the rules on standing. Although it was held that the association of small businesses making the application in the instant case did not have standing, the House of Lords nevertheless envisaged an approach in which potentially any government decision was open to challenge by any individual or group, where the fuller context suggested sufficiency of interest. The point was put at its highest by Lord Diplock, who considered that:

it would . . . be a grave lacuna in our system of public law if a pressure group, like the federation, or even a single public-spirited taxpayer, were prevented by outdated technical rules of *locus standi* from bringing the matter to the attention of the court to vindicate the rule of law and get the unlawful conduct stopped.[97]

---

94 [1982] AC 617.
95 See also, e.g., *R v Somerset County Council, ex p Dixon* [1997] COD 323.
96 [1982] AC 617, 656.
97 Ibid, 644.

Such comments made clear that the emphasis in the law was on the need to control illegality in the field of public law, and, equally, to safeguard the interests of an individual if their interests were directly affected. It followed that sufficiency of interest would arise in a case where such rights were affected or, alternatively, where the court considersed that government action should be reviewed irrespective of the absence of a directly affected party. This approach was accepted by other members of the court, albeit in words that were less robust than those used by Lord Diplock.

In the case before them their Lordships found that a coalition of taxpayers could not satisfy a legal test of standing that one taxpayer acting alone could not satisfy. In other words, one taxpayer ordinarily would not have an interest in the tax affairs of another taxpayer, and it followed that the requisite sufficiency of interest could not be established simply by amalgamating individual interests that, in and of themselves, did not satisfy the test. However, it was recognised that the applicants may have succeeded had it been shown that the Inland Revenue had yielded to improper pressure, or had committed a grave breach of duty. Indeed, in other circumstances, taxpayers have subsequently been recognised as having standing to challenge decisions. For instance, in *R v HM Treasury, ex p Smedley*[98] a taxpayer was considered to have sufficient standing to challenge an Order in Council allowing expenditure from the consolidated fund to (what was then) the European Community budget. This was because the Order in Council was potentially unlawful.[99] Moreover, in *R v Attorney General, ex p Imperial Chemical Industries plc*[100] the applicant was allowed to challenge a decision by the Revenue concerning the valuation of ethane. The applicant was considered to have standing on the ground that it was in competition with other companies and was not just raising it concerns as a taxpayer. This case therefore illustrates clearly the contextual nature of the approach adopted by the courts and the inherent flexibility in the new standing rules.

Another important point that follows from *Inland Revenue Commissioners* is that the test for standing now no longer varies according to the remedy sought (as was the case prior to the reforms) but fastens instead upon the nature of the claimant's interest in the case. Although there were some differences of opinion in the House of Lords, it has since become axiomatic that the test is the same irrespective of the remedy (i.e., whether a prerogative order or a declaration or injunction). The point is illustrated by *R v Felixstowe Justices, ex p Leigh*.[101] This case was brought by a journalist who was neither present at a trial before a bench of magistrates, nor was he directly concerned in the proceedings. Nevertheless, he sought a declaration that the justices were acting *ultra vires* when deciding that their own identities should not be disclosed, and he also sought *mandamus* to compel disclosure of the names of magistrates who heard the cases. A declaration was granted because there was, given the legal and factual context, a public interest in the matter raised. However, it was held that the journalist's interest in the case was not such that an order of *mandamus* should be made, as his investigative purposes would be served by the grant of a declaration. The approach of the court was therefore to look to the nature of the applicant's interest in the case rather than to the remedy. In other words,

---

98 [1985] QB 657.

99 For an historical comparator see the position of ratepayers in *Prescott v Birmingham Corporation* [1955] Ch 210.

100 [1987] 1 CMLR 72.

101 [1987] QB 582.

while some of the remedies were previously available only to certain applicants, availability is now determined on a case-by-case and context-sensitive basis.[102]

The nature of the relationship between a claimant's interests and remedies has also been explored recently by the Supreme Court in the case of *Walton v Scottish Ministers*.[103] This case involved a challenge to the lawfulness of ministerial approval for the construction of a road network outside Aberdeen, which was argued to have been granted in breach of consultation requirements imposed by EU law (specifically by the Strategic Environmental Assessment (SEA) Directive).[104] When the case came before the Supreme Court the main issues on appeal were: (i) whether the applicant had standing to bring the proceedings; (ii) whether the SEA Directive was of application in the case; and (iii) whether the applicant should be denied a remedy even if the SEA Directive did apply. Holding that the applicant did have standing but that the SEA Directive was not engaged on the facts, the Supreme Court emphasised that the remedies that are available in public law are discretionary and that the courts can refuse relief where, for instance, an applicant has suffered no substantial prejudice as a result of a procedural error and where the broader public interest or some private interest would be disadvantaged by the grant of a remedy. In that circumstance, the Supreme Court was of the view that a remedy may be withheld at the discretion of the Court, even in cases where it is argued that an individual's rights under EU law are in issue. The Court's ruling on this point was of some significance as it marked a departure from the former position whereby it was expected that remedies would be granted in all EU law cases because of the doctrine of the supremacy of EU law.[105]

8.10.2 Group interests and/or the public interest: 'open' or 'closed' access

In turn, the emergence of the more liberal approach to standing in *Inland Revenue Commissioners* prompted an active debate—both among academics and members of the judiciary—about the model of public law emerging in the UK. The underlying emphasis in *Inland Revenue Commissioners* on controlling public law wrongs had, in short, raised the question of whether access to the courts should now be regarded as more 'open' than 'closed'. Open approaches to access would be synonymous with Lord Diplock's judgment in *Inland Revenue Commissioners*: that is, that it is more important to prevent government illegality and that it does not matter who is the corresponding claimant so long as the issue is brought to the court. However, a potential problem with trends towards open access is a tendency to promote judicial activism and the involvement of courts in policy matters that are better left to the political arena. The potential for such activism is particularly pronounced in relation to representative applications.[106] Although some representative actions

---

102 See also on this point *Gillick v West Norfolk and Wisbech Area Health Authority* [1986] AC 112, a decision that has been criticised on the grounds that Mrs Gillick lacked *locus standi* because she was essentially acting to protect her private law rights as a parent.

103 [2012] UKSC 44, [2013] 1 CMLR 28.

104 Directive 2001/42/EC.

105 For the earlier position see *Berkeley v Secretary of State for the Environment* [2000] UKHL 36, [2001] 2 AC 603, 616, Lord Hoffmann; and for subsequent application of *Walton* see, e.g., *R (Champion) v North Norfolk DC* [2015] UKSC 52, [2015] 1 WLR 3710. On remedies in EU law see 3.2.4.

106 See P Cane, 'Open Standing and the Role of Courts in a Democratic Society' (1999) *Singapore Law Review* 23.

will be in the form of class actions whereby, for instance, a trade union brings proceedings on the part of each of its directly affected members,[107] other actions may be taken by groups that claim to represent the 'public interest' (or a section of it). Such groups will often be politically motivated and they may regard litigation as merely one aspect of their wider activities.[108] Well-resourced groups may simply calculate that there is much to be gained from the publicity that a full hearing may generate, even if the case itself is unlikely to succeed, although the position of such applicants may now be complicated by section 31(3C)–(3F) of the Senior Courts Act 1981, at note 91 above: this requires the court, save in cases of 'exceptional public interest', to refuse permission where it considers that it is 'highly likely' that the outcome for the applicant would not have been 'substantially different' if the conduct complained of had not occurred. So, should the courts be willing to permit such claims, particularly if they facilitate participation in the wider democratic process by allowing access to a forum that can overturn government preferences? Or should the courts instead adopt a 'closed' approach to access, thereby avoiding the prospect of becoming involved in essentially political disputes?

The cases in the years immediately after *Inland Revenue Commissioners* pointed in both directions. On the one hand, there were a number of judgments that quite clearly preferred the open approach and where standing was accorded to, among others, Covent Garden residents, local objectors to a planning scheme, and the Child Poverty Action Group.[109] However, a more closed approach was preferred in *R v Secretary of State for the Environment, ex p Rose Theatre Trust Co.*[110] The facts were that a property development in central London on the site of the Rose Theatre unearthed some archaeological remains of the original construction of a theatre used by Shakespeare during the Elizabethan period. A trust company that had been established for the purpose of protecting the site applied to the Secretary of State to have the monument listed under section 1 of the Ancient Monuments and Archaeological Areas Act 1979. Although the remains were acknowledged as being of national importance, the Secretary of State refused to list them for the reason that compensation might have to be paid and that the site was under no immediate threat. The Rose Theatre Trust applied for judicial review of the decision. Although leave was granted to apply for review, the application itself was refused for the reason of the applicant's lack of standing. First, Schiemann J considered that the mere gathering together of people with a common interest did not, in itself, achieve standing. It was reasoned that it would be remarkable if two persons without such standing should be able to acquire such standing by the simple fact of incorporating themselves as a company or trust. Second, it was emphasised that this was a case concerned with a governmental decision in respect of which the ordinary citizen does not have a sufficient interest to entitle him to challenge the decision. The application was dismissed.

Rose Theatre Trust was, however, to prove something of an exception to an emerging rule (although the logic of the closed approach was not without influence).[111]

107 See, e.g., *R v Secretary of State for the Home Department, ex p Fire Brigade's Union* [1995] 2 AC 513.

108 See G Anthony, 'Public Interest and the Three Dimensions of Judicial Review' (2013) 64 *Northern Ireland Legal Quarterly* 125.

109 Respectively, *Covent Garden Community Association Ltd v GLC* [1981] JPL 183; *R v Hammersmith and Fulham London Borough Council, ex p People Before Profit* (1982) 80 LGR 322; and *R v Secretary of State for Social Services, ex p Child Poverty Action Group* [1990] 2 QB 540.

110 [1990] 1 QB 504.

111 See, e.g., *R v Secretary of State for Defence, ex p Sancto* [1993] COD 144; *R v Darlington Borough Council, ex p Association of Darlington Taxi Owners* [1994] COD 424; and *R v Secretary of State for the Home Department, ex p Bulger* [2001] EWHC Admin 119, [2001] 3 All ER 449.

There were, during the 1990s, a number of high-profile cases in which the courts accepted controversial representative applications. The reasons for accepting that the applicants had standing in the cases in question sometimes varied. For example, in *R v HM Inspectorate of Pollution, ex p Greenpeace Ltd (No 2)*,[112] it was held that Greenpeace had the necessary standing to challenge (albeit unsuccessfully) the variation of existing authorisations for the Sellafield nuclear processing site because of its membership in the area, because of its access to expert information, and because it was likely that failure to accord standing to Greenpeace would result in 'a less well informed challenge [which might stretch] unnecessarily the court's resources and which would not afford the court the assistance it requires in order to do justice between the parties'.[113] And in *R v Secretary of State for Employment, ex p Equal Opportunities Commission*,[114] it was held by the House of Lords that the Equal Opportunities Commission had standing by virtue of its statutory powers to challenge the compatibility of the Employment Protection Consolidation Act 1978 with EU law. Lord Keith was clearly in no doubt about the development of the rules when he stressed that:

In my opinion it would be a very retrograde step now to hold that the EOC has no *locus standi* to agitate in judicial review proceedings questions related to sex discrimination which are of public importance and affect a large section of the population.[115]

The outstanding example of a pressure group application—and one that was both successful and controversial— perhaps remains *R v Secretary of State for Foreign and Commonwealth Affairs, ex p World Development Movement Ltd*.[116] The applicant here was a non-partisan pressure group that had been established for more than 20 years and had an interest in ensuring that aid budgets were put to good use to fund worthy overseas projects. The application in question challenged the Secretary of State's decision to grant aid to the building of a dam in Malaysia. The applicant argued that the project in question was not economically viable, and that the Overseas Development and Co-operation Act 1980 permitted the Secretary of State to make awards of aid only where they would help to develop the recipient economy. In granting the application—this notwithstanding that none of the members of the association had a direct personal interest in the matter—the court listed a number of considerations that were determinative of the issue. Rose LJ pointed in particular to the need to vindicate the rule of law and that, in the absence of the applicant coming forward, it was likely that the issue would have escaped judicial attention. The application was thus allowed and the decision to award the aid package in question was found to be *ultra vires*.[117]

The move towards increasingly liberal standing has not been limited to England and Wales, as the Northern Ireland courts have long also adopted an open approach, and the law in Scotland—where a petitioner has historically had to have 'title and

---

112 [1994] 4 All ER 329.

113 Ibid, 350.

114 [1995] 1 AC 1.

115 [1995] 1 AC 1, 26. See also, e.g., *R v Traffic Commissioner for the North West Traffic Area, ex p Brake* [1996] COD 248 where 'Brake', a pressure group and unincorporated association with the aim of promoting greater safety in the use of lorries on public roads, was granted leave to apply.

116 [1995] 1 WLR 386.

117 For a recent example of a successful application by a pressure group see *R (Child Poverty Action Group) v Secretary of State for Work and Pensions* [2012] EWHC 2579 (Admin).

interest'—has recently aligned itself with that in the rest of the UK.[118] But are representative actions beneficial and democratically legitimate? It is certainly true that one reason for increased judicial activism has been a perception that Parliament is relatively weak as a counter-weight to executive action, and cases such as *World Development Movement* arguably allow the courts to fill, in part, the accountability void. However, in the absence of a constitutional court, the liberal approach to standing which has given many single-issue pressure groups access to the courts has been questioned as undermining the democratic process of representative government. In a carefully argued critique, it has been pointed out by Harlow that judicial review has become a political tactic, with permission being routinely granted to a broad range of organisations without regard to whether they have consulted their membership. This raises the issue of whether such groups have a legitimate right or justification to challenge the decisions of elected public bodies either in their own right, or on the basis of their understanding of the public interest. Harlow has argued that the relaxed approach to standing should be modified to prevent judicial review from becoming a free for all, and that the courts should, in effect, tend towards the *Rose Theatre* approach rather than that in *World Development Movement*. It remains to be seen whether any such shift occurs.

8.10.3 Standing under the Human Rights Act

In the light of the points made by Harlow, it is interesting to note that the standing rules under the Human Rights Act 1998 have the clear effect of limiting the scope for public interest applications in human rights cases.[119] In line with the approach taken at Strasbourg, section 7(1) of the Human Rights Act 1998 adopts a 'victim' test that incorporates Article 34 of the ECHR.[120] This is intended as a much narrower standard and, since the Human Rights Act 1998 came into force in October 2000, there have been some strict rulings on the victim requirement.[121] On the other hand, it is perhaps important not to overstate the point about public interest actions being 'written out' of the Act, as groups will in some cases be able to provide financial backing for an individual who is a victim for the purposes of the Act. It is also to be noted that some discrete pieces of legislation enable organisations to bring proceedings under the Human Rights Act 1998 even though the organisations would not themselves come within the section 7 definition of victims.[122] Finally, it is possible for public interest groups to gain access to courts as third party interveners in human rights cases, albeit that this option requires that a victim has already initiated proceedings.[123]

118 On Northern Ireland see *Re D's Application* [2003] NI 295; and on Scottish law see *Axa General Insurance v Lord Advocate* [2011] UKSC 46, [2012] 1 AC 868.

119 See further 4.4.5.

120 Art 34 ECHR reads: 'The [European Court of Human Rights] may receive applications from any person, non-governmental organisation, or group of individuals claiming to be a victim of a violation . . .'

121 See, e.g., *Re CAJ's Application* [2005] NIQB 25—human rights NGO not allowed to rely on Art 2 ECHR when seeking information on the ongoing police investigation into the murder of one of its members.

122 e.g., s 71 of the Northern Ireland Act 1998 as relates to the powers of the Northern Ireland Human Rights Commission; and see *Re Northern Ireland Human Rights Commission's Application* [2014] NI 263.

123 For an example of such an intervention see *R (Nicklinson) v Ministry of Justice* [2014] UKSC 38, [2015] AC 657, discussed at 4.4.3, 'Care Not Killing' intervening.

Before leaving section 7, there are two further points that we should make. The first concerns the circumstance where an individual who has successfully brought proceedings against the UK in Strasbourg initiates a further claim for judicial review in the domestic courts, seeking remedies that may include damages. Is that person no longer a victim, that is, because he or she has already been given a remedy in Strasbourg? The answer here—found in the House of Lords judgment in *In Re McKerr*—is that they may still be a victim, and that all will depend on the circumstances of the case.[124] For instance, in the *McKerr* case itself, the son of a man who had been killed in 1982 by undercover police officers sought additional remedies in the Northern Ireland courts after the European Court of Human Rights (ECtHR) had found a violation of the Article 2 ECHR right to life.[125] Although the point about standing was ultimately rendered secondary by the House of Lords finding that the Human Rights Act does not have retrospective effect—a finding that has since been overtaken in Article 2 cases by the Supreme Court ruling in *Re McCaughey*[126]—the House emphasised that the applicant would otherwise have been a victim within the meaning of section 7. This was because the ECtHR ruling had not resolved all issues relevant to Article 2 of the ECHR, in particular those related to the proportionality of the force used by the police. The case on that basis suggests that individuals will remain as victims for so long as their interests are affected by the state's failure to discharge its obligations under international law.

The second point concerns public authorities. Article 34 of the ECHR, noted above, refers to actions being brought by 'any person, non-governmental organisation or group of individuals', and this wording has long been understood to preclude proceedings brought by a state and/or by its manifestations. However, while it is clear that 'core' public authorities for the purposes of section 6 of the Human Rights Act 1998 cannot be victims for the purposes of section 7, the position in respect of 'mixed function' public authorities is less well-established (mixed function authorities are those persons 'certain of whose functions are functions of a public nature' and who are bound by the Human Rights Act 1998 when performing public functions but not when they are performing private acts).[127] Some commentators have argued that the courts should be slow to recognise bodies such as charities, privatised utilities, and companies as section 6 mixed function authorities, as this would mean that the bodies would not be able to rely on the ECHR in other cases as they would no longer exist as 'non-governmental organisations' etc.[128] At the same time, the logic of that argument has since been doubted by the House of Lords, where it was suggested that a body may be classified as a mixed function authority in one case but still be able to avail itself of its rights under the ECHR in another when it is acting in a private capacity.[129] Nevertheless, the comments were made *obiter* and there is not yet any definitive statement on the interplay between sections 6 and 7.

---

124 [2004] 1 WLR 807. See, too, the different circumstance presented by parallel negligence and Art 2 ECHR claims as in *Rabone v Pennine Care NHS Trust* [2012] 2 WLR 381 discussed at 20.5.

125 See *McKerr v UK* (2002) 34 EHRR 20.

126 [2011] 2 WLR 1279. But see also *Keyu v Secretary of State for Foreign and Commonwealth Affairs* [2015] UKSC 69, [2015] 3 WLR 1665 and 4.4.6.

127 See 4.4.4 and 9.2.3.

128 D Oliver, 'The Frontiers of the State: Public Authorities and Public Functions Under the Human Rights Act' [2000] *Public Law* 476.

129 *Aston Cantlow v Wallbank* [2003] 3 WLR 283, 288, para 11, Lord Nicholls.

8.11 **Time limits and delay**

The final aspect of the procedure to be noted is that concerned with the time limit for initiating proceedings. Under the rules in England and Wales, a claim for judicial review generally has to be made '(a) promptly and (b) in any event not later than 3 months after the grounds to make the claim first arose' (the outer time limit is shorter in planning law cases and cases under the Public Contracts Regulations 2015, *viz* six weeks, and 30 days, respectively).[130] This is because time is very often of the essence in public law matters, and 'undue delay' in applying for judicial review, even within the three-month time limit, can legitimately be used as a reason for the court not to grant permission to proceed (or, if permission is granted, for refusing relief at the end of the full hearing).[131] Lord Diplock summarised the underlying logic in *O'Reilly v Mackman* when he said that:

The public interest in good administration requires that public authorities and third parties should not be kept in suspense as to the legal validity of a decision the authority has reached in purported exercise of decision-making powers for any longer than is absolutely necessary in fairness to the person affected by the decision.[132]

Bearing in mind this need for speed, the promptly/three-month time limit may appear at first glance to be perfectly adequate, especially as the court can extend the limit in exceptional cases, for example, if an alternative remedy has been pursued or for delays in obtaining legal aid. On the other hand, it might be suggested that restrictive time limits have the effect of encouraging misconceived applications rather than allowing time for matters to be resolved by the parties to a dispute.

How have the courts approached the need for observance of the time limit? Inevitably, there is a large body of case law, some of which has adopted a strict approach to tardy claims. This has been notably true of some planning cases, where there can be an overlap with statutory challenges and where the courts have tended towards a rigid application of the rules. For instance, *R v Cotswold District Council, ex p Barrington* concerned a challenge to a grant of planning permission which had been approved on 7 November 1996.[133] The applicant was informed on 10 December 1996 and judicial review proceedings were set in train on 31 December 1996, that is, within three weeks of receiving notice. Nevertheless, this was eight weeks after the grant of permission and therefore outside a statutory six-week period for bringing High Court proceedings to challenge the validity of permission. In dismissing the application Keene J held that time ran, not from the time of notification of the decision, but from the date of the decision itself. This safeguard was important in planning situations to protect the interests of third parties likely to be adversely affected if subsequent challenges were allowed. In *R v Newbury District Council, ex p Chievely Parish Council* there was further support in the Court of Appeal for a strict approach in planning cases.[134] Pill LJ pointed out that important decisions are often taken on the strength of planning decisions,

---

130 CPR Part 54.5. For judicial consideration of time-limits see *R (Burkett) v Hammersmith and Fulham London Borough Council* [2002] 1 WLR 1593.
131 *R v Criminal Injuries Compensation Board, ex p A* [1999] 2 WLR 974.
132 [1983] 2 AC 237, 280–1.
133 (1998) 75 P & CR 375.
134 (1998) 10 Admin LR 676.

setting in motion a chain of events. The clear implication is that tardy claims might negatively affect that chain and militate against the considerations that Lord Diplock outlined in *O'Reilly*.[135]

On the other hand, we have noted that the courts have discretion as to the extension of the time limit and that delayed claims can still be heard. For instance, in *R v Secretary of State for Foreign and Commonwealth Affairs, ex p World Development Movement Ltd*,[136] discussed above, the action was allowed nearly three years after the initial decision because of the importance of the issue in question and because some of the relevant evidence emerged only at a late stage. In *R v Director of Passenger Rail Franchising, ex p Save Our Railways*,[137] the court stated that it would be detrimental to good administration to grant *certiorari* or *mandamus* in the context of the case, but relief was granted by declaration because a delay of five weeks was not regarded as excessive. In contrast, in *R v Customs & Excise Commissioners, ex p Eurotunnel plc*,[138] relief was refused when Eurotunnel applied for judicial review to challenge the sale of certain duty-free goods on ferries and aircraft in accordance with EC (now EU) directives. This was because extending the time limit in the case might have a prejudicial effect on third parties (in this instance the operators of ferries or aircraft).

Of course, taken together, the above examples indicate that there is an element of flexibility in the procedure and that the courts can use this according to the perceived public interest in any given case. That flexibility can, however, also generate uncertainty in the law, and concern about that uncertainty has led the Court of Justice of the European Union (CJEU) to rule that the 'promptly' requirement is inconsistent with the general principles of EU law. The ruling was made in the case of *Uniplex*,[139] which arose in the related field of public procurement law and which concerned a statutory requirement that challenges to decisions be made 'promptly and in any event within 3 months from the date when grounds for bringing the proceedings first arose'.[140] The High Court in England and Wales had referred a number of questions to the CJEU, including whether this formulation was consistent with the general principles of EU law. In holding that it was not consistent, the CJEU focused upon the principle of legal certainty and noted that 'a duration which is placed at the discretion of the competent court is not predictable in its effects' and that 'the possibility cannot be ruled out that such a provision empowers national courts to dismiss an action as being out of time even before the expiry of the three-month period'.[141] The CJEU on this basis held that the need for certainty within EU law's public procurement regime precluded national provisions from including the word 'promptly'.

Uniplex has since been the subject of much discussion and the courts have apparently accepted that the term 'promptly' should no longer be used in any EU law case, whether arising in the area of public procurement or elsewhere.[142] Less straightforward, however, has been the matter whether the courts should allow *Uniplex* to 'spill

---

135 See also, e.g., *Re Doyle's Application* [2014] NIQB 82.

136 [1995] 1 WLR 386.

137 [1996] CLC 596.

138 [1995] COD 291.

139 Case C-406/08, *Uniplex (UK) Ltd v NHS Business Services Authority* [2010] 2 CMLR 47. See, too, Case 456/08, *Commission v Ireland* [2010] 2 CMLR 42.

140 *Per* Regulation 47(7)(b) of the Public Contracts Regulations 2006.

141 [2010] 2 CMLR 47, paras 41–42.

142 See, most notably, *R (Berky) v Newport County Council* [2012] EWCA Civ 378 and *R (Buglife) v Medway Council* [2011] EWHC 746.

-over' into non-EU law cases and to displace use of the 'promptly' requirement in judicial review proceedings more generally.[143] Certainly, it is true that some judges had noted that the promptly requirement may be inconsistent with EU law's conception of legal certainty even before the CJEU's ruling in *Uniplex*,[144] and it may be that those *dicta* could provide a bridging point for a recasting of the common law approach. However, it is also true that EU administrative law and the common law are driven by different assumptions and the UK courts may be reluctant to jettison the element of flexibility that inheres in the current judicial review procedure.[145] If that is so, the courts may well choose to limit *Uniplex* to the realm of EU law.[146]

8.12 **Conclusion**

In this chapter we have sought to introduce the reader to some of the essential functions and characteristics of the judicial review procedure. We have done so by considering the nature of governmental power and how the courts position judicial review in relation to that power. We have seen how judicial review has grown in importance both in doctrinal and statistical terms, albeit that the courts have had some difficulties with the question of when the judicial procedure should be used. We have finally seen how the courts have approached the different elements of the judicial review procedure—standing, delay, etc—and some of the doctrinal and theoretical issues that have arisen in the case law.

In the following chapters (10–17) we will be building upon this analysis when examining the reach of judicial review and the grounds for challenging the decisions and other measures of public authorities. As we will see, most of the developments in these areas have been led by the judges, who have reinvented principles on the basis of the common law and in the light of EU law and the ECHR. The grounds for review, in particular, are regarded as evolutionary in form, and this is something that can be seen in how they are now categorised in academic and practitioner texts. In short, while they have historically been examined under the three-way distinction used by Lord Diplock in the *GCHQ* case—*viz* 'illegality', 'irrationality', and 'procedural impropriety'[147]—it is now generally accepted that the Diplock taxonomy no longer encapsulates the complexity of the grounds for review. At the same time, it should be pointed out that Lord Diplock did not, himself, consider that his summary of the law would remain definitive and that we have since seen the much-anticipated development of proportionality and legitimate expectation.

However, before leaving this chapter we should make one final point about the importance that the doctrine of the separation of powers has for our analysis of judicial review. When considering that doctrine above, we pointed out that judicial review is structured around the understanding that the courts should not take decisions in the place of public bodies that Parliament has entrusted with a particular

---

143 On 'spill-over' see 3.3.4.

144 *R (Burkett) v Hammersmith and Fulham LBC* [2002] 3 All ER 97, 114, Lord Steyn.

145 On the nature of EU law see P Craig, *EU Administrative Law*, 2nd edn (Oxford: Oxford University Press, 2012).

146 For application of the 'promptly' requirement in a non-EU law case see *Re Quinn's Application for Leave* [2010] NIQB 100, para 14.

147 *Council of Civil Service Unions v Minister for Civil Service* [1985] AC 374, 410–11.

power of decision. While the courts often emphasise that the imperative of judicial restraint remains, we will see that ongoing developments in judicial review can raise searching questions about the constitutional role of the courts. This is because, to the extent that the courts may wish to respect the constitutional balance within the state when developing judicial review, they equally wish to ensure that individuals are protected against the abuse of power by public decision-makers. There is thus an inherent tension in judicial review that not only defines debates about the role of the courts but gives rise to much controversy in the case law.

FURTHER READING

Anthony, G (2013) 'Public Interest and the Three Dimensions of Judicial Review' 64 *Northern Ireland Legal Quarterly* 125.

Anthony, G (2014) *Judicial Review in Northern Ireland*, 2nd edn (Oxford: Hart Publishing).

Bondy, V and Sunkin, M [2008] 'Accessing Judicial Review' *Public Law* 647.

Bowes, A and Stanton, J [2014] 'The Localism Act 2011 and the General Power of Competence' *Public Law* 392

Cane, P (2003) 'Accountability and the Public-Private Law Distinction' in Bamforth, N and Leyland, P (eds), *Public Law in a Multi-Layered Constitution* (Oxford: Hart Publishing).

Craig, P (2015) *UK, EU and Global Administrative Law: Foundations and Challenges* (Cambridge: Cambridge University Press).

Elliott, M (1999) 'The *Ultra Vires* Doctrine in a Constitutional Setting: Still the Central Principle of Administrative Law' *Cambridge Law Journal* 129.

Fordham, M (2012) *Judicial Review Handbook*, 7th edn (Oxford: Hart Publishing).

Forsyth, C (1996) 'Of Fig-Leaves and Fairy Tales: the *Ultra Vires* Doctrine. The Sovereignty of Parliament and Judicial Review' 55 *Cambridge Law Journal* 122.

Forsyth, C [1998] 'Collateral Challenge and the Foundations of Judicial Review: Orthodoxy Vindicated and Procedural Exclusivity Rejected' *Public Law* 364.

Forsyth, C (ed) (2000) *Judicial Review and the Constitution* (Oxford: Hart Publishing).

Griffiths, T [2000] 'The Procedural Impact of Bowman and Part 54 of the CPR' *Judicial Review* 209.

Halliday, S [2000] 'The Influence of Judicial Review on Bureaucratic Decision-Making' *Public Law* 110.

Harris, BV (2007) 'The "Third Source" of Authority for Government Action Revisited' 123 *Law Quarterly Review* 225.

Himsworth, CMG (1997) 'No Standing Still on Standing' in Leyland, P and Woods, T (eds), *Administrative Law Facing the Future: Old Constraints and New Horizons* (London: Blackstone Press).

Jowell, J (1997) 'Restraining the State: Politics, Principle and Judicial Review' in *Current Legal Problems*, vol 50 (Oxford: Oxford University Press), 189–212.

Laws, Sir John [1995] 'Law and Democracy' *Public Law* 72.

Miles, J (2003) 'Standing in a Multi-Layered Constitution' in Bamforth, N and Leyland, P (eds), *Public Law in a Multi-Layered Constitution* (Oxford: Hart Publishing).

Nason, S and Sunkin, M (2013) 'The Regionalisation of Judicial Review: Constitutional Authority, Access to Justice and Specialisation of Legal Services in Public Law' *Modern Law Review* 76(2), 223–53.

Oliver, D [2000] 'The Frontiers of the State: Public Authorities and Public Functions Under the Human Rights Act' *Public Law* 496.

Oliver, D [2002] 'Public Law Procedures and Remedies—Do We Need Them?' *Public Law* 91.

Woolf, Lord [1995] 'Droit Public—English style' *Public Law* 57.

9

Extending the reach of judicial review: the public–private divide and the Royal prerogative

9.1 Introduction

We have already seen in the previous chapter that administrative and executive decision-makers will, in the vast majority of cases, derive their power of decision from statute. Historically, this coincided with the *ultra vires* doctrine whereby judicial review exists as a remedy to ensure that decision-makers observe the boundaries of statutory powers and duties that have been delegated to them. However, to the extent that this suggests that powers and duties can always be traced to the sovereign legislature,[1] we also know from chapter 5 that it would be misleading to say that *all* public law powers and duties are found in statute. As we explained in that chapter, there are a number of ways in which non-statutory powers pervade the workings of the modern administrative state, whether at the level of local authorities or the devolved or central governments. One such way is through the privatisation and contracting-out of government functions, where decision-makers in the 'private' sector can now take decisions in realms that many would regard as 'public'. Another way—and one that has much more of an historical pedigree—is through decision-making on the basis of the Royal prerogative. The prerogative powers are, of course, non-statutory in form, yet government ministers can use them to take decisions that have direct and indirect implications for individuals. A further way is where non-statutory bodies have acquired unique positions of influence, often as a result of historical accident, in fields of human activities such as sports and commerce.

For the *ultra vires* doctrine, such varied forms of decision-making present an obvious problem: if judicial review exists as a check on the exercise of statutory powers and duties, then it follows that non-statutory powers and duties can never be subject to the supervisory jurisdiction of the courts. In real terms, this means that certain decisions could potentially be taken without any possibility of judicial control over the decision-maker, and we will see that the courts have long since moved beyond the *ultra vires* doctrine when extending the reach of judicial review.[2] However, in doing so, the courts have encountered some apparent conceptual limits to the supervisory jurisdiction, and these continue to cause (admittedly exceptional) difficulties in the context of the contracting-out of government functions. This, in turn, is an out-working of the public–private

---

1 On the importance of which see ch 2.

2 The seminal article on the point is D Oliver, 'Is the *Ultra Vires* Rule the Basis of Judicial Review' [1987] *Public Law* 543.

divide that we discussed in the previous chapter, and we will explain here how the courts try to identify 'public law decisions' that can be challenged by way of the judicial review procedure. We also consider the courts' approach to decisions based upon the prerogative powers and how they have identified decisions that are suited to judicial control and those that are matters for parliamentary oversight.

We begin the chapter by examining the range of tests that the courts now use when deciding whether decisions are matters of public law. The focus in this part of the chapter is very much on the approach to decisions of non-statutory bodies with unique positions of influence and the decisions of privatised utilities and private bodies performing contracted-out government functions. The remainder of the chapter considers the leading case law on the review of the prerogative, together with the significance of the Constitutional Reform and Governance Act 2010 that has recently placed a number of prerogative powers on a statutory footing. We conclude with some evaluative comments about the current state of the law.

One final point by way of introduction concerns other factors that govern the reach of judicial review, notably public interest immunity certificates and so-called 'ouster clauses'. These are mechanisms that can be used either to prevent certain evidence being disclosed during the course of proceedings (public interest immunity) or to prevent the courts enquiring into the lawfulness of a decision (ouster clauses). While these are also important to understanding the limits to the reach of judicial review, they raise a number of complex issues that would only complicate the analysis that is to be given in this chapter. We have, for ease of reading, therefore separated off public interest immunity and ouster clauses for consideration in chapter 10.

9.2 Identifying public law decisions: the public–private divide

It will be recalled from the previous chapter that a fundamental problem with the public–private divide is deciding whether a legal dispute should/must be pursued by way of the judicial review procedure. In our discussion at that time, we focused largely on the procedural difficulties that can arise where a private law matter is collateral to a public law decision, and we emphasised how the courts have moved towards a position of increased flexibility to ensure that disputes are not dismissed on account of procedural formalism. The issue we now wish to examine is, in some senses, anterior to those procedural difficulties, as we are asking whether there is even a public law decision that would engage the judicial review procedure. If there is no such decision, this means that the judicial review procedure cannot be used, come what may. However, as we have outlined above, the nature of public power has changed in recent decades, and this likewise means that there are some decisions that could escape control in the absence of judicial creativity, particularly if private law does not offer a remedy. So what, then, are the tests that the courts now employ, and what are their limits?

9.2.1 **The 'source of power' test**

We must start with the source of power test as, in almost all cases, this will continue to provide the answer to the question whether a matter of public law arises. This returns us to the *ultra vires* doctrine and the historically central role of statute, as constitutional orthodoxy would hold that all public law powers derive from the sovereign Parliament, which delegates a power of decision, or imposes a duty to act, through legislation. Although this does not mean that all statutory powers will be regarded as public law in form,[3] it does mean that the judicial role centres upon the review of decisions etc. for compliance with Parliament's intentions as expressed in legislation. Of course, the corollary of this is that non-statutory powers are not subject to judicial review precisely because Parliament has not delegated the powers in question to the decision-maker. Hence, where a dispute arises within the framework of, for instance, contract, this will *par excellence* be regarded as a dispute that is subject to the rules of private law. In those circumstances, the orthodox view is that judicial review can have no relevance.

The leading case on contractual relations being excluded from judicial review remains *R v Disciplinary Committee of the Jockey Club, ex p Aga Khan*.[4] The applicant sought to challenge by judicial review a decision of the Jockey Club's disciplinary committee following the disqualification of one of his horses. Although the applicant had agreed to be contractually bound by the rules of racing administered by the Jockey Club as the organisation which controls and regulates horse racing, it was argued on his behalf that the regulation of a major national industry (horse racing) was essentially governmental in nature and thus ought to be subject to judicial review. The monopoly enjoyed by the Jockey Club over regulation was acknowledged by the Court of Appeal, which also said that future cases may raise different considerations for the courts. However, in the instant case Sir Thomas Bingham MR held that judicial review was not available:

[T]he Jockey Club is not in its origin, its history, its constitution or (least of all) its membership a public body . . . It has not been woven into any system of governmental control of horse racing, perhaps because it has itself controlled horse racing so successfully that there has been no need for any such governmental system and such does not therefore exist. This has the result that while the Jockey Club's powers may be described as, in many ways, public they are in no sense governmental.[5]

It should be obvious that an insistence on the difference between *contractual* and *governmental* powers in this case greatly restricted the reach of judicial review. Moreover, in doing so, the case revealed in sharp form the 'either/or' nature of the source of power test and, as we will see below, the existence of contract continues to provide difficulties for judicial review even though case law has since progressed beyond the *ultra vires* doctrine. That said, we should add that, just because judicial review is unavailable, this does not necessarily mean that the affected individual will be without any remedy. In other words, if there is a contract, the individual will be able to rely upon contractual remedies, where it is well known that the

---

3 *YL v Birmingham City Council* [2008] 1 AC 95, 131, para 101, Lord Mance.

4 [1993] 2 All ER 853. See, too, e.g., *R v Football Association, ex p Football League* [1993] 2 All ER 833 and *R (West) v Lloyd's of London* [2004] 3 All ER 251.

5 [1993] 2 All ER 853, 867.

courts may apply what amount to public law principles in the context of private disciplinary proceedings.[6] The point to be noted at this stage is therefore one that is primarily normative: if public power takes various forms, and if judicial review is the supposed means to supervise such power, is it not counter-intuitive to hold that judicial review cannot be available simply because of the existence of a contract?

9.2.2 The 'public function' test

The test that is synonymous with judicial review's departure from the *ultra vires* doctrine is the 'public function' test, which emerged in *R v Panel on Take-overs and Mergers, ex p Datafin*.[7] In that case, the Court of Appeal held that the decisions of a self-regulating unincorporated association that oversees the takeovers of listed public companies could be subject to judicial review, notwithstanding that the body had no direct statutory, prerogative, or common law powers (statute did, however, play an indirect role relative to sanctions for breach of the Panel's code). For the Court, it was no longer appropriate to consider solely the source of a body's power, but also its nature. On this basis the Court held that, where a body is 'exercising public law functions, or if the exercise of the functions have public law consequences, then that may . . . be sufficient to bring the body within the reach of judicial review'.[8] This was an open-ended test that was premised upon the need to identify 'a public element, which can take many different forms',[9] and it was to give rise to a number of related tests and questions that include: 'whether (the body) operates as an integral part of a system which has a public law character, is supported by public law . . . and performs what might be described as public law functions';[10] whether there is sufficient statutory penetration of the decision-maker's functions;[11] whether the body is under an express or implied public duty to perform its tasks;[12] or whether government would, 'but for' the existence of the non-statutory body, create a statutory body to oversee the area in question.[13]

Datafin is rightly regarded as a seminal case, and it ushered in a much-needed element of flexibility on the question of the reach of judicial review. For instance, in *R (Beer t/a Hammer Trout Farm) v Hampshire Farmers Markets Ltd*[14] the claimant wished to challenge a private company's refusal to grant him a licence to participate in the company's markets. The proceedings were brought by way of judicial review, as the private company had been set up by Hampshire County Council

---

6 See, e.g., *Lee v Showmen's Guild of Great Britain* [1952] 2 QB 329. See further D Oliver, *Common Values and the Public-Private Divide* (London: Butterworths, 1999).

7 [1987] QB 815.

8 Ibid, 847, Lloyd LJ.

9 Ibid, 838, Sir John Donaldson MR.

10 Ibid, 836, Sir John Donaldson MR; and see, e.g., *R (Beer) v Hampshire Farmers Market Ltd* [2004] 1 WLR 233 and *R (Al Veg Ltd) v Hounslow London Borough Council* [2004] LGR 536.

11 *R v Governors of Haberdashers' Aske's Hatcham College Trust, ex p T* [1995] ELR 350 and *R v Cobham Hall School, ex p S* [1998] ELR 389. Cf *R v Muntham House School, ex p R* [2000] LGR 255 and *R v Servite Houses, ex p Goldsmith* [2001] LGR 55.

12 *R v Panel on Take-overs and Mergers, ex p Datafin* [1987] QB 815, 852, Nicholls LJ.

13 Ibid, 835, Sir John Donaldson MR. And see, e.g., *R v Advertising Standards Authority Ltd, ex p The Insurance Service* Plc (1990) 2 Admin LR 77, 86 (government inevitably would intervene); *R v Chief Rabbi of the United Hebrew Congregations of Great Britain and the Commonwealth, ex p Wachmann* [1992] 1 WLR 1036, 1041 (government would not intervene); and *R v Football Association, ex p Football League Ltd* [1993] 2 All ER 833, 848 (no evidence that government would intervene).

14 [2004] 1 WLR 233.

when it decided to hand over its running of farmers' markets to stall-holders (the Council also gave some logistical support to the company). Holding that the decision of the company was susceptible to judicial review, the Court of Appeal noted that the essential feature of the markets was that they were held on publicly owned land to which the public had access, and that there thus existed the necessary element of public law which opened the door to judicial review. The Court also noted that the company owed its existence to the authority and that it had, in effect, stepped into the authority's shoes and was 'performing the same functions as had previously been performed by [the council], to the same end and in substantially the same way'.[15] Judicial review was therefore available.[16]

On the other hand, the test has not proven so flexible as to allow the supervisory jurisdiction to extend into the realm of contractual relations. We have already noted above the approach that the Court of Appeal adopted in *Aga Khan*—which was decided after *Datafin*—and an even more stark illustration of the point was given in the case of *R v Servite Houses, ex p Goldsmith*.[17] Wandsworth Council had here entered into a contractual relationship with Servite under which the Council paid Servite to provide residential care for elderly citizens in respect of whom the Council had statutory care obligations (section 21 of the National Assistance Act 1948 imposed a duty to provide suitable residential accommodation for eligible citizens, while section 26 allowed the authority to contract out the service). The applicants in the case were two elderly women who lived in a home that Servite had decided to close. While the judge expressed his sympathy with the applicants, he nevertheless considered that Servite's decision—which had been taken in accordance with the terms of the contract—was not amenable to review. The applicants had argued: (a) that the wider statutory context gave the decision the necessary public law qualities; and (b) that the decision in any event sounded in public law as the provision of care to those in need is 'the very essence of the business of government'.[18] However, both arguments were rejected. On the point about statutory underpinnings, Moses J thus considered that they were not sufficiently far-reaching in this case as the legislation did not add a public function to Servite's existing private functions, but merely empowered the local authority to enter into contractual relationships for the purposes of discharging its public law obligations (Servite's powers were thereby purely contractual). And in respect of the argument that Servite was performing a classic governmental function, the judge considered that he was restrained by earlier case law that had established that 'the courts cannot impose public law standards upon a body the source of whose power is contractual and absent sufficient statutory penetration'.[19] Although the judge acknowledged the force of arguments about the need for increased flexibility in the face of contractualisation (the judge also noted the fact that the applicants were without any other remedy), he held that judicial review did not lie:

15 Ibid, 248.

16 See also, e.g., *R (Agnello) v Hownslow London Borough Council* [2004] LGR 536 (decision not to include former tenants of market units within a new, smaller market was amenable to judicial review). Compare, e.g., *R (Boyle) v Haverhill Pub Watch* [2010] LLR 93 (local pub watch scheme's decision to ban an individual from all participating licensed premises was not amenable to judicial review as it did not have the requisite public law element).

17 [2001] LGR 55.

18 Ibid, 78.

19 Ibid, 81.

I have been unable to find any legislative underpinning, but have been faced merely with a statute which appears to permit the local authority to enter into private arrangements for the provision of community care . . . In those circumstances, it seems to me wrong for a court of first instance to identify Servite's function as a public function absent any of the features upon which courts have in the past relied. That is not to say that a fresh approach ought not to be adopted so that the court can meet the needs of the public faced with the increasing privatisation of what were hitherto public law functions. But any advance can, in my judgment, only be made by those courts which have the power to reject the previous approach enshrined in past authority.[20]

9.2.3 The Human Rights Act and 'public functions'

The question of the reach of judicial review has since been further complicated—rather than resolved—by the Human Rights Act 1998. We have already seen in chapter 4 that section 6(3)(b) of the Human Rights Act defines public authorities as including 'any person certain of whose functions are functions of a public nature'. This phrase was included to try to ensure that the Act would have an expansive reach *vis-à-vis* government activity, notwithstanding changes in the nature of the state and public service provision. Under the Act, there are therefore two categories of public authorities: 'core' authorities such as the police, central government departments, and local authorities; and 'mixed function' authorities that may sometimes perform public functions in addition to their other non-public activities. The significance of the distinction lies in the fact that, while core public authorities must act consistently with the European Convention on Human Rights (ECHR) in all that they do (whether of a public or private law nature), mixed function authorities must act consistently with the ECHR only when they perform public functions.[21] This distinction was criticised from the outset as having the potential to limit the reach of human rights protection.[22] However, it was also argued that bringing mixed function authorities under the ambit of the Act when performing public functions would help to delimit more clearly the reach of judicial review.[23] In short, it was thought that use of the term 'public function' in the Human Rights Act would allow the Act to cover the performance of contracted-out government functions and that this would lead to analogous developments in judicial review.[24] The resulting case law has, however, failed to live up to this expectation.

The principal reason for the failure has been the tendency of the courts to give section 6 a restrictive interpretation. Although there have been some judicial *dicta* to the effect that the courts should adopt a broad view of mixed function authorities,[25] the courts have focused on the nature of the relationship that the government has with the provider of a service that has, for instance, been contracted out, rather than on

---

20 Ibid, 81.

21 Section 6(5).

22 GS Morris, 'The Human Rights Act and the Public-Private Divide in Employment Law' (1998) 27 *Industrial Law Journal* 293.

23 N Bamforth, 'The Application of the Human Rights Act 1998 to Public Authorities and Private Bodies' (1999) 58 *Cambridge Law Journal* 159.

24 Although note that the courts may not automatically accept that questions about the reach of s 6(3) (b) and judicial review are coterminous: see, e.g., *R (Weaver) v London and Quadrant Housing Trust* [2010] 1 WLR 363, 374, para 37, Elias LJ.

25 e.g., *Aston Cantlow and Wilcote with Billesley Parochial Church Council v Wallbank* [2004] 1 AC 546, 554-5, Lord Nicholls.

the nature of the 'function' being performed.[26] The first case that revealed the restrictive approach was *R (Heather) v Leonard Cheshire Foundation*.[27] The facts concerned a number of claimants who were long-stay patients in a residential care home owned and run by the Foundation, most of whom had been placed there by local authority social services departments, or by their health authorities acting under statutory powers and duties. The Foundation, one of the voluntary sector's leading providers of care services to the old and disabled, took a decision to close the home and transfer the residents to smaller units based in the surrounding community. In holding that the Foundation was not performing a public function for the purposes of the Human Rights Act, the Court of Appeal emphasised that, while public funding for an activity was an important consideration, the question of the reach of the Act ultimately depended on a number of variables that went to the question of whether the service provider was in effect 'standing in the shoes of the local authority'. Quoting from the Court of Appeal's earlier judgment in *Poplar Housing v Donoghue* it stated:

What can make an act, which would otherwise be private, public, is a feature or a combination of features which impose a public character or stamp on the act. Statutory authority for what is done can at least help to mark the act as being public; so can the extent of control over the function exercised by another body which is a public authority. The more closely the acts that could be of a private nature are enmeshed in the activities of a public body, the more likely they are to be public. However, the fact that the acts are supervised by a public regulatory body does not necessarily indicate that they are of a public nature. This is analogous to the position in judicial review, where a regulatory body may be deemed public but the activities of the body which is regulated may be categorised private.[28]

Applying these considerations to the facts of the case, the Court concluded that the Leonard Cheshire Foundation was not performing a public function, and that the local authorities had not divested themselves of their responsibilities under domestic law and the ECHR (the individuals' remedy therefore lay against the local authority).[29] This approach is to be contrasted with that in the *Donoghue* case itself, in which it was held that a Housing Association that was linked to a local authority was performing public functions for the purposes of section 6 when seeking repossession of a property. This was because Tower Hamlets London Borough Council had created the association for the purposes of managing the council's housing stock; because there was an overlap in membership of the council and association; and because the association was subject to guidance by the local council. The position was therefore different to that in *Leonard Cheshire*, where the charity did not owe its existence to the local authority but rather was a freestanding organisation that had voluntarily entered into a contractual relationship.[30]

26 See further the Joint Committee on Human Rights Report, *The Meaning of Public Authority under the Human Rights Act*, Seventh Report of Session 2003-04, HL 39, HC 382; see, too, the Ninth Report of Session 2006-2007, *The Meaning of Public Authority Under the Human Rights Act*, HL 787/HC 410.

27 [2002] 2 All ER 936.

28 Ibid, 942. The *Donoghue* case is reported at [2002] QB 48.

29 For critical commentary see P Craig, 'Contracting Out, the Human Rights Act, and the Scope of Judicial Review' (2002) 118 *Law Quarterly Review* 551.

30 Some of the other early case law on s 6 includes *R (A) v Partnerships in Care Ltd* [2002] 1 WLR 2610 (where managers of a private psychiatric hospital were held to be performing a public function when making decisions about the focus of a ward in which a mental health patient was detained); *Aston Cantlow and Wilcote with Billesley Parochial Church Council v Wallbank* [2004] 1 AC 546 (held that, although the Church of England has special links with central government and performed certain public functions, it was neither acting as a core nor a mixed function public authority in the context of a property dispute); and *R (West) v Lloyd's of London* [2004] 3 All ER 251 (Business Conduct Committee of Lloyds was neither embraced by s 6(3)(b) nor amenable to judicial review).

The underlying logic of the restrictive approach was confirmed by a majority of the House of Lords in the leading case of *YL v Birmingham City Council*.[31] An individual who had been placed with a care home under the terms of a contract between the home and a local authority that had a statutory duty to make arrangements for accommodation for the individual sought to rely upon the ECHR when challenging the care home's decision to move her from the home. The key issue on appeal was whether the private care home was embraced by section 6(3)(b) and, in holding that it was not embraced, the majority in the House of Lords emphasised that there was an important distinction to be drawn between the act of the local authority in making arrangements for the accommodation of the individual (which corresponded with the performance of a public function under the Act) and the subsequent actions of the care home in providing the accommodation under the terms of the contract (which had a commercial basis and thereby fell outside section 6(3)(b)). This therefore placed the activities of the care home squarely on the private law side of the public–private divide and, moreover, did so in a manner that was reminiscent of the source of power test that had previously predominated in public law. Thus, even though the minority in the House felt that the existence of public funding and the wider public interest in the provision of care services meant that the care home was performing a public function, the majority was of the view that the Human Rights Act did not extend to the care home in question. Any further protection for individuals was therefore said to be a matter for the legislature, not the courts.

We have already criticised this judgment in chapter 4 for the reason that it conflicts with Parliament's apparent intentions in enacting section 6(3)(b), and we noted there that legislation was introduced to reverse the effect of the ruling.[32] Of course, in relation to judicial review it can also be criticised for the reason that it represents an 'opportunity lost' in terms of developing a broader and more nuanced understanding of the reach of public law principles in the modern polity. The judgment has, in short, suggested again that the existence of contract will automatically problematise any recourse to public law principles and proceedings, and that remedies should be found in private law. While we have noted above that contract will often give affected individual access to a remedy, cases like *YL* reveal that there can still be cases where, in the absence of legislative intervention, individuals may have no effective remedy in the face of a contract between a private company and a public authority (albeit that the individual in *YL* did make a partial contribution to the costs of care and therefore had a limited contractual relationship). Given the point, would it not be preferable for the courts to redraw the boundaries of public law both for normative and practical reasons?

---

31 [2008] 1 AC 95; followed in, e.g., *R (Weaver) v London and Quadrant Housing Trust* [2010] 1 WLR 363.

32 *Viz*, the Health and Social Care Home Act 2008, s 145; considered in *R (Broadway Care Centre) v Caerphilly CBC* [2012] EWHC 37 (care home wishing to challenge, by way of judicial review, the local council's decision to terminate a contract for provision of care facilities: held that it could not proceed by way of judicial review as s 145 gives public law protections to individuals within care homes, not to private companies in contractual relationships with local authorities). Note the s 145 has since been repealed by para 90 of Sch 1 to SI 2015/914 but that substantially the same provision has been enacted in s 73 of the Care Act 2014.

9.2.4 **The 'emanation of the state' test**

In addition to the public function test, the courts have occasionally borrowed from EU law's 'emanation of the state' doctrine when asking whether some private bodies can be regarded as public authorities. This has proven to be a particularly effective approach when dealing with the decisions of privatised utilities. For instance, in the Northern Ireland case of *Re Sherlock and Morris' Application*,[33] the question was whether judicial review was available to challenge a decision of Northern Ireland Electricity (NIE) to disconnect the permanent electricity supply to two residences. Having held that the decision was amenable to review on the basis of the public function test, Kerr J held that the 'emanation of the state' doctrine also suggested a positive answer to the question. Under this doctrine, individuals can invoke the terms of directly effective directives in proceedings against the state or a body 'which has been made responsible, pursuant to a measure adopted by the State, for providing a public service under the control of the State and has for that purpose special powers beyond those which result from the normal rules applicable in relations between individuals'.[34] In cross-referring to the doctrine, Kerr J noted that a privatised water utility in England had already been held to be an emanation of the state for the purposes of EU law.[35] Given that he considered NIE to discharge similar duties to those of the water authority, Kerr J reasoned that it 'would be anomalous if NIE . . . were to be regarded as a state authority but was considered to be immune from judicial review'.[36] EU law thereby 'spilled-over' in *Sherlock and Morris* and influenced the judgment of the court in a purely national law dispute.[37]

The emanation of the state test should, however, be part distinguished from the 'public function' test that can otherwise be used by the courts. This is because the question whether a body is an emanation of the state is, in one sense, logically prior to the question whether a decision taken by the body has implications in public law. In other words, while the emanation of the state test may help to determine whether a body is, in effect, a repository of public power, the body will still make a variety of public law and private law decisions (e.g., to cut off the electricity supply, and to discipline an employee respectively). In relation to a discrete decision taken by, for instance, a private company, it is thus likely that the key question will remain whether the decision is in the nature of a public law decision or comes within the terms of the public function test. It is, moreover, significant that the courts have, in any event, emphasised the need for judicial caution when reviewing the 'public law' decisions of such bodies:[38] while judicial review is available, the courts plainly wish to avoid over-active invigilation of decisions taken in quasi-commercial contexts where such invigilation may have unforeseen implications for parties beyond those before the court.

---

33 [1996] NIJB 80.
34 Case C-188/89, *Foster v British Gas* [1990] ECR I-3313, 3348–9, para 20.
35 *Griffin v South West Water Services Ltd* [1995] IRLR 15.
36 [1996] NIJB 80, 87.
37 On 'spill-over' see 3.3.4.
38 See, e.g., *R v Panel on Take-overs and Mergers, ex p Datafin* [1987] QB 815, 842.

9.2.5 **Northern Ireland and Scotland**

One final point that we would make in relation to the public–private divide is that all of the above cases, with the exception of *Sherlock and Morris*, have arisen in England and Wales. While we have seen that the existence of a contract has presented a conceptual barrier to the further development of judicial review, it is interesting to note that the law in Northern Ireland and in Scotland has been less constrained by the out-workings of the source of power test. Although the law of judicial review is largely similar across all of the United Kingdom, especially at the level of the grounds for review,[39] the approach to the public–private divide is one area in which there have been some differences. This has led some commentators to argue that the law of England and Wales may have much to learn from the law of Scotland in particular.[40]

Taking first the position in Northern Ireland, the courts have already held that the decisions of, for instance, private societies[41] are susceptible to review when the decision in issue 'has characteristics which import an element of public law'.[42] The question of whether the matter imports an element of public law—and thereby falls on the 'public law' side of the public–private divide—is answered with reference to a 'public interest' test that is potentially very wide in its reach. The test, as originally formulated by the High Court, holds that:

> an issue is one of public law where it involves a matter of public interest in the sense that it has an impact on the public generally and not merely on an individual or group. That is not to say that an issue becomes one of public law simply because it generates interest or concern in the minds of the public. It must affect the public rather than merely engage its interest to qualify as a public law issue. It seems to me to be equally clear that a matter may be one of public law while having a specific impact on an individual in his personal capacity.[43]

The Northern Ireland Court of Appeal has since cited this test with approval,[44] and it has become central to the workings of judicial review. This has thus led to the judicial review procedure being available when a cooperative society which had an historical and exclusive right to grant commercial licences for eel fishing refused to grant a licence to the applicant;[45] when the Northern Ireland Railways Company Ltd excluded a taxi driver from a designated rank at Belfast's Central Station;[46] and when there was a dispute between a property company and the Department of Social Development about costing for the development of lands owned by the Department.[47]

The approach in Scotland is, in turn, very different again, as Scottish law does not even recognise a substantive public–private divide for the purposes of judicial

---

[39] See generally G Anthony, *Judicial Review in Northern Ireland*, 2nd edn (Oxford: Hart Publishing, 2014) and C Himsworth, 'Judicial Review in Scotland' in M Supperstone, J Goudie, and P Walker (eds), *Judicial Review*, 5th edn (London: Butterworths, LexisNexis, 2014), ch 22.

[40] Oliver, n 6.

[41] *Re Patrick Wylie's Application* [2005] NI 359 (decision of the Lough Neagh Fisherman's Co-operative Society).

[42] *Re Phillips' Application* [1995] NI 322, 334.

[43] *Re McBride's Application* [1999] NI 299, 310, Kerr J.

[44] *Re McBride's Application (No 2)* [2003] NI 319, 336, Carswell LCJ.

[45] *Re Alan Kirkpatrick's Application* [2004] NIJB 15. See also *Re Mulholland's Application* [2010] NIQB 118.

[46] *Re Ronald Wadsworth's Application* [2004] NIQB 8.

[47] *Re City Hotel (Derry) Ltd's Application* [2004] NIQB 38.

review.[48] While judicial review will generally not be available where an individual has an alternative remedy in statute or, for instance, in contract law,[49] the Court of Session's competence to hear petitions for judicial review does not ultimately depend upon the existence of some 'public law' element. Petitions for judicial review may instead be brought where there is a 'tripartite relationship' within which (1) power is conferred (2) on a party who is entrusted with a decision-making power and (3) whose decision affects the rights and obligations of another person.[50] Although the tripartite test has been criticised for its lack of clarity[51]—it has also been doubted whether the test need always be satisfied[52]—it is beyond doubt that it is broader in its scope than is case law on the reach of judicial review in England and Wales. There have consequently been cases in Scotland in which the disciplinary decisions of private sporting bodies have been considered amenable to judicial review (the tripartite relationship existing between the sporting organisation, its disciplinary panel, and the affected individual),[53] and case law has also established that a private landlord's refusal to make a statutory payment to a tenant who was displaced during building work was reviewable.[54] On the other hand, there have been some cases in which limits have been placed on the test, for instance where a public sector employee sought to argue that the tripartite relationship could be completed simply by placing the legislature at the apex of his relationship with his employer.[55]

We will return to the significance of the different approaches to the public–private divide in the conclusion to this chapter. However, one point that we would make at this stage concerns the argument that the absence of a public–private divide in Scotland is to be preferred to the system that pertains in England and Wales and, in apparently less problematic form, in Northern Ireland. Academic and legal opinion on the merit of the divide has sometimes become polarised with some commentators being of the view that is incongruent with English historical experience and others arguing that it is necessary because the corresponding judicial review procedure offers protections to public bodies who act in the broader public interest.[56] We do not propose to add either way to those arguments at this stage, but we would refer once more to the problem presented by the contracting out of government functions and the possibility that individuals can, in exceptional circumstances, be left without remedies. Given the point, we would suggest that the Scottish model would appear to rule out that possibility and that a petition for judicial review would be available. This is surely an outcome that each of the jurisdictions in the United Kingdom would wish to achieve.

---

48 *Axa General Insurance v Lord Advocate* [2011] UKSC 46, [2012] 1 AC 868, 915, para 56, citing *West v Secretary of State for Scotland* 1992 SC 385.

49 For statute law see, e.g., *McCue v Glasgow City Council* 2014 SLT 891; and for contract see, e.g., *Ronald McIntosh v Aberdeenshire Council* 1999 SLT 93.

50 *West v Secretary of State for Scotland* 1992 SC 385, 413.

51 See, e.g., C Himsworth, 'Judicial Review in Scotland' in B Hadfield (ed), *Judicial Review: A Thematic Approach* (Dublin: Gill & Macmillan, 1995), 288, 290ff.

52 See, e.g., *Naik v University of Stirling* 1994 SLT 449 and *Crocket v Tantallon Golf Club* 2005 SLT 663.

53 e.g., *St Johnstone Football Club Ltd v Scottish Football Association* 1965 SLT 171 and *Irvine v Royal Burgess Golfing Society of Edinburgh* 2004 SCLR 386. Compare, in England and Wales, e.g., *Law v National Greyhound Racing Club* [1983] 1 WLR 1302 and *ex p Aga Khan* [1993] 1 WLR 909, n 4.

54 *Boyle v Castlemilk Housing Association* [1998] SLT 56.

55 *Blair v Lochaber District Council* [1995] IRLR 135.

56 Compare and contrast JWF Allison, *A Continental Distinction in the Common Law* (Oxford: Oxford University Press, 1996) and Lord Woolf, *Protection of the Public-A New Challenge* (London: Steven and Sons, 1990).

9.3 Judicial review and the prerogative powers

The corresponding development of the law in relation to the prerogative powers has been driven by a tension between two considerations. On the one hand, the courts have been concerned with the basic democratic principle whereby public decision-makers—here, government ministers—should be held to account when they take decisions that have implications for the rights or interests of individuals. As we outlined in chapter 5, there is considerable scope for such decision-making on the basis of the non-statutory prerogative powers, and the courts have sought to ensure that the exercise of those powers is subject to at least some degree of judicial control. However, this has, on the other hand, raised the question of when judicial invigilation of the prerogative powers should cease in favour of parliamentary oversight of ministerial decision-making. As we also outlined in chapter 5, some of the prerogative powers concern political matters of what have been termed 'high policy',[57] and it is clearly inappropriate for the courts to trespass into that territory. We will thus see that the watchword that has guided the courts has been 'justiciability': is the matter before the court one that is suited to control through the judicial process?[58]

We begin our analysis of the law in this area by considering the leading historical case on the status of the prerogative, namely *A-G v De Keyser's Royal Hotel Ltd*.[59] On that basis, we examine how the law has developed up to the present day in the light of the above tension. We finally note the importance of the Constitutional Reform and Governance Act 2010 that has placed a number of important prerogative powers on a statutory footing.

9.3.1 Statute law and the prerogative powers

It has long been recognised by the courts that Parliament has the power expressly to modify, limit, or replace (abrogate) prerogative powers through the enactment of statute.[60] However, a more difficult matter, historically, has been what the courts should do where prerogative powers appear to be in conflict with those contained in a statute. This was the central issue in the *De Keyser's* case. In 1916, the government, acting in the name of the Crown under the Defence of the Realm Regulations, took control of a hotel to house the headquarters of the Royal Flying Corps. It then denied the legal owners any right to compensation that was apparently available to them under the statutory provisions of the Defence Act 1842. It was argued by the Crown that compensation for requisition of a hotel was within its discretion, acting under the prerogative in wartime. However, it was decided by the court that requisition and compensation were now governed by statute, which had superseded the prerogative's control of these matters where there was any inconsistency

---

57 *R v Secretary of State for Foreign and Commonwealth Affairs, ex p Everett* [1989] 1 All ER 655, 660.

58 *Council of Civil Service Unions v Minister for the Civil Service* [1985] 1 AC 374.

59 [1920] AC 508.

60 See *R (Munir) v Secretary of State for the Home Department* [2012] 1 WLR 2192, 2203, para 33, Lord Dyson. One example of abrogation concerns MI5 and MI6 which were established under the prerogative but which were placed on a statutory footing by the Security Service Act 1989 and the Intelligence Service Act 1994, respectively.

with the legislation. To this extent, the prerogative power was placed in abeyance in favour of the exercise of the statutory power. Lord Atkinson said:

It was suggested that when a statute is passed empowering the Crown to do a certain thing which it might theretofore have done by virtue of its prerogative, the prerogative is merged in the statute. I confess I do not think the word 'merged' is happily chosen. I should prefer to say that when such a statute, expressing the will and intention of the King and of the three estates of the realm, is passed, it abridges the Royal prerogative while it is in force to this extent: that the Crown can only do the particular thing under and in accordance with the statutory provisions, and that its prerogative power to do that thing is in abeyance . . . after the statute has been passed, and while it is in force, the thing it empowers the Crown to do can thenceforth only be done by and under the statute, and subject to all the limitations, restrictions and conditions by it imposed, howsoever unrestricted the Royal prerogative may theretofore have been.[61]

This approach was wholly consistent with the doctrine of the sovereignty of Parliament and it was qualified only to the extent that legislation may include a reservation preserving, or partly preserving, a prerogative power. Of course, in *De Keyser's* case the issue was relatively easy to resolve, as there was an inconsistency between the statute and the prerogative in a given area and the courts held that the statutory provision enjoyed primacy. Subsequent case law on the relationship between statute law and the prerogative has not, however, always been so straightforward, and there have been some controversial decisions. One such example is *R v Secretary of State for the Home Department, ex p Northumbria Police Authority*.[62] In this case, the Home Secretary issued a circular to all chief officers of police advising them that he would be maintaining a central store of riot equipment and that the officers would be able to obtain equipment from that store either with or without the approval of their police authorities. A police authority challenged the circular for the reason that section 4(4) of the Police Act 1964 did not give the Home Secretary the authority to maintain a central store but rather made police authorities responsible for the maintenance of policing equipment and so on. When the matter came before the Court of Appeal, the central issue was whether there was a prerogative power corresponding to that which underpins the power to make war and peace, namely a power to enforce the 'Queen's peace within the realm'. It was contended by the applicant police authority that, since no such prerogative was in existence at the time of Peel's reforms in 1829, it followed that all powers that police forces exercised, and also those exercised by the Home Secretary, emanated from statute. Croom-Johnson LJ rejected this argument: ' . . . I have no doubt that the Crown does have a prerogative power to keep the peace, which is bound up with its undoubted right to see that crime is prevented and that justice is administered'.[63] Crucial to this conclusion was the view that section 4(4) did not give local police authorities an express monopoly over the supply of such equipment, that is, section 4(4) had not replaced the prerogative.

There are two points to be made about *ex p Northumbia Police Authority*. First, it would seem that, following *De Keyser*, where a statutory provision is enacted which covers the same grounds as a prerogative power, the latter is not destroyed but falls only into abeyance. Of course, it would follow from this that, if the statutory provision in question were subsequently repealed, it

---

61 *A-G v De Keyser's Royal Hotel Ltd* [1920] AC 508, 539–40.
62 [1988] 1 All ER 556.
63 Ibid, 598–601.

would seem that the prerogative power could be used again at some stage in the future. As we will see below, the remaining question whether those powers would in turn be reviewable by the courts is one that would be answered in the light of the facts of any particular case and the prerogative powers in issue.

Secondly, *ex p Northumbria Police Authority* raises the crucial issue of how broadly or narrowly the courts view the Royal prerogative when there are ambiguities within a statute. The Home Office plainly believed that it was competent to act in the area in question, as the Police Act 1964 did not expressly restrict the prerogative in every circumstance and recourse was therefore had to an ancient prerogative power to keep the peace. By agreeing with that approach, and by reading the imprecision within the statute in a way that allowed the prerogative to prevail, the court here seemed to be implying that the constitutional principle enunciated in *De Keyser* was very much narrower than had generally been supposed. Does this then allow the use of the prerogative in almost any ambiguous circumstances where national security or the keeping of peace is an issue? Subsequent case law had not yet provided any definitive answer to this question.

9.3.2 The prerogative and the supervisory role of the courts

We have already pointed out that the prerogative often involves the exercise of powers that are central to executive action in crucial areas such as foreign policy, defence, national security, and the prerogative of mercy. Historically, the courts had denied that they had any power to review exercises of the prerogative power in these areas precisely because of the political nature of the substantive choices that were often being made. However, while it is true that the courts still regard some policy areas as ill-suited to the judicial process—or 'non-justiciable'—it is also true that the modern approach has been characterised by an incremental expansion of the supervisory role. Indeed, at its height, some recent case law has taken the courts to the very fringes of what may be regarded as matters of 'high policy'.

9.3.2.1 The traditional approach

The essence of the traditional approach has been stated as follows:

The courts will inquire into whether a particular prerogative power exists or not and, if it does exist, into its extent. But once the existence and extent of a power are established to the satisfaction of the court, the court cannot inquire into the propriety of its exercise.[64]

As in *De Keyser's* case, the courts were therefore willing to intervene to clarify only the existence and ambit of powers, where it was sometimes said that the common law would not permit any expansion of the prerogative powers.[65] But beyond performing this scoping exercise, the orthodox view was that exercises of the prerogative powers could not be reviewed by the courts. Control was instead to be achieved through the parliamentary process or by Parliament intervening through the enactment of legislation.

There were many cases in which the orthodox view proved dispositive of issues that came before the courts. For instance, in *Blackburn v A-G*,[66] Mr Blackburn's

---

64 *Council of Civil Service Unions v Minister for the Civil Service* [1985] 1 AC 374, 398, Lord Fraser.
65 *BBC v Johns* [1965] Ch 32, 79, Diplock LJ.
66 [1971] 2 All ER 1380.

challenge to the legality of the government's decision to sign the Treaty of Rome failed because the treaty-making powers 'cannot be challenged or questioned in these courts'.[67] Likewise, in *Hanratty v Lord Butler*, an attempt to sue a former Home Secretary in negligence for decisions taken in respect of the prerogative of mercy while in office was not allowed to proceed because the prerogative of mercy is 'one of the high prerogatives of the Crown'.[68] And in *Gouriet v Union of Post Office Workers*,[69] the issue was whether the courts could review a decision of the Attorney General whereby he had refused consent for relator proceedings. In the Court of Appeal, Lord Denning MR believed this could be the subject of review, but the House of Lords held that, in this instance, the Attorney General's discretion was part of the prerogative and unreviewable. One of the factors that guided the House was that the Attorney General was responsible to Parliament for his actions, *viz* there was a political control mechanism.

That said, there were also cases in which departures from orthodoxy were hinted at. One example was *Burmah Oil v Lord Advocate*,[70] where compensation was sought for acts carried out by British troops in Burma acting under the prerogative in war-time. In deciding that compensation was payable as of right in respect of property destroyed and seized, the House of Lords omitted to discuss whether the underlying exercises of the prerogative had been unlawful. This case was decided against the conventional wisdom of the time, and the War Damage Act 1965 was subsequently passed by Parliament to overturn retrospectively the decision of the House of Lords. *Obiter* comments in the case of *Chandler v DPP*[71] also presaged a change in approach, albeit that the case was decided in accordance with orthodox principles. The issue in the case was whether CND protestors who had been convicted under section 1 of the Official Secrets Act 1911 of having conspired to enter a military base were entitled to contest whether this was prejudicial to the safety of the state. While the House of Lords held that the defence was not open to them—the case concerned the disposition and armament of the armed forces, matters that had for centuries been in the exclusive discretion of the Crown—Lords Devlin and Reid indicated that aspects of the prerogative powers may be reviewable in the future. In *Laker Airways Ltd v Department of Trade*,[72] Lord Denning likewise suggested, *obiter*, that exercises of the prerogative may be reviewable (the case itself concerned a decision, taken within the framework of a treaty, to cancel permission for an airline route). As he expressed it:

The law does not interfere with the proper exercise of discretion by the executive in those situations; but it can set limits by defining the bounds of the activity; and it can intervene if the discretion is exercised improperly or mistakenly. That is a fundamental principle of our constitution . . . Seeing that the prerogative is a discretionary power to be exercised for the public good, it follows that its exercise can be examined by the courts just as any other discretionary power which is vested in the executive.[73]

---

67 Ibid, 1382, Lord Denning MR. See, too, e.g., *R v Secretary of State for Foreign and Commonwealth Affairs, ex p Rees-Mogg* [1994] QB 552, reaffirming the essentially non-justiciable nature of the treaty-making power in a dispute over the ratification of the Treaty on European Union.

68 (1971) 115 SJ 386.

69 [1978] AC 435.

70 [1965] AC 75.

71 [1964] AC 763.

72 [1977] QB 643.

73 Ibid, 705.

A case that proved particularly influential when the law finally moved to review prerogative powers was *R v Criminal Injuries Compensation Board, ex p Lain*.[74] A police widow here wished to challenge a determination that she should be given a compensatory award of nil for the death of her husband who had been injured while on duty and who subsequently committed suicide. The Board had been set up under the prerogative and it was contended, in response, that *certiorari* did not lie since the Board was not a body amenable to the supervisory jurisdiction of the court. However, the court drew a distinction between the decision to set up the Board, which had been taken on the basis of the prerogative, and decisions that were thereafter taken by the Board, which were not decisions taken on the basis of the prerogative and which should be subject to judicial review. This was because judicial review had already been extended to tribunals and other such bodies and because the Board was taking quasi-judicial decisions that affected individual members of the public. The court, in the result, was not persuaded by the original role played by the prerogative powers.

9.3.2.2 *GCHQ*: towards the modern view of the law

We come now to what is widely considered to be the most significant modern decision on the prerogative powers, namely *Council of Civil Service Unions v Minister for the Civil Service* (the *GCHQ* case).[75] The facts of this case were that a number of strikes at government communication headquarters at Cheltenham led the government to use powers under a prerogative Order in Council[76] to limit the union rights of civil servants working at the headquarters (the case was therefore not concerned with a direct exercise of the prerogative, but rather with the exercise of powers delegated on the basis of the prerogative). The limitations had been imposed without any prior consultation with the trade unions who argued that there had been a breach of their legitimate expectation of prior consultation.[77] The House of Lords thus had to decide upon the scope of the prerogative powers and whether judicial review was available in the circumstances. Although the unions ultimately lost the case, it was unanimously agreed by their Lordships that executive action was not immune from judicial review merely because it was carried out in pursuance of a power derived from common law, or the prerogative, rather than a statutory source. It was, instead, the *subject matter* that counted, not the *source*, and the trade unions would have had an enforceable legitimate expectation of consultation had the government not been able to highlight national security considerations. However, given those considerations, the House of Lords held that it had been permissible for the government to truncate the common law rules of fairness.[78]

The judicial opinions that were expressed within the case varied considerably. Lord Fraser regarded the regulation of the civil service through an Order in Council as an indirect exercise of prerogative power, and, while he saw no obvious reason why the mode of exercise of that power should be immune from review, he did recognise that to open it up to review would be against the weight of accepted

---

74 [1967] 2 All ER 770.

75 [1985] AC 374.

76 Civil Service Order in Council 1982.

77 On which dimension to the case see 15.3.1.

78 On which rules see ch 17. Note that the rights of the applicants in *GCHQ* to join a trade union were restored by the government in May 1997.

authority (his Lordship also declined to discuss the matter further given that national security considerations had determined the outcome of the case). Lord Brightman joined Lord Fraser in expressing caution, while Lord Roskill was of the view, *obiter*, that certain prerogative powers such as the exercise of the prerogative of mercy, the making of treaties, the granting of honours, and the defence of the realm were not suited to judicial review because of their nature and subject matter. Nevertheless, he joined the majority in thinking that some other decisions taken on the basis of the prerogative powers should be subject to judicial scrutiny. Lord Scarman cited case law that included *Chandler* and *ex p Lain* when stressing that the developing law of judicial review had overtaken many of the restrictions imposed by orthodoxy:

> . . . the law relating to judicial review has now reached the stage where it can be said with confidence that, if the subject matter in respect of which prerogative power is exercised is justiciable, that is to say if it is a matter [i.e., subject matter] upon which the court can adjudicate, the exercise of the power is subject to review in accordance with the principles developed in respect of the review of the exercise of statutory power. . . . Today . . . the controlling factor in determining whether the exercise of prerogative power is subject to judicial review is not its source but its subject matter.[79]

This was, of course, a far-reaching departure as, in theory at least, many areas once considered unreviewable were now potentially open to judicial scrutiny. However, some of the cases that followed in the wake of *GCHQ* did not develop the common law position to any great extent. For instance, in *R v Secretary of State for the Home Department, ex p Harrison*,[80] the applicant was convicted of conspiracy to defraud and sentenced to three years' imprisonment. He later successfully appealed on the ground that he should originally have been granted full legal aid at his trial. Subsequently, he applied for compensation from the Home Office. When this was refused, without reasons being given, the applicant sought judicial review, claiming that the refusal by the Home Secretary to grant compensation was unfair. *Ex gratia* payments in these circumstances were made under the prerogative and, in the instant case, the court held that decisions of this kind could not be called into question in the absence of bias or fraud on the part of the Home Secretary and, moreover, that the applicant was not entitled to reasons for the decision.[81] A conservative approach to the emerging law was arguably also adopted in the *Northumbria Police Authority* case that we considered above.[82]

In contrast, a case that sought to build upon the change in direction in *GCHQ* was *R v Secretary of State for Foreign and Commonwealth Affairs, ex p Everett*.[83] The facts involved the refusal of the British embassy in Spain and the Foreign Office to renew a passport because there was a warrant out for Everett's arrest in the UK. It was held by O'Connor LJ, citing the comments of Lords Scarman, Roskill, and Diplock in *GCHQ*, that the High Court had the jurisdiction to review this administrative decision and that, although the government's policy was sound, Everett should have been given detailed reasons for the refusal of his passport.[84] Taylor LJ

---

79 [1985] AC 374, 407.
80 [1988] 3 All ER 86.
81 On the common law duty to give reasons see 17.3.5
82 See also Lord Keith's opinion in *Lord Advocate v Dumbarton District Council* [1990] 2 AC 580.
83 [1989] 1 All ER 655.
84 Compare *Secretary of State for the Home Department v Lakdawalla* [1972] Imm AR 26.

also sought to give greater coherence to the concept of justiciability that had been noted in *GCHQ*. Drawing a distinction between prerogative powers that concern 'matters of high policy', which are non-justiciable, and other matters such as the power to issue passports, which are justiciable, he said:

I am in no doubt that the court has the power to review the withdrawal or refusal to grant or renew a passport. The House of Lords in (GCHQ) . . . made it clear that the powers of the court cannot be ousted merely by invoking the word 'prerogative'. The majority of their Lordships indicated that whether judicial review of the exercise of the prerogative is open depends on the subject matter and in particular whether it is justiciable. At the top of the scale of executive functions under the prerogative are matters of high policy, of which examples were given by their Lordships: making treaties, making law, dissolving Parliament, mobilizing the armed forces. Clearly those matters, and no doubt a number of others, are not justiciable. But the grant or refusal of a passport is in quite a different category. It is a matter of administrative decision, affecting the rights of individuals.[85]

Significant, too, was the decision in *ex p Bentley*, which was a case concerning an exercise of the prerogative of mercy.[86] Judicial review was here granted for Iris Bentley to seek a declaration that the Home Secretary's refusal to grant a posthumous pardon to her brother, hanged for the murder of a policeman in 1953 despite his having the mental capacity of an 11-year-old at the time, was an error of law. This was because the court regarded the prerogative of mercy as an important feature of the criminal justice system, which meant that decisions of the Home Secretary that may be wrong in law should, in principle, be open to challenge. Moreover, in making this finding, the court emphasised that the category of justiciable decisions should not be seen as closed. As we saw above, Lord Roskill was of the view in *GCHQ* that the prerogative of mercy fell beyond the scope of judicial review. However, the court in *Bentley* thought otherwise on the facts and, in so doing, it highlighted the fluid and adaptable nature of the supervisory jurisdiction:

We conclude therefore that some aspects of the royal prerogative are amenable to the judicial review process. We do not think that it is necessary for us to say more than this in the instant case. It will be for other courts to decide on a case-by-case basis whether the matter in question is reviewable or not.[87]

One further case that might be discussed in this context is *R (Sandiford) v Secretary of State for Foreign and Commonwealth Affairs*.[88] This was a disturbing case in which a British woman had been sentenced to death, in Indonesia, for drugs offences committed on the island of Bali. She requested financial assistance from the British government to support her appeals within the Indonesian system, but her request was refused on the basis of the government's policy not to provide assistance for overseas criminal trials, including death penalty cases. The policy in question had been adopted on the basis of the prerogative, and the claimant argued that it fettered the Secretary of State's discretion and was contrary to human rights law. While the Supreme Court plainly had some sympathy for the claimant, it held that it was unable to grant a remedy on the facts of the case. This was because the law on

---

85 [1989] 1 All ER 655, 660.

86 [1993] 4 All ER 442. And see, e.g., *R (Shields) v Secretary of State for Justice* [2010] QB 150 and *McGeough v Secretary of State for Northern Ireland* [2013] NI 143.

87 [1993] 4 All ER 442, 453, Watkins LJ. See, to like effect, *Re McBride's Application (No 2)* [2003] NI 319, 334.

88 [2014] UKSC 44, [2014] 1 WLR 2697.

the fettering of discretion had been developed in relation to statutory powers and could not extend into the realm of non-statutory prerogative powers.[89] The Court was also of the view that the claimant's human rights arguments failed because the Secretary of State had no extra-territorial obligations on the facts.

9.3.2.3 *Fire Brigade's Union* and *Bancoult*

Of the remaining cases heard post-*GCHQ*, the two most important have undoubtedly been *R v Secretary of State for the Home Department, ex p Fire Brigades Union* and *R (Bancoult) v Secretary of State for Foreign and Commonwealth Affairs (No 2)*.[90] Final judgment in both cases was given by the House of Lords and, to the extent that the former judgment was regarded as something of a high-water mark in terms of judicial control of the prerogative, the latter has been described as 'a disappointing statement of contemporary judicial attitudes to the prerogative'.[91] The cases thus reveal, in different ways, the parameters within which the prerogative powers are now constrained.

Fire Brigades Union arose when the government sought to revise provisions in the Criminal Justice Act 1988 that enabled changes to be made to the structure of the Criminal Injuries Compensation Scheme. The Scheme had first been introduced in the UK under the prerogative powers and it had, until 1988, existed solely on that basis (on the reviewability of decisions of the Criminal Injuries Compensation Board see *ex p Lain*, noted earlier). In 1988, however, Parliament enacted legislation to place the scheme on a statutory footing, with the relevant provisions being set to come into force when the Home Secretary made an order to that effect. Instead of making such an order, the Home Secretary indicated in 1993 that the statutory scheme would not be brought into force and, acting on the basis of the prerogative powers, he replaced the existing non-statutory scheme with a less generous tariff scheme that likewise was to be non-statutory. As his decision meant that many individuals would likely receive considerably reduced compensation packages, a number of trade unions applied for judicial review on the ground that the Home Secretary had acted unlawfully by using the prerogative powers to by-pass statutory provisions which were not yet in force and which he was required by statute to activate.

The House of Lords held by a 3:2 majority that the new scheme was *ultra vires* and an abuse of the Secretary of State's power. Although the majority rejected the applicants' argument that the Home Secretary was under a legally enforceable duty to activate the relevant statutory provisions at a particular time, it held that he was under a continuing duty to consider whether to bring the statutory scheme into force. The lead judgment was delivered by Lord Browne-Wilkinson who, having noted *De Keyser's* case, held that it would be 'most surprising if . . . prerogative powers could be validly exercised so as to frustrate the will of Parliament as expressed

---

89 On fettering of discretion see ch 12.

90 [1995] 2 AC 513 and [2009] 1 AC 453 respectively. Other notable cases include *R v British Coal Corporation and the Secretary of State for Trade and Industry, ex p Vardy* [1993] ICR 720 (concerning the legality of the closure of a number of coal pits) and *R v Ministry of Defence, ex p Smith* [1996] QB 517 (concerning the legality of a policy that prohibited gays and lesbians from serving in the armed forces—but see too *Smith & Grady v UK* (2000) 29 EHRR 493, finding a violation of, among other rights, the Art 8 ECHR right to respect for private and family life).

91 M Elliott and A Perreau-Saussine, 'Pyrrhic Public Law: *Bancoult* and the Sources, Status and Content of Common Law Limitations on Prerogative Power' (2009) *Public Law* 697.

in statute and, to an extent, to pre-empt the decision of Parliament whether or not to continue with the statutory scheme'.[92] His Lordship's findings in this regard were vigorously opposed in the House's dissenting judgments, with Lord Mustill suggesting that '(S)ome of the arguments addressed would have the court push to the very boundaries of the distinction between court and Parliament established in, and recognised ever since, the Bill of Rights 1689'.[93] But the majority of the House maintained that there existed the imperative of ensuring that the executive did not use the prerogative powers to usurp law-making functions which properly belong to Parliament. For that reason, 'the decision to introduce the tariff scheme at a time when the statutory provisions and his power . . . were on the statutory book was unlawful and an abuse of the prerogative power'.[94]

It is clear that this case raised significant constitutional issues and, moreover, that it led to sharp divisions of opinion between the Lords. For instance, while Lords Lloyd and Nicholls agreed with the reasoning of Lord Browne-Wilkinson in finding that there had been an abuse of power, Lords Keith and Mustill delivered strong dissenting judgments and stated that any judicial interference with the decision of the Secretary of State was to overstep the boundary that separated the judicial from the executive and Parliamentary powers. As Ganz commented:

> The fundamental difference between them is that the majority regarded the Home Secretary's decisions as giving rise to legal issues subject to judicial review, whereas the dissenters treated them as political decisions for which he was answerable to Parliament but not to the courts.[95]

Here, then, the majority apparently positioned itself at the very margin between law and policy.[96]

The constitutional issues arising out of *Bancoult* were equally controversial, as were the facts that gave rise to them. In broad terms, the case concerned the legality of government attempts to use Prerogative Orders in Council—prerogative legislation—to prevent the Chagos Islanders returning to the homeland that they had been compulsorily removed from in the 1970s (the removal had been made because Diego Garcia, the principal island in the archipelago, was to be used as a US military base). The legal basis for the removal was found to be unlawful and was quashed in 2001,[97] and the government initially stated that it would abide by the ruling of the court and allow the islanders to return to their homeland (with the exception of Diego Garcia). However, the government later changed its mind and, without consulting the islanders, laid before Her Majesty two Orders in Council that would have had the effect of preventing return to the islands. The corresponding claim for judicial review thus raised a number of important questions that included: (a) whether the House of Lords could review prerogative legislation, and, if it could, (b) whether the Orders in Council in this case were unlawful.

The House of Lords answered (a) with reference to *GCHQ* and held that there was no reason in principle why prerogative legislation should not, like other prerogative acts, be reviewable by the courts. This, in turn, was a significant finding, as

---

92 [1995] 2 AC 513, 552.
93 Ibid, 568.
94 Ibid, 554, Lord Browne-Wilkinson.
95 G Ganz, 'Criminal Injuries Compensation: The Constitutional Issues' (1996) 59 *Modern Law Review* 95, 97.
96 See, too, e.g., *R (Abassi) v Secretary of State for Foreign and Commonwealth Affairs* [2003] UKHRR 76.
97 *R (Bancoult) v Secretary of State for Foreign and Commonwealth Affairs* [2001] 2 WLR 1219.

it marked yet a further expansion of the supervisory jurisdiction into realms that were previously considered immune from review. However, it was in answering (b) that the ruling was to attract criticism, as the House of Lords held that the legislation was not unlawful. The reasoning of the House here ranged across complex issues of the nature and status of colonial laws and, crucially, whether the legislation offended common law principles of unreasonableness, abuse of power, and legitimate expectation.[98] In finding that it did not offend those principles, the House of Lords emphasised that the decision to enact the legislation had been taken in the light of factors such as the feasibility of resettlement, the demands on public expenditure, and the implications for the state's security and diplomatic interests. Noting that these were matters that 'lay peculiarly' within the competence of the executive, the House concluded that the legislation could not be characterised as unreasonable or as amounting to an abuse of power. Nor, in the context of the case, could the claimants have had a legitimate expectation of resettlement, as the government statements made in the light of the court ruling of 2001 were not clear and unambiguous.

Does the ruling in *Bancoult* merit criticism? Certainly, the development of the logic of *GCHQ* is to be welcomed, as it provides further safeguards against executive excess even in the context of the making of legislation (which is, at least within the terms of the Human Rights Act 1998, a form of primary legislation).[99] On the other hand, the judicial refusal to look closely at the government's justification for the legislation has led Elliott and Perreau-Saussine to describe the case as 'a pyrrhic victory for those who regard executive power as constrained by the rule of law'.[100] The point they make is that, to the extent that the House of Lords held that prerogative legislation is subject to review, restraint on the resulting question of its legality arguably undermined the value of subjecting it to review in the first instance. An example, perhaps, of how developments that are doctrinally significant in judicial review can be of only limited practical utility?

9.3.3 The Constitutional Reform and Governance Act 2010

We turn, finally (and briefly), to consider the importance of the Constitutional Reform and Governance Act 2010, which has placed a number of prerogative powers on a statutory footing. As we have already discussed in chapter 5, the powers in question relate to the management of the civil service and the ratification of treaties.[101] While exercises of the prerogative in these areas were already subject to parliamentary oversight, the Act has consolidated the link to parliamentary control. To take the example of the ratification of treaties, the essence of what was previously known as the 'Ponsonby rule' has been enacted in section 20, which provides, among other things, that:

a treaty is not to be ratified unless (a) a Minister of the Crown has laid before Parliament a copy of the treaty (b) the treaty has been published in a way that a Minister of the Crown thinks appropriate and (c) [21 days have] expired without either House having resolved, [within 21 days], that the treaty should not be ratified.

---

98 On which see chs 13 and 15.
99 Section 21.
100 Elliott and Perreau-Saussine, n 91, 717.
101 Parts I and II, respectively.

The decision to put these powers on a statutory footing was driven by a concern to increase the levels of democratic control over the prerogative.[102] Of course, in this context, 'democratic control' is to be equated with 'parliamentary control' rather than with any control that the courts have exercised through the medium of judicial review. Indeed, while we have described above how the courts have taken significant steps to ensure accountability in respect of aspects of the prerogative powers, the case law has at no time engaged the courts in the matters of 'high policy' associated with the ratification of treaties. The Act, in that sense, can be said to pursue a level of democratic control that has long been recognised as beyond the constitutional role of the courts.

9.4 Conclusion

We began this chapter by noting judicial review's historical emphasis on the control of statutory powers and duties and the importance of the related source of power test. In the pages that followed, we explained how the courts have moved beyond the source of power test in an attempt to ensure that there is a degree of judicial control of public power in areas where such control would otherwise be absent. When doing so, we have emphasised that the reach of judicial review still remains limited by a number of factors, some of which are desirable, and others less so. Hence, in relation to the Royal prerogative, we have seen that the expansion of the review jurisdiction has remained sensitive to wider separation of powers concerns and to the role to be played by Parliament. We have also seen that the judicial approach to the contracting-out of government functions has been constrained by the remnants of the source of power test, at least in England and Wales, and that this arguably is an unnecessary obstacle to the protection of individual interests (particularly when compared with the position in Scottish law).

On a cautionary note we would add that, while the expansion of judicial review in recent decades has indeed been remarkable, there is sometimes a tendency to overstate the significance of what this actually means. Our point here is that, just because the departure from the source of power test has increased the range of decisions that are susceptible to judicial review, it does not follow that the courts will always find that a decision was unlawful. Whether a decision is unlawful will, instead, depend on a range of considerations that guide the courts, such as the nature and extent of discretion, whether rights are engaged by a decision, whether a decision has implications for the public purse, and so on. This, ultimately, is what determined the final approach of the House of Lords in *Bancoult*, and Elliott and Perreau-Saussine's critical comments merely underlined that reality. A decision may therefore be subject to judicial review, but it should always be remembered that it may well be one that is allowed to stand.

---

102 See the *Governance of Britain White Paper*, Cm 7170, available at <http://www.official-documents. gov.uk/document/cm71/7170/7170.pdf>.

FURTHER READING

On the public–private divide

Anthony, G (2008) 'Human Rights and the Public-Private Divide in the UK's Multi-level Constitution' in Pavlopoulos, P and Flogaitis, S (eds), *Multilevel Governance and Administrative Reform in the 21st Century* (London: Esperia Publications), 237.

Anthony, G (2014) *Judicial Review in Northern Ireland*, 2nd edn (Oxford: Hart Publishing).

Bamforth, N (1997) 'The Public-Private Law Distinction: A Comparative and Philosophical Approach', in Leyland, P and Woods, T (eds), *Administrative Law Facing the Future: Old Constraints and New Horizons* (London: Blackstone Press).

Bamforth, N (1999) 'The Application of the Human Rights Act 1998 to Public Authorities and Private Bodies' 58 *Cambridge Law Journal* 159.

Craig, P (1997) 'Public Law and Control Over Private Power' in Taggart, M (ed), *The Province of Administrative Law* (Oxford: Hart Publishing).

Elliott, M (1999) 'The *Ultra Vires* Doctrine in a Constitutional Setting: Still the Central Principle of Administrative Law' *Cambridge Law Journal* 129.

Harlow, C (1980) '"Public" or "Private" Law: Definition Without Distinction' 43 *Modern Law Review* 241.

Meisel, F [2004] 'The Aston Cantlow Case: Blots on English Jurisprudence and the Public/Private Law Divide' *Public Law* 2.

Oliver, D [1987] 'Is the *Ultra Vires* Rule the Basis of Judicial Review' *Public Law* 543.

Oliver, D [1997] 'Common Values in Public and Private Law and the Public-Private Divide' *Public Law* 630.

Oliver, D [2000] 'The Frontiers of the State: Public Authorities and Public Functions under the Human Rights Act' *Public Law* 476.

On the prerogative

Billings, P and Pontin, B [2001] 'Prerogative Powers and the Human Rights Act: Elevating the Status of Orders in Council' *Public Law* 21.

Craig, P (1998) 'Prerogative, Precedent and Power' in Forsyth, C and Hare, I (eds), *The Golden Metwand and the Crooked Cord* (Oxford: Clarendon Press).

Elliott, M and Perreau-Saussine, A [2009] 'Pyrrhic Public Law: *Bancoult* and the Sources, Status and Content of Common Law Limitations on Prerogative Power' *Public Law* 697.

Ganz, G (1996) 'Criminal Injuries Compensation: The Constitutional Issues' 59 *Modern Law Review* 95.

Hadfield, B (1999) 'Judicial Review and the Prerogative Powers of the Crown' in Sunkin, M and Payne, S (eds), *The Nature of the Crown: A Legal and Political Analysis* (Oxford: Oxford University Press), chapter 8.

Leigh, I (1995) 'The Prerogative, Legislative Power and the Democratic Deficit: the *Fire Brigades Union* case' 3 *Web Journal of Current Legal Issues*.

Loughlin, M (1999) 'The State, the Crown and the Law' in Sunkin, M and Payne, S (eds), *The Nature of the Crown* (Oxford: Oxford University Press).

Pollard, D (1997) 'Judicial Review of Prerogative Powers in the United Kingdom and France' in Leyland, P and Woods, T (eds), *Administrative Law Facing the Future: Old Constraints and New Horizons* (London: Blackstone Press).

Sunkin, M and Payne, S (eds) (1999) *The Nature of the Crown: A Legal and Political Analysis* (Oxford: Oxford University Press).

Tomkins, A [2001] 'Magna Carta, Crown and Colonies' *Public Law* 571.

10

....

Limiting judicial review: ouster clauses and public interest immunity

10.1 Introduction

We have already seen that the expansion of judicial review has been one conspicuous feature of our administrative law over recent decades. However, the focus of this
chapter is somewhat different in that it considers the question of when judicial review can be subject to limitations. In the first instance, we will examine how far it is
possible to exclude the jurisdiction of the courts by the careful drafting of objectively
worded statutory ouster provisions, and by the use of subjective language allowing
considerable discretion to the decision-maker. Second, we will focus on an area where
implied, rather than *express*, limits are central to the law: the use of public interest immunity by government and other bodies. This is important because, if in advance
of any action it is recognised that the exclusion of the courts has been achieved, this
is a clear signal to decision-makers that they may operate without fear of intervention by the courts at a later stage. However, judges are aware of their constitutional
position, and particularly of the doctrine of the rule of law. The result is that they
have been unwilling to permit any subordinate authority to obtain uncontrollable
power which would exempt public authorities, or other bodies, from the jurisdiction
of the courts, as this would be, theoretically, tantamount to opening the door to
potentially dictatorial power. For example, strong opposition was expressed in political, judicial, and academic circles to a proposal by the then government to insert
an ouster clause in the Asylum and Immigration Bill 2004 whereby the legislation
would have excluded entirely the jurisdiction of the courts in relation to the operation of the Asylum and Immigration Tribunal.[1] The measure was intended to rule out
the established grounds of judicial review and by so doing it would have taken away
an important constitutional safeguard. In the face of strong resistance, especially in
the House of Lords, the government relented and the clause was dropped from what
became the Asylum and Immigration (Treatment of Claimants etc) Act 2004. Indeed,
the courts have, since the 1960s, taken a strong, even, on occasion, rebellious, stand
against the creation of pockets of power which they hold to be in violation of the rule
of law and an abuse of power. As is stated in Wade and Forsyth:

Although lawyers appearing for government departments may argue that some Act confers unfettered discretion they are guilty of constitutional blasphemy, for unfettered discretion cannot
exist where the rule of law reigns. The same truth can be expressed by saying that all power is
capable of abuse, and that the power to prevent abuse is the acid test of effective judicial review.[2]

---

1 e.g., Lord Woolf Squire Centenary Lecture (2004) 63 *Cambridge Law Journal* 310.
2 W Wade and C Forsyth, *Administrative Law*, 11th edn (Oxford: Oxford University Press 2014), 27.

This is clearly in line with one strongly held view of the role of the judiciary, working within the parameters set by the constitutional convention of the separation of powers, although a number of judges have historically appeared to agree with the view that the courts should always accede to the wishes of Parliament, or the decisions of ministers, however controversial.[3] However, as differing judicial *dicta* indicate, the question of how far decisions made by governmental and other administrative bodies should be subject to control by the courts is far from being an uncontroversial one. Ousters, for example, may well be regarded as a useful device to keep at bay a conservatively inclined judiciary. Griffith, articulating an essentially 'green light' view,[4] recognised and encouraged the need for specialist bodies to act as adjudicators in certain areas of administration. Considered from this perspective, precisely the same type of ouster restrictions may, with significant qualifications, satisfy the desire of administrators for consistency and finality in the implementation of policy decisions.[5]

It will become apparent as we work through this chapter that this is one area in which the language of the law can become very complex, largely because of historical distinctions that were previously made by the courts. We return to some of the corresponding definitional issues later,[6] but before beginning our analysis we should clarify one point about use of the term 'jurisdiction'. In short, judicial review used to fasten upon what may be termed a 'jurisdictional' theory of law, whereby the courts spoke of a decision-maker's 'jurisdiction' over a matter as a synonym for what would now be called 'legal power'. On this basis, the courts drew a distinction between 'errors of law that went to jurisdiction' (essentially, an error about whether the decision-maker had the power it purported to have) and 'errors of law that were made within jurisdiction' (i.e., an error that did not take the decision-maker outside the four corners of its power). While errors of law that went to jurisdiction were always subject to judicial control—any other approach would allow a decision-maker to assume for itself power beyond that delegated by Parliament—the courts were less willing to intervene in relation to errors within jurisdiction. However, to the extent that the jurisdictional theory limited the reach of review, it should be noted that the courts no longer rely on the old distinction and that they now regard *any* error of law as reviewable. As will be seen below, this is widely regarded to be the result of the *Anisminic* case that is often credited with the emergence of *ultra vires* doctrine.[7]

10.2 **Ouster and time limit clauses**

10.2.1 **Finality**

Finality clauses are sometimes inserted in statutes to indicate that the decision of a particular decision-maker, for instance a tribunal, cannot be challenged in any court. However, there is now an overwhelming body of case law that suggests that

---

3 See, e.g., Viscount Simonds in *Smith v East Elloe Rural District Council* [1956] 1 All ER 855.

4 See 1.4.

5 J Griffith, *The Politics of the Judiciary*, 5th edn (London: Fontana, 1997), 340ff.

6 See 10.4.

7 See discussion of grounds of judicial review in chs 11–17 and *Boddington v British Transport Police* [1999] 2 AC 143.

such finality clauses will not be recognised by the courts as excluding judicial review. *R v Medical Appeal Tribunal, ex p Gilmore*[8] is regarded as a leading decision on this point. Here, section 36(3) of the National Insurance (Industrial Injuries) Act 1946 provided that 'any decision of a claim or question . . . shall be final'. The applicant sought the remedy of *certiorari* (a quashing order) when there had been an error of law on the face of the record.[9] Although the remedy was refused in the Divisional Court, it was allowed in the Court of Appeal. Denning LJ held that, while these words may have been enough to exclude an appeal, they did not prevent judicial review—'I find it very well settled that the remedy by *certiorari* is never to be taken away by any statute except by the most clear and explicit words'—and he was in no doubt that such a formulation as 'shall be final' was not sufficient to achieve this objective. With regard to 'no *certiorari*' clauses, the case for not readily accepting exclusion was explained with reference to old statutes and cases which established that ' . . . the court never allowed those statutes to be used as a cover for wrongdoing by tribunals. If tribunals were to be at liberty to exceed their jurisdiction without any check by the courts, the rule of law would be at an end'.[10] Despite express words taking away *certiorari*, therefore, it was held (in these older cases) that *certiorari* could still lie if that was necessary to vindicate the rule of law.

Similarly, there is well-established authority to suggest that a finality clause will be ineffective when there is error which goes to the jurisdiction. For example, in *Pearlman v Harrow School*,[11] the decision of a county court judge on the matter in question was to be 'final and conclusive'. In addition, section 107 of the County Court Act 1959 contained a non-*certiorari* clause, but this did not apply and affect the supervisory jurisdiction of the High Court. Moreover, it was suggested, more controversially, in Lord Denning's *obiter* remarks in this case, that a finality clause may not even exclude more general appeals on points of law. Although *ex p Gilmore* and *Pearlman v Harrow School* are concerned with applications for the remedy of *certiorari*, it should be noted that, whatever remedy is being sought, a finality clause will not exclude judicial review when an error is deemed to go to the jurisdiction of the decision-maker.

10.2.2 Total ouster clauses and the *Anisminic* case

We shall see below[12] that the decision in *Smith v East Elloe Rural District Council*[13] exemplified a view of time limitation clauses reached towards the end of a recognised period of judicial quietism. In this instance the House of Lords interpreted a statutory provision which limited the court's jurisdiction to review a compulsory purchase order on land so broadly that even fraud by public servants would not entitle the owner to a remedy by way of *certiorari*. In striking contrast, we can now consider the landmark decision of the House of Lords in *Anisminic Ltd v Foreign Compensation Commission*.[14] This case is regarded as one of the high points

---

8 [1957] 1 QB 574.
9 See 10.4.
10 [1957] 1 QB 574, at 586.
11 [1979] QB 56.
12 10.2.3.
13 [1956] 1 All ER 855.
14 [1969] 2 AC 147.

of judicial intervention. Before becoming involved with the finer details raised, it is useful to keep in mind that the two central issues for our purposes were:

(a) the applicability of statutory exclusion clauses contained in the Foreign Compensation Act 1950; and

(b) the extent to which judicial review was confined to errors going to the jurisdiction of the decision-maker.

The background of the case needs to be outlined briefly in order to highlight the claim that was to give rise to the eventual House of Lords decision. Anisminic Ltd was a British mining company which had owned property in Egypt, but during the Suez Crisis in 1956 the property was taken over by Israeli troops and £500,000 worth of damage was caused to it. It was then sequestrated in November 1956 by the Egyptian government. In 1957 the Egyptian government authorised the sale of the property, including a substantial quantity of manganese ore, for less than its real value to TEDO, an Egyptian corporate body that had acquired Anisminic's assets under an agreement with the Egyptian government. As part of that agreement, Anisminic also received £500,000 in compensation from the Egyptian government, albeit that the arrangement deliberately left open the question of compensation from other sources. In 1959, a treaty was negotiated between the UAR (Egypt) and the British government, which provided for £27.5 million compensation to be paid to the UK for any property confiscated in Egypt in 1956. Responsibility for distributing these funds was vested in the Foreign Compensation Commission. Anisminic Ltd duly submitted a compensation claim.

The Commission operated under the Foreign Compensation (Egypt) (Determination and Registration of Claims) Order 1962. A claim could be established under the order if:

(a) the applicant was the person referred to in the relevant part of Annex E of the order as the owner of property or their successor in title;

(b) the person referred to in the relevant part of Annex E and any person who became successor in title of such person on or before 28 February 1959 were British nationals on 31 October 1956 and 28 February 1959.

The Commission interpreted the order (which their Lordships criticised as being very badly drafted) as meaning not only that the applicant had to be British but also that its successors in title had to be British. Such an interpretation of the clause appeared to defeat almost any claim, since it was most unlikely that a successor in title would be British; and in any event, once such a deal (sale to a non-British company) had been reached by Anisminic (or any other company) it was powerless to do anything about it. (We should not lose sight of the fact that the object of these provisions was to ensure that only persons of British nationality would be entitled to compensation, be they the original owners or their successors in title.) The Commission found that Anisminic failed in its claim for compensation solely on the grounds that TEDO, its successor in title, was not a British national. Anisminic sought a declaration that the order had been misconstrued by the Commission.

A major obstacle to overcome was whether a statutory ouster clause could prevent the intervention of the courts. The House of Lords considered the meaning of section 4(4) of the Foreign Compensation Act 1950, which had provided in

unequivocal language that 'the determination by the Commission of any application made to them under this Act shall not be called into question in any court of
law'. Taken at face value this provision would appear to indicate that any consideration in a court was excluded by the clause, including any action to establish that
the determination was itself a nullity. The logical consequences of this are plain
enough, that is, that a decision may well have been a nullity, but there was no way
of knowing this because the statutory exclusion clause prevented the courts from
reviewing the matter. However, Lord Reid asked, in his judgment:

Does such a provision require the court to treat that order as a valid order? It is a well established principle that a provision ousting the ordinary jurisdiction of the court must be construed strictly—meaning, I think, that, if such a provision is reasonably capable of having
two meanings, that meaning shall be taken which preserves the ordinary jurisdiction of the
court . . . No case has been cited in which any other form of words limiting the jurisdiction
of the court has been held to protect a nullity. (See [1969] 2 AC 147, 170.

The exclusion therefore related to valid determinations only. It was held that, because the Commission was acting *ultra vires*, its determination in this case was void
ab initio and thus judicial intervention could not be excluded by any such clause.

The case depended upon the way an inadequately drafted order in council had
been interpreted when the Commission was deciding who were successors in title.
This in itself raised questions about the jurisdiction of the decision-maker. Lord Reid
stated that: 'If they [the Commission] base their decision on some matter which is
not prescribed for their adjudication, they are doing something which they have no
right to do and . . . their decision is a nullity.' ([1969] 2 AC 147, 174). The Commission
had in effect considered the questions it had been granted jurisdiction to determine
by recourse to totally irrelevant considerations. Lord Reid added that:

In themselves the words 'successor in title' are . . . inappropriate in the circumstances of this
Order to denote any person while the original owner is still in existence, and I think that it
is most improbable that they were intended to denote any such person. There is no necessity
to stretch them to cover any such person. I would therefore hold that the words 'and any
person who became successor in title to such person' in article 4(1)(b)(ii) have no application
to a case where the applicant is the original owner. It follows that the commission rejected
the appellants' claim on a ground which they had no right to take into account and that their
decision was a nullity. ([1969] 2 AC 147, 175).

As an *ultra vires* determination was regarded as not being a determination at all, the
decision was a nullity which could have no effect. Their Lordships unanimously
held that such exclusion clauses only protected determinations which were *intra
vires*. The determination in this case was, however, *ultra vires* as it was based upon
a misconstruction of the scope of the relevant Order; in other words the decision-
maker had made an error that went to the basis of its jurisdiction.[15] It is worth
remembering (as is implicit from Lord Reid's first statement above) that, even when
there is any such clause purporting to exclude judicial review (total ouster), the determination of whether the decision is valid will inevitably be made by a judge on
an application for judicial review. In this sense the courts are not excluded.

An almost immediate response was that the relevant legislation was amended by
the passing of the Foreign Compensation Act 1969, with provision for appeals to

15 On errors that go to jurisdiction see further 10.4.

the Court of Appeal on a question of law concerning the construction of the Order in Council. In turn, this raises the question of whether limitation clauses will ever be read as having the effect of ousting the jurisdiction of the courts.

10.2.2.1 The impact of *Anisminic*

At first encounter it appears that *Anisminic* could be taken to mean that virtually any action committed in error by an administrative agency/body might be regarded as being fundamental, in the sense that the error will go to jurisdiction and thus render the resulting decision, or other administrative action, beyond that body's powers. But it is important to consider whether the decision went too far by providing almost an open door for intervention by the courts in many situations where the judges had previously been reluctant to tread (see, e.g., Lord Morris's dissenting judgment in *Anisminic*). In fact the dangers of over-eager judicial involvement were subsequently raised in *Pearlman v Governors of Harrow School*,[16] briefly mentioned earlier. The County Court was given the right to determine a matter, with paragraph 2(2) of Schedule 8 to the Housing Act 1974 providing that any determination by the court 'shall be final and conclusive'. Furthermore, section 107 of the County Courts Act 1959 provided that 'no judgment or order of any judge of county courts . . . shall be removed by appeal, motion, or *certiorari* or otherwise into any other court'. Lord Denning held that even if section 107 did apply, it would only exclude *certiorari* for error of law on the face of the record and it would not limit the power of the High Court to issue *certiorari* for absence of jurisdiction. His Lordship considered that, by misconstruing the words in the statute, the judge had made an error of law that went to jurisdiction. However, Lane LJ strongly dissented from the majority view:

The judge is considering the words (in the Schedule) which he ought to consider . . . [he] is not embarking on some unauthorised or extraneous or irrelevant exercise. All he has done is to come to what appears to this court to be a wrong conclusion on a difficult question. It seems to me that, if this judge is acting outside his jurisdiction, so then is every judge who comes to a wrong decision on a point of law.[17]

This raises the question of whether Lord Denning's solution is blurring the distinction between law and fact, a distinction that we consider in chapter 12.

Lane LJ's dissenting view in *Pearlman* was ultimately endorsed by the House of Lords in *Re Racal Communications*.[18] The statutory exclusion in this case had been provided under section 441(3) of the Companies Act 1948. This stated that a decision by a High Court judge on an application 'shall not be appealable'. Nevertheless, the Court of Appeal entertained an appeal on the grounds that the section had been misconstrued by the judge and that this error went to jurisdiction, as it had in *Anisminic*. Accordingly, the Court of Appeal reversed the decision of the High Court. On final appeal, however, the House of Lords rejected this approach for several reasons. First, it held that the jurisdiction of the Court of Appeal itself was entirely appellate and therefore it had no power to deal with an original application for judicial review, which this amounted to. (The court was acting beyond its own powers!). Secondly, Lord Diplock explained that judicial review, as a remedy that relates to the decisions of courts, is available

---

16 [1979] QB 56.
17 Ibid, 76.
18 [1981] AC 374.

for mistakes of law made by inferior courts and tribunals only, although it was acknowledged that errors of law by these bodies would go to jurisdiction and thus be reviewable. In other words, no public body has the right to act unlawfully under Dicey's doctrine so that, where there is a mistake of law, the public body concerned is in a sense acting outside its jurisdiction, even if there is an ouster clause (the important point here is to distinguish mistakes of fact where the final determination can rest with the decision-maker—by 'fact' we mean the issues that the inferior body is meant to decide, for example the level of a pension or benefit, to grant or refuse planning permission, etc). Further, it was pointed out that in some cases such as *Pearlman*, above, it would still be possible to isolate questions of fact, which Parliament had intended should be determined entirely by the inferior tribunal (not by an appellate body). Thirdly, Lord Diplock was satisfied that the clause excluding the appeal should be taken at face value as excluding jurisdiction. Lastly, his Lordship believed that corrections of mistakes of law in the High Court were to be achieved by appeal alone (not review). If a statute excludes an appeal, as this one did, then there can be no correction at all. This judgment of Lord Diplock can be considered to have set boundaries to the impact of *Anisminic*.[19]

Another case of note is *R v Secretary of State for the Home Department, ex p Fayed*,[20] where the Fayed brothers appealed against a decision by the Home Secretary who had refused to grant them naturalisation. In order to provide a remedy, the court had to override section 44(2) of the British Nationality Act 1981 whereby 'the Secretary of State . . . shall not be required to assign any reason for the grant or refusal of any application under this Act . . . and the decision of the Secretary of State . . . on any such decision shall not be subject to appeal to, or review in, any court'. It was held that this clause did not oust jurisdiction and prevent the court from reviewing the decision on procedural grounds. *Attorney General v Ryan*[21] was cited as authority in support of the inference that Parliament was not intending to exclude from review a decision which failed to comply with the need for fairness.

On the other hand, ostensibly weaker 'conclusive evidence' clauses have been recognised as excluding review. In *R v Registrar of Companies, ex p Central Bank of India*,[22] the Court of Appeal was of the opinion that the Registrar, operating under the Companies Act 1948, had made an error of law; but it went on to hold that no evidence could be brought before the court to prove this because of a clause in section 98(2) containing the words 'and the certificate shall be conclusive evidence that the requirements of [Part III] of the Act as to registration have been complied with'. A successful challenge to the Registrar's decision on these grounds would effectively undermine the certainty offered by a scheme of statutory regulation which specifically allowed the Registrar to make decisions on issues of mixed law and fact.

10.2.2.2 The *Cart* case and the Tribunals Courts and Enforcement Act 2007

The Tribunals, Courts and Enforcement Act 2007, which sets the seal on the Leggatt reforms of tribunals, reorganises most of the important statutory tribunals

---

19 See also, e.g., *South East Asia Fire Bricks Sdn Bhd v Non-Metallic Mineral Products Manufacturing Employees Union* [1981] AC 363.

20 [1997] 1 All ER 228.

21 [1980] AC 718.

22 [1986] 1 All ER 105.

into a single system with a revised appellate structure.[23] Section 11 provides a right of appeal to the Upper Tribunal (UT) from the First-Tier Tribunal (FTT) which will redirect cases that would previously be heard in the High Court, while section 13(1) of the Act allows for a right of appeal to the Court of Appeal. Such appeals are restricted to points of law of general importance. A further innovation under section 19 is to grant the UT (presided over by a High Court judge) a limited jurisdiction to hear judicial reviews that would previously have been directed to the Administrative Court. Although the Act contained no ouster clause, it was not clear whether decisions of the UT as a superior court of record were intended to be subject to judicial review. This was an issue that needed to be resolved against a background of limited judicial resources.

R (Cart) v The Upper Tribunal[24] arose from unsuccessful appeals to the FTT, where subsequently there was refusal of permission to appeal to the UT by both the First and Upper Tier Tribunals.[25] The question for the Supreme Court was whether this refusal could be challenged by way of judicial review. The Court of Appeal considered that unappealable decisions were amenable to judicial review, but only if there had been an error of jurisdiction or a gross procedural irregularity. This approach, while restricting access, ran the risk of reinstating the highly technical distinction between error of law and excess of jurisdiction, which had been removed by the *Anisminic* decision. A balance needed to be reached between setting limits on the number of times that a judge should have another look at a decision, but without imposing unwarranted restrictions upon judicial review. As Baroness Hale, giving the leading judgment in the Supreme Court, explained: 'The real question . . . is what level of independent scrutiny outside the tribunal structure is required by the rule of law'.[26] The UT is empowered to set precedents for lower tribunals, often in a highly technical and fast-moving area of law, and could become the final arbiter of the law contrary to the wishes of Parliament. The answer to this question in the Supreme Court's opinion 'must be a principled but proportionate approach'. It was held that judicial review should be limited to the grounds upon which permission to make second-tier appeals are made, namely: (a) that the proposed appeal would raise some important point of principle or practice; or (b) there is some other compelling reason for the relevant appellate court to hear the appeal. The Court felt that this approach would ensure that errors on important points of principle or practice, in Lord Dyson's words, 'do not become fossilised within the UT system'.[27]

10.2.3 Time limit clauses (partial ousters)

While finality clauses have not generally been successful in barring the courts, partial ouster clauses have managed to achieve this objective much more effectively. A method that is frequently employed to limit intervention is specifying a restricted period of time after which no remedy will be available. For example, this is especially popular in planning and compulsory purchase statutes. The Acquisition of Land Act 1981 now deals with compulsory purchase orders and provides that a

23 See further ch 7.
24 [2011] UKSC 28, [2012] 1 AC 663.
25 See 7.5.
26 [2012] 1 AC 663, 687, para 51.
27 [2012] 1 AC 663, 708, para 130.

person may apply within six weeks for the order to be quashed, and that this time runs from the date of the order being made.

A significant decision regarding the justiciability of a case where a specified time limit had not been observed was *Smith v East Elloe Rural District Council*,[28] mentioned at 10.2.2. This concerned a challenge to a compulsory purchase order under the Acquisition of Land (Authorisation Procedure) Act 1946. The Act allowed a court to quash an order in cases in which the order was beyond the powers of the enabling Act itself or outside the procedural requirements contained in the Act, as long as substantial prejudice had been caused to the applicant. However, the statute had stipulated that any challenge was to be made within a six-week period of the order being made, and that otherwise a compulsory purchase order 'shall not be questioned in any legal proceedings whatsoever'. No challenge was made during the specified period. In fact, some five-and-a-half years elapsed before the plaintiff, Mrs Smith, claimed that the order had been wrongly confirmed; but crucially she claimed that it had been made in bad faith. It was therefore contended that in these circumstances, that is, where there had been bad faith, the time limit clause did not apply. Their Lordships concluded by a majority that they could not impugn the order because, according to Viscount Simmonds, notwithstanding the alleged fraud, 'plain words must be given their plain meaning' ([1956] 1 All ER 855, 859). The consequences of such an approach were recognised in a dissenting judgment by Lord Reid (perhaps a pointer to later developments) in which he doubted whether such an order that had been obtained by corrupt or fraudulent means could be protected from being questioned or attacked in any court. His Lordship stated in his judgment: 'In every class of case that I can think of the courts have always held that general words are not to be read as enabling a deliberate wrongdoer to take advantage of his own dishonesty.' (See [1956] 1 All ER 855, 868). Notwithstanding these remarks, the validity of the order was allowed to remain intact. (Incidentally, it was unanimously held by the House of Lords that Mrs Smith's related claim against the clerk to the council could proceed on the ground of bad faith, etc.) As we shall see, there are obvious practical advantages to setting such a limitation in this kind of area, and this may go some way to accounting for the much later decision of the Court of Appeal in *R v Secretary of State for the Environment, ex p Ostler*.[29]

By way of introducing ex p Ostler, we would note again that the *Anisminic* case, and certain other authorities that followed in its wake, appeared to suggest that complete ouster clauses would not be a safeguard against errors of law. However, the decision of the Court of Appeal in *ex p Ostler* confirmed that there can be a very different approach when time limit clauses are included in the legislation. In *ex p Ostler*, there had been an inquiry and publication of proposals for a ring road scheme in Boston, but it was not until the publication of supplementary plans that the applicant realised that the first set of proposals was also likely to affect his business premises in the centre of the town. Paragraph 2 of Schedule 2 to the Highways Act 1959 set a time limit of six weeks for applications to the High Court, and the Act further stipulated (by paragraph 4 of Schedule 2) that an order, once it had been confirmed, should not be questioned in any legal proceedings. The applicant sought *certiorari* to have the scheme quashed. No objections were allowed because the time limit in respect of the first proposals

---

28 [1956] 1 All ER 855.
29 [1976] 3 All ER 90.

was regarded as being final. It is noteworthy that the challenge was on grounds of bad faith and breach of natural justice, since it was said that secret assurances had been given to a trader behind the back of the applicant.

The facts of *ex p Ostler* were distinguished from *Anisminic* on several grounds, some of which were not wholly convincing. First, it was decided that the questionable authority of *Smith v East Elloe Rural District Council* could be followed because this was not a complete ouster clause but approximated to a limitation period, and thus a potential six-week period to make a challenge was available under the statute (although, of course, Ostler did not know of the defect until long after the six weeks had elapsed and therefore no remedy was in reality obtainable). Secondly, it was distinguished on the now-discredited basis that the determination in *Anisminic* was judicial, while the present question was considered more in the nature of an administrative decision.[30] Lastly, the Court of Appeal believed that a distinction could be drawn here because the matter did not go to jurisdiction as it had in *Anisminic*. The decision, the court maintained, was made within the statutory jurisdiction.

Although this case shows that the strict rule was still applicable, the judgment, and particularly the reasoning that distinguished *Anisminic* on this point, was the focus of much criticism, not least by Lord Denning who (extra-judicially) drew back from some of his reasoning in the case.[31] The point was that time limit clauses were invented for the purpose of public interest, and if the courts were to allow plaintiffs to come to them for a remedy long after the time limit had expired (i.e., retrospectively) it would be productive of much disruption to the public good, in that property would have been acquired and demolished. It is important to note that Mr Ostler's case was finally referred to the Parliamentary Commissioner for Administration, who found serious deficiencies in the manner in which the matter had been handled by the department. As a result he eventually received an *ex gratia* payment of compensation from the department.

This general reluctance of the courts to intervene in planning cases is vividly demonstrated by other decisions. In *R v Secretary of State for the Environment, ex p Kent*,[32] *Ostler* was followed and applied. Racal Vodafones had here applied for planning permission to construct a radio base and transmitter. K was not informed by the council about this application as he should have been. Planning permission was refused at this stage and the company appealed to the Secretary of State. Under the appeals procedure an inquiry was set up and the Secretary of State wrote to the council asking it to notify local residents. Once again, because of the inefficiency of the council in contacting and informing local people, K, the applicant, was not informed about the appeal. Some two months later he did find out about the plans and set about challenging the grant of planning permission on grounds of natural justice. This was after the statutory period of six weeks had elapsed. The application for judicial review relied on *Anisminic* as authority. It was maintained that this error went to jurisdiction. However, *Anisminic* was again distinguished on the ground that it had been concerned with a total ouster provision, whereas here Parliament did allow challenges to be made within a specific time limit. The result was that

---

30 On the now discredited judicial/administrative distinction see further ch 17 on natural justice.

31 See the discussion in M Beloff, 'Time, Time, Time It's On My Side, Yes it is' in C Forsyth and I Hare (eds), *The Golden Metwand and the Crooked Cord* (Oxford: Clarendon Press, 1998), 286.

32 [1990] COD 78.

a faultless applicant was left without a remedy because of a partial ouster clause, despite the ineptitude of a public authority.

In another example, *R v Cornwall County Council, ex p Huntington*,[33] the applicant's farm had been affected by a public right of way under section 53(2)(b) of the Wildlife and Countryside Act 1981. It was specified by paragraph 12(3) of Schedule 15 to the Act that a challenge had to be made within 42 days, after which the validity of the order 'shall not be questioned in any legal proceedings whatsoever'. *Certiorari* was applied for outside the statutory period, on the ground that the council had acted beyond the statutory powers conferred upon it by Parliament. Once again, this led the court to consider the argument for fundamental invalidity advanced in the House of Lords in *Anisminic*. Assuming the grounds to be correct, and that the council was acting *ultra vires* in a quasi-judicial capacity, it was submitted for the applicants that the decision was a nullity, thus defeating any statutory exclusion. Mann LJ, whose decision was upheld in the Court of Appeal, rejected any suggestion of degrees of invalidity linked to the functions being exercised by the decision-making body. Parliament had followed a standard formula in drafting the legislation, which provided an opportunity to challenge on specified grounds, and this had been combined with an ouster clause limiting the time allowed. In such cases, any challenge must be within the time laid down in the Act. It was held that any jurisdiction to grant review had been ousted by the above clause and the application for judicial review failed. Mann LJ pointed out that the principle in *Smith v East Elloe Rural District Council* has been affirmed as binding authority in a number of other cases. Mann LJ had further stated in the Divisional Court that:

The intention of Parliament when it uses an *Anisminic* clause is that questions as to validity are not excluded . . . [W]hen paragraphs such as those considered in *ex p Ostler* are used, then the legislative intention is that questions as to invalidity may be raised on the specified grounds in the prescribed time and in the prescribed manner, but otherwise the jurisdiction of the court is excluded in the interests of certainty.[34]

However, it is important to note that the reasoning in *Huntington* has not always been followed. For instance, in *R v Wiltshire County Council, ex p Nettlecombe Ltd*,[35] the case was distinguished on a challenge to an 'antecedent step' and for simple error of law. We would also note that time-limited ouster clauses may be open to attack under Article 6 of the European Convention on Human Rights (ECHR) (the right to a fair trial): while such clauses will not automatically breach Article 6 of the ECHR, they must be proportionate in all the circumstances and not interfere unduly with an individual's right of access to justice.

10.2.4 **Final comments on ouster and time limit clauses**

The crucial issue to resolve in respect of partial exclusion and time limit clauses has been whether, following the landmark judgment in *Anisminic*, the courts would be prepared to go beyond the strict statutory provision to allow an applicant a remedy. It appears that the position adopted in *ex p Ostler* and *ex p Kent* marked at least a qualified return to *Smith v East Elloe Rural District Council*. However, we should

---

33 [1992] 3 All ER 566 (Divisional Court); [1994] 1 All ER 694 (Court of Appeal).
34 *R v Cornwall CC, ex p Huntington* [1992] 3 All ER 566, 575.
35 [1998] 96 LGR 386.

remember that the underlying reason for accepting these clauses is the complication that would be caused by making a retrospective finding of illegality. In other words, there can be good policy reasons that lead the courts to adhere to strict time limits. For example, it would clearly be unsatisfactory if the prospect of some future challenge caused public development schemes to be suspended or delayed on a prolonged basis. Accordingly, the reluctance of the courts to intervene in these circumstances has not simply been because of judicial deference to parliamentary provisions, but because of the widespread potential disruption to administrative decision-making that would result if they did so.

10.3 Subjective words

One other method of restricting review by the courts has been to cast statutory language in a subjective form. For example, it is a fairly standard drafting practice to find a discretion granted to a minister, local authority, or other agency in the following terms: 'If the minister in any case so directs'[36] or 'such . . . wages as [the Council] may think fit'.[37] This might seem to suggest that the discretion rests entirely with the minister, local authority, or agency. The question will be, therefore, whether the failure to exercise the discretion contained in an Act will be considered a ground for review. We will see that, while the courts are generally willing to review an apparent failure to exercise a power, they can be reluctant to assess how a power has been exercised once the decision to exercise the power has been taken.

One of the most celebrated cases is *Padfield v Minister of Agriculture*.[38] Section 19 of the Agricultural Marketing Act 1958 provided that complaints could be heard against the milk-marketing scheme 'if the minister in any case so directs'. A farmer complained after the minister had refused to refer a complaint to the relevant committee of investigation. The minister claimed an absolute discretion and suggested that any reference to this committee would oblige him to follow its recommendations because those investigations would raise wider issues, thereby limiting the discretion given to him by statute. The House of Lords rejected this argument and held that, by not acting, he was effectively frustrating the intentions of the statute, read as a whole. This landmark decision has been regarded as extending the scope of judicial review into areas where statutory powers define, in very wide terms, the parameters of ministerial or administrative action.[39]

The criteria for the exercise of subjective powers have also been discussed in other cases. In *R v Secretary of State for Trade and Industry, ex p Lonrho plc*,[40] the challenge was based on whether the minister had acted unlawfully by, first, not publishing the inspector's report pursuant to powers under section 437 of the Companies Act 1985, which gave the minister the power to publish the report 'if he thinks fit'; and, secondly, by not referring a takeover of the Harrods shop to the Monopolies and Mergers Commission pursuant to his powers under section 64(4)(b) of the

36 See *Padfield v Minister of Agriculture* [1968] AC 997.
37 *Roberts v Hopwood* [1925] AC 578, discussed at 11.5.2.
38 [1968] AC 997.
39 See further ch 11.
40 [1989] 2 All ER 609.

Fair Trading Act 1973 (whereby the Secretary of State could make a reference 'if it appeared to him that there were new material facts about the merger'). In accepting that the minister had acted within the discretion allowed by these statutes, Lord Keith, in the House of Lords, rejected the approach of the Divisional Court, which his Lordship believed had led them into considering questions of merits rather than simple *vires*. He explained that the question is not whether the minister came to the correct solution or made the right decision, but simply whether the discretion is properly exercised. In other words, was the decision-making process conducted in accordance with the statutory procedure? The discretion under the legislation could not be converted into a duty to act.

In *R v Secretary of State for the Environment, ex p Hammersmith and Fulham London Borough Council*,[41] very similar sentiments were expressed in the judgment of the court. The challenge here had arisen because, under section 100 of the Local Government Finance Act 1988, the minister was empowered to decide if local budgets were excessive as part of the determination of the level of the community charge (local taxation). The Act stated that 'the Secretary of State may designate a charging authority if in his opinion . . . '. Although in his pace-setting judgment in *Padfield* Lord Reid had not been prepared to accept the subjective wording contained in the statute at face value, this decision by the House of Lords provides further confirmation that, where policy implications are present, the courts can be reluctant to intervene. This is notably so where the court is, in effect, being asked to force a *particular* exercise of a minister's subjective powers under a statute. The appeal by the councils was unsuccessful; moreover, Lord Bridge held that once it is established that ministerial action does not contravene the requirements of a statute dealing with national economic policy it will not be open to challenge for irrationality short of extremes of bad faith, improper motive, or manifest absurdity (so-called 'super *Wednesbury*' grounds).[42]

10.4 Error of law on the face of the record

10.4.1 Historical background

We turn now to consider the (historical) significance of the term 'error on the face of the record'. In short, this was an ancient device for quashing the decision of a body by *certiorari* even though it was acting within its jurisdiction. A mistake of law (not of fact) was revealed by perusal of the record of the proceedings. Such errors—which might, perhaps counter-intuitively, be regarded as *intra vires* errors—normally related to the blatant misconstruction of a statute and, in limited circumstances, the courts could intervene to correct the erroneous decision. Error on the face re-emerged in the early 1950s, following a period in which it had rarely been used, after it had been held that reasons for decisions could form part of the record of the tribunal.[43]

---

41 [1990] 3 All ER 589.

42 See also *Secretary of State for Education and Science v Tameside Metropolitan Borough Council* [1977] AC 1015; and ch 13.

43 See *R v Northumberland Compensation Appeal Tribunal, ex p Shaw* [1952] 1 All ER 122.

The *Anisminic* case—discussed earlier—raised important questions about how far the courts could review errors of law that were 'within' the jurisdiction of the decision-maker. The decision in *Anisminic* itself had been one that went to the question of whether the decision-maker had jurisdiction to make the impugned decision, although the various judgments delivered in the House of Lords pointed to the possibility of judicial review lying for any error of law (whether 'going to jurisiction' or 'within' jurisdiction). Was judicial review now available in respect of all errors of law, or were the courts limited to reviewing errors within jursidiction on the basis of error on the face of the record? Uncertainty as to the answer to this question was reflected in a significant division of judicial opinion in *Anisminic* on the scope for the courts to intervene to correct errors within certain jurisdictions. However, in an important decision, *R v Lord President of the Privy Council, ex p Page*,[44] the House of Lords once more turned its attention to this issue and appeared finally to resolve it. The facts concerned a university lecturer who was made redundant after having worked for the university since 1966. It was held that the decision of the university visitor (an individual appointed to hear disputes within the university in respect of its own internal rules) was not amenable to judicial review in respect of any ruling in fact or law that he might make in exercising that jurisdiction in a judicial capacity.[45] Nevertheless, Lord Browne-Wilkinson affirmed that the decision in *Anisminic* meant that it was no longer possible to distinguish errors of law on the face of the record and other errors of law because:

Parliament had only conferred a decision-making power on the basis that it was to be exercised on the correct legal basis: a misdirection in law in making the decision therefore rendered the decision *ultra vires*. Therefore . . . in general any error of law made by an administrative tribunal or inferior court in reaching its decision can be quashed for error of law.[46]

Another issue is that, following the decision in *Anisminic*, the position was clarified for administrative bodies; but some doubt persisted concerning the capacity to intervene to correct the decisions of inferior courts. Certain problems had been identified by Lane LJ in his dissenting judgment in *Pearlman v Harrow School*.[47] In particular, as we have seen, he pointed out the difficulties involved with the distinctions Lord Denning drew in his judgment in *Pearlman* between matters within and outside the court's jurisdiction. Difficult questions also arose about whether errors of law should be approached in the same way depending on whether the error had been made by the High Court or by a lower tribunal.[48]

However, in *Re Racal Communications*,[49] the House of Lords brought some clarity and certainty to the law. Lord Diplock, in particular, held that a distinction could be made between situations where Parliament intended a matter to be determined by an inferior tribunal and to decisions of the High Court, which in no circumstances would be amenable to judicial review. In *ex p Page* Lord Browne-Wilkinson referred specifically to Lord Diplock's reasoning when noting that:

---

44 [1993] AC 682.

45 See *Re Racal* at 10.2.2.1.

46 [1993] AC 682, 701.

47 [1979] QB 56 and see 10.2.2.1.

48 For discussion see, e.g., *South East Asia Fire Bricks Sdn Bhd v Non-Metallic Mineral Products Manufacturing Union* [1981] AC 363.

49 [1981] AC 374.

In my judgment, therefore, if there were a statutory provision that the decision of a visitor on the law applicable to internal disputes of a charity was to be 'final and conclusive', courts would have no jurisdiction to review the visitors' decision on the grounds of error of law made by the visitor within his jurisdiction (in the narrow sense). For myself, I can see no relevant distinction between a case where a statute has conferred such final and conclusive jurisdiction and the case where the common law has for 300 years recognised that the visitor's decisions on questions of fact and law are final and conclusive and are not to be reviewed by the courts. Accordingly, unless this House is prepared to sweep away long-established law, there is no jurisdiction in the court to review a visitor's decision for error of law committed within the jurisdiction.[50]

On this basis, it was held in *Page* that decisions by a visitor within jurisdiction merely apply the internal law of the body concerned and cannot therefore be unlawful in the wider sense (i.e., in terms of the laws of the land) and are thus immune from review. While it is to be noted that decisions of visitors are subject to challenge under the Human Rights Act 1998,[51] *Page* still offers them a significant degree of freedom in terms of their decision-making. That said, it is to be noted that the powers of visitors, at least as these relate to students, have since been limited through the use of the Office of the Independent Arbitrator as the means to resolve disputes under the Higher Education Act 2004.

In sum, once it was accepted that the interpretation of *Anisminic* that had been followed by Lord Denning and Lord Diplock, which holds that every error of law by a tribunal and inferior court is a possible excess of jurisdiction, then the technical distinction between some errors of law which were taken to go to the jurisdiction, and other errors of law which were not, is removed. It is now apparent that the categorical assertion by Lord Browne-Wilkinson in *ex p Page* has settled the issue and has rendered any distinction between jurisdictional errors and errors of law on the face of the record obsolete. We can therefore conclude that error on the face of the record is merely of continuing historical interest, and that any error of law is reviewable (subject to the exception of decisions about the 'internal' law of a body or organisation).

10.5 Implied limits on judicial review: public interest immunity

10.5.1 What is public interest immunity?

In order to appreciate fully the significance of public interest immunity (PII), a doctrine of the law of evidence (formerly known as Crown privilege), it is first necessary to recognise the function of discovery of documents as part of the trial process. In civil litigation this procedure enables the parties to the action to examine information and documents from the other side. Normally, the court will order the disclosure of documents that are not voluntarily produced and this exchange of documents serves to speed up the trial process by allowing a person to know the nature of the case that is to be presented against him or her. This also permits a case

---

50 [1993] AC 682, 703.
51 See, e.g., *Re CS' Application* [2015] NIQB 36.

to be prepared thoroughly in advance, and tends to reduce the possibility of either side being surprised or ambushed by the production of unexpected evidence. In criminal cases, there is an even stronger right to be notified in advance of the prosecution's case because of the desire to acquit the innocent.

In private civil actions, the counterpart to discovery in public law arises when evidence is protected by qualified privilege, preventing certain sources from being revealed. Accordingly, if a party refuses to disclose documents, a dispute can take place on recognised grounds and the judge may order the production of the documents. However, it had long been recognised that the Crown occupied a special position and, latterly, that this now extends to certain other public bodies. Such bodies are able to invoke PII if it is considered contrary to the public interest for the document(s) to be released on specified grounds, for example, doing harm to national security or revealing the name of a police informer. It is these grounds and others that will be the main concern of this chapter.

It should be noted that one feature of the Crown Proceedings Act 1947 is that section 28 provides that the courts can make an order for the discovery of documents against the Crown. But section 28 is subject to the major qualification that it does not affect the rule that evidence can still be withheld if the wider public interest so demands. As we shall soon see, the courts are, in effect, called upon to strike a balance between defining this public interest on the one hand and, on the other hand, ensuring that the power to withhold information is not abused by public authorities to shield them against legitimate claims from aggrieved members of the public.

The constitutional context against which this area of law applies has been transformed over the past 20 years or so. First, the Human Rights Act 1998 requires UK domestic courts to uphold rights under the ECHR including the right to a fair trial under Article 6(1). Secondly, the Freedom of Information Act 2000 (FOI), which came fully into force on 1 January 2005, introduces a 'general right to know'. Despite its limitations, the Act has a far-reaching impact on the way official bodies handle information. Public authorities, including the courts, the Crown Prosecution Service, and the police, are required to supply the citizen with information they hold on demand (not the actual documents but information contained in documents). Although Part II of the FOI sets out numerous exempted categories and imposes many qualifications to this right, this regime makes a substantial difference to the types of official information placed in the public domain. Also, publication schemes have become a routine requirement for public authorities. An Information Commissioner and staff oversee the operation of the Act and ensure compliance with its principal requirements. The FOI allows the citizen to request information without any need to state the reasons for wishing to have the material released, which is fundamentally at variance with the targeted approach required under rules of disclosure at trial. The availability of information on a broader basis from public authorities, coupled with this new right to request information, can facilitate litigation against public bodies by allowing parties to obtain documents more widely, in particular from public bodies not directly involved in private litigation, and also when making a claim of judicial review against a public authority.[52]

---

52 On the Freedom of Information Act see further 5.10.

10.5.2 **Why is public interest immunity important?**

For our purposes PII must be considered in the context of the general accountability (or lack of it) of government and public bodies. In the absence of a written constitution (albeit that we have the Human Rights Act 1998 and a Freedom of Information Act 2000) we shall see that defining the extent of immunity touches on some fundamental questions. For example, how far should official bodies be allowed to cloak their activities in a veil of secrecy by preventing the release of information when matters are being disputed in open court? Should high-level government and cabinet documents be regarded differently to the mundane communications of official bodies? Perhaps more specifically, should mundane communications by official bodies, including government departments, be afforded any immunity at all? Should the rules for disclosure be different for civil and criminal matters?

It will become apparent that it is frequently the judges who are called upon to decide which matters can remain outside the consideration of the courts, despite the suggestion by some that judges are not well suited or even sufficiently independent of the state to perform this function. Whatever the merits of these arguments, it is important to stress, before we proceed, that there are potentially far-reaching implications if certain types of document are kept out of the public domain. This is, in part, because the government or public officials may be assuming (sometimes inadvertently, but at other times knowingly) considerable licence to make up their own rules in secret; and in part, because decisions about immunity, once reached, can mean that an aggrieved citizen or a defendant in a criminal trial is then confronted with what appears to be an impenetrable barrier of secrecy. Most disturbing of all is the realisation that, as a result of such secrecy, a person may be denied a remedy, and consequently may be denied justice. Indeed, towards the end of this discussion, it will become clear why there was such general concern following the collapse of the Matrix Churchill trial in November 1992. The result of the signing of immunity certificates by ministers, withholding information from the court that the defendants had been acting in collusion with the security services, might have resulted in their imprisonment. Public concern about this matter led to the Scott Inquiry being set up, and the subsequent report will be discussed in more detail later.[53]

10.5.3 **The development of the modern law**

10.5.3.1 *Duncan v Cammell Laird*

The judicial benchmark on this subject was set by the House of Lords in *Duncan v Cammell Laird and Co Ltd*.[54] The House reached a decision which indicated that the courts were prepared to allow the Crown general immunity from disclosing documents, whenever the protection of the public interest was raised by them. The case came in the aftermath of the sinking of the submarine *Thetis* in Liverpool bay, while on sea trials, with the loss of all hands in 1939. The widow of one of the victims wanted to sue Cammell Laird, the shipyard that had built the submarine, for negligence, and alleged that the design itself had been defective. To prove this,

---

53 See 10.5.5.1.
54 [1942] AC 624.

the plans of the submarine would have to be produced in open court. It should be remembered that the litigation arising from the tragedy took place during the course of the Second World War, and the First Lord of the Admiralty swore an affidavit claiming that it was in the public interest not to disclose the plans. Bearing this in mind, the House of Lords refused to allow discovery and accepted that the documents were protected by Crown privilege (as it was then known).

The outcome of the case in wartime conditions was perhaps inevitable. It was accepted that these plans might well have given valuable information to the skilled eye of the agent of a foreign power, and that the plans should therefore clearly be protected. However, the House of Lords considered that, more generally, there were two alternative grounds for claiming Crown privilege:

(a) That the content of particular documents would harm the public interest. This became known as a *contents* claim (in *Duncan v Cammell Laird* the plans of the submarine fell into this category).

(b) That the document belonged to a class that was injurious to 'the proper functioning of the public service'. This became known as a *class* claim. More significantly, class claims recognised a much broader category into which a large proportion of the routine communications of public bodies could, in principle, fit (see later).

Although their Lordships considered that it was for the judge in any case to make the decision about whether particular documents should be made available, they also held that a properly executed affidavit from the minister claiming non-disclosure for any category of public documents was to be regarded as final and conclusive. This was a remarkable and controversial approach, although it should be remembered that *Duncan v Cammell Laird* was a civil action and Viscount Simon LC indicated that the position might be different in a criminal trial.[55]

10.5.3.2 **The aftermath of** *Duncan v Cammell Laird*

The case was interpreted for 25 years as meaning that any ministerial certificate was to be taken at face value, unquestioned by the courts, with the result that the public interest was firmly identified as being in the suppression of government information. This approach is illustrated very well by the decision in *Ellis v Home Office*.[56] In this case, a prisoner sought to take action against the Home Office, maintaining that injuries to him were caused because another mentally disturbed prisoner, who was known to be dangerous and violent, had been inadequately supervised. However, his claim for negligence failed because the documents that might have demonstrated lack of care on the part of the Home Office were accepted by the court as being protected by PII. This was on the ground that it would be detrimental to the proper functioning of the prison service to have released them. The rule in *Duncan v Cammell Laird and Co Ltd*[57] was strictly applied. Wade and Forsyth comment: 'It is not surprising that the Crown having been given a blank cheque, yielded to the temptation to overdraw.'[58] The decision was heavily criticised on

---

55 See 10.5.5.
56 [1953] 2 QB 135.
57 [1942] AC 624.
58 W Wade and C Forsyth, *Administrative Law*, 11th edn (Oxford: Oxford University Press, 2014), 713.

the ground that far too little attention was paid to achieving justice for the victim in such situations. Meanwhile, the Scottish courts were already showing signs of moving away from this overly restrictive interpretation.[59] However, the most significant concession to the criticism levelled at such a wide exclusionary rule came from the Lord Chancellor, Viscount Kilmuir, in 1956. Acting on behalf of the government, he announced that a number of categories of information would no longer be protected by Crown privilege, including documents required by the defence in criminal cases.[60]

10.5.3.3 *Conway v Rimmer*

In one of the crucial judgments marking a shift to greater judicial activism, *Conway v Rimmer*,[61] the House of Lords departed from their earlier position in *Duncan v Cammell Laird*. The case arose after a probationary police constable had been acquitted of theft. Subsequently, he sought to take an action for malicious prosecution against the superintendent who had been responsible for bringing the charges against him in the first place. He sought discovery of four reports made during the probationary period, and of a report made by the superintendent to the Chief Constable on the subject of the investigation into the offence. The first four reports fell into a category of documents which comprised confidential reports by police officers to chief police officers relating to the competence, efficiency, and fitness for employment of individual police officers under their command. The other report fell within a class of documents comprising reports by police officers to their superiors concerning investigations into the commission of crime. Both parties were in favour of disclosure of these documents, but the Home Office objected because it maintained that the documents would be injurious to the public interest. To justify suppression, the argument advanced was the desirability of candour. It was suggested that the likelihood of documents being revealed at a later stage would influence the degree of candour with which reports were prepared, and that this, in turn, would influence the quality of serious investigations of this type to the detriment of the public interest. (It will soon be obvious to the reader that this argument has been employed repeatedly over the years to justify non-disclosure of information.)

Breaking with earlier precedents, their Lordships in *Conway v Rimmer* were unwilling to accept the unqualified use of the candour argument, and held that the court had the power to inspect the disputed documents. After so doing in private, they declared that the documents should be made available to the plaintiff. In reaching this conclusion, Lord Reid found that it was necessary to balance the interests of the government in secrecy against the demands of the public interest in disclosure. Although he acknowledged that greater weight must be placed behind a minister's claims for immunity, His Lordship departed from Lord Simon's judgment in *Duncan v Cammell Laird and Co Ltd* and made a clear distinction between routine reports and matters that were truly prejudicial to national security. A wide-ranging exception to Crown privilege that had already been established was concerned with documents that were relevant to the defence in criminal proceedings. This was

---

59 See *Glasgow Corporation v Central Land Board* 1956 SC 1.
60 See 10.5.5 on PII in criminal cases.
61 [1968] AC 910.

accepted following Viscount Kilmuir's statement in 1956. In the instant case, however, it was being argued that suppression was nevertheless justified in subsequent civil proceedings. But according to Lord Reid, the test to be applied was to ask whether it was really 'necessary for the proper functioning of the public service'. Ministers should be required to clarify their reasons for non-disclosure. If in doubt, the judge should also perform an important role by inspecting the documents in the absence of the parties to ascertain, first, whether the documents are required, and, secondly, to assess the impact of disclosure on the public interest. In order for judges to inspect the documents, however, it was necessary to establish a relevance threshold for those documents. And even if disclosure was ordered by the judge, the minister should have a right of appeal. Lord Reid believed that there were some important exceptions to the much more general rule allowing for judicial inspection and possible disclosure. For instance, some classes of documents should not be disclosed, including cabinet minutes. The upshot was that it was no longer to be thought of in terms of Crown immunity but whether the public interest overrode the ordinary rights of litigants.

10.5.3.4 'Crown privilege' becomes 'public interest immunity'

In *Rogers v Home Secretary*,[62] the House of Lords broadly followed the approach taken in *Conway v Rimmer*. Significantly, Lord Reid shifted the terminology away from Crown privilege, on the ground that it was misleading, to the use of the term 'public interest immunity'. The scope of this immunity was extended from governmental to non-governmental bodies in *D v National Society for the Prevention of Cruelty to Children*.[63] In particular, the principle that certain sources needed to be protected (to uphold the system of criminal justice) was widened by the House of Lords to include an authorised body (rather than an organ of the government) recognised under the Children and Young Persons Act 1969. On this occasion a person who had been wrongly accused of child abuse was not permitted access to documents in order to sue the NSPCC. It was held that the wider public interest would be served by the identity of informants remaining anonymous so that the Society could expect full cooperation when investigating future complaints of alleged child abuse.

We have so far observed that the decision in *Conway v Rimmer* qualified the principle of PII and expressed the claims of justice by no longer accepting the wholesale exclusion of a class of documents. This was because circumstances were recognised where a wider public interest might be served by disclosure than would be served by suppression. Nevertheless, further important questions remained to be answered. First, could high-level government documents, such as cabinet papers, be produced at a trial? Lord Reid had indicated earlier in *Conway v Rimmer* that they would be protected except in the most exceptional circumstances. Secondly, what was to be the mechanism for determining whether such documents are released? These questions were considered in *Burmah Oil v Bank of England*.[64] In order to pursue an action against the Bank of England, Burmah Oil submitted a list of some 62 documents it wished to obtain. The bank was instructed by the Crown

---

62 [1973] AC 388.
63 [1978] AC 171.
64 [1980] AC 1090.

not to produce these documents because, it was stated in the certificate issued by the minister, they would be injurious to the public interest. Two sets of documents were involved. Group A included communications between ministers, and between ministers and senior departmental officials, and related to the formulation of government policy at the highest level. Another set of documents, Group B, concerned advice given by businessmen to the Bank of England. By a majority, the House of Lords held that it was necessary to inspect the documents, if there was a reasonable probability that they would be helpful to the applicant's case. This inspection was to take place before a final decision was taken on whether the failure to disclose was in the public interest. In *Burmah Oil* inspection took place but there was no disclosure, because ultimately the objections to disclosure were stronger than any value as evidence the papers were said to have. It is also notable that Lord Keith expressed strong disapproval of the candour argument, stating that 'the notion that any competent and conscientious public servant would be inhibited at all in the candour of his writings by consideration of the off-chance that they might have to be produced in a litigation is in my opinion grotesque . . .'. ([1980] AC 1090, 1133; see also Lord Wilberforce's dissenting judgment on the argument for candour.)

Although *Burmah Oil* went further than *Conway v Rimmer* in discussing the procedures to follow when immunity is claimed, there is an obvious difficulty for an applicant who wishes to demonstrate that a document will in fact be beneficial to his or her case. It is a classic 'Catch 22' dilemma: if the material is not first examined because it is protected, how can a litigant be sure that it is necessary? Yet at the same time, the danger of relaxing the rules was to introduce the possibility of speculative fishing for documents. Their Lordships held that a relevance threshold must be reached; but should this be 'reasonable probability', as a majority in the case found? Or was even this too strong, as the minority noted, requiring a 'strong positive belief' before disclosure of the documents?

In *Air Canada v Secretary of State for Trade*,[65] there was further consideration of the difficulties presented when classes of documents, including ministerial minutes and cabinet documents, are subject to PII certificates. The British Airports Authority (BAA), the statutory body that owns and manages Heathrow Airport, wished to develop the airport, but the Secretary of State refused to allow any money to be raised by borrowing for this purpose, and he gave a direction under the Airports Act 1975 that the funding was to come from revenues that the BAA itself was to raise. Accordingly, substantial increases of 35 per cent in landing charges were imposed. However, a group of 18 airlines sought to challenge the new charges as being *ultra vires* the Airports Act 1975. It was argued that the dominant motive behind the exercise of the power was to reduce the public sector borrowing requirement. In pursuit of their action, the airlines successfully obtained discovery of one group of documents that had passed between the Secretary of State and the BAA. However, they also sought to obtain another group of documents relating to discussions between ministers at cabinet level. PII was claimed in respect of the ministerial documents.

It was held in the House of Lords that a case for inspection of these documents by the courts had not been established. Lord Fraser stated that even cabinet minutes were not completely immune from disclosure—for instance, in a case involving

65 [1983] 2 AC 394.

serious misconduct by a cabinet minister—but that documents of this type are generally entitled to a high degree of protection. It was not enough to establish that the documents were relevant to the matters at issue and necessary for disposing fairly with the case. Because PII had been claimed, there was an onus on the plaintiffs to show why the documents ought to be produced for inspection by the court in private. It needed to be established how they would help their own case, the test being:

> . . . in order to persuade the court even to inspect the documents for which public interest immunity is claimed, the party seeking disclosure ought at least to satisfy the court that the documents are very likely to contain material which would give substantial support to his contention on an issue which arises in the case, and that without them he 'might be deprived of the means of . . . proper presentation' of his case.[66]

It was further suggested that inspection should not take place unless the court was *likely* to order production. Equally, although Lord Wilberforce placed considerable emphasis on the court doing, and being seen to do, justice as between the parties in the instant case, he also stressed that *likely*, in relation to any benefit to the plaintiff's case, must mean more than a mere 'fishing' expedition. (Note also the divergence in the approaches of Lords Scarman and Templeman, who favoured private inspection of the documents by the court.)

10.5.4 **What is the public interest? The candour argument**

There have been a number of notable decisions which have required the courts to consider whether it is truly 'necessary for the proper functioning of the public service' for a class of documents containing confidential information to continue to be protected. In essence, it is a question of deciding whether the public interest is being served by preserving the anonymity of the source of information. As we have seen, the candour argument in support of non-disclosure is founded in part on the assumption that important information that official bodies, such as the police, rely on will not be forthcoming if those volunteering information face the prospect of having their identity unmasked. In *Alfred Crompton Amusement Machines Ltd v Customs and Excise Commissioners*,[67] a company believed that its assessment for purchase tax was too high. In reaching its assessment, the Customs and Excise Commissioners had obtained information from the company's customers and other sources regarding the value of its machines. The company required this information to contest its assessment for tax before the arbitrator. After weighing the considerations, it was held in the House of Lords that disclosure would be harmful to the efficient working of the Act of Parliament. Unless they remained anonymous, such sources would be less willing to come forward and cooperate with the Commissioners of Customs and Excise, leading to a less effective discharge of the Commissioners' duties. This ruling was, however, delivered before *Burmah Oil* and *Air Canada* and it should be read alongside these later decisions.

Williams v Home Office (No 2)[68] allows us to compare another important decision in which, after the judge had examined the relevant documents, the candour

---

66 [1983] 2 AC 394, 435.
67 *(No 2)* [1974] AC 405.
68 [1981] 1 All ER 1151.

argument was overridden and the public interest was considered to be best served by disclosure. It concerned a long-term prisoner who wanted to bring an action against the Home Office, after he had spent time in an experimental control unit at Wakefield prison. A large stack of documents was produced, but the Home Office objected, in particular, to the production of 23 documents which involved communications to and from ministers, and between ministers and officials. These documents were in a class that involved the formulation of policy, and it was claimed that immunity here was required for the proper functioning of the public service. Nevertheless, it was held that it appeared that the rights of the applicant may have been interfered with and that there was a reasonable probability that these documents contained relevant material, which was essential to prove that such a policy existed. McNeill J examined the documents and then ordered six of them to be disclosed at the trial. In this case, it is clear that the needs of the prisoner outweighed the possibility that the Home Office might be subjected to ill-judged and unfair comment.

10.5.5 Public interest immunity in criminal cases

In *Duncan v Cammell Laird and Co Ltd* Viscount Simon LC stated that:

the judgment of the House in the present case is limited to civil actions and the practice as applied in criminal trials where an individual's life or liberty may be at stake, is not necessarily the same.[69]

The rules discussed so far have developed in and been limited to civil proceedings, which is the context within which the vast majority of administrative law matters will arise. However, it would paint an incomplete picture of PII were we not to make mention of the approach in criminal law, as important questions about human rights can arise in criminal proceedings. In such proceedings, the central question about PII can be put very simply: can a situation ever be envisaged where the public interest in non-disclosure of documents outweighs the public interest in ensuring that, in a criminal trial, justice is both done and seen to be done? It is not all that unusual for criminal cases to involve documents to which a PII claim might attach. For example, evidence might arise which the state, in the form of the police or security services, might wish to suppress, in particular where an informer has been used and the individual's identity might be revealed. As Lord Taylor CJ put it in *R v Keane*: 'If the disputed material may prove the defendant's innocence or avoid a miscarriage of justice, then the balance comes down resoundingly in favour of disclosing it.'[70] In circumstances where the public interest requires that disclosure should be withheld, the result may be that the prosecution cannot proceed. This is because of the prospect of a miscarriage of justice if the evidence is not disclosed. In such cases, the judge will normally have a role in examining the documents to ascertain their sensitivity and relevance. If they are examined and found crucial to establishing the innocence of the defendant, the prosecution will be faced with a choice—they can either decide to release the document, or they can drop the prosecution.[71] However, an additional dimension will be present

---

69 [1942] AC 624, 633.
70 (1994) 99 Cr App R 1, 6.
71 See *R v H, R v C* [2004] UKHL 3, [2004] 1 All ER 1269, where the House of Lords addressed this issue.

when the immunity is claimed on the grounds of national security. The telling example of *Matrix Churchill*, a criminal prosecution that we consider below, vividly illustrated many of the dangers that can arise from claims of PII in a criminal trial.

In *R v H, R v C*[72] the House of Lords clarified the position where the prosecution claims PII in a criminal trial, while also taking account of the requirements of Article 6 of the ECHR and the Strasbourg jurisprudence. In the instant case the defendants had been charged with conspiracy to supply heroin. In order to establish a defence based on the planting of evidence and the falsification of observations by the police, the defendants made far-reaching requests for disclosure, including of material relating to covert human intelligence sources relating to the investigation. Without first fully considering the evidence, the trial judge sought to appoint special counsel to consider this evidence. The House of Lords rejected the general contention that, 'it was [now] incompatible with Article 6 for a judge to rule on a claim to PII in the absence of adversarial argument on behalf of the accused where the material which the prosecution is seeking to withhold is, or may be, relevant to a disputed issue of fact . . . .'[73] Rather their Lordships recognised that there were circumstances where some derogation from the golden rule of full disclosure may be justified and, adopting the language of proportionality, they stated that any 'such derogation must always be the minimum derogation necessary to protect the public interest in question and must never imperil the overall fairness of the trial' ([2004] 2 AC 134, 148—it was also acknowledged that very occasionally the evidence in question might be so sensitive that even its existence could not be disclosed). A series of related questions were set out at paragraph 36 of the ruling to assist the court in determining the risk of serious prejudice likely to be caused to the defence where PII was claimed by the prosecution. In cases of exceptional difficulty, where there would be a risk of serious prejudice to the defence and where the court also identified a public interest to be protected, their Lordships recognised the need to appoint a special counsel to represent the interests of the defence without disclosing the disputed evidence.

10.5.5.1 *Matrix Churchill*, the Scott Report, and public interest immunity

PII was central to the *Matrix Churchill* trial that we mentioned above, the collapse of which prompted the government to set up a wide-ranging public inquiry chaired by Sir Richard Scott into the use of PII and the conduct of ministers and civil servants in relation to Parliament.[74] The original case concerned the trial of the directors of a machine tool company which had been responsible for exporting to Iraq tools and components that had possible military uses. Trading in such materials was in flagrant breach of the export guidelines published by the government. After certain parts (for a 'super gun') had been seized by customs officers, three directors of Matrix Churchill were prosecuted by HM Customs and Excise for being involved with these illegal exports. Even greater prominence was given to the matter as it surfaced almost coincidentally with the outbreak of the Gulf War in 1990. However, the defence case was founded on the contention that the government

---

72 [2004] UKHL 3, [2004] 2 AC 134.

73 [2004] 2 AC 134, 154, considering submissions centred on *Edwards and Lewis v United Kingdom*, 22 July 2003, unreported, Application Nos 39647/98 and 40461/98.

74 *Report of the Inquiry into the Export of Defence Equipment and Dual-Use Goods to Iraq and Related Prosecutions*, HC (1995–96) 115.

and the intelligence services had known about the sales to Iraq from the outset. The trial threatened to, and in the event did, unmask a tangled web of conflicting engagements between government departments. The Foreign Office was assuming an appearance of impartiality. The Department of Trade was promoting British business, manufacturing, and exports vigorously. The Ministry of Defence was considering the strategic and intelligence situation. The political sensitivity of the trial was pronounced because the defence case would reveal that certain ministers at the Department of Trade had been flouting the government's own policy guidelines. Behind the scenes, companies supplying defence equipment had not only been encouraged to trade with Iraq, but the business executives involved were at the same time being useful by feeding vital information to the intelligence services. The extent of this collusion would be revealed if the relevant documents entered the public domain. Category A documents constituted a couple of pieces of paper from a confidential informant. Category B were ministerial and departmental documents, and were covered by a certificate, signed by a junior minister on behalf of the Foreign Secretary. This certificate claimed they were concerned with high-level policy formulation and included the advice given to ministers. It was strongly maintained that it would be against the public interest to release this information, as being prejudicial to the giving of honest and candid advice. Category C documents were to do with security and secret intelligence matters, signed by three ministers, because it was asserted that these documents would identify members of the intelligence services and their deployment.

There was surprisingly little direct authority on PII in criminal cases to guide the *Matrix Churchill* trial, which pre-dated *R v H* by some years. Smedley J, who presided over the trial, turned to *R v Governor of Brixton Prison, ex p Osman (No 1)*,[75] and was of the opinion that class immunity had been rightly claimed by ministers. After the certification of documents, the judge believed the protection for the accused lay with the appropriate judicial scrutiny. Mann LJ had stated in *ex p Osman* that it is the judge who must weigh the competing interests in the administration of justice and determine if the documents can be used. He had further stated that: 'Where the interests of justice arise in a criminal case touching and concerning liberty . . . the weight to be attached to the interests of justice is plainly very great indeed'.[76] It inevitably follows from this *dictum* that in a criminal case a class claim is only rarely likely to survive the judicial balancing of interests.[77] Judge Smedley's robust approach to disclosure, at least on one view of the proceedings, resulted in the collapse of the *Matrix Churchill* trial.

Subsequently, it became a matter of great controversy whether a class of documents must be automatically certified because of a duty resting on ministers. Certain Conservative ex-ministers maintained in public that their reason for signing PII certificates was, despite clear misgivings, entirely the result of following (what turned out to be erroneous) advice of the Attorney General to the effect that ministers were under a duty to sign PII certificates falling within a protected class without questioning their contents. They were told by the Attorney General they had no choice in the matter.

---

75 [1991] 1 WLR 281.

76 [1991] 1 WLR 281, 288.

77 Simon-Brown LJ emphasised the same point regarding class claims in *R v Horseferry Road Magistrates' Court, ex p Bennett (No 2)* [1994] 1 All ER 289.

If this position is accepted, it is still essential to ask how it is decided by a minister when this duty arises. The fact that there is no mechanism dealing with this question, suggests that there is a wide discretion in defining the grounds on which immunity can actually be claimed. Bearing this in mind, it is not at all surprising that charges of abuse of process gained momentum. For example, how could ministers possibly reconcile their willingness to suppress information with regard to the *Matrix Churchill* trial on the basis that they were slavishly following the Attorney General's advice, when in July 1993 the same government authorised the disclosure of letters written by the Attorney General (whose advice is always regarded as confidential) with regard to the questionable conduct of Michael Mates MP in his dealings with businessman Asil Nadir? Presumably, disclosure was deemed to be expedient, so that the apparently strict rule that a class claim should always be asserted was conveniently overlooked. (The fact that ministers exercise discretion on whether to sign certificates was acknowledged by Kenneth Clarke MP in his evidence to the Scott Inquiry.) Furthermore, we should remember Lord Kilmuir's statement, in 1956, that the government would not invoke PII in criminal trials. Had this escaped the notice of the Attorney General when he proffered his advice? In his findings, Sir Richard Scott attached great importance to providing a fair trial. The court had a role in protecting the fundamental rights of the accused which would include insistence on disclosure of prosecution evidence that might be favourable to the defence. This was regarded as a basic safeguard necessary to uphold the rule of law, but the Scott Report itself failed to recommend any legislative steps that might lead to root and branch reform to codify this principle.

In fact, in relation to PII claims in criminal cases, it is doubtful whether 'the efficient functioning of the public service' (the test set out in *Conway v Rimmer*: see 10.5.3.3) can ever provide a satisfactory justification for refusing to release documents necessary for the defence. If we accept that the considerations of justice are likely to be viewed by the trial judge as overwhelming in criminal cases, it seems pointless for such claims to be asserted by ministers in the first place.

After the collapse of the *Matrix Churchill* trial, the Court of Appeal in *R v Ward*[78] confirmed that the prosecution in a criminal case has a duty generally to disclose all the evidence which it has gathered. This involves giving notice to the defence of the categories of material that are held and allowing the defence to make representations to the court. It was for the court to make the ultimate decision about disclosure to avoid the prosecution being the judge in its own cause. However, Lord Taylor CJ chose to qualify these guidelines and referred to situations where even disclosing the existence of a category of material might be going too far.[79]

In line with the recommendations of the Scott Report, the distinction between class and contents claims was abolished in respect of central government in England and Wales in December 1996.[80] In consequence, blanket immunity through class claims no longer applies and ministers can claim PII only when they consider that the content of a specific document (or documents) will cause 'real damage or harm' to the public interest. Although no definition of 'real damage to the public interest' is provided, this includes preventing harm to individuals (informants), or

---

78 [1993] 1 WLR 619.
79 See *R v Davis* [1993] 1 WLR 613 and *R v Keane* (1994) 99 Cr App Rep 1.
80 See Hansard HL Deb, vol 576, col 1507 and HC Deb, vol 287, col 949, 18 December 1996.

damaging the regulatory process, international relations, or economic interests. We would note that there is a clear overlap here with the sort of considerations that the European Court of Human Rights (ECtHR) regards as permissible justifications for limiting rights, including the right to a fair trial under Article 6 of the ECHR.

10.5.6 Public interest immunity: the current law

Returning to civil proceedings, the principles of PII were revised once more by the House of Lords in *R v Chief Constable of West Midlands Police, ex p Wiley,*[81] another case involving the police. The difficulty for the courts policing cases lies in the fact that the police clearly occupy a special position. They must conduct investigations into serious crime and, in general, a strong case can be made for their operations and tactics being kept strictly confidential. But prior to *ex p Wiley* there were occasions when the courts were arguably too ready to grant immunity. For example, *Gill and Goodwin v Chief Constable of Lancashire*[82] was a civil action for negligence by police officers against their local force. They had sustained injuries during a riot training course by being burnt when a pool of petrol was ignited by an instructor. In order to prove their case, they sought disclosure of the Public Order Manual used by the police, but the Chief Constable objected to this being revealed on the ground of PII. The trial judge had ordered disclosure, but this decision was overruled by the Court of Appeal because the manual belonged to a class of documents which (at that time) could be protected by PII. The confidentiality of police strategies in dealing with demonstrations and public order was considered to be of the highest importance, even though it appeared that much of the information in the manual was already widely available. In contrast, *Peach v Commissioner of Police of the Metropolis*[83] was a civil case in which it was alleged that police action had been responsible for unlawfully killing a demonstrator. On this occasion the Court of Appeal decided that documents relating to the incident ought to be released. This was on the grounds that the public interest in determining the cause of death at a public inquiry outweighed the need for the maintenance of confidentiality. In *Neilson v Laugharne,*[84] it was held by the Court of Appeal that statements made as part of an investigation which had taken place under section 49 of the Police Act 1964 could not be used in subsequent civil proceedings; and in *Makanjuola v Commissioner of Police of the Metropolis,*[85] the Court of Appeal, in allowing an appeal by the Police Commissioner, adopted the same reasoning as in *Neilson v Laugharne* (accepting the candour argument). Bingham LJ, in a judgment later referred to critically in the Scott Report, stated that the Commissioner was under a duty to claim immunity because PII is not a privilege that can be waived by the Crown or by any party:

Public interest immunity is not a trump card vouchsafed to certain privileged players to play when and as they wish. It is an exclusionary rule, imposed on parties in certain circumstances, even when it is to their disadvantage in the litigation.[86]

---

81 [1995] 1 AC 274.
82 *The Times,* 3 November 1992.
83 [1986] QB 1064.
84 [1981] QB 736.
85 [1992] 3 All ER 617.
86 [1992] 3 All ER 617, 623.

In *ex p Wiley*,[87] the House of Lords overruled *Neilson v Laugharne, Makanjuola v Commissioner of Police of the Metropolis,* and the other cases based upon these previous authorities. Their Lordships held that documents coming into existence during police complaints proceedings do not fit into a class covered by PII (the case again pre-dated the departure from class-based claims post-*Matrix Churchill*). Indeed, a surprising feature of the appeal was that the Chief Constables themselves contended that PII did not attach to this class of documents. In his judgment, Lord Woolf dismissed any contention that the balance of public interest had altered and maintained that a class claim should be rejected because such a claim could only be justified in exceptional circumstances, thereby indicating that the reasoning of previous cases was flawed (although a contents claim could still be made with regard to police disciplinary investigations). Another point discussed by Lord Woolf was the assumption of 'a level playing field' in cases where a claim for PII has been made. In other words, if documents are unavailable to one side, they would be equally unavailable to the other side.

A further case of note is *Al-Rawi v The Security Service*,[88] which involved allegations that the Security Services may have been complicit in the ill treatment of prisoners at Guantanamo Bay. When the matter came before the Supreme Court, the central issue was whether the common law could fashion a closed material procedure given that there would otherwise be an extensive and very time-consuming PII exercise.[89] On this point, the Supreme Court held that the common law would not facilitate such a procedure because of the principle of open justice and that any such procedures were a matter for Parliament (which has since legislated to this effect).[90] However, the case was also interesting insofar as Lord Clarke summarised the current law on PII, established in *ex p Wiley*, as follows:

(i) A claim for PII must ordinarily be supported by a certificate signed by the appropriate minister relating to the individual documents in question.

(ii) Disclosure of documents which ought otherwise to be disclosed under CPR Part 31 may only be refused if the court concludes that the public interest which demands that the evidence be withheld outweighs the public interest in the administration of justice.

(iii) In making that decision, the court may inspect the documents. This must necessarily be done in an ex parte process from which the party seeking disclosure may properly be excluded. Otherwise the very purpose of the application for PII would be defeated.

(iv) In making its decision, the court should consider what safeguards may be imposed to permit the disclosure of the material. These might include, for example, holding all or part of the hearing in camera; requiring express undertakings of confidentiality from those to whom documents are disclosed; restricting the number of copies of a document that could be taken, or the circumstances in which documents could be inspected (eg requiring the claimant and his legal team to attend at a particular location to read sensitive material); or requiring the unique numbering of any copy of a sensitive document.

(v) Even where a complete document cannot be disclosed it may be possible to produce relevant extracts, or to summarise the relevant effect of the material.

---

87 [1995] 1 AC 274.
88 [2011] UKSC 34; [2012] 1 AC 531.
89 On closed material procedures see 17.3.2.
90 Justice and Security Act 2013.

(vi) If the public interest in withholding the evidence does not outweigh the public interest in the administration of justice, the document must be disclosed unless the party
who has possession of the document concedes the issue to which it relates.[91]

10.5.7 Conclusion on public interest immunity

The clash between the executive and the judiciary which can arise in claims of PII
by central government has certain parallels with the Watergate Affair in the 1970s.
After the revelations following on from the break-in at Democratic Party headquarters, attention shifted to the President's claim to protect his own position from
accusations of wrongdoing by preventing the disclosure of executive documents
and tape recordings. *Nixon v United States*[92] can still be regarded as an historic decision which may be referred to in support of the view that there is, in the words of
Burger CJ, no 'unqualified Presidential privilege of immunity from judicial process
under all circumstances'. We should both take heed of these words and demand
candour from our politicians and civil servants. The introduction of the Freedom
of Information Act 2000 has gone some way to fulfilling these demands. Indeed,
while the Act contains a manifest limitation by providing for executive override of
rulings that information should be disclosed, the important case of *Evans* makes
clear that that power cannot easily be exercised over a judicial determination of
the Upper Tribunal.[93] In this complex area, our courts are therefore determined to
safeguard the separation of powers as a doctrine that complements the idea of the
rule of law that underlies administrative law.

In determining questions of PII, it has been apparent that judges occupy a difficult position, as they are required to decide between the executive organs of the
administrative state and the citizen. There have been many situations in the past
where the government and other public bodies have exerted pressure on the courts
to identify the public interest in maintaining confidentiality in their activities. In
what circumstances is this really justified? Clearly, there are times when national
security and other such considerations arise, and when the sensitivity of information means that the public interest does ultimately lie in withholding information
from a person seeking a remedy in the courts. In those circumstances, can there
really be any objection to immunity being granted after the interests have been
balanced, the one with the other, by a judge?

FURTHER READING

Birkinshaw, P (2010) *Freedom of Information: The Law, the Practice and the Ideal*, 4th edn
(Cambridge: Cambridge University Press).

Hare, I (1998) 'Separation of Powers and Judicial Review for Error of Law' in Forsyth, C and
Hare, I (eds), *The Golden Metwand and the Crooked Cord* (Oxford: Oxford University Press).

Tomkins, A (1998) *The Constitution after Scott: Government Unwrapped* (Oxford: Clarendon
Press), chapter 5.

Wade, HWR (1969) 'Constitutional and Administrative Aspects of the *Anisminic* Case' 85
Law Quarterly Review 198.

---

91 [2012] 1 AC 531, 607, para 145.
92 418 US 683 (1974).
93 *Evans v Attorney General* [2015] UKSC 21, [2015] AC 1787; and 5.10.

11

....

Illegality I

11.1 **Introduction**

This is the first of two chapters dealing with illegality as a ground for judicial review. Returning to Lord Diplock's original three-way classification in the *GCHQ* case, this ground is defined as meaning 'that the decision-maker must understand correctly the law that regulates his decision-making power and must give effect to it'.[1] At its most obvious, illegality thus allows decisions and other measures to be challenged where the decision or other measure has no legal basis, for instance where the decision-maker did not have the power that it purported to have. However, beyond such straightforward cases—we describe them below as 'simple *ultra vires*' cases—the ground also allows challenges to be made to the way in which discretion is exercised or, depending on circumstance, to a public authority's failure to do something. Consistent with more general developments in judicial review, the ground furthermore permits of challenges to decisions etc for the reason that they are contrary to EU law and/or the European Convention on Human Rights (ECHR).[2]

Our analysis begins with a brief word on statutory interpretation, which is often of importance in relation to the grounds for review. Thereafter, the chapter focuses upon claims for judicial review that are based upon arguments of 'simple *ultra vires*', 'improper purpose', 'relevant and irrelevant considerations', and/or 'bad faith'. In analytical terms, we have grouped these sub-headings together in the present chapter for the reason that they typically involve the exercise—or at least the purported exercise—of discretion in any given case. On the other hand, there may be cases where it is argued that an authority has 'fettered its discretion' in the sense that it has previously done something that has the effect of preventing the public authority from exercising its discretion in the light of an individual's circumstances. In constitutional terms, this is unlawful as the body which has been entrusted with discretion by Parliament must retain for itself the option of exercising that discretion on a case-by-case basis. We consider this aspect of illegality—and a number of others—in chapter 12.

One final point to be made at this stage is that case law under the heading of illegality almost always concerns decisions etc that are taken within the framework of statute (the point is also true of case law on the other grounds for review). This reminds us again that the vast majority of the public law powers and duties

---

1 *Council of Civil Service Unions v Minister for the Civil Service* [1985] AC 374, 410–11.
2 See chs 3 and 4.

of decision-makers in the modern administrative state remain sourced in statute, whether enacted at Westminster or at the level of the devolved authorities.[3] At the same time, it should be noted that judicial review is now also available in respect of a range of decisions that might be taken on the basis of the Royal prerogative, as well as the decisions of some non-statutory and private bodies.[4]

11.2 The importance of statutory interpretation

Because the vast majority of claims for judicial review centre upon the legality of decisions and other measures that are taken within the framework of statute, the interpretation that is given to the relevant statute can be all important. Traditionally, it has been said that courts choose between a 'literal' interpretation of an Act (whereby they do not look beyond the dictionary meaning of the words in question) and a 'purposive' interpretation (whereby the courts look to the broader objectives that underlie the legislation). However, in reality the judicial approach to interpretation is often much more complex than this 'either/or' choice, and there is a range of techniques that is open to the courts in any given dispute. Hence the courts may interpret sections in a statute with part reference to the corresponding headings in the legislation;[5] use the age-old 'mischief rule' to look to the pre-existing common law position when deciding what the objective of legislation is;[6] consult Hansard when trying to ascertain Parliament's intention in enacting certain provisions;[7] read legislation in the light of its historical context;[8] give words their broader meaning where this enables two decision-makers to exercise their powers in a complementary fashion that is consistent with the intention of the legislation;[9] and protect common law fundamental rights by requiring that any statutory interference with those rights is provided for either in express terms or by necessary implication.[10] Moreover, where a case falls under the European Communities Act 1972, the courts must interpret legislation creatively where this is necessary to guarantee the primacy of EU law, for instance where there is national legislation in an area occupied by a directive that has not been implemented in domestic law.[11] An interpretive obligation is likewise imposed by section 3 of the Human Rights Act 1998, which requires courts, 'so far as it is possible to do so', to interpret legislation 'whenever enacted' in a manner that it is compatible with the rights in the ECHR that have effect under the Act.[12]

In terms of illegality as a ground of review—in particular simple *ultra vires*, below—one further interpretive technique that can be of particular relevance is

---

3 See 5.6 and 9.2.

4 See 5.6 and ch 9.

5 See *DPP v Schildkamp* [1971] AC 1.

6 *Heydon's Case* (1584) 3 Co Rep 7b.

7 *Pepper v Hart* [1993] AC 593—but see, too, *R v Secretary of State for the Environment, Transport and the Regions, ex p Spath Holme Ltd* [2001] 2 AC 349.

8 *R (Quintavalle) v Secretary of State for Health* [2003] 2 AC 687, 695, para 8, Lord Bingham.

9 *Re Shield's Application* [2003] NI 161.

10 See, e.g., *R v Lord Chancellor, ex p Witham* [1998] QB 975; see also 4.2.2.

11 *Webb v EMO Air Cargo (UK) Ltd (No 2)* [1995] 4 All ER 577.

12 See 4.4.2.

the 'reasonably incidental' rule. Under this rule, the courts will permit bodies to undertake not only those tasks that are expressly authorised by the statute, but also those tasks that are regarded as 'reasonably incidental' to the original tasks (although note that some statutes already recognise the need for implied power, e.g., section 111 of the Local Government Act 1972). A famous example here is *Attorney General v Crayford Urban District Council*.[13] This case concerned the interpretation to be given to section 111(1) of the Housing Act 1957, which granted powers of 'general management' of houses provided by local authorities. Using this power, Crayford Urban District Council agreed to recommend to its tenants that they insure themselves with the Municipal Mutual Insurance Ltd (this followed an agreement between the council and the company). A competing insurance company brought an action against the council, maintaining that the scheme was *ultra vires* the statute. However, the court decided that the scheme was within the general management remit of the council. If tenants did not insure themselves, and then suffered uninsured loss, they would be likely to default on the rent. In view of this, a prudent authority would be concerned to safeguard its rent receipts by having its tenants take out insurance policies.[14]

11.3 Simple *ultra vires*

Now we turn to consider more closely the various sub-grounds of review that can be used to challenge the decisions and actions of public authorities and which fall under the general umbrella of illegality identified by Lord Diplock in the *GCHQ* case. The first of these can be termed 'simple *ultra vires*'. As we indicated above, this sub-heading can be used when it is considered that the decision-maker did not have the power that it purported to have and that there was therefore no basis in law for the impugned action. Of course, the idea of 'simplicity' here is perhaps a little misleading, as we have seen above that the answer to the question whether the decision-maker has a particular power can depend upon, among other things, judicial recourse to the 'reasonably incidental' rule.[15] However, where the courts decide that there is neither an express nor an implied power to make a decision or other measure, a finding of illegality should follow. Under those circumstances, the remaining question for the court will be the nature of the remedy that should issue.

Attorney General v Fulham Corporation[16] is an important early decision that revealed the nature of the simple *ultra vires* doctrine. Fulham Corporation, a statutory body, was empowered under the Baths and Washhouses Acts (1846–78) to establish washhouses and baths in order that the residents of the borough would have a facility to wash their clothes adequately. However, the corporation subsequently decided to introduce a new scheme whereby a laundry service would be

---

13 [1962] 2 All ER 147.

14 For a further example, see *Re Northern Ireland Human Rights Commission* [2002] NI 236—statutory body with responsibility for, among other things, promoting 'understanding and awareness of the importance of human rights in Northern Ireland', had an implied power to apply to intervene in ongoing legal proceedings—and see now Northern Ireland Act 1998, s 71.

15 See 11.2.

16 [1921] 1 Ch 440.

operated by the municipality for the benefit of the community. All this occurred at a time of prevailing *laissez-faire* assumptions about non-intervention in business affairs, and the court held that this was 'a completely different enterprise' (see [1921] 1 Ch 440, 453). The statute did not empower the corporation to spend monies on a laundry facility. This was because the purpose of the Act was to enable residents who did not have, and could not afford, their own washing facilities to do their washing at facilities provided by the corporation. The council therefore had no power to establish a municipal laundry and was acting *ultra vires* in purporting to do so.

Another high-profile case involving simple illegality—amounting to an abuse of power—is *Congreve v Home Office*.[17] The Home Secretary had here announced that the colour television licence fee would be increased from £12 to £18 on 1 April 1975, and he made an Order to that effect under section 2(1) of the Wireless Telegraphy Act 1949. The Home Office, in accordance with its administrative practice, thereafter prepared special instructions for its agents, who included post office counter clerks, telling them that anyone applying in advance for the 'renewal' of a licence which did not expire until 31 March 1975 or later should be told to reapply on or after 1 April 1975. However, when the plaintiff applied for renewal of his licence in March 1975, the counter clerk at the post office did not follow the Home Office instruction and issued him with a £12 licence that was valid until 29 February 1976 (some 24,500 licence holders were likewise issued with overlapping licences at the lower price). The Home Office wrote to the plaintiff stating that unless the additional £6 was paid, the licence he obtained in March 1975 would be revoked. No offer was made to refund any part of the £12 should that be done and, on the plaintiff's action for a declaration, the court held that this was an improper exercise of the Home Secretary's discretionary powers of revocation. This was because taxation should not be levied without clear statutory authority and also because the threat of exercising the power was used as a means of extracting money. The Court of Appeal issued a declaration that the revocation was unlawful, invalid, and of no effect, the point being that: 'In effect, the Home Office had tried to use their licensing powers to obtain taxing powers which had not been conferred on them.'[18]

11.4 'Improper' purpose

The basic principle that is applied by the courts here is very easy to explain: where statute grants a power for purpose (a) it is unlawful for the decision-maker to exercise the power for purpose (b). Of course, in practice much will again depend on the judicial interpretation given to the parent statute, as purposes will be found in either the express terms of the statute or be read as implicit in the overall statutory scheme. However, once the purposes are identified by the courts, the task is to determine whether the decision-maker has used its power in a manner that is *intra* or *ultra vires* the Act. In making its determination, a court may couch the questions for itself in terms of 'illegality' and assess whether the decision complained of is

---

17 [1976] 1 All ER 697.
18 W Wade and C Forsyth, *Administrative Law*, 11th edn (Oxford: Oxford University Press, 2014), 301.

ultra vires within the above meaning of that term.[19] On the other hand, we have also noted that the grounds for judicial review overlap with one another, and a court may therefore alternatively ask whether there has been an 'abuse of power' or an 'unreasonable' exercise of power by the decision-maker.[20] Depending on circumstance, arguments based on purposes may also overlap with those made with reference to relevant and irrelevant considerations.[21]

There are many examples of challenges based upon purposes in the case law, and we consider some of the classic authorities below. However, before doing so, it is important to make a further definitional point about overlapping terminology in this area. In short, while we have used 'improper purposes' in the general heading, the wider body of case law may instead refer to purposes that are 'collateral', 'extraneous', and/or 'ulterior' to the statute. At one level, such use of different terminology is essentially inconsequential, as all the cases are ultimately concerned with the question whether the purpose pursued by the decision-maker is outside that which is permitted by statute. However, it has also been suggested by some commentators that the term 'improper' should be regarded as different from 'collateral' etc in so far as the former term connotes moral impropriety and an intention to use a power unlawfully.[22] At the same time, it is unclear how far the courts actually use the term 'improper' for this reason, as there does not appear to be a definitive judicial statement on the point.[23] For the present, it is therefore perhaps sufficient to note that use of the term 'improper' implies that the courts view, as particularly grave, an alleged misuse of power.

11.4.1 The case law

Perhaps the most celebrated 'purposes' case is *Padfield v Minister of Agriculture*.[24] The facts were that, under section 19(3) of the Agricultural Marketing Act 1958, complaints could be heard against a milk marketing scheme 'if the minister in any such case so directs'. South-eastern producers complained that a fixed price scheme would result in their being treated unfairly, but the minister refused to refer the complaint to a committee of investigation. In doing so, the minister maintained that the statute required him only to consider a complaint fairly and otherwise conferred on him what amounted to an unfettered (subjective) discretion. The minister further argued that reference to this committee might make it necessary to follow its recommendations and thereby potentially undermine the unfettered discretion that he claimed to have under the Act. However, the House of Lords held this was not a legally valid reason and that he was effectively frustrating the objectives of the statute as his exercise of the power was based on a misunderstanding of the purpose for which the power had been given to him. The meaning of the statutory provision had to be viewed in the context of the legislation as a whole and the minister was on this basis ordered to consider the complaint in accordance

---

19 See 11.1.

20 On the meaning of unreasonableness see ch 13.

21 See *Hanks v Minister of Housing and Local Government* [1963] 1 QB 999, 1020; and on relevance and irrelevant considerations see 11.5

22 See H Woolf et al, *De Smith's Judicial Review*, 7th edn (London: Thomson/Sweet & Maxwell, 2013), 290.

23 But for consideration of ideas of impropriety see *Porter v Magill* [2002] 2 AC 357.

24 [1968] AC 997, HL.

with the correct understanding of the law as indicated by the court. This the minister duly did, although it should be noted that he subsequently disregarded the recommendations of the committee. *Padfield* thus exemplifies not just the essential elements of the improper purpose principle but also some of the limitations of the remedy of judicial review.

The decision of the Divisional Court in *R v Secretary of State for Foreign Affairs, ex p World Development Movement*[25] arguably developed the principle still further by imposing strict limits on the decision-making powers of ministers under statute. Under section 1 of the Overseas Development and Cooperation Act 1980 the Foreign Secretary could grant financial aid 'for the purposes of promoting the development or maintaining the economy of a country'. The government had here decided to lend significant financial support to a project that would build the Pergau Dam in Malaysia, even though some economic reports indicated that such use of monies would not benefit the poorer sections of Malaysia's population. The decision was challenged by a pressure group that sought to raise awareness of poverty in the developing world, and the court granted a declaration that the government's decision was unlawful. It was held that, whatever the intentions of the Foreign Secretary, the court had to determine whether the grant was within his statutory powers. Looking to the wording of the statute, the court held that Parliament had intended that aid could be given only in respect of development projects that were economically 'sound'. This was a highly controversial decision since the allegations at the time were that the real reasons why the government had allocated funds to this scheme in Malaysia were not to promote overseas aid but to ensure that the UK received a number of lucrative armaments contracts for the British defence industry. Rose LJ stated that:

Whatever the Secretary of State's intention or purpose may have been, it is, as it seems to me, a matter for the courts and not for the Secretary of State to determine whether, on the evidence before the court, the particular conduct was, or was not, within the statutory purpose.

In this instance the minister had exercised his discretion for an improper diplomatic purpose and he had taken account of irrelevant considerations. It was held that the wider issue of Anglo–Malaysian relations could only be taken into account as a relevant consideration if a genuine developmental purpose lay behind the grant. From a different perspective, it might be argued that the court has come perilously close to interfering with ministerial discretion in the crucial area of foreign policy. It remains a matter of debate whether the soundness of the scheme fell under (statutory) purpose or whether it should instead have been regarded as merely a relevant consideration (we pause to note here the overlap between improper purpose and relevant/irrelevant considerations). The result was that the government continued to support the project but from a different budgetary source.

In addition to *World Development Movement* and *Padfield* there are many more purposes cases that can be used to illustrate the core principles of law.[26] However, of particular interest are some of the cases concerned with 'political' decision-making, race relations, and planning. Also of interest are so-called 'mixed purpose'

---

25 [1995] 1 WLR 386; and 8.10.2.

26 See, e.g., *R v Greenwich London Borough Council, ex p Lovelace* [1990] 1 All ER 353.

cases, which can raise difficult questions about the relationship between the 'rule of law' and 'administrative convenience'.

11.4.1.1 **Political purpose cases**

The extent to which statutory duties resting on public authorities may be influenced by political events yet remain within discretion has been a contentious issue in a range of contexts. A leading case here is *Meade v Haringey London Borough Council*.[27] The council had sent out an instruction during a strike by its manual workers and ancillary staff, to the effect that all schools would be closed from the date of the strike and that no one should attempt to open a school. After the strike had lasted for four weeks, some of the parents of children complained to the minister under section 99(1) of the Education Act 1944, requesting her to make the education authority discharge its statutory duty under section 8 of the same Act. The minister refused to do so and a parent acting on his own behalf and on behalf of other parents in the area and ratepayers brought proceedings seeking a declaration and a mandatory injunction to compel the authority to perform its duties. Although the proceedings were ultimately dismissed both at first instance and by the Court of Appeal, some important points of principle were rehearsed. These were that a decision by an authority to close schools in sympathy with a trade union's claim when the closure could have been avoided would be *ultra vires* if the decision was affected by considerations not relevant to the educational field and was a positive misuse of the authority's powers for an improper purpose. On the other hand, the authority was entrusted with the duty of running the schools and, if it genuinely took the view that in order to perform that duty it was better to close the schools or if they had compelling and reasonable grounds for failing to keep the schools open, they would not be in breach of duty. While the plaintiff had, on the facts, made out a clear *prima facie* case of a breach of duty based on the authority's alleged *ultra vires* action, it was right to refuse to grant the injunction sought because the issue was strongly contested and on the balance of convenience it would be difficult to enforce. The Court of Appeal moreover held that this was not a case in which the court should interfere in an industrial dispute by granting an injunction.

R v Somerset County Council, ex p Fewings[28] is a controversial decision that illustrates further the workings of public law principle in this area. The case concerned a ban on stag hunting on council land. At first instance, Laws J held the ban could not be introduced simply because the majority of the councillors considered the activity to be morally wrong, but rather could be introduced only where it was necessary for the 'benefit, improvement or development of (the) area' (Local Government Act 1972, section 120(1)(b)). Laws J thus construed the authority's role very restrictively, as existing merely in respect of specified duties and not including the ability to make decisions based upon free-standing moral perceptions. On appeal, Sir Thomas Bingham MR accepted that too narrow a construction had been put on the words 'benefit of the area' by the trial judge and indicated that the ban might have been made lawfully. However, in dismissing the appeal his Lordship concluded that the ban was unlawful because the council had expressly

27 [1979] 2 All ER 1016.
28 [1995] 1 WLR 1037.

failed to take account of the governing statutory provisions in taking its decision. The debate ranged over many emotive ethical issues and in doing so lost sight of what was of benefit to the area as required by the statute. It is noteworthy that, in a dissenting judgment, Simon Brown LJ expressed the view that ethical issues could be regarded as decisive by councillors in reaching their decision. This illustrates some of the difficulties the courts can have in wrestling with such charged issues.[29]

11.4.1.2 Race relations

Wheeler v Leicester City Council[30] is a seminal case on race relations, which also illustrates, doctrinally, the difficulty of separating out the various grounds of review, for example, *Wednesbury* unreasonableness, improper purpose, and relevant considerations. A local authority, using discretionary powers pursuant to section 10 of the Open Spaces Act 1906, section 76 of the Public Health Amendment Act 1907, and sections 52(2) and 56 of the Public Health Act 1925, had banned a rugby club from using a recreation ground. The ban was introduced because the club had ignored a number of requirements stipulated by the council; in particular, it had not attempted to prevent its members from visiting South Africa (which was at that time under apartheid rule). The council maintained that it was acting, *inter alia*, under the Race Relations Act 1976, section 71, with due regard to the need 'to promote good relations between persons of different racial or ethnic groups' in an area with a large ethnic population. In finding that the council's ban was *ultra vires* the House of Lords held that local authorities were entitled to take into account race relations matters in exercising their powers but that it was perhaps 'unfair', and certainly unreasonable, for the council to impose what amounted to a punishment on those who acted contrary to the council's preferences. Lord Templeman was clear that the council had acted wrongly by misusing its statutory powers for the purpose of punishing the club when it had done no wrong.[31]

11.4.1.3 Planning cases

Planning is an area in which authorities have significant discretionary powers, for instance they are sometimes able to impose 'such conditions as (they) think fit' when considering grants of planning permission. At the same time, such power may be constrained by a range other statutes that impact upon the planning process and any exercise must be consistent with that legislation and its purposes. For instance, in *Hanks v Minister of Housing and Local Government*[32] the court had to consider whether the dominant purpose of a compulsory purchase order fell within the terms of the Housing Act 1957.[33] The applicants maintained that the true and dominant purpose of the order was improper as it related to general development and highway improvement, which were planning considerations rather than considerations related to the supply of housing within the meaning of section 97 of the 1957 Act. There was much detailed discussion in the judgment about the

---

29 Compare and contrast *R v Sefton Metropolitan Borough Council, ex p British Association of Shooting and Conservation* [2000] LGR 628, where the court held that the council was entitled under s 120(1)(b) of the Local Government Act 1972 to refuse to renew shooting rights over a nature reserve on the grounds that the refusal was for the benefit, improvement, or development of its area.

30 [1985] AC 1054.

31 See also on this point *R v Lewisham London Borough Council, ex p Shell UK Ltd* [1988] 1 All ER 938.

32 [1963] 1 QB 999.

33 On dominant purposes see 11.4.1.4.

difficulties in distinguishing between housing matters and motives and planning matters and motives, and Megaw J doubted whether a strict distinction could be made in these circumstances. Nevertheless, it was held on the facts that the correct procedure under the Housing Act 1957 had been followed for a scheme of this type and that, in any event, any such scheme would necessarily involve some planning considerations. Under those circumstances, it was held that the authority was entitled to build a road incidental to the purpose of a scheme.[34]

R v Hillingdon London Borough Council, ex p Royce Homes Ltd[35] illustrates the use of planning permission for an ulterior purpose in circumstances where the applicant, Royce Homes, had asked the council for permission to build houses. The local authority granted this but imposed conditions which, among other things, specified that the houses that were built should be occupied for the first ten years by persons who were on the council's waiting list. The planning permission was challenged on the grounds that the attached conditions were *ultra vires* the planning authority. An order of *certiorari* was made, as the council was, in effect, using its powers in respect of planning permission as a means to overcome its housing shortage.

Hall & Co Ltd v Shoreham-by-Sea Urban District Council[36] provides a further example of an abuse of discretionary powers. The company had applied for planning permission to develop an industrial site, and permission was granted under section 14 of the Town and Country Planning Act 1947. However, the Act appeared to allow the council to attach conditions for regulating the development or use of land for which any grant of planning permission was made, and the council stipulated as a condition that the company was not only to build an ancillary road over the whole site at its expense, but further provided that this road should give right of passage from such ancillary roads that might be constructed on adjoining sites. It was clear that, by imposing the conditions under this Act and not using its powers under the Highways Act 1959, the council was avoiding having to pay compensation for the road building. On appeal, these conditions were found to be unduly onerous and unreasonable and therefore *ultra vires*.[37]

11.4.1.4 **Mixed purpose cases**

We now need to consider situations where power has been exercised for 'mixed' purposes (or motives). Clearly, as we have already observed, if a power has been given for one purpose it cannot be used for another. However, a problem for the court arises when a decision pursues a number of purposes, only some of which are lawful. Under those circumstances, the court has to decide if the unlawful purpose is incidental to the exercise of the power or, in other words, if the dominant purpose is lawful.

Of course, in reality there is no simple way to assess which purpose dominates and it may come down to a question of judicial preference in the face of the evidence. The point can be illustrated with reference to *Westminster Corporation v London and North Western Railway Co.*[38] Under section 44 of the Public Health

---

34 Compare *Meravale Builders Ltd v Secretary of State for the Environment* (1978) 77 LGR 365.

35 [1974] 2 All ER 643.

36 [1964] 1 All ER 1.

37 See also *Virgin Cinema Properties Ltd v Secretary of State* [1998] 2 PLR 24, DC for a case concerning the alleged misapplication of planning policy guidance by the Secretary of State.

38 [1905] AC 426.

(London) Act 1891, Westminster Corporation had the power to build lavatories, but it designed them to be accessed by a subway passage that also served as a means of crossing a busy street. An action was brought to prevent the work going ahead on the ground that the real reason for the project was to provide the crossing and not the lavatories. It was held that to establish that the improper purpose dominated, it had to be shown that the authority had constructed the subway 'under the colour and pretence of providing public conveniences not really wanted' ([1905] AC 426, 432). In other words, it was not enough to show that the corporation contemplated that the public might use the subway for crossing the street. On the question whether the lavatories were the primary purpose or not, it was thus held that the lawful one was the most important. The subway was a 'mere incidental advantage' and the scheme was allowed to proceed.

A different result was reached in *R v Minister of Health, ex p Davis*.[39] An improvement scheme concerning a site in the centre of Derby purported to be made under the provisions of the Housing Act 1925 that provided for the purchase and clearing of an unhealthy area. The scheme was held to be *ultra vires* the statute because some of the land was being compulsorily purchased for the purpose of resale, and the Act did not authorise an improvement scheme which contained an unrestricted power to sell or lease the cleared area without also containing particulars of the proposed development. It was held that the minister had no jurisdiction to consider the scheme in the first instance.

Webb v Minister of Housing and Local Government[40] provides an example of the misuse of compulsory purchase powers. The coastal protection authority, wishing to carry out necessary works, prepared a scheme under section 6 of the Coast Protection Act 1949. Subsequently, the scheme was amended to include the acquisition of a further strip of land for the construction of a paved access way. A compulsory purchase order was then executed in accordance with the Act to acquire the necessary land, and the minister approved the scheme and the purchase order. However, on a challenge brought by the owners of the land, the scheme and the order were quashed since the authority could not demonstrate that the scheme was necessary in order to exercise its powers under the Act. The acquisition of the land was for purposes not within the powers conferred by the Act, involving as it did mixed motives and an abuse of discretion. Accordingly, this was a clear case of improper purpose.

11.5 Relevant and irrelevant considerations

We turn now to consider the principles that the courts give effect to in cases in which decisions and other measures are challenged for the reason that the decision-maker has failed to take into account all relevant considerations and/or to disregard irrelevant considerations. Considerations for these purposes will ordinarily be identified expressly or impliedly in the statute that underpins the decision, although the courts may also intervene where there are, as Lord Scarman explained,

---

39 [1929] 1 KB 619.
40 [1965] 1 WLR 755.

'matters so obviously material to a decision on a particular project that anything short of direct consideration of them . . . would not be in accordance with the intention of the Act'.[41] In cases brought under this heading, there can sometimes be an overlap with the language of purposes (and vice versa), as the taking of a decision in the light of a particular consideration may equate to taking the decision for an improper purpose. Indeed, the overlap can become so pronounced that it has been suggested previously that the language of purposes should be subsumed with that of relevant and irrelevant considerations.[42] However, this has not happened formally in the case law and the two sub-headings continue to exist separately from one another.

The basic approach of the courts under this heading is to enquire whether all relevant considerations have been taken into account by the decision-maker and irrelevant ones have been ignored and, if so, to allow the decision to stand subject to arguments of unreasonableness, perversity etc.[43] This approach is consistent with the 'supervisory/appellate' distinction that underpins judicial review,[44] as the courts are not concerned with the merits of a decision but only with the question whether it accords with the Act (illegality) and does not contravene accepted standards of rational decision-making (irrationality/*Wednesbury* unreasonableness). At the same time, we will see below that case law on relevant considerations can occasionally take the courts to the fringes of difficult social and economic choices and that (arguably) the courts have not always adopted a position of self-restraint. On the other hand, we will see in chapter 13 that the courts sometimes also emphasise that there is an enhanced imperative of restraint when challenges are made to decisions that have been taken in the face of resource considerations and/or where the decision is essentially political. For example, in *ex p B* the court would not intervene in a health authority's decision to refuse further treatment to a child cancer patient where the decision had been taken both for medical and resource-related reasons.[45] Under those circumstances—and notwithstanding that an individual's fundamental rights may be at stake—the courts may highlight how the decision-maker has a 'discretionary area of judgement' into which the judiciary should not intrude.[46]

11.5.1 'Target' duties—are resources a relevant consideration?

The question under this heading is how far public authorities can take into account the resources available to them when making discretionary choices in respect of the performance of 'target' duties. Such duties, which are imposed by legislation in the field of public service provision, are often read as giving authorities discretion as to how to meet an Act's demands while working within the framework of a finite budget. However, while the link between resources and public service provision may be self-evident in a practical sense, it does not follow that resources will, in law, always be a relevant consideration that should be taken into account by

---

41 *Re Findlay* [1985] AC 318, 333–4.
42 See, e.g., Megaw J in *Hanks v Minister of Housing and Local Government* [1963] 1 QB 999, 1020.
43 See ch 13.
44 See 8.3.
45 *R v Cambridge Health Authority, ex p B* [1995] 1 WLR 898.
46 See, e.g., *R (Pro-life Alliance) v BBC* [2004] 1 AC 185.

the decision-maker when exercising its discretion. Much will, instead, depend on how the courts read the overall legislative scheme that imposes the duty of service provision upon the public authority. Resources may therefore be a relevant consideration; and, equally, they may not be.

One case in which it was held that resources were a relevant consideration is *R v Gloucestershire County Council, ex p Barry*.[47] The local council informed the applicant that, following a £2.5 million budget cut, it had to review its priorities and could no longer provide the care to which he had been assessed as being entitled. Mr Barry was 82 years old, chronically sick, partially sighted, and, after fracturing his hip, was able to get around only with a walking frame. The Court of Appeal interpreted section 2 of the Chronically Sick and Disabled Persons Act 1970 as meaning that a local authority was not entitled to take into account the availability of resources when deciding whether to meet the needs of a disabled person under the Act, since it was under a duty to make such a provision. At the same time, it was held that, once the assessment of need had been made, the authority could exercise discretion in deciding how resources were deployed to meet it, for example, by providing home care or residential care. However, on appeal to the House of Lords, the majority held that the need for services could not sensibly be assessed without first having some regard to the cost of providing them. The criterion for assessment adopted might be what constituted an acceptable standard of living, and the eligibility criteria for services could be adjusted in line with the availability of funds. Costs, in this way, were a relevant consideration.

No matter which way it had been decided, *ex p Barry* was a case with significant implications. The Court of Appeal had identified the principal relevant consideration as a target duty under the statute; while another consideration was the overall funding constraints placed on the authority. The discretion lay with the decision-maker only after having fulfilled its statutory obligations to meet the assessed needs, with the discretionary element then sounding on the manner of deployment of resources to fulfil the duty. By finding a strict duty in a statute when the decision-making body is faced with obvious resource limitations, the court was thus preserving a basic safety net provision. However, under this sort of approach it might well turn out that the needs of certain categories of disabled people had been protected at the expense of funding for other groups, also arguably in priority need. The Court of Appeal's approach is thus one example of how judicial decision-making can have political ramifications even where that may not be intended.

The wisdom of the House of Lords' approach can also be doubted, albeit from a different perspective. In short, it had afforded a democratically elected public authority more scope to decide how to exercise its discretion in allocating resources between deserving groups in need. This seems to have been based on the assumption that the imposed limits on funding by central government are unchallengeable. But the problem with this decision is that, against a background of dwindling resources provided for local authorities, it would appear to send a signal to public service providers that priority needs, which have never been lavishly met, can be constantly trimmed at the edges (subject to a residual test of reasonableness or, if rights under the ECHR are in issue, proportionality). The question therefore remains how such statutory obligations can adequately be fulfilled if public bodies

---

47 [1996] 4 All ER 421 (CA), [1997] AC 584 (HL).

are deprived of the financial means by central government. As Lord Lloyd pointed out in his dissenting judgment, 'Having willed the end, Parliament must be asked to provide the means' ([1997] AC 584, 604).

The decision in *ex p Barry* can be contrasted with that in *R v East Sussex County Council, ex p Tandy*.[48] From July 1995 Miss Tandy had had five hours per week home tuition provided by the council, under section 298 of the Education Act 1993 (subsequently replaced by section 19 of the Education Act 1996), because she was suffering from ME. This was a statutory duty which required a local education authority (LEA) to make arrangements for children who have special needs. However, in October 1996 the LEA informed Miss Tandy's parents that, following an expenditure review, and a review of home tuition services, the maximum hours of home tuition provided would be reduced from five hours to three (this was despite the fact that Miss Tandy's circumstances had not changed). On an application for judicial review it was held in the High Court that the council had taken into account an irrelevant factor, namely, its financial resources. This decision was reversed in the Court of Appeal, and then appealed to the House of Lords. Holding that the decision of the High Court had been correct, the House of Lords stated that the local authority, in performing its statutory duty to provide suitable education to children of school age, could not take into account the availability of financial resources. There were a number of reasons for this, included among which was the interpretation to be given to the statute. Relatedly, their Lordships were concerned that the authority would, in effect, be able to reduce a statutory duty to the level of a discretionary power. As Lord Browne-Wilkinson put it: 'Parliament has chosen to impose a statutory duty, as opposed to a power, requiring the local authority to do certain things. In my judgment the courts should be slow to downgrade duties into what are, in effect, mere discretions over which the court would have very little real control.'[49]

In *R v Birmingham City Council, ex p Mohammed*[50] the High Court followed *ex p Tandy* and distinguished *ex p Barry*. Moreover, such duties have been discussed in a number of related contexts including community care needs,[51] housing offered to homeless people,[52] and in respect of a special educational needs tribunal considering a home authority's resources but not those of a neighbouring authority when determining provision for a child.[53]

However, the Supreme Court has since considered—or certainly noted—the implications of *Barry* in two important cases about the provision of care and assistance for the ill and disabled. In the first case, *R (McDonald) v Royal Borough of Kensington and Chelsea*,[54] the Court was called upon to decide whether a claimant with limited mobility could challenge a care package provided by the authority. In this instance, the substitution of incontinence pads for personal assistance to use a commode at night for a patient who was not in fact incontinent had the effect of reducing the cost of care by an estimated £22,000 per year. Lord Brown, giving

---

48 [1998] AC 714.
49 [1998] AC 714, 749.
50 [1999] 1 WLR 33.
51 *R v Bristol City Council, ex p Penfold* [1998] 1 CCLR 315, DC.
52 *R v Lambeth London Borough Council, ex p Ekpo-Wedderman* [1998] 3 FCR 532.
53 *B v London Borough of Harrow* [2000] 1 WLR 223.
54 [2011] UKSC 33, [2011] 4 All ER 881.

the lead judgment, stressed that, following *ex p Barry*, needs for services cannot sensibly be assessed without having some regard to the cost of providing them. The majority accepted that the guidance allowing substitution of pads could be seen as a practical and appropriate solution. Baroness Hale, dissenting, was of the view that it was irrational for the authority to maintain that the claimant had a need different from the one that she in fact had.[55]

The second case was *R (KM) (by his mother and litigation friend JM) v Cambridgeshire CC*.[56] The claimant here was a profoundly disabled man who suffered from a range of physical and mental difficulties and required help in feeding and caring for himself. Under section 2(1) of the Chronically Sick and Disabled Persons Act 1970 the Council had a duty to make arrangements for his care, including the provision of specified services for him. On the claimant's challenge to the Council's assessment of the amount of a direct payment that should be awarded for his care needs, Lord Wilson once again recognised that the availability of resources can be a relevant consideration for a public authority when it is making determinations about levels of assistance. However, beyond this, his Lordship was reluctant to fully endorse *Barry* as he noted that the House of Lords may have fallen into error on the question of precisely *when* resources may be taken into account in the decision-making process.[57] Baroness Hale likewise cautioned that *Barry* may need to be revisited, and it would therefore seem that the line of case law running through *Barry*, *Tandy*, and *McDonald* has yet to reach its terminus. That said the point was ultimately irrelevant to the resolution of *KM* as it became clear in the case that resource limitations had not informed the authority's decision and that the challenge instead centred upon the mechanisms that had been used to determine the level of direct payment (the so-called 'resource allocation system' and the 'upper banding calculator'). Holding that the claimant's challenge should fail, the Supreme Court concluded that the method of calculation used by the defendant authority could not be classified as irrational even if it was not wholly at one with the method used by some other authorities. The authority's decision should stand even if 'the unpalatable result is that exactly the same level of presenting need will be eligible for services in one authority area but not in another . . . that is currently the law'.[58]

11.5.2 Fiduciary duty/electoral mandate cases

Useful comparisons can also be made between 'resources' case law and that concerning what are often referred to as 'fiduciary duties'. This is a term that has been used by the courts in relation to the performance of local government functions in circumstances where a local authority (a) has a duty to provide a service or range of services to the local community, but where (b) it must also have due regard for the interests of the taxpayers or council taxpayers resident in the area. In effect,

---

55 Ibid, paras 61–79. See also *McDonald v UK* (2015) 60 EHRR 1: while Art 8 ECHR had been violated at one certain stage in the decision-making process, states enjoy a wide margin of appreciation when taking decisions about the allocation of resources and the application to the ECtHR otherwise was manifestly ill-founded.

56 [2012] UKSC 23, [2012] 3 All ER 1218.

57 Ibid, paras 5–7.

58 Ibid, para 47, Baroness Hale.

the concept of a 'fiduciary duty' owed to taxpayers acts as a (potential) limit on the statutory powers of the decision-maker where the decision-maker wishes, for instance, to increase revenue so as to provide more effective local services. When apparent conflicts between (a) and (b) arise, the courts must thus find a meeting point between the two, and they have, at least historically, sometimes appeared to have made politically loaded judgments.

Roberts v Hopwood[59] can be regarded as the leading case on this point. A decision was made by Poplar Borough Council to pay its employees uniform pay increases considerably higher than the rate of inflation and unrelated to the sex of the employee and to the nature of the work done. The authority had a wide statutory power to pay its employees such salaries and wages as it thought fit. Following a challenge by the district auditor, this action was held to be wrong in law. In the first place, the council had acted on the basis of irrelevant considerations in seeking to set itself up as a model employer. The council had allowed itself, according to Lord Atkinson, 'to be guided by some eccentric principle of socialistic philanthropy or by a feminist ambition to secure equality of the sexes in the matter of wages in the world of labour' ([1925] AC 578, 594). Secondly, at a time when wages were actually falling, it had taken insufficient account of ratepayers' interests.[60]

However, where the expenditure is deemed to be reasonable, the courts will not interfere. *Pickwell v Camden Council*[61] can clearly be contrasted with *Roberts v Hopwood*. During a national strike involving the National Union of Public Employees (NUPE), Camden Council negotiated a local pay settlement more favourable than the national agreement which had been reached from negotiations embarked upon during the strike. This was challenged by the district auditor, who considered that the agreement had resulted in extra expenditure for which the council members were liable to be surcharged if the item of expenditure was *ultra vires*. In effect, the court thus had to consider and reconcile the legality of two exercises of discretion. On the one hand, there was the council, which owed fiduciary duties to ratepayers, but which had also entered into local negotiations with the union and reached a separate settlement. On the other hand, there was an exercise of discretion by the auditor, who had applied for a surcharge on the council for having entered this agreement far too readily and with the result of additional and unnecessary expenditure. The court held that the council had not acted unlawfully—there had not been any collusion between the council and strikers, and it was not possible to draw the inference that the council had ignored relevant material or had been guided by improper motives.

Bromley London Borough Council v Greater London Council[62] is one of the most celebrated cases of this kind, and points to the very clear difficulties which can arise for the courts in such cases. The Greater London Council (GLC), acting under section 1 of the Transport (London) Act 1969, sought to implement a supplementary rate in order to put into operation its clear manifesto promise to lower fares on public transport by 25 per cent (section 1 required the GLC 'to develop policies . . . which

---

59 [1925] AC 578.

60 It has been pointed out on numerous occasions that, even allowing for the context of the times, the political prejudices of at least some elements of the judiciary are plainly displayed by this decision. See, e.g., J Griffith, *Judicial Politics since 1920: A Chronicle* (Oxford: Blackwell, 1993), 1–11.

61 [1983] 1 All ER 602.

62 [1983] 1 AC 768.

will promote the provision of integrated, efficient and economic transport facilities and services for Greater London'). This was challenged in the courts by Bromley London Borough Council, and the GLC was declared to have exceeded its powers. The House of Lords held, *inter alia*, that the GLC was under a 'fiduciary duty' towards ratepayers to maintain a balance between services and costs to the ratepayer, which it had failed to do. Its decision to pursue such a policy was therefore unlawful as it had not taken these relevant considerations into account. Lord Diplock held that 'a local authority owes a fiduciary duty to the ratepayers from whom it obtains moneys needed to carry out its statutory functions, and . . . this includes a duty not to expend those moneys thriftlessly but to deploy the full financial resources available to it to the best advantage'.[63] Once again the issue of political policy emerges as a boundary which the courts are in danger of transgressing, as how can one balance the different community interests discussed in this case without raising moral and political considerations? How are the boundaries to be drawn? And at what point does the expenditure, deemed to be excessive, become unlawful? Addressing such matters, John Griffith argued that the courts are substituting their own value judgements for those of the rightful decision-maker, and that this raises fundamental questions about the legitimacy of such judicial decision-making.[64] So should the courts never intervene in such political disputes? Or must they intervene to ensure that Parliament's intentions in delegating power are being observed? Or does this then lead the courts to make assumptions about the legislature's intentions, at which stage they resort to a construct such as fiduciary duty by way of resolving disputes?

In turn, electoral mandate cases are often concerned with disputes between central and local government, and some decisions have raised doubts about the consistency with which the courts approach such disputes. For instance, *Secretary of State for Education and Science v Tameside Metropolitan Borough Council*[65] is a well-known case which appears to conflict with the approach to manifesto commitments taken in *Bromley London Borough Council*. It concerned the refusal of a Conservative-held local authority to accept the Labour Government's policy on comprehensive education. Arrangements had already been made to allow for a changeover when the council was under Labour control but, after the Conservatives had been elected, the authority modified its plans to abandon selective education in favour of comprehensive education by deciding to retain five selective grammar schools. Although the Conservatives had pledged to review the situation in their local election manifesto, the change of policy was likely to be highly disruptive. In attempting to impose the previously approved scheme for comprehensive education, the minister acted under section 68 of the Education Act 1944, which gave him power, if he felt an authority was acting unreasonably, to give 'such directions . . . as appear to him expedient'. However, the House of Lords decided in favour of the council and refused to grant the Secretary of State a mandatory order. In so doing, they construed 'unreasonably' to mean behaving in a manner in which no reasonable authority would behave; in other words, behaving in a manner that was *Wednesbury* unreasonable.[66] 'Unreasonably' did not mean simply disagreeing on

---

63 Ibid, 829.
64 J Griffith, *The Politics of the Judiciary*, 5th edn (London, Fontana, 1997), 126–33.
65 [1977] AC 1014.
66 See ch 13.

a matter of principle, but rather that the Secretary of State had to point to some objective conduct that was unreasonable (in this strong sense) before exercising his discretion under this section. It was recognised by Lord Wilberforce in particular that the council was entitled to make a policy change of this kind, based on political considerations and beliefs. The importance of the mandate created by the electorate's approval of a manifesto policy of the winning Conservative party in the local election was noted because it endorsed the change of policy. Given the very different sentiments that were discernible in Lord Wilberforce's judgment in *Bromley London Borough Council v GLC—viz* where it was in effect held that a fiduciary duty should trump the Labour party's local electoral mandate—one might wonder how, if at all, these two judgments are to be reconciled.[67]

11.5.3 European Union law as a relevant consideration?

The above case law has been centrally concerned with challenges to exercises of discretion within the framework set by Acts of Parliament. Of course, in some cases, it may be that provisions of EU law are also directly or indirectly engaged by a decision-making process, and the question thereby arises whether the decision-maker should take EU law into account as a relevant consideration.[68] Certainly, the doctrine of the supremacy of EU law would suggest that EU law should have to be taken into account where EU law rights are directly in issue, as a failure to prioritise those rights in the overall decision-making process would run contrary to the core obligations of EU membership. On the other hand, it might also be said that a decision-maker need not give express consideration to rights under EU law where the final decision itself is incidentally compliant with any supranational norm. The point would perhaps have an added force when EU law rights are only peripheral to the matter before the decision-maker.

One case which suggests that EU law should be taken into account is *R v Human Fertilisation and Embryology Authority, ex p Blood*.[69] This case, which concerned the interpretation to be given to the Human Fertilisation and Embryology Act 1990, arose when Diane Blood's husband died suddenly of meningitis before having the opportunity to give written consent for his sperm to be used for his wife's insemination.[70] The Court of Appeal upheld the decision of the Family Division of the High Court in finding that the Human Fertilisation and Embryology Authority had been within its power in refusing to license fertilisation in the UK. It also ruled that taking and storing sperm without consent was unlawful, but this meant that the case before them was unique and unlikely to recur. Despite recognising that written consent was an absolute requirement under the Human Fertilisation and Embryology Act 1990, the Court of Appeal went on to consider whether, in the case before it, the applicant's right to receive cross-border medical treatment

---

67 For a subsequent case on fiduciary duties see *R (on the application of Structadene Ltd v Hackney London Borough Council* [2001] 2 All ER 225; and for a case that considered the moral, as opposed to legal weight, to be given to electoral promises see *R v Department for Education and Science, ex p Begbie* [2000] 1 WLR 1115.

68 Note the framework is set here by an Act of Parliament, namely, the terms of the European Communities Act 1972; see 3.3.1.

69 [1997] 2 All ER 687, CA.

70 On the Act of 1990 see further *R (Quintavalle) v Secretary of State for Health* [2003] 2 AC 687; *Evans v Amicus Healthcare* [2004] 3 WLR 681; and *Evans v UK* (2008) 46 EHRR 34.

under (what were then) Articles 59 and 60 of the EC Treaty had been infringed by the Authority's decision.[71] Such a right is directly enforceable as part of EU law, and treatment might therefore lawfully be obtained in another Member State (Belgium was the example argued in the case). It followed that a refusal to permit the export of the husband's sperm in effect prevented the applicant from travelling abroad for such treatment. The Court of Appeal thus held that the Authority was required to take the Treaty into consideration when reaching its decision and, because it had not done so, Mrs Blood's appeal was allowed (note that the Authority subsequently ruled (27 February 1997) that she would be able to take her husband's sperm to a clinic in Belgium and, in 1998, Mrs Blood conceived a child).

One further point to be made here is that EU law apparently permits authorities to take resources into account when determining how to discharge their obligations under those provisions of the Treaty that permit the state, in narrowly defined circumstances, to place limitations upon EU law rights. The point can perhaps best be made with reference to *R v Chief Constable of Sussex, ex p International Traders' Ferry Ltd*,[72] which arose when animal rights protestors sought to prevent the export of live calves from England to the European continent. On the pretext of budgetary limitations, the Chief Constable decided that he would provide policing to escort lorries to and from the port terminal on only two days a week. This decision was successfully challenged in the Divisional Court by the International Traders' Ferry Ltd as being contrary to the free movement of goods under EU law. The applicants based their argument on a distinction between, on the one hand, the deployment of police resources, which was a matter for the discretion of the Chief Constable, and, on the other, the Chief Constable's duty to keep the peace and uphold the law. However, the distinction was not accepted in the Court of Appeal, where Kennedy LJ recognised as undeniable the fact that the manpower and fiscal resources available were finite. Bearing this in mind, the Chief Constable's decision to restrict policing could not be regarded as unreasonable as long as it could be shown that, in reaching his decision, he had balanced competing interests and acted proportionately. Moreover, on the facts of the case the Chief Constable was said to have a 'margin of appreciation' in relation to his decisions about how best to use resources. The House of Lords agreed, Lord Slynn of Hadley noting that the Chief Constable's decision was one that was reasonable under both English law and EU law.

11.5.4 Human rights as a relevant consideration?

In contrast to the (apparent) position under EU law, decision-makers are not required to take rights arising under the Human Rights Act 1998 into account as relevant considerations (it might be assumed, by analogy, that the point is also true of common law fundamental rights). This is the result of the House of Lords judgment in *R (on the application of SB) v Headteacher and Governors of Denbigh High School*.[73] The issue here was whether a school uniform policy which prevented a

---

71 The corresponding provisions are now Arts 56 and 57 of the Treaty on the Functioning of the European Union (TFEU).

72 [1998] QB 477 (CA), [1999] 2 AC 418 (HL).

73 [2007] 1 AC 100. See, too, *Belfast City Council v Miss Behavin' Ltd* [2007] 1 WLR 1420; and 4.4.4. But compare *Manchester City Council v Pinnock (Nos 1 & 2)* [2011] 2 AC 104, 134, where Lord Neuberger noted that it was 'common ground' that the housing authority 'must take into account a demoted tenant's article 8 rights when taking possession proceedings under' the Housing Act 1996.

Muslim school girl, Shabina Begum (SB), from wearing a *jilbab* was a violation of her religious beliefs under Article 9 of the ECHR (Article 9 protects both the right to hold a belief, which is absolute, and a right to manifest religious belief, which is qualified). The school in Luton, which had approximately 80 per cent Muslim students, had adopted its uniform policy after consultation with the governing body. Under this policy, cultural and religious diversity were recognised to a considerable extent, as girls were allowed to wear a skirt, trousers, or a *shalwar kameez*. SB, who had changed her religious beliefs since being admitted to the school, was then excluded for not wearing the correct uniform. Although her original claim was unsuccessful, the Court of Appeal found that her freedom to manifest her beliefs in public had been limited and the decision-making process had been flawed. Brooke LJ suggested that, in deciding whether restrictions on the claimant's religious freedom were lawful, the school should have taken the decision in the manner of a court by establishing, first, if the claimant had a relevant Convention right and, if so, by balancing the inteference with the right against a legitimate aim in order to establish if the infringement was justified, thereby in effect holding that the school was required to apply a proportionality test. However, this approach, which placed rights at the heart of the decision-making process, was rejected in the House of Lords. Giving the lead judgment, Lord Bingham explained that the purpose of the Human Rights Act 1998 had not been to enlarge the rights or remedies of those in the UK, but to enable those rights and remedies to be asserted and enforced in the UK domestic courts. Referring to Strasbourg case law, his Lordship said that there was no support in the international case law for challenges based upon argued defects in the decision-making process beyond those centred on the fairness of the process.[74] What mattered instead was the actual outcome of the decision-making process and, if the outcome was compliant with the rights of the individual, then there was no anterior obligation to reason with reference to those rights. Put differently, the rights of the individual were minimum requirements for the courts to protect rather than relevant considerations for the decision-maker to assess.

It should be noted that there are different views on the correctness of this approach. For example, as we have already been seen in chapter 4, the Human Rights Act 1998 was intended to herald a cultural shift in UK public law through, among other things, the section 6 requirement that public authorities act in a manner that is compatible with the ECHR. Given that reference point, it might be said that the Lords were incorrect to hold that authorities need not reason with reference to the very rights that they are supposed to observe. On the other hand, Lord Bingham was rightly concerned that such an approach could result in 'a new formalism and be a recipe for judicialisation on an unprecedented scale' as decision-makers would be required to take into account technical legal principles such as proportionality (see [2007] 1 AC 100, 116). It may therefore be that the Supreme Court will have to revisit this issue in the future.[75]

---

74 On this point the analysis by T Poole, 'Of Headscarves and Heresies: The Denbigh High School Case and Public Authority Decision Making under the Human Rights Act' [2005] *Public Law* 685, was cited with approval by Lord Bingham at paras 28 and 29; and on procedural impropriety/unfairness see chs 16 and 17.

75 M Fordham, 'Judicial Review: The Future' [2008] 13 *Judicial Review* 66. See also M Mazher Idriss, 'The House of Lords, Shabina Begum and Proportionality' [2006] *Judicial Review* 23.

11.5.5 **Equality duties**

One final matter that should be addressed in relation to relevant considerations is the public sector equality duty that decision-makers are placed under by section 149 of the Equality Act 2010.[76] We deal with the principle of equality in more detail in chapter 14, and it is sufficient, for present purposes, to note that the duty in section 149 requires public bodies to seek to eliminate discrimination on grounds such as race, religion, and sex, and to ensure that there is equality of opportunity for individuals irrespective of their race, religion, and so on. The pursuit of such duties can, in turn, require public bodies to carry out equality impact assessments that will help them to understand what effects a decision might have, and the results of such assessments may factor into the final decisions that are taken by public bodies. However, to the extent that this would suggest that the duties and assessments are relevant considerations and that it would be unlawful for a public authority not to have regard to them—a position that is more in keeping with that in relation to EU law than the Human Rights Act 1998—what should a court do where, for example, no regard has been had for the duty, or where an individual challenges the weight that has been given to an equality impact assessment? Can a public body be said fully to have discharged its equality duty only where it has prior regard for the duty and for the outcome of an equality impact assessment? Or is it enough for a public body simply to note the matter of its equality duties and to consider whether it is even necessary to conduct an equality impact assessment?

The answer to these questions is that a public body must always have 'due regard' for its equality duty, as any other approach would undermine the value of having the duties in the first instance. However, quite what constitutes due regard will thereafter depend on the context of the decision in question, and equality duties—and equality impact assessments—may be more or less relevant. For instance, in one of the leading cases on equality duties—*Elias*—it was said that, 'No doubt in some cases it will be plain even after a cursory consideration that [a duty] is not engaged, or at least is not relevant. There is no need to enter into time consuming and potentially expensive consultation exercises or monitoring when discrimination issues are plainly not in point'.[77] On the other hand, there will clearly be cases where the equality duty is engaged and where a decision must be closely tailored to the context and the requirements of equality law. In such instances, it might be thought that a failure to consider the results of an equality impact assessment would fatally affect a decision, as it could be argued that that a relevant consideration of far-reaching importance has simply not been taken into account. In situations where an equality impact assessment is taken into account, the remaining matter may then be whether, in the context of the case, it has been given sufficient weight.[78] This is an enquiry that would take a court unavoidably towards the *Wednesbury* and proportionality principles, where there can often be related—and

---

76 See T Hickman, 'Too Hot, Too Cold, or Just Right? The Development of the Public Sector Equality Duties in Administrative Law' [2013] *Public Law* 325.

77 *R (Elias) v Secretary of State for Defence* [2005] EWHC 1435 (Admin), para 96. Note that the duty at issue in this case was that contained in the Race Relations Act 1976, s 71, subsequently repealed by the Equality Act 2010.

78 See further, e.g., *R (Baker) v Secretary of State for Communities and Local Government* [2008] EWCA Civ 141 and *R (Brown) v Secretary of State for Work and Pensions* [2008] EWHC 3158. See, too, *Re JR 1's Application* [2011] NIQB 5, considering, by analogy, the nature and reach of the Northern Ireland Act 1998, s 75.

difficult—questions about the institutional competence of the courts and whether they should second-guess the decision of a public body. We return to those principles and the nature of the questions about them in chapter 13.

11.6 **Bad faith**

We can deal with this sub-heading for review very briefly. In sum, bad faith is a ground that can be used where an individual considers that a decision-maker has intentionally abused its power or was reckless as to whether it did so. At its highest, bad faith will thus vitiate a decision where it can be shown that the decision-maker has acted dishonestly or has taken action which it knew to be improper. Indeed, while there is clearly some potential here for overlap between bad faith, purposes, and relevant/irrelevant considerations, it is perhaps best to view bad faith as distinct insofar as it links to the intention of the decision-maker.[79] As Megaw LJ said in *Cannock Chase District Council v Kelly*, bad faith 'always involves a grave charge. It must not be treated as a synonym for an honest mistake'.[80]

It should, however, be noted that arguments of bad faith are rare in the case law. This is likely as much because of the difficulties involved in sustaining an argument as it is a result of the practical absence of ill-motive. Nevertheless, the sub-heading remains as an important safeguard against the abuse of power by decision-makers, and it can in that sense be compared to other little used administrative law headings such as 'actual bias' and 'misfeasance in public office' (on which see chapters 17 and 20 respectively).

11.7 **Conclusion**

In this chapter—the first of two on illegality—we have sought to introduce key elements of the ground for review as originally defined by Lord Diplock in the *GCHQ* case. Given the breadth of topics covered, it would be neither beneficial nor desirable to attempt to summarise each of the main points, and we will instead highlight two that are of more general importance to subsequent chapters. The first is that judicial intervention under this heading can sometimes be controversial in so far as it raises questions about the limits to the judicial role in review proceedings. As will become apparent, in particular in the chapters on proportionality and legitimate expectations, this is a tension that runs through each and all of the grounds for review.

The second point, already noted above and previously in chapter 9, is that the grounds for review overlap with one another, as indeed do sub-headings within the grounds. For instance, we have referred several times in this chapter to the cross-over between illegality and the standard of reasonableness that has historically suffused UK administrative law;[81] and we have likewise seen that a case that is

---

79 See, e.g., *Webb v Minister of Housing and Local Government* [1965] 1 WLR 755.
80 [1978] 1 All ER 152, 156.
81 See ch 13.

argued under purposes may also, or alternatively, be argued on the basis of relevant and irrelevant considerations (which ground can, in turn, also run into arguments about 'reasonableness'). When reading the remaining chapters on the grounds for review it is thus important to recall that the facts of any one case may give rise to arguments under one or all of the grounds for review and that the courts develop those grounds for the common reason of constraining unlawful governmental action. Viewed from this perspective, it is the judicial pursuit of that objective that can result in questions about the legitimacy of judicial decision-making and the importance or otherwise of the supervisory/appellate distinction.

FURTHER READING

Allan, TRS (1985) 'Rugby, Recreation Grounds and Race Relations: Punishment for Silence' *Modern Law Review* 448.

Bennion, F (2002) *Statutory Interpretation* (London: Butterworths).

Dignom, T (1983) 'Policy-making, Local Authorities and the Courts: the "GLC Fares" Case' *Law Quarterly Review* 605.

Hare, I (1995) 'Judicial Review and the Pergau Dam' 54 *Cambridge Law Journal* 227.

Hickman, T [2013] 'Too Hot, Too Cold, or Just Right? The Development of the Public Sector Equality Duties in Administrative Law' *Public Law* 325.

Mazher Idriss, M [2006] 'The House of Lords, Shabina Begum and Proportionality' *Judicial Review* 23.

Mead, D [2012] 'Outcomes Aren't All: Defending Process-Based Review of Public Authority Decisions Under the Human Rights Act' *Public Law* 661.

Palmer, E (2000) 'Resource Allocation, Welfare Rights—Mapping the Boundaries of Judicial Control in Public Administrative Law' *Oxford Journal of Legal Studies* 63.

Poole, T [2005] 'Of Headscarves and Heresies: The Denbigh High School Case and Public Authority Decision Making under the Human Rights Act' *Public Law* 685.

See also further reading for chapter 12.

12

···

Illegality II

12.1 Introduction

We turn, in this chapter, to consider three further issues related to illegality. The first is the approach that the courts adopt when it is argued that an authority has acted illegally because it has done something that has the effect of preventing it exercising its discretion in the light of new circumstances. The basic position here is very easy to state: where Parliament, through statute, gives discretion to a subordinate decision-maker, the decision-maker cannot fetter its discretion as to do so would be contrary to Parliament's intention in granting the discretion. However, in practice, the case law can become much more complex than this, as the courts have to determine the extent of discretion and also whether an authority has actually fettered it powers. This can require courts to make important assumptions not only about the respective needs of individuals and decision-makers (and how those are to be reconciled), but also about the meaning of the legislation that confers the power of decision.[1] As we have already seen in the previous chapter, the performance of either or both of those tasks can raise difficult questions about the judicial role in review proceedings.

In considering this first issue—the so-called rule against fettering discretion—we begin our analysis with a section that examines the relationship between policies and discretion (we return to the meaning of the term 'policy' below). Thereafter, we consider the role that the private law doctrine of estoppel previously played in administrative law (the doctrine has since been replaced by the doctrine of legitimate expectation), and we then examine case law on 'contract and the fettering of discretion' and 'the principle of non-delegation'. In illustrative terms, contract provides a particularly strong example of how arguments of illegality can arise, as it is sometimes said that the terms and conditions of a contract that an authority has entered into will have the future effect of preventing the authority from performing its statutory duties and/or exercising its statutory powers. Thus we will see how the courts here seek to reconcile the pragmatic need for authorities to be able to enter into contracts with the need for those authorities to observe the limits to their statutory powers.[2] We will likewise see in the section on 'non-delegation' how practical realities can inform the case law there too.

The two remaining aspects of illegality that will be discussed are those concerned with (1) review for 'errors of law' and 'errors of fact' and (2) challenges to delegated

---

1 On statutory interpretation see 11.2.
2 See also 19.3.

legislation. As will become apparent, each of these matters present significant challenges for the courts, both in terms of ensuring that judicial 'review' does not become an 'appeal' (*viz* errors of law and of fact) and in terms of the separation of powers more generally (delegated legislation). We will thus see here that there are some important distinctions in the case law that correspond to traditional constitutional assumptions about the public law role the courts. At the same time, it will become apparent that some of those assumptions are being challenged as judicial review evolves to address complex issues of illegality.

12.2 Fettering discretion: deciding by reference to a policy

Where public authorities are given discretion under statute—for instance, to allocate licences or to admit individuals to government-run schemes—they will often adopt policies to guide them in the exercise of their discretion. Use of the term 'policy' here does not carry the connotation of a 'political' choice that would otherwise prompt judicial restraint, as the authority is instead mapping out key considerations and priorities that will inform its decision in any given case.[3] In general terms, the courts accept that it is legitimate for public authorities to formulate policies that are 'legally relevant to the exercise of (their) powers, consistent with the purpose of the enabling legislation, and not arbitrary, capricious or unjust'.[4] However, the courts equally emphasise that authorities must remain free to depart from their policies in individual cases and that they should not adopt policies that are so rigid that they become a rule to be applied in any given case. Should such a policy be adopted, the corresponding decisions of the authority may be challenged either on the ground that they are *ultra vires* the empowering statute or, depending on circumstance, on the ground that the individual has not been given a fair hearing on the matter.[5] This latter point corresponds to a requirement that decision-makers must not pre-judge a matter or 'shut their ears' to individual applications simply because the authority has a particular policy in place.

R v Port of London Authority, ex p Kynoch Ltd[6] is perhaps the leading early authority on some of these principles. Kynoch Ltd was challenging the decision of the port authority not to grant a licence to build a deep-water wharf on the Thames. This was because the authority had a policy to carry out such works itself under powers conferred by the Port of London Act 1908 and the Thames Conservancy Act 1894. While finding that the authority had properly heard and determined licensing applications in this instance, Bankes LJ sets out basic principles in his judgment that are relevant to the understanding of later cases. He explained that:

There must be something in the nature of a refusal to exercise jurisdiction by the tribunal . . . conveyed in one of two ways: there may be an absolute refusal in terms, or there may be conduct amounting to a refusal. In the latter case it is often difficult to draw the line

---

3 For use of the term within its more political meaning see, e.g., *R v Secretary of State for the Environment, ex p Nottinghamshire County Council* [1986] AC 240, where the court emphasised the need for restraint in the context of a challenge to economic measures.

4 Halsbury's Laws of England, Vol 1 (1) para 32.

5 On the requirements of a fair hearing, see ch 17.

6 [1919] 1 KB 176.

between those cases where the tribunal or authority has heard and determined erroneously upon grounds which it was entitled to take into consideration and those cases where it was heard and determined upon grounds outside and beyond its jurisdiction; but this conclusion may be drawn from decided cases, that there is no refusal to hear and determine unless the authority has in substance shut its ears to the application which was made to it, and has determined upon an application which was not made to it.[7]

The principles set out in *ex p Kynoch* were considered and developed in *British Oxygen Co Ltd v Minister of Technology*.[8] British Oxygen was involved in the manufacture and distribution of medical gases that were stored in special cylinders. Over three years the company purchased £4 million worth of these containers at an average of £20 each. Under the Industrial Development Act 1966, the Board of Trade had a discretion to award investment grants for new plants. They had adopted a rule not to approve grant expenditure on items costing less than £25, whatever the numbers of the item. At first instance, the company was awarded a declaration to the effect that this was an abrogation of the discretion conferred on the minister. This was reversed in the Court of Appeal. In the House of Lords, Lord Reid noted that it was difficult to see the difference between a 'rule' and a 'policy' and, while upholding the decision of the Board, he reiterated the general principle whereby anyone who has a statutory discretion must not 'shut his ears to an application' thereby excluding discretion in any particular case on its merits. The decision-maker must instead always be prepared to consider anything new and relevant to the application.

In *R v Secretary of State for the Environment, ex p Brent London Borough Council*,[9] we have a good example of an *ultra vires* fettering of discretion. Prior to issuing an order reducing the rate support grant made available to local authorities, the minister refused to hear representations from councils. When doing so, he maintained that nothing the councils could say would cause him to alter his proposed course of action. This was considered to be *ultra vires*, as he had clearly fettered his discretion by adopting a policy which had been formulated earlier to tackle 'overspending' by councils. It was plain that he was obliged not to declare his unwillingness to listen and that he had to keep an open mind. As the court put it: '[The minister is] entitled to have in mind his policy. To this extent the reference to keeping an open mind does not mean an empty mind. His mind must be kept ajar'.[10] In the absence of his doing so, one can also see a breach of principle that the parties to be affected by a decision should have a right to a fair hearing/to be consulted.

H Lavender & Son Ltd v Minister of Housing and Local Government[11] is another important example. The minister had here dismissed an appeal for planning permission to extract sand, gravel, and ballast from a site on the Thames in the following terms:

. . . it is the Minister's present policy that land in the reservations should not be released for mineral working unless the Minister of Agriculture, Fisheries and Food is not opposed to the working. In the present case the agricultural objection has not been waived, and the Minister has therefore decided not to grant planning permission for the working of the appeal site.

---

7 Ibid, 183.
8 [1971] AC 610.
9 [1983] 3 All ER 321.
10 [1983] 3 All ER 321, 355.
11 [1970] 3 All ER 871.

In fact, the only objection to the application had come from the Ministry of Agriculture and this, without more, had apparently proved determinative of the appeal. This led the court to quash the decision for the reason that the minister had fettered his discretion and improperly delegated his powers. While Willis J pointed out that the courts have no authority to interfere with the way in which a minister carries out his planning policy, and that he is entitled to obtain views from other departments,[12] he was still required to consider objections for himself and not disable himself from exercising his discretion. On the facts before the court, he had failed to observe these minimum requirements.

A further case that illustrates some of the general principles that apply in relation to policies, in particular the requirement that they should not be 'arbitrary', is *R (Rogers) v Swindon NHS Primay Care Trust*.[13] The appellant here was a woman who was suffering from the early stages of breast cancer and wished to challenge the respondent authority's refusal to fund treatment with Herceptin, an unlicensed drug which had not yet been appraised by the National Institute for Clinical Excellence. She had already started treatment with the drug which she had been paying for privately, but she now needed funding from the trust to allow the treatment to continue. However, while the trust had funding available for such treatment, it had formulated a policy of refusing funding unless each patient concerned could demonstrate exceptional circumstances. Accepting the appellant's argument that this policy was irrational, the Court of Appeal held that the policy of withholding the treatment save in exceptional circumstances would be rational only if it was possible to envisage what those exceptional circumstances might be. On the other hand, if it were impossible to envisage such circumstances, the policy would, in practice, amount to a complete refusal of funding, which had been the effect in this case. The court on this basis held that, once the trust had decided that it would fund Herceptin for some patients and that cost was irrelevant, the only reasonable approach was to focus on the patient's clinical needs and to fund patients within the eligible group who were properly prescribed Herceptin by their physician. It followed that the trust's decision to refuse to fund the claimant's treatment with Herceptin had to be quashed and the authority should formulate a new and lawful policy upon which to base future decisions in particular cases. Incidentally, such a decision on narrow legal grounds favouring an individual claimant over the collective interest in the allocation of finite health resources, raises a wider question, namely, whether the courts should be routinely drawn into decisions concerning the rationing of healthcare.[14]

Lastly under this heading, it should be noted that the rule whereby policies cannot fetter discretion does not apply where the source of a power is the Royal prerogative, rather than statute. This is one of the primary points to come out of the Supreme Court's ruling in *R (Sandiford) v Secretary of State for Foreign and Commonwealth Affairs*.[15] The claimant in this case was a British woman who had been sentenced to death, in Indonesia, for drugs offences committed on the island

---

12 For more recent arguments about the unitary nature of the Crown and its ministers see *R (Bapio) v Home Secretary* [2008] 1 AC 1003, discussed later.

13 [2006] 89 BMLR 211.

14 K Syrett, 'Opening Eyes to the Reality of Scarce Health Care Resources? (R (on the application of Rogers) v Swindon NHS Primary Care Trust and Secretary of State for Health' [2006] *Public Law* 664, 669.

15 [2014] UKSC 44, [2014] 1 WLR 2697.

of Bali. She requested financial assistance from the British government to support her appeals within the Indonesian system, but her request was refused on the basis of the government's policy not to provide assistance for overseas criminal trials, including death penalty cases. The policy in question had been adopted on the basis of the Royal prerogative, and the claimant argued, among other things, that it fettered the Secretary of State's discretion. Rejecting that submission, the Supreme Court held that, while policies adopted on the basis of statute cannot be allowed to fetter discretion, the same is not true of policies that are adopted on the basis of the Royal prerogative. Lord Sumption, using the term 'common law power' in place of 'prerogative power', explained the point in the following way:

A common law power is a mere power. It does not confer a discretion in the same sense that a statutory power confers a discretion. A statutory discretionary power carries with it a duty to exercise the discretion one way or the other and in doing so to take account of all relevant matters having regard to its scope. Ministers have common law powers to do many things, and if they choose to exercise such a power they must do so in accordance with ordinary public law principles, that is, fairly, rationally and on a correct appreciation of the law. But there is no duty to exercise the power at all. There is no identifiable class of potential beneficiaries of the common law powers of the Crown in general, other than the public at large. There are no legal criteria analogous to those to be derived from an empowering Act, by which the decision whether to exercise a common law power or not can be assessed. It is up to ministers to decide whether to exercise them, and if so to what extent. It follows that the mere existence of a common law power to do something cannot give rise to any right to be considered, on the part of someone who might hypothetically benefit by it. Such a right must arise, if at all, in other ways, usually by virtue of a legitimate expectation arising from the actual exercise of the power.[16]

On this reasoning, the claimant was unable to advance her case, and related arguments that were centred upon human rights were also dismissed.[17]

12.2.1 Deciding by reference to a policy: the status of circulars and guidance

Beyond the basic principles that govern the use of policies by public authorities, a related issue that can cause difficulty in the case law is the legal status of codes, circulars, and/or guidance that purport to influence how discretion should be exercised. Certainly, if guidance is adopted with reference to statute, issues as to the *vires* of the guidance or other measure may arise, as too may questions about whether the guidance fetters the discretion of the decision-maker. But what of the position where the guidance, or a circular, does not have an identifiable legal basis? Are these simply to be regarded as measures that do not have legal consequences? Indeed, is it even accurate to speak of the guidance as a 'policy' within the sense used above, as 'policies' are there conceived of as frameworks to guide exercises of discretion under statute.

Laker Airways Ltd v Department of Trade[18] is a classic case where there was a sharp distinction drawn between statutory directions (usually to be regarded as mandatory) and statutory guidance (regarded as merely indicative). In *Laker* the guidance

---

16 [2014] UKSC 44, [2014] 1 WLR 2697, 2720, para 83.
17 See further 9.3.2.2.
18 [1977] QB 643.

issued by the minister was considered unlawful since it conflicted with (or cut across) the objectives of the Civil Aviation Act 1971. The facts concerned the right of an airline (Laker's Skytrain) to operate over transatlantic routes. The Civil Aviation Authority (CAA) had powers over the operation of scheduled air services under the Civil Aviation Act 1971, but under section 3(2) the Secretary of State was able to issue circulars giving written guidance to the CAA regarding its functions. The Court of Appeal found that the government's action in cancelling the designation of an airline under a treaty made in 1946 with the USA was unlawful, since the cancellation nullified a licence that had earlier been granted under statutory powers. This was held to be *ultra vires* the Civil Aviation Act 1971. Drawing the above distinction, the court noted that, while the minister had *authority to offer guidance* to the CAA, he could not *direct* it. On this basis, the court held that the guidance was unlawful as it was contrary to the objectives of the Civil Aviation Act 1971. Indeed, while section 4 gave the Secretary of State the power to give directions, his ability to do so was limited to circumstances which were inapplicable here. As Lord Denning put it:

The word direction in section 4 is in stark contrast with the word 'guidance' in section 3. . . . It denotes an order or command which must be obeyed, even though it may be contrary to the general objectives and provisions of the statute. But the word 'guidance' in section 3 does not denote an order or command. It cannot be used so as to reverse or contradict the general objectives of the statute. It can only be used so as to explain, amplify or supplement them. So long as the 'guidance' given by the Secretary of State keeps within the due bounds of guidance, the Authority is under a duty to follow his guidance. Even so the authority is allowed some degree of flexibility. It is to perform its function 'in such a manner as it considers in accordance with the guidance'.[19]

This would therefore suggest that, while an authority is obliged to follow the guidance, the manner of doing so is for the authority itself.

In contrast to a statutory circular, a non-statutory circular offering guidance will often be regarded as being no more than advisory in its effect. Nevertheless, it is now also acknowledged that such guidance can produce legal effects and be challenged as such. An example is provided by *R (Bapio) v Home Secretary*.[20] In this case, the Department of Health was worried that immigrant doctors who were benefiting from special immigration arrangements were occupying posts that would otherwise be open to UK or European Economic Area (EEA) nationals. The arrangements in question had been introduced at a time when there was a shortage of junior doctors but, as that situation had since changed, the Department of Health asked the Home Department to make the relevant rules more restrictive. When the Home Department declined to so, the Department of Health issued employment guidance to the NHS which effectively sought to prioritise the employment prospects of UK and EEA nationals. Holding that the guidance was unlawful, the House of Lords considered that an unwritten and formally unauthorised term was being added to the terms and conditions under which a number of immigrant doctors had been admitted to the UK. Moreover, that term had implications for the ability of the doctors to stay in the UK beyond the initial period granted, and the guidance in that way interfered with their legitimate expectations. The non-statutory 'advice' was thus unlawful.

19 Ibid, 700.
20 [2008] 1 AC 1003.

A further case of interest is that of *Alvi*,[21] which also arose in the immigration context and concerned the status of changes to the Immigration Rules that are made under the Immigration Act 1971 (the rules are not secondary legislation in the classic sense but exist somewhere between the realms of 'hard' and 'soft' law). The particular issue in the case was the relationship between rules, guidance, and administrative practices within the meaning of section 3(2) of the Immigration Act 1971 and the requirement that 'statements of the rules, or of any changes in the rules' must be laid before Parliament in accordance with that section. On the facts of the case, the Home Secretary had introduced a code of practice that contained qualifying thresholds for skilled jobs under the Immigration Rules and according to which the applicant had been refused leave to remain in the UK as a physio-therapy assistant. It was accepted in the case that the relevant code of practice had not been laid before Parliament, and the question was whether the code—which contained detailed information about the qualifying criteria to be applied when making immigration decisions—was in the form a 'rule' under section 3(2). The Supreme Court unanimously dismissed the Secretary of State's appeal from the decision of the Court of Appeal whereby it had quashed the original decision to refuse the applicant's leave to remain in the UK. In doing so the Court held that the code of practice did take the form of a rule as it had the effect of meaning that an application for leave to remain would be refused where an applicant was unable to meet the qualifying thresholds contained therein. The Home Secretary should therefore have laid the code before Parliament in accordance with the Act since guidance that creates a rule requires parliamentary oversight.[22]

12.2.2 Legitimate expectations, legal certainty, circulars, and policies

The doctrine of legitimate expectation, which partly informed the House of Lords judgment in *Bapio*, discussed earlier, is also of a more general importance to case law on policies. We deal with the emergence and nature of the doctrine in much more detail in chapter 15, and it is sufficient to note here that an individual may assert a legitimate expectation by way of trying to prevent an authority from act-ing in a particular way. In many cases, the individual's expectation may be based upon some prior practice of an authority or a representation that it has made, although expectations may also be generated by the existence of a policy. This was the essence of the argument that was made in *R v Secretary of State for the Home Department, ex p Asif Mahmood Khan*,[23] where a husband and wife who were domi-ciled in the UK wished to adopt their nephew who was living in Pakistan. Before applying to do so, they obtained a Home Office circular letter which stated that, although there was no provision in the immigration rules for bringing a child into the UK for adoption, the Secretary of State may exceptionally permit such adop-tion where there was a genuine intention to adopt and the welfare of the child was assured. However, different criteria were then applied to the applicants, who were

---

21 *R (Alvi) v Secretary of State for the Home Department* [2012] UKSC 33, [2012] 1 WLR 2208.

22 Compare *R (Munir) v Secretary of State for the Home Department* [2012] UKSC 32, [2012] 1 WLR 2192, where it was held that there was no requirement to lay before Parliament statements about the granting of concessions in individual cases to those seeking leave to enter or remain in the UK because the state-ments did not amount to a 'practice to be followed' and were not therefore a rule for the purposes of the Immigration Act 1971, s 3(2).

23 [1984] 1 WLR 1337.

informed that their application had been refused because there were no serious or compelling family considerations or other grounds in their case. Finding that the Secretary of State had acted unlawfully, Parker LJ stated that the Secretary of State has a duty to exercise his common law discretion fairly, and that this had not happened here. Although the court accepted that the Secretary of State could change the policy for entry, it said that there must be evidence of that change and that the letter sent out in this case did not indicate that there had been any such change. The officials therefore appeared not to have followed the declared policy, and there had been unfairness to the individuals who had a legitimate expectation that the criteria in the letter would be applied to them. The decision was quashed.

The reference to the doctrine of legitimate expectations in *Khan* raises a further and important point about policies and when decision-makers may depart from them. In general terms, an individual will invoke the doctrine of legitimate expectation where an authority purports to change an earlier policy which the individual has already relied upon. However, while the individual is in such circumstances plainly aware of the policy in question, there have been cases in which the courts have held that an individual can rely upon a policy even when he or she was initially unaware of it. This is the result of *R (Rashid) v Secretary of State for the Home Department*,[24] which concerned the government's failure to apply its policy on Iraqi asylum seekers to the applicant. Although Mr Rashid was originally unaware of the policy—the policy had also since been replaced by a new one—it was accepted that he could have a legitimate expectation that the original policy would apply to him save where there was good reason for it not doing so. In the absence of such reason, it was an abuse of power to take a decision without reference to the relevant policy.

Finally, it should be readily apparent that there is the potential for tension between legitimate expectation and the rule against the fettering of discretion.[25] In short, while the latter rule entails that public authorities should retain for themselves the option of exercising their discretion (whether by way of changing policies or departing from a policy in a particular case), the legitimate expectation doctrine purports to constrain such exercises of discretion by tying the authority to its earlier policies. However, while it might appear that the rule against fettering and the doctrine of legitimate expectation are incompatible, it has recently been suggested that the interplay between them need not be seen in that way. Suggesting that they can, instead, easily be reconciled, Chris Hilson has linked the workings of the rule and doctrine to the wider values of legality, flexibility, and legal certainty that guide the courts on any claim for judicial review.[26] Hence, noting that the rule against fettering is about the values of legality and flexibility, Hilson argues that the flexible application of a *new* policy in the light of legitimate expectation generated by an *old* policy serves to complement the value of legal certainty that is at the very heart of legitimate expectation.[27] In other words, Hilson suggests that the question should not be whether a decision-maker is being tied to an earlier policy,

---

24 [2005] Imm AR 608.

25 For judicial recognition of the point see, e.g., *Findlay v Secretary of State for the Home Department* [1985] AC 318, 338.

26 C Hilson, 'Policies, the Non-Fetter Principle of Substantive Legitimate Expectations: Between a Rock and a Hard Place' [2006] 11(4) *Judicial Review* 289.

27 See further 15.2; and *R (Bhatt Murphy) Independent Assessor* [2008] EWCA Civ 755.

but rather whether it is being required to apply its new policy flexibly in the light of an individual's circumstances. On this view *Khan* provides authority for the proposition that the court is not requiring the decision-maker to apply its previous policy, but rather to consider whether the individual's legitimate expectation merits the making of an exception to the revised policy it has now adopted.

12.2.3 **Human rights and policies**

One final point about policies concerns the judicial approach to the protection of human rights. Although decision-makers are not themselves legally required to take rights into account when formulating their policies, any policy adopted must be compliant with human rights standards.[28] Where a policy is adopted in an area covered by human rights law, it must therefore neither violate the rule against the fettering of discretion nor have an impact that is contrary to an individual's rights. At the same time, if an authority is voluntarily turning its mind to rights considerations and it appears to it that the application of the policy might violate a right, the rule against fettering will be all the more important as the authority could then exercise its discretion to avoid any potential violation.

An example of a policy being adopted in breach of the rule against fettering, in a pre-Human Rights Act context where there were implications for fundamental rights, is *R v Secretary of State for the Home Department, ex p Venables*.[29] The central issue here was the legality of the Home Secretary's decision to fix a minimum 15-year period of detention for the child killers of a two-year old boy called Jamie Bulger. This 'tariff', which was considerably in excess of that originally fixed by the judiciary, had been set by comparative reference to the mandatory life sentences given to adults who were convicted of murder. Holding that the Secretary of State had acted unlawfully, the House of Lords stated that a sentence of detention during Her Majesty's pleasure passed on a young offender under section 53(1) of the Children and Young Persons Act 1933 was not properly to be equated with a mandatory sentence of life imprisonment for an adult. Their Lordships also held that a sentence under section 53(1) required the Secretary of State to consider from time to time whether the continued detention of the young offender was justified. While the House of Lords accepted that the Secretary of State had discretion as regards matters of punishment and deterrence, it held that a policy adopted by him in 1993 whereby he said that the period to be served would in no circumstances be varied was overly rigid. In the result, the Secretary of State had fettered his discretion (and note that the House of Lords later held that it was inconsistent with Article 6 of the European Convention on Human Rights (ECHR) for the Secretary of State to play any role in the sentencing process).[30]

In contrast, *R v Chief Constable of the North Wales Police, ex p AB*[31] is a case in which it was held that a policy was compliant with human rights standards. The central issue here was when it was lawful for the police to disclose information about the whereabouts of paedophiles who had been released from prison having

---

28 See *R (SB) v Headteacher and Governors of Denbigh High School* [2006] UKHL 15; and see 4.4.4 and 13.6.1.

29 [1998] AC 407, HL.

30 *R (Anderson) v Home Secretary* [2003] 1 AC 837.

31 [1999] QB 396.

served sentences for sexual offences committed against children. The offenders moved to accommodation at a number of locations at which they were attacked by the press and members of the public, before they eventually obtained a caravan and moved to a caravan site in North Wales. The North Wales police received a report from another force that the men concerned were very dangerous and presented a considerable risk to children. The police asked them to move on and, when the applicants refused to do so, the police, acting with reference to a policy on the risks presented by paedophiles, showed the camp-site owner material which had appeared in the local press. This led the owner to ask the applicants to move on and, on having done so, the applicants challenged the lawfulness of the police decision to disclose information about them to the owner. Their application was dismissed by both the High Court and the Court of Appeal. Both courts accepted that a broader community interest was engaged on the facts and the police could lawfully disclose the identity of the paedophiles in accordance with its policy. Such disclosures were said to be permissible only where, as here, they were necessary in the public interest (although the Court of Appeal also noted that, before making such disclosures, the police should learn as much about the individuals as they could and, where possible, give the individuals concerned a chance to comment on the information concerned). In the instant case, the original policy of the police was not unlawful, and nor was their action in giving effect to that policy.

Recognition that policies should be compatible with the ECHR can then be seen in a number of cases arising in the prison context. For instance, in *R v Secretary of State for the Home Department, ex p Simms*,[32] which pre-dated the coming into force of the Human Rights Act 1998, a policy restricting access by prisoners to journalists was declared unlawful because such a policy was regarded as an unjustified interference with the right to freedom of expression. Similarly, in *R v Governor of Frankland Prison, ex p Russell*[33] it was held that, while a prison governor was entitled to lay down conditions which regulated access to food by protesting prisoners, the policy had to be administered flexibly to ensure that the prisoner was adequately nourished. Finding that the policy in question in that case did not meet these requirements, the court referred to *Simms* when holding that, in the absence of express statutory authorisation, 'prison regulations expressed in general terms were presumed to be subject to fundamental human rights'.[34] In *R v Home Secretary, ex p Daly*, one of the first House of Lords cases under the Human Rights Act 1998, it was held that a prison policy on the searching of cells was disproportionate and contrary to the Article 8 ECHR right to respect for correspondence.[35]

12.3 Estoppel and the fettering of discretion

We turn now to address the significance of the estoppel doctrine that was previously of some importance in administrative law, but which has become less so due to the ongoing development of the doctrine of legitimate expectation. Estoppel,

---

32 [2000] 2 AC 115.
33 [2000] 1 WLR 2027.
34 [2000] 1 WLR 2027, 2034.
35 [2001] 2 AC 532; and 13.6.1.

which has equitable origins, can for these purposes be defined as the doctrine that prevents one party (a public authority) from going back on a representation made to another party (the individual) where the individual has relied upon the earlier representation to his or her detriment. While the doctrine would, on this definition, appear to have much in common with legitimate expectation,[36] its role in administrative law was different insofar as it related to representations that were either *ultra vires* the authority or, while *intra vires* the authority, made by unauthorised officers. Where an authority subsequently sought to exercise its discretion in a manner that was contrary to, for instance, its earlier unlawful representation, the individual would thus argue that the authority should be estopped from doing so for reasons of fairness. However, arguments of this kind also raised important questions about the rule of law, as a ruling in favour of the individual would mean that the authority would be bound to a representation that went beyond the powers that Parliament had originally delegated to it. A ruling in favour of the individual would also serve to fetter the authority's discretion in the sense that it would be held to an earlier *ultra vires* representation and not be allowed to make a new—and lawful—choice.

The corresponding body of case law on estoppel is complex and sometimes contradictory. However, the first fundamental principle to be derived from it is that the courts would not allow arguments based upon estoppel to validate illegal action by public bodies, or to extend their powers beyond those given by statute. Hence in *Rhyl Urban District Council v Rhyl Amusements Ltd*,[37] the relations between the parties had been governed by a lease since 1932, and it was argued by the company that the council was therefore estopped from denying the validity of the lease. Nevertheless, the court issued a declaration that a lease which had been granted to the defendant company was void. This was because under the relevant statute the granting of a lease required the consent of the minister and this consent had not been obtained.[38]

A second cardinal principle was that estoppel could not be employed to stop the performance of a duty by a body where that duty had been imposed on it by statute. The main authority here is *Maritime Electric Company Ltd v General Dairies Ltd*,[39] which concerned a private electricity supply company that was under a statutory duty to supply electricity at a controlled price. Due to its own error the company had charged only a tenth of the correct amount to General Dairies over more than a two-year period, and General Dairies, in turn, had acted on the incorrect amount charged in setting their own prices. It was held that the electricity company was still under a statutory duty to collect the full amount notwithstanding its mistake. Lord Maugham stated, 'it cannot therefore avail in such a case to release the plaintiff from an obligation to obey such a statute, nor can it enable the defendant to escape from a statutory obligation of such a kind on his part' ([1937] 1 All ER 748, 753).

More difficult was the circumstance where the aggrieved individual sought to enforce a representation that was *intra vires* the authority but which had been made by an employee who was not authorised to make the representation. If we take a

---

36 See ch 15.

37 [1959] 1 All ER 259.

38 See also *R v Secretary of State for the Home Department, ex p Naheed Ejaz* [1994] QB 496, per Stuart-Smith LJ, at 504c–e: 'The Secretary of State cannot, by mistaking his own powers, enlarge them beyond what Parliament has granted and he cannot be estopped from asserting that he lacked the necessary power, if that be the case.'

39 [1937] 1 All ER 748.

typical example, a member of the public would approach a public body for information in regard to a matter that is normally the concern of that body, for instance
the need for planning permission. The individual then enters into communication
with an officer of the planning authority, who tells the individual that planning
permission is to be granted. However, in reality the decision on permission is a
matter for another decision-maker within the authority and, when the relevant
decision subsequently is taken, it is a decision to refuse permission. Would the
doctrine of estoppel provide the individual with any protection, or was the fact
that the original communication was not authorised decisive?

The answer here was that estoppel could offer some protection to the individual
where he or she had been misled by the actions of officials. The leading early case
on the point is *Robertson v Minister of Pensions*.[40] This was a case that concerned an
army officer who had been injured in December 1939. His entitlement to a pension
depended upon whether a disability from which he suffered was caused by his
period of military service. He wrote to the War Office inquiring about a pension
and received a reply stating that 'your disability is attributable to military service'.
On the basis of this letter he did not bother to have an independent medical consultation. Some time later the Ministry of Pensions, which now dealt with military pensions, decided that the disability was due to an injury sustained in 1927.
Robertson appealed against that decision. His appeal was allowed by Denning J
(as he then was) who stated that, if a government department takes it on itself to
assume authority on a matter, a person is entitled to rely on that authority and cannot be expected to know the limits of the authority. Indeed, the judge was to make
substantially the same point in the later case of *Howell v Falmouth Boat Construction
Co Ltd*,[41] where he said: when 'government officers, in their dealings with a subject,
take on themselves to assume authority in a matter with which (the subject) is
concerned, the subject is entitled to rely on their having the authority which they
assume . . . and he ought not to suffer if (the officers) exceed it'.[42]

This view did not, however, enjoy widespread judicial support, and subsequent
case law narrowed the Denning approach. For instance, in *Western Fish Products Ltd
v Penwith District Council*,[43] a company had started building work on the basis of
representations made to it, and it had later been told by an official that an application for planning permission was necessary only as a formality. However, the application for permission was subsequently rejected, and the issue was whether the
authority could be estopped given the earlier representations and correspondence.
In his judgment, Megaw LJ said that there were only two exceptions to the rule that
public authorities could not be estopped from exercising their powers. The first was
where the authority had the power to delegate some of its functions to the officer
and there were special circumstances to justify the applicant in believing that the
officer could bind the authority.[44] The second exception was where the authority
had waived a procedural requirement relating to the matter before it. Under those
circumstances, it could be stopped from relying upon the lack of formality.[45]

---

40 [1949] 1 KB 227.
41 [1950] 2 KB 16.
42 Ibid, 26.
43 [1981] 2 All ER 204.
44 The judge cited *Lever Finance Ltd v Westminster (City) London Borough Council* [1971] QB 222.
45 The judge here cited *Wells v Minister of Housing and Local Government* [1967] 2 All ER 104.

This more narrow approach was clearly conditioned by a concern to prioritise legality as a defining value in administrative law, and the case law remains important for that reason. However, as we have noted above, the corresponding judicial pronouncements are also of less contemporary value, as the courts have said that the issues addressed by estoppel should now be resolved with reference to the legitimate expectation doctrine. This is because the legitimate expectation doctrine is a purely public law doctrine that has been developed with reference to considerations of legality, fairness, and the public interest.[46] Given the point, it is thought that an equitable doctrine is ill-suited to the resolution of public law matters and that it should for that reason be placed in abeyance in the administrative law context. As Lord Hoffmann put it in *R v East Sussex County Council, ex p Reprotech (Pebsham) Ltd*:

In any case, I think that it is unhelpful to introduce private law concepts of estoppel into planning law . . . There is of course an analogy between a private law estoppel and the public law concept of legitimate expectation created by a public authority, the denial of which may amount to an abuse of power [see *ex p Coughlan*]. But it is no more than an analogy because remedies against public authorities also have to take into account the interests of the general public which the authority exists to promote. Public law can also take into account the hierarchy of individual rights which exist under the Human Rights Act 1998 [e.g., see *Coughlan*], . . . while ordinary property rights are in general far more limited by considerations of public interest [e.g., see *R (Alconbury Developments Ltd) v Secretary of State for the Environment, Transport and the Regions* [2001] 2 WLR 1389 (HL)]. It is true that in early cases . . . Lord Denning MR used the language of estoppel . . . At that time the public law concepts of abuse of power and legitimate expectation were very undeveloped and no doubt the analogy of estoppel seemed useful. In the *Western Fish* case the Court of Appeal tried its best to reconcile these invocations of estoppel with the general principle that a public authority cannot be estopped from exercising a statutory discretion or performing a public duty. But the results did not give universal satisfaction: see the comments of Dyson J in the *Powergen* case [2000] JPL 629, at 638. It seems to me that in this area, public law has already absorbed whatever is useful from the moral values which underlie the private law concept of estoppel and the time has come for it to stand upon its own two feet.[47]

In other words, in public law the principle of estoppel has been superceded by the development of legitimate expectation, and the case law now draws upon legitimate expectation when previously it may have been decided with reference to estoppel.[48]

12.4 Fettering discretion by contract

We now need to consider whether public bodies can enter into contracts if the terms of the contract may conflict with the lawful exercise of power and thereby potentially fetter the exercise of discretion. There are several questions for the courts to answer in this area. For instance, how far can a public body go in binding itself by contract or other undertaking? Will there be any contractual liability if a

---

46 See ch 15.

47 [2002] UKHL 8, [2002] 4 All ER 58, 66.

48 See further W Wade and C Forsyth, *Administrative Law*, 10th edn (Oxford: Oxford University Press, 2009), 283–4.

body, when exercising its statutory powers, acts so as to breach an earlier contractual undertaking it has given? What will be the position if a body believes itself to be bound by a contract and as a result leaves itself in the position where it fails to exercise, because of this restriction, an important duty or a discretionary power? Of course, in trying to answer these questions the courts are inevitably involved in something approaching a balancing exercise and the resulting case law is often confused and lacking in clarity.

An early authority which illustrates the point that a contract may be broken if it substantially interferes with the exercise of a statutory power is *Ayr Harbour Trustees v Oswald*.[49] The harbour trustees had statutory powers under the Ayr Harbour Act 1879 compulsorily to purchase land which was to be used, as need might arise, for the construction of works to the coastline of the harbour. To reduce the amount of compensation payable to one particular landowner, the trustees agreed to a covenant that they would never construct works on the land acquired which might have the effect of cutting him off from access to the waters or the harbour. In holding this to be *ultra vires* the court stated that, irrespective of motive, a contract purporting to bind the trustees and their successors would be void, since it would inevitably be incompatible with the objectives of the statute. Parliament's intention was to vest the trustees of the harbour with power for the public good without limitation.

Dowty Boulton Paul Ltd v Wolverhampton Corporation[50] can be usefully compared with *Ayr Harbour*, as it confirms that the courts will not readily allow authorities to escape from their contractual obligations. In 1936 the corporation conveyed an aerodrome on a 99-year lease to the plaintiffs. As part of the agreement the plaintiffs contracted to erect a factory for manufacturing aircraft and parts, and they were also allowed to use the aerodrome for flights in connection with their business. In addition, the lease for the land provided that it could be repurchased by the council if it was not being used for this original purpose. By 1957 the factory was no longer manufacturing aircraft in accordance with the terms of the lease but the aerodrome was still in use. The council sought to reacquire the land under the lease for local needs in housing, shops, and schools under section 163(1) of the Local Government Act 1933. It was held that, despite the change in circumstances, the local authority could not now override the rights of the first conveyance. The original agreement, as a whole, did not constitute an unlawful fetter on the council and could not simply be set aside.

Stringer v Minister of Housing and Local Government[51] is an example of a contract being held to be *ultra vires* the powers of the authority. Cheshire County Council and Congleton Rural District Council entered into a contract with Manchester University, which entailed that the councils would no longer be in a position to approve development schemes in a particular area. This was in order to protect the operation of the radio telescope at Jodrell Bank from interference. The court held that the protection of the telescope was a factor which the authorities were entitled to take into account as a relevant consideration in grants of planning permission. However, the above agreement was judged to have been *ultra vires* section 17(1)

---

49 (1883) 8 App Cas 623.
50 [1971] 2 All ER 277.
51 [1971] 1 All ER 65.

of the Town and Country Planning Act 1962 since it led the authorities to ignore other statutory obligations, in particular the proper exercise of their discretion in relation to other applications for planning permission. Thus, the contract was likely to have adverse effects on third parties and was therefore fundamentally incompatible with the councils' obligations under the Town and Country Planning Act 1962.

Restrictive covenants are discussed in relation to a local authority's discretionary powers in *R v Hammersmith and Fulham London Borough Council, ex p Beddowes*.[52] After a dispute over policy the council resolved to sell to a private company some of an estate that was in a state of disrepair. Only a proportion of the estate was to be sold, but the sales included covenants to indicate to the developer that further blocks were to be sold on similar terms in the future to the same developer for owner occupation. Following a change in the political control of the council, the covenants were challenged as a fetter on the discretion of the council as a housing authority. It was held that an authority cannot extinguish its statutory powers by way of covenants; however, if a scheme is consistent with the legislative objective of providing housing accommodation within the purposes of existing legislation, then covenants will be *intra vires*. Kerr LJ stated, in a dissenting judgment, that the covenants that were intended to ensure the irrevocable maintenance of these policies in the event of political change were indeed *ultra vires* and unreasonable.

12.5 Fettering discretion by wrongful delegation

12.5.1 General principle

Where statute gives a decision-maker a discretionary power, whether of a judicial, legislative, or administrative nature, it is generally unlawful for the decision-maker to delegate that power of decision to another person or body unless the statute itself expressly provides for such delegation. This notion is sometimes expressed in the Latin maxim *delegatus non potest delegare*, which means that a body or person to whom power has been delegated by Parliament cannot itself delegate the power. However, it should be noted at the outset that this does not necessarily mean that civil servants or local government officials are prevented from taking executive decisions on behalf of ministers or local authorities. Central government powers are always vested in the Secretary of State, and it is obvious that he or she cannot make every individual decision and that reliance on others is inevitable (a commonplace that has been approved of in the case law). However, more difficult is the position in respect of large organisations that may have to divide responsibilities between various departments, committees, and officers, and the courts will here be required to decide by reference to the statute whether unlawful delegation has occurred.[53] Moreover, it appears that the nature of the functions that have been delegated will be of particular relevance in determining whether the body has

---

52 [1987] 1 All ER 369.

53 See, e.g., as regards the police, *DPP v Haw* [2007] EWHC 1931, [2008] 1 WLR 379: power to delegate Police Commissioner's functions under the Serious Organised Crime and Police Act 2005, s 134, as read with the Police Act 1996, ss 9C and 9F.

acted beyond its powers as, to the extent that certain administrative functions can be carried out by others, the same may not be true when it comes to decisions that have implications for an individual's fundamental rights.[54]

12.5.2 Central and local government

The leading judicial authority for the proposition that it is not unlawful for a civil servant to take a decision on behalf of a minister is *Carltona Ltd v Commissioner of Works*.[55] This case famously set out the general position that, even when the statute uses the term 'minister', Parliament will expect only that the power is to be exercised by an appropriate official. In the case, the Commissioner for Works had been given powers to requisition property under regulation 51(1) of the Defence Regulations 1939, which were in operation during the Second World War. Carltona's factory had been taken over under this provision, but the notice had been issued by a civil servant of the rank of assistant secretary, acting on behalf of the minister. In holding that there had been no illegality Lord Greene MR, in a classic statement about the principle of delegation and ministerial responsibility, said:

functions which are given to ministers (and constitutionally properly given to ministers because they are constitutionally responsible) are functions so multifarious that no minister could personally attend to all of them . . . It cannot be supposed that [the particular statutory provision] meant that in each case, the minister in person should direct his mind to the matter. The duties imposed upon ministers and the powers given to ministers are normally exercised under the authority of the ministers by responsible officials of the department. Public business could not be carried on if that were not the case. Constitutionally, the decision of such an official is of course the decision of the minister, the minister is responsible. It is he who must answer before Parliament for anything his officials have done under his authority, and, if for an important matter he selected an official of such junior standing that he could not be expected competently to perform the work, the minister would have to answer for that in Parliament.[56]

Lord Greene is here making it plain that, from a constitutional standpoint, the act of the official is considered to be the act of the minister, and that there are convincing pragmatic reasons for allowing decisions to be taken in this way. This has been termed the 'alter ego' principle and, in considering the reach of the principle in *R v Secretary of State for the Home Department, ex p Oladehinde*,[57] Woolf LJ was of the opinion that it should be regarded as implicit in statute in the absence of any clear contrary indication by Parliament. Lord Donaldson MR also indicated that the constitutional power to take decisions in this way could be negatived or confined only by express statutory provision.[58] On the other hand, there has been some discussion as to the circumstances in which the minister will be expected to exercise powers in person, and it has been suggested that this should be the case where the matters under consideration concern issues of personal liberty.[59]

---

54 For judicial consideration of this point see, e.g., *Re Henry's Application* [2004] NIQB 11, paras 37–9.

55 [1943] 2 All ER 560.

56 Ibid, 563.

57 [1991] 1 AC 254.

58 See also *R v Secretary of State for the Home Department, ex p Doody* [1994] 1 AC 531, HL.

59 See, e.g., *Liversidge v Anderson* [1942] AC 206, where a detention order was signed during wartime by the minister himself; and on the alter ego principle see further D Lanham, 'Delegation and the Alter Ego Principle' (1984) *Law Quarterly Review* 587.

In a recent prison case, it has also been held that the roles of Prison Governors and the Secretary of State for Justice are not to be confused when segregation decisions are taken under section 47 of the Prison Act 1952 and the Prison Rules 1999. Governors hold an independent statutory office and, when they make segregation decisions, the Secretary of State has a distinct role in reviewing those decisions that only he or his officials can perform as persons who are independent of the internal management of prisons.[60]

In matters concerning local government, section 101 of the Local Government Act 1972 allows local authorities to delegate functions to officers and to committees. In these matters the courts have also acknowledged the need for some degree of flexibility. For example, in *Provident Mutual Life Assurance v Derby City Council*,[61] it was accepted that administrative matters necessary for the collection of rates, which had been placed in the hands of the treasurer, could be exercised by the treasurer's staff. However, it has been established that delegation under section 101 of the 1972 Act does not allow the power to be exercised by a single member.[62]

12.5.3 Statutory bodies

We can return now the basic principle about non-delegation, which can be illustrated with reference to *Barnard v National Dock Labour Board*.[63] The Dock Workers (Regulations) Order 1947 set up a National Dock Labour Board to administer a Scheme under which powers and relevant functions were to be delegated to local boards. Amongst these functions were disciplinary powers. The London Dock Labour Board passed a resolution which delegated to the port manager such disciplinary powers. Subsequently, the port manager suspended a number of dockers as part of an industrial dispute. In the High Court this was considered to be an administrative function that could be delegated, but this view was unanimously rejected in the Court of Appeal. Denning LJ held that it was a judicial function because it affected the rights of individuals, and that it was a basic principle that no tribunal could delegate a judicial function. This principle was approved by the House of Lords in a similar case, *Vine v National Dock Labour Board*.[64] On this occasion a dock worker had been dismissed by a disciplinary committee set up by the South Coast Local Dock Labour Board: this was a judicial power too important to delegate.

On the other hand, where functions are considered to be administrative in nature delegation may remain *intra vires*. For instance, in *R v Race Relations Board, ex p Selvarajan*,[65] it was accepted that the Race Relations Board could establish a committee in order to investigate and conduct preliminary inquiries into a claim of racial discrimination. The court held that the Board was master of its own procedure

---

60 *R (Bourgass) v Secretary of State for Justice* [2015] UKSC 54, [2015] 3 WLR 457.

61 (1981) 79 LGR 297.

62 See *R v Secretary of State for Education and Science, ex p Birmingham City Council* (1984) 83 LGR 79. See also *R v Servite Houses and Wandsworth London Borough Council, ex p Goldsmith* [2000] 3 CCLR 325, regarding an arrangement made between the council and a housing association to provide a residential home—the housing association could not be regarded as the agent of the council because the council had no power to delegate beyond its committees and officers.

63 [1953] 1 All ER 1113.

64 [1957] AC 488.

65 [1975] 1 WLR 1686.

and that it could delegate particular tasks to staff members. This was because it would not be practical for the whole body to be engaged in these activities.

The issue of delegation was also considered in *R v Admiralty Board of the Defence Council, ex p Coupland*.[66] Here the applicant, in taking a complaint before the Board, argued that it could not base its judgment upon material gathered during an investigation. The Board had relied on a series of summaries of the material prepared by an officer. Dyson J held the Board could delegate responsibility for the conduct of the investigation and the preparation of summaries, but it could never delegate its duty to determine the case by means of a fair hearing. This duty had been undermined by the failure of the Board to consider carefully whether summaries of the evidence of controversial witnesses of fact, where a view needed to be formed as to their credibility, could be relied upon. The decision of the Board was quashed.

12.6 **Errors of law and errors of fact**

The next issue to consider is 'error of law' and 'error of fact'. It should already be evident that judicial review is primarily concerned with the legality of decisions, not with their merits.[67] While the courts will therefore regard errors of law as within their province, evidently correctable by review, they show a great deal more reluctance to intervene in alleged errors of fact (although note that it may not always be easy to distinguish matters of fact and law, for instance are inferences drawn from established facts to be regarded as matters of law, matters of fact, or matters of mixed law and fact?).[68] This reluctance is essentially conditioned by separation of powers concerns and the understanding that the courts may not have the necessary expertise to assess factual situations[69] (although note that the courts are also reluctant to intervene for the reason that doing so might invite vexatious litigation). Indeed, where a matter can be described as one of 'fact and degree' the emphasis on the limited nature of the judicial role can become even more pronounced. A matter of degree is one upon which reasonable people may arrive at different conclusions given the same evidence and, as conclusions on such matters will often be reached by decision-makers who are more experienced in the area than are judges, the courts accept that the decision-makers are better placed to make corresponding value judgements. As Lord Scarman put it in *R v Barnet London Borough Council, ex p Nilish Shah*: 'If (the decision-maker) gets the law right, or, as lawyers would put it, directs itself correctly in law, the question of fact . . . is for the authority, not the court, to decide. The merits of the application are for the (decision-maker) subject only to judicial review to ensure that the authority has proceeded according to the law'.[70]

Nevertheless, it would be misleading to suggest that all errors of fact lie beyond the reach of courts in judicial review proceedings, as the courts will now review

---

66 [1999] COD 27.

67 See further 8.3 on the 'supervisory/appellate' distinction.

68 On the difficulties see, e.g., *R (Jones) v First Tier Tribunal (Social Entitlement Chamber)* [2013] UKSC 19, [2013] 2 AC 48.

69 See *R v Hillingdon London Borough Council, ex p Pulhofer* [1986] AC 484, 518, Lord Brightman.

70 [1983] 2 AC 309, 341.

for: (a) error of precedent fact; (b) the taking into account of irrelevant considerations/failure to take account of relevant considerations; (c) 'no evidence'; and (d) error of material fact. As we will see below, case law under these sub-headings has sometimes been highly inventive and has tested the strength of the supervisory/appellate distinction.

12.6.1 Error of precedent fact

An error of precedent fact is made when a decision-maker takes a decision in the absence of facts which must exist objectively before the decision-maker has the power of decision under legislation (such facts were previously also described as 'jurisdictional', although that term has fallen into disuse in the years after the *Anisminic* case).[71] Review for error of precedent fact can, as such, be linked directly to the ground of illegality as defined by Lord Diplock in the *GCHQ* case,[72] as the courts are here enquiring whether the decision-maker has the power to make the decision that it has purported to make. In other words, the courts are not concerned with the decision-maker's evaluation of facts or the respective weight that has been given to a particular fact, but rather with the question whether the required facts exist so as to allow the decision-maker to exercise the power entrusted by the legislature. In the absence of the facts there can therefore be no lawful exercise of the power.

One of the leading cases on precedent fact is *White & Collins v Minister of Health*.[73] Ripon Borough Council issued a compulsory purchase order affecting 23 acres of land owned by White & Collins, who maintained that the land was protected under section 75 of the Housing Act 1936. This provided that powers were not to be exercised over land forming any 'part of any park, garden or pleasure ground required for the amenity or convenience of any house'. After a public inquiry had taken place the minister confirmed the compulsory purchase order, but this was quashed. This was because the issuing of the order depended on a finding of fact; that is, the statute provided that the order could only be made if it was clear that the land in question was not part of a park, or not to be required for the amenity or convenience of any house. In the context of the case the key words were 'part of a park' and, as there was no legal definition of the phrase, the court had to resort to the *Oxford English Dictionary*. Having done so, the court concluded that the land was part of a park and that the minister's order should be quashed. Were it to be otherwise, the minister would have been able to extend his power beyond that authorised by the statute.

It should also be noted that the courts will look closely at issues of precedent fact where any corresponding administrative decision could have implications for an individual's fundamental rights. The foremost authority here remains *R v Secretary of State for the Home Department, ex p Khawaja*,[74] which involved a challenge to the

---

71 *Anisminic Ltd v Foreign Compensation Commission* [1969] 2 AC 147; and 10.2. But for more recent use of the term see, e.g., *R (A) v Croydon LBC* [2009] UKSC 8, [2009] 1 WLR 2557 (question whether a person was a child for the purposes of the Children Act 1989 variously described as a question of jurisdictional and/or precedent fact).

72 See *Council of Civil Service Unions v Minister for the Civil Service* [1985] AC 374, 410–11.

73 [1939] 2 KB 838.

74 [1983] 1 All ER 765.

Home Secretary's power under the Immigration Act 1971 to detain and remove persons from the UK once they had been designated an 'illegal entrant'. It was held that all the evidence should be before the court so that it could determine as a matter of precedent fact whether an individual was or was not an illegal entrant, as the resulting implications for the individual could be very far-reaching. In other words, their Lordships were reluctant to allow an individual's rights to be affected by the decision of an official acting alone, and great emphasis was placed on the judicial role in safeguarding the individual's rights.

12.6.2 Relevant and irrelevant considerations

We have dealt with relevant and irrelevant considerations in much more detail elsewhere,[75] where we provided examples of case law and comment on this important aspect of review. However, for present purposes it is sufficient to state that the courts are, in effect, reviewing for error of fact here insofar as they ask whether the decision-maker has failed to take into account all relevant considerations and/or to disregard irrelevant considerations. Considerations for these purposes will ordinarily be identified expressly or impliedly in the statute that underpins the decision, and a decision-maker who fails to accord with the terms of the statute will thus act illegally within the meaning of the *GCHQ* formulation.[76] At the same time, the courts may also intervene where there are 'matters so obviously material to a decision on a particular project that anything short of direct consideration of them . . . would not be in accordance with the intention of the Act'.[77] While it could be possible to speak of 'illegality' here too, it is also possible to couch a failure to have regard for such considerations as unreasonable. The question, in other words, would be whether the failure to take account of the considerations was so unreasonable that no reasonable authority could have acted in that way.[78]

The orthodox judicial approach to arguments of relevancy is one that (a) enquires whether all relevant considerations have been taken into account by the decision-maker and irrelevant ones ignored and, if so, (b) allows the decision to stand subject to arguments of unreasonableness, perversity, etc. The rationale for this approach is that it prevents courts becoming involved in disputes about the respective weights given to relevant/factual considerations, albeit that it is an approach that is not without exception. For instance, the courts have long been willing to subject decisions that impact upon fundamental rights to a common law test of 'anxious scrutiny' where arguments of relevancy arise;[79] and the proportionality principle may also entail some modification of approach. This principle, which applies in Human Rights Act 1998 cases but which is of increasing importance in judicial review more generally,[80] requires that courts set a decision against the interests affected by it and assess whether the decision-maker has struck the appropriate balance between the two. As we will see in chapter 13, this raises difficult questions about the role of the courts, as they can, in effect, start to make determinations

---

75 See 11.5.
76 [1985] AC 374, 410–11.
77 See Lord Scarman in *Re Findlay* [1985] AC 318, 333–4.
78 On unreasonableness see ch 13.
79 See *Bugdaycay v Secretary of State for the Home Department* [1987] AC 514; and 4.2.1.
80 See ch 13.

about matters of fact and degree that would otherwise be matters for the decision-maker. It is perhaps not surprising that the proportionality principle has therefore been aligned to a 'discretionary area of judgement' doctrine that seeks to ensure judicial self-restraint in accordance with the context of discrete cases.[81]

12.6.3 'No evidence'

The basis for intervention here is very simple to explain: if a decision is unsupported by any evidence, or the evidence taken as a whole is not reasonably capable of supporting the decision, it cannot stand. For example, in *Coleen Properties Ltd v Minister of Housing and Local Government*[82] two rows of houses in Clark Street and Sidney Street were declared by Tower Hamlets Council to be clearance areas under the Housing Act 1957. In addition, the council sought to use its powers under section 43(2) of the Act to acquire further property which was considered 'reasonably necessary' for the satisfactory development of the cleared area. This further property included the 'first class' Clark House, but at a public inquiry no evidence had been brought by the council to support the need for this acquisition and the inspector had reported to the minister that the acquisition was not reasonably necessary for the scheme. Nevertheless, the minister, who had before him only the inspector's report and no other evidence (neither had the minister seen Clark House), confirmed that the property should be included in the compulsory purchase order. In the Court of Appeal, Lord Denning held that the minister was in error in reversing the inspector's recommendation as the property could come within section 43(2) of the Act only where there was evidence to support that finding. Having regard to the absence of such evidence before the inspector and to the inspector's clear opinion that the acquisition of Clark House was not reasonably necessary, there was therefore no material on which the minister could properly overrule the inspector's recommendation. In other words, the question of reasonable necessity was not a question of planning policy but was an inference of fact on which the minister could not overrule the inspector's recommendation unless there was material sufficient to justify that outcome.

12.6.4 Error of material fact

Finally, it is possible to challenge a decision as vitiated by an error of material fact. Such errors are made where there is 'misunderstanding or ignorance of an established and relevant fact' and/or where the decision-maker acts 'upon an incorrect basis of fact'.[83] Although it was originally thought that this sub-heading existed merely as one aspect of relevant and irrelevant considerations, it now appears that it allows the courts to intervene where an error of fact causes 'unfairness' to an individual, as this is said to be a matter of law. This is the result of *E v*

---

81 See 13.6.2.

82 [1971] 1 WLR 433.

83 See *Secretary of State for Education and Science v Tameside Metropolitan Borough Council* [1977] AC 1014, 1030, Lord Scarman, and 1047, Lord Wilberforce; see too *R (Alconbury) v Secretary of State for the Environment, Transport and the Regions* [2003] 2 AC 295, para 53, Lord Slynn.

Home Secretary,[84] which arose in the asylum context and concerned the question whether the decision of a tribunal could be appealed on a point of law where the tribunal had refused to admit new evidence when hearing an appeal. Holding that intervention would be justified, 'at least in those statutory contexts where the parties share an interest in co-operating to achieve the correct result',[85] the Court of Appeal equated the role of the court in an appeal on a point of law (as in the instant case) with the role of the court on a claim for judicial review. Viewing 'unfairness' as a question of law, the Court held that it was permissible for the courts to intervene where a mistake of fact had that legal consequence for the individual. However, the Court also said that before a finding of unfairness could be made it would have to be shown that the tribunal whose decision was under appeal had made a mistake as to an established fact which was uncontentious and objectively verifiable, including a mistake as to the availability of evidence on a particular matter. The Court of Appeal moreover said that it would have to be established that the appellant or his advisers had not been responsible for the mistake, and that the mistake had played a material though not necessarily decisive part in the tribunal's reasoning. Only then could the Court legitimately intervene and consider whether the tribunal had made a mistake of fact giving rise to unfairness such as amounted to an error of law.[86]

The emergence of this species of review for error of fact is both potentially problematic and very significant for public law.[87] Its potentially problematic aspect concerns the apparent scope for judicial intervention that now exists, as it is difficult to identify with certainty where the boundaries of intervention for reasons of 'fairness' are to be found. This is because fairness is an open-ended common law construct and, while the courts may wish to use the logic of *E* primarily when fundamental rights are in issue (as in *E* itself), it may be that fairness could be used to justify intervention in an ever more broad range of cases. At the same time, such broadening review may be necessary to enable the courts to meet the demands of Article 6 of the ECHR, and it is here that error of material fact is significant. As we will see in chapter 17, Article 6 of the ECHR requires that an individual whose 'civil rights' are in issue should have access to an independent and impartial tribunal with 'full jurisdiction' in the matter before it. However, as the grounds for judicial review have not traditionally allowed the High Court to substitute its own decision for that of the decision-maker—*viz* the 'supervisory/appellate' distinction—it was initially thought that judicial review may not be able to satisfy the demands of Article 6 of the ECHR when the High Court is the forum within which to protect civil rights. The emergence of review for error of material fact has, however, since gone some way towards addressing those concerns and the European Court of Human Rights (ECtHR) has accepted that judicial review will be sufficient in some (though not necessarily all) cases. We return to this matter at 17.4.5.

---

84 [2004] 2 WLR 1351.

85 Ibid, para 66.

86 For commentary see P Craig, 'Judicial Review, Appeal and Factual Error' [2004] *Public Law* 788.

87 For application of *E* see, e.g., *Re Gracey's Application* [2014] NIQB 131; *R (Pharmacy Care Plus Ltd) v Family Health Services Appeals Unit* [2013] EWHC 824 (Admin); and *Jobson v Secretary of State for Communities and Local Government* [2010] EWHC 1602 (Admin).

12.7 **Delegated (or subordinate) legislation**

The last issue to be addressed in this chapter is the position of delegated legislation; that is 'an instrument made by a person or body (the delegate) under legislative powers conferred by Act (the enabling Act)'.[88] Such legislation, which can alternatively be called 'subordinate' legislation,[89] will typically be published (in Westminster) as Statutory Instruments that take the form of, among other things, regulations, schemes, or orders. The legislation is ordinarily subject to some level of parliamentary control before it has final force of law (Statutory Instruments Act 1946), and it is in this way constitutionally different from other acts and measures taken, or adopted, on the basis of primary legislation. However, its different constitutional positioning should not be taken to mean that the making of delegated legislation does not give rise to difficult questions, as it has long been doubted whether parliamentary controls work fully and efficiently.[90] The point is all the more important given both the amount of such legislation and the fact that it can, in some instances, be used to amend primary legislation (through use of so-called Henry VIII clauses).[91]

In terms of illegality, the basic rule is that delegated legislation will be *ultra vires* the enabling Act if it does not comply with the terms of the Act as read, where appropriate, with the European Communities Act 1972 and the Human Rights Act 1998. However, beyond this basic position—which is at one with that which applies more generally in respect of statutory powers and duties—there are some important points of difference about the review of delegated legislation. These relate to: (1) the limits to procedural and substantive challenges to *vires*; (2) the *fora* in which delegated legislation may be challenged; and (3) the problem of subsequent acts/decisions.

12.7.1 **Procedural and substantive *ultra vires***

Procedural challenges to delegated legislation are brought on the ground that the legislation has been made in breach of a procedure specified in the parent statute, while substantive challenges may variously argue that the delegated legislation conflicts with the objectives of the Act, unlawfully sub-delegates the power of decision, is substantively unfair, is unreasonable, or has a disproportionate impact on the rights of those affected by it. In terms of procedural challenges, the starting point here is, of course, the interpretation to be given to the parent statute, as the courts accept that breach of a procedural requirement need not invalidate delegated legislation where that outcome is inconsistent with the intentions of the legislature (see further chapter 16 for discussion of the—now out-dated—distinction between 'mandatory' and 'directory' requirements). However, where the courts consider that failure to observe a particular requirement should render

---

88 F Bennion, *Statutory Interpretation* (London: Butterworths, 2002), 197.

89 Although note the specific meaning of the latter term under s 21 of the Human Rights Act 1998.

90 For analysis of this and related issues see E Page, *Governing by Numbers: Delegated Legislation and Everyday Policy-making* (Oxford: Hart Publishing, 2001).

91 See C Forsyth and E Kong, 'The Constitution and Prospective Henry VIII Clauses' [2004] *Judicial Review* 17.

the delegated legislation invalid, a remedy will usually issue. This is what happened in *Agricultural, Horticultural and Forestry Industry Training Board v Aylesbury Mushrooms*,[92] where an industrial training order had been made without consulting the Mushroom Growers Association. Section 1(4) of the Industrial Training Act 1964 provided that the minister should consult any representative of organisations to be affected by the order, and the Association thus sought exemption from the order and a declaration that the minister had failed to comply with the duty to consult. Although the Association was a specialist branch of the National Farmers Union, which had been consulted, the court held that the Association should have been consulted too. In the absence of consultation, the order therefore had no application to the Association.

Outside of procedural requirements in statute, it should be noted that delegated legislation cannot generally be challenged with reference to common law requirements of procedural fairness.[93] The underlying rationale for this approach is simply that a common law requirement to, for instance, consult when making delegated legislation would, given the numbers of people potentially affected by a measure, be unduly burdensome both for the relevant authority and for the courts should the failure to consult be challenged in judicial review proceedings. However, this position is not absolute, and there are some (exceptional) circumstances in which the courts will accept that the common law rules of fairness may require that an individual or organisation should be consulted, or be allowed to make representations, before delegated legislation is made. For instance, one apparent exception is where a claimant can demonstrate that he or she had a legitimate expectation of consultation, for example as a result of pre-existing government practice or of a statement made to them (albeit subject to arguments about when legitimate expectations may lawfully be frustrated).[94] Another apparent exception is where delegated legislation that is to be made will, in reality, have effects on only one party who will suffer serious detriment if the legislation is made within the terms that are envisaged. This is one outcome of the *Bank Mellat* ruling of the Supreme Court, which concerned the lawfulness of an Order in Council made under the Counter-Terrorism Act 2008.[95] The Order, which was intended to stifle Iran's pursuit of nuclear weapons, prohibited organisations in the UK financial sector from having any dealings with the claimant Iranian bank, and it was made without the bank being allowed to make representations about the terms of the Order. The Supreme Court held that the Order was disproportionate because it had been made with reference to risks in international banking more generally rather than with reference to the particular circumstances of the claimant bank. A majority also held that there had been a breach of the common law rules of fairness. This was not only by virtue of the fact that the Order was draconian in it is effects but also because it applied only to the claimant bank and because there was nothing in the parent legislation expressly to exclude consultation. In those circumstances, it was only fair that the bank should have been allowed to make representations before the Order was made.

---

92 [1972] 1 All ER 280.

93 See *Bates v Lord Hailsham* [1972] 3 All ER 1019. On common law fairness see ch 17.

94 See, e.g., *Re General Consumer Council's Application* [2006] NIQB 86, para 36, Weatherup J; and on legitimate expectation see ch 15.

95 *Bank Mellat v Her Majesty's Treasury (No 2)* [2013] UKSC 39, [2014] AC 700.

Substantive challenges, in contrast, may be brought when it is considered that delegated legislation is, for instance, in conflict with the objectives of the Act or some general constitutional principle. For instance, regulations have previously—and successfully—been challenged on the ground that they have levied taxation in the absence of express statutory authorisation for so doing (under the Bill of Rights 1688 only Parliament can authorise the raising of taxes). One such case is *Daymond v South West Water Authority*,[96] where it was held that a demand for payment for sewerage and sewage disposal services that was made to an individual whose property was not connected to the main drainage was unlawful. This was because section 30 of the Water Act 1973 envisaged that charges would be made only to those who were connected to the main system, and delegated legislation that purported to extend the scope for charging—the Water Authorities (Collection of Charges) Order 1974—was unlawful to that extent. Similarly, in *Commissioners of Customs and Excise v Cure and Deeley Ltd*,[97] the Finance Act 1940 had given the Commissioners authority to draw up regulations providing for any matter which appeared to them to be necessary for giving effect to the statutory provisions relating to purchase tax. The regulations that were made stipulated that if proper tax returns were not submitted the Commissioners could determine the amount of tax due for payment unless, within seven days, the taxpayer satisfied the Commissioners that some other sum was due. Despite the attempt at judge-proofing, the court found the regulation to be invalid as it appeared to prevent the taxpayer from proving in court the amount of tax actually due. An amount arbitrarily determined by the Commissioners was in effect replacing the tax authorised by Parliament for collection.

Substantive challenges may also be brought where it is considered, among other things, that the instrument unlawfully sub-delegates the power of decision, is substantively unfair, is unreasonable, or has a disproportionate impact on the rights of those affected by it. In such contexts, the principles applied by the courts are again at one with those applied in cases involving challenges to administrative decisions, albeit that the context set by the subordinate legislative process may complicate matters. The point can perhaps best be made with reference to reasonableness as a ground for review, as the courts may be reluctant to intervene given the width of discretion involved in designing legislation. This may be true, for instance, where delegated legislation is made in the realm of socio-economic policy;[98] and it may also be true where measures are adopted for reasons of national security. The leading historical example perhaps remains *McEldowney v Forde*,[99] where the minister had acted under section 3(1) of the Civil Authorities (Special Powers) Act (Northern Ireland) 1922 (now repealed) and issued a regulation in March 1967 whereby it was an offence to be a member of 'Republican clubs or any like organisation howsoever described'. This regulation was challenged by a person who was a member of a Republican club, who argued that the measure was vague and thereby unlawful. Although the House of Lords acknowledged that the provision was vague, it nevertheless held by a majority that it was valid. This is thus one case that illustrates how

---

96 [1976] AC 609, HL.
97 [1962] 1 QB 340.
98 See, e.g, *R v Secretary of State for the Environment, ex p Hammersmith London Borough Council* [1991] 1 AC 521.
99 [1971] AC 632, HL.

far the courts tend towards restraint in the context of national security cases, albeit that the restraint in such contexts has become more conditional in recent years.[100]

Finally, delegated legislation can be challenged for the reason that it is contrary to human rights standards and/or EU law. Hence in respect of human rights guarantees, we have already seen in chapter 4 how challenges may be made on the basis of the common law;[101] and we have also considered in that chapter how delegated legislation can, subject to section 4(4) of the Human Rights Act 1998, be invalidated where it is contrary to one or other provisions of the ECHR that have effect under the Act.[102] In respect of EU law, it is also axiomatic that delegated legislation can be quashed for reasons associated with the primacy of EU law. Thus, in the seminal *Factortame* case the House of Lords not only disapplied an Act of Parliament but also set aside related regulations.[103]

12.7.2 When can delegated legislation be challenged?

In most instances, challenges to the legality of delegated legislation will be made by way of claim for judicial review, where the issues for the court will include whether the claimant has an arguable case and has satisfied the requirements of delay, standing, etc.[104] However, it is important to note that challenges may also be made collaterally, that is, within other proceedings.[105] Such challenges will typically be made in criminal proceedings where an individual who has been charged with an offence under subordinate legislation argues in their defence that the legislation itself is unlawful (although note that collateral arguments may also be made in respect of decisions that preceded prosecution, that is, that they were unlawful and that the prosecution is in that way flawed). While such challenges will generally not be permitted where the defendant had prior opportunity to challenge the legislation or decisions taken under it,[106] the position is different where the individual becomes aware of the legislation only once charged with an offence. Under these circumstances, the criminal proceedings will provide the first chance to challenge the legislation and the courts presume that Parliament did not intend to deprive the defendant of an opportunity to defend him or herself in this way. The challenge will thus be permitted to proceed, save where there is express language in the statute to rebut the presumption in respect of Parliament's intentions.

The leading authority on these principles is *Boddington v British Transport Police*.[107] The facts were that a railway company had banned smoking in its carriages after research into passengers' views, and had widely advertised its decision to do so. The appellant subsequently smoked a cigarette in one of the company's carriages and, when he was charged with an offence contrary to bye-law 20 of the Railways

---

100 See, e.g., *Secretary of State for the Home Department v Rehman* [2003] 1 AC 153, 187, para 31, Lord Steyn; and 17.2.6.

101 e.g., *R v Lord Chancellor, ex p Witham* [1998] QB 575, at 4.2.2.

102 See 4.4.3.

103 See *R v Secretary of State for Transport, ex p Factortame Ltd (No 2)* [1991] 1 AC 603, considered at 4.4.3; and see too, e.g., *Bourgoin SA v Ministry of Agriculture, Fisheries and Food* [1986] QB 716, where a ministerial order was held unlawful.

104 See ch 8.

105 On the idea of collateral challenge see 8.7.

106 *R v Wicks* [1998] AC 92.

107 [1999] 2 AC 143.

Byelaws 1965 made under section 67 of the Transport Act 1962, he sought to challenge collaterally both the legality of the bye-law and the administrative decision to implement the ban. The stipendiary magistrate hearing the case rejected the defendant's collateral challenge, and the Divisional Court dismissed an appeal for the reason that the public law issues raised fell outside the jurisdiction of a criminal tribunal. However, the House of Lords held that collateral challenges were possible within criminal proceedings where this was consistent with Parliament's presumed intentions in relation to rights of defence. While the appeal was ultimately dismissed for the reason that the impugned measures were valid, a challenge to them had been permissible.

12.7.3 The problem of subsequent acts/decisions

The remaining point to note about delegated legislation concerns the problem of subsequent acts/decisions. In short, delegated legislation may provide the basis for a range of other administrative decisions that derive their legal authority from the original delegated legislation. Should that original delegated legislation later be deemed unlawful, this can raise difficult questions about whether decisions taken on the basis of the instrument are likewise to be regarded as unlawful. In other words, if the earlier measure is without legal validity, it would seem to follow that any subsequent measures should, in relative terms, also be regarded as without validity. For the hypothetical government department that made the instrument and took the subsequent decisions, a finding of this kind could, of course, create very significant complications indeed.

The courts are clearly aware of the difficulties that a finding of illegality can generate and, whilst always wishing to uphold the rule of law,[108] they may grant remedies in a way that is intended to minimise disruption. For instance, one option is to make a declaration that delegated legislation is *ultra vires* rather than to grant a quashing order. Declarations, in contrast to quashing orders, do not affect the legal force of the legislation in respect of which they are made and, while it would be expected that legislative and administrative amendments would follow the judgment of the court, there would be no coercive remedy to enforce the point (although a coercive remedy may subsequently be sought should the decision-maker continue to act unlawfully).[109] However, should the court decide that the appropriate remedy is a quashing order, this will have the effect of rendering the delegated legislation as *void ab initio*. Under those circumstances, significant administrative disruption may follow.

Another option is 'severance'. This option is open to a court where it makes a finding of illegality in respect of only some of the provisions in delegated legislation. Under those circumstances, it may be possible for the court to separate off and quash the offending provisions while allowing the remainder of the legislation to continue in force. Whether this is possible will very much depend on the structure of the legislation in question, and it may be that the 'good' cannot be separated from the 'bad' (through use of the so-called 'blue pencil' test). However, where it is possible to sever, this can have the dual benefit of protecting an individual from an

---

108 See, e.g., *HM Treasury v Ahmed* [2010] AC 534, discussed at 18.3.1.
109 *Webster v Southwark London Borough Council* [1983] QB 698.

illegality while at the same time allowing significant parts of a legislative scheme to remain in place. Cast in terms of the problem of subsequent acts, the 'good' provisions will thus continue to provide a basis for lawful administrative action.

An example of severance is provided by *Dunkley v Evans*.[110] The issue here was whether the West Coast Herring (Prohibition of Fishing) Order 1978 which had been made under the Sea Fish (Conservation) Act 1967 should be invalidated because it purported to include within its terms an area of sea adjacent to the coast of Northern Ireland which, by virtue of section 23(1) of the 1967 Act (as amended) was to be excluded from the Act. Holding that the Order need not be invalidated, the court said that, where it is possible to sever an invalid part of delegated legislation from the valid, the court is entitled to set aside or disregard the invalid part and to leave the rest intact so long as the invalid part is not inextricably interconnected with the valid. On the court's reading of the Order no such nexis between between the parts existed.[111]

12.8 **Conclusion**

This chapter has analysed the leading case law on 'fettering of discretion'; 'error of law' and 'error of fact'; and challenges to delegated legislation. Given the complexity of the issues involved there would be little merit in trying to summarise the key points, and we will limit ourselves to one comment. In short, the judicial approach to questions of illegality here, as in the areas considered in chapter 11, is guided both by principle and by the need for pragmatism. Hence in terms of principle it should be apparent that the courts have become increasingly anxious to constrain the abuse of governmental power and that they have developed the ground of illegality accordingly (a feature of the law that will also be seen in subsequent chapters on the remaining grounds). However, in terms of pragmatism the courts have further recognised that decision-makers may have to, for instance, adopt policies and enter into contracts as they seek to provide services to the public. By allowing them to do so, subject to legal constraints, the courts thus clearly accept the needs of decision-makers and tend towards the amber light view of administrative law referred to in our introductory chapter.[112]

FURTHER READING

Blundell, D [2004] 'Material Error of Fact—Where are we Now?' *Judicial Review* 36.

Costello, K (2015) 'The Scope of Application of the Rule Against Fettering in Administrative Law' *Law Quarterly Review* 354.

Craig, P [2004] 'Judicial Review, Appeal and Factual Error' *Public Law* 788.

---

110 [1981] 3 All ER 285.

111 Compare *DPP v Hutchinson* [1990] 2 AC 783 which provides an illustration of the limits of severence. The convictions of anti-nuclear protestors who were charged under the RAF Greenham Common Byelaws 1985 quashed as provisions in the bye-laws were *ultra vires* and it was not feasible to effect severance.

112 See 1.4.3.

Forsyth, CF and Kong, E [2004] 'The Constitution and Prospective Henry VIII clauses' 9 *Judicial Review* 17.

Hilson, C [2002] 'Judicial Review, Policies and the Fettering of Discretion' *Public Law* 111.

Knight, CJS [2009] 'A Framework for Fettering' *Judicial Review* 73.

Lanham, D (1984) 'Delegation and the Alter Ego Principle' *Law Quarterly Review* 587.

Page, EC (2001) *Governing by Numbers: Delegated Legislation and Everyday Policy-making* (Oxford: Hart Publishing).

Syrett, K [2006] 'Opening Eyes to the Reality of Scarce Health Care Resources? (R (on the application of Rogers) v Swindon NHS Primary Care Trust and Secretary of State for Health' *Public Law* 664.

13

Unreasonableness, irrationality, and proportionality

13.1 Introduction

We might start by asking an obvious question, that is, whether it can ever possibly have been the intention of Parliament that a body of any kind should behave unreasonably or irrationally? The answer is of course 'No', and it is just this presumption on the part of the courts which provides the foundation for the review jurisdiction. The courts, as we will see, presume that Parliament does not intend that public power should be exercised capriciously, and reasonableness therefore becomes a ground of possible intervention against an abuse of power under the *ultra vires* doctrine. But why has it arisen as a ground for review in its own right? To answer this question, and others which will emerge during the course of our discussion, we must have recourse to the history of the *ultra vires* doctrine. In particular, we must consider the principle of unreasonableness enunciated by Lord Greene in the seminal *Wednesbury* case and Lord Diplock's related formulation of irrationality in the *GCHQ* case.[1]

Before we proceed, it is worth reiterating once again that there are very often overlapping grounds of review in the case law, and new grounds are developing all the time, for example, proportionality, discussed below. Primarily, this is because the facts of any given case are likely to introduce degrees of complexity which may require a number of grounds to be considered as appropriate for use by the court when arriving at a judgment. It is immediately evident from a glance at numerous decisions in this field that unreasonableness commonly features among such principles of review.[2] However, the question might well be posed: when judges use the term 'unreasonableness', or 'irrationality', what exactly do they mean? Is it simply that there is a general duty for a public body to act reasonably, or is unreasonableness used to describe manifestly outrageous behaviour? What criteria do the courts employ in order to determine the degree of unreasonableness? Are these criteria clear, or is there imprecision in the case law? Further, the term 'irrationality' has sometimes been used since Lord Diplock's judgment in the *GCHQ* case to refer to strong unreasonableness as a head of review. Is irrationality to be preferred to strong unreasonableness, or does it essentially mean much the same thing? Moreover, what is the relationship between these variants of *Wednesbury*/irrationality and the balancing test associated with the proportionality principle? To answer these questions we must first start with an overview of the *Wednesbury* case itself.

---

1 Respectively, *Associated Provincial Picture Houses v Wednesbury Corporation* [1948] 1 KB 223 and *Council of Civil Service Unions v Minister for the Civil Service* [1985] AC 374.

2 See, for instance, chs 11 and 12, which provide several examples of overlap with illegality.

13.2 *Wednesbury* unreasonableness and general unreasonableness distinguished

Associated Provincial Picture Houses v Wednesbury Corporation[3] remains one of the most commonly cited decisions in administrative law (it is sometimes also cited in private law disputes).[4] This case marks the occasion when the basic principles of unreasonableness were reaffirmed and elaborated. The facts are straightforward. Wednesbury Corporation had discretionary power under section 1(1) of the Sunday Entertainments Act 1932 to grant licences to allow picture houses to open on Sundays, subject to 'such conditions as the authority should think fit to impose'. The authority introduced a condition that no children under the age of 15 should be admitted to Sunday performances. It was contended that this condition was unreasonable and, as a consequence, that it exceeded the scope of the statutory authority and was *ultra vires*. Nonetheless, the condition was not set aside, as this was the type of case in which the courts have never been very willing to interfere, for the reason that such decisions lie within the discretion of local authorities.[5] In his judgment Lord Greene pointed out that the statute had given local authorities a discretionary power to impose conditions which were, in its terms, without limitation. He also pointed out that the statute did not provide an appeal from a decision of the local authority on any ground. He therefore had to go on to consider the extent of the court's power to intervene. In doing so, it was made clear that an act taken within the framework of legislation will only be set aside if it can be shown that, in exercising its discretion, a decision-maker has 'contravened the law'. Lord Greene went on to explain when a contravention of the law could be on grounds of 'unreasonableness':

For instance, a person entrusted with a discretion must . . . direct himself properly in law. He must call his own attention to the matters which he is bound to consider. He must exclude from his consideration matters which are irrelevant to what he has to consider. If he does not obey these rules, he may truly be said . . . to be acting 'unreasonably'.[6]

His Lordship then proceeded, in the course of his discussion, to identify another sense in which the concept of unreasonableness might apply:

Similarly, there may be something so absurd that no sensible person could ever dream that it lay within the powers of the authority. Warrington LJ in *Short v Poole Corporation* [1926] Ch 66, 90, 91 gave the example of the red-haired teacher, dismissed because she had red hair. That is unreasonable in one sense. In another sense it is taking into consideration extraneous matters. It is so unreasonable that it might almost be described as being done in bad faith; and, in fact, all these things run into one another.[7]

It is worth paying close attention to the words chosen by Lord Greene in his judgment. If we turn to the first (general) sense in which 'unreasonableness' is used, we can see that what is meant by the terms purpose, relevancy, and reasonableness

---

3 [1948] 1 KB 223.

4 e.g., *Braganza v BP Shipping* [2015] UKSC 17, [2015] 1 WLR 1661.

5 For an historical and contextual analysis of the case see M Taggart, 'Reinventing Administrative Law' in N Bamforth and P Leyland (eds), *Public Law in a Multi-Layered Constitution* (Oxford: Hart Publishing, 2003), 311.

6 [1948] 1 KB 223, 229.

7 Ibid.

are the general considerations that should be uppermost in the minds of a decision-maker. The failure to adhere to such considerations can contribute to a decision being challenged. These grounds have elsewhere been termed weak, broad, or general unreasonableness. It will be apparent that they are very similar, if not identical, to what in the previous chapters was regarded as constituting different types of illegality. They would include improper purpose, relevant and irrelevant considerations, and bad faith.[8] It is established in the case law that all these factors can contribute to general unreasonableness and by themselves, or in different combinations, form the basis for a challenge in the courts.

Later Lord Greene describes another, quite specific and distinct type of (strong) unreasonableness. In fact, at the end of the judgment he summarises the position by suggesting that, if the court is satisfied that there is no general unreasonableness attached to the decision-making process, what has now come to be termed as *Wednesbury* (strong) unreasonableness could still come into play as a last resort as a ground for invalidating a decision. He suggests that this would be the case if it turns out to be a decision that 'is so unreasonable that no reasonable authority' could have come to it. Although he casts this restatement in slightly different words, it is clear that in setting these grounds for intervention he is referring to something narrow and focused, something that has to be overwhelming to be activated, not just in the everyday sense wrong or mistaken:

It is true to say that, if a decision on a competent matter is so unreasonable that no reasonable authority could ever have come to it, then the courts can interfere. That I think, is quite right; but to prove a case of that kind would require something overwhelming.[9]

Although the facts came nowhere near this standard in the *Wednesbury* case itself, an earlier case, *Roberts v Hopwood*, provides just such an example.[10] The minimum wage of £4 set by the authority had been disallowed by the district auditor as contrary to the law, despite the fact that Poplar Borough Council (known as 'Red Poplar' because of its radical politics) was empowered by statute to pay its employees such wages as it 'may think fit'. Lord Sumner reflected the sentiments of the House of Lords when he stated that 'such salaries and wages as . . . [the Council] may think fit' conferred not an unbounded discretion, but one that implied honesty and reasonableness. The fact that the authority chose to ignore market rates when setting its wage levels was, in the eyes of the court, totally unreasonable. It altogether ignored the predominant fiduciary interests of local ratepayers. Thus the findings of the auditor in setting aside the council's decision were unanimously upheld by the House of Lords.[11]

This 'strong unreasonableness principle', or *Wednesbury* test, as formulated in these passages of Lord Greene's judgment, is a standard that has been widely adopted when considering the status of the actions of public bodies in many varying contexts. But, as we have already indicated, in employing this definition of unreasonableness, the courts will only interfere with the exercise of a discretion when an authority has come to a conclusion *so unreasonable that no reasonable*

8 See ch 11.

9 [1948] 1 KB 223, 230.

10 [1925] AC 578; and see 11.5.2.

11 See also, e.g., *Secretary of State for Education and Science v Tameside Metropolitan Borough Council* [1977] AC 1014, considered below.

authority could ever have come to it. This is a much more exacting standard than just suggesting that a person or body in whom a discretionary power is vested must exercise that power reasonably. It is, in fact, so high a threshold for review as to be almost impossible to prove on its own. This is because Lord Greene was not proposing that it is part of a court's task to replace the discretionary power of local authorities with its own decisions, simply because such a decision is in some way thought to be suspect, or can be contested for being undesirable or unpopular. Although, arguably, a real extension of the *ultra vires* principle, the courts must be attentive to the possibility of becoming embroiled in debates about the quality or merits of a decision, something which will inevitably involve them in politics.[12] It is perhaps with this in mind that what has come to be termed the *Wednesbury* test for unreasonableness may have been regarded by Lord Greene as arising as a principle of last resort, to be relied on only in certain limited circumstances. Basically, it can come into play only if other principles of review fail for judicial review purposes, albeit that the courts can be reluctant to rely upon it. In this sense it is synonymous with judicial restraint.

However, it is significant that Lord Greene ends this famous passage by stating that all the grounds run into one another. This suggests that they are not necessarily distinct, either in theory or in practice. Indeed, as has already been stated, *Wednesbury* unreasonableness rarely occurs on its own, and is nearly always associated in the case law with other grounds of review. For example, as we have seen in *Roberts v Hopwood*, where the council's decision to pay above the market level for wages was found to be unreasonable, apparently in the *Wednesbury* sense, the finding of the court was also partly based on the view that the council's philanthropic purposes were irrelevant considerations. On the other hand, it was felt that giving the ratepayers value was a relevant consideration that was *not* taken into account in the exercise of the discretion. In the course of this chapter, we will show that other such grounds are almost always cited together with *Wednesbury* unreasonableness. It is therefore debatable whether unreasonableness, in this sense, should properly be regarded as a separate head of review at all. Arguably, it is so narrowly defined as to be almost superfluous. We might add that there is a certain circularity in the argument. Thus, a decision is deemed to be unreasonable if no reasonable person could arrive at it. If we accept the above assumptions, then conduct that is likely to be regarded as falling under this definition of strong unreasonableness would be more or less part of a continuum with other grounds—grounds which themselves introduce questions of *general* unreasonableness or procedural impropriety, thereby confusing what might otherwise have appeared to be clear distinctions.

Lastly, if we do assume that irrationality/*Wednesbury* unreasonableness can be considered as a self-standing ground in its own right—Lord Greene seemed to envisage that it should have such status; subsequent case law has made clear that it is self-standing—it becomes a real extension of the *ultra vires* doctrine, since unreasonableness is ultimately concerned not just with *vires* but with the quality and merits of a decision. This is a point that will be seen to have an added significance when we turn, below, to consider the relationship between *Wednesbury* and the proportionality principle.

---

12 On which possibility see JAG Griffiths, *The Politics of the Judiciary*, 5th edn (London: Fontana Press, 1997).

13.3 **History of unreasonableness**

It is widely recognised that unreasonableness has long been established as one of the traditional grounds of review in administrative law which pre-date *Wednesbury* by many years. In fact, there are judicial statements going back to Sir Edward Coke CJ's *dicta* in *Rookes Case*.[13] This general principle remains fundamentally the same to this day. But, returning to *Wednesbury*, the decision is interesting not simply because it can be set against this historical backdrop; another aspect of this judgment is that it was made during a period of what we have referred to as 'judicial quietism', that is, from 1914 to the early 1960s, during which time judicial attitudes to intervention were generally limited by a restrained conception of the judicial role. One immediate question is: were the strict limits to the court's powers to set aside decisions envisaged by Lord Greene the same as those that applied after the succession of judgments in the 1960s, which heralded a more interventionist judicial mood? Our review of the case law will answer this question for us, but it is interesting to observe that other commentators believe that unreasonableness was only genuinely revived in *Padfield v Minister of Agriculture, Fisheries and Food*.[14]

There has also been a history of judicial reticence when a power is delegated to an elected public body. A good early example is *Kruse v Johnson*, which concerned a bye-law introduced by Kent County Council prohibiting anyone from playing music or singing in a public place within 50 yards of a dwelling house.[15] Lord Russell CJ stated that the courts would be reluctant to condemn bye-laws made by a representative political authority as being invalid because of unreasonableness. He suggested that, when considering a challenge to delegated legislation, unreasonableness would be relevant:

> If for instance they were found to be partial and unequal in their operation as between classes; if they were manifestly unjust; if they disclosed bad faith; if they involved such oppressive or gratuitous interference with the rights of those subject to them as could find no justification in the minds of reasonable men, the court might well say, 'Parliament never intended to give authority to make such rules; they are unreasonable and *ultra vires*'. But it is in this sense, and this sense only, as I conceive, that the question of unreasonableness can properly be regarded. A by-law is not unreasonable merely because judges may think it goes further than is prudent, necessary or convenient . . . [16]

In arriving at his formula Lord Russell is describing a standard that is virtually identical to *Wednesbury* unreasonableness, and spelling out the danger of judges merely ending up by substituting their own views in such situations.

13.3.1 **The boundaries of *Wednesbury* unreasonableness**

Even where, as we see in the case law, *Wednesbury* unreasonableness is frequently used, it may appear to be applied imprecisely, and not as Lord Greene himself probably intended. The courts have sometimes used it as a convenient shorthand

---

13 (1598) 5 Co Rep 99b.

14 e.g., W Wade and C Forsyth, *Administrative Law*, 11th edn (Oxford: Oxford University Press, 2014), ch 11.

15 [1898] 2 QB 91.

16 Ibid, 100.

to stand for conduct ranging from relatively insignificant degrees of unreasonableness through to something manifestly irrational. For example, the meaning of 'unreasonable' in this context was elaborated upon in *Secretary of State for Education and Science v Tameside Metropolitan Borough Council*.[17] Lord Diplock stated that 'unreasonable' denotes conduct which no sensible authority acting with due appreciation of its responsibilities would have pursued. This may be contrasted with the words used by Lord Greene in the *Wednesbury* case.

As will now be apparent, unreasonableness is a variable standard that is difficult to pin down or to confine to objective criteria. Indeed, it seems clear from decided cases that there are certain areas, particularly those where political discretion is being exercised by elected representatives, where the courts will be very reluctant to intervene. This is particularly true where the matter has been considered by Parliament. For instance, in *R v Secretary of State for the Environment, ex p Nottinghamshire County Council*,[18] a challenge was made to 'expenditure guidance' that the minister had issued to local authorities. Addressing the availability of unreasonableness as a ground of review, Lord Scarman stated that there are constitutional limits to the reviewability of such decisions:

> I cannot accept that it is constitutionally appropriate, save in very exceptional circumstances for the courts to intervene on the grounds of unreasonableness to quash guidance framed by the Secretary of State and by necessary implication approved by the House of Commons, the guidance being concerned with the limits of public authorities and the incidence of the tax burden between ratepayers and public authorities.[19]

However, his Lordship continued by saying that if *Wednesbury* unreasonableness was evident and the decision was itself perverse the court could still intervene. Lord Scarman is stating plainly that only this type of unreasonableness will allow a remedy in these situations, that it is a last resort. In another case involving what amounted to a challenge to government policy in the area of local government finance, the *dicta* of Lord Scarman in *ex p Nottinghamshire County Council* were strongly endorsed by Lord Bridge in the House of Lords.[20] Another aspect, discussed in *British Airways Board v Laker Airways*,[21] was that it would be very difficult for the courts to intervene on grounds of unreasonableness if the matter concerned relations between this country and some other state. Political decisions, properly arrived at, cannot be judged on objective grounds by the courts and they would therefore interfere only in extreme circumstances (under what is sometimes termed as the 'super-*Wednesbury*' test).

13.3.2 The effect of statutory language

A further matter is whether the use of the word 'reasonable' in a statute that grants a discretionary power adds anything or whether it makes no material difference. For example, we have already seen above how the local authority in *Roberts v*

---

17 [1977] AC 1014.

18 [1986] AC 240.

19 Ibid, 247.

20 *R v Secretary of State for the Environment, ex p Hammersmith and Fulham London Borough Council* [1991] 1 AC 521.

21 [1984] 3 All ER 39.

Hopwood[22] was empowered to pay its employees reasonable wages, and in *Luby v Newcastle-under-Lyme Corporation* a local authority was likewise required to charge a reasonable rent for council tenancies.[23] However, in neither of these cases did the word 'reasonable' in the statute affect in any way the court's ability to intervene, as the court was willing to grant a remedy only where the authority had acted irrationally or abused its power in some other way, for instance, by taking irrelevant considerations into account. Thus, it seems in such cases that the law presumes that public authorities will always act reasonably and that that presumption will remain unaffected unless and until the contrary is proved.

At other times, statutes may grant discretion by using words such as 'If the Secretary of State has reasonable cause to believe . . . '.[24] This will introduce a standard that requires the minister not simply to act on his own beliefs, but to have regard to evidence of a factual nature on which he should base his decision. If it is reasonable for the minister to have reached this decision from this evidence, the courts will not interfere. *Liversidge v Anderson* was an exceptional case which provides a controversial—and now dated—example of the subject matter affecting the decision at hand.[25] The minister did not have to show 'reasonable cause to believe the person was of hostile origin', as he was apparently required to do by the Defence (General) Regulations 1939, simply because it was held that the sufficiency of grounds was a matter solely to be determined by the minister without reference to the courts. In *Secretary of State for Education and Science v Tameside Metropolitan Borough Council*,[26] Lord Wilberforce suggested that each section of the Education Act 1944 had to be examined in the context of the Act as a whole. The case is also a good example because it was as much concerned with the relationship between central and local government, as it was with that between the courts and the executive. It also illustrates well the concept of unreasonableness and the merits/*vires* argument, as they have recently evolved. In particular, it reveals the power that courts have to intervene in cases where there is subjective language and thereby to, in effect, involve themselves in moral and political questions. The facts centred on the refusal of a Conservative-held local authority to accept the Labour Government's provisions for comprehensive education. The minister was acting according to section 68 of the Education Act 1944, which gave him power, if he felt an authority was acting unreasonably, to give 'such directions . . . as appear to him expedient'. The court ruled in favour of the council, and in doing so, construed 'unreasonably' to mean *Wednesbury* unreasonableness. In other words, the court was of the view that the minister's capacity to intervene depended upon the education authority doing something that was so extreme that no reasonable authority would contemplate it. Acting unreasonably did *not* simply mean disagreeing on a matter of policy, nor could it include the disruption that might ensue from an abrupt change of education policy. On the other hand, taking into account the importance of the mandate created by the electorate's approval of a manifesto policy, to act as the council did was regarded as a reasonable course of action.

---

22 [1925] AC 578.
23 [1964] 2 QB 64.
24 On discretion and statutory language see 8.4.
25 [1942] AC 206; and see 17.2.6.
26 [1977] AC 1014.

13.3.3 **Unreasonableness as a sliding scale/varying standards**

In *Tameside*, we can see the distinction alluded to above between 'general' un-reasonableness and 'strong' unreasonableness: indeed it might be said that the House of Lords had recourse to both dimensions of the principle. This raises the question whether the interplay of the 'general' and 'strong' dimensions means that unreasonableness in effect exists on a sliding scale of judicial intervention. In other words, if there are several standards available, and if the courts are reluctant to substitute their views for those of the decision-maker, how far does the outcome of particular cases depend upon other considerations such as the subject matter of the case and its general context? In addressing this point, we might start with *Wheeler v Leicester City Council*, which involved an application of what is termed the 'sub-*Wednesbury*' test.[27] The case concerned a challenge to a ban that had been imposed by the local authority on Leicester Rugby Club, which prevented it from using council playing fields in a public park. The ban had been introduced be-cause some of the Leicester players intended to participate in a tour of South Africa (South Africa was at that time under the apartheid regime and boycotts were the norm). It was held that this ban was an improper exercise of statutory power and had the effect of punishing the club unfairly. In addition, the House of Lords found the ban to be *Wednesbury* unreasonable, since it brought to bear on the rugby club illegitimate pressure from the council to coerce the club into agreeing with the council's policy. According to Lord Roskill, although the decision was *Wednesbury* unreasonable, it was far from clear that it was illogical or immoral. This, he pointed out, was a matter about which reasonable people might well disagree. It was con-ceded that the council could claim to be properly motivated by a desire to pro-mote harmonious race relations in the city, in accordance with section 71 of the Race Relations Act 1976. However, this reasonable objective could not justify the pursuit of a policy that was, in itself, unreasonably punitive. Lord Roskill's ap-proach thereby sat in direct contrast with that adopted by Ackner LJ in the Court of Appeal, where he had held not only that the authority was lawfully entitled to take into account section 71 of the Race Relations Act 1976, but also that it would be quite wrong to categorise the council's action as perverse.[28]

Similarly, in *West Glamorgan County Council v Rafferty*,[29] the council, which was under a statutory duty by virtue of the Caravans Sites Act 1968 to provide adequate accommodation for travellers, attempted to evict travellers from its land without providing alternative accommodation. The travellers sought to prevent the evic-tion, whereupon it was held by Ralph Gibson LJ that the order was unreasonable in the *Wednesbury* sense and would remain so until an alternative site was found. This was despite the fact that there were a number of points in favour of eviction, for example, the council wished to develop the site, there was a nuisance caused by the travellers, and they were trespassers. Nevertheless, it was held that the over-riding factor was that their trespassing came down to the failure of the council to provide alternative accommodation. The decision of the council was thus held to have been unreasonable, notwithstanding the existence of certain 'relevant con-siderations' that lent support to its decision.

---

27 [1985] AC 1054; and 11.4.1.2.
28 See C Turpin, 'Race Relations, Rugby Football and the Law' (1985) 44 *Cambridge Law Journal* 333.
29 [1987] 1 All ER 1005.

On the other hand, we have already seen above that the courts are reluctant to become involved where matters of public expenditure or government policy are involved; that is, only perversity or absurdity amounting to bad faith or misconduct (of an extreme kind) will satisfy the threshold of unreasonableness. This standard, sometimes referred to as the 'super-*Wednesbury* test', therefore represents the high-water mark of judicial self-restraint.[30] It is, however, equally important to note again the importance of 'sub-*Wednesbury*' review, which was partly in issue in *Tameside* and which can also be used when fundamental human rights are at issue (albeit that such cases will typically fall under the Human Rights Act 1998, below, where the proportionality principle applies). For example, adopting such an approach, the courts have taken a closer look at decisions that have had implications for the right to life[31] and freedom of expression,[32] among others. While this raises questions about how far the courts should modify their position *vis-à-vis* the discretionary choices of decision-makers, the point to be noted here is that a sub-*Wednesbury* standard of review reveals again the potential elasticity of the courts' approach under the *Wednesbury* heading.[33] Moreover, it will be important to have grasped the meaning of the concept of sub-*Wednesbury* review when we turn, below, to discuss the relationship between *Wednesbury* and the proportionality principle.

13.4 Irrationality: Lord Diplock's reformulation in *GCHQ*

When setting out the grounds for judicial review in the *GCHQ* case,[34] Lord Diplock preferred to employ the term 'irrationality' to describe '*Wednesbury* unreasonableness'. In doing so, he explained that 'It applies to a decision which is so outrageous in its defiance of logic or of accepted moral standards that no sensible person who had applied his mind to the question to be decided could have arrived at it'.[35] The important point is that he suggests that it could stand on its own as an accepted ground of review, and so become a genuine extension of the *ultra vires* doctrine. At the same time, he also hints at the problems involved in defining its parameters, when he suggests that this category can be recognised by judges applying their training and experience to the task. However, there is some doubt as to whether *Wednesbury* unreasonableness and irrationality *indeed* are the same thing. As we have seen, it has been suggested that *Wednesbury* unreasonableness has become judicial shorthand for the kind of conduct in decision-making that falls below the standard that public bodies are expected to display. Nevertheless, despite some doubts about the superiority of the term 'irrationality' as a ground of

---

30 See Lord Scarman's remarks in *R v Secretary of State for the Environment, ex p Nottinghamshire County Council* [1986] AC 240, 247.

31 *Re Officer L* [2007] 4 All ER 965; *R v Cambridge Health Authority, ex p Child B* [1995] 25 BMLR 5; and *R v Home Secretary, ex p Bugdaycay* [1987] AC 514.

32 *R v Home Secretary, ex p Brind* [1991] 1 AC 696.

33 For recent judicial discussion of the point see *Pham v Home Secretary* [2015] UKSC 19, [2015] 1 WLR 1591, in particular the judgments of Lords Sumption and Reed.

34 *Council of Civil Service v Minister for Civil Service* [1985] AC 374.

35 [1985] AC 374, 410.

review over *Wednesbury* unreasonableness, it, like *Wednesbury* unreasonableness, has nevertheless been used in its own right.

R v Secretary of State for the Environment, ex p Fielder Estates (Canvey Ltd) is an example of a case illustrating behaviour of a kind that was deemed irrational.[36] After a planning application to build houses close to Canvey Island had been refused, a public inquiry was set up which was expected to last for three days. During the inquiry, one of the objectors, the Canvey Ratepayers Association, was to present its evidence on the second day. When it turned up to do so, the Association found that the inquiry had already been closed by the inspector. After a complaint had been made to the Secretary of State, another inquiry was set up. But this time, the other parties who had been present at the first inquiry, including Fielder Estates, were not notified about the second inquiry. It was held that the conduct of the Secretary of State was so unreasonable as to verge on the irrational and absurd. It also amounted to a failure to act with procedural fairness, thereby exemplifying once more how the grounds for review can overlap.[37]

Another case of note is *R v Secretary of State for Trade and Industry, ex p Lonrho plc*,[38] which concerned the failure of the minister to refer the Harrods takeover to the Monopolies and Mergers Commission. The question was whether the minister's failure to use his discretion to act on the report of inspectors, following the advice of the Director General of Fair Trading, and not to provide reasons for his refusal to refer, would, in itself, amount to irrationality. It is important to note that this was the sole ground for the challenge on this point. The outcome here appears to follow from the reasoning of Lord Scarman in *ex p Nottinghamshire County Council*, above, by offering a very narrow construction of irrationality as a ground for intervention, when controversial political factors are present. In this regard, it is interesting to note that the Divisional Court found the minister's conduct to be unlawful, and that the court was itself criticised in the House of Lords for 'wrongly though unconsciously, substituting their own view, for the views of the decision maker'.[39] The interpretation of the court's role set out by Lord Keith may indicate that even a very poor quality decision should not be challenged, if it means that the court is thereby dragged into the political process and effectively becomes the decision-maker. The problem is that it is often not possible to disentangle the *political* aspects of a decision while examining how it has been arrived at. The seminal case of *Padfield v Minister of Agriculture*[40] was distinguished, with Lord Keith stating that the absence of reasons, when there is no duty to give them, could not by itself provide support for irrationality, except by the inference that there were no rational reasons. His Lordship then proceeded to speculate on good reasons that might have been uppermost in the minister's mind. However, this again shows the complexity that can be involved with such review, as surely the issue was the quality of the decision itself.

It was also argued in *ex p Lonrho* that the minister had acted perversely in failing to publish the report of the department's inspectors. This argument was rejected because the minister was entitled to take the view that publication might prejudice a fair trial. Lord Keith found there to be nothing wrong with

---

36 (1989) 57 P & CR 424.
37 On procedural fairness see chs 16 and 17.
38 [1989] 1 WLR 525.
39 [1989] 1 WLR 525, 535.
40 [1968] AC 997, considered at 11.4.1.

this decision, since there had been no attack on the good faith of the Secretary of State. The implication was that, even if the decision-making process had been correct, but bad faith was found to be involved, then irrationality might be employed as a supplementary ground, as it was in *Nottinghamshire County Council*, mentioned above.[41]

13.5 Proportionality

13.5.1 Nature of the principle of proportionality

The related principle of proportionality is widely accepted in Continental Europe, where it plays an important part not only in the domestic law of Germany and France, but also in European Union (EU) law and in the European Convention on Human Rights (ECHR) (although it is to be noted that the principle that applies in EU law and the ECHR, while very similar, is not identical).[42] The concept has its origins in German administrative law and is in some respects closely related to irrationality, improper purpose, and relevant and irrelevant considerations.[43] Proportionality works on the assumption that administrative action ought not go beyond that which is necessary to achieve its desired result (in everyday terms, that one should not use a sledge-hammer to crack a nut) and, in contrast to irrationality, is often understood to bring courts much closer to reviewing the merits of a decision. In other words, if measures are considered to do more harm than good in reaching a given objective, they are liable to be set aside. Sedley LJ thus stated in *B v Secretary of State for the Home Department*, a deportation case in which the Home Secretary's decision to deport the appellant was so severe as to be disproportionate, that:

In essence it amounts to this: a measure which interferes with a Community or human right must not only be authorised by law but must correspond to a pressing social need and go no further than strictly necessary in a pluralistic society to achieve its permitted purpose; or, more shortly, must be appropriate and necessary to its legitimate aim.[44]

This is a useful approach to adopt when seeking to balance exercises of discretion with the rights of individuals affected by any corresponding decisions. Proportionality may be regarded as an extra safeguard which is activated only after it has been established that a public body has the legal power to act, or that the body is not pursuing an improper purpose; that is, even if these grounds do not apply, it may still be relevant to consider whether the body concerned is acting proportionately. At its simplest, the court may be called upon to perform a kind

---

41 See also *R v Ealing London Borough Council, ex p Times Newspapers* (1986) 85 LGR 316. And for other cases using 'unreasonableness' and/or 'irrationality' as headings of review see, e.g., *Re Duffy's Application* [2008] UKHL 4, para 31, Lord Rodger; *R v Bow Street Metropolitan Stipendiary Magistrate, ex p DPP* [1992] COD 267; *R v Secretary of State for the Home Department, ex p Handscomb* (1988) 86 Cr App R 59; and *R v Secretary of State for the Home Department, ex p Norney* (1995) Admin LR 861.

42 See generally E Ellis (ed), *Proportionality in the Laws of Europe* (Oxford: Hart Publishing, 1999); and on the subtle differences between the principle in EU law and the ECHR see *R (Lumsdon) v Legal Services Board* [2015] UKSC 41, [2015] 3 WLR 121.

43 On purposes and relevant and irrelevant considerations see ch 11.

44 [2000] UKHRR 498, 502.

of balancing exercise to assess if the objective of an official decision necessitates (the 'necessity test') the means employed to achieve it, or whether the means can be deemed to be disproportionate. A measure will therefore typically be proportionate only where: (i) the measure's objective is sufficiently important to justify the limitation of a right or interest; (ii) the measure is rationally connected to the objective; (iii) there is no less intrusive measure that could have been used; and (iv) 'having regard to these matters and to the severity of the consequences, a fair balance has been struck between the rights of the individual and the interests of the community'.[45] We will return to the nature of this test—which is now synonymous with the Human Rights Act 1998—below.

In terms of the principle's place in domestic administrative law, Lord Diplock recognised the potential importance of proportionality in the *GCHQ* case.[46] The principle's place was later considered by the House of Lords in another important case pre-dating the Human Rights Act 1998, one which was charged with political controversy, *R v Secretary of State for the Home Department, ex p Brind*.[47] In response to violence in the conflict that was at that time ongoing in Northern Ireland, the Home Secretary had introduced broadcast directives which banned the use of live or recorded speech by proscribed organisations and their political affiliates, including the IRA, Sinn Fein, and the Ulster Defence Association (the Broadcasting Act 1981, section 29(3), allowed the Home Secretary to restrict matters that could be broadcast by the BBC and the IBA). This action was challenged by the National Union of Journalists (NUJ), which applied for judicial review, contending that the ban was unlawful for a number of reasons. First, they argued that it appeared to frustrate the objectives of the 1981 Act; secondly, that it was in breach of the right to freedom of expression under Article 10 of the ECHR; and, thirdly, it was irrational in the *Wednesbury* sense. Most significantly for us here, the NUJ also maintained that the action was disproportionate.

In his judgment, Lord Templeman pointed out that any interference with freedom of expression must be assessed in the light of the damage which the restriction is designed to prevent. It was also noted that there clearly were competing public interests that had to be balanced in this situation, and that nothing less than a pressing public interest would justify such a ban as that which had been imposed. Nevertheless, it was decided by their Lordships that the Secretary of State had not exceeded the bounds of his discretion because he had been influenced by important considerations such as the offence that terrorists might cause to viewers, the publicity and standing given to proscribed organisations, which was against the public interest, the effect of intimidation that broadcasts might have, and so on.[48] However, some other members of the House—notably Lords Ackner and Lowry— were very concerned by the merits question visible just beneath the surface of a proportionality inquiry, and they emphasised how constitutional propriety demanded that they remain at the outer-reaches of the decision-making process. In other words, their Lordships were concerned that, by considering whether the ban

---

45 *Bank Mellat v HM Treasury (No 2)* [2013] UKSC 38 and 39, [2014] AC 700, 771, para 20, Lord Sumption.

46 [1985] AC 374.

47 [1991] 1 AC 696.

48 Note that the measures were subsequently also found to be justified in Strasbourg: *Brind v UK*, App No 18714/91, 77 DR 42.

corresponded to a pressing need, the court would itself be addressing a matter that Parliament had decided ought to be left to the Secretary of State. While their Lordships were therefore arguably close to accepting a test of proportionality, they foresaw the danger of assuming an appellate function as opposed to exercising their accepted supervisory jurisdiction. The House of Lords therefore refused to accept that proportionality was a free-standing ground of review in domestic law, although they did leave open the possibility of future recognition of the principle.

13.5.2 **Proportionality and the intensity of review**

Brind was to set a forceful precedent and the courts remained reluctant to develop proportionality in domestic law in the years preceding the enactment and coming into force of the Human Rights Act 1998.[49] This reluctance was criticised by some commentators, who argued not only that the courts already gave effect to the principle in cases involving EU law, but also that the principle was well established in areas of English law (for instance, there is a fundamental principle embodied in the Bill of Rights 1689 that a punishment or penalty should not be excessive).[50] Nevertheless, the prevailing judicial view was that recognition of the principle as a free-standing ground of review would mark an undesirable shift in the constitutional role of the courts. As Lord Irvine of Lairg suggested, 'There is no escape from an acceptance that a proportionality test would lower the *Wednesbury* "threshold of unreasonableness"'.[51]

That said, it was also argued by some commentators that the proportionality principle was misunderstood and that a fuller analysis of the jurisprudence of the Court of Justice of the European Union (CJEU) and the European Court of Human Rights (ECtHR) revealed that it could be applied in a flexible and context-sensitive way.[52] Here, it was argued that the proportionality principle can correspond with a 'margin of appreciation' that is given to legislative and administrative decision-makers and that the intensity of judicial review will depend on a range of factors that will, in some circumstances, demand judicial restraint. In essence, therefore, the judicial task under the principle is not simply one of asking whether the right balance has been struck by an original decision-maker, but of adapting the test to suit the needs of the situation in hand. For example, it has been pointed out in regard to EU law that the threshold for proportionality is not necessarily lower and that, if it were, the CJEU would be called upon to second guess the policy choices that have been made. The difficulties that this would involve for the Court have been examined in great depth by Paul Craig, both when discussing EU law and developments in UK administrative law itself.[53]

---

49 See, e.g., *R v Secretary of State for the Environment, ex p NALGO* [1993] Admin LR 785.

50 On the position in EU law see ch 3 and, e.g., *R (Rotherham MBC) v Secretary of State for Business, Innovation and Skills* [2015] UKSC 6, [2015] 3 CMLR 20 (discussed at 14.3). On its place in English law see J Jowell and A Lester, 'Beyond *Wednesbury*: Substantive Principles of Administrative Law' [1987] *Public Law* 368.

51 Lord Irvine of Lairg, 'Judges and Decision-Makers: The Theory and Practice of *Wednesbury* Review' [1996] *Public Law* 59, 74.

52 See, e.g., G de Búrca, 'Proportionality in EC Law' (1993) 13 *Yearbook of European Law* 105; and for leading case law, e.g., Case C-331/88, *FEDESA* [1990] ECR I-4023 and *Handyside v United Kingdom* [1976] 1 EHRR 737.

53 See P Craig, *Administrative Law*, 7th edn (London: Sweet and Maxwell, 2012), ch 21; and P Craig, *UK, EU and Global Administrative Law: Foundations and Challenges* (Cambridge: Cambridge University Press, 2015), 375ff. See also *R (Lumsdon) v Legal Services Board* [2015] UKSC 41, [2015] 3 WLR 121.

On the other hand, it has been suggested that, when it comes to fundamental rights, proportionality (as with the *Wednesbury* unreasonableness and irrationality tests) should be employed on a different basis, with a different intensity. Indeed, it is axiomatic that such rights ought not to be needlessly interfered with. Thus the 'margin of appreciation' allowed to public authorities might be correspondingly reduced in this context. In fact, Laws J, as he then was, argued, extra-judicially, that fundamental rights are embodied in the common law and that, if they are worthy of distinct protection, a decision-maker ought not to be left to order priorities without due regard for such rights. He noted: 'What is therefore needed is a preparedness to hold that a decision which overrides a fundamental right without sufficient objective justification will, as a matter of law, necessarily be disproportionate to the aim in view'.[54] In certain categories of case it is therefore envisaged that the judge will end up balancing executive action against any interference with those rights. This is precisely what occurred in *R v Cambridgeshire Health Authority, ex p B*,[55] where Laws J himself regarded the right to life as inviolable and as presenting an irreducible constraint on the power of the health authority to decide how to allocate its resources. The controversial outcome of the case—the decision was overturned on appeal—perhaps serves as a salutary illustration of the dangers alluded to above by their Lordships in *ex p Brind* and by Lord Irvine. The problem is that such cases are, if anything, less suitable matters for judicial determination because they are liable to confront the most difficult and subjective moral and political issues, presenting enormous scope for disagreement at a philosophical level. Are judges, for example, any better placed by training, experience, and knowledge to know where to draw the line than professional administrators?

Nevertheless, it is clear that the proportionality principle can result in the courts attaching a relatively high value to considerations such as those relating to fundamental rights. In *R v Ministry of Defence, ex p Smith*, Sir Thomas Bingham MR accepted that 'The more substantial the interference with human rights, the more the court will require by way of justification before it is satisfied that the decision is reasonable'.[56] The implication here is that, where an administrative decision has implications for fundamental rights, the courts will subject the decision to 'anxious scrutiny' in appropriate cases (albeit that the approach adopted in *ex p Smith* was subsequently criticised by the ECtHR as falling beneath the ECHR's standards of protection).[57] However, the recognition of a need to be somewhat more vigilant in protecting certain rights over others is very different from regarding them as automatically having priority over other relevant and important considerations, such as matters of public order, or security. For instance, *R v Coventry City Council, ex p Phoenix Aviation* involved a matter of public controversy where the terminology of proportionality was referred to in the judgment (largely because of an EU law element to the case).[58] The applicants sought judicial review to challenge the action of local councils in banning the export of live animals, ostensibly to prevent trouble from animal rights' demonstrators. Simon Brown LJ held that the courts were entitled to intervene to uphold the rule of law, because to allow the port authorities

54 J Laws, 'Is the High Court the Guardian of Fundamental Rights?' [1993] *Public Law* 59, 74.
55 [1995] 1 FLR 1055.
56 [1996] QB 517, 554.
57 *Smith and Grady v UK* (2000) 29 EHRR 493.
58 [1995] 3 All ER 37.

to implement the ban would encourage widespread unlawful action by protesters. In addition, the court had to consider wider interests, which, in this case, included protecting the livelihood of farmers faced with financial ruin caused by the disruption. It was held that the council's resolution to ban the export of live animals was wholly disproportionate to the security risk presented at the time.[59]

13.6 The Human Rights Act and proportionality

Since the coming into force of the Human Rights Act 1998 in October 2000, the proportionality principle has of course played a much more central role in domestic law (we return to the question of just how central that role is below—but note that *Wednesbury* can still also play a role in fundamental rights cases).[60] Nevertheless, the central problem remains how to reconcile its emphasis on balancing respective interests with traditional public law understandings of the role of the courts. Indeed, this is now true not just in the context of the review of administrative and executive decisions, but also in the context of assessing whether Acts of the Westminster Parliament are compatible with the ECHR. As we saw in chapter 4, the courts are required, 'so far as it is possible to do so', to interpret Acts of Parliament (and other measures) in a manner that is compatible with the ECHR (in the event that such harmonious interpretation is not possible they may make a declaration of incompatibility under section 4 of the Act). However, even before the courts reach the interpretive obligation, they must first consider whether the legislation in question would violate the rights that are said to be engaged by it. Under those circumstances, the courts must thus ask whether any legislative interference with rights is proportionate and, for instance, 'necessary in a democratic society'.

The courts' approach to the problems presented by the principle can best be evaluated by using three sub-headings that deal with: the principle's emergence; its calibration; and its application.

13.6.1 The emergence of proportionality

Proportionality was formally recognised as a freestanding ground of review under the Human Rights Act in the first case on the point to come before the House of Lords, *R v Home Secretary, ex p Daly*.[61] In one sense, the ruling should have been regarded as unremarkable, as section 2 of the Act requires that courts 'take into account' the body of ECHR case law that includes the proportionality principle.[62] However, the judgment had an added significance as it resolved judicial uncertainty about how the principle should relate to *Wednesbury* review, at least under the Human Rights Act (on the position in cases outside the Act, see 13.7). A number of judgments that preceded *Daly* had suggested that the courts should continue to

59 See also on these issues and on the issue of proportionality in EU law/domestic law *R v Chief Constable of Sussex, ex p International Trader's Ferry Ltd* [1998] 3 WLR 1260.

60 As in, e.g., *In re Officer L* [2007] 1 WLR 2135 and *Keyu v Secretary of State for Foreign and Commonwealth Affairs* [2015] UKSC 69, [2015] 3 WLR 1665 (noted at 4.4.6).

61 [2001] 2 AC 532.

62 See 4.4.1.

couch their approach to substantive review in the language of reasonableness, as such an approach was more in accord with orthodox understandings of the judicial role. For example, in *R (Mahmood) v Home Secretary*,[63] the claimant sought leave to remain in the UK on the basis of marriage after an initial application for asylum had been rejected. After the application for leave to remain was also rejected, the claimant challenged the decision on the ground that it interfered with his right to respect for family life under Article 8 of the ECHR. However, the Court of Appeal was not prepared to intervene, Lord Phillips MR stating: 'the court will ask the question, applying an objective test, whether the decision-maker could *reasonably* have concluded that the interference was necessary to achieve one or more of the legitimate aims recognised by the convention' (emphasis added).[64] The Court of Appeal thereby avoided engaging in the kind of balancing exercise that sets the degree of interference with the ECHR guarantee against the importance of the objective being pursued.[65]

This approach was not approved in *Daly*, where the House of Lords pronounced that proportionality is central to review in cases where the ECHR is in issue.[66] *Daly* concerned a challenge to regulations made under section 47(2) of the Prison Act 1952, which affected the rights of prisoners. In this situation there was a conflict between the need to protect the rights of individuals in prison who might be exposed to regulations that could be regarded as oppressive and unnecessary and the state's interest in interfering with certain rights to ensure that prisons can be a secure and safe environment. It was pointed out by Lord Bingham that the prison population includes a core of dangerous, disruptive, and manipulative prisoners, hostile to authority, and ready to exploit for their own advantage any concession granted to them. The question was therefore whether new prison rules permitting staff to read the correspondence of a prisoner when searching cells without the prisoner being present constituted a breach of Article 8 of the ECHR—in other words whether the rule was disproportionate. In a unanimous judgment the House of Lords accepted the view that the policy contained in this rule breached the ECHR and that a prisoner should be entitled to be present when privileged correspondence is examined. Lord Bingham, giving the leading judgment, held that Article 8(1) of the ECHR gave the applicant a right to respect for his correspondence. This right was subject to the qualification forming part of the ECHR that interference with such a right by a public authority may be permitted in the interests of national security, public safety, the prevention of disorder or crime, or for protection of the rights and freedoms of others. Nevertheless, it was held that the policy adopted by the Home Office was a disproportionate interference with the claimant's exercise of his right under Article 8(1) of the ECHR as it went much further than necessity required.

Other members of the House of Lords elaborated further upon the proportionality principle and its relationship with *Wednesbury*. For instance, Lord Steyn stated that proportionality should now be used in cases of this type, and he was in no

---

63 [2001] 1 WLR 840.

64 Ibid, 857.

65 See also, e.g., *R v Home Secretary, ex p Turget* [2001] 1 All ER 719 and *R v Home Secretary, ex p Isiko* [2001] FLR 930.

66 For affirmation of the point see *Re E (A child)* [2009] 1 AC 536.

doubt that the differences in approach between the traditional grounds of review and proportionality may sometimes lead to different results:

The starting point is that there is an overlap between the traditional grounds of review and the approach of proportionality. Most cases would be decided in the same way whichever approach is adopted. But the intensity of review is somewhat greater under the proportionality approach making due allowance for important structural differences between various convention rights . . . [67]

His Lordship thereby emphasised the importance of analysing Human Rights Act cases in the correct way, something that required use of proportionality. His Lordship was, however, also very clear that this did not mean that there had been a shift to merits review. He explained that the roles of judges and administrators are fundamentally distinct and will remain so, since under the proportionality test administrators are afforded a 'margin of appreciation' within which they can be allowed to set the restrictions necessary to satisfy pressing social need. This concern for the separation of powers reflects the traditional logic of *Wednesbury*, and Lord Steyn's words have since been prominent in more general debates about whether proportionality plus the margin of appreciation (or domestic equivalent) should now displace the traditional unreasonableness ground in all cases (whether under the Act or not). Although Lord Steyn was silent on this wider point, other members of the House were much more vocal in forecasting an end to *Wednesbury*. Lord Cooke in particular was of the opinion that:

the day will come when it will be more widely recognised that *Associated Provincial Picture Houses Ltd v Wednesbury Corporation* . . . was an unfortunately retrogressive decision in English administrative law, in so far as it suggested that there are degrees of unreasonableness and that only a very extreme degree can bring an administrative decision within the legitimate scope of judicial invalidation.[68]

The significance of this more general debate is returned to at 13.7.

Daly proved to be a highly significant judgment in terms of clarifying how courts should apply the proportionality principle in cases under the Human Rights Act 1998, and we examine some of the subsequent leading case law below. However, we need to pause here to make two further points about the proportionality principle post-*Daly*. The first is about who should have to apply the proportionality principle, and when. While *Daly* established that courts in Human Rights Act cases should give effect to the principle, it left open the question whether administrative decision-makers more generally should have to consider the proportionality of any of their decisions or policies that may have implications for rights under the ECHR. The answer to that question was given by the House of Lords in its judgment in *R (SB) v Headteacher and Governors of Denbigh High School*,[69] which held that section 6 of the Human Rights Act 1998 does not require decision-makers expressly to take human rights principles into account during decision-making processes. This is because their Lordships, referring to Thomas Poole's analysis, believed that this would 'be a recipe for judicialisation on an unprecedented scale' in the sense that decision-makers would be required to apply legal principles more suited to the

---

67 [2001] 2 AC 532, 547.
68 Ibid, 549.
69 [2007] 1 AC 100.

courts.[70] As Lord Bingham put it, 'what matters in any case is the practical outcome [in terms of conformity with the ECHR] not the quality of the decision-making process that led to it'.[71] Whether the impugned decision is proportionate is therefore a question of law for the courts to determine in the light of *ex p Daly*.[72]

The second point concerns the structure of the test that is used by the courts when assessing proportionality. At the time of *Daly*, it was regarded as a three-stage test whereby the courts would ask whether: '(i) the . . . objective is sufficiently important to justify limiting a fundamental right; (ii) the measures designed to meet the . . . objective are rationally connected to it; and (iii) the means used to impair the right or freedom are no more than is necessary to accomplish the objective'.[73] While all of these elements remain within the test that is applied by the courts, the test has since been amended to include a further element that makes express mention of the interests of the wider community within any balancing process. This revised test, which we referred to earlier, was fashioned by Lord Sumption in the *Bank Mellat* case, and it is now to be regarded as the authoritative statement of the law. The *Bank Mellat* case itself concerned the lawfulness of financial restrictions that the government had imposed upon an Iranian bank for reasons of national security, and Lord Sumption, after having surveyed case law that included *Daly*, stated:

Their [i.e., *Daly*, etc] effect can be sufficiently summarised for present purposes by saying that the question depends on an exacting analysis of the factual case advanced in defence of the measure, in order to determine (i) whether its objective is sufficiently important to justify the limitation of a fundamental right; (ii) whether it is rationally connected to the objective; (iii) whether a less intrusive measure could have been used; and (iv) whether, having regard to these matters and to the severity of the consequences, a fair balance has been struck between the rights of the individual and the interests of the community. These four requirements are logically separate, but in practice they inevitably overlap because the same facts are likely to be relevant to more than one of them.[74]

We would add that, on the application of this test to the facts before it, the Supreme Court held that the government's financial restrictions were disproportionate in their effects.

13.6.2 Calibrating the principle

The attempts by the courts to calibrate the principle have focused in large part on their parallel use of 'due deference' or the 'discretionary area of judgment' doctrine. The conceptual underpinnings of the doctrine have led to criticism from some commentators,[75] although its essential objective remains constitutionally

---

70 [2007] 1 AC 100, 116. Poole's article is 'Of Headscarves and Heresies: The Denbigh High School Case and Public Authority Decision Making under the Human Rights Act' [2005] *Public Law* 685.

71 [2007] 1 AC 100, 116.

72 See also *Belfast City Council v Misbehavin' Ltd* [2007] 1 WLR 1420. But compare *Manchester City Council v Pinnock* [2011] 2 AC 104 134, Lord Neuberger.

73 [2001] 2 AC 532, 547, Lord Steyn, citing *de Freitas v Permanent Secretary of Ministry of Agriculture, Fisheries, Lands and Housing* [1999] 1 AC 69.

74 *Bank Mellat v HM Treasury (No 2)* [2013] UKSC 38 and 39, [2014] AC 700, 771, para 20.

75 For early criticisms see RA Edwards, 'Judicial Deference Under the Human Rights Act' (2002) 5 *Modern Law Review* 859. See also, e.g., T Allan, 'Judicial Deference and Judicial Review: Legal Doctrine and Legal Theory' (2011) 127 *Law Quarterly Review* 96.

sound. Put shortly, the doctrine acknowledges that there will be certain circumstances in which it is entirely appropriate for courts to exercise restraint in the face of the lawful preferences of decision-makers (the decision-maker may be the legislature, a central government minister, a locally elected body, or, more controversially, an unelected recipient of delegated power, e.g., a Chief Constable). The case in which the doctrine was first introduced was *R v DPP, ex p Kebilene*,[76] which was decided before the Human Rights Act was in force. The facts were that the two co-accused, who were suspected members of the Armed Islamic Group that was engaged in terrorism, had been faced with a possible trial. One issue for the House was whether judicial review was available to challenge a decision of the DPP to prosecute where such prosecution would be contrary to Article 6 of the ECHR. In accepting that judicial review should be available, the House nevertheless emphasised the importance of judicial caution. As Lord Hope pointed out:

> By conceding a margin of appreciation to each national system, the [ECtHR] has recognised that the Convention, as a living system, does not need to be applied uniformly by all states but may vary in its application according to local needs and conditions. This technique is not available to the national courts when they are considering Convention issues arising within their own countries. But in the hands of the national courts also the Convention should be seen as an expression of fundamental principles rather than as a set of mere rules. The questions which the courts will have to decide in the application of these principles will involve questions of balance between competing interests and issues of proportionality. In this area difficult choices may have to be made by the executive or the legislature between the rights of the individual and the needs of society. In some circumstances it will be appropriate for the courts to recognise that there is an area of judgment within which the judiciary will defer, on democratic grounds, to the considered opinion of the elected body or person whose act or decision is said to be incompatible with the Convention.[77]

Further guidance on when judicial caution might be appropriate was provided by Laws LJ in *International Transport Roth GmbH and others v Secretary of State for the Home Department*.[78] This was a case that concerned the compatibility with the ECHR of a scheme that imposed fixed penalties on carriers who were suspected of facilitating the clandestine entry into the UK of illegal immigrants (property such as vehicles could also be impounded). The scheme had been introduced on the basis of section 32 of the Immigration and Asylum Act 1999, and the foremost issue for the court was whether the scheme was compliant with Article 6 of the ECHR (it was held that the scheme was not consistent with ECHR principles and a declaration of incompatibility was made). In identifying some core principles, Laws LJ (dissenting) surveyed the existing case law and presented a spectrum of possible scenarios that would determine the appropriate degree of judicial self-restraint (the spectrum was not intended to be definitive, but rather indicative). Laws LJ's first principle was that greater restraint would be required where questions were raised about measures introduced by the sovereign legislature. While this did not mean that the courts should accept parliamentary choices without question, it was here that constitutional tension would be 'at its most acute'.[79] After this, Laws LJ distinguished cases 'Where the decision-maker is not Parliament,

---

76 [2000] 2 AC 326.
77 Ibid, 380–1.
78 [2003] QB 728.
79 Ibid, 765.

but a minister or other public or governmental authority exercising power conferred by Parliament'.[80] Here, a degree of restraint would also be due on democratic grounds, as the decision-maker is Parliament's delegate, although the approach should vary on a case-by-case basis. Factors that will help courts to decide how closely they should scrutinise secondary decisions and acts include whether the rights in question are qualified or absolute, whether the subject matter at hand falls more under the 'constitutional responsibility' of the 'democratic-powers' or the courts, and whether a decision is concerned with macro-economic policy which 'will be relatively remote from judicial control'.[81] When discussing this final consideration, Laws LJ noted how previous case law in UK courts had not concerned human rights, but that the issue of institutional balance was nevertheless of more general concern. The criteria listed are therefore of potential relevance not just in the human rights context, but also beyond.

We will turn shortly to consider how such criteria have influenced the courts in practice. However, before doing so, it is important to note that the discretionary area of judgment doctrine has taken debate about the constitutional role of the courts in a different direction from that which was dominant prior to the coming into force of the Human Rights Act 1998. While all commentators accept the need for judicial caution when using the proportionality principle, some doubt that the discretionary area of judgment doctrine offers a satisfactory intellectual basis for structuring judicial restraint. For instance, Murray Hunt has previously been critical of the use of the term 'area', as he considers that this suggests spatial zones into which the judiciary may never enquire and that this can frustrate the balancing of interests demanded by the proportionality principle.[82] Hunt argued instead for a doctrine of 'due deference', as he considered that this would allow the courts to look much more closely at the basis for decisions and then to accept or reject the decisions in the light of their full legal and constitutional context. The language of due deference has, however, since been criticised by some senior members of the judiciary, who consider that 'deference' suggests judicial servility in the face of administrative choices. Lord Hoffman has in particular been critical of the term, stating:

I do not think that its overtones of servility, or perhaps gracious concession, are appropriate to describe what is happening. In a society based upon the rule of law and the separation of powers, it is necessary to decide which branch of government has in any particular instance the decision-making power and what the legal limits of that power are. That is a question of law.[83]

Moreover, in its judgment in *Huang* the House of Lords said that, when a court exercises restraint, it is not 'apt' to say that the court is 'deferring' to a decision-maker, but rather that it is performing 'the ordinary judicial task of weighing up the competing considerations on each side and according appropriate weight to the judgment of a person with responsibility for a given subject matter and access to special sources of knowledge and advice'.[84] While some subsequent Supreme Court case law has since made mention of the courts according 'due deference' to the view of a government decision-maker—something that is not easy to reconcile with

---

80 Ibid, 765.
81 Ibid, 766–7.
82 See M Hunt, 'Sovereignty's Blight: Why Contemporary Public Law Needs the Concept of "Due Deference"' in Bamforth and Leyland, n 5, 337.
83 *R (Pro-life Alliance) v BBC* [2004] 1 AC 185, 240.
84 *Huang v Home Secretary* [2007] 2 AC 167, 185, Lord Bingham.

Huang—that same case law has also emphasised that the Court should not simply 'genuflect' in the face of executive choices. As Lord Neuberger has said: 'there is a spectrum of types of decision, ranging from those based on factors on which judges have the evidence, the experience, the knowledge, and the institutional legitimacy to be able to form their own view with confidence, to those based on factors in respect of which judges cannot claim any such competence, and where only exceptional circumstances would justify judicial interference'.[85] On this reading, it would appear that the courts will jealously guard their constitutional function of review, where appropriate, and will perform this task irrespective of the particular form of words employed in the case before them.

13.6.3 Proportionality in practice

13.6.3.1 Primary legislation and proportionality

In feeling their way with the proportionality principle, the courts have inevitably had to address highly controversial issues, and the corresponding case law has sometimes been marked by a close judicial examination of legislative choices and, at other times, by restraint. Perhaps the best example of close judicial examination of a legislative scheme remains that provided by *A v Home Secretary*.[86] The central issue in this case—the *'Belmarsh detainees'* case—was the proportionality of the legislature's response to the threat posed by global terrorism after the attacks in New York, Washington, and Pennsylvania on 11 September 2001. The Anti-terrorism, Crime and Security Act 2001 was a far-reaching piece of legislation that, among other things, empowered the Home Secretary to authorise the indefinite detention, without trial, of non-British nationals who were suspected of involvement in terrorism. Such detention, which was ordered in respect of a number of individuals who were suspected of involvement with Islamic terror groups, interfered with the Article 5 ECHR guarantee of the right to liberty. That guarantee can, however, be derogated from under Article 15 of the ECHR where there is 'a public emergency threatening the life of the nation', and the government had entered a derogation with the Council of Europe and made the Human Rights Act 1998 (Designated Derogation) Order 2001. While the majority in the House of Lords did not formally reject the government's assessment that such an emergency existed—Lord Hoffmann dissented on this point and was highly critical of the derogation—it did reject the argument that indefinite detention represented a proportionate response to the perceived threat. This is because Article 15 of the ECHR requires that any measures introduced should be strictly in proportion to the mischief pursued, and the House felt that the relevant provisions of the 2001 Act failed that test in relation to the liberty rights of the individuals (the House also considered that, as only non-British nationals could be detained, the measures were discriminatory and contrary to Article 14 of the ECHR).[87] Lord Bingham, for example, considered that the threat presented by suspected terrorists could have been countered in much less intrusive ways that included the requirement that the individuals should report regularly to police stations. The Human Rights Act 1998 (Designated Derogation) Order 2001 was thus quashed on account of its

---

85 *R (Lord Carlile) v Secretary of State for the Home Department* [2014] UKSC 60, [2015] AC 945, para 68 (Lord Neuberger). The term 'genuflect' was used by Lord Kerr at para 150.
86 [2005] 2 AC 68.
87 See 14.4.

incompatibility with Article 15 of the ECHR, and a corresponding declaration of incompatibility was made *vis-à-vis* the relevant provisions of the 2001 Act.

Another example of close judicial scrutiny is provided by *R (F) v Home Secretary.*[88] This was a case involving two individuals who were, respectively, a child who had been convicted of rape while aged 11, and an adult who had been convicted of indecent assault and sentenced to five years' imprisonment. Under the Sexual Offences Act 2003 both individuals were automatically subject to notification requirements for an indefinite period, which meant that they had to notify the police of, among other things, certain personal details and also of any foreign travel plans. The 2003 Act did not, however, provide a review mechanism for periodically assessing whether the notification requirements should remain in place, and the individuals brought claims for judicial review whereby they argued that the legislation constituted a disproportionate interference with their rights to private and family life under Article 8 of the ECHR. Agreeing with that argument, the Supreme Court noted that there was a clear interference with Article 8 of the ECHR and that such interference should no longer be necessary where an individual who was subject to notification requirements could demonstrate that he or she no longer presented any risk of re-offending. While the Court acknowledged that it was for the legislature to set the threshold at which an independent decision-maker could conclude that a risk of a future offence should be discounted, it held that the total absence of any such review mechanism within the extant legislative scheme could not be reconciled with Article 8 of the ECHR. The legislation thus constituted a disproportionate interference with Article 8 of the ECHR and a declaration of incompatibility issued.

On the other hand, restraint has been evident in cases that include *R (Animal Defenders International) v Secretary of State for Culture, Media and Sports.*[89] The claimant was a non-profit-making company that lobbied to prevent the suppression of all forms of cruelty to animals and to protect animals and their environment. In 2005, it launched a campaign titled 'My Mate's a Primate', which had the objective of bringing attention to the negative uses of primates by humans. As part of its campaign it wished to broadcast a number of advertisements and, in advance of doing so, it submitted a proposed advertisement to the Broadcast Advertising Clearance Centre. The Clearance Centre subsequently declined to clear the advertisement for the reason that it would breach the prohibition on political advertising in section 321(2) of the Communications Act 2003, and Animal Defenders International brought a claim for judicial review seeking a declaration that section 321(2) was incompatible with the Article 10 ECHR right to freedom of expression. Refusing the claim, the House of Lords noted that the issue of political advertising was particularly contentious and that Parliament's measured views on the matter should be accorded great weight. On this basis, the House observed that restrictions on political advertising could be said to protect the rights of others by shielding them from the mischief of partial political advertising and that Parliament was entitled to regard such advertising as a real danger. The House of Lords also noted the immediate impact that advertising can have on the public and that Parliament had adjudged that it was not possible to design a more limited scheme

---

88 [2011] 1 AC 331.
89 [2008] 1 AC 1312.

for restricting the rights under Article 10 of the ECHR. Given these considerations, the prohibition in section 321(2) was justified.[90]

A preference for judicial restraint can also be apparent even where the courts consider that a provision in an Act of the Westminster Parliament is disproportionate, as the courts may refuse to grant a declaration of incompatibility. We have already discussed in chapter 4 how the declaration of incompatibility is a discretionary remedy, and one (admittedly exceptional) case in which the Supreme Court refused to grant the remedy was *R (Nicklinson) v Ministry of Justice*.[91] One of the main issues in this case was whether the Supreme Court should make a declaration of incompatibility as between section 2(1) of the Suicide Act 1961—which makes it an offence to assist a person to commit suicide—and the right to private and family life under Article 8 of the ECHR. The issue had arisen because the claimant wished to end his life but was unable to do so because of his physical condition, and he argued that the blanket nature of section 2(1) was disproportionate in its effects on his Article 8 rights. While there was detailed discussion within the case about whether Article 8 of the ECHR was breached by the legislation—Lady Hale and Lord Kerr, dissenting, agreed that the legislation was disproportionate and that a declaration should be made—the other members of the Court were concerned about the limits to their powers in an area of such religious and moral complexity. The majority were thus of the view that it would not be appropriate for them to make a declaration of incompatibility and that Parliament could reconsider the matter at its own speed.[92]

Another important case on restraint—this time in the face of the legislative choices of the Scottish Parliament—is *Axa General Insurance v Lord Advocate*.[93] The Scottish Parliament had here enacted the Damages (Asbestos-related Conditions) (Scotland) Act 2009 to allow individuals to sue for damages where they had suffered the onset of pleural plaques as a result of their exposure to asbestos while working in Scotland's heavy industries (the legislation thereby reversed the effects of the *Rothwell* ruling of the House of Lords which had held that pleural plaques did not constitute physical harm and were not actionable).[94] In real terms, this meant that Axa and a number of other insurance companies would have to meet a large number of claims against employers, and they challenged the legislation on the basis that it was a disproportionate interference with their Article 1 Protocol 1 ECHR property rights and thereby *ultra vires* section 29(2)(d) of the Scotland Act 1998. Rejecting that argument, the Supreme Court noted that property rights are qualified rights under the ECHR and that the case law of the ECtHR accords states a wide margin of appreciation when making legislative choices that are in 'the public interest'.[95] Emphasising that the impugned legislation had been introduced to remedy what the Scottish Parliament perceived to be a 'social injustice', the Supreme Court was of the view that it should use ECHR principles to interfere with such choices only where they were absent any 'reasonable foundation' or were 'manifestly unreasonable'. As Lord Hope put it:

---

90 And note that a subsequent petition to the ECtHR was dismissed: *Animal Defenders International v UK* (2013) 57 EHRR 21.

91 [2014] UKSC 38, [2015] AC 657; and 4.4.3.

92 The case was subsequently deemed inadmissible by the ECtHR: see *Nicklinson v UK* (2015) 61 EHRR SE7.

93 [2011] UKSC 46, [2012] 1 AC 868.

94 *Rothwell v Chemical Insulating Co* [2008] 1 AC 281.

95 Citing, most prominently, *James v UK* (1986) 8 EHRR 123.

Can it be said that the judgment of the Scottish Parliament that this was a matter of public interest on which it should legislate to remove what was regarded as a social injustice was without reasonable foundation or manifestly unreasonable? I do not think so. There is no doubt that the negligence of employers whose activities were concentrated in socially disadvantaged areas such as Clydebank had exposed their workforce to asbestos and all the risk associated with it for many years. The anxiety that is generated by a diagnosis of pleural plaques is well documented . . . The numbers of those involved, and the fact that many of them live in communities alongside people who are known to have developed very serious asbestos-related illnesses, contributed to a situation which no responsible government could ignore. It seems to me that the Scottish Parliament were entitled to regard their predicament as a social injustice, and that its judgment that asbestos-related pleural plaques should be actionable cannot be dismissed as unreasonable.[96]

One other point to note about *Axa* is that the Supreme Court also rejected the argument that decisions of the Scottish Parliament could be reviewed with reference to the common law ground of unreasonableness/irrationality. The argument that it could be so reviewed had been advanced in addition to that centred on proportionality and, in dismissing the argument, the Supreme Court emphasised that the Scottish Parliament is a democratically legitimated body that commands wide-ranging powers within the framework of the Scotland Act 1998. While the Supreme Court at the same time made clear that the Scottish Parliament is not legally sovereign in the sense that is associated with the Westminster Parliament, it was firmly of the view that the courts should exercise the fullest possible restraint when assessing the *vires* of Acts of the Scottish Parliament with reference to the common law. Unreasonableness, in the result, is not available as a ground for review, and the courts will intervene on the basis of the common law only where legislation purports to abolish common law fundamental rights.[97]

13.6.3.2 Proportionality and discretion

There are, in turn, many cases in which the proportionality principle has been used to gauge the lawfulness of decisions taken by the recipients of statutory discretion/ powers. A useful starting point is provided by one of the earliest House of Lords rulings on the issue, *R v British Broadcasting Corporation, ex p Pro-Life Alliance*.[98] This case concerned a challenge to a decision of the BBC and other broadcasters not to transmit in Wales a party election broadcast which had been made by the Pro-Life Alliance. The broadcast used material that the broadcasters considered to be sensational and disturbing, and the Alliance challenged the decision as a breach of their right to freedom of expression under Article 10 of the ECHR (the decision was taken on the basis of an Agreement with the Secretary of State for National Heritage and under section 6(1) of the Broadcasting Act 1990). The Court of Appeal adopted an approach to proportionality review which posited that freedom of political speech enjoyed by an accredited party at a public election, especially a general election, must not be interfered with save on the most pressing grounds. It was stated by Laws LJ (in holding the decision not to broadcast unlawful) that the courts owed a special responsibility to the public as the constitutional guardian of freedom of political debate. While it was acknowledged that broadcasters enjoyed

96 [2011] UKSC 46, [2012] 1 AC 868, 907–8, para 33. Compare *Recovery of Medical Costs for Asbestos Diseases (Wales) Bill* [2015] UKSC 3, [2015] AC 1016.

97 [2011] UKSC 46, [2012] 1 AC 868, 913, para 51 (Lord Hope) and 946, para 153 (Lord Reed).

98 [2004] 1 AC 185.

wide editorial discretion in entertainment and news reporting, they did not do so where political free speech was concerned. However, the majority in the House of Lords took a radically different view of the court's role in such matters, thereby revealing different judicial understandings of the constitutional limits of the principle. For example, Lord Nicholls commented:

As it was, the Court of Appeal in effect carried out its own balancing exercise between the requirements of freedom of political speech and the protection of the public from being unduly distressed in their own homes. That was not a legitimate exercise for the courts in this case. Parliament has decided where the balance shall be held.[99]

There was nothing to indicate that the BBC had applied an inappropriate standard in assessing whether the broadcast was offensive. Prior to this refusal to broadcast it had been pointed out to the Pro-Life Alliance by the BBC (as would be the case with others proposing to make election broadcasts) that a significant proportion of their programme would not comply with the relevant provisions of the BBC's Producers' Guidelines and the Programme Code of the Independent Television Commission in respect of matters of taste and decency. The Court of Appeal did not hesitate to express its opinion on whether the broadcast met the relevant criteria of taste. However, for the House of Lords the question was whether this was something for the court to decide, or a matter for the decision-maker. Their Lordships found that the decision by the Court of Appeal had gone too far and that determining the issue of what could be broadcast in these circumstances amounted to a form of merits review.

Differing judicial approaches have been in evidence in other cases too. *R (Farrakhan) v Home Secretary* was a case in which Louis Farrakhan, the leader of the Nation of Islam in the USA, challenged the Home Secretary's refusal to grant him entry clearance to come to the UK to address his followers.[100] The Home Secretary's decision was based upon public order concerns, as the claimant had previously made anti-Semitic statements and it was thought that his presence in the UK might inflame inter-community tensions. In challenging the refusal as an unjustified interference with his Article 10 ECHR right to freedom of expression, the claimant argued that he had since retracted and apologised for the anti-Semitic comments, and also that he had signed a form that listed conditions of behaviour that would bind him for the duration of his stay in the UK. The claimant's arguments were initially successful in the Administrative Court, where the judge concluded that the Home Secretary's belief that there was a threat to public order was not supported by sufficient evidence. However, the Secretary of State was successful on appeal to the Court of Appeal, where it was emphasised that decision-makers in such cases enjoy a discretionary area of judgment. Highlighting how the Secretary of State is democratically accountable for his decisions and in the best position to make value judgements in cases of this kind, the Court of Appeal said that it was thereby, and legitimately, required to 'confer a wide margin of discretion upon the Minister'. The Court on this basis decided that the Secretary of State was entitled to rely upon public order concerns.

A similar case, this time heard by the Supreme Court, is *R (Lord Carlile) v Secretary of State for the Home Department*.[101] The issue here was whether the Home

---

99 Ibid, 226, para 16.
100 [2002] QB 1391.
101 [2014] UKSC 60, [2015] AC 945.

Secretary had acted unlawfully when refusing the entry to the UK of a dissident Iranian politician. The individual in question was resident in Paris and had been invited to address a group of Parliamentarians at Westminster. Lord Kerr, dissenting was of the view that the Court could itself form a view as to the proportionality of the Home Secretary's decision. In consequence, his Lordship held, on the facts of the case, that there had been a breach of the applicant's rights under Article 10 of the ECHR. However, the majority disagreed and considered that the Home Secretary had been entitled to make the decision at hand. The evidence before the Court was that the Home Secretary had had regard for international relations and the UK's historically difficult relationship with Iran when making her decision. Further, she had been concerned that permission to enter might have negative implications for British overseas interests. While the majority acknowledged that freedom of expression is particularly important in the context of political debate, it also accepted that Article 10 of the ECHR is a qualified right that can be made subject to countervailing concerns of national security and so on. On this reasoning, and bearing in mind the limits to the judicial role, it was held that the Secretary of State's decision was not unlawful.

There are, inevitably, many other cases outside the context of freedom of expression where the courts have had to (re)assess the limits of their role when using the proportionality principle.[102] Little would be gained from our trying to summarise even the essence of those cases here, and we would simply reiterate that the case law is often defined by divisions such as those seen in *Pro-lifeAlliance*, *Farrakhan*, and *Lord Carlile*. While those divisions were perhaps initially attributable to the novelty of giving effect to the case law of the ECHR, the differences that persist today are consistent with the fact of competing philosophies about the limits to the judicial role. As we have outlined above, those philosophies envisage more or less judicial intervention in public decision-making, and the proportionality principle has certainly offered an increased scope for judicial control of public authorities. To understand when—or whether—that intervention is legitimate, we would refer once more to Laws LJ's broad and impressive statement of principle in *International Transport*,[103] considered above.

13.7 *Wednesbury* and proportionality outside the Human Rights Act

Of course, all of the cases considered in the above section are examples that have arisen under the Human Rights Act 1998. So what, then, is the relationship between *Wednesbury* and proportionality in case law that arises outside the Human Rights Act 1998? If proportionality is applied in EU law cases and in Human Rights

---

102 e.g., *Re E (A child)* [2009] 1 AC 536 (in the context of policing and positive obligations and the prohibition of inhuman and degrading treatment under Art 3 ECHR); *Chikwamba v Home Secretary* [2008] 1 WLR 1420 (on the Art 8 ECHR right to family life and immigration decisions); and *R (Clays Lane Housing Co-operative Ltd) v The Housing Corporation* [2005] 1 WLR 2229 (Art 1 Prot 1 property rights and the compulsory transfer of property).

103 *International Transport Roth GmbH and others v Secretary of State for the Home Department* [2003] QB 728.

Act cases, what role does this leave for *Wednesbury*? Is *Wednesbury* obsolete, or can it, as a principle that exists on a sliding scale, co-exist with a proportionality principle that likewise provides a variable standard of review?

There are two main approaches to this issue, each having some judicial and academic support. The first proposes that the courts should retain the traditional grounds of review and allow those traditional grounds to continue to function in cases that are not embraced by EU law and/or the ECHR.[104] This approach is founded upon an apparent understanding that domestic canons of review should not automatically be displaced by European standards, as *Wednesbury* has a robustness that gives it an enduring quality.[105] This approach also envisages that *Wednesbury* and proportionality will often achieve similar outcomes as a matter of practice and that there is therefore nothing prejudicial in using the principles within their respective spheres of influence or, indeed, together.[106]

The second view favours the development of a single test of public law illegality founded upon the proportionality principle. This approach, which considers that *Wednesbury* should now be regarded as of historical rather than contemporary worth, initially enjoyed strong support among some members of the judiciary. For instance, Lord Slynn stated how he considered that:

> [E]ven without reference to the Human Rights Act 1998 the time has come to recognise that (proportionality) is part of English administrative law, not only when judges are dealing with [EU] acts but also when they are dealing with acts subject to domestic law. Trying to keep the *Wednesbury* principle and proportionality in separate compartments seems to me to be unnecessary and confusing.[107]

In an even more robust statement, Lord Cooke suggested, in the *Daly* case, that the *Wednesbury* test should be consigned to history and receive its 'quietus' in favour of the proportionality principle.[108] Moreover, in *R (British Civilian Internees—Far Eastern Region) v Secretary of State for Defence*, the Court of Appeal suggested that proportionality should be available outside the EU and ECHR contexts, albeit that the Court observed that such availability was a matter for the highest appellate court.[109] However, the Supreme Court, for its part, has yet to take that step and recently declined the invitation to do so in the significant case of *Keyu*:[110] while the Court did not close off the possibility that *Wednesbury* would be jettisoned, it did caution that a decision of such importance should be taken by a panel of seven or nine Justices as opposed to the panel of five that heard *Keyu*.

Which approach is to be preferred? The answer here ultimately depends on one's viewpoint of the respective merits of the *Wednesbury* and proportionality principles. Certainly, it is true that proportionality has sometimes been regarded

---

104 M Elliott, 'The Human Rights Act 1998 and the Standard of Substantive Review' (2001) 60 *Cambridge Law Journal* 301.

105 An argument originally made, extra-curially, by Sir John Laws: see, 'Wednesbury', in C Forsyth and I Hare (eds), *The Golden Metwand and the Crooked Cord* (Oxford: Clarendon Press, 1998).

106 See further *Pham v Home Secretary* [2015] UKSC 19, [2015] 1 WLR 1591, 1624ff, Lord Sumption, and *Kennedy v Information Commissioner* [2014] UKSC 20, [2015] AC 455, paras 51–5, Lord Mance.

107 *R (on the application of Alconbury Developments Ltd) v Secretary of State for the Environment Transport and the Regions* [2003] 2 AC 295, 321, para 51.

108 *R v Secretary of State for the Home Department, ex p Daly* [2001] 2 AC 532, 549, para 32.

109 [2003] QB 1397.

110 *R (Keyu) v Secretary of State for Foreign and Commonwealth Affairs* [2015] UKSC 69, [2015] 3 WLR 1665. See also *R (Youssef) v Foreign Secretary* [2016] UKSC 3, [2016] 2 WLR 509 paras 55–6.

as a superior concept to *Wednesbury* unreasonableness/irrationality, as the principle's emphasis on balance and justification is taken to offer a 'more structured methodology'. For instance, Jowell and Lester have long held that 'proportionality advances a relatively specific legal principle—one that is at any rate far more specific than 'unreasonableness' or 'irrationality'—it focuses more clearly than those vaguer standards on the precise conduct it seeks to prevent'.[111] Nevertheless—and despite considerable academic and judicial support for the fuller emergence of the proportionality principle—it has been emphasised by senior members of the judiciary that it is vital that the courts remain distanced from direct involvement in legitimate decision-making by representative public bodies and that they avoid being drawn into the political process. This point was at the heart of the 2011 FA Mann lecture that was given by one of the Supreme Court's most high-profile Justices, Lord Sumption, where much of the language that was used was evocative of the constitutional logic of *Wednesbury*.[112] While not all judges will agree with the judicial conservatism that marked the Mann lecture, it is perhaps no coincidence that *Wednesbury* seems to be enjoying growing support among members of the judiciary and, to a limited extent, in the academic community.[113] Proof, perhaps, of the durability of common law principles even at a time of increased Europeanisation and globalisation.[114]

13.8 Conclusion

In this chapter we have seen that, as grounds of review, the principles of *Wednesbury* unreasonableness and proportionality have been of fundamental importance in determining judicial approaches to challenges to the discretionary decision-making powers of public bodies. The *Wednesbury* test, at least in its original form, deliberately established a high threshold reflecting a judicial perception of the need to exercise self-restraint. At the same time, we have noted that theory and practice have not always elided and that the courts have sometimes engaged in more or less intensive review, for instance, through the development of 'sub' and 'super' standards of *Wednesbury* review. We have also considered how the emergence of the proportionality principle, since the introduction of the Human Rights Act, has presented a very different challenge for the courts, as that principle often posits 'closer look' review as an inevitability. While such review would not be wholly inconsistent with prior experience (*viz* sub-*Wednesbury* review), a wholesale shift towards 'merits' review would be regarded as problematic in terms of the separation of powers. To safeguard that latter doctrine, the courts have thus developed a parallel 'discretionary area of judgment' doctrine that seeks to ensure appropriate judicial restraint in Human Rights Act cases.

---

111 J Jowell, 'Proportionality: Neither Novel nor Dangerous' in J Jowell and D Oliver (eds), *New Directions in Judicial Review* (London: Sweet & Maxwell, 1988), 61, 68.

112 'Judicial and Political Decision-making: the Uncertain Boundary' [2011] 16 *Judicial Review* 301.

113 See *Pham* and *Kennedy*, n 106, and, e.g., P Daly, '*Wednesbury's* reason and structure' [2011] *Public Law* 238.

114 On which concepts see ch 2.

One final point concerns the desirability of the use of such apparently variable public law principles. Although it is within the nature of the common law for the courts to use principles creatively and responsively, it might be argued that there is too much inconsistency in this area of the law. For instance, we have seen above how there may be significantly different judicial opinions as to the 'reasonableness' or 'proportionality' of particular choices, with arguments being allowed on normative points rather than on technical points of detail. So, is this to be regarded as problematic? Certainly, there is an argument in favour of greater coherence in the overall process of judicial reasoning, for the simple fact that this lends itself to greater predictability and clarity. But, on the other hand, it is important not to lose sight of the reasons why there may be differing judicial opinions as to the appropriate standard of review in any given case. Not only are cases heard by judges who may have very different judicial philosophies; the cases may also raise highly complex and context-specific issues. It is thus here that the scope for variable application of principle becomes apparent and, indeed, reveals fault-lines in ongoing debates about the respective constitutional weights of concepts such as the 'rule of law' and the 'separation of powers'.

FURTHER READING

Allan, T (2011) 'Judicial Deference and Judicial Review: Legal Doctrine and Legal Theory' 127 *Law Quarterly Review* 96.

Amos, M (2007) 'Separating Human Rights Adjudication from Judicial Review—*Huang v Secretary of State for the Home Department*' *European Human Rights Law Review* 679.

Arden, M (2015) *Human Rights and European Law: Building New Legal Orders* (Oxford: Oxford University Press).

Carnwath, R (2014) 'From Rationality to Proportionality in Modern Law' 44 *Hong Kong Law Journal* 1.

Craig, P (2015) *UK, EU and Global Administrative Law* (Cambridge: Cambridge University Press), 256ff.

Craig, P [2015] 'Judicial Review and Anxious Scrutiny: Foundations, Evolution and Application' *Public Law* 60.

Daly, P [2011] '*Wednesbury's* Reason and Structure' *Public Law* 238.

Elliott, M (2001) 'The Human Rights Act 1998 and the Standard of Substantive Review' 60 *Cambridge Law Journal* 301.

Goodwin, J [2012] 'The Last Defence of Wednesbury' *Public Law* 445.

Hickman, T [2008] 'The Substance and Structure of Proportionality' *Public Law* 694.

Irvine of Lairg, Lord [1996] 'Judges and Decision-Makers: The Theory and Practice of *Wednesbury* Review' *Public Law* 59.

Laws, Sir J (1998) '*Wednesbury*', in Forsyth, C and Hare, I (eds), *The Golden Metwand and the Crooked Cord* (Oxford: Clarendon Press).

Poole, T [2005] 'Of Headscarves and Heresies: The Denbigh High School Case and Public Authority Decision Making under the Human Rights Act' *Public Law* 685.

Sales, P (2013) 'Rationality, Proportionality and the Development of the Law' 129 *Law Quarterly Review* 223.

Taggart, M (2003) 'Reinventing Administrative Law' in Bamforth, N and Leyland, P (eds), *Public Law in a Multi-Layered Constitution* (Oxford: Hart Publishing).

14

Equality

14.1 Introduction

The focus of this chapter is the principle of equality or, as it is otherwise termed, non-discrimination. For our purposes, the principle can be defined as that which requires public decision-makers to treat like situations alike and different situations differently, unless there is good reason for them not to do so.[1] In terms of the structure of this book, we have placed our chapter on equality directly after that on *Wednesbury* and proportionality because there is a very close link between the various principles in the sense that judicial approaches to equality often mirror those in respect of reasonableness and so on. Although we will see that the equality principle has a number of dimensions, it is ultimately defined by an expectation of consistency in public decision-making and, as with *Wednesbury* and proportionality, an absence of the abuse of power. However, while this provides one linkage between the principles, we will also see that claims that individuals have been treated unfairly will often involve arguments about how a public decision-maker has exercised discretionary powers and whether any alleged discriminatory treatment can be justified. A challenge to the manner of the exercise of those powers will thus bring with it familiar questions about the intensity of review that is appropriate—should the courts look closely at the decision, or should they intervene only where the impugned decision is so unreasonable that no reasonable decision-maker could have taken it?

Of course, it will be apparent from having read the previous chapter that all will depend on the context within which a decision has been taken and whether, for instance, the matter is considered under common law principles or whether EU law and/or the European Convention on Human Rights (ECHR) apply. Where the matter is considered solely on common law principles the starting point for review will be *Wednesbury* unreasonableness.[2] Nevertheless, we have already seen that the *Wednesbury* principle exists on a sliding scale and that there is an ongoing debate about whether it should be subsumed by proportionality review. However, should a challenge be brought under the European Communities Act 1972 and/or the Human Rights Act 1998, it is axiomatic that the proportionality principle should guide the courts and that this can—though not necessarily will—result in a closer look review of any discretionary choice. All will, again, depend upon the context

---

1 *Re Coroner for South Down's Application* [2004] NIQB 86, para 33, Weatherup J.
2 *Matadeen v Pointu* [1999] 1 AC 98, 109, Lord Hoffmann.

within which the decision has been taken and whether the courts consider that it falls within the decision-maker's 'discretionary area of judgment'.

We begin our analysis in the chapter by looking at how arguments about equality can arise in the case law and the issues this presents for review based upon common law principles. There then follow two sections that consider, respectively, the nature of the equality principle in EU law and in the law of the ECHR. In those sections, we provide a number of examples from the case law that reveal both how the proportionality principle interacts with the equality principle and how the reception of the European standards have impacted upon constitutional orthodoxy in the UK.[3] The final section of the chapter looks briefly at the role that discrete legislative schemes can play in relation to the elimination of discrimination,[4] and how those schemes relate to judicial review's equality principle.

One final point that should be made by way of introduction is that this chapter is concerned with equality in a *substantive* sense, not in a *formal* sense. The formal sense is one that is associated with the Diceyan conception of the rule of law that we examined in chapter 2; that is, the understanding that all persons, whether public or private, should be equally subject to the ordinary law of the land. The corresponding formalism follows from Dicey's related doctrine of legislative supremacy, which entails that the Westminster Parliament can enact discriminatory legislation that will be applied equally to all those affected by it, irrespective of any argument of the need for substantive equality among different groups in society.[5] However, while it remains theoretically and practically possible for the Westminster Parliament to enact such discriminatory legislation, judicial acceptance of that legislation is now moderated by the demands of EU law and the ECHR, as read with the European Communities Act 1972 and the Human Rights Act 1998. As we have already explained elsewhere, Acts of Parliament that are contrary to EU law's equality requirements can thus be disapplied by the courts (save where there are words that repudiate EU law either expressly or by 'irresistible' implication),[6] while legislation that cannot be read in a manner that is compatible with the ECHR may be the subject of a declaration of incompatibility under section 4 of the Human Rights Act 1998.[7]

14.2 Equality and the common law

There are perhaps two main ways in which common law arguments centred upon the equality principle can arise in judicial review proceedings. The first is where it is argued that the principle has been offended by an administrative or executive decision-maker's application of a policy.[8] Here, an individual may point to an

3 See further chs 2–4.

4 See J Wadham et al (eds), *Blackstone's Guide to the Equality Act 2010* 2nd edn (Oxford: Oxford University Press, 2012) and N Bamforth, M Malik, and C O'Cinneide, *Discrimination Law: Theory and Context, Text and Materials* (London: Sweet and Maxwell, 2008).

5 See J Jowell, 'Is Equality a Constitutional Principle?' (1994) 2 *CLP* 1.

6 See 3.3.2 and, e.g., *R v Secretary of State for Transport, ex p Factortame Ltd (No 2)* [1991] 1 AC 603 and *Thoburn v Sunderland CC* [2003] QB 151.

7 See 4.4.3 and e.g., *A v Secretary of State for the Home Department* [2005] 2 AC 68.

8 On the nature of policies see 12.2.

extant policy and argue that the decision-maker has chosen not to resolve the matter before it in the light of that policy and that it has thereby acted unlawfully. In such circumstances, arguments based upon the equality principle may be particularly persuasive precisely because policies are intended to guide the decision-maker and, in doing so, to generate certainty and consistency in the decision-making process. Hence in *R v Home Secretary, ex p Urmaza*,[9] a Filipino seaman who had 'jumped ship' while in the UK and subsequently married within this country challenged a decision to detain him with a view to deportation. The application for judicial review succeeded because the Secretary of State had decided not to determine the applicant's immigration status in the light of a policy that would have entitled the applicant to remain in the UK. It was held that there was no reason not to apply this policy to the applicant and that the decision of the Secretary of State was unlawful.[10]

The second way in which the principle may arise is where an individual argues that the decision-maker has discriminated when making a discretionary choice in an area that is not actually covered by any policy. In this scenario—and in contrast to that above—it might be expected that the individual would face a steeper climb when seeking to convince the court that there has been an unlawful decision. This is because decisions here may be taken on the basis of a wide discretion that necessarily involves the authority in making value judgements about whether two discrete matters are, in fact, the same and to be treated as such. Judicial acceptance of arguments about the need for equality in such circumstances could thus result in the courts becoming involved in matters that are, on a separation of powers analysis, matters for the authority. In consequence, a judicial ruling to the effect that two cases should have been treated the same could result in the court making choices that are, in law, matters for the relevant authority.

The corresponding link between the equality principle and *Wednesbury* and/or proportionality is made when a court must determine whether any difference in treatment between individuals, or groups of individuals, is justified. Certainly, it is well-established that the courts view the need to treat 'like cases alike and unlike cases differently [as] a general axiom of rational behaviour',[11] and it can therefore be expected that the courts will intervene where the justification for a decision is unreasonable within the strong meaning of the *Wednesbury* principle (i.e., the justification is 'so unreasonable that no reasonable decision-maker' could have offered it). But more difficult is the circumstance where a justification does not exhibit such unreasonableness. While orthodoxy would dictate that the courts should not intervene in the absence of strong unreasonableness,[12] we know that the law can be much more complex and that the context to a case may lead to more or less intervention. Considerations that might guide the courts towards closer look review would include the extent of any discretion and whether common law

---

9 [1996] COD 479.

10 See too *R v Home Secretary, ex p Gangadeen* [1998] 1 FLR 762 and *R (Gurung) v Ministry of Defence* [2002] EWHC Admin 2463.

11 *Matadeen v Pointu* [1999] 1 AC 98, 109, Lord Hoffmann.

12 As in, e.g., *Kruse v Johnson* [1898] 2 QB 91 (a bye-law that prohibited the playing of music in certain localities would be deemed unlawful only where it was manifestly partial and unequal in its operation between different classes, or unjust, or made in bad faith, or clearly involved an unjustifiable interference with the liberty of those subject to it).

fundamental rights are affected by the impugned decisions. On the other hand, considerations that might lead the courts towards a position of restraint would include whether a decision was essentially political in nature or one that was informed by social policy.[13]

14.3 Equality and EU law

The principle of equality in EU law exists at a number of levels that intersect with one another and can require the courts to engage in closer look review of even Acts of the Westminster Parliament.[14] First, the principle is found in the Equality Chapter of the EU Charter of Fundamental Rights[15] and in a range of Treaty provisions that prohibit discrimination on grounds of nationality;[16] that pursue the elimination of discrimination based on sex, racial or ethnic origin, religion or belief, disability, age, or sexual orientation;[17] and that require equal pay for equal work between the sexes.[18] Secondly, the principle can be found in a large number of legislative acts of the EU institutions that have been adopted on the basis of the above Treaty Articles and which will often be directly enforceable in UK courts. Where those legislative acts are in the form of directives, it is of course incumbent upon the UK legislature(s) to achieve the objectives of the acts, and this is frequently done by introducing specific legislative schemes that allow individuals to bring tribunal proceedings in the face of alleged discrimination (see 14.5). Thirdly, equality exists as a general principle of EU law, which means that national decision-makers working within the realm of EU law must treat like cases alike and different cases differently unless there is an objective justification for not doing so.[19] As proportionality is also a general principle of EU law, it follows that the legality of any discretionary choice must be assessed using that principle, albeit that EU law has a 'margin of appreciation' doctrine that may lessen the scope for judicial intervention in certain contexts.[20]

The intersection of the above levels has been central to some of the seminal case law on the constitutional implications of UK membership of the EU. For instance, the *Factortame* case that we discussed in chapter 3 was brought by Spanish fishing boat operators who argued that the Merchant Shipping Act 1988 was, among other things, contrary to the (then) EC Treaty's prohibition on discrimination on grounds of nationality.[21] And a case of comparable constitutional significance was *R v Secretary of State for Employment, ex p Equal Opportunities Commission*.[22] The applicant in this case was a statutory body with responsibility for monitoring

---

13 *Matadeen v Pointu* [1999] 1 AC 98, 109, Lord Hoffmann.

14 See 3.2.1.2.

15 Arts 20–26.

16 Art 18 TFEU.

17 Art 19 TFEU.

18 Art 157 TFEU.

19 Cases 117/76 and 16/77, *Ruckdeschel v Hauptzollamt Hambourg-St Annen* [1977] ECR 1753, 1811.

20 See 3.2.2.1; and on the margin of appreciation doctrine in EU law see, e.g., Case C-265/95, *Commission v French Republic* [1997] ECR I-6959, 6999, para 33.

21 *R v Secretary of State for Transport, ex p Factortame Ltd (No 2)* [1991] 1 AC 603.

22 [1995] 1 AC 1.

matters of equality, and it here challenged the validity of various provisions of the Employment Protection (Consolidation) Act 1978 relative to EU law's equal pay requirements (then contained in Article 119 EEC; now contained in Article 157 TFEU). The applicant's central argument was that the Act discriminated indirectly against women because it granted preferential employment protection rights to full-time workers, a majority of whom were men, as opposed to part-time workers, a majority of whom were women (indirect discrimination can be said to occur where apparently neutral rules/conditions have a disadvantageous impact on particular individuals or groups). Agreeing with that argument, and that the discrimination could not be justified, the House of Lords considered the significance of the *Factortame* case when addressing the remedies that it had available to it when dealing with an Act of the Westminster Parliament. In the event, it took the unprecedented step of making a declaration that the Act of 1978 was incompatible with the relevant provisions of EU law.[23]

A recent case in which the Supreme Court accepted that measures that were indirectly discriminatory were lawful is *Patmalniece v Secretary of State for Work and Pensions*.[24] The central issue in the case was whether the conditions governing entitlement to State Pension Credit were contrary to EU law's prohibition of discrimination on grounds of nationality and, if they were, whether they could be justified. The case had been brought by a Latvian women who had lived in—but not worked in—the UK since 2000. When Latvia acceded to the EU in 2004, Mrs Patmalniece applied for State Pension Credit as an entitlement that she said followed from Regulation 1408/71 EC (which applies to social security schemes). However, her claim for the Credit was refused for the reason that she did not satisfy the qualifying residence requirements under the relevant national legislation. Accepting that the legislation was thereby indirectly discriminatory, the Supreme Court was of the view that nevertheless it was justified. This was because the legislation sought to protect the public purse against so-called 'benefit' or 'social' tourism and because this objective was independent of the question of nationality. As Lord Hope put it, the wording of the legislation shows:

that the Secretary of State's purpose was to protect the resources of the United Kingdom against resort to benefit or social tourism by persons who are not economically or socially integrated with this country. This is not because of their nationality or because of where they have come from. It is because of the principle that only those who are economically or socially integrated with the host member state should have access to its social assistance system.[25]

Another case of note is *R (Rotherham MBC) v Secretary of State for Business, Innovation and Skills*.[26] This case involved use of EU law's equality principle to challenge the Secretary of State's decisions about the allocation of EU structural funds amongst the UK's regions, including Northern Ireland and the Highlands and Islands in Scotland. The claimant council argued that the Secretary of State had adopted an unfair method of calculation in making the allocation as between the countries

---

23 For some of the other leading EU law equality cases see, e.g., *Duke v GEC Reliance Ltd* [1988] AC 618; *Pickstone v Freemans plc* [1989] AC 66; *Finnegan v Clowney Youth Training Ltd* [1990] 2 AC 407; and *Webb v EMO Cargo (UK) Ltd* [1995] 1 WLR 1454.

24 [2011] 1 WLR 783. The legislation in question was the State Pension and Credit Act 2002, s 1(2)(a) and the Pension Credit Regulations 2002.

25 [2011] 1 WLR 783, 803, para 52.

26 [2015] UKSC 6, [2015] 3 CMLR 20.

and regions within the UK and that this had caused it to suffer a greatly reduced level of funding. In dismissing the argument that there had been a breach of the equality principle, the Supreme Court began by noting that the issues in the case—concerning the allocation of funding—were such that the Secretary of State had a wide 'margin of judgement' and that the Court should be slow to intervene. On the specific question of whether there had been discrimination as between the regions, the Court held that the Secretary of State had been entitled to have regard to the constitutional settlement in the UK so long as his approach did not discriminate unjustifiably between the four countries or place him in breach of the relevant EU legislation on structural funds. On the facts before the Court, a majority was of the view that the Secretary of State's actions were lawful.

14.4 **Equality and the ECHR**

The starting point in relation to the equality principle under this heading is Article 14 of the ECHR, which provides:

[T]he enjoyment of the rights and freedoms set forth in this Convention shall be secured without discrimination on any ground such as sex, race, colour, language, religion, political or other opinion, national or social origin, association with a national minority, property, birth or other status.

Although Article 14 of the ECHR does not thereby enshrine a free-standing prohibition of discrimination—*viz* its reference to 'the enjoyment of the rights and freedoms in the Convention'[27]—the case law of the European Court of Human Rights (ECtHR) has established that there need not be a breach of one of the other rights and freedoms for there to be a breach of Article 14 of the ECHR.[28] It is, instead, sufficient for the decision or other measure under challenge to come 'within the ambit' of one of the other Articles, at which stage a court may determine whether there has been a violation of Article 14 of the ECHR.[29] Where an individual is making an argument under Article 14 of the ECHR, as read with one of the other rights and freedoms, he or she must be able to identify a comparator who has, or would have, been treated more favourably. Discrimination for these purposes may be direct or indirect in form and, if a reviewing court is of the view that the comparison that has been made is a valid one, it must decide whether the less favourable treatment of the applicant can be justified.[30] Justification, in this context, also requires the public authority to identify a legitimate objective that the less favourable treatment pursues and to satisfy the court that the treatment is proportionate in all the circumstances. Should the court conclude that no legitimate objective has been

---

27 Cf Protocol 12 ECHR, not yet ratified by the UK government: '1. The enjoyment of any right set forth by law shall be secured without discrimination on any ground such as sex, race, colour, language, religion, political or other opinion, national or social origin, association with a national minority, property, birth or other status. 2. No one shall be discriminated against by any public authority on any ground such as those mentioned in paragraph 1.'

28 e.g., *Abdulaziz, Cabales and Balkandali v UK* (1985) 7 EHRR 471.

29 e.g., *Van der Mussele v Belgium* (1984) 6 EHRR 163, 178, para 43.

30 *Larkos v Cyprus* (2000) 30 EHRR 597, 608, para 29; and *R (Carson) v Secretary of State for Work and Pensions* [2006] 1 AC 173.

pursued and/or that there has been a lack of proportion, a violation of Article 14 of the ECHR will be made out and a remedy should be granted. On the other hand, the courts will also take account of the overall context to a dispute and may exercise restraint in the face of the decision-maker's choice. Under those circumstances, they may emphasise that the impugned decision or other measure falls within the decision-maker's 'discretionary area of judgment'.[31]

There have been a great number of cases about the reach of Article 14 of the ECHR under the Human Rights Act 1998, and some of these have touched upon matters of considerable controversy. One example, which has already been discussed in previous chapters, is *A v Home Secretary*,[32] the famous *'Belmarsh detainees'* case. It will be recalled that Parliament had here enacted the Anti-terrorism, Crime and Security Act 2001, which provided, among other things, for the indefinite detention without trial of non-British nationals who were suspected of involvement in international terrorism. While the outcome of the case is perhaps most famously associated with the finding that there had been a disproportionate interference with liberty rights under Article 5 of the ECHR, as read with Article 15 of the ECHR, the House of Lords also held that the measures were discriminatory and unjustified within the meaning of Article 14 of the ECHR. The government had argued on this point that the measures fell within the field of immigration and asylum and that detention was the only meaningful option, as there was no power to deport the individuals to their countries of origin given threats, there, to their well being.[33] However, the House of Lords disagreed that the measures concerned immigration and asylum and held, instead, that they had been adopted in the field of national security. Noting that terror attacks equally could be perpetrated by British nationals—a point subsequently borne out by the tragic events of 7 July 2005—the House of Lords concluded that the measures were unjustified and discriminatory in form. A declaration of incompatibility with Article 14 of the ECHR, as well as Article 5 of the ECHR, was made.

A case in which discriminatory measures were held to be lawful under Article 14 of the ECHR is *Re Parsons' Application*.[34] The applicant in this case was a Protestant man who wished to join the Police Service of Northern Ireland but who was refused a place because of a 50/50 recruitment quota that meant, on the facts, that some applications from Catholics had been preferred to his. The quota, which was sourced in section 46(1) of the Police (Northern Ireland) Act 2000, had been introduced in an effort to increase the levels of Catholic representation in the Police Service in post-conflict Northern Ireland. Accepting that that was a legitimate objective—policing in Northern Ireland had historically been very divisive and the vast majority of officers had been Protestant—Kerr J held that the impugned measures were proportionate and that they were not contrary to Article 14 of the ECHR, as read with the Article 9 ECHR guarantee of religious freedom. This was because, among other

---

31 For the leading judicial statements of principle see *R (Hooper) v Secretary of State for Work and Pensions* [2005] 1 WLR 1681; *R (Carson) v Secretary of State for Work and Pensions* [2006] 1 AC 173; and *R (M) v Secretary of State for Work and Pensions* [2009] 1 AC 311. And for application of the principle see, e.g., *Humphreys v Revenue and Customs Commissioners* [2012] UKSC 18, [2012] 1 WLR 1545 and *(SG) v Secretary of State for Work and Pensions* [2015] UKSC 16, [2015] 1 WLR 1449.

32 [2005] 2 AC 68. See 4.4.3 and 13.6.3.1.

33 This was the result of the ECtHR ruling in *Chahal v UK* (1996) 23 EHRR 413.

34 [2002] NI 378 (Northern Ireland High Court) and [2004] NI 38 (Northern Ireland Court of Appeal).

things, the measures that had been put in place were time-limited in the sense that their operation was to be reviewed after a period of five years. An appeal to the Court of Appeal was dismissed.

Another case of note is *R (Hurley) v Secretary of State for Business, Innovation and Skills*.[35] The issue here, among others, was whether regulations that permit universities in England to charge up to £9,000 per year for tuition fees are contrary to Article 14 of the ECHR, as read with the right to education under Article 2 of Protocol 1 of the ECHR.[36] The regulations had been made after a panel recommended that the higher amount be introduced but in a manner that provided greater assistance to students from low-income backgrounds. In challenging the regulations, the claimant argued that the higher fee level discriminated indirectly against individuals from lower socio-economic groups, as there was evidence that the new fee cap would act as a disincentive to such individuals entering third-level education. However, while the court accepted that there was evidence that the fees would act as a disincentive for some students, it was not satisfied that these students would necessarily come from lower income backgrounds, particularly given the availability of measures intended to increase university access for poorer students. The court also noted the need for judicial restraint in cases of this kind, as 'this is an area of macro-economic judgment, where decisions have to be taken about prioritizing public resources . . . significant leeway must be given to the democratically accountable Secretary of State as to how the objective of providing sustainable and quality higher education can best be secured'.[37] The Article 14 ECHR argument therefore failed, albeit that the claimant obtained a declaration about a point of detail concerning the Secretary of State's equality duties under statute and his analysis of the overall package of measures (but not the fees level).

14.5 Equality and statute law

The final issue to be addressed is the relationship between the equality principle and a range of statutory schemes that have been enacted in addition to the European Communities Act 1972 and Human Rights Act 1998 and which seek to eliminate discrimination. As we have already indicated at 14.3, some of these schemes have historically been enacted to give effect to legislative acts of the EU institutions,[38] while others, such as that at issue in *Re Parsons' Application*, have been aimed at mischiefs more specific to (parts of) the UK. Other schemes have sought to address discrimination on the basis of characteristics such as race and disability, albeit that the Equality Act 2010 has now consolidated many of those schemes within England and Wales and, for the most part, Scotland[39] (it might also

---

35 [2012] HRLR 13.

36 The regulations are the Higher Education (Basic Amount) (England) Regulations 2010, SI 2010/3021, and the Higher Education (Higher Amount) (England) Regulations 2010, SI 2010/3020.

37 [2012] HRLR 13, para 63.

38 e.g., the Sex Discrimination Act 1975, since repealed by Sch 27 to the Equality Act 2010.

39 On the Act see Wadham et al, n 4. The Act does not generally apply to Northern Ireland: see s 217(3).

be noted that equality duties of the kind mentioned in *Hurley*, above, are found in this legislation and that decision-makers must have 'due regard' for the duties through, for instance, assessing the likely impact that measures will have on identified societal groups).[40]

In terms of judicial review, the key question about legislation will often be whether it provides for alternative remedies in the event of discrimination, for instance through proceedings in the County Court or before a tribunal.[41] If that is the case, it is well known that courts will require an individual to avail him or herself of that remedy not just for reasons of fidelity to legislative intention but also because the remedy will likely be more effective in the circumstances.[42] However, where legislation does not provide a suitable remedy, a claim for judicial review will be appropriate. Depending on context, that claim would be likely to centre upon the argument that the public body in question has acted illegally/*ultra vires* by discriminating contrary to the terms of the relevant legislation.

A leading example of just such a claim for judicial review is *R (E) v Jewish Free School Governing Body*.[43] Under the Equality Act 2006, discrimination on religious grounds was prohibited, but faith schools were granted an exemption. This meant that schools were allowed to select pupils by preferring those of the faith adopted by the school. However, this exemption did not permit discrimination on other prohibited grounds, for example, on grounds of race. The claimant was a Masorti Jew who had sought admittance to an over-subscribed Jewish school that refused him a place for the reason that his mother was not of Jewish descent (his father was) and had converted to Judaism within a non-Orthodox synagogue. The decision was taken on the basis of the school's over-subscription policy and, in challenging the policy, the claimant alleged direct discrimination on the basis of his ethnicity (contrary to section 1(1)(a) of the Race Relations Act 1976) and/or indirect discrimination on the same ground (contrary to section 1(1A) of the same Act). The Supreme Court, by a majority of five to four, held that the school policy was directly discriminatory as it was clear that the victim's ethnic origins were the factual basis for the refusal to admit him to the school and that such discrimination was thereby unlawful—in other words, that the admission had been taken not with reference to the religion that was practised but rather the matter of descent through the mother's line. The corresponding difficulty for the school was that the criterion of descent from a Jewish mother fell squarely within the scope of the Race Relations Act 1976 and the 'faith school' exemption did not apply. While this initial finding could have been dispositive of the case—direct discrimination cannot be justified under the Act of 1976—a majority also held that the policy was indirectly discriminatory and could not be justified. This was because it was apparent that applicants with different ethnic origins would be treated less favourably under the policy, and also because the criteria attached no weight to matters of

---

40 On the 'due regard' obligation see 11.5.5.

41 Equality Act 2010, Part 9. On tribunals see ch 7. For a case of seminal importance that began as a County Court action see *Hall v Bull* [2013] UKSC 73, [2013] 1 WLR 3741 (a decision by the Christian owners of a bed and breakfast establishment to refuse a double room to a same-sex couple in a civil partnership was discrimination contrary to the Equality Act (Sexual Orientation) Regulations 2007).

42 e.g., *Re Kirkpatrick's Application* [2004] NIJB 15.

43 [2010] 2 AC 728. And see C McCrudden, 'Multiculturalism, Freedom of Religion, Equality, and the British Constitution: The JFS Case Considered' (2011) 9 *International Journal of Constitutional Law* 200.

religious practice. Given that the school had argued that the policy was intended to preserve the ethos of a 'faith school', the Court concluded that the criteria lacked the necessary quality of proportionality.[44]

14.6 **Conclusion**

We began this discussion by noting that the principle of equality is inextricably linked to the principles of *Wednesbury* and proportionality that were examined in chapter 13. Returning to those linkages, we would make two points by way of concluding the present chapter. The first—outlined at 14.2—is that the tension that runs through the *Wednesbury* and proportionality debate can be present in cases about the common law's equality principle. As we have seen, that principle requires the courts to ask whether decision-makers have acted lawfully when making distinctions between individuals and, if they have not, whether the courts should grant a remedy. We would note simply that, while intervention in cases of strong unreasonableness should always be unremarkable, intervention beneath that threshold is potentially more problematic in constitutional terms.

The second point concerns the scope for challenges to decisions and so on that are based upon legislative schemes that seek to eliminate discrimination. As several of the examples given above will have made clear, the language of proportionality can often underpin such challenges, as can the language and logic of the illegality principle considered in chapters 11 and 12. Referring back to our earlier discussion of the grounds for judicial review, this is thus one further area in which the overlapping nature of the grounds can frequently be seen.

FURTHER READING

Bamforth, N, Malik, M, and O'Cinneide, C (2008) *Discrimination Law: Theory and Context, Text and Materials* (London: Sweet and Maxwell).

Bell, M (2002) *Anti-discrimination Law and the European Union* (Oxford: Oxford University Press).

Jowell, J (1994) 'Is Equality a Constitutional Principle' 2 *Current Legal Problems* 1.

Mancini, S [2009] 'The Power of Symbols as Power: Secularism and Religion as Guarantors of Cultural Convergence' 30 (6) *Cardozo Law Review* 2629.

McCrudden, C (2011), 'Multiculturalism, Freedom of Religion, Equality, and the British Constitution: The JFS Case Considered' 9 *International Journal of Constitutional Law* 200.

Wadham, J et al (eds) (2012) *Blackstone's Guide to the Equality Act 2010* 2nd edn (Oxford: Oxford University Press).

---

44 See G Bindman, 'When Freedoms Collide' (2010) 160 *New Law Journal* 320.

15

Legitimate expectations

15.1 **Introduction**

We turn in this chapter to consider the doctrine of legitimate expectation. This is a doctrine that has become increasingly prominent in case law in the past 20 years or so, and it is now regarded as central to the workings of public law.[1] The origins of the doctrine lie in common law fairness and the idea that an individual who will be affected by a decision can expect that he or she will be consulted in advance of the decision being taken—a so-called 'procedural legitimate expectation'.[2] However, the doctrine has since evolved to embrace a substantive dimension whereby a decision-maker may be prevented from going back on, for instance, a lawful representation that an individual will receive, or continue to receive, a substantive benefit of some kind (a 'substantive legitimate expectation'). This latter dimension has prompted wide-ranging debate about the limits to the judicial role in a claim for judicial review, as any decision that frustrates a substantive expectation will typically have been taken within the framework of statute that has delegated discretionary powers to the decision-maker. The corresponding debate has thus centred upon familiar concerns about the separation of powers doctrine, *viz* how closely the courts should scrutinise discretionary choices; and consideration has also been given to the apparent tension between the legitimate expectation doctrine and the rule against the fettering of discretion. As we saw in chapter 12, the rule against fettering entails that decision-makers may not place limitations upon discretionary powers that have been delegated to them, as to do so would run contrary to the legislature's intention in granting the discretion. At the same time, the legitimate expectation doctrine, which is founded upon the principle of legal certainty, allows an individual to argue that a decision-maker should be bound by an earlier policy in respect of the individual's circumstances or required to give effect to a promise that has earlier been made to the individual. At its simplest, this thus suggests that an exercise of discretion which ignores previous policy and/or a representation might be deemed unlawful.[3]

---

1 *R v East Sussex County Council, ex p Reprotech* [2002] 4 All ER 58, 66, Lord Hoffmann. On its position in EU law, where it exists as a 'general principle of law', see 3.2.2.3. On its position under the ECHR see, e.g., M Sigron, 'Legitimate Expectations Under Article 1 of Protocol No. 1 to the European Convention on Human Rights' (2014) 32 *Netherlands Quarterly of Human Rights* 338.

2 On the doctrine's basis in fairness see *R (Bapio) v Home Secretary* [2008] 1 AC 1003, 1016, para 29, Lord Scott; and on common law fairness, see ch 17.

3 See further C Hilson, 'Policies, the Non-Fetter Principle and the Principle of Substantive Legitimate Expectations: Between a Rock and a Hard Place?' [2006] 11 *Judicial Review* 289. And for judicial consideration of the point see *Re Loreto Grammar School's Application* [2013] NI 41.

We will see that the case law in this area is developing and that the courts continue to work through the relationship that the legitimate expectation doctrine has with principles such as *Wednesbury* unreasonableness and proportionality.[4] Nevertheless, there are two generally valid points that can be made with reference to the existing case law, and these should be borne in mind when reading what follows. The first is that, where an expectation is procedural in form, the courts may be much more demanding when identifying what fairness requires in any given case.[5] This is because the courts have long been willing to scrutinise decisions for procedural impropriety, as such an enquiry is not understood to engage the courts in assessing the merits of a decision but rather the manner in which it has been reached. On the other hand, it can be said that matters of procedure and substance cannot always or easily be disentangled and that a 'procedural' development may have 'substantive' implications. One might think here of the common law duty to give reasons: while the duty can be described as a facet of procedural fairness,[6] any reasons given may subsequently be used to found an application for judicial review that centres on arguments of, among other things, relevancy, unreasonableness, lack of proportion, or abuse of power.

The second point is that the courts are more willing to look closely at a decision that frustrates a substantive legitimate expectation where a representation has been made to 'one or a few people giving the promise or representation the character of a contract . . . it is more likely to be held binding if made to a smaller number of people, on discrete facts, with no implications for an innominate class of persons'.[7] Although we will see that a willingness to look closely at decisions in such instances can give rise to controversy,[8] the need for fairness towards individuals can here be said to be at its highest. This is because an individual will typically have relied upon the representation to his or her detriment—whether by spending money or making fresh life choices—and the courts will be anxious to avoid the 'abuse of power' by a decision-maker who suddenly resiles from the earlier representation. However, the corresponding difficulty with intervention in such cases is that it may be difficult to determine whether a representation that has been made to one person (or small group of persons) has implications only for that person (or group). Indeed, the problem can become particularly pronounced where the challenged public authority decision concerns the allocation of resources, for instance where there has been a refusal to grant social housing to a person who has previously received assurances about such housing. Should that person successfully challenge the decision, a judicial remedy could have an impact on the affairs of many other people who are not before the court. Hence we will see that disputes of this kind are sometimes described as 'polycentric' and that there are strong arguments in favour of judicial restraint where the issues raised could have 'knock-on' effects on individuals whose interests are not represented in court.[9]

---

4 On which see ch 13.

5 On procedural legitimate expectation see further 17.2.5.

6 See ch 17.

7 *R v North and East Devon Heath Authority, ex p Coughlan* [2000] 2 WLR 622, 646, para 59.

8 M Elliott, '*Coughlan*: Substantive Protection of Legitimate Expectations Revisited' [2000] 5 *Judicial Review* 27.

9 J Allison, 'The Procedural Reason for Judicial Self-restraint' [1994] *Public Law* 452.

We begin our analysis in the chapter with a section that explains how legitimate expectations are created and recognised in law. There then follow two sections that examine (1) the relationship between the procedural and substantive dimensions of the doctrine, and (2) the manner in which the courts now protect substantive legitimate expectations. The analysis here, it should be emphasised, will be concerned with legitimate expectations that are created by public authority representations and other measures that are lawful, or *intra vires*, the authority concerned (these may be described as 'lawfully created expectations'). As will become apparent, it is also possible (albeit exceptionally) for an individual to argue that he or she has a legitimate expectation arising from a representation that is *ultra vires* the authority or, alternatively, a representation that has been made by an officer who was not authorised to make the representation (these may be termed 'unlawfully created expectations'). Cases of this kind raise difficult questions about how to reconcile the need for fairness with the constitutional demands of the legality doctrine, and we thus consider those questions in a final section on the protection of unlawfully created expectations. The conclusion offers some more general, evaluative comments on the current state of the law.

15.2 **When are legitimate expectations created?**

The question whether an individual has a legitimate expectation is a matter of law that is answered objectively and with reference to the full legal and factual context of a case.[10] In the first instance, the courts look to the actions of the public authority, as an individual can have a legitimate expectation only in the light of the conduct of the decision-maker.[11] This is consonant with public law's more general emphasis on preventing the 'abuse of power' in circumstances where one party (the public authority) is able to take decisions that have implications for another party (the individual), which second party does not have a comparable power of decision in respect of the first party.[12] Should an authority indicate that it will or will not act in a particular way, the courts have thus said that they may recognise a legitimate expectation as having been created even in the exceptional circumstance where the individual has not relied upon the authority's earlier indications to his or her detriment.[13] The imperative of preventing the abuse of power has also led the courts to accept that an individual may have a legitimate expectation where he or she was initially unaware that the authority had indicated that it would act in the manner that the individual subsequently asks the court to order.[14]

---

10 *Re Findlay* [1985] AC 318, 338.

11 See *R (Bapio) v Home Secretary* [2008] 1 AC 1003, 1017, para 29, Lord Scott.

12 See D Oliver, *Common Values and the Public–Private Divide* (London: Butterworths, 1999), ch 1.

13 *R v Secretary of State for Education and Employment, ex p Begbie* [2000] 1 WLR 1115, 1123–4 and *R (Bibi) v London Borough of Newham* [2002] 1 WLR 237, 246, para 31.

14 See *R (Rashid) v Secretary of State for the Home Department* [2005] Imm AR 608; 12.2.2; and M Elliott, 'Legitimate Expectation, Consistency and Abuse of Power: the *Rashid* case' [2005] 10 *Judicial Review* 281.

In broad terms, there are three ways in which the conduct of a public authority can give rise to a legitimate expectation.[15] The first—and strongest foundation for a legitimate expectation—is where the public authority makes a representation that it will, or will not, act in a particular way (representations for these purposes may be found in one or more of an individual statement, a circular, a report, or some other official document). Although it may be difficult to establish that a representation has been made to a particular individual and that it sounds in law—for example, where government makes a pre-election statement on a matter,[16] or where a representation is subject to a changing financial environment[17]—it is clear that the courts will recognise an expectation as having been created where there has been a promise or a 'clear and unambiguous' representation to an individual. This is what happened in the seminal *Coughlan* case that we examine below, where a severely disabled individual moved to a residential care facility on the public authority's promise that it would be her 'home for life'. In those circumstances, the Court of Appeal accepted that the specific and individualised nature of the representation had given the representation 'the character of a contract' and that the authority could resile from it only where there was a compelling public interest justification for doing so. On the facts, no such justification was found.

Secondly, legitimate expectations may be grounded in the practices of a public authority. For instance, an expectation of consultation may be engendered where an authority has previously consulted the affected individuals about decisions of the kind to be taken;[18] and a public authority cannot, without warning, change a long-standing practice that it is aware an individual has acted in the light of and from which the individual has derived a benefit.[19] In cases of this latter kind there will clearly be reliance on the practice, and the courts have held that it may amount to an abuse of power to allow the practice to be changed without giving the individual a corresponding opportunity to prepare for the change. On the other hand, the fact that an individual has previously received a grant or a licence from an authority cannot, of itself, give rise to an expectation that a future application for a grant or licence will be successful. While the position may be different where an authority has made a clear and unambiguous representation to the effect that a grant will be made, the fact that there will often be more applications for grants/licences than there are resources available would mean that the individual could not have a legitimate expectation of success. The individual could, instead, expect only that his or her application for a grant or licence would be determined in a procedurally fair manner.[20]

Thirdly, an individual may argue that he or she has a legitimate expectation of being treated in accordance with a policy that an authority has adopted to guide it in the exercise of its discretion.[21] Such arguments may arise (a) where an authority decides to depart from its existing policy *vis-à-vis* the individual or (b) where an

---

15 For fuller analysis see S Schønberg, *Legitimate Expectations in Administrative Law* (Oxford: Oxford University Press, 2000) and F Ahmed and A Perry, 'The Coherence of the Doctrine of Legitimate Expectation' (2014) 73 *Cambridge Law Journal* 61.

16 See *R v Secretary of State for Education and Employment, ex p Begbie* [2000] 1 WLR 1115.

17 As in, e.g., *Re Loreto Grammar School's Application* [2013] NI 41.

18 *Council of Civil Service Unions v Minister for the Civil Service* [1985] AC 374, discussed at 9.3.2.2.

19 *R v Inland Revenue Commissioners, ex p Unilever* [1996] STC 681.

20 On the requirements of fairness and licences see *McInnes v Onslow Fane* [1978] 3 All ER 211.

21 On policies see 12.2.

authority changes its policy and the individual considers that the previous policy should still be applied to him or her. In respect of (a), it appears that an individual may legitimately expect that their circumstances will be dealt with in accordance with the policy of the respondent and that any departure from the policy must be reasoned and conform with the principle of equality.[22] Case law under (b) likewise suggests that an individual can have a legitimate expectation of a particular outcome in the light of the original policy but that the weight of the expectation will vary according to the context to the dispute. Hence, where the operation of the original policy was accompanied by a clear and unambiguous representation to the individual that the policy would be applied to him or her, the courts will recognise the expectation as having its greatest weight. Where, in contrast, there was no promise or representation the expectation will be weaker and the corresponding judicial protection less exacting.[23]

One final point about recognition of legitimate expectations concerns unincorporated international treaties and conventions. There have been several cases in which it has been argued that, where the government has signed and ratified an international instrument, this creates a legitimate expectation that ministerial decisions will be taken in accordance with the state's obligations under the instrument.[24] However, this argument, which has been developed with reference to Australian authority,[25] is problematised by constitutional dualism and the understanding that international law can become a part of the domestic system only where Parliament enacts legislation for that purpose.[26] There is thus case law to the effect that ratification of an international treaty cannot give rise to enforceable expectations in domestic law, as that would provide for incorporation of the treaty by the 'back door'.[27] The courts have also held that there cannot be a legitimate expectation that decision-makers will act in accordance with a Treaty where Parliament has enacted legislation to give effect to the Treaty but where the legislation is yet to enter into force.[28]

15.3 **The development of the doctrine**

We will now examine more fully how the legitimate expectation doctrine has evolved from being one that was originally only procedural in form to one that includes an important substantive dimension. As we indicated above, this development in the law has not been without controversy, as the courts can now review decisions for the reason that they are substantively unfair. On the other hand, it

---

22 See *R v Home Secretary, ex p Urmaza* [1996] COD 479 and *R v Home Secretary, ex p Gangadeen* [1998] 1 FLR 762; and on the equality principle see ch 14 (*Urmaza* is noted at 14.2).

23 *R v North and East Devon Heath Authority, ex p Coughlan* [2000] 2 WLR 622.

24 See, e.g., *R v Home Secretary, ex p Ahmed and Patel* [1999] Imm AR 22.

25 *Minister for Immigration and Ethnic Affairs v Teoh* (1995) 128 ALR 353.

26 For the application of dualist orthodoxy see, e.g., *R (Hurst) v London Northern District Coroner* [2007] 2 WLR 726. And see, more recently, *Public Law Project v Secretary of State for Justice* [2015] EWCA Civ 1193, para 27 Laws LJ.

27 *Re T's Application* [2000] NI 516, 537, citing *Thomas v Baptiste* [2000] AC 1.

28 *R v DPP, ex p Kebeline* [2000] 2 AC 326—DPP not required to act in accordance with ECHR until Human Rights Act 1998 entered into force.

can be argued that the distinction between procedure and substance has always been (at least part) unsatisfactory in so far as it hides the true reason for judicial intervention on procedural grounds. The point here is simply that an individual who claims that they had a legitimate expectation of consultation will do so only because he or she has some concrete interest that has been, or will be, affected by the decision under challenge. It can therefore be said that procedural protections never existed in isolation from substantive interests; and it can also be argued that the move towards more open protection of those substantive interests is only a logical progression in the law.

15.3.1 **The doctrine's early years**

The case in which the courts first used the term legitimate expectations was *Schmidt v Secretary of State for Home Affairs*.[29] The plaintiffs, who were American students studying at the Hubbard College of Scientology, had been granted residence permits for a limited period of time for the purpose of studying at a 'recognised educational establishment'. During their period of study the Home Secretary announced that the Hubbard College would no longer be accorded the status of a 'recognised educational establishment' and, when the plaintiffs applied to have their residence permits renewed, the applications were refused (the change in status had followed growing concern about the practice of Scientology). The plaintiffs thereupon alleged that there had been a denial of natural justice, as they had not been given a hearing before the decision was reached. Lord Denning, who delivered the lead judgment of the Court of Appeal, rejected this argument, finding that the original permits had been issued only for a limited time which had since expired. But beyond this, Lord Denning stated that, had the plaintiffs' residence permits been revoked *before* they had expired, the court's approach would have been different. Under those circumstances the plaintiffs: 'ought . . . to be given an opportunity of making representations: for (they) would have a legitimate expectation of being allowed to stay for the permitted time' ([1969] 2 Ch 149, 171). As Christopher Forsyth has since put it, the court was here envisaging *procedural* protection of a *substantive* expectation of being allowed to stay in the UK.[30]

In terms of more general developments in public law at this time, *Schmidt* was consistent with an increasing judicial emphasis on fairness and ideas of natural justice in the years after the seminal case of *Ridge v Baldwin*.[31] That said, Lord Denning's use of the term 'legitimate expectation' did not apparently enjoy universal judicial support, and there was even some unease with the idea that there was anything new in the concept. For instance, in *Lloyd v McMahon*,[32] where the House of Lords rejected the argument that surcharged councils should have been given oral hearings because they had previously been given such hearings, Lord Templeman stated that he did not consider that the concept added to the existing common law requirements of fairness. His Lordship made the point in respect of the argument that a legitimate expectation of an oral hearing was to be regarded as

---

29 [1969] 2 Ch 149.
30 C Forsyth, '*Wednesbury* Protection of Substantive Legitimate Expectations' [1997] *Public Law* 375, 377.
31 [1964] AC 40; and see 17.2.3.
32 [1987] AC 625.

a right and that a failure to observe the right should automatically invalidate any resulting decision. Describing this argument as 'extravagant', Lord Templeman said that the test in any case remained one of 'fairness' and that the court need not look beyond established common law standards. Put differently, his Lordship did not wish to turn a 'catch-phrase' into 'a principle'.[33]

The case that is often credited with elevating legitimate expectation to a more prominent position in common law fairness is *Council of Civil Service Unions v Minister for the Civil Service*.[34] The facts here were that civil servants at the Government Communication Headquarters (GCHQ) had engaged in a number of strikes, which had led the government to become increasingly concerned about the potential threat to national security. The government thus used the prerogative powers to make the Civil Service Order in Council under which the Minister for the Civil Service (the Prime Minister) limited the union rights of employees at GCHQ to membership of a number of government-approved unions. This change in employment conditions had occurred without any consultation with the civil service unions, who argued that they should have been consulted because of a long-standing practice of doing so. While the House of Lords ultimately held that the government action was not unlawful for reasons of national security, it agreed that there was a legitimate expectation on the facts and that, had the circumstances been otherwise, the application for judicial review would have been granted (see, e.g., the opinion of Lord Scarman). At the same time, the emphasis in their Lordships' opinions was very much on the notion of procedural fairness, and there was no indication that the unions could have had any substantive expectation in respect of the outcome of consultation. Nevertheless, the *GCHQ* case established firmly the proposition that fairness includes the doctrine of procedural legitimate expectation and it in that sense provided a reference point for all subsequent development of the law.[35]

It thereafter became commonplace for the courts to relate legitimate expectations solely to procedure,[36] and there were some robust judicial statements to the effect that the doctrine did not have a substantive dimension.[37] However, there were also some cases which, while centred on the language of procedure, could be said to belie the early existence of substantive legitimate expectations. One such example is *R v Secretary of State for the Home Department, ex p Khan*,[38] where the applicant had relied upon a government circular (in the form of a letter) when arguing that the government had failed to apply the criteria which the circular identified as determining when a family could adopt children who lived outside the UK. While the court emphasised again the importance of the relationship between legitimate expectations and procedure, it equally said that limiting the doctrine to procedural requirements may not be appropriate in all cases. As Parker LJ put it:

---

33 [1987] AC 625, 714.

34 [1985] AC 374.

35 For recent recognition of the link between common law fairness and legitimate expectation see *R (Moseley) v Haringey LBC* [2014] UKSC 56, [2014] 1 WLR 3947, 3956–7, para 23, Lord Wilson.

36 e.g., *Re Police Association of Northern Ireland's Application* [1990] NI 258.

37 e.g., *R v Secretary of State for Transport, ex p Richmond upon Thames London Borough Council* [1994] 1 WLR 74.

38 [1984] 1 WLR 1337, noted at 12.2.2 and 17.2.5.

There can . . . be no doubt that the Secretary of State has a duty to exercise his common law discretion fairly. Furthermore, just as (other cases have established that public authorities cannot) resile from an undertaking and change (their) policy without giving a fair hearing so, in principle, the Secretary of State, if he undertakes to allow in persons if certain conditions are satisfied, should not in my view be entitled to resile from that undertaking without affording interested persons a hearing *and then only if the overriding public interest demands it* . . . The Secretary of State is, of course, at liberty to change the policy but in my view, *vis-à-vis* the recipient of such a letter, a new policy can only be implemented after such recipient has been given a full and serious consideration whether there is some overriding public interest which justifies a departure from the procedures stated in the letter.[39]

It is important to be clear just what the court was saying here. In short, it had suggested that there could be cases in which the courts would consider whether a change in policy was justified even where there had already been consultation with those individuals to be affected by any change in policy. This shift is, in turn, key to understanding the significance of the emergence of substantive legitimate expectations, as the court was indicating that it would look beyond what the individual could expect in terms of procedures and ask whether the public interest would be better served by requiring the authority to honour an undertaking than to frustrate it.[40] As we will see below, the prospect of such review continues to raise difficult questions about the appropriate threshold for judicial intervention.

One further point about *Khan* is that it is sometimes said to have been the first case in which it was recognised that an individual might rely upon a more general policy, rather than a specific representation or a policy formulated with reference to a closed class of individuals, as the basis for their expectation of a particular outcome or benefit.[41] As we have already indicated in the introduction to this chapter, this led to additional criticism of the judgment insofar as it was thought that the legitimate expectation doctrine had the potential to contradict the rule against the fettering of discretion.[42] Under that rule, public authorities are allowed to adopt policies to guide them in the exercise of their discretion, but they are not allowed to follow the policy to the extent that they disable themselves from exercising their discretion in the light of the circumstances of individual cases. Given this, *Khan* was said to have the potential to prevent public authorities making lawful discretionary choices through tying them to earlier policies, and other case law thus adopted a more restrictive approach to legitimate expectations and policy changes. For instance, in *Findlay v Secretary of State for the Home Department*,[43] the issue was whether the government had acted unlawfully when changing a prison parole policy whereby prisoners would have been released at an earlier date had it not been for the introduction of the new scheme. Finding that 'the most that a convicted prisoner can legitimately expect is that his case will be examined individually in the light of whatever (lawful) policy the Secretary of State sees fit to adopt', the House of Lords emphasised that there was a public interest in ensuring that

---

[39] Ibid, 1344, emphasis added. See also *R v Secretary of State for the Home Department, ex p Ruddock* [1987] 2 All ER 518.

[40] See, too, *R v Liverpool Corporation, ex p Liverpool Taxi Fleet Operators' Association* [1972] 2 QB 299, 308, Lord Denning.

[41] B Hadfield, 'Judicial Review and the Concept of Legitimate Expectation' (1988) 39 *Northern Ireland Legal Quarterly* 103, 114.

[42] And see, e.g., *Re Loreto Grammar School's Application* [2013] NI 41.

[43] [1985] AC 318.

the Home Secretary could exercise his discretion in relation to the administration of parole:

Any other view would entail the conclusion that the unfettered discretion conferred by the statute in the Minister can in some cases be restricted so as to hamper, or even prevent, changes of policy . . . I cannot think that Parliament intended the discretion to be restricted in this way.[44]

15.3.2 **Towards substantive legitimate expectations**

The nascent substantive dimension to the doctrine was to be developed much more fully—and controversially—in the High Court judgment in *R v Ministry of Agriculture, Fisheries and Food, ex p Hamble (Off-shore) Fisheries Ltd.*[45] In that case, Sedley J (as he then was) sought to move the doctrine beyond the understanding that expectations could only ever be procedural in form (as in *GCHQ*) and/or offer procedural protection of a substantive expectation (as in *Schmidt*), towards the understanding that there might also be 'substantive protection of a substantive legitimate expectation' (which idea underlay *Khan*; the phrase is Mark Elliott's).[46] The corresponding controversy followed from Sedley J's suggestion as to how such protection was to be achieved. In short, the judge considered that the courts should look closely at decisions in some cases and balance the requirements of fairness against the reasons for any change in policy. That approach, which was developed with part reference to the proportionality case law of the Court of Justice of the European Union (CJEU),[47] was subsequently criticised because it was thought to have the potential to involve the courts too closely in the review of discretionary choices. The case thus brought into sharp focus, in a different context, the elements of the *Wednesbury* and proportionality debate that we have considered in chapter 13.

The case arose when the Ministry for Agriculture, Fisheries and Food placed a moratorium on the transfer and aggregation of certain types of licences for fishing vessels (the policy change in question was taken to fall generally within the reach of the Common Agricultural Policy; hence Sedley J's reference to EU case law). Prior to the moratorium, licence transfers were permissible, and Hamble Fisheries Limited had purchased two vessels with the intention of transferring the licences for those vessels to a larger vessel. As the change in policy meant that it was now unable to do so, the applicant argued that the change in policy had breached its legitimate expectations (the application to the court was ultimately dismissed). In accepting that the applicant should, in principle, be able to argue for the substantive protection of a substantive legitimate expectation, Sedley J not only doubted the strength of the fettering of discretion argument that had been influential in earlier case law; he also rejected forcefully the suggestion that legitimate expectations could be only procedural in form:

. . . the real question is one of fairness in public administration. It is difficult to see why it is any less unfair to frustrate a legitimate expectation that something will or will not be done

---

44 Ibid, 338; see, too, e.g., *Hughes v Department of Health and Social Security* [1985] 1 AC 776.

45 [1995] 2 All ER 714.

46 See M Elliott, 'The Human Rights Act 1998 and the Standard of Substantive Review' (2001) 60 *Cambridge Law Journal* 301.

47 On which see 3.2.2.1.

by the decision-maker than it is to frustrate a legitimate expectation that the applicant will be listened to before the decision-maker decides whether to take a particular step. Such a doctrine does not risk fettering a public body in the discharge of public duties because no individual can legitimately expect the discharge of public duties to stand still or be distorted because of that individual's peculiar position.[48]

Having made the initial point, Sedley J turned to the question of how and when substantive protection could be ensured. In the first instance, the judge drew a distinction between expectations raised by a public promise made by government, and expectations raised by the existence of a policy or an ongoing practice. Where the expectation arose from the former, the judge considered that, so long as enforcement of the promise did not interfere with the public authority's discharge of its statutory duties, enforcement could be justified simply on account of the interests of good administration. But where the expectation arose from the existence of a policy or the continuation of a practice, the position was necessarily more complex, and it was here that Sedley J introduced his balancing test:

if the outcome is challenged by way of judicial review, I do not consider that the court's criterion is the bare rationality of the policy-maker's conclusion. While policy is for the policy-maker alone, the fairness of his or her decision not to accommodate reasonable expectations which the policy will thus thwart remains the court's concern . . . To postulate this is not to place the judge in the seat of the minister . . . It is the court's task to recognise the constitutional importance of ministerial freedom to formulate and to reformulate policy; but it is equally the court's duty to protect the interests of those individuals whose expectation of different treatment has a legitimacy which in fairness outtops the policy choice which threatens it.[49]

Sedley J's approach was, of course, controversial, and it was to be several years before it was accepted in the case law. This was because the Court of Appeal in *R v Secretary of State for the Home Department, ex p Hargreaves*[50] initially rejected the argument that the courts could perform a substantive review function beyond that permitted by *Wednesbury*. The issue in *Hargreaves* was whether prisoners could have a legitimate expectation of home leave after signing a compact apparently entitling them to this privilege and, in rejecting the application on its facts, the Court of Appeal emphasised that matters of substance could be reviewed only with reference to the *Wednesbury* threshold.[51] *Hamble*, on that rationale, was to be regarded as 'heresy'.[52]

At the same time, it was clear that *Hamble* had taken the debate about substantive legitimate expectations onto a new level. Thus, while it had become axiomatic that the doctrine should offer procedural protections to individuals, Sedley J envisaged substantive protection of the individual as a necessary corollary of any procedural guarantees. This, in turn, posited increased judicial intervention on substantive grounds beyond *Wednesbury* or, at the very least, within the framework offered by modified *Wednesbury* review.[53] It was therefore to be only a matter of time before

48 [1995] 2 All ER 714, 724.
49 Ibid, 731.
50 [1997] 1 All ER 397.
51 See, too, *R v Inland Revenue Commissioners, ex p Unilever* [1996] STC 681, linking 'abuse of power' to 'irrationality'.
52 [1997] 1 All ER 397, 412.
53 See ch 13.

the question of how to protect substantive legitimate expectations again came be-fore the Court of Appeal, which used its judgment in *R v North and East Devon Heath Authority, ex p Coughlan*[54] to refashion the doctrine around the reasoning both in *Hamble* and in *Hargreaves*.

15.4 *Coughlan* and the protection of substantive legitimate expectations

The facts of *Coughlan* were that the claimant, Pamela Coughlan, had been seriously injured in a traffic accident in 1971, after which she became a long-term patient in Newcourt Hospital. In 1993, the defendant authority's predecessor moved the claimant and a number of other residents to a new purpose-built premise (Mardon House), promising that this would be their 'home for life'. However, in 1998, the authority decided that the facility had become 'prohibitively expensive' to run and that it wished to close it. The claimant challenged this decision in the High Court, which granted a quashing order because of the promise that had previously been made. The authority's resulting appeal to the Court of Appeal was dismissed and the order of the High Court upheld.

The Court of Appeal—which had among its members Sedley LJ—began by sur-veying the earlier case law on legitimate expectations, and noted that there was still 'some controversy' about the role of the reviewing court. Nevertheless, it stated that the case law had reached the stage where there were now:

> ... at least three possible outcomes. (a) The court may decide that the public authority is only required to bear in mind its previous policy or other representation, giving it the weight it thinks right, but no more, before deciding to change course. Here the court is confined to reviewing the decision on *Wednesbury* grounds ... This has been held to be the effect of changes in policy in cases involving the early release of prisoners: see *Findlay* ... (and) ... *Hargreaves* ... (b) On the other hand the court may decide that the promise or practice induces a legitimate expectation of, for example, being consulted before a particular decision is taken. Here it is uncontentious that the court itself will require the *opportunity for consultation* to be given unless there is an overriding reason to resile from it ... in which case the court will itself judge the adequacy of the reason advanced for the change of policy, taking into ac-count what fairness requires. (c) Where the court considers that a lawful promise or practice has induced a legitimate expectation of a *benefit which is substantive*, not simply procedural, authority now establishes that here too the court will in a proper case decide whether to frustrate the expectation is so unfair that to take a new and different course will amount to an abuse of power. Here, once the legitimacy of the expectation is established, the court will have the task of weighing the requirements of fairness against any overriding interest relied upon for the change of policy.[55]

The key parts of this passage are those concerning the approach to be adopted in categories (a) and (c). In short, both categories govern the substantive protection of substantive legitimate expectations, albeit that they prescribe significantly dif-ferent roles for the reviewing court. Hence, in cases that fall under category (a), the

---

54 [2000] 2 WLR 622.
55 Ibid, 645 (emphasis in the judgment).

courts will adopt a position of self-restraint and be reluctant to engage in any form of 'closer look' review. In contrast, category (c) cases will be characterised by the type of balancing exercise that was first suggested in *Hamble* and which requires closer look review almost by definition. Indeed, while category (c) is couched in the language of 'fairness' and 'abuse of power', the approach to be adopted is, in reality, very close to that associated with the application of the proportionality principle. In that sense, *Coughlan* provides one further example of the growing influence of proportionality and of the lesser role that *Wednesbury* unreasonableness now plays in domestic law.[56]

Of course, *Coughlan* was to be the subject of lively debate. For instance, Mark Elliott criticised the judgment on separation of powers grounds, noting that the decision on the facts of the case—which had been taken to fall within category (c)—had obvious implications for the allocation of resources.[57] This criticism returns us to the point that was made in the introduction about the polycentric nature of resource disputes and the question of the role that the courts should play when faced with challenges to the spending choices of public decision-makers. John Allison has previously written that a dispute about resources can have consequences for parties who are not represented before the reviewing court and that restraint is, for that reason, mandated (the argument being that the authority has been entrusted with making decisions about the allocation of resources in the public interest).[58] However, the approach contained in *Coughlan* category (c) could clearly provide a template for more active invigilation of such choices, and it is in that way that the logic of the separation of powers was said to be threatened. From this perspective, *Coughlan* (arguably) represented a problematic development of the law.

A second criticism concerned the question of which category—(a) or (c)—a particular dispute about substantive legitimate expectations should fall into. Certainly, it was clear that cases that lie 'in what may inelegantly be called the macro-political field'[59] would be expected to fall within category (a), and that category (c) cases would be 'likely in the nature of things to be cases where the expectation is confined to one person or a few people, giving the promise or representation the character of a contract'.[60] However, beyond cases that would 'self-evidently' fall within (a) or (c) (query: where are the boundaries of the macro-political field?), there was scope for uncertainty in judicial reasoning precisely because the *Coughlan* categories were not regarded as 'hermetically sealed'.[61] While a case involving national prison policy may therefore be expected to fall within category (a), what of the circumstance where specific and individualised representations had been made to prisoners on the basis of the policy?[62] Moreover, where a representation had been made to a small group of individuals, would that automatically bring the case within category (c)? And when would a representation to a 'small' group of individuals become a representation with implications for an innominate

---

56 On which see 13.7.

57 Elliott, n 8.

58 J Allison, 'The Procedural Reason for Judicial Self-restraint' [1994] *Public Law* 452.

59 *R v Secretary of State for Education and Employment, ex p Begbie* [2000] 1 WLR 1115, 1131, Laws LJ.

60 *Coughlan* [2000] 2 WLR 622, 646.

61 *R v Secretary of State for Education and Employment, ex p Begbie* [2000] 1 WLR 1115, 1130, Laws LJ.

62 See, e.g., *R (Vary) v Home Secretary* [2004] EWHC 2251: prison decisions that affect only a small number of prisoners are still governed by *Findlay* and *Hargreaves*, at least in the absence of an express undertaking.

class of persons, thereby taking the facts of a dispute out of category (c) and into category (a)?[63]

A third criticism, which was closely related to the second, concerned the use of *Wednesbury* in category (a) and the 'fairness/abuse of power' formulation in category (c). In short, it was doubted whether it would be necessary to retain two standards for review when both standards pursue the objective of substantive protection of substantive legitimate expectations. This then raised the question of which standards should be displaced and, given broader trends in judicial review, it was expected that *Wednesbury* might cede its position.[64] However, this, in turn, raised the question whether the 'fairness/abuse of power' formulation would have the necessary conceptual foundations for resolving all legitimate expectations disputes, and it was here that overlap with the proportionality principle was potentially significant. Although it was said that the category (c) formulation lacked the structure and precision of a proportionality enquiry,[65] it was also said to incorporate the element of balance that defines the workings of the European standard.[66] Given this, it was argued that category (c) should be openly structured around the proportionality principle[67] and that, were that to happen, it would (arguably) require only a small development in the law to allow the principle to apply in category (a) cases too. This was because it was noted that the proportionality principle can be applied in a context-sensitive way that permits of more or less intensive review as the facts of a case demand.[68] In the event that a challenge were to be brought to a decision in the 'macro-political field', there would, on this reasoning, be sufficient flexibility within the proportionality principle to allow for judicial self-restraint of the kind associated with *Wednesbury* unreasonableness.

The post-*Coughlan* case law quickly gave some indication of how the courts regarded such criticisms.[69] For instance, in *R (Bibi) v Newham London Borough Council*,[70] the Court of Appeal was clearly influenced by separation of powers considerations and polycentricity when deciding upon the appropriate form of the relief in the case before it. The issue in the case was whether, and to what extent, a local authority could be required to fulfil a promise to provide permanent housing for a number of homeless families (the promise had been made on the prior and ultimately erroneous belief that the authority was under a duty to provide permanent accommodation). The applicants had argued that the promise gave them a substantive legitimate expectation of housing, and the High Court, agreeing, made a declaration that the authority was 'bound to treat the duties originally owed by them to both

---

63 Compare and contrast the approaches of the Court of Appeal and the House of Lords in *R (Bancoult) v Secretary of State for Foreign and Commonwealth Affairs (No 2)* at [2007] 3 WLR 768 and [2009] 1 AC 453 respectively. While the Court of Appeal held that the Chagos Islanders had a legitimate expectation of being allowed to return to their homeland given the content of government statements—the islanders had previously been forcibly removed so that Diego Garcia could be used as a US base—the House of Lords held that no legitimate expectation arose on the facts. On this case see further 9.3.2.3.

64 P Craig and S Schønberg, 'Legitimate Expectations after *Coughlan*' [2000] *Public Law* 684. On *Wednesbury*'s influence see 13.7.

65 See Craig and Schønberg, n 64.

66 See Elliott, n 46.

67 Craig and Schønberg, n 64.

68 See ch 13.

69 P Sales and K Steyn, 'Legitimate Expectations in English Public Law: An Analysis' [2004] *Public Law* 564.

70 [2002] 1 WLR 237.

applicants . . . as not discharged until the applicants be provided with suitable accommodation on a secure tenancy'. However, while the Court of Appeal accepted
that the applicants had a substantive legitimate expectation, it emphasised that
'it is often not adequate to look at the situation purely from the point of view of
the disappointed promisee who comes to court'. Noting that promises will often
have been made to many different people, the Court stated that 'where decisions
are informed by social and political value judgments as to priorities of expenditure
the court will start with a recognition that such invidious choices are essentially
political rather than judicial . . . (and that) . . . the appropriate body to make that
choice in the context of the present case is the authority.' Where, as here, an earlier
representation had given rise to a substantive legitimate expectation, that expectation was then a factor to be considered during the decision-making process. On
the other hand, the Court also accepted that there may be other factors that might
inhibit the fulfilment of an expectation and that decision-making may have to
take account of those too. The Court thus varied the terms of the High Court's
declaration so that it read: 'the authority is under a duty to consider the applicants'
applications for suitable housing on the basis that they have a legitimate expectation that they will be provided by the authority with suitable accommodation on
a secure tenancy'.[71]

The 'which category' and 'which principle' points also received some consideration in the case law. For instance, in *Nadarajah v Home Secretary*[72]—a case that concerned the application of immigration and asylum policy—Laws LJ said that the
legitimate expectation doctrine centres upon a 'requirement of good administration, by which public bodies ought to deal straightforwardly and consistently with
the public'. This was said to mean that a public body could resile from its promise
or practice as to future conduct only 'in circumstances where to do so is the public
body's legal duty, or is otherwise, to use a now familiar vocabulary, a proportionate
response (of which the court is judge, or the last judge) having regard to the legitimate aim pursued by the public body in the public interest'. Laws LJ thus envisaged
a proportionality enquiry irrespective of whether an expectation was procedural
or substantive in form or, indeed, whether a substantive expectation is engendered
by an individualised representation or wide-ranging or 'macro-political' issues of
policy. In either instance, the task for the courts was said to be constant and guided
by the question whether denial of the expectation is *in the circumstances* proportionate to a legitimate aim pursued. Hence where 'the representation relied on
amounts to an unambiguous promise; where there is detrimental reliance; where
the promise is made to an individual or specific group; these are instances where
denial of the expectation is likely to be harder to justify as a proportionate measure . . . On the other hand where the government decision-maker is concerned to
raise wide-ranging or macro-political issues of policy, the expectation's enforcement in the courts will encounter a steeper climb'.[73]

Such statements make clear that *Coughlan's* three-way distinction is not written in stone and, even though the case remains central to the subject, *Nadarajah*

---

71 See ibid, 247 and 251.
72 [2005] EWCA Civ 1363.
73 Ibid, all quotes at paras 68–9. For further analysis see *R (Bhatt Murphy) v Independent Assessor* [2008]
EWCA Civ 755.

and other cases have revealed that legitimate expectations are now to be regarded as 'rooted in the [overalapping] principles of fairness, good administration, legal certainty, and the proper exercise of power'.[74] So what does all this mean for the different ways in which legitimate expectations can arise and how the courts will protect them? Are there emerging themes in the case law?

We would suggest that the best way to conceive of the current state of the law is to return to the analytical framework provided by 'representations', 'practices', and 'policies'. Taking representations first, it would appear that, where there is a representation or promise to the effect that an individual or small group of persons will receive a substantive benefit, the logic of *Coughlan* category (c) will retain its full vigour and the courts will be particularly anxious to avoid abuses of power (but see our discussion, above, on the difficulty of drawing the boundaries of a group for the purposes of category (c)). Indeed, the only change might be at the level of terminology. This is because case law including *Nadarajah* suggests that the prevailing language is now 'proportionality' (as wedded to ideas of 'abuse of power'), and it might therefore be anticipated that the courts will intervene on the basis of that principle where there is an insufficient public interest to justify a decision to resile from a promise. On this point, it should also be noted that a public authority must adduce sufficient evidence to support its argument of public interest and that, in the event that it fails to do so, the reviewing court may conclude that no such interest exists.[75]

In relation to 'practices', all will depend, initially, on whether the practice generates a legitimate expectation that is procedural or substantive in form. Where the practice generates an expectation that is procedural, the public authority will be expected to consult affected parties before any change of practice and any departure from the requirement to consult must comport with fairness (this point would also be true where the authority has promised to consult). On the other hand, if a practice has generated an expectation that is substantive in nature, any departure from it will be gauged with reference to the proportionality principle. The considerations that will guide the courts when using the principle will include the legitimacy of the objective pursued by the change in practice; the nature of the interests affected by the change; whether the change in practice is necessary given the impact on interests; and the extent to which the courts should be cognisant of the decision-maker's discretion on the matter.

The starting point in respect of policies is that decision-makers are constrained by a legal duty to be fair.[76] Within this, a public authority may be required to consult before changing a policy; and it may also be required to adhere to a particular policy that affects certain individuals where it has promised that it will adhere to the policy in relation to them (see the overlap with 'representations/promises', above). Should it wish to depart from a policy in this latter instance, the principle of proportionality will again come into play and the authority must be able to identify a public interest that trumps the interests of those who legitimately expected

---

74 *Re Board of Governors of Loretta Grammar School's Application* [2011] NIQB 30, para 95, McCloskey J. Although note that the ruling of the High Court on the issues in this case was overturned by the Northern Ireland Court of Appeal: [2013] NI 41.

75 *Paponette v Att Gen of Trinidad and Tobago* [2010] UKPC 32, [2012] 1 AC 1, 14, paras 37–8, Sir John Dyson SCJ.

76 *R (Bhatt Murphy) v Independent Assessor* [2008] EWCA Civ 755, para 50.

to be governed by the original policy. Where the public authority cannot identify such a public interest, the court may either require the public authority to adhere to the original policy or, alternatively, to adopt transitional measures that have due regard for the interests of those who expected that the original policy would apply to them.[77] Either way, the principle of proportionality becomes the driving element of substantive fairness.

15.5 Unlawfully created legitimate expectations

The final issue to be discussed in this chapter is 'unlawfully created legitimate expectations'. As we indicated in the introduction, these may be created (a) where an authority makes a representation that it will do something that it cannot lawfully do (an *ultra vires* representation), or (b) where an official who has not been authorised to make a representation purports to make a representation on behalf of the authority (it can be said here that the representation is *intra vires* the authority but made by an unauthorised official). We will return to the corresponding principles in the case law below, but before doing so it may help to provide illustrative examples of what each scenario might look like in practice. In short, an expectation may arise under (a) where an authority says that it will, for instance, accept an individual's claim to a property right over a piece of land where statute in fact specifies that the land is for public use.[78] And in relation to (b) an expectation might arise where an individual enters into communication with an officer in a public authority, who advises the individual that a decision in their favour has already been taken or is imminent. The prototypical example here is to be found in the planning context, where an officer may indicate to an individual that planning permission has been granted but where no such decision has been taken and is, moreover, a matter for a committee within the authority.

It should also be emphasised at the outset of this section that, although such issues are rare in the case law, they raise difficult questions about how to reconcile the demands of fairness with the doctrines of Parliamentary sovereignty and legality. This tension is at its most pronounced in relation to scenario (a), as recognition and enforcement of an expectation here would effectively mean that the authority had been able to redraw the boundaries of its own power by making an *ultra vires* representation. Given the UK constitution's emphasis on legislative supremacy,[79] the courts have, in such circumstances, historically limited the scope for protection of the individual by holding that public authorities cannot be bound by such representations (albeit that the Human Rights Act 1998 has since required a slight modification of approach). In contrast, the judicial approach to scenario (b) has been less absolute, as there is here no *ultra vires* representation that would take the authority beyond the powers that have been delegated to it. The resulting tension has instead been that generated by the need to ensure fairness towards individuals

---

77 Compare and contrast the approaches of Laws and Sedley LJJ in *R (Bhatt Murphy) v Independent Assessor* [2008] EWCA Civ 755, para 50.

78 See, e.g., *Rowland v Environment Agency* [2004] 3 WLR 249.

79 See ch 2.

with the requirement that statutory powers be exercised only by those to whom the powers have been entrusted. As we will see below, the courts have in this instance previously offered some protection to individuals through use of the estoppel doctrine that has, in the public law context, since been subsumed within legitimate expectation.[80]

15.5.1 *Ultra vires* representations

The understanding that *ultra vires* representations cannot bind an authority rests upon constitutional orthodoxy and, in particular, the understanding that decision-makers may act only within the parameters of the powers that are granted to them, or the duties that are imposed upon them, by statute.[81] This position follows from the fact that a decision-making function will typically, though not exclusively, be delegated to an authority under legislation enacted by the Westminster legislature or, alternatively, the devolved legislatures. While the extent of any statutory power or duty will depend upon judicial interpretation of the statute, the basic understanding is that a decision-maker may do only that which the legislature has authorised. This principle, which is central to illegality as a ground for review,[82] would therefore clearly be offended if an authority were able to extend its powers through a misapprehension of, and representation about, the basis of those very powers.[83] Even where an individual relies upon the representation to his or her detriment, orthodoxy would thus entail that he or she could not obtain a remedy in the courts. Under those circumstances, the matter may better be regarded as one of maladministration that should be brought to the attention of the relevant ombudsman.[84]

The position is, however, more complex where a representation is made to the individual in circumstances that fall under the Human Rights Act 1998. While the European Court of Human Rights (ECtHR) accepts that it is important that public authorities act in accordance with their legal powers, it has also emphasised that arguments of legality should not always override the rights of individuals in the manner that orthodoxy dictates. The point is now most readily associated with the ECtHR's judgment in *Stretch v UK*, where the right at issue was a property right centred upon an (unlawfully created) expectation that the individual would have the benefit of a renewal of a lease.[85] In short, the ECtHR stated that the question whether an individual's rights should be overridden must be answered on a case-by-case basis in the light of the proportionality principle and that it is possible that the context of a case may mean that the individual should be able to enforce an unlawfully created expectation. While the domestic courts have not, in turn, yet acted on this understanding to the extent of holding that the demands of legality should yield to a right, they have suggested that public authorities should seek to

---

80 On estoppel see 12.3.

81 On statutory powers and duties see 8.4.

82 See chs 11 and 12.

83 For judicial discussion see further *R (Bibi) v Newham London Borough Council* [2002] 1 WLR 237 and *Rowland v Environment Agency* [2004] 3 WLR 249.

84 Ch 6.

85 (2004) 38 EHRR 12. See further *Pine Valley Developments Ltd v Ireland* (1991) 14 EHRR 319; and on the question of when a legitimate expectation can come within Art 1 Protocol 1 ECHR, see *Bryer Group Plc v Department of Energy and Climate Change* [2015] 2 All ER 44.

exercise their powers benevolently where a previous representation has given rise to an expectation of a particular outcome.[86] It has since also been suggested that the benevolent exercise of power might take the form of an award of compensation to an individual who has suffered loss and that, where such an award is not made, the individual might alternatively seek redress in an action for negligent misstatement.[87]

15.5.2 Statements made by unauthorised officers

We have already considered how the estoppel doctrine was used to offer limited protection to individuals in chapter 12. There, we referred to Lord Denning's understanding that individuals who liaise with officers in public authorities are entitled to assume that officers are empowered to make the representations that they make and that an individual should not have to bear a loss if an officer was not so empowered.[88] Of course, as was so often the case with Lord Denning, not all judges agreed with his approach, and the broad role he envisaged for estoppel was to be narrowed considerably in subsequent case law. For instance, in *Western Fish Products Ltd v Penwith District Council*,[89] a company had started building work on the basis of representations made to it, and it had later been told by an official that an application for planning permission was necessary only as a formality. However, the application for permission was subsequently rejected, and the issue was whether the authority could be estopped given the earlier representations and correspondence. In his judgment, Megaw LJ said that there were only two exceptions to the rule that public authorities could not be estopped from exercising their powers. The first was where the authority had the power to delegate some of its functions to the officer and there were special circumstances to justify the applicant in believing that the officer could bind the authority.[90] The second exception was where the authority had waived a procedural requirement relating to the matter before it. Under those circumstances, it could be estopped from relying upon the lack of formality.[91]

Since *Western Fish*, the courts have gone even further when saying that it is 'unhelpful' to use private law concepts such as estoppel in the public law sphere and that 'public law has already absorbed whatever is useful from the moral values which underlie [private law] . . . and the time has come for it to stand upon its own two feet'.[92] This, of course, is a reference to the emergence of the legitimate expectation doctrine and public law's corresponding attempts to reconcile the pursuit of fairness with the demands of legality and the broader public interest in public

---

86 *Rowland v Environment Agency* [2004] 3 WLR 249, 300, paras 153ff, Mance LJ. But for a more recent statement of the need for the courts to 'be slow to weaken the principle of legality', see *Rainbow Insurance Company Ltd v The Financial Services Commission* [2015] UKPC 15, para 53, Lord Hodge.

87 M Elliott, *Beatson, Mathews and Elliott's: Administrative Law Text and Materials*, 4th edn (Oxford: Oxford University Press, 2011), 219–20; W Wade and C Forsyth, *Administrative Law*, 11th edn (Oxford: Oxford University Press, 2014), 284–5; and Y Vanderman, 'Ultra Vires Legitimate Expectations: An Argument for Compensation' [2012] *Public Law* 85.

88 See *Robertson v Minister of Pensions* [1949] 1 KB 227 and *Howell v Falmouth Boat Construction Co Ltd* [1950] 2 KB 16.

89 [1981] 2 All ER 204.

90 The judge here cited *Lever Finance Ltd v Westminster (City) London Borough Council* [1971] QB 222.

91 The judge here cited *Wells v Minister of Housing and Local Government* [1967] 2 All ER 104.

92 *R v East Sussex County Council, ex p Reprotech* [2002] 4 All ER 58, 66, Lord Hoffmann.

decision-making. So, if estoppel has been placed in abeyance, does this mean that the legitimate expectation doctrine will now afford protection to individuals who have received unauthorised advice? Certainly, if the courts accept that an unauthorised representation can generate a legitimate expectation this would raise the question of how the expectation is to be protected. However, it is at this stage that the distinction between estoppel and legitimate expectation may become apparent, in particular the fact of their respective origins in private law and public law. Thus, while a private law doctrine of estoppel would focus primarily on the interests of the two parties directly affected by a dispute, the legitimate expectation doctrine has evolved in the light of the need to reconcile individual interests with those of the wider public (as represented by the public body). In assessing whether an unauthorised representation should be allowed to bind the authority, a court would thus have to consider whether there would be merit in preventing an authority from exercising its powers, or performing its duties in the public interest. Given that any proposed or actual public authority action would be lawful, it may be that the courts will only ever be willing to intervene in cases of extreme hardship for the individual and, moreover, if there is no other way to alleviate the hardship.

15.6 Conclusion

This chapter has focused primarily on how the doctrine of (lawfully created) legitimate expectations has evolved from being one that was originally only procedural in form, through to the position where it now includes procedural and substantive dimensions that permit of increasingly intensive judicial scrutiny of public authority choices. It has been emphasised throughout that this development of the law has not been without difficulty or controversy, and that it raises fundamental questions about the judicial role on an application for judicial review. On the other hand, we have also sought to emphasise how the courts are here concerned with fairness towards individuals and overall levels of consistency in public decision-making. Therefore, while a decision-maker may still go back on (for instance) a representation where doing so accords with its legal duty or where there is a public interest justification for doing so, the courts have become evermore anxious to protect individuals against the abuse of power. The point can still best be illustrated with reference to the Court of Appeal's original judgment in the seminal *Coughlan* case that we analysed above.

One final point that might be made by way of conclusion concerns the relationship between the substantive legitimate expectation doctrine and the doctrine against the fettering of discretion. We have mentioned several times in this chapter that there is sometimes said to be a clash between the two doctrines in the sense that legitimate expectation seeks to tie an authority to an earlier policy while the non-fettering doctrine entails that decision-makers should be free to depart from their policies in any given case. So, is there truly a clash, or are the two doctrines reconcilable? The answer here, it seems, is to be found in the wider values of legality, flexibility, and legal certainty that guide the courts on any claim for judicial review. Arguing that the two doctrines are not contradictory, Chris Hilson has said that the fettering doctrine is about the values of legality and flexibility, and that the flexible application of a *new* policy in the light of legitimate expectation generated by an *old* policy complements the value of legal certainty that is at the very heart of legitimate expectation.[93] Seen from this perspective, the question is therefore not whether a decision-maker is being tied to an earlier policy but rather whether the new policy is being applied flexibly. If it is, legitimate expectations can be protected in tandem with exercises of discretion in the light of any new conditions.

FURTHER READING

Ahmed, F and Perry, A (2014) 'The Coherence of the Doctrine of Legitimate Expectation' 73 *Cambridge Law Journal* 61.

Craig, P and Schønberg, S [2000] 'Legitimate Expectations After *Coughlan*' *Public Law* 684.

Elliott, M [2000] '*Coughlan*: Substantive Protection of Legitimate Expectations Revisited' 5 *Judicial Review* 27.

Elliott, M (2001) 'The Human Rights Act 1998 and the Standard of Substantive Review' 60 *Cambridge Law Journal* 301.

Elliott, M [2005] 'Legitimate Expectation, Consistency and Abuse of Power: the *Rashid* Case' 10 *Judicial Review* 281.

Forsyth, CF [1997] '*Wednesbury* Protection of Substantive Legitimate Expectations' *Public Law* 375.

Forsyth, C [2011] 'Legitimate Expectation Revisited' *Judicial Review* 429.

Hadfield, B (1988) 'Judicial Review and the Concept of Legitimate Expectation' 39 *Northern Ireland Legal Quarterly* 103.

Hilson, C [2006] 'Policies, the Non-Fetter Principle and the Principle of Substantive Legitimate Expectations: Between a Rock and a Hard Place?' *Judicial Review* 289.

Reynolds, P [2011] 'Legitimate Expectations and the Protection of Trust in Public Officials' *Public Law* 330.

Sales, P and Steyn, K [2004] 'Legitimate Expectations in English Public Law: An Analysis' *Public Law* 564.

Schønberg, S (2000) *Legitimate Expectations in Administrative Law* (Oxford: Oxford University Press).

Vanderman, Y [2012] 'Ultra Vires Legitimate Expectations: An Argument for Compensation' *Public Law* 85.

---

93 C Hilson, 'Policies, the Non-Fetter Principle and the Principle of Substantive Legitimate Expectations: Between a Rock and a Hard Place?'[2006] 11 *Judicial Review* 289.

16

Procedural impropriety I: statutory requirements

16.1 Introduction

Having discussed the principles and doctrines of legality, unreasonableness, and legitimate expectations (among others), we can now turn to the third type of unlawful action that Lord Diplock referred to in his judgment in the *GCHQ* case. He used the term 'procedural impropriety' when explaining that a public authority could be acting unlawfully if it commits a procedural error of some kind. This encompasses two things:

(1) decisions and so on that are *ultra vires* a legislative scheme (i.e., procedural *ultra vires*). Such decisions will have been taken in breach of statutory rules of procedure such as relate to, among other things, time limits, notification, consultation, the right to appear before a body, the right to be represented, and the duty to give reasons for a decision; and

(2) decisions taken in breach of the common law rules of natural justice/fairness. These also include components such as the right to hearing, the right to be represented, the duty to give reasons, etc.

In this chapter we will deal with procedural *ultra vires*, and we will then consider the origins and nature of the rules of natural justice/fairness in chapter 17. However, before turning to the detail of the law, we should say a few words about why it is that the law imposes procedural obligations upon decision-makers. Although this perhaps begs the question of the type of modeling that underpins administrative law—discussed in chapter 1—we would suggest that there are three interlocking justifications for procedural requirements. The first is that the law can in this way perform a democratic function in the sense that it allows those who will be affected by a decision to participate in the decision-making process through, for instance, the making of representations at a hearing.[1] Secondly, and by providing for such hearing rights, the law can provide for transparency in decision-making, as the obligation to receive representations from the individual will often (though not always) be coupled with a duty to give reasons for the decision that is reached in the light of those representations. This, in turn, will allow the individual to assess how far the representations that he or she has made have been taken into account by the decision-maker and given weight in the decision-making process. The third

---

[1] See further *R (Moseley) v Haringey LBC* [2014] UKSC 56, [2014] 1 WLR 3947, 3957, para 24, Lord Wilson.

justification focuses upon the value of accountability that can be achieved where the reasons for a decision point to a legal flaw that may be remedied through the individual bringing an appeal (if available) or a claim for judicial review.[2]

We should add that each of the above justifications can likewise be found in case law under Article 6 of the European Convention on Human Rights (ECHR). That Article, which has effect under the Human Rights Act 1998, imposes a range of procedural obligations that are intended to protect the individual whenever there is a 'determination of his civil rights and obligations or of any criminal charge against him' (and note that other Articles of the ECHR can also impose procedural obligations).[3] We will therefore make many references to it as we consider the role of statutory and common law requirements.

16.2 **Procedural** *ultra vires*

We will now concentrate on situations where an administrative decision or other measure is challenged as defective because basic statutory requirements have been overlooked altogether, or have been improperly observed. Once again, judges inevitably assume a significant role in performing this function, as difficult questions about the parameters of the judicial role can arise. Statutes, and their accompanying delegated powers, are often of some complexity and may be contradictory in their demands. A procedural oversight may be of a minor nature only and thus be considered of limited importance. Setting aside a decision on this ground alone could well cause greater injustice than leaving the decision in place. Therefore, in dealing with alleged procedural impropriety, the courts will take particular account of the established rules of statutory interpretation, which require consideration of the overall aims and purposes of Parliament in enacting the legislation in question.[4] Indeed, in *Howard v Bodington*, Lord Penzance stated that, 'in each case you must look to the subject-matter; consider the importance of the provision that has been disregarded and the relation of that provision to the general object intended to be secured by the Act'.[5] This has been accepted as the test for when a court has to decide between what are often referred to as 'mandatory' and 'directory' requirements, albeit that that distinction is no longer central to the law. At the same time, in assessing the importance of a procedural requirement, regard must be paid to basic principles of effectiveness and fairness, as well as to the interests of third parties and the broader public. Would a failure to follow the procedure result in serious injustice or prejudice to the complainant, or to the public interest?

---

2 See also *Re Reilly's Application* [2013] UKSC 61, [2014] AC 1115, 1149–50, Lord Reed noting the values of participation, the rule of law, and efficient use of sources.

3 e.g., Art 2 ECHR imposes a procedural obligation to investigate the use of force by states and, among other things, to give reasons for decisions about whether or not prosecutions will be brought: see, among others, *McKerr v UK* (2002) 34 EHRR 20.

4 See further 11.2.

5 (1877) 2 PD 203, 211.

16.2.1 **Mandatory and directory requirements**

It is common for statutes and regulations to lay down procedures that are to be followed in administrative matters (note that primary legislation may also specify procedural requirements that are to be observed when making delegated legislation). Sometimes, as in planning law, these are complex. To take some typical examples, there may be provisions requiring that persons should be given notice of action to be taken within a specified period; that particular bodies should be consulted before a decision is made; that reasons for a decision should be given; and that affected parties should be notified of any statutory rights of appeal. A basic difficulty is that the Act will rarely state what should occur if, in practice, the procedure is not strictly adhered to. This means that the courts may have to decide on the effect of non-compliance or substantial compliance and, to help them do so, they have used a number of terms and distinctions. Perhaps the most important of these has historically been the above-mentioned distinction between 'mandatory' and 'directory' requirements. Although the courts no longer regard this distinction as definitive of questions of legality,[6] a failure to observe a 'mandatory' term will generally render invalid what has been done. In contrast, a provision that is read as 'directory' should ordinarily be observed by the decision-maker, albeit that a failure to do so may not render the resulting decision invalid. All will depend on context and whether, for instance, a mistake is found to be trivial or whether individual rights are obviously prejudiced by the failure to observe the requirement. As Lord Hailsham LC said in *London & Clydeside Estates v Abberdeen DC*,[7] labels such as 'mandatory' and 'directory' may be useful, but they should always be applied in context.

It should also be noted that the courts may read a provision as both mandatory and directory; that is, mandatory as to substantial compliance but directory as to precise compliance. The idea of substantial compliance is one that can work very much to the advantage of decision-makers, as the courts will not allow matters of mere technicality to trump a decision and to cause 'unjust and unintended consequences' where the decision has been taken in a manner that, overall, is compliant with the legislative scheme.[8] On the other hand, it is important to be aware that the need for substantial compliance can have the opposite implication for decision-makers where it can be said that there has been only formal adherence to a requirement during the decision-making process. Under these circumstances, formal adherence could serve to defeat the purpose of the requirement, as the decision-maker may be able to avoid the legislation's actual procedural objectives. Hence, where statute imposes, for example, a duty of consultation, or a duty to give reasons for a decision (see below), the consultation that is held must be adequate and the reasons given meaningful within their statutory context. Failing this, the decision may be deemed unlawful.

Of course, it is also possible for an authority to argue that an individual has failed to observe procedural requirements and that any challenge to a decision of the

---

6 See *R v Immigration Appeal Tribunal, ex p Jeyeanthan* [1999] 3 All ER 231; and *R v Soneji* [2005] UKHL 49, [2006] 1 AC 340.

7 [1980] 1 WLR 182.

8 *R v Immigration Appeal Tribunal, ex p Jeyeanthan* [1999] 3 All ER 231, 238–9, Lord Woolf CJ; and see, e.g., *R v Dacorum Gaming Licensing Committee, ex p EMI Cinemas and Leisure Ltd* [1971] 3 All ER 666, where it was held that a misprint in a notice in a local newspaper could not make the notice ineffective as the mistake was a 'trifling typographic error'.

authority is thereby precluded. However, ideas of substantial compliance can here, too, be invoked by the individual. A good example is found in *Howard v Secretary of State for the Environment*.[9] A right of appeal was provided by section 16 of the Town and Country Planning Act 1968 against an enforcement notice issued by the local planning authority. The appeal, which was made to the minister, had to be in writing, within a specified time, and had to indicate the grounds of the appeal. An appeal letter was sent by H's solicitor on 6 November 1970 against an enforcement notice from Havering Council, but no indication of the grounds of appeal were included, as required by the statute. The ministry replied, pointing out that grounds had to be indicated. The solicitor wrote again on 16 November, specifying the grounds, but this time the letter was delayed through an office error and did not reach the ministry until 24 November. After receiving this letter, the ministry informed H that no action could be taken since it was received out of time. A declaration was sought stating that the original letter, or that letter considered together with the later letter, amounted to a valid notice of appeal. In the Court of Appeal, Lord Denning MR considered the section to be imperative, that is, mandatory, in respect of the need for the appeal to be in writing and to be made within the specified time, but only directory in respect of its contents, that being the grounds of appeal. The effect of lodging an appeal was to suspend an enforcement notice, so evidently time was of the essence on this question. However, once notification had taken place, the appeal would not fail simply because the grounds were not stated, as these could be provided later. Accordingly, it was unanimously held that the letter of 6 November was a valid notice of appeal.[10]

It should finally be noted that legislation that specifies procedural requirements falls to be interpreted in the light of the ECHR where decision-making processes have implications for an individual's rights under the ECHR.[11] In terms of the mandatory and directory distinction, this thus means that a mandatory provision that may have negative implications for an individuals' rights should, 'so far as it is possible to do so', be read as directory if that would ensure ECHR compatibility. An example here may be where an individual would be prohibited from bringing an appeal for failing to observe a mandatory rule of court procedure. Under these circumstances, the courts may need to read the rule as directory so as to ensure that Article 6 ECHR rights of access to court are not subject to a disproportionate interference.[12]

16.3 Statutory requirements: indications from the case law

We can now consider some of the most frequently recurring types of procedural requirements, together with leading case law on the approach to be taken to them.

---

9 [1974] 1 All ER 644.

10 On substantial compliance see too, e.g., *Berkeley v Secretary of State for the Environment* [2000] 3 WLR 420 (HL); *Haringey London Borough Council v Awaritefe* (1999) 32 HLR 517; and *Secretary of State for Trade and Industry v Langridge* [1991] Ch 402.

11 See Human Rights Act 1998, s 3, as read with Sch 1 to the Act; and 4.4.2.

12 See, e.g., *Foyle, Carlingford and Irish Lights Commission v McGillion* [2002] NI 86.

16.3.1 **Prior notification**

A statute may require the notification of affected individuals or groups before a body acts, thereby allowing the affected individuals to make representations and so on to the public body before any action is taken. We can see how the historical distinction between mandatory and directory was arrived at in two contrasting cases, both involving prior notice under the Education Act 1944. A conventionally strict view was adopted by the Court of Appeal in *Bradbury v Enfield LBC*.[13] Enfield Council was on the point of introducing a scheme for reorganising its schools for comprehensive education, but the notice of its intentions had not been submitted for examination by the public. Because of this failure, local ratepayers managed to obtain an injunction to delay the authority from making the changeover from selective to comprehensive secondary education until the prescribed statutory procedure had been followed. Lord Denning MR held that this was a mandatory requirement and that there was an obligation to give prior notice under section 13 of the Education Act 1944 so that representations may be made. Further, he stated that the injunction would be granted even if it caused some chaos during an enforced period of consultation in line with the statutory requirement. Dankwerts LJ added:

[I]n cases of this kind it is imperative that the procedure laid down in the relevant statute should be properly observed. The provisions of the statutes in this respect are supposed to provide safeguards for Her Majesty's subjects. Public bodies and ministers must be compelled to observe the law; and it is essential that the bureaucracy be kept in its place.[14]

Despite this strict approach, there was a very different outcome in *Coney v Choyce*, which also concerned plans for the reorganisation of schools, this time in Nottinghamshire.[15] The authority was obliged to comply with the same section of the Education Act 1944 (section 13), which provided that notices about plans should be posted at or near the main entrance of schools and in local newspapers. Although the plans were well publicised by meetings, newsletters, and in churches, no notices had been posted at two schools in Worksop. Templeman J held that the general requirement to provide notice was mandatory. However, a remedy was refused because the plans had been sufficiently well publicised to allow for objections. In other words, there had been 'substantial compliance' with the Act. This meant that the specific requirements were found to be only directory. It was apparent that the publication had been in such a manner that a representative number of people were able to see what the plans were, and thus no substantial prejudice would be suffered by those for whom the measure had been introduced. Omitting these schools was considered too trivial in its consequences for the scheme to be set aside. It is also worth making the point that the battle against reorganisation had already been lost on its merits, and a challenge on this procedural point was being pursued as a last-ditch means of having the plans invalidated.

---

13 [1967] 1 WLR 1311.
14 Ibid, 1325.
15 [1975] 1 All ER 979.

16.3.2 **Right of appeal**

It appears that the courts view a provision granting a right of appeal made available under a statute as of fundamental importance. Any failure to inform an individual of his or her right of appeal might therefore be expected to render a decision unlawful.

In *Agricultural, Horticultural and Forestry Industry Training Board v Kent*, a notice was sent out which neglected to indicate clearly that the recipient had a right of appeal, or the address to which appeals should be sent.[16] It was held that this failure was sufficient to invalidate the notice, as the right of appeal was of first importance. This point was again illustrated in *London & Clydeside Estates v Aberdeen DC*.[17] In this instance, there was a breach of a statutory requirement under the Land Compensation (Scotland) Act 1963, taken in conjunction with the Town and Country Planning (General Purposes) (Scotland) Order 1959, in that a decision from the local authority contained in a certificate delivered to the applicant omitted to make any reference to a statutory right to appeal. Despite it being apparent that the company involved was aware that it had a right of appeal, it was held that proper notice of this right was mandatory. The certificate was set aside by the courts on the ground that it was a breach of a mandatory requirement, even though no prejudice had been suffered by the applicant. This was an interesting outcome, as the substantial prejudice rule would normally mean that a body would have to have faced some detriment as a result of the failure to adhere to the procedural requirement. On the other hand, it appears that notification of the possible grounds for appeal, rather than the right to appeal itself, will only be regarded as directory requirements.[18]

16.3.3 **The duty to consult**

The duty to consult is almost invariably regarded as mandatory and, where there is consultation, it must be adequate.

Agricultural, Horticultural and Forestry Industry Training Board v Aylesbury Mushrooms is a leading authority on the imperative nature of the duty to consult.[19] The Industrial Training Act 1964, section 1(4), provided that, before making an industrial training order, the minister should consult organisations appearing to him to be representative of substantial numbers of persons employed in the industry. There had been a press notice summarising the functions of the new training board, and the National Farmers Union itself was consulted. However, the relevant subsidiary body, the Mushroom Growers Association, was sent a circular containing details of the scheme, which it did not receive. When an order came into force, Aylesbury Mushrooms, on behalf of the Mushroom Growers Association, applied for complete exemption from it on the ground that they had not been consulted in accordance with the Act. It was agreed by both parties that under the terms of the Act some consultation by the minister was mandatory. It was held that there had been a failure to consult and, as a result, that the order had no application to mushroom growers.

---

16 [1970] 1 All ER 304.
17 [1980] 1 WLR 182.
18 See also *Button v Jenkins* [1975] 3 All ER 585 and *Chief Adjudication Officer v Foster* [1993] AC 754.
19 [1972] 1 All ER 280.

Another example is *Grunwick Processing Laboratories Ltd v Advisory Consultation and Arbitration Service* (ACAS), where workers at Grunwick sought recognition of their union by their employers.[20] When this was refused, they applied to ACAS under section 11 of the Employment Protection Act 1975. ACAS proceeded to act under sections 12 and 14 of the Act. Section 14(1) provided that, in the course of its inquiries into a recognition issue, ACAS was to ascertain the opinions of the workers to whom the issue related. However, only a minority of employees, namely, union members, could be contacted because Grunwick refused to disclose the names and addresses of the rest of its workers, that is, non-union. Despite this, ACAS recommended recognition of the union. The decision was challenged by the company on the ground that ACAS had failed to consult all the workers. The question was whether ACAS was subject to a mandatory duty to consult all those involved in a trade union recognition dispute. In finding that there was a mandatory duty to consult, Lord Diplock stated: 'In the context of this part of the Act it is unthinkable that Parliament should have left it to the discretion of ACAS whether they should or should not consult those to whom the decision relates before coming to their conclusion.'[21] Moreover, the court refused to accept the qualification that the requirement was only mandatory in so far as it was 'reasonably practicable', as this would give ACAS far too wide a discretion. But, it might be asked, how could ACAS consult those whose names and addresses had been withheld? This decision, coming as it did in the course of a bitter industrial dispute, has been regarded as being highly political in nature. Incidentally, it had the effect of making union recognition dependent on the cooperation of the employers, and thereby frustrated one of the aims of the Employment Protection Act 1975.

We should also refer to the seminal case of *R v Brent LBC, ex p Gunning*,[22] where it was held that the respondent had acted unlawfully by failing properly to consult in advance of proposals being made about the amalgamation and closure of schools within its area. In his judgment Hodgson J set out four basic requirements of the duty to consult: (i) consultation must be at a time when proposals are at a formative stage; (ii) the proposer must give sufficient reasons for any proposal to permit of intelligent consideration and response; (iii) adequate time must be given for consideration and response; and (iv) the product of consultation must be conscientiously taken into account in finalising any statutory proposals. These requirements have since become known as the '*Gunning* criteria' and they have recently been endorsed by the Supreme Court in its ruling in *R (Moseley) v Haringey LBC*.[23] The issue in this case was whether the local authority had discharged its statutory duty to consult by inviting submissions on only one option for a council tax reduction scheme rather than on the wider range of options that had been open to it but which it had discarded. Holding that the authority had acted unlawfully, Lord Wilson referred to the *Gunning* criteria and observed that, 'It is hard to see how any of [the] four suggested requirements could be rejected or indeed improved'.[24] On the facts before the Court, this meant that consultation should have

---

20 [1978] AC 655.

21 Ibid, 677.

22 (1985) 84 LGR 168.

23 [2014] UKSC 56, [2014] 1 WLR 3947. For application of the criteria see also, e.g., *R (Wainwright) v Richmond upon Thames London Borough Council* [2001] All ER (D) 422.

24 [2014] 1 WLR 3947, 3957, para 25.

been extended to include the wider range of options and that the process had been deficient by reason of its more narrow focus. In the event, the Court granted relief by way of a declaration because the scheme that had been adopted had since been in operation for two years and the Court was of the view that it would have been disproportionate to require a fresh consultation to be completed.[25]

16.3.4 **Duty to give reasons**

Although it is very often desirable, in the interests of good administration, for reasons to be advanced in support of decisions, there is no general common law duty to give reasons.[26] However, statute may impose a duty to give reasons on specified decision-makers such as ministers and tribunals.[27] For instance, section 10 of the Tribunals and Inquiries Act 1992 allows reasons for decisions to be requested from almost all tribunals. The point to stress here is that the statutory duty to provide reasons will be held to be mandatory and that non-compliance will ordinarily result in a decision being either quashed or sent back to the deciding authority.

In *Mountview Court Properties Ltd v Devlin*, a case concerning the assessment of rents by a committee under the then extant tribunals legislation (the Tribunals and Inquiries Act 1958), it was held that any reasons must be sufficient and adequate in the context of the decision, and that sufficiency in any particular case would depend upon the facts before the tribunal.[28] However, Lord Parker CJ considered that a failure to provide sufficient reasons did not, in itself, give the court a right to quash a decision. On the facts of the instant case, the matter was thus remitted with a request for further reasons concerning the point at issue.

One related issue that has featured in the case law is the question of how far a public authority can add to its original reasons in the context of judicial review proceedings. This is essentially a matter concerned with the admissibility of evidence and the starting position is that the courts may allow the authority to supplement or explain its decision, but not to contradict or provide an *ex post facto* rationalisation for the decision.[29] Much will, however, again depend on the statutory context to the decision and the basic position can become more complex given the nature of the duty. For instance, where there is a duty to give reasons as part of the notification of the decision to the parties, the courts will normally regard the provision of adequate reasons at the time of the decision as a condition of the decision's validity (fuller explanation of the reasons would therefore not be possible). Where, in contrast, adequate reasons are not regarded as a condition of the decision's validity the courts may be willing to accept delayed reasons, albeit that they will be cautious about doing so. In such cases, the courts will enquire whether the late reasons are consistent with the earlier ones, whether they

---

25 Compare *R (United Co Ruscal plc) v London Metal Exchange* [2014] EWCA Civ 1271, [2015] 1 WLR 1375: common law recognises public bodies as having a wide degree of discretion as to the options on which to consult and there is no general obligation to consult on options which have been discarded unless there are very specific reasons for doing so.

26 See 17.3.5.

27 See further, e.g., *R v London Borough of Southwark, ex p Dagou* [1996] 28 HLR 72; *South Bucks District Council v Porter (No 2)* [2004] 1 WLR 1953; and *Uprichard v Scottish Ministers* [2013] UKSC 21, 2013 SC (UKSC) 219.

28 (1970) 21 P & CR 689.

29 See *R v Westminster City Council, ex p Ermakov* [1996] 2 All ER 302.

appear to be genuine, and whether they amount to an *ex post facto* rationalisation of the decision. In the event that the delayed reasons are found to be inadmissible, the court must decide whether the legislature intended that the decision should thereby be deemed unlawful.

It should finally be noted that the ECHR can require that reasons be given for a decision, even where statute does not (although the fact that the ECHR has effect under the Human Rights Act may mean that any duty can be said to have its origins in a domestic statute). For instance, Article 6 of the ECHR may require that reasons be given as an aspect of a fair hearing;[30] and an obligation can also arise under Article 2 of the ECHR when decisions are taken in the context of ongoing investigations into controversial deaths caused by the state. In such cases, the European Court of Human Rights (ECtHR) has identified a particular need for transparency and said that, if the prosecuting authorities decide not to charge the state officers involved with an offence, reasons should ordinarily be given.[31] Articles 3 and 8 of the ECHR can likewise require that reasons be given where, for instance, a mental health patient is to be administered medication contrary to his or her stated wishes.[32]

16.3.5 **Time limits**

Statutes will often also prescribe time limits for the making of decisions. Whether time limits are mandatory or directory will again depend on the wider statutory and factual context. In general, where the interests of individuals are directly affected, the courts will be more inclined to regard time limits as mandatory. For instance, in the above noted case of *Howard v Bodington*, a complaint against a clergyman fell because the bishop who received the complaint failed to forward it to the clergyman within the statutory 21 days.[33] The correctness of such an approach was confirmed in *R (Dawkins) v Standards Committee of the District Council of Bolsover*.[34] Here, it was held that a decision to suspend a local councillor from his position for three months was unlawful because it had been taken outside a three-month time limit specified in regulations. While the court accepted that a decision to suspend could be taken outside the limit, it held that the Committee needed to do more than demonstrate that the difficulties it had faced in convening within the time limit were 'understandable'. The test was to consider whether unforeseen and unexpected events had prevented compliance.

The approach in *Howard* and *Dawkins* can be contrasted with that adopted in the very different case of *Robinson v Secretary of State for Northern Ireland*.[35] One of the main issues in this case was whether the Northern Ireland Assembly could lawfully elect the First and Deputy First Ministers after the expiry of a statutory six-week time limit for electing persons to the posts. In finding that the Assembly could elect the ministers outside the time limit, a majority of the House of Lords considered that the elections were valid, as this outcome was consistent with the overall

---

30 See 17.3.5.
31 See *Jordan v UK* (2003) 37 EHRR 2, para 124.
32 See *R (Wooder) v Feggetter* [2003] QB 219.
33 (1877) 2 PD 203.
34 [2004] EWHC 2998.
35 [2002] NI 390.

constitutional objective of the Northern Ireland Act 1998, namely, the creation a stable system of devolved government. Under those circumstances, the statutory time limit did not need to be rigidly adhered to even if it was written in terms that were apparently mandatory.

16.3.6 **Financial measures**

Procedural requirements will be strictly enforced in respect of measures introducing a financial burden. For example, in *Sheffield City Council v Graingers Wines Ltd*, a resolution enabling the authority to impose rates was set aside for failing to specify the precise day on which it was to be operative.[36]

16.4 **Conclusion—a common sense approach?**

The review of the above cases indicates that, although there is a fairly clear distinction to be made between mandatory and directory requirements, in practice the courts now adopt a broad common sense approach that takes cognisance of all the circumstances of a case. If faced with a breach of a procedural requirement that is found in statute, judges therefore now appear simply to ask whether the requirement is important, and whether it would be fair, just, and convenient to set the offending government action aside. In *R v Lambeth LBC, ex p Sharp* it was thus said that:

When the provisions of (procedural) regulations are contravened, almost invariably it is unhelpful to consider what are the consequences of non-compliance with the regulations by classifying them as containing mandatory or directory provisions, or as containing a condition precedent, or as containing a provision which renders a decision void or voidable, or by considering whether they contain a provision that goes to jurisdiction. What has to be considered is: what is the particular provision designed to achieve?[37]

This statement points clearly to the need for a contextual approach in procedural *ultra vires* cases, and, as we have already noted above, the courts now regard the mandatory/directory dichotomy as only one tool among many in the hands of the courts. The point was made by Lord Woolf MR in *R v Immigration Appeal Tribunal, ex p Jeyeanthan*, where the Home Secretary had failed to comply with the requirements of the Asylum Appeals (Procedure) Rules 1993 in that he had not included a declaration of truth in an application for leave to appeal from a special adjudicator to the immigration appeal tribunal (it was ultimately held that the failure did not affect the validity of the Secretary of State's actions and that the failure could be addressed on appeal).[38] Stating that an over-concentration on distinctions can distract attention from the central task of ascertaining legislative intent in enacting a provision, Lord Woolf MR said that it is more important to consider the language of the Act and to remember that procedural requirements serve the interests of justice and that any result that would be contrary to those interests should be treated

---

36 [1978] 2 All ER 70.
37 (1986) 55 P & CR 232, 239, Woolf LJ.
38 [1999] 3 All ER 231.

with reservation. The question whether a requirement is mandatory or directory is therefore to be asked only as a first step, as it is likely that other considerations will also be of assistance in the majority of cases. Lord Woolf noted that these include: (a) whether the statutory requirement would be fulfilled if there were substantial compliance with the requirement, even if there has not been strict compliance (the substantial compliance consideration); (b) whether the non-compliance is capable of being waived and, if so, whether it should be waived in the particular case (the discretionary consideration); and (c) if the non-compliance cannot be waived, whether the consequence of non-compliance is such that a remedy should be granted (the consequences consideration) (see [1999] 3 All ER 231, 238–9).

Of course, the manner in which these or other matters will be addressed in any given case will depend upon the facts of the case and the nature of the particular requirement at issue. However, in general terms, it can be seen that considering such matters has the advantage of allowing the courts to marry the need for principle in public law to the corresponding need for pragmatism and flexibility in governmental processes. Indeed, the quest for balance between principle and pragmatism that now seems to define cases about the interpretation of statute might be said to complement much more fully the logic of the common law principles of natural justice and fairness. As we will see in the next chapter, those principles have long been applied variably and on the understanding that context is all important in any dispute about procedural impropriety. The approach considered above is thus arguably now much more at one with that adopted in circumstances where statute is partly or altogether silent on the issue of procedural protection.

For **further reading** on procedural fairness see chapter 17.

17

Procedural impropriety II: common law rules

17.1 Introduction

We turn now to consider the common law rules of fairness or, as they are often also described, the rules of natural justice. At the outset, we should emphasise that the rules—'the right to a hearing' and 'the rule against bias'—have long been central to administrative law where they are synonymous with the common law's historical protection of the individual. For instance, in *McNab v United States*,[1] Frankfurter J said that 'The history of liberty has largely been the history of the observance of procedural safeguards'; and in *R v Chancellor of the University of Cambridge*,[2] Fortescue J identified the basics of natural justice with the Garden of Eden when saying that 'even God himself did not pass sentence upon Adam, before he was called upon to make his defence'. Such statements indicate that there are minimum procedural guarantees that the common law expects decision-makers to observe, and the law, in its modern form, imposes a whole range of requirements that are intended to ensure that individuals can participate meaningfully in decision-making processes that affect their rights and interests.[3] Should a decision-maker fail to adhere to any of the common law requirements, this may—though not necessarily will—mean that its decision is unlawful.

In considering the common law rules, we divide this chapter into two main sections that describe, respectively, the historical development of the rules and their content. However, before turning to those sections, we would make four overarching points that are key to understanding the dynamics of the rules. The first concerns the relationship between the rules and procedural requirements that are found in statute. As we have already seen in the preceding chapter, legislation often contains procedural requirements and, where a decision-maker fails to act in accordance with those, any corresponding decision may be deemed *ultra vires*. This is wholly consonant with the doctrine of legislative supremacy, although it is important to note that, even if a decision-maker has observed all statutory requirements, it does not necessarily follow that their decision is procedurally sound. This is because the courts have long held that the question whether there has been procedural unfairness is a question of law for the courts, which may use the common law to imply 'so much and no more . . . by way of additional procedural

---

1 318 US 332 (1943).

2 (1723) 1 Str 557.

3 On the rationale for procedural fairness see further 16.1; and, e.g., *Re Reilly's Application* [2013] UKSC 61, [2014] AC 1115, 1149–50, Lord Reed.

safeguards as will ensure the attainment of fairness'.[4] That said, it is equally important to note that such judicial comments do not challenge the constitution's emphasis on legislative supremacy as the courts have also stated that, when they scrutinise the fairness of decision-making processes closely, they do so on the presumption that Parliament implicitly requires that decisions be made in accordance with the demands of fairness.[5] It does, of course, follow from this that Parliament may legislate, either expressly or by necessary implication, to place common law guarantees in abeyance, albeit that there would remain the possibility of a declaration of incompatibility if the legislation was incompatible with Article 6 of the European Convention on Human Rights (ECHR).[6] Some case law has similarly held that, where legislation lays down an exhaustive procedural code, it may be neither necessary nor legitimate for the courts to imply further safeguards.[7]

The second point concerns the context-sensitive nature of the rules, in particular the right to a hearing. As will become apparent below, the precise requirements of fairness vary according to the context of any given case—that is, there is a 'sliding scale' of fairness which entails that different cases may attract more or less procedural protection, depending on their facts. For instance, where a decision is essentially 'judicial' in character, the procedures will of necessity be required to have more in common with court proceedings (disclosure of information; right to legal representation; right to be given reasons; etc). On the other hand, lesser standards might be expected to apply for what might be regarded as 'administrative' decisions, albeit that the decision-maker will always be required to act fairly. All will therefore depend on context and what the court considers to be appropriate to a given factual matrix. As Lord Bridge expressed it in *Lloyd v McMahon*:

The so-called rules of natural justice are not engraved on tablets of stone. To use the phrase which better expresses the underlying concept, what the requirements of fairness demand when any body, domestic, administrative or judicial, has to make a decision which will affect the rights of individuals depends on the character of the decision-making body, the kind of decision it has to make and the statutory or other framework in which it operates.[8]

The third point is that the rules of fairness/natural justice, as with the other grounds for judicial review, continue to develop in the light of the ECHR and, in particular, the right to a fair trial under Article 6 of the ECHR (and, to a lesser extent, Article 47 of the Charter of Fundamental Rights of the European Union).[9] The manner of that influence is explained in much more detail below, but it is important to be aware at this stage that the common law developments described in this chapter do not—if they ever did—occur in a vacuum. The common law is, instead, influenced by legal considerations that are both internal and external to

---

4 *Lloyd v McMahon* [1987] AC 625, 702, Lord Bridge.

5 *R v Secretary of State for the Home Department, ex p Pierson* [1998] AC 539, 573–4.

6 For recognition of the point about Parliament's powers see ibid; but compare Lord Hodge's comments in *Re Moohan* [2014] UKSC 67, [2015] AC 901, 925, para 35. On declarations of incompatibility see 4.4.3.

7 *Furnell v Whangarei High School's Board* [1973] AC 660 and *R v Secretary of State for the Environment, ex p Hammersmith and Fulham LBC* [1991] 1 AC 521.

8 [1987] AC 625, 702.

9 Article 47 guarantees, among other things, the 'right to an effective remedy' and 'a fair and public hearing within a reasonable time by an independent and impartial tribunal previously established by law'. On the reach of the Charter see 3.2.3 and 4.5; and, e.g., Case C-300/11, *ZZ v Secretary of State for the Home Department* [2013] 3 WLR 813.

the domestic system,[10] and we shall see that external considerations such as the ECHR can sometimes require modification of long-standing common law wisdom. Perhaps the leading example that we discuss below is that of bias, where the common law approach to 'apparent bias' was modified in the light of the case law of the European Court of Human Rights (ECtHR).[11]

The fourth, and final, point concerns the use of the terms 'fairness' and 'natural justice' throughout the chapter. In short, it will become apparent on reading the chapter that the term 'natural justice' was preferred in the earlier case law largely because the courts considered that the rules applied only to judicial decision-makers, rather than those who were administrative (the term 'justice' thereby corresponding with court hearings). However, the case law has since moved far beyond any distinction between judicial and administrative decision-makers, and the principles of 'natural justice' are now regarded as subsumed within the common law rules of 'fairness' that apply whenever '(anyone) decides anything'.[12] When reading this chapter, it should therefore be remembered that the rules of natural justice and fairness are essentially indistinct and that they should be regarded as such. Where we use one or other of the terms in certain sections or when discussing certain cases, this is thus merely consistent with the language that prevailed at the time or was used in the corresponding law reports.

17.2 History

17.2.1 Establishing the rules

As we have noted above, the principles on which the modern concept of natural justice is based go back many centuries. Many of the early cases were to do with the deprivation of offices, for example, *Baggs Case*, where it was held that there was a requirement of notice and a hearing.[13] The importance attached to the idea can be gauged from the fact that it was stated in *Dr Bonham's Case*[14] by Coke CJ, and repeated by Holt CJ in *City of London v Wood*[15] a hundred years later, that if it made a man a judge in his own cause the court would go so far as to declare an Act of Parliament void (an approach that the courts have also hinted at in the modern era, the doctrine of parliamentary sovereignty notwithstanding).[16] However, in more general terms, there is a greater historical link between the development of the rules of natural justice and the expansion of state activity and institutions. In this context, the courts became ever more aware that the greater the powers conferred on such public bodies, the greater would be the commensurate need for the observance and enforcement of safeguards. Indeed, it will become apparent as we examine the cases that the rules of natural justice/fairness have evolved mainly over the last

---

10 See chs 2–4.
11 *Porter v Magill* [2002] 2 AC 357.
12 *Board of Education v Rice* [1911] AC 179, 182, Lord Loreburn.
13 (1615) 11 Co Rep 93b; and see 4.2.1.
14 (1610) 8 Co Rep 113a.
15 (1701) 12 Mod 669.
16 See, e.g., *R (Jackson) v Attorney-General* [2006] 1 AC 262, 318, Baroness Hale stating the courts might reject an Act of Parliament that purported to abolish rights of access to judicial review.

150 years or so in response to some of the consequences of the type of legislation that was passed from the late nineteenth century onwards, for example, the Public Health Acts of 1872 and 1875, or the Artisans and Labourer's Dwellings Improvement Acts of 1875 and 1879. A leading case of that era is *Cooper v Wandsworth Board of Works*,[17] which emphasised the importance of the right to a hearing even when there was no such provision in the statute. In this instance it was provided by section 76 of the Metropolis Local Management Act 1855 that a person erecting new housing should give seven days' notice in writing to the Board and that, if they failed to do so, the Board could alter or demolish the property. The plaintiff in this case later claimed to have sent such a notice under section 76, but this was denied by the Board. In any event, he admitted that the work commenced within five days of when he claimed to have given notice. This question of notice is an important one since, had there been a hearing, what Erle CJ described as a default may have been explained. The Board, without itself giving any notice, sent some workmen out late in the evening to demolish the building, which had by this time reached the second floor level. It is interesting to note here that the Board had conformed with all the designated statutory requirements but, in doing so, it had also deprived someone of their property. In other words, for a person to find that their premises had been demolished was, in the circumstances, grossly disproportionate, even if the correct procedures had been followed. A remedy in the form of damages was granted, as it was held that the Board had no power to act without granting the plaintiff a hearing.

Another early landmark case showing the willingness of the courts to intervene is *Board of Education v Rice*.[18] This concerned a dispute about pay for teachers. The local authority was remunerating teachers in church schools at a lower rate than in its own schools. This had a serious impact on morale and many teachers were on the point of leaving their jobs. At the same time, the policies were controversial and the managers claimed that the authority was failing to keep the schools efficient. To deal with the problem, a public inquiry was set up under the chairmanship of a local barrister. The inquiry had reported in favour of the managers, but the Board of Education still proceeded to find in favour of the local authority, which raised some serious doubt as to the conduct of the Board in determining the dispute. The House of Lords granted writs of *certiorari* and *mandamus* (now quashing and mandatory orders) to overturn the decision and make the Board fulfil its duties. However, the significance of this case lies in Lord Loreburn's words, which have already been referred to above, and which came to be regarded as a classic statement of the duty of any decision-maker:

[T]hey must act in good faith and fairly listen to both sides, for that is a duty laying upon every one who decides anything. But I do not think they are bound to treat such a question as though it were a trial.[19]

17.2.2 Natural justice in abeyance: the distinction between 'judicial' and 'administrative' decisions

The potential implications of the above judgments were wide-ranging but, for a period of time, the development of the law became hindered by a misunderstanding

---

17 (1863) 14 CB(NS) 180.
18 [1911] AC 179.
19 Ibid, 182.

of Lord Loreburn's statement that there is no need to treat all matters 'as though it were a trial'. In broad terms, his Lordship's comments were taken to mean that there was a distinction to be drawn between 'judicial' decisions (which attracted the full protections of natural justice) and 'administrative' decisions (which did not attract the protections). In every day administration this came to mean that, even though there had been a marked increase in decision-making by departments and executive bodies, individuals would not enjoy procedural protections unless the decision in question could be classified as 'judicial'. Of course, deciding where to draw the line would often prove problematic, and the development of natural justice suffered as administrative law retreated into conceptual abstraction.

A leading case that marked the retreat was *Local Government Board v Arlidge*.[20] The House of Lords here inserted certain qualifications as prerequisites to judicial intervention, which had the effect of limiting the application of natural justice to government and non-government administrative procedures alike for many years to come. The central matter that had to be determined was the extent to which the courts should allow the rules of natural justice to override 'the needs of practical administration' (this can be referred to as the 'efficiency of administration' argument). *Arlidge* itself concerned the role of a local authority in inspecting housing and, on the facts, Mr Arlidge's house had been declared unfit for human habitation. He appealed, submitting reports by experts that his house was, in fact, fit for habitation. The inspector at a public inquiry that was later set up to determine the question visited the premises and, after he had summarised the evidence, the clearance order was again upheld. This occurred without Arlidge being able to appear before this officer, or being given an opportunity to examine his evidence. However, the House of Lords refused to accept that this inquiry, before a housing inspector, had been inadequate simply because it had not been held in open session, with the publication of a report. Their Lordships considered that there was no expectation that an administrative (as opposed to judicial) procedure should operate like a court of law, and there was therefore no requirement that the inspector's report be disclosed.

A case that illustrated the difficulties in drawing the line between judicial and administrative decisions was *Errington v Minister of Health*,[21] where a remedy was granted but only after the nature of the functions had been established to the satisfaction of the court. The facts were that a slum clearance order was challenged because civil servants, acting on behalf of the minister, had conferred with local officials and heard additional evidence after a public inquiry had ended (some officials had also visited the site after the inquiry without informing the owner). The point that was raised was that this information was accepted without the other side being given the opportunity to respond, which amounted to communicating with one side behind the back of the other. The court proceeded by first deciding whether the minister had been acting in a judicial or an administrative capacity when confirming the closing order; and it was emphasised by Maugham LJ that the rules of natural justice would not apply if the minister was classified as acting in a purely administrative capacity. It was found that the minister had been acting in a quasi-judicial capacity, and that there had been a breach of natural justice. Today, the term 'quasi-judicial' is probably best avoided, as we shall see.

---

20 [1915] AC 120.
21 [1935] 1 KB 249.

Nakkuda Ali v Jayaratne[22] is another important case, which is now commonly regarded as exemplifying both a narrow definition of 'acting judicially' and the high watermark of what we have referred to as the departure from earlier standards of natural justice. The controller of textiles in Sri Lanka (then Ceylon) had a power under a defence regulation to cancel the licence of a dealer in textiles if he had 'reasonable grounds to believe' that the dealer was unfit to continue in business. It had been alleged that a particular dealer had behaved fraudulently and the controller duly exercised the power. The Privy Council noted that the controller in withdrawing the dealer's licence was not acting judicially, and held that he was not determining a question of right but was taking executive action to remove a privilege. Lord Radcliffe stated that, as there was nothing in the words of the relevant statute or regulations to indicate that the controller was acting in a judicial or quasi-judicial capacity, there were no grounds for granting relief. It is widely considered that this judgment went beyond upholding the distinction between administrative and judicial action, and simply ignored the fact that the court would intervene, where necessary, to supply the omission of the legislature. As William Wade said in an earlier edition of his seminal book: 'Primary principles of law were abandoned in favour of the fallacious doctrine, devoid alike of logic, equity and authority, that a licence was a mere privilege and that therefore the holder could be deprived of his livelihood without ceremony.'[23]

17.2.3 **Modern development of the rules: *Ridge v Baldwin***

The rules of natural justice were then to be reborn in *Ridge v Baldwin*,[24] which is the starting point for any study of natural justice/fairness in the modern administrative state. Indeed, the case marked not only a return to a vibrant body of natural justice case law, but it was also one of the landmark decisions that reflected a more general shift in judicial attitudes during the 1960s towards a broader, more activist intervention in administrative decision-making. The case concerned Charles Ridge, the Chief Constable of Brighton, who had been charged with conspiracy to obstruct the course of justice. He was acquitted at his trial. However, Ridge had been heavily criticised by the judge for his conduct, which was regarded as revealing, *inter alia*, a lack of probity, responsibility, and leadership. As a result of this criticism, his continued tenure in the office of Chief Constable appeared to be unsustainable. The consequence was that the local watch committee dismissed Ridge on the day after the trial. They claimed to be acting under section 191(4) of the Municipal Corporations Act 1882, which allowed them to dismiss 'any borough constable whom they think negligent in the discharge of his duty, or otherwise unfit for the same'. However, there were further regulations that set out the procedures to be followed in the event of allegations being made against a Chief Constable. The upshot was that Ridge was dismissed not only without any notice of the proposal to dismiss him, but also without being allowed any kind of hearing. Further, he was not given particulars of the grounds for the committee's decision.

---

22 [1951] AC 66.

23 *Administrative Law*, 6th edn (Oxford: Oxford University Press, 1988), 515. And see also, e.g., *R v Metropolitan Police Commissioner, ex p Parker* [1953] 2 All ER 717.

24 [1964] AC 40.

Following a request by his solicitor, the committee reconvened several days later, only to confirm their original decision. An appeal to the minister followed, and was rejected. The underlying issue in this case was the loss of pension rights, which would be forfeited in the case of dismissal, but not if Ridge was allowed to resign. He applied for a declaration that the dismissal had been *ultra vires*.

In his judgment in the House of Lords, Lord Reid referred to three types of dismissal: dismissal of a servant by his master; dismissal from an office held during pleasure; and dismissal from an office (again, note the importance of context and the sliding scale of fairness). Holding that Ridge's case fell into this last category, the judge said that there must be something against a person to warrant dismissal. His Lordship also considered why the law in this area had become confused and, in a particularly famous passage that presaged the need for change, said, 'We do not have a developed system of administrative law—perhaps because until fairly recently we did not need it'.[25] His Lordship traced the source of some of the confusion to the *dictum* of Lord Atkin in *R v Electricity Commissioner, ex p London Electricity Joint Committee (1920)*, where it was said that: 'Wherever any body of persons having legal authority to determine questions affecting the rights of subjects, and having the duty to act judicially, act in excess of their legal authority, they are subject to the controlling jurisdiction of the King's Bench Division exercised in these writs.'[26] Lord Hewart CJ, in the later case of *R v Legislative Committee of the Church Assembly, ex p Haynes-Smith*,[27] had construed the passage to mean that there *had* to be a duty to act judicially, with the result that a line of authority developed that sought to confine intervention by the courts to what was defined as judicial or quasi-judicial decision-making only. Lord Reid rejected this distinction and moved towards the understanding that any power that affects a person's rights, in the sense of having consequences for them, must be exercised fairly. Failure to do so will give rise to a remedy. Accordingly, it was held in *Ridge v Baldwin* that the dismissal was void because the appellant should have been informed of the charges against him, as required by the Municipal Corporations Act 1882, and he should have been given a hearing on the ground that what he had to say was of substance to the case.

It should be noted that it was sometimes also argued that a hearing was unnecessary because nothing that could be said in it would alter the outcome of the decision-making process. Although this approach was rejected by Lord Reid in *Ridge v Baldwin*—and would be contrary to the weight of the modern authorities that we consider below—some case law did support the view that a person has not only to demonstrate a right to make a representation, but must also show that there is a case of substance to make. This is because, as Lord Wilberforce put it, 'The court does not act in vain'.[28] However, to the extent that such arguments can be made with reference to ideas of administrative efficiency (i.e., the need not to overburden decision-makers with procedural requirements), it might also be asked how far a decision-maker can make a truly informed choice without first hearing from

---

25 [1964] AC 40, 72.

26 [1924] 1 KB 171, 205.

27 [1928] 1 KB 411.

28 *Malloch v Aberdeen Corporation* [1971] 1 WLR 1578, 1595. And see, too, e.g., *R v Secretary of State for the Environment, ex p Brent London Borough Council* [1982] QB 593.

those who will be affected by a decision. Megarry LJ encapsulated the problem with this neat logic in *John v Rees*:

As everybody who has anything to do with the law well knows, the path of the law is strewn with examples of open and shut cases which, somehow, were not; of unanswerable charges which, in the event, were completely answered; of inexplicable conduct which was fully explained; of fixed and unalterable determinations that, by discussion suffered a change.[29]

Bearing these points in mind, we can see that *Ridge v Baldwin* exposed the obsolescence of the previous conceptual distinction between administrative decisions, to which the rules of natural justice did not apply, and judicial decisions, to which they did. The rules of natural justice were thus liberated from the rigid limitations which had been imposed in earlier decisions by dispensing with the requirement that the decision-making body was under a duty to act judicially. This is where fairness receives an interpretation which now becomes almost synonymous with natural justice. For example, following *Ridge v Baldwin*, a failure to afford a hearing will sometimes—though certainly not always—mean that a decision-maker will have acted unlawfully, whether for reasons of fairness and/or a failure to take relevant considerations into account (i.e., the views of those who will be affected by a decision). It is perhaps surprising that the courts ever managed to place themselves in what was to prove an ultimately unsustainable position. The test advocated by Lord Reid in *Ridge v Baldwin* is to assess what a reasonable person would regard as fair procedure in any given circumstances.

We would also add that the principles enunciated in *Ridge v Baldwin* have since been applied in a very large number of cases and that it is, for that reason, one of the seminal cases in administrative law. There are many examples that could be used to illustrate the point, but the one that we will use here is the Court of Appeal's decision in *R (Shoesmith) v OFSTED and Others*.[30] This case arose out of the tragic death of 'Baby P', which led the Secretary of State to issue a Direction under the Education Act 1996 which had the effect of removing the claimant—the Director of Children's Services in Haringey LBC—from her post with immediate effect. The Secretary of State also expressed the view that the claimant should not receive any compensation from her employer local authority and, after a hearing was held, she was summarily dismissed on the basis of the Secretary of State's Direction and breach of trust and confidence. The claimant brought proceedings and, in a ruling that was full of the language and logic of *Ridge v Baldwin*, succeeded. Focusing primarily on the failings in the role of the Secretary of State, the Court of Appeal found that, although the claimant was ultimately responsible and accountable for children's services, she was entitled to procedural protections including the opportunity to offer an explanation in respect of matters falling under her ultimate control. The Court was also of the view that, as it had been more than a year since Baby P had died in circumstances where the claimant was not a front-line social worker, there was no reason of urgency to justify denying the claimant the opportunity to answer the charge against her. The Court likewise found that the Secretary of State had wrongly assumed that the claimant had been given more opportunity to explain her case than she had in fact been allowed, and also that

---

29 [1970] Ch 345, 402.
30 [2011] PTSR 1459.

the case against her was not so clear that any representations she made would make no difference to the Secretary of State's decision. On the facts, a declaration that the Direction of the Secretary of State was unlawful would be made.

17.2.4 Aftermath of *Ridge v Baldwin*: the sliding scale of fairness

Post-*Ridge v Baldwin*, the courts have, as we have already noted above, sought to apply the rules of fairness in the light of the different factual circumstances of individual cases. Take the position of a person who has the intention of studying at university. As an applicant to the institution, any general expectation of fair treatment would naturally be lower than if he or she were already part of the institution, that is, he or she could expect only that his or her application to the university would be processed on the same basis as those of other applicants. On the other hand, in the situation where an enrolled student has a contractual relationship with the university, and is then for some reason subjected to internal disciplinary action, he or she might well be entitled to certain procedural safeguards. In the most extreme situation, in circumstances involving an allegation that might lead to the student being expelled from the institution (e.g., if there were an accusation that he or she had stolen from the library), then one might expect that something approaching a full hearing, with some form of representation, would be required to ensure fairness.

An important ruling that broadly acknowledges and applies this approach was given in the immigration case of *Re HK (an infant)*.[31] HK was an immigrant under the Commonwealth Immigration Act 1962, whose entry depended upon being able to prove that he was under the age of 16. On this occasion, entry had been refused because the immigration officer suspected that HK was well above 16 and sent the boy to the duty medical officer at Heathrow. The officer estimated his age as 17. A challenge could only be mounted on the basis that the rules of natural justice had not been complied with. It was recognised that there clearly had to be limits to the amount of time that could be spent on processing individual cases of this kind. The court held that the person ought to be told that he or she was suspected of being over age, and be given a chance to explain his or her position. But even if the officer was acting judicially or quasi-judicially, this did not extend to allowing a full-scale hearing: 'That is not, as I see it, a question of acting or being required to act judicially but of being required to act fairly' ([1967] 1 All ER 226, 231, per Lord Parker CJ). Thus, *Re HK* can be regarded as a decision leaning towards recognition of a general duty to act fairly.[32]

This trend towards recognising the idea of a duty to act fairly was reinforced in *Re Pergamon Press*.[33] This was a case involving a Board of Trade inquiry into a company in circumstances where the inspectors were not themselves empowered to make a decision that directly affected the rights of the parties. It was held that even though the inspectors were acting in an administrative capacity alone, they were under a duty to act fairly. This was because, as Lord Denning explained in his judgment, the report involved might have had very wide repercussions which

---

31 [1967] 1 All ER 226.
32 And see, to like effect, *Schmidt v Secretary of State for Home Affairs* [1969] 1 All ER 904.
33 [1970] 3 All ER 535.

could have led to criminal proceedings and ruined the reputations and careers of the directors and others. Although Lord Denning concluded that the inspectors must act fairly, by giving the parties a proper opportunity of correcting or contradicting what was said against them, there was also a recognition that this had to be balanced against other factors, since the inquiry itself was in the public interest. If, as the directors demanded, the names of witnesses were revealed, and these witnesses were to be subject to cross-examination at this early stage, it might impede the inquiry by discouraging people from coming forward to present evidence.

In another important case on fairness measured against the extent of harm to an individual, *McInnes v Onslow-Fane*,[34] the principles in *Ridge v Baldwin* were considered and developed by Megarry V-C. First, there was an attempt to relate, more precisely, rules that were to apply (on a sliding scale) to the rights or interests that were to be affected, and, secondly, Megarry V-C developed the use of the term 'legitimate expectation'.[35] The plaintiff applied for a declaration against the British Boxing Board of Control, maintaining that the Board had neglected to follow the correct procedures when considering his application for a licence. He was neither informed of the case against him nor given the opportunity of an oral hearing. He had in fact previously held a licence that enabled him to engage in a number of activities in the sport of boxing, including training, promotion, and acting as master of ceremonies. Megarry V-C held that, despite the fact that the situation was not governed by statute or by contract, the court could intervene:

> . . . if one accepts that 'natural justice' is a flexible term which imposes different requirements in different cases, it is capable of applying to the whole range of situations indicated by terms such as 'judicial', 'quasi-judicial' and 'administrative'. Nevertheless, the further the situation is away from anything that resembles a judicial or quasi-judicial situation . . . the more appropriate it is to reject an expression which includes the word 'justice' and to use instead terms such as 'fairness' or the 'duty to act fairly'.[36]

Megarry V-C discussed the very different requirements for, on the one hand, 'forfeiture cases', that involve the taking away of some existing right or position, and, on the other hand, 'application cases', where a person applies for but is denied the application to a position. He also identified an intermediate category of what he called 'expectation cases', or 'renewal' cases, where the applicant, on the basis of a previous practice, for example, the holding of the licence for some time, has a legitimate expectation that his application will be granted. This amounts to a sliding scale according to how much is at stake for the plaintiff. To achieve 'fairness' in the forfeiture cases there is a general right to an unbiased tribunal, to be given notice of charges, and to be heard in answer to those charges. For application cases, including the one under consideration, there is no general right to be heard, since nothing is being taken away and there are no charges being made against the person concerned. In these circumstances a 'duty to act fairly' meant that the Board (or other body) had to reach an honest conclusion, without bias, and not in pursuance of a capricious policy. It did not, however, extend as far as requiring them to give reasons for the refusal. This was because there was no slur on the character of

---

34 [1978] 3 All ER 211.
35 On which doctrine see ch 15.
36 [1978] 3 All ER 211, 219.

the applicant by the refusal. There was only a duty on the Board to consider the application fairly.

This emphasis on context has since become the defining feature of the judicial approach, and there have been a number of important judicial statements about the significance of the circumstances of individual cases. For instance, we have already made reference in our introduction to Lord Bridge's famous dictum in *Lloyd v McMahon*, and Lord Lane CJ likewise explained in *R v Commission for Racial Equality, ex p Cottrell and Rothon* that:

It seems to me that there are degrees of judicial hearing, and those degrees run from the borders of pure administration to the borders of the full hearing of a criminal cause or a matter in the Crown Court. It does not profit one to try to pigeon-hole the particular set of circumstances either into the administrative pigeon-hole or into the judicial pigeon-hole. Each case will inevitably differ, and one must ask oneself what is the basic nature of the proceeding which was going on here.[37]

Of course, when thinking of context, one of the most important considerations in any case is whether the fundamental rights of an individual will be affected by a decision. *R v Army Board of the Defence Council, ex p Anderson* illustrates that, where such rights are affected, the common law will be demanding in terms of procedural protection.[38] Anderson, who was the only black soldier in his platoon in the army, went absent without leave after suffering alleged racial abuse from other soldiers. He was eventually arrested and sent back to his unit. In response to his complaints, there was an inquiry by the military police into the allegations of racial discrimination. However, the report resulting from the inquiry was not made available to Anderson. At his court martial he pleaded guilty and was given a sentence of detention. Some time after the court martial he was provided with a summary of the report, which confirmed the allegation that he had suffered verbal abuse, but not other allegations of assault. Following this disclosure from the report, he made a complaint of discrimination under the Race Relations Act 1976. This was investigated by the commanding officer and rejected, but Anderson was told that disciplinary action had been taken against two soldiers. Finally he complained to the Army Board. The procedure involved the relevant documents being sent to two members of the Board, who reached their conclusion independently. Their decision was that, although there was some evidence to substantiate the complaint, they considered that it was insufficient to warrant an apology or any compensation. However, despite his requests, Anderson was denied an oral hearing or access to the relevant documents. As a last resort he applied for judicial review.

In a significant judgment, Taylor LJ, quoting Lord Bridge in *Lloyd v McMahon*, again resisted any attempt to revive or sustain a distinction between administrative and judicial functions. He also referred to Professor Wade in support of the view established in *Ridge v Baldwin*, and thereafter in other notable cases, that the crucial fact in determining what was judicial was simply whether a decision affects the rights and interests of an individual: 'The Army Board as the forum of last resort, dealing with an individual's fundamental statutory rights, must by its procedures achieve a high standard of fairness.' This included, in his Lordship's

---

37 [1980] 3 All ER 265, 271.
38 [1992] QB 169.

view, the right to a proper hearing which need not necessarily be oral. It was plain that the Board had fettered their discretion by deciding, whatever the circumstances, never to hold an oral hearing. It was further held that the nature of the complaint was such that the applicant was also entitled to have full disclosure of the material that was considered by the Board. This is the sliding scale in practice.[39]

Of course, since the Human Rights Act 1998 came into force, it has also been true that Article 6 of the ECHR has been of (potential) relevance in cases that engage an individual's fundamental rights. That Article, so far as is relevant, provides:

In the determination of his civil rights and obligations or of any criminal charge against him, everyone is entitled to a fair and public hearing within a reasonable time by an independent and impartial tribunal established by law.[40]

We return to some of the procedural obligations that are contained in Article 6 of the ECHR, below, but the point to be made here is that the Article can augment and in some instances supplant the common law's procedural guarantees. On the other hand, it is also true that 'civil rights' has a Convention specific meaning that is narrower than might be expected and that this can limit the reach of Article 6 in cases where the common law still applies. In short, the term has historically been associated with the concept of private law rights as used in civil law systems, with Article 6 of the ECHR applying where there is a 'dispute' about those rights.[41] This historical reference point has, in turn, given rise to considerable difficulty in the international and domestic case law, as it is not always clear whether administrative determinations are embraced by Article 6 of the ECHR (the case law on social and welfare benefits, discussed at 17.4.5, has become notably complex).[42] The ECtHR has, however, tended to adopt a broad approach to the interpretation of the term, and 'civil rights' have been taken to be engaged in disputes involving land use,[43] monetary claims against public authorities,[44] licences (whether to be applied for or to be revoked),[45] social security benefits,[46] and disciplinary proceedings.[47] On the other hand, there are categories of decisions that apparently remain outside the scope of the Article, for instance those relating to immigration and asylum[48] (although it can apply in extradition proceedings in UK courts that involve UK citizens)[49] and some public sector employment disputes.[50]

---

39 See also, e.g., *R v Secretary of State for the Home Department, ex p Moon* (1996) 8 Admin LR 477 and *R v Secretary of State for the Home Department, ex p Fayed* [1998] 1 All ER 228.

40 On the question of when the Article is engaged by a decision-maker see *R (G) v X Governors School* [2011] UKSC 30, [2011] 3 WLR 237.

41 See *H v Belgium* (1988) 10 EHRR 339, 346, para 40.

42 See most recently *Ali v Birmingham City Council* [2010] 2 AC 39, as read in the light of *Fazia Ali v UK*, judgment of 20 October 2015.

43 e.g., *Ringeisen v Austria* (1979-80) 1 EHRR 455 and *Skarby v Sweden* (1990) 13 EHRR 90.

44 *Editions Periscope v France* (1992) 14 EHRR 597.

45 *Benthem v Netherlands* (1986) 8 EHRR 1 and *Pudas v Sweden* (1988) 10 EHRR 380.

46 *Feldbrugge v The Netherlands* (1986) 8 EHRR 425; *Salesi v Italy* (1998) 26 EHRR 187; *Mennitto v Italy* (2002) 34 EHRR 48.

47 *Le Compte, Van Leuven and De Meyere v Belgium* (1982) 4 EHRR 1.

48 *Maaouia v France* (2001) 33 EHRR 42 and *Algar v Norway* (2012) 54 EHRR SE6.

49 *Pomiechowski v District Court of Legnica* [2012] UKSC 20, [2012] 1 WLR 1604, 1623–4, paras 31–3, Lord Mance.

50 *Pellegrin v France* (2001) 31 EHRR 651 and *Eskelinen v Finland* (2007) 45 EHRR 43.

17.2.5 **Legitimate expectation of fairness**

We have already seen above how, in *McInnes v Onslow-Fane*,[51] Megarry V-C made a link between fairness and the doctrine of legitimate expectation. That doctrine, which we have considered in depth in chapter 15, has procedural and substantive dimensions that seek to ensure fairness to individuals both in terms of decision-making processes and, more controversially, their outcomes (albeit that public authorities can seek to rely upon a point of public interest by way of frustrating an expectation). Of course, in the context of the present chapter, we are concerned only with the procedural dimension to the doctrine, which emerged very much as a part of the more general development of the rules of natural justice/fairness. Indeed, as we noted in chapter 15, it is with the procedural dimension that the story of legitimate expectation begins.

Given that we have already examined the evolution of the doctrine in detail, little would be gained from examining the case law again here. However, in terms of understanding the significance of the doctrine within the rubric of natural justice/fairness, there are two key points that we would make. The first is that the doctrine broadened the scope of procedural fairness by offering individuals a means of procedural protection even in circumstances where they did not have a recognised legal right that was to be affected by a decision. It is important to be clear here just what this means. In sum, where an individual had a recognised right—for instance, a property right (as in *Cooper*, above)—the common law already required that the individual be given a hearing, subject, as always, to context. However, with the emergence of the legitimate expectation doctrine, it became accepted that individuals may expect to be heard—or consulted—even in instances where they had no comparable common law right. In other words, the courts, with the doctrine, started to focus less on vindicating established rights, and more on ensuring fairness towards individuals who may have had some other reason to expect fairness. A good example from the case law is *Schmidt v Secretary of State for Home Affairs*, which is discussed in the legitimate expectation chapter.[52]

The second point concerns the question when a legitimate expectation of a hearing, or consultation, will be created in law. Here, the courts have again been highly flexible, and they have accepted that expectations may be engendered by express undertakings, policies, and/or practices. *Attorney-General for Hong Kong v Ng Yuen Shiu* is an example of an expectation being generated by an express undertaking.[53] The facts, here, were that an illegal immigrant had come to Hong Kong from Macau and had established a business in Hong Kong. In order to address a problem that existed with illegal immigration, it was officially announced that any persons presenting themselves to the authorities would have their individual cases dealt with on their merits. However, when the applicant came forward he was detained while a deportation order was applied for. Following this, his appeal against deportation was dismissed without a hearing. *Certiorari* (quashing order) was sought on the ground that the applicant had not been allowed to present his case against deportation to the authorities. Although it was held that an alien as a rule does not

---

51 [1978] 3 All ER 211.
52 [1969] 2 Ch 149 at 15.3.1.
53 [1983] 2 AC 629.

have a right to a hearing in this situation, it was held that there was a legitimate expectation that he would be accorded a hearing after the announcement had been made. As Lord Fraser put it:

'legitimate expectations' . . . are capable of including expectations which go beyond enforceable legal rights, provided they have some reasonable basis . . . The expectations may be based upon some statement or undertaking by, or on behalf of, the public authority which has the duty of making the decision, if the authority has, through its officers, acted in a way that would make it unfair or inconsistent with good administration for [the applicant] to be denied such an inquiry.[54]

An example of a policy giving rise to an expectation is provided by *R v Secretary of State for Home Office, ex p Asif Mahmood Khan*.[55] Rules for adoption had been set out in a circular letter which was received by the applicants. The information they entered on the relevant forms had been supplied to the department with this letter in mind. It was argued that the letter, in itself, generated a legitimate expectation which had not been realised. In considering the application, different criteria had been applied to those specified in the circular, and the applicants had their application for adoption refused. This was compounded by the fact that an unsatisfactory reason for refusal had been advanced by the Secretary of State. The Khans wanted to rely on an existing policy in the form that had been communicated to them, and not be treated as an exception to it. They were able to establish this by maintaining that the department had acted contrary to a legitimate expectation which had been created by its own published circular. It was made clear that only an overriding public interest would allow the minister to resile from this commitment.[56]

Finally, and turning to the example of practices giving rise to expectations of consultation, we have the seminal *GCHQ* case.[57] The facts here were that civil servants at the Government Communication Headquarters (GCHQ) had engaged in a number of strikes, which had led the government to become increasingly concerned about the potential threat to national security. The government thus used the prerogative powers to make the Civil Service Order in Council under which the Minster for the Civil Service (the Prime Minister) limited the union rights of employees at GCHQ to membership of a number of government-approved unions. This change in employment conditions had occurred without any consultation with the civil service unions, who argued that they should have been consulted because of a long-standing practice of doing so. While the House of Lords ultimately held that the government action was lawful for reasons of national security, it agreed that there was a legitimate expectation on the facts and that, had the circumstances been otherwise, the application for judicial review would have been granted. As Lord Diplock explained:

Prima facie . . . civil servants employed at GCHQ who were members of national trade unions had, at best, in December 1983, a legitimate expectation that they would continue to enjoy the benefits of such membership and of representation by those trade unions in any consultations and negotiations with representatives of the management of that government department as to the changes in any term of their employment. So, but again prima facie

---

54 Ibid, 636.
55 [1984] 1 WLR 1337.
56 The case is discussed further at 15.3.1.
57 *Council of Civil Service Unions v Minister for the Civil Service* [1985] AC 374; and see 9.3.2.2.

only, they were entitled, as a matter of public law under the head of 'procedural impropriety', before administrative action was taken on a decision to withdraw that benefit, to have communicated to the national trade unions by which they had theretofore been represented the reason for such withdrawal, and for such unions to be given an opportunity to comment on it.[58]

17.2.6 Fairness and national security

The importance of national security considerations in *GCHQ* overlaps with another issue that should be addressed before we turn to the content of the rules of natural justice/fairness, namely the limits to the application of the rules. Again, this is always a function of context and, to the extent that individuals may be given increased protection in some circumstances, there equally will be circumstances where the courts accept that procedural protections should be more limited or even placed in abeyance.[59] Taking national security as the strongest and most frequently invoked reason for limiting the reach of the rules, the dominant judicial view in such cases has historically been that the sensitivity of such matters demands that the courts should not look closely at governmental decisions to limit procedural rights.[60] However, while it remains true that the courts will often exercise restraint in the face of executive choices,[61] it is also true that the demands of Article 6 of the ECHR have greatly complicated case law in recent years, causing the courts to revisit key questions about the limits of procedural fairness. The result is a fluid state of affairs in which the common law, under the influence of the ECHR, is almost continually redrawing the boundaries of what is deemed acceptable in the interests of national security.

The historical reluctance to examine executive choices is most famously associated with the wartime case of *Liversidge v Anderson*.[62] The Home Secretary was empowered under regulation 18B of the Defence (General) Regulations 1939 to make an order for the detention of any person whom he had 'reasonable cause to believe' was of hostile origin or association. This was a wide-ranging power and the question was whether it could be exercised without qualification. The appellant, who had been detained, took an action for false imprisonment, seeking a declaration that the detention had been unlawful. The House of Lords found that there could be no inquiry into whether there were reasonable grounds for this detention. Under the legislation, this was a subjective matter for the Home Secretary to determine. The decision could not be challenged unless bad faith had been proved, and the minister was not obliged to reveal the particulars of the grounds for his decision. However, in his celebrated dissenting judgment, Lord Atkin declined to endorse this reading of the law. He stated:

I view with apprehension the attitude of judges who . . . when face to face with claims involving the liberty of the subject show themselves more Executive-minded than the

---

58 Ibid, 412. See further 15.3.1.

59 See, e.g., *R v Davey* [1899] 2 QB 301, where the interests of public health required that a person with an infectious disease was removed to hospital without a hearing.

60 Although there have been some notable exceptions to national security questions: see, e.g., Lord Hoffmann's dissenting opinion in *A v Home Secretary* [2005] 2 AC 68 (the *Belmarsh detainees* case).

61 For a particularly notorious example see *R v Ponting* [1985] Crim LR 318.

62 [1942] AC 206.

Executive . . . In this country, amid the clash of arms, the laws are not silent. They may be changed, but they speak the same language in war as in peace. It has always been one of the pillars of freedom, one of the principles of liberty for which on recent authority we are now fighting, that the judges are no respecters of persons and stand between the subject and any attempted encroachments on his liberty by the Executive.[63]

Lord Atkin further remarked that he had listened to arguments from the government, 'which might have been addressed acceptably to the Court of King's Bench in the time of Charles I . . . I protest, even if I do it alone, against a strained construction put on words with the effect of giving an uncontrolled power of imprisonment to the minister'.[64] The majority decision in this case is now regarded as being wrong and Lord Atkin as correct, not only on the construction of regulation 18B, but also as to English legal principle, *viz* that every imprisonment is on the face of it illegal until justified by the arresting authority.[65]

Liversidge should be considered in conjunction with *R v Secretary of State for the Home Department, ex p Cheblak*,[66] which also involved executive authority being exercised during wartime emergency powers. The Gulf War between the allied nations under the UN flag and Iraq, in 1991, led to a series of detentions of foreign nationals. The appellant was a Lebanese citizen who had been resident in the UK for 15 years. After his arrest a deportation order was issued on the ground of its 'being conducive to the public good' under section 18(1)(b) of the Immigration Act 1971. It was indicated by the authorities that he might have had links with Middle Eastern terrorist organisations. Although the appellant had been given the right to put his case to a non-statutory panel of 'three wise men', appointed by the Secretary of State, he sought judicial review on the grounds that he did not know the case against him, that he was not provided with any representation, and that he thus had been unable to present his case adequately. A Home Office official signed an affidavit to the effect that disclosure of further details pertaining to the case would be prejudicial to national security. In rejecting the appellant's application, Lord Donaldson MR in the Court of Appeal made it plain that matters of this kind were better left in the hands of the government of the day. The courts had a limited role and would intervene in such cases only if the minister had either overstepped the limitations of his legal authority, or had acted in bad faith. Natural justice sometimes had to be sacrificed in such circumstances, and the appellant should trust the Home Secretary's independent advisory panel to arrive at an impartial decision in deportation cases of this kind.[67]

The reasoning in *Cheblak* has not, however, survived the impact of Article 6 of the ECHR, and it is in cases of that kind that the law is continuing to change.[68] We consider the relevant Article 6 ECHR case law in much more detail below, but the point to be noted here is that fairness—whether at common law and/or

---

63 Ibid, 244.

64 Ibid, 244.

65 See the speeches of Lord Diplock and Lord Denning in *R v Inland Revenue Commissioners, ex p Rossminster Ltd* [1980] AC 952.

66 [1991] 1 WLR 890.

67 For a similar approach in 'peacetime' see *R v Secretary of State for Home Affairs, ex p Hosenball* [1977] 3 All ER 452.

68 In-roads had already been made even before the Human Rights Act came into force: see, e.g., *R v Secretary of State for the Home Department, ex p McQuillan* [1995] 4 All ER 400. See also *Secretary of State for the Home Department v Rehman* [2003] 1 AC 153.

under Article 6 of the ECHR—is becoming increasingly demanding of the need for some degree of transparency in national security cases. This is notably true of the requirement that individuals be given sufficient information about any national security case they may have to answer as, to the extent that Article 6 of the ECHR permits of limitations on procedural rights, any limitations must be proportionate and must not set fair trial guarantees at nought.[69] This principle has been at the heart of a number of cases arising from the so-called post-9/11 'war on terror', where government attempts to use 'closed material' when seeking to limit the activities of suspected terrorists has sometimes been condemned as defeating the very idea of a fair hearing.[70] While we will see that this does not mean that 'closed material' can never be used in terrorism cases—all depends on context, including the relevant legislative setting[71]—it does mean that use of such material must adhere to minimum standards of fairness. In the event that the government is not able so to adhere, it follows that information contained in closed material cannot be relied upon to justify government action.

17.2.7 Waiver

We would note, finally, that it is possible for an individual to waive their procedural entitlements, both at common law and under Article 6 of the ECHR.[72] However, before a court will accept that an individual has waived their procedural protections, it must be satisfied that the waiver was 'clear and unequivocal, and made with full knowledge of all the facts relevant to the decision whether to waive or not'.[73] That said, where it is established that a waiver has freely been made, the individual will not be able subsequently to argue that there has been procedural unfairness. The individual's choice will instead be dispositive of the matter, save where there is some countervailing argument of 'public interest, where some greater public concern arises'.[74]

17.3 The right to a hearing

We turn now to consider in more detail the requirements of the right of a hearing. As we have already indicated above, the common law right to a hearing is centuries old and has historically sought to ensure that individuals who will be affected by a decision are able to make informed representations to the decision-maker in advance of the decision being taken.[75] The right corresponds, at its highest, with

---

69 On Art 6 ECHR see, e.g., *Tinnelly v UK* (1999) 27 EHRR 249.

70 *Home Secretary v AF (No 3)* [2010] 2 AC 269 and, e.g., *AT v Home Secretary* [2012] EWCA Civ 42. Compare *Tariq v Home Office* [2012] 1 AC 452.

71 See, e.g., Sch 4 to the Terrorism Prevention and Investigation Measures Act 2011 and Part 2 of the Justice and Security Act 2013.

72 *Millar v Dickson (Procurator Fiscal, Elgin)* [2002] 1 WLR 1615.

73 *Re Glasgow's Application* [2006] NIQB 42, para 12, Weatherup J, citing *Locabail (UK) Ltd v Bayfield Properties Ltd* [2000] 1 All ER 65, 73, para 15, Lord Bingham.

74 *Re Glasgow's Application* [2006] NIQB 42, para 13.

75 *Baggs Case* (1615) 11 Co Rep 93b.

a constitutional right of access to a court[76] and, more generally, with the right to have a decision taken in the absence of actual or apparent bias on the part of the decision-maker (we discuss bias at 17.4). In terms of the content of the right to a hearing, the common law and Article 6 of the ECHR can each impose obligations before a decision is taken (for instance, notification of the issue to be addressed), during the hearing itself (as to the type of hearing, evidence, and so on), and after a decision has been reached. However, as we have emphasised above, the particulars of the common law right in any given case will depend on context, and the levels of protection for an individual may vary according to the right, interest, or expectation affected. Moreover, where an initial decision is reached in apparent breach of the applicable common law requirements and/or Article 6 of the ECHR, this may—but need not necessarily—mean that the decision is unlawful. All will depend on whether it is possible for the defect in the original decision to be 'cured' on appeal (at common law) or through 'composite' compliance with Article 6 of the ECHR (i.e., where the individual has a right of recourse to a court or tribunal that is independent, impartial, and so on).

It is important to note at the outset of our analysis that the requirement of a hearing can be linked to a peculiarly common law view that starts with an assumption about the virtue of an adversarial style procedure. However, it should also be recognised that, as is suggested by the sliding scale approach elaborated by Megarry V-C above, there may be situations where an adversarial approach is not appropriate. One might think here of an increased trend towards alternative dispute resolution (ADR) and proportional dispute resolution, where proceedings are characterised more by consensual resolution of contested issues.

With this in mind, we suggest that the content of the right to a hearing, both at common law and under Article 6 of the ECHR, can be examined with reference to six complementary headings. These are: pre-hearings and applications; the right to know the opposing case; the nature of the hearing and evidence; representation; reasons; and appeals and rehearings.

17.3.1 Pre-hearings and applications

Preliminary decisions—for instance, a determination as to whether there is a *prima facie* disciplinary case for an individual to answer—can have a detrimental impact on individuals and it has for this reason been argued that the rules of natural justice should apply to such determinations. The argument in favour of observing the rules in such circumstances is that they would act as a safeguard against the danger that preliminary decisions might have a telling influence on any final decision and thereby have an adverse effect on the individual. However, such arguments have not automatically prevailed, as the context to a particular determination is something else that must (of course) also be taken into account. The resulting question for the courts is therefore one that can be posed in accordance with the sliding scale of fairness: is the nature of a preliminary determination such that fuller procedural safeguards are required at that stage, or can the demands of fairness be satisfied by a later hearing?

---

76 *R v Lord Chancellor, ex p Witham* [1998] QB 575.

The case law on this issue is complex and has not always spoken with one voice. For instance, in *Wiseman v Borneman*[77] a taxpayer challenged a decision of a taxation tribunal, which, at the pre-hearing stage, had refused to allow him to make any representations or to examine the evidence before it (the stage in question decided whether there was a *prima facie* case about tax affairs that needed to be answered). Lord Reid considered the situation analogous to that of a prosecution in a criminal trial, where the evidence has to be assessed to decide whether there is a *prima facie* case. It was pointed out by his Lordship that there is no obligation to consult the accused when performing this task. The House of Lords dismissed the appeal because they were satisfied that, in this instance, there would be a full opportunity to contest the case at a later stage in the proceedings. Although their Lordships made a strong endorsement of the general right to a fair hearing, and said that this right would not necessarily be excluded from preliminary determinations, it was held that fairness did not have to be satisfied at every stage so long as there was fairness in all the circumstances of the case. Other cases have, for similar reasons, held that there will not be a right to a hearing when a body is making only a recommendation.[78]

Wiseman can, however, be contrasted with *Re Pergamon Press*,[79] which concerned a formal investigation by the Board of Trade under the Companies Act 1948. Lord Denning started by observing that the functions of the inspectors were neither judicial nor even quasi-judicial because they decided nothing themselves, not even whether there was a *prima facie* case. Their role was merely to investigate and then issue a report. Nevertheless, because of the repercussions that a report might well have on company directors and employees, it was incumbent on the inspectors to act fairly within the context of the case, even if they were only an administrative body.

Lord Denning was to reach a different conclusion on the facts of *R v Gaming Board for GB, ex p Benaim and Khaida*,[80] a well-known application case. Here the statutory procedure operated so that, prior to being able to apply for a licence under the Gaming Act 1968, a person was required to obtain a certificate of consent from the Gaming Board. Crockfords, a long-established gambling club, had their application for a certificate refused without being allowed a hearing and without any reasons being given. The Act, which also gave powers to the board to regulate its own procedures, only required it to have regard to the question whether the applicant was capable of, and diligent in, securing the provisions of the Act. In doing so, it was to take into account the applicant's character, reputation, and financial standing. However, it was argued by the club that the hearing of evidence for one side behind the back of the other was unfair. Lord Denning rejected this contention and considered that the Gaming Board could receive information from the police and other reliable sources without the disclosure of this information. Although his Lordship considered that rules of natural justice did apply to the extent that the board was required to act fairly, he considered that the duty to act

---

77 [1971] AC 297.
78 e.g., *Herring v Templeman* [1973] 3 All ER 569; and in *Norwest Holst Ltd v Secretary of State for Trade* [1978] Ch 201.
79 [1971] Ch 388.
80 [1970] 2 All ER 528.

fairly amounted to no more than giving the applicants an opportunity to satisfy the board in respect of the matters required by the Act. In addition, the board should let the applicants know the impressions it had gained about them so that they could be contested. However, Lord Denning was careful to distinguish *Ridge v Baldwin* and other cases where a person is being deprived of an office. It was an error to see this application as a right being deprived; it was a privilege or franchise to carry out gaming for a profit. The challenge by the applicants failed because, in the court's opinion, the Board had acted with complete fairness even though their sources were deemed to be confidential.

The approach in *Benaim and Khaida* can be contrasted with that in *R v National Lottery Commission, ex p Camelot Group plc*, another application case.[81] The National Lottery Commission (NLC), using its discretion, had here established a competitive procedure for the award of a new licence. 'Camelot', the existing holder, and the 'People's Lottery Ltd' both applied. However the Commission announced, following a lengthy evaluation of the two final bids, that it (i) would end the current competitive process, and (ii) begin a new process of exclusive negotiation with the 'People's Lottery' (this would have the effect of allowing the People's Lottery, but not Camelot, to allay the Commission's reservations about granting the licence). Camelot applied for a judicial review on a number of grounds, including lack of fairness. The court held that, although the Commission had a wide discretion under the National Lottery Act 1993, as amended by the National Lottery Act 1998, this discretion had to be exercised without offending basic public law principles. The apparent lack of even-handedness between the two rival bidders would need compelling justification by the Commission, and the reasons they had advanced for their decision came nowhere near the level required. Indeed, the Commission's decision to enter into exclusive negotiations with the People's Lottery was so unfair as to amount to an 'abuse of power'. The decision was accordingly deemed unlawful and was quashed.

Equally complex is the question of when Article 6 of the ECHR applies to preliminary determinations, where the leading authority is the Supreme Court ruling in *R (G) v Governors of X School*.[82] The facts of the case were that the claimant, a teaching assistant within a school, had been suspended pending an investigation into allegations that he had had an inappropriate sexual relationship with a pupil. Under the school's disciplinary procedure, the claimant was entitled to be represented at a hearing by a friend or his trade union, but not by a lawyer. In the event of the hearing, the school found that the claimant had formed an inappropriate relationship with the pupil and, having dismissed him, referred the matter to the Secretary of State under the Safeguarding Vulnerable Groups Act 2006 so that a decision could be made about whether the claimant should be added to the 'children's barred list'. Any decision in that regard, which would have serious implications for the claimant's employability, would also be taken after a hearing before the Independent Safeguarding Authority (ISA), but this time one at which legal representation would be allowed. However, before that hearing was held, the claimant sought a declaration that there had been a violation of his rights under Article 6 of the ECHR as the outcome of the school hearing would inevitably have a bearing on the outcome of

---

81 [2001] EMLR 43.
82 [2011] UKSC 30, [2012] 1 AC 167.

the ISA hearing and he should therefore have been afforded legal representation at the initial hearing. Rejecting that argument, the Supreme Court held that the question whether legal representation was required at the school hearing depended on whether that hearing would have a 'substantial influence' on the outcome of the proceedings before the ISA. Having considered the statutory and factual context within which the ISA's decision would be taken, the Supreme Court concluded that such substantial influence would not be exerted. The school and the ISA had to conduct essentially distinct processes and the absence of legal representation at the school hearing did not amount to a violation of Article 6 of the ECHR.

17.3.2 **The right to know the opposing case**

It is sometimes said to be a 'first principle'[83] of the common law that an individual who may be adversely affected by a decision is given advance notification of information that is held against him or her and of the corresponding issues that the decision-maker must address. The underlying justification for this is simply that: 'If the right to be heard is to be a real right which is worth anything, it must carry with it a right in the accused man to know the case which is to be made against him.'[84] While the language of 'accused' and a 'case being made against' is perhaps more evocative of, for instance, criminal or disciplinary proceedings, the idea of notification is also germane to administrative decision-making processes that may have implications for an individual's rights (such as property rights) or interests (such as employment).[85] The right to be given notification of the opposing case may, in other instances, be linked to a legitimate expectation of a fair hearing.

The corollary of the right to notification is, of course, the opportunity to respond, as 'procedural fairness requires that a party has the right to know the case against him and the right to respond to that case'.[86] The right to respond, in turn, requires disclosure of material facts to the party affected and adequate time to prepare a response (the right to respond need not necessarily include the right of the party to cross-examine witnesses, although such a right may exist within the nature of the hearing, below). While the presumption in favour of disclosure can at the same time be subject to arguments of public interest immunity (PII) or of the need to maintain confidence/protect witnesses—urgent cases may also have implications for the 'adequate time' requirement—the common law here seeks to 'facilitate participation and involvement in the decision-making process' and to 'accommodate the strong impulse for practical justice'.[87] It is therefore likely that there will be breach of the rules of common law fairness where the procedure adopted by the decision-maker prejudices the individual 'to the extent that his opportunity to participate effectively is seriously handicapped, certainly if it is in effect stultified'.[88]

---

83 *Re D (Minors) (Adoption Reports: Confidentiality)* [1996] AC 593, 603, Lord Mustill. See also *Bank Mellat v HM Treasury (No 2)* [2013] UKSC 38 and 39, [2014] AC 700, 774, para 29, Lord Sumption, noting advance notification as 'one of the oldest principles'.

84 *Kanda v Government of the Federation of Malaysia* [1962] AC 322, 337, Lord Denning.

85 See, e.g., *R v Chief Constable of North Wales Police, ex p Evans* [1982] 3 All ER 141, concerning the fairness of the procedure for the discharge of a police constable.

86 *Re McBurney's Application* [2004] NIQB 37, para 14, Weatherup J.

87 *Re A & Ors Application* [2007] NIQB 30, paras 40 and 41, Gillen J.

88 *R v Thames Magistrates Court, ex p Polemis* [1974] 2 All ER 1219, 1223, Lord Widgery CJ.

The right to notification and to respond are likewise found in Article 6 ECHR's guarantees in respect of civil rights. The starting point here is the ECtHR's 'equality of arms' principle, which entails 'that each party must be afforded a reasonable opportunity to present his case under conditions that do not place him at a substantial disadvantage vis-à-vis his opponent'.[89] Where a decision is to be made in respect of an individual's 'civil rights', the equality of arms principle can thus impose a duty to disclose documents to individuals, albeit that disclosure may be limited where there is good reason for doing so.[90] The case law of the ECtHR has similarly established that the principle can by implication require that the individual should have adequate time to prepare his or her case[91] (Article 6(3) of the ECHR contains an express requirement to that effect in the context of criminal proceedings).

The out-workings of the above principles have been evident in a number of controversial national security cases that we mentioned above and which now merit closer attention. The first is the very important case of *Home Secretary v AF (No 3)*,[92] which was about the use of 'control orders' as a means to contain the perceived and actual terror threat within the UK. Under the Prevention of Terrorism Act 2005, it was possible for the government to interfere with an individual's qualified rights under the ECHR through the use of 'non-derogating orders' (which were made by the Home Secretary, subject to subsequent judicial scrutiny) or to interfere with an individual's right to liberty under Article 5 of the ECHR through the use of 'derogating orders' (which could be made only by the courts on the application of the Home Secretary). The issue in *AF* was the nature of the Home Secretary's disclosure obligation when a challenge was made to a non-derogating order, as the legislation provided that 'closed material' could be used in circumstances in which the affected individual did not have access to the material but where a Special Advocate was allowed to make representations on the individual's behalf. However, the corresponding difficulty was that the Special Advocate was able to consult with the individual only before the 'closed material' was considered and, once submissions had been made, the Special Advocate was not allowed to consult with the individual again save with the leave of the court. There was thus a potentially serious shortfall in the overall process: while the Special Advocate was meant to query evidence, etc, on the part of the individual, he or she could receive only very limited, if any, instructions from the individual given that there could be no prior knowledge of what was within the material in question.

The resulting ruling of the House of Lords, which followed the ECtHR's ruling in *A v UK*,[93] represented something of a high-water mark in terms of the reception of the principles of the ECHR. Although the House of Lords had earlier ruled that the Special Advocates procedure could ensure fairness where there was recourse to 'closed material',[94] the ECtHR had later said, in *A v UK*, that use of the procedure would violate the ECHR where the decision of a court was based solely or to a decisive degree upon the 'closed material'. Adopting that logic in *AF*, the House of Lords held that the scheme under the 2005 Act could transgress the boundaries of

---

89 *De Haes and Gijsels v Belgium* (1998) 25 EHRR 1, 57, para 53.
90 e.g., *McGinley and Egan v UK* (1999) 27 EHRR 1, 41, para 86.
91 *Albert and Le Compte v Belgium* (1983) 5 EHRR 533, 546, para 39.
92 [2010] 2 AC 269.
93 (2009) 49 EHRR 29.
94 *Home Secretary v MB* [2008] 1 AC 440.

Article 6 of the ECHR, albeit that it need not always have that effect. Having noted that it might still be appropriate not to disclose sources of evidence in some cases, the Lords nevertheless emphasised that, to remain compatible with Article 6 of the ECHR, a controllee had to be given the 'gist' of the allegations against him or her to enable him or her to give effective instructions to his or her Special Advocate (the term 'gisting' is now often used in the case law; the Lords also spoke of the need for 'sufficient information' to be given). The Lords on that basis held that, so long as that requirement was satisfied, there could be a fair hearing without the need for detailed disclosure of the sources of evidence on which the allegations were based. However, where the disclosed material consisted of only general assertions and the case against the controllee was based solely or to a decisive extent upon undisclosed materials, the requirements of a fair trial under Article 6 of the ECHR would not be satisfied and any control order would be unlawful.[95]

It is important to be clear just how profound the implications of this ruling were, as it cast doubt over the long-term sustainability of the system of control orders and ultimately led to the repeal of the underlying legislative provisions and the introduction of a new scheme.[96] The doubt about their sustainability followed from the fact that the 'gisting'/'sufficient information' requirement will vary from case to case and that, where a court considers that a high level of detail is needed, this may act as a disincentive to pursue an order. As Lord Hope expressed it:

[T]here are bound to be cases where . . . the procedure will be rendered nugatory because the details cannot be separated out from the sources or because the judge is satisfied that more needs to be disclosed than the Secretary of State is prepared to agree to. Lord Bingham used the phrase 'effectively to challenge' . . . [This] sets a relatively high standard. It suggests that where detail matters, as it often will, detail must be met with detail . . . There may indeed be . . . a significant number of cases of that kind. If that be so, the fact must simply be faced that the system is unsustainable.[97]

On the other hand, there have been cases that have held that the principle enunciated in *AF* does not automatically transfer over to other factual scenarios. For instance, *Tariq v Home Office*[98] was a race and religious discrimination claim brought by a man of Pakistani and Muslim heritage who had been suspended from his position as an immigration officer because some of his relatives had been involved in terrorism. The government sought to reply upon 'closed material' and Special Advocates in accordance with provisions of the applicable tribunal legislation, and Mr Tariq argued, with reference to *AF*, that this would amount to, among other things, a violation of Article 6 of the ECHR. Rejecting that argument, the Supreme Court distinguished control order cases that could have implications for the liberty of the individual from the very different circumstances of an employment dispute. To quote once more from Lord Hope:

There cannot, after all, be an absolute rule that gisting must always be resorted to whatever the circumstances. There are no hard edged rules in this area of the law. As I said at the beginning, the principles that lie at the heart of the case pull in different directions. It must be a

---

95 As in, e.g., *AT v Home Secretary* [2012] EWCA Civ 42. Compare, by analogy, *Re Corey's Application* [2014] NI 49. See also the related ruling of the Supreme Court on other issues in *In re Corey* [2013] UKSC 76, [2014] AC 516.

96 The Terrorism Prevention and Investigation Measures Act 2011.

97 [2010] 2 AC 269, para 87.

98 [2011] UKSC 35, [2012] 1 AC 452.

question of degree, balancing [fairness] on one side with [national security] on the other, as to how much weight is to be given to each of them. I would hold that, given the nature of the case, the fact that the disadvantage to Mr Tariq that the closed procedure will give rise to can to some extent be minimized and the paramount need to protect the integrity of the security vetting process, the balance is in favour of the Home Office.[99]

Two further cases should be mentioned under this heading. The first is *Al-Rawi v Security Services*,[100] which was delivered by the Supreme Court on the same day as *Tariq*, but which was concerned with common law approaches to arguments about national security. The proceedings here had been brought by a number of individuals who alleged that they had been tortured overseas as a part of the war on terror and that the UK government had been complicit in that torture. At the beginning of the trial, the government argued that there were very large portions of evidence that would attract PII and it invited the court, in the absence of a legislative scheme that allowed for 'closed material', etc, to use its inherent jurisdiction to create a parallel 'closed hearing' at which such evidence could be assessed.[101] This raised the question whether the common law would tolerate such wholescale procedural change, and the Supreme Court was robust in holding that it would not. Although the Court noted that it was open to Parliament to enact legislation that would provide for use of closed material—the Justice and Security Act 2013 now has that effect in 'relevant civil proceedings'[102]—the Court emphasised that open justice is a key component of the common law and that there should be no limitation upon that form of justice save to the extent that could occur through PII claims. *Al-Rawi* in that way provided a strong reassertion of core common law principles, even if the approach that was adopted did not appear to complement that taken in relation to Article 6 of the ECHR in *Tariq*.

The other case is *W (Algeria) v Home Secretary*.[103] This case is particularly interesting as it raised the question whether an individual appellant to the Special Immigration Appeals Commission (SIAC) could keep the identity of one of his or her witnesses secret, where the witness had important evidence to give but would face danger if their identity became known. The issue arose in the context of an appeal against a deportation order that had been made against a number of Algerians who were suspected of involvement in terrorism but who claimed that they would be subjected to torture if deported to their country of origin. One of the appellants proposed to call a witness who could attest to the probability that the appellant would be tortured, but the witness was concerned about a possible, subsequent threat to his or her wellbeing. Holding that the witness could be given anonymity in this case, the Supreme Court emphasised that it was imperative that SIAC could maximise its capacity to arrive at the correct decision regarding the risk of torture in Algeria. While the Supreme Court made clear that appellants would always be obliged fully to disclose to SIAC the circumstances surrounding, among other

---

99 Ibid, para 83. See too, e.g., *Re Davidson's Application* [2011] NICA 39, rejecting the argument that *AF* was applicable to prison disciplinary proceedings.

100 [2011] UKSC 34, [2011] 3 WLR 388.

101 On PII see 10.5; *Al-Rawi* is discussed at 10.5.6.

102 Section 6. See also *Bank Mellat v HM Treasury (No 2)* [2013] UKSC 38 and 39, [2014] AC 700: majority of the Supreme Court holding that it has a general statutory power under the Constitutional Reform Act 2005, s 40(2) and (5) to hold closed hearings where the lower court judgment that is subject to appeal is based partly upon closed material.

103 [2012] UKSC 8, [2012] 2 AC 115.

things, the witness's fear of reprisals, there was nothing inherently objectionable to hearing evidence in the manner proposed. It would therefore appear that 'closed material' is not just the preserve of government.

17.3.3 The nature of the hearing and evidence

We have already discussed above, with reference to *McInnes v Onslow-Fane* (see 17.2.4), how the nature of the hearing that is required by the common law will depend on the context that is set by the individual's right, interest, or expectation, and by the corresponding nature of the decision to be taken. At its highest, the full protection of the individual would require that there is an oral hearing at which the individual is both present and able fully to participate (although it is also open to an individual to decline the offer of a hearing). However, there is at the same time no fixed requirement for an oral hearing and it may be that written submissions will suffice where, for instance, an individual is making an application for the first time for a licence for an economic activity. On the other hand, the common law may impose an obligation to grant an oral hearing in the very different circumstances where a prisoner who has been released early from prison on licence resists recall to prison for an alleged breach of the terms of the licence.[104] While the right to an oral hearing here is not absolute—the decision-maker is also tasked with protecting society from the risk of re-offending—the courts have emphasised that an oral hearing is to be preferred even in cases where there is no dispute as to primary facts. This is because facts not in dispute might still be open to explanation or mitigation, or because they might lose some of their significance in the light of other new facts. It is also because an oral hearing can bolster a prisoner's right of response in the sense that it may otherwise be difficult for the prisoner to know which points are troubling the decision-maker and to address those points effectively.[105]

The common law rules of fairness do not, however, require that the strict rules of evidence have to be followed during a hearing;[106] and neither do they necessarily require that there is an opportunity to test evidence through the cross-examination of witnesses.[107] Nevertheless, the overall procedure adopted during the hearing must be fair, and the more adversarial the hearing, the more that will be expected by way of procedural safeguards. At its most rigorous, the common law may therefore require that:

> Where there is an oral hearing, a tribunal must . . . consider all relevant evidence submitted, inform the parties of the evidence taken into account, allow witnesses to be questioned and allow comment on the whole case . . . a [tribunal] should not rely on points not argued or private enquires made.[108]

Article 6 ECHR's guarantees in respect of civil rights likewise emphasise the importance of oral hearings at which the individual is able to participate, albeit that

---

104 *R (Smith and West) v Parole Board* [2005] 1 All ER 755.

105 Ibid. See also *Re Reilly's Application* [2013] UKSC 61, [2014] AC 1115 for a statement of guiding principles that apply when prisoners have become eligible to be considered for release by the Parole Board.

106 *R v Deputy Industrial Injuries Commissioner, ex p Moore* [1965] 1 QB 456, 487, Diplock LJ.

107 *R v Commission for Racial Equality, ex p Cottrell & Rothon* [1980] 3 All ER 265.

108 *Re J's Application* [2004] NIQB 75, para 15, Gillen J.

there is a stronger presumption in favour of such hearings in civil disputes where the dispute is centred upon, for example, the conduct of the individual[109] (other Articles may also require hearings, for instance Article 5 of the ECHR in the context of prisoner release disputes).[110] This emphasis on oral hearings corresponds not only with the 'equality of arms' principle that we outlined above, but also with Article 6 ECHR's textual requirement that an individual be afforded a 'fair and public hearing'. While the rules of evidence are, in turn, a matter for the national system, those rules must accord with the ECHR's conception of what is fair in all the circumstances,[111] and this may require that there is an opportunity for cross-examination of witnesses even in civil disputes.[112] Article 6 of the ECHR also requires that the hearing is held within a 'reasonable time' given the nature of dispute, *viz* the complexity of the issues, the nature of the individual's interests, and so on.[113]

17.3.4 **Representation**

Another fundamentally important requirement of the common law is that each side should have an equal capacity to present its case (this is also the essential logic of Article 6 ECHR's 'equality of arms' principle). It is stating the obvious to point out that there are many individuals who will be affected by decisions but who will not be capable of arguing their case in its most favourable light.[114] Moreover, research into tribunals has shown that representation will contribute to a person's success in the outcome of a case.[115] In nearly every situation involving courts and tribunals, representation is, in principle, allowed, but the problem is that entitlement to legal aid to pay for it is strictly limited. Nevertheless, despite the fact that access to representation might serve to redress the balance in some contexts, critics have been guarded about suggesting that legal representation is a necessary condition in every case. This is mainly because of a desire to avoid the formality and protracted nature of court proceedings. The expense and delay that a more judicial process might involve could well outweigh the advantages, especially in areas such as that of benefit appeals. However, taking into account the overriding consideration of fairness, it appears that, on the question of representation, the courts will be inclined to consider legal representation as an imperative requirement when the proceedings are unmistakably judicial, or where the proceedings could lead to the loss of a person's livelihood, or have other serious adverse consequences.

The corresponding common law approach is that there is no right to be legally represented in all cases and that the matter is one for the discretion of the decision-maker.[116] It is, however, often said that any such discretion is to be exercised in the light of the so-called '*Tarrant* criteria',[117] and these, as with all aspects of the rules

---

109 *Muyldermans v Belgium* (1993) 15 EHRR 204.

110 *R (Smith and West) v Parole Board* [2005] 1 All ER 755 and *Re Reilly's Application* [2013] UKSC 61, [2014] AC 1115.

111 *Miailhe v France (No 2)* (1997) 23 EHRR 491, 511, para 43.

112 *X v Austria*, App 5362/72, 42 CD 145 (1972).

113 See, e.g., *H v UK* (1988) 10 EHRR 95, 111, para 86 (period of 31 months to decide whether a mother should have access to her child in the care of the authorities unreasonable).

114 *Pett v Greyhound Racing Association* [1968] 2 All ER 545, 549, Lord Denning.

115 See ch 7.

116 *Enderby Town FC v FA* [1971] 1 All ER 215.

117 *R v Secretary of State for the Home Department, ex p Tarrant* [1985] QB 251.

of fairness, are context-sensitive. Under the criteria, decision-makers should thus consider: the seriousness of the decision to be taken; whether any points of law are likely to arise; whether the individual will be able to present his or her own case; whether there may be procedural difficulties; the need for reasonable speed in reaching a decision; and the need for fairness as between the individual and other parties to the dispute. Those same criteria are also to be considered where an application is made to the decision-maker by a party who wishes to attend the hearing as the friend or adviser of the individual to be affected by the decision.

Where an individual's civil rights within the meaning of Article 6 of the ECHR will be determined by a decision, there is similarly no automatic entitlement to representation[118] (on the question of when a right will be determined, and the link to the need for representation, see *R (G) v Governors of X School*[119] considered above; and note that there is an automatic right to representation in respect of criminal charges).[120] The ECHR is, however, premised on the need for rights to be effectively protected, and representation will therefore be deemed necessary for the purposes of protecting the right to a hearing where, among other things, a dispute is legally and factually complex. In those circumstances, questions about the need for legal aid may also arise.[121]

17.3.5 **Reasons**

We have already touched upon the importance of reasons in the previous chapter and, cast in terms of the common law right to a fair hearing, they can allow the individual to determine whether the decision-maker has taken account of the arguments made by the individual and, if not, whether to challenge the decision. Where statute does not impose a duty to give reasons, it therefore falls to the common law to resolve whether a duty should be imposed in respect of a particular decision (reasons given under the common law must, as with those given under statute, be 'adequate and intelligible').[122] Historically, the common law has not imposed a general duty to give reasons, largely because of the burden that it was thought this might place upon decision-makers, *viz* it may 'demand an appearance of unanimity where there is diversity; call for the articulation of sometimes inexpressible value judgments; and offer an invitation to the captious to comb the reasons for previously unsuspected grounds of challenge'.[123] However, while there is still no general duty to give reasons,[124] the common law has developed so as to impose duties in a wide range of circumstances in which fairness is taken to demand that reasons be given.[125] It might now also be said that there will be more circumstances than not in which the common law will expect reasons to be given.

---

118 *Webb v UK* (1984) 6 EHRR 120, 123ff, Eur Comm.

119 [2011] UKSC 30; [2011] 3 WLR 237.

120 Art 6(3)(c) reads: 'Everyone charged with a criminal offence has the following human rights: (c) to defend himself in person or through legal assistance of his own choosing or, if he has not sufficient means to pay for legal assistance, to be given it free when the interests of justice so require.'

121 *Airey v Ireland* (1979) 2 EHRR 305; and, in the criminal setting, *Re Brownlee's Application* [2014] UKSC 4, [2014] NI 188.

122 *R v Mental Health Tribunal, ex p Pickering* [1986] 1 All ER 99, 102, Forbes J.

123 *R v Higher Education Funding Council, ex p Institute of Dental Surgery* [1994] 1 All ER 651, 665, Sedley J.

124 e.g., *R (Hasan) v Secretary of State for Trade and Industry* [2008] EWCA 1312 and *Martin v Secretary of State for Communities and Local Government* [2015] EWHC 3435 (Admin), para 51.

125 For judicial recognition of the point see, e.g., *Re Kavanagh's Application* [1997] NI 368, 381; and *Re Tucker's Application* [1995] NI 14, 26.

There have been many important cases in the development of the common law's approach to reasons as a facet of fairness, but we will focus upon three as key to the current state of the law. The first is the case of *R v Civil Service Appeal Board, ex p Cunningham*,[126] which arose when a prison officer had been dismissed after accusations that he had assaulted a prisoner. This was later found by the Civil Service Board to have been an unfair dismissal, and the board recommended reinstatement of the officer. However, when the Home Office refused to act upon this recommendation, the Board awarded a payment of £6,500 as compensation, a sum which the applicant considered to be grossly inadequate. He applied for judicial review so that he could be informed of the reasons for the decision, and it was held that, although there was no statutory duty to give reasons, there was a common law requirement of natural justice to outline *sufficient* reasons to indicate whether the decision had been lawful. Lord Donaldson MR cited the decision in *Public Service Board of New South Wales v Osmond*[127] to support a view that there should be 'sufficient reasons for [a] decision to enable the parties to know the issues to which [the decision-maker] addressed its mind and that it acted lawfully'.[128] The case was thus driven by the demands not only of fairness, but of the need for some degree of transparency in public decision-making.[129]

The second—seminal—case is that of *R v Secretary of State for the Home Department, ex p Doody*,[130] which concerned a prisoner who had been sentenced to a mandatory term of life imprisonment. Although life imprisonment is the only available sentence in cases of murder, it is axiomatic that most prisoners will not remain incarcerated for the rest of their natural lives. Sentences are, instead, divided between a penal component, consisting of the period that the trial judge considers necessary, and an additional risk component, which is the period after the penal element has been served that is considered necessary before the risk to the public is sufficiently reduced to justify release. At the time of the *Doody* case, the risk component was determined by the Home Office, which was accepted as having a wide discretion in the matter.[131] In broad terms, the Home Office had pursued a policy whereby the Home Secretary would, after consultation with the judiciary, set the penal element of a prisoner's sentence, thereby simultaneously establishing the date on which the Parole Board would review the prisoner's sentence. However, the applicant considered that the Home Office had in his case increased the penal element of his sentence as originally recommended by the judiciary, and he argued that he should have been given the reasons for the increase. In agreeing that reasons should have been given, the House of Lords held that, where Parliament confers an administrative power, there exists a corresponding presumption that the power will be exercised in a manner that is fair in all the circumstances. Applying this principle to the Home Office procedure in question, the House of Lords concluded that 'the continuing momentum in administrative law towards openness

---

126 [1992] ICR 816.
127 [1986] ALR 559.
128 [1992] ICR 816, 828.
129 And see *Re Officer O's Application* [2009] NI 55, para 50, Gillen J.
130 [1994] 1 AC 531.
131 Note that the executive no longer plays any role in the sentencing of mandatory life prisoners, as it was held by the House of Lords that such a role was incompatible with Art 6 ECHR: see *R (Anderson) v Home Secretary* [2003] 1 AC 837 and Criminal Justice Act 2003, ss 303 and 332, and Sch 37, Part 8.

of decision-making' obliged the Home Secretary to conduct a more transparent procedure. As Lord Mustill put it:

It is not, as I understand it, questioned that the decision of the Home Secretary on the penal element is subject to judicial review. To mount an effective attack on the decision, given no more material than the facts of the offence and the length of the penal element, the prisoner has virtually no means of ascertaining whether this is an instance where the decision-making process has gone astray. I think it is important that there should be an effective means of detecting the kind of error which would entitle the court to intervene and in practice I regard it as necessary for this purpose that the reasoning of the Home Secretary should be disclosed.[132]

It is important to be aware just what the import of a case such as *Doody* is. In short, if an authority does not have to give reasons for a decision, this means that determinations can be made without any of the possible shortcomings in the decision-making process being revealed by the authority. However, if reasons should be given in a wider range of cases, this means that there should be increased scope for judicial review of decisions precisely because the affected individuals will have a much better grasp of what occurred during the decision-making process. To the common law values of 'fairness' and 'transparency', we might therefore say that *Doody* added 'accountability' to the workings of the common law.[133]

The third case is *R v Ministry of Defence, ex p Murray*, which, while reported in 1998, provides a list of guiding principles on the duty to give reasons that remains reflective of the current state of the common law.[134] The case itself concerned the question whether a court martial which had sentenced a long-serving soldier of exemplary character to a term of imprisonment after he had pleaded guilty to an offence of wounding—he had attributed this action to the effects of an anti-malarial drug—should provide reasons for its decision. Holding that it should provide reasons, Lord Bingham CJ noted a perceptible trend towards an insistence on greater openness and transparency in the making of administrative decisions. While the judge at the same time accepted that there is no general duty to give reasons— he also noted that it is for an applicant to raise the matter to the satisfaction of the court—he identified a number of considerations that should guide the courts when forming a view as to whether reasons should be given in any particular case. These were: whether there is a right of appeal (the absence of which may be a factor in deciding that reasons should be given); the nature of the individual's interest that is affected by the decision (that is, the more important the interest the more likely it is that reasons will be required); and the corresponding function performed by the decision-maker. A court should also consider whether there are public interest considerations that militate against the giving of reasons. The judge further noted that reasons may not be required if the procedures of the particular decision-maker would be frustrated by the imposition of such a requirement.

Article 6 of the ECHR likewise imposes a duty to give reasons for decisions that affect civil and criminal rights, notwithstanding that the obligation is not imposed in express terms. The justification for the obligation is, again, the need for

---

132 [1994] 1 AC 531, 565–6.

133 And see, e.g., *R v Secretary of State for the Home Department, ex p Duggan* [1994] 3 All ER 277; *R v East Yorkshire Borough of Beverley Housing Benefits Review Board, ex p Hare* (1995) 27 HLR 637; *Stefan v General Medical Council* [1999] 1 WLR 1293; and *Home Secretary v Thakur* [2011] Imm AR 533.

134 [1998] COD 134.

fairness and to enable an individual to decide whether to challenge a decision (reasons, to this end, should be sufficient to aid the individual in understanding the essence of the decision).[135] A duty to give reasons can, moreover, be imposed by other Articles of the ECHR. For instance, in *R (Wooder) v Feggetter*,[136] the question for the court was whether a mental health patient who was to be administered a form of treatment to which he objected should be given the reasons for the decision that the treatment should proceed. In finding that reasons should be given, Sedley LJ relied upon the idea of personal autonomy in Article 8 of the ECHR to emphasise that the patient was entitled to reasons 'not as a matter of grace or of practice, but as a matter of right'.[137] In doing so, the judge also held that, while the common law, too, would have required that reasons be given, the developing common law position nevertheless had a distance to travel before it would provide 'a principled framework of public decision-making'.[138] A suggestion, perhaps, both that on-going development of the common law remains imperfect, and that there is much to be learned from the elements of European human rights law.

One final point to be considered under this heading concerns a somewhat finely drawn distinction between a duty to give reasons for a particular decision and a duty of adequate disclosure towards an individual affected by a decision. In truth, the latter duty is one that has featured in only very few cases that have involved particular statutory schemes and, as with the former duty, it is underpinned by the common law's pursuit of fairness. The leading case on the duty is *R v Secretary of State for the Home Department, ex p Fayed*.[139] Here, the Fayed brothers—well-known Egyptian business men with long-standing links in the UK— appealed against a decision of the Home Secretary to refuse to grant them naturalisation certificates despite the fact that they had satisfied the formal application requirements. The relevant legislation—the British Nationality Act 1981—did not impose any duty on the Home Secretary to give reasons for his decision, although it became apparent that he had concerns about the applicants' 'good character'. The applicants thereupon argued that they should have been given an indication of the information that had been held against them and also that they should have been given an opportunity to comment on any areas of concern. Lord Woolf MR approached the issues by first asking whether there would be a requirement of fairness in the absence of the provisions of the statute, and found that this was a situation where high-profile public figures were being deprived of the substantial benefits of citizenship. Referring to *ex p Benaim*[140] and *ex p Doody*[141] as examples of cases where the production of reasons might have resulted in a different outcome, his Lordship stated: 'The fact that the Home Secretary might refuse an application because he was not satisfied that the applicant fulfilled the rather nebulous requirement of good character . . . underlined the need for an obligation of fairness'.[142] He concluded that, unless the applicants were made aware of the areas of

---

135 *Helle v Finland* (1998) 26 EHRR 159.
136 [2003] QB 219.
137 [2003] QB 219, 232.
138 [2003] QB 219, 229.
139 [1998] 1 WLR 763.
140 [1970] 2 QB 417.
141 [1994] 1 AC 531.
142 [1998] 1 WLR 763, 773.

concern, the consequence could be grossly unfair. While it was recognised that the Home Secretary was not required to give reasons, it was said that this did not prevent him from so doing. In Lord Woolf's view, administrative convenience could not justify unfairness. This meant that the British Nationality Act 1981 still required the Home Secretary 'to identify the subject of his concern in such terms as to enable the applicant to make such submissions as he could'.[143] Moreover, to the extent that the Act of 1981 did not require that reasons be given for a decision, the Court was of the view that this did not oust its jurisdiction and prevent the Court from reviewing the decision on procedural grounds.[144] *Attorney-General v Ryan*[145] was cited as authority in support of the inference that Parliament was not intending to exclude from review a decision which failed to comply with the need for fairness. The result was a robust judicial decision that revealed a willingness to intervene where issues of procedural fairness arose in regard to basic rights.

17.3.6 Appeals and rehearings

Where a decision is reached in apparent breach of the common law's fair hearing requirements and/or the equivalent aspects of Article 6 of the ECHR, this may, but need not necessarily, mean that the decision is unlawful. Much will here depend on whether there is a remedy by way of an appeal and whether that remedy can cure the defects in the original decision-making process (the so-called 'curative' principle—note that there is no common law right to an appeal as all appeals are statutory).[146] A cure, for the purposes of the common law, is more likely to be achieved where the individual has a full right of appeal against the decision, as the appellate body will be able to rehear all issues and, if appropriate, substitute its own decision for that of the original decision-maker. However, where an appeal is only partial, it may be that the original defect cannot be cured by that remedy and that the decision thereby remains tainted by impropriety. Under those circumstances, an application for judicial review may thus be appropriate and the High Court may, for instance, quash the decision and require that it be retaken. On the other hand, there may be cases where the High Court in its discretion declines to grant a remedy because it is of the opinion, on the facts, that the impropriety had no bearing on the final decision and that a new decision would be no different to that under challenge.[147]

The leading case on the common law's 'curative' principle remains the decision of the Privy Council in *Calvin v Carr*.[148] The case concerned an investigation by the Australian Jockey Club into a racehorse at short odds finishing fourth. The owner of the horse and the jockey were found guilty of improper conduct at an initial hearing, and a penalty was imposed that disqualified the plaintiff and jockey from racing for a year. There followed an appeal to the disciplinary committee of the Jockey Club during which the owner and jockey were fully represented and al-lowed to cross-examine witnesses, but their appeals were dismissed. The owner

---

143 [1998] 1 WLR 763, 776.
144 On ouster clauses, etc see 10.2.
145 [1980] AC 718.
146 *Ward v Bradford Corporation* (1972) 70 LGR 27.
147 On the discretionary nature of the remedies see ch 18.
148 [1980] AC 574.

subsequently challenged the disqualification in court, seeking both a declaration and an injunction on the basis that there was nothing here against which to appeal, since the first decision should be regarded as a nullity. Lord Wilberforce stated that the principles of natural justice ought to have been observed and, while recognising that no absolute rules existed, he went on to outline three types of situation. In the first, the initial hearing is by an incompletely constituted version of the body that hears the appeal. In these cases, which often involve social clubs with agreed procedures under contractual rules, the general rule is that defects can be cured by a subsequent hearing. In the second situation, there is a requirement for a proper procedure at the hearing and at the appeal. If this is not to be insisted upon by the court, the individual will be deprived of having 'two cracks of the whip', as it follows that, if the first hearing has already proved to be invalid, in effect the appeal is turned into a first hearing. In the third situation, it is necessary to look back at the whole process to assess whether the process has been fair overall. Lord Wilberforce indicated that there were situations where the rules had been so flagrantly breached, with severe consequences, that even a perfect appeal could not correct the situation. This was not such an occasion, since the owner and the jockey were aware of the appeals procedure and had in any event accepted standards that have always applied to their sport. The requirements of a fair hearing had been satisfied and the action was dismissed.

Article 6 of the ECHR likewise accepts that a defect in the original decision-making process that affects civil rights can be remedied on appeal or by an application for judicial review where the body hearing the issue has 'full jurisdiction' in the matter that comes before it[149] (the so-called 'composite' approach to compliance). Compliance for these purposes will be achieved most readily where there is a full right of appeal, as the appellate body will be able to rehear all the issues and substitute its own decision for that of the original decision-maker. However, the European Court of Human Rights has at the same time held that the question of what constitutes 'full jurisdiction' depends on context and that it may, in some circumstances, be sufficient for an individual to have an appeal on a point of law or a remedy by way of an application for judicial review. The significance of this point as relates to judicial review under the Human Rights Act 1998 is considered in more detail at 17.4.5.

17.4 The rule against bias

We turn now to consider the rule against bias. This rule, which is normally of stricter application than the elements of the right to a hearing, entails that a decision-maker should not be judge in his or her own cause (*nemo judex in causa sua*), irrespective of whether he or she is named as a party to the dispute. The rule, which can apply to decision-makers acting in either a judicial or an administrative capacity,[150] in this way complements the right to a hearing, as it could not be expected

---

149 *Bryan v UK* (1995) 21 EHRR 342.
150 *R v Secretary of State for the Environment ex p Kirkstall Valley Campaign Ltd* [1996] 3 All ER 304, 323, Sedley J.

that a hearing would be fair if the decision-maker had an interest in the outcome of a dispute beyond an interest in the administration of justice between the parties. In terms of the values that underlie the common law rules of fairness (as well as procedural requirements in statute), the rule against bias thus seeks to eliminate arbitrariness in decision-making by requiring those who are, or who may appear to be, partial to recuse themselves or 'step aside'. While the common law at the same time recognises that the rule should be of variable application depending on the nature of the decision-maker and any corresponding interest—it is also possible for an individual to waive his or her objection to any perceived bias—the overall objective of the rule is the attainment of transparency in decision-making processes and the safeguarding of public confidence in those processes. The rule against bias in this way has both an internal and external dynamic: internal as concerns the interests of the individual affected by the decision; and external as concerns the public perception of the manner in which that decision is reached.

The corresponding body of case law identifies two types of bias, namely 'actual' bias and 'apparent' bias. Each of these is examined more fully below, although one point of more general importance concerns the test for apparent bias. Until fairly recently, the test was that laid down by the House of Lords in *R v Gough*,[151] whereby the reviewing court would determine, with reference to the information available to it, whether there was a 'real danger of bias' on the part of the decision-maker. The test was not, at the same time, formulated in terms of the 'reasonable man', both because the court itself was taken to personify the reasonable man and because it was thought that the court would have available to it evidence that may not be available to the ordinary observer. However, this court-centred approach was criticised in other common law jurisdictions for the reason that it placed insufficient emphasis on public perception of the issue under challenge,[152] and it was thought in the UK that it may be incompatible with Article 6 ECHR's approach to bias[153] (*viz* to ask whether there was an objective risk of bias in the light of the circumstances identified by the court).[154] The House of Lords in *Porter v Magill* thus adopted a revised test that requires a reviewing court, once it has ascertained all the circumstances that have a bearing on the suggestion of bias, to ask 'whether the fair-minded and informed observer, having considered the facts, would conclude that there was a real possibility' of bias.[155] The modern test, while not always easy to apply, is thus more closely aligned with the approach to apparent bias both in other common law systems and in the ECHR.[156]

One other introductory point about Article 6 ECHR's impact on bias concerns the requirement that determinations about an individual's 'civil rights and obligations' be made by an 'independent and impartial tribunal established by law'. This requirement has raised important questions about the workings of judicial review, as determinations about civil rights in the field of administration may often

---

151 [1993] AC 646.

152 See, e.g., in Australia *Webb v R* (1994) 181 CLR 41.

153 *Re Medicaments and Related Classes of Goods (No 2)* [2001] 1 WLR 700.

154 *Piersack v Belgium* (1983) 5 EHRR 169, 179–80.

155 [2002] 2 AC 357, 494, paras 102–3, Lord Hope. See too the HL judgments in *Lawal v Northern Spirit Ltd* [2004] 1 All ER 187, and *Davidson v Scottish Ministers* [2004] HRLR 34.

156 For discussion see P Havers QC and A Henderson, 'Recent Developments (and Problems) in the Law of Bias' [2011] 16 *Judicial Review* 80.

be taken by decision-makers who are neither 'independent' of the executive nor 'impartial' (for instance, ministers who are giving effect to central or devolved government policy, or local authority officers who may be conducting a review of a decision taken by the same authority). Under such circumstances, Article 6 of the ECHR is not automatically violated so long as the affected individual has a means of recourse to an independent and impartial tribunal that has 'full jurisdiction' in the matter in question[157] (this is the realm of the ECHR's 'curative' principle that we referred to earlier). In terms of the workings of judicial review, difficult questions have been raised about whether the High Court can be said to have full jurisdiction when the judicial review procedure has historically fastened upon a 'review, not appeal' distinction that precludes judicial assessment of the merits of a decision. However, the greater weight of the case law on this point now accepts that judicial review will often (though not always) be sufficient for the purposes of Article 6 of the ECHR because of, among other things, developments in relation to error of fact as a ground for review.[158] We return to the corresponding case law—and what it reveals about the interaction between the common law and the ECHR—below.

17.4.1 **Actual bias**

We can deal with the question of actual bias in only a very few words. In sum, actual bias is taken to exist where the decision-maker is 'either (1) influenced by partiality or prejudice in reaching the decision, or (2) actually prejudiced in favour of or against a party'.[159] Whether a decision is vitiated by such bias is a question of fact, and the courts have said that a claim of actual bias will succeed only 'when supported by the clearest evidence'.[160] The courts have, moreover, said that a claim of actual bias is 'an extremely serious allegation'[161] and it is therefore clear that any claim should not be made lightly (there have been very few in the case law).[162] Nevertheless, the ground remains an important, if little-used, safeguard against the potential abuse of power and it in that sense corresponds with other little-used headings such as bad faith.[163]

17.4.2 **Apparent bias**

The test for apparent bias, as we have noted above, is centred on the question whether 'the fair-minded and informed observer, having considered the facts, would conclude that there was a real possibility' of bias.[164] In some instances, the test is applied on the basis of a presumption that the nature of the decision-maker's interest in the matter before it is such that the common law requires automatic disqualification from the decision-making process. However, in many other cases there is no automatic requirement of disqualification, and the issue will fall to be

---

157 *Bryan v UK* (1995) 21 EHRR 342.

158 On error of fact see 12.6.

159 *Re Medicaments and Related Classes of Goods (No 2)* [2001] 1 WLR 700, 711, para 38, Lord Phillips MR.

160 *Re Foster's Application* [2004] NI 248, 265, para 66, Kerr J.

161 Ibid.

162 For an example see *Catalina SS (Owners) v Norma* (1938) 61 Ll L Rep 360.

163 On which see 11.6.

164 *Porter v Magill* [2002] 2 AC 357, 494, paras 102–3, Lord Hope.

determined with reference to context. Here, the reviewing court must first ascertain all the circumstances that have a bearing on the suggestion of bias and, on that basis, decide whether the fair-minded and informed observer would conclude that there was a real possibility of bias. This emphasis on context is all-important, as the courts accept that the rule against bias should be applied variably and in the light of the nature of the decision-maker and its corresponding interests. On the other hand, the courts have emphasised that they will not allow old distinctions in the law—for instance, as between judicial and administrative decision-makers—to limit the reach of the rule.[165] The modern starting point is thus that context is key but that '(anyone) who decides anything'[166] must do so fairly.

We will look more closely at the reasonably informed observer test below. However, before turning to it, we will provide some examples of how and when arguments of apparent bias can be made out.

17.4.2.1 Automatic disqualification: direct pecuniary interests

As a first principle, it appears that a decision will automatically be set aside if the adjudicator had a pecuniary interest in a case (no matter how small). *Dimes v Grand Junction Canal Proprietors* is the leading authority here.[167] Land adjoining a canal towpath was subject to litigation between the Grand Junction proprietors and Dimes, a local landowner. This action had gone on for over 20 years from 1831 and culminated in the Lord Chancellor affirming decrees that had been made in favour of the proprietors. It was later discovered by Dimes that Lord Cottenham, the Lord Chancellor, had several thousand pounds worth of shares in the canal company. Because he was a shareholder in one of the companies that was party to the proceedings, the ruling was set aside, with the result that the Lord Chancellor was disqualified as a judge in the case. This was not because it created a real probability of bias on the part of the Lord Chancellor, but because it might lead to a more general concern about the perceived fairness of the proceedings. As Lord Campbell said:

No one can suppose that Lord Cottenham could be, in the remotest degree, influenced by the interest that he had in this concern; but, my Lords, it is of the last importance that the maxim that no man is to be a judge in his own cause should be held sacred . . . This will be a lesson to all inferior tribunals to take care not only that in their decrees they are not influenced by their personal interest, but to avoid the appearance of labouring under such an influence ((1852) 3 HL Cas 759, 793–4).

On the other hand, it should be noted that there are clear—if rarely observed—exceptions to this aspect of the rule against bias. For example, proceedings may continue if the parties are made aware of the interest and agree to waive their objections; where there is special statutory dispensation on the matter; or where all the available adjudicators are affected by the same disqualifying interest and there is no option other than to proceed. There is also authority to suggest that, if the financial interest is very remote and no suspicion of bias could occur to a reasonable person, then the decision-maker will not be disqualified.[168] It has also been said

---

165 *R v Secretary of State for the Environment ex p Kirkstall Valley Campaign Limited* [1996] 3 All ER 304, 323, Sedley J.
166 *Board of Education v Rice* [1911] AC 179, 182.
167 (1852) 3 HL Cas 759.
168 *R v Mulvihill* [1990] 1 WLR 438.

that, while any pecuniary interest would be sufficient to lead to disqualification, the approach to other interests might be less strict.[169]

17.4.2.2 Bias and the judiciary

A similar approach is adopted where the decision-maker is a party to the dispute in which he or she adjudicates. At its broadest, an individual decision-maker (typically a judge) may be held to be a party where he or she is a member of an organisation that is one of the named parties to the proceedings, or where he or she has a close institutional link to the party or organisation. However, there is also authority to suggest that simple membership is not enough to justify automatic disqualification and that the decision-maker must have been actively involved in the initiation of the proceedings in question.[170] In the event that the decision-maker is merely a member of an organisation, automatic disqualification may not follow.[171]

The leading example of the broader approach being adopted was *R v Bow Street Metropolitan Stipendiary Magistrate, ex p Pinochet Ugarte (No 2)*.[172] This was an unprecedented decision in which the House of Lords set aside one of its own previous judgments on the grounds of maintaining the absolute impartiality of the judiciary. The decision to set aside was taken because Lord Hoffmann, one of the five members of the Appellate Committee who heard the appeal of General Pinochet, the ex-Chilean dictator, against extradition, had connections with one of the interveners in the case, namely Amnesty International. These were such as to give the appearance that he might have been biased against General Pinochet. This was all the more important as the case was not one of civil litigation but concerned criminal proceedings (General Pinochet was to face charges of human rights violations). The House of Lords held that it was unnecessary to determine the precise nature of the common law test to be applied (we consider the different approaches below). This was because it was enough to say that Lord Hoffmann should have played no part in the deliberations in the case. As Lord Hope of Craighead put it: 'There has been no suggestion that [Lord Hoffmann] was actually biased . . . But his relationship with Amnesty International was such that he was, in effect, acting as a judge in his own cause'.[173] In other words, he had some kind of interest, however indirect, in the outcome, and the court thus acted to extend the principle of automatic disqualification by setting aside its own previous judgment. In the event, the Lords issued another judgment that resulted with the extradition of the General, albeit that he never faced trial on account of ill health.[174]

17.4.2.3 Bias and intermingling of functions

Decisions may also be challenged for bias where a party who has been involved in a case at an earlier stage, for instance in investigating an individual, has some subsequent involvement in the decision about whether to impose a penalty on

---

169 *R v Cambridge Recorder* (1857) 8 E & B 637.

170 *Meerabux v Attorney-General of Belize* [2005] 2 AC 513.

171 But see, e.g., *R (Northamptonshire DC) v Secretary of State for Communities and Local Government* [2012] EWHC 4377 (Admin) (judge who was a member of the National Trust automatically disqualified from hearing a planning case in which the National Trust was a party).

172 [2000] 1 AC 119.

173 [2000] 1 AC 119, 144.

174 For other cases concerning judges see, e.g., *Hoekstra v HM Advocate* [2001] 1 AC 216 and *Davidson v Scottish Ministers* [2004] HRLR 34 and *Helow v Home Secretary* [2008] 1 WLR 2416.

the individual. Such later involvement need not be formal and/or direct, as even the mere presence of the party at the later stage of proceedings may be enough to render the decision invalid. A memorable decision that illustrates the point is *R v Barnsley Metropolitan Borough Council, ex p Hook*.[175] Harry Hook was a street trader who had traded for six years without any sort of complaint being made against him. One evening, after the public lavatories had already closed, he urinated in a side street near to the market where he had a stall. Two council employees witnessed this event. There was a heated exchange between Harry Hook and the council workmen, who reported Hook to the market manager. The manager considered the matter to be a serious incident and wrote to Hook informing him that his licence had been revoked (this had the effect of barring him permanently from trading at the market). Hook was granted further hearings by the council but, while the committee allowed a union representative and an articled clerk to represent him, they were not allowed to address the committee and they were not given particulars of the charges against Hook. Furthermore, the market manager who had taken the original decision was present at all the hearings, and he was in a position to tell the committee in private his view of the evidence, without being cross-examined. After Hook's case had been heard, the committee took the decision to uphold the ruling, with the market manager remaining in attendance while the committee deliberated. In the Court of Appeal, Lord Denning ruled that the decision could not stand as the market manager's presence and hearsay evidence breached the rule of natural justice whereby a prosecutor should not be present during deliberations.[176]

Two other cases help to map out the limits to the principle in *Hook*. In the first—*R (Bennion) v Chief Constable of Merseyside Police*[177]—an officer had been found guilty of an offence by the Chief Constable following disciplinary proceedings. These proceedings were to be heard by the Chief Constable unless he had an interest in the case, in which event they were to be passed on to another force for hearing. The officer concerned brought an action against the Chief Constable in which he argued that, although the Chief Constable was not himself personally involved, he was vicariously liable for acts of sexual discrimination and victimisation, that is, that these were conflicting functions. The court held that the Chief Constable had no disqualifying interest from his involvement in different capacities. His role was not the same as a judge because he had overall operational responsibility for discipline within the force, and his decision not to pass on his role in the proceedings to another force was not wrong. However, a different outcome can be seen in *R (McNally) v Secretary of State for Education and Metropolitan Borough of Bury*.[178] Here a teacher had been suspended from all teaching duties following an allegation of inappropriate physical contact with a pupil. Subsequently, a disciplinary hearing before a number of school governors was held, during which the Chief Education Officer of the local education authority was present, as was his statutory entitlement under paragraph 8(9) of Schedule 3 to the Education Act 1996. However, the governors excluded the Chief Education Officer from their deliberations, following the hearing, on the grounds that he might well be considered part of the

175 [1976] 3 All ER 452.
176 See also, e.g., *R (Agnello and others) v Hounslow LBC* [2003] EWHC 3112.
177 [2002] ICR 136.
178 [2001] ELR 773.

team for the prosecution, while the Chief Education Officer contended that he was entitled to attend under the 1996 statute. The Secretary of State intervened, acting under Schedule 3 to the Act, and concluded that the Chief Education Officer should have been involved. On a claim for judicial review of that decision brought by the teacher it was held, *inter alia*, that, although the Chief Education Officer was entitled to attend, this was not true under any/all circumstances. Dyson LJ further stated that the presence of the Chief Education Officer would in any event have contravened the principles of natural justice, as the teacher could reasonably have regarded the Chief Education Officer as one of the prosecution team.

17.4.3 The test for apparent bias

Turning, then, to the test for apparent bias that would govern cases of the kind discussed above, we have already seen that it is formulated in terms of the 'fair-minded and informed observer'. But what is the significance of this test, and why was it considered necessary to change the 'real danger of bias' test that had previously been used?

Taking first the 'real danger of bias' test, this is associated with the House of Lords ruling in *R v Gough*.[179] *Gough* was a case where a juror realised after the defendant had been convicted that she occupied the house next door to the defendant's brother. The House of Lords held that, after ascertaining all the relevant circumstances, the correct test to be applied was whether there was a 'real danger' that the appellant had not had a fair hearing. This meant deciding whether there was a real danger in the sense of a real possibility, but less than a probability, of bias on the part of a magistrate or member of a tribunal. Lord Goff said: 'I prefer to state the test in terms of the real danger rather than real likelihood, to ensure that the court is thinking in terms of possibility rather than probability of bias.'[180] This was considered to be equivalent to asking if there was a real danger that injustice would result from the alleged bias. His Lordship thought it unnecessary in formulating the test to look at the matter through the eyes of the reasonable man, because the court was taken to personify the reasonable man in such cases. He also pointed out that the test was not concerned with the actual state of mind of the person who was alleged to be biased, as bias is insidious and may not be present in the conscious mind. Public confidence demanded that justice had to be seen to be done. This meant that the court should examine all the necessary material so as to be satisfied that there was no danger that the alleged bias had created injustice.[181]

The subsequent reformulation of the test occurred, as we noted above, in the light of Article 6 of the ECHR and the experience of some Commonwealth systems. The origins of the change lie in the Court of Appeal's judgments in *Locabail (UK) Ltd v Bayfield Properties Ltd* and *Re Medicaments and Related Classes of Goods (No 2)*,[182] albeit that the leading authority is the House of Lords judgment in *Porter v Magill*.[183]

---

179 [1993] AC 646. Note that the *Gough* test had in turn replaced an earlier test of 'reasonable suspicion' of bias, on which see *R v Sussex Justices, ex p McCarthy* [1924] 1 KB 256.

180 [1993] AC 646, 670.

181 For application of the test see, e.g., *R v Inner West London Coroner, ex p Dallaglio* [1994] 4 All ER 139; and *R v Secretary of State for the Environment, ex p Kirkstall Valley Campaign Ltd* [1996] 3 All ER 304.

182 Respectively [2000] QB 451 and [2001] 1 WLR 700.

183 [2002] 2 AC 357.

In *Locabail*, the Court of Appeal had an opportunity to review and provide guidance on what constitutes bias by a judge in five applications heard together by the Lord Chief Justice, the Vice Chancellor, and the Master of the Rolls. Two basic rules were distinguished. The first was the test of automatic disqualification, as seen above in *Dimes v Grand Junction Canal*, where the judge should recuse him or herself from the case before any objection is raised. However, the court also stressed that any further extension of this rule beyond the limited class of non-financial interests (as in *Pinochet*, above) was undesirable 'unless plainly required to give effect to the important underlying principles upon which the rule is based', and also that a judge 'would be as wrong to yield to a tenuous or frivolous objection as he would to ignore an objection of substance'.[184] The second rule was based on the real danger or possibility of bias test (as in *R v Gough*), one which the Court of Appeal felt bound to apply here, since it was decided in the House of Lords (although the court noted that English law was, in applying the test, at variance both with the approach in Scotland and with the 'reasonable apprehension' test applied in most other Commonwealth jurisdictions[185]). Regarding the real danger test, it was impossible to conceive of every situation in which it might apply, but the court stated that objections would not succeed if based on, for instance, the religion, ethnic or national origin, gender, age, class, means, or sexual orientation of the judge. Nor would they be sound if based on social or educational background, previous political affiliations, or membership of other bodies, such as masonic associations. By way of contrast, strongly held views previously expressed about something connected to the case before the judge or a close personal connection to a member of the public involved in the case may well constitute a real danger or possibility of bias. Every application must be decided on the facts and circumstances of the individual case.

The Court of Appeal in *Locabail* also addressed the issue whether an alternative test for bias to that of *Gough* was now needed given the demands of the ECHR. In *Re Medicaments and Related Classes of Goods (No 2)* the Court of Appeal took the further opportunity to review and adapt the test in the light of the coming into force of the Human Rights Act 1998. The live issue here was whether the Restrictive Practices Court should have recused itself given the apparent bias of one its members and, in deciding that it should, the Court of Appeal outlined what it considered to be necessary for compliance with Article 6 of the ECHR. In this regard it said that, where a court was considering the question of bias, it should first ascertain all the circumstances which had a bearing on the suggestion of bias. However, rather than ask whether the court, as the personification of the reasonable man, considered that there was a real danger of bias, it said that the court should ask whether those circumstances would lead a fair-minded and informed observer to conclude that there was a 'real possibility', or a 'real danger', of bias. Those formulations, in turn, were said to be 'the same', and the judgment of the Court of Appeal in that way did not doubt the suitability of *Gough* in its entirety, but only that part that omitted to structure the test around the reasonable man. At the same time, the problems with *Gough* had become apparent, and the House of Lords in *Porter v Magill* subsequently adopted and refined the language of the Court of Appeal when deleting any reference to 'real danger'. The issue in this case was an allegation of bias against an

---

184 [2000] QB 451, 475, and 479.
185 Citing, e.g., the Australian case *Webb v Queen* (1994) 181 CLR 41.

auditor who had found that local councillors had misused their powers for party political advantage and at considerable cost to their council (Westminster City Council). Stating that the *Gough* test was no longer appropriate as it could in effect amount to a test for actual bias, Lord Hope sought to achieve conformity with the Strasbourg case law and the test applied in most Commonwealth jurisprudence and in Scotland by simply deleting any reference to 'real danger'. Under the revised test the question is thus:

whether the fair-minded and informed observer, having considered the facts, would conclude that there was a real possibility that the tribunal was biased.

Before leaving this point, we should note that guidance has since been given on the question of what the 'fair minded and informed observer' might look like. Of course, in reality this is an attempt to identify the impossible as there is always an element of fiction with the role that such characters play in the law—and this is something that can generate difficulty on a case-by-case basis.[186] Nevertheless, the observer has been elevated to a position of increased prominence in administrative law and Lord Hope took the opportunity to expound upon some of his/her qualities in the case of *Helow v Home Secretary*.[187] This was a case in which a Palestinian asylum seeker argued that the Court of Session judge who had heard (and dismissed) her appeal had been biased because she was, among other things, a founding member of the International Association of Jewish Lawyers and Jurists. Rejecting the argument that the 'fair minded and informed' observer would have detected a real possibility of bias, Lord Hope said:

The fair minded and informed observer is a relative newcomer among the select group of personalities who inhabit our legal village and are available to be called upon when a problem arises that needs to be solved objectively. Like the reasonable man whose attributes have been explored so often in the context of the law of negligence, the fair-minded observer is a creature of fiction. Gender neutral (as this is a case where the complainer and the person complained about are both women, I shall avoid using the word 'he'), she has attributes which many of us might struggle to attain to.

The observer who is fair-minded is the sort of person who always reserves judgment on every point until she has seen and fully understood both sides of the argument. She is not unduly sensitive or suspicious . . . Her approach must not be confused with that of the person who has brought the complaint. The 'real possibility' test ensures that there is this measure of detachment. The assumptions that the complainer makes are not to be attributed to the observer unless they can be justified objectively. But she is not complacent either. She knows that fairness requires that a judge must be, and must be seen to be, unbiased. She knows that judges, like anybody else, have their weaknesses. She will not shrink from the conclusion, if it can be justified objectively, that things that they have said or done or associations that they have formed may make it difficult for them to judge the case before them impartially.[188]

17.4.4 Policy bias and decision-making

Notwithstanding the above authorities, there have been certain situations in which it has been held that it would be inappropriate to apply the rule against bias

---

186 See Havers and Henderson, n 156.
187 [2008] 1 WLR 2416.
188 Ibid, 2417–18. And see, e.g., *O'Neill v HM Lord Advocate* [2013] UKSC 36, [2013] 1 WLR 1992.

rigidly. For instance, *Franklin v Minister of Town and Country Planning*[189] illustrates the difficulty that arises when there is a conflict between a stated policy and an implied requirement to act without bias and according to the rules of fairness. After the Second World War ended in 1945, there had been a clear political commitment to the construction of a number of new towns on the fringes of London, and to the development of Stevenage in particular. However, this policy was contentious as there were many objections to individual proposals. Before the legislation had completed its passage through Parliament, the minister stated at a public meeting that, in spite of any objections, the project for Stevenage would go ahead. Soon afterwards, the New Towns Act 1946 was passed, and, in line with its provisions, a public inquiry was set up to hear objections before any final designation of Stevenage as a new town. It was undeniably the case that, in approving the scheme for Stevenage, the minister had made a decision which, in view of his earlier pronouncements, inevitably imported a suggestion of bias. However, the House of Lords decided the question by regarding this as an administrative rather than a judicial matter, and by asking simply whether the decision had been arrived at by following the correct procedures. This allowed them to conclude that an earlier ministerial pronouncement to the effect that the project was going to go through anyway did not invalidate the decision. They adopted the reasoning that, because it amounted to a purely administrative decision, there was no need to follow the rules of natural justice. While that line of reasoning would not, of course, survive the change in the law heralded by *Ridge v Baldwin*, the case still indicates that there are occasions when it is permissible for decision-makers to take political (policy) considerations into account.[190]

We can contrast this with the decision in *Steeples v Derbyshire County Council*.[191] In this instance, the council had entered into a contractual agreement with KLF Ltd, which stipulated that the company would develop a site owned by the council by building a leisure complex. This was agreed on the understanding that the authority gave the company planning permission. Indeed, as part of the agreement, £116,000 was payable in the event of planning permission not being granted. The decision of the planning committee was declared void by Webster J. Principally, this was because the contract that had been entered into suggested that the council had prejudged the situation, albeit we should note that it was pointed out by counsel in the case that the local authority was perfectly entitled to grant itself planning permission and that it would, in that circumstance, be a judge in its own cause. Nevertheless, Webster J made it plain where the council had gone wrong, as it should have avoided committing itself by making its contract subject to planning permission. Had it done so, the rule against bias may not have been applied so strictly.

When considering bias in the wider policy context, it is also important to note that a distinction may be made between 'predetermination' and 'predisposition'. Predetermination is where the decision-maker has already made up its mind in advance and, in *R v Secretary of State for the Environment, ex p Kirkstall Valley*

---

189 [1948] AC 97.

190 See also *R v Amber Valley District Council, ex p Jackson* [1984] 3 All ER 501 and *R v Sevenoaks District Council, ex p Terry* [1985] 3 All ER 226.

191 [1984] 3 All ER 468.

Campaign Ltd, Sedley J said that there is: 'a different although equally important principle: that the decision of a body, albeit composed of disinterested individuals, will be struck down if its outcome has been predetermined whether by the adoption of an inflexible policy or by the effective surrender of the body's independent judgment.'[192] On the other hand, predisposition arises where a person on a decision-making body may have expressed opinions which are unfavourable to an individual, but where the decision-maker may still be prepared to listen to the arguments. Such might be the situation where there has been a manifesto commitment to a particular policy. In order to decide the matter, the court will have to assess whether, considering all the facts, a fair-minded and informed observer would conclude that there was a real possibility of bias. For example, in *Condron v National Assembly for Wales*,[193] a decision of the planning decision committee of the Welsh Assembly was challenged because one of its members had stated orally that he was 'going to go with the inspector's report' in regard to a proposed application for opencast mining. Given that non-judicial decision-makers are entitled to have predispositions, it was concluded in *Condron* that there had been no apparent bias on the facts.[194]

17.4.5 Article 6 of the ECHR, bias, and 'independent and impartial tribunals'

The final matter that we must consider is the complex question of the interaction between judicial review and Article 6 of the ECHR when decisions that affect 'civil rights' are taken by decision-makers who are neither 'independent' nor 'impartial' when making the decisions. We gave some prototypical examples of such decision-makers above, where we noted the role of ministers in giving effect to central or devolved government policy and of local authority officers who are conducting reviews of decisions taken by their employing local authority. Under such circumstances, Article 6 of the ECHR is not automatically violated so long as the affected individual subsequently has a means of recourse to an independent and impartial tribunal that has 'full jurisdiction' in the matter in question (whether there is full jurisdiction depends on context and, in particular, 'the subject-matter of the decision appealed against, the manner in which that decision was arrived at and the content of the dispute, including the desired and actual grounds of appeal').[195] This, again, is the so-called 'curative' approach to compliance, and it will clearly be satisfied where statute gives the individual a full right of appeal to a tribunal or court. However, much more difficult is the circumstance where judicial review is the only available remedy. This is because judicial review has historically fastened upon a 'review not appeal' distinction that precludes the courts from considering the merits of a decision under challenge and, for instance, disputed questions of fact. Put at its height, the concern is thus that a judicial review court

---

192 [1996] 3 All ER 304, 321.
193 [2006] EWCA Civ 1573.
194 See also, e.g., *R (On the Application of Lewis) v Redcar and Cleveland BC* [2009] 1 WLR 83 and *R v Local Commissioner for Administration in the North and North East England, ex p Liverpool CC* [2001] 1 All ER 462.
195 *Bryan v UK* (1995) 21 EHRR 342.

can never have the requisite 'full jurisdiction' and that Article 6 of the ECHR will be open to violation.

The corresponding law on this point has developed over three main stages. The first emphasised the context-dependent nature of the 'full jurisdiction' requirement when holding that judicial review would often suffice for the purposes of Article 6 of the ECHR. For instance, in *R (Alconbury) v Secretary of State for Environment, Transport and the Regions*,[196] the question was whether planning legislation was incompatible with Article 6 of the ECHR by virtue of empowering the Secretary of State—who is responsible for formulating planning policy—to, among other things, 'call in' and determine certain planning applications. The government accepted that, while this meant that the Secretary of State could not be regarded as independent and impartial when making a decision, recourse to judicial review on ordinary grounds (illegality; irrationality; procedural impropriety) remedied any shortcomings. In accepting the argument, the House of Lords noted that the Secretary of State's role in the planning regime was legitimated by the existence of parliamentary control and accountability; and their Lordships also noted the Secretary of State's powers were governed by procedural requirements that were supported by his accountability to Parliament and amenability to judicial review on traditional grounds. A framework for dealing with applications based on the separation of powers was thus in operation, and this was sufficient, given the overall circumstances of the case.

A similar reasoning drove the House of Lords judgment in *Runa Begum v Tower Hamlets LBC*.[197] The local authority had here offered housing to the claimant as a homeless person, but the offer was refused because the claimant considered that the house was in an area where there was racism and drug abuse. After an officer of the local authority had reviewed the refusal and decided that the offer was suitable, the claimant appealed to the County Court, arguing that the authority had breached Article 6 of the ECHR by failing to refer the matter to an independent tribunal. The issue, on appeal to the House of Lords, was whether the problems created by the role of the local officer were remedied through an appeal to the county court (which, under the relevant legislation, had essentially the same powers of review in such cases as the High Court in judicial review proceedings). On this point, the individual had argued that the traditional grounds were insufficient precisely because they did not enable the County Court to substitute its finding of fact for that of a local authority official who had been deputed to conduct a review of the authority's original decision. However, in holding that Article 6 of the ECHR did not require an independent fact-finder in the case, the House of Lords emphasised that 'the question is whether, consistently with the rule of law and constitutional propriety, the relevant decision-making powers may be entrusted to administrators'.[198] Situating the case within its welfare context, the House of Lords concluded that it was perfectly legitimate for the legislature to entrust decisions of the kind at hand to administrators with specialist expertise in the area, as they would be

---

196 [2003] 2 AC 295.
197 [2003] 2 AC 430.
198 Ibid, 454, Lord Hoffmann.

required to reach their decisions in accordance with particular procedures and their decisions would thereafter be subject to review on the traditional grounds. This, it was held, would avoid an over-judicialisation of the workings of the welfare state and, by analogy, other regulatory areas, such as those concerned with licensing and planning. In contrast, a more involved role for the courts was envisaged where decisions had implications for the private rights of individuals or where they were concerned with alleged breaches of the criminal law.

The second stage was led by the ECtHR and its ruling in *Tsfayo v UK*,[199] which established that judicial review would be insufficient for the purpose of Article 6 of the ECHR in some cases, the reasoning in *Alconbury* and *Runa Begum* notwithstanding. *Tsfayo* itself was a case which arose out of a local authority housing benefit review board's decision that the individual had not shown good cause for a delay in making a claim for welfare entitlements (the review board was comprised of three councillors from the local authority and was therefore neither independent nor impartial). In finding that there had been a violation of Article 6 of the ECHR, the ECtHR drew a distinction between cases involving disputed questions of fact that 'required a measure of professional knowledge or experience and the exercise of administrative discretion pursuant to wider policy aims' (as in *Alconbury* and *Runa Begum*) and those, such as the instant case, in which the decision-maker 'was deciding a simple question of fact, namely whether there was 'good cause' for the applicant's delay in making a claim'.[200] In cases of this latter kind, the ECtHR considered that a reviewing court should be able to substitute its findings for those of the original decision-maker as 'no specialist expertise [is] required to determine this issue . . . [Nor] . . . can the factual findings in the present case be said to be merely incidental to the reaching of broader judgments of policy or expediency which it was for the democratically accountable authority to take'.[201] However, the ECtHR noted that there had been no possibility of such review in the instant case, as the domestic error of fact doctrine does not extend so far as to permit the High Court to substitute its own findings of fact for those of the original decision-maker. There was, in the result, no composite compliance with Article 6 of the ECHR.[202]

The implications of *Tsfayo* were much commented upon, and some authors suggested that the reasoning of the ECtHR even undermined the essential logic of *Alconbury* and *Runa Begum*. This was certainly the view of John Howell QC, who said that while 'it may appear that the ECtHR simply distinguished the decisions in the *Alconbury* and *Runa Begum* cases . . . [*Tsfayo*] is more significant in its implications and it is inconsistent with the decisions in those cases'.[203] However, to the extent that this suggested further problems in reconciling judicial review with the 'full jurisdiction' requirement, that has not proven to be the reality. While we will see that part of the reason for this was an (apparently wrong) narrowing of the reach of Article 6 of the ECHR by the Supreme Court in the subsequent case of *Ali v Birmingham City Council*, the ECtHR seemed to suggest,

---

199 (2009) 48 EHRR 18. See too, e.g., *Kingsley v UK* (2002) 35 EHRR 177.

200 (2009) 48 EHRR 18, para 45.

201 Ibid, para 45.

202 For domestic application of *Tsfayo* see, e.g., *Re Bothwell's Application* [2007] NIQB 25. And on error of fact see 12.6.

203 J Howell, '*Alconbury* Crumbles' [2007] 12 *Judicial Review* 9, at 11.

when the *Ali* case later came before it by way of petition, that *Tsfayo*'s implications are to be narrowly drawn.[204] This is thus the third stage in the development of the law and it may yet prove to be the most decisive.

The applicant in *Ali* was a single mother who wished to challenge, before the County Court, Birmingham City Council's determination that it had discharged its statutory duties to her under the Housing Act 1996 when offering her accommodation which the applicant had rejected. The powers of the County Court were, again, essentially the same as those of the High Court on a claim for judicial review, and the applicant argued, among other things, that she did not have access to a court of 'full jurisdiction' for the purposes of Article 6 of the ECHR. However, rather than resolve that issue, the Supreme Court focused upon the anterior question whether Article 6 of the ECHR was even engaged by the housing decision, and it was here that it took an apparent wrong turning.[205] Holding that Article 6 of the ECHR was not engaged, the Supreme Court drew a distinction between the class of social security and welfare benefits whose substance was defined precisely, and which could therefore amount to an individual right of which the applicant could consider herself the holder, and those benefits which were, in their essence, dependent upon the exercise of judgement by the relevant authority. The Court on that basis said that cases in the latter category, where the award of services or benefits in kind was dependent upon a series of evaluative judgements by the provider, did not amount to a 'civil right' within the autonomous meaning of Article 6 of the ECHR (on the content of 'civil rights' see further 17.2.4). As the right to accommodation in this case fell into the latter category, it followed that no issue arose under Article 6 of the ECHR.[206]

The ECtHR's ruling in *Ali* then centred upon two main findings. The first was that the accommodation entitlement under the Housing Act 1996 was a 'civil right' within the meaning of Article 6 of the ECHR, notwithstanding that it was a contingent upon an exercise of discretion and could be classified as a 'benefit in kind'. Of course, this finding was very different from that which had been made by the Supreme Court (hence its apparent error), and the ECtHR emphasised that its case law takes a broad approach to the nature of civil rights in the welfare setting. However, its second finding concerned the demands of 'full jurisdiction' in the welfare setting, and it was here that the ECtHR seemed to recognise the limitations of *Tsfayo*. Distinguishing the facts of *Tsfayo* from those that were before it, the ECtHR referred to the House of Lords reasoning in *Runa Begum* when noting that the Housing Act 1996 covers 'a multitude of small cases and is intended to bring as great a benefit as possible to needy persons in an economical and fair manner . . . when due enquiry into the facts has already been conducted at the administrative adjudicatory stage, [Article 6 of the ECHR] cannot be read as requiring that the judicial review before a court should encompass a reopening with a rehearing of witnesses'.[207] Approaching the matter in this way, the ECtHR concluded that the

---

204 For the Supreme Court's ruling see [2010] UKSC 8, [2010] 2 AC 39; the ECtHR's judgment was delivered on 20 October 2015 and is reported at [2015] HRLR 46.

205 And for a forerunner see *R (A) v Croydon LBC* [2009] UKSC 8; [2009] 1 WLR 2557.

206 For subsequent application of the Supreme Court's ruling outside the housing context see *R (Saava) v Kensington and Chelsea RLBC* [2010] EWHC 414 (Admin) (High Court noting *obiter* that the creation of personal budgets for sick and disabled persons falls outside Art 6 ECHR).

207 [2015] HRLR 46, para 85.

option of County Court proceedings that had been open to the applicant had been compliant with Article 6 of the ECHR because 'the applicant could—and initially did—argue that in reaching the decision the Officer had taken into account irrelevant considerations and/or acted under a fundamental mistake of fact; that the Council had failed to make adequate inquiries to enable it to reach a lawful decision; that the decision was one which no rational Council could have made; that it had fettered its discretion; and that it had acted in breach of natural justice'.[208] By deciding the case in this way, the ECtHR was thus able to safeguard its own understanding of 'civil rights' whilst at the same time accepting the parameters of judicial review in the UK's contemporary administrative state.

17.5 Conclusion

Procedural impropriety, in the form of the rules of natural justice or fairness, has been discussed in this chapter against the backdrop of an enormous increase in decision-making by public bodies, especially since 1945. Although it might be argued that the reassertion of judicial activism marked in this area by the leading decision of *Ridge v Baldwin* has been an inadequate, and perhaps belated, judicial response to the scale of the problems that have arisen, nevertheless it does appear that there has been greater willingness to intervene to correct decisions, whatever their nature or type, if appropriate procedures have not been followed by the decision-making body. Presently, the guiding principle (if there is one) is that of fairness and, broadly speaking, the potential effects of a decision on an individual or a group will determine how closely the procedures will be expected to resemble an adversarial model. In fact, we can see that in the 50 years or so since *Ridge v Baldwin* the expectation of the courts with regard to many procedures has evolved to a considerable extent. For example, there has been an increasing willingness by the courts to insist that reasons be given for decisions, and the phrases 'proportionality' and 'legitimate expectation' have become settled at the centre of the judicial vocabulary.[209] As already observed in other chapters, the emergence of these—and other—principles has been aided by the influence of European law.

We would lastly reiterate that the discussion of the rules of fairness in this chapter has been broken down into sub-categories which correspond to important questions that continually arise with regard to the out-workings of the rules. We should bear in mind that procedural defects, when they do occur, will often involve a combination of factors, and that accordingly the categories are imprecise. Indeed, it will have become apparent that the rules of natural justice/fairness are not applied in a strict manner, and it may for that reason be said that they are not even rules at all. They are, perhaps, better thought of as guidelines that have been developed to provide safeguards against possible injustice. They thus provide excellent illustrations of the flexibility of the common law, both in terms of how it evolves to meet new demands and in terms of how it gives the courts discretion as to whether to grant a remedy.

---

208 Ibid, para 83.
209 See chs 13 and 15.

FURTHER READING

Attrill, S (2003) 'Who is the "Fair-Minded Observer"? Bias after *Magill*' *Cambridge Law Journal* 279.

Clayton, R and Tomlinson, H (2010) *Fair Trial Rights* (Oxford: Oxford University Press).

Craig, P [2003] 'The Human Rights Act, Article 6 and Procedural Rights' *Public Law* 753.

Elliott, M [2011] 'Has the Common Law Duty to Give Reasons Come of Age Yet?' *Public Law* 56.

Havers, P and Henderson, A [2011] 'Recent Developments (and Problems) in the Law of Bias' 16 *Judicial Review* 80.

Howell, J [2007] '*Alconbury* Crumbles' 12 *Judicial Review* 9.

Le Sueur, A (1999) 'Legal Duties to Give Reasons' 54 *Current Legal Problems* 150.

Maher, G (1986) 'Natural Justice as Fairness' in Birks, P and MacCormick, N (eds), *The Legal Mind* (Oxford: Oxford University Press).

Mallinson, K (2000) 'Judicial Bias and Disqualification after *Pinochet (No 2)*' 63 *Modern Law Review* 119.

Maurici, J [2007] 'The Modern Approach to Bias' *Judicial Review* 251.

Olowofoyeku, AA [2000] 'The *Nemo Judex* Rule: The Case Against Automatic Disqualification' *Public Law* 456.

Williams, Sir D, QC [2000] 'Bias; the Judges and the Separation of Powers' *Public Law* 45.

18

Remedies in judicial review

18.1 Introduction

Having considered in depth the grounds upon which administrative decisions and so on may be challenged, we turn to examine the remedies that *may* be granted by the courts. The word 'may' has been emphasised, as we will see that the remedies that are available on a claim for judicial review are discretionary.[1] This means that, even if the court is satisfied that a public authority has acted unlawfully, it may decide not to grant a remedy to the claimant. This may be because the court considers that the individual has acted in some way that means that he or she is not deserving of a remedy, or it may be because the court considers that a remedy would be of only limited practical utility. An example here would be where the court concludes that a decision-maker has failed to follow some point of procedure but that, even if it had observed its procedural obligations, it would still have made the same decision.

We will also see that the remedies are designed and used in such as way as to ensure, at least theoretically, that the courts do not substitute their decisions for those of the original decision-maker.[2] This is wholly consistent with the 'review, not appeal' distinction that runs through the grounds for judicial review, and we will see that the remedies are more limited in their effect than might be expected. For instance, the so-called prerogative remedies allow the courts either to quash a decision (historically *certiorari*, now a quashing order), to prevent a public body from acting in a particular way (historically *prohibition*, now prohibiting order), or to compel a public body to perform its public duties (historically *mandamus*, now mandatory order). While the use of these remedies can sometimes have far-reaching implications, they are not intended to allow the courts to take discretionary choices in the place of a public body. The same is true of the private law remedies that were consolidated with the prerogative remedies under the procedure that was introduced in 1977.[3] Injunctions will thus usually be granted to prevent a course of

---

1 See Sir T Bingham, 'Should Public Law Remedies be Discretionary?' [1991] *Public Law* 64.

2 Although note the exception contained in the Tribunals, Courts and Enforcement Act 2007, s 141, summarised at 18.3.1.

3 See ch 8. The procedure, in England and Wales, is now found in Part 54 of the Civil Procedure Rules as read with the Senior Courts Act 1981, s 31. Substantially the same remedies are available in Northern Ireland, where the governing procedure is contained in the Judicature (Northern Ireland) Act 1978, ss 18–25 and Order 53 of the Rules of the Court of Judicature. On Scotland see Chapter 58 of the Rules of the Court of Session.

action being taken or from continuing, while the declaration has no effect beyond identifying the respective legal rights and duties of the parties to a dispute.

We begin our analysis with a section that looks in more detail at the origins of the remedies and at their discretionary nature. Next, we consider each of the remedies in the order that they have been noted above, discussing some of the leading case law as we proceed. Finally, we make some comments about the availability of remedies under the European Communities Act 1972 and the Human Rights Act 1998.

Two further points that should be made by way of introduction concern the position of Ministers of the Crown, and damages claims. Regarding Ministers of the Crown, it is to be emphasised that all of the remedies are available in proceedings against ministers, whether the remedy is prerogative in form or of private law origin. The point here is really one about injunctions as, prior to the House of Lords' seminal ruling in *M v Home Office*[4] (discussed below), it was thought that section 21 of the Crown Proceedings Act 1947 precluded the grant of such relief in civil proceedings. However, in *M*—a case concerning the breach of an undertaking that an asylum seeker would not be deported pending a judicial ruling—the House of Lords ruled that this was not the correct position. Holding, first, that section 21 does not apply to judicial review proceedings because they are not 'civil proceedings', the House noted that injunctions were available against Ministers of the Crown in cases under the European Communities Act 1972 and that it was desirable that they should be available in non-EU law cases too (an injunction had been issued in the celebrated *Factortame* case).[5] The House of Lords also emphasised that injunctions should be available given that the prerogative orders and declarations are available against ministers and that the procedural reforms of the late 1970s had been intended to consolidate the remedies.

The point about damages is that they are rarely granted in judicial review proceedings. Although it is possible to claim damages, a court will award them only where it is satisfied that there would have been a corresponding claim in private law or where there would be an entitlement to damages under the European Communities Act 1972 and/or the Human Rights Act 1998. However, the related case law on the liability of public authorities, particularly in tort law, can become very complex and we have therefore made only brief mention of it in this chapter. A fuller account of the applicable legal principles is provided in chapters 19 and 20 on, respectively, the contractual and tort liability of public authorities, where we also consider the scope for damages actions under the European Communities Act 1972 and the Human Rights Act 1998.

18.2 **The origins and discretionary nature of the remedies**

It will be recalled from chapter 8 that the prerogative orders (formerly writs) were historically issued by the Crown and that they enabled the monarch to exercise control both over courts and over local and non-royal decision-makers. Through

---

4 [1994] 1 AC 377.

5 *R v Secretary of State for Transport, ex p Factortame Ltd* (No 2) [1991] AC 603; and see 3.2.4.

time, however, the prerogative orders became judicialised as individuals increasingly sought redress in the King's Court rather than from the King himself, and the courts began to grant the remedies in accordance with common law principles. Declarations and injunctions, in contrast, have equitable origins and this historically entailed that they were more flexible than the common law prerogative orders. In other words, while the prerogative orders were to develop in the light of highly technical distinctions that could render it difficult for individuals to gain access to them,[6] declarations and injunctions were originally unconstrained by strict rules of precedent and were defined more by equity's emphasis on flexibility in the face of injustice.[7] On the other hand, a judicial aversion towards solely declaratory relief meant that use of the declaration remained under-developed in cases involving public bodies, at least until the legislature intervened to encourage such relief.[8]

The introduction of the composite judicial review procedure in the late 1970s means that historical distinctions between the remedies are no longer relevant, and the most remarkable aspect of them remains their discretionary nature (the prerogative orders and equitable remedies have always been discretionary). The historical approach of the courts was one that depended on the context to a given case and the motivation and actions of the individual, and these continue to be guiding considerations in the modern case law (although different considerations can apply in cases under the European Communities Act 1972 and/or the Human Rights Act 1998—see below). For instance, the courts today may decline to grant a remedy where: the applicant has not exhausted alternative remedies; the illegality is a technical irregularity that has caused the applicant no substantial wrong; the applicant has failed to bring proceedings within the requisite time-frame; the applicant does not have standing to seek a remedy; or the applicant has acted without candour and integrity.[9] A remedy may also be refused in the circumstance that we noted above, *viz* where the court concludes that a decision-maker has failed to follow some point of procedure but that, even if it had observed its procedural obligations, it would still have made the same decision.[10]

The courts may also decline to grant a *particular* remedy in a given case because of the wider ramifications that the grant of the remedy might have. The point here is that a claim for judicial review may frequently seek more than one of the remedies, but that the court may consider that the grant of one specific remedy would be inappropriate in the circumstances. The point can perhaps best be seen in relation to a mandatory order, as this remedy has the effect of compelling a decision-maker to perform a public—usually a statutory—duty (the nature of that remedy is considered in more detail below). Should the performance of that duty involve discretionary choices in respect of, for instance, resource allocation, the courts may consider that an order of *mandamus* should not issue, as it may have the effect of dictating a resource choice in circumstances that could have implications for other

6 See, e.g., the discussion of standing at 8.10.

7 J Glister and J Lee, *Hanbury & Martin: Modern Equity*, 20th edn (London: Sweet & Maxwell, 2015), ch 1.

8 e.g., through the Chancery Procedure Act 1852, s 50.

9 On some of these elements of the judicial review procedure and the corresponding case law see 8.6ff.

10 See, e.g., *Re National Union of Public Employers and Confederation of Health Service Employees' Application* [1988] NI 255. See also s 31(2A) of the Senior Courts Act 1981, which requires, save in cases of 'exceptional public interest', that relief be refused where it is 'highly likely that the outcome for the applicant would not have been substantially different if the conduct complained of had not occurred'; and, e.g., *Hawke* [2015] EWHC 3599 (Admin).

parties not before the court (for instance, other NHS patients[11] or other applicants for a licence for an economic activity).[12] Rather than grant a remedy that would strain the logic of the separation of powers doctrine insofar as it would involve the court in making a choice that should be left to others, a court may thus prefer to make a declaration in respect of the rights and obligations of the parties.[13] A court may alternatively decline to grant any formal remedy for the reason that the judgment of the court itself has, in effect, declared the respective rights of the parties.

18.3 **The remedies**

We can turn now to consider in more detail the principal remedies that are available on a claim for judicial review, namely quashing order/*certiorari*; prohibiting order/*prohibition*; mandatory order/*mandamus*; injunctions; and declarations. Damages are noted only briefly below, as a fuller account of that remedy is provided in chapters 19 and 20. The remedy of *habeas corpus*—discussed in chapter 8—is not available under the judicial review procedure but rather under its own rules of procedure.[14]

18.3.1 **Quashing order (formerly *certiorari*)**

A quashing order is the most commonly sought of the prerogative remedies and it will often be the remedy of most value to the claimant. As its name makes clear, the order serves to quash a decision or other measure and, where it is granted, the decision or other measure in respect of which it is granted is regarded as having never had legal effect.[15] The remedy is coercive, which means that a failure to observe it may be regarded as a contempt of court and result in the imposition of a penalty such as a fine.[16] Historically, it has its origins in the context of the control of inferior courts, but it is now potentially available in respect of any decision of a subordinate decision-maker that is making public law decisions.[17] There are, in turn, many examples of cases where the remedy has been granted, and these include *R v Criminal Injuries Compensation Board, ex p Lain*,[18] where it was held that the remedy may be sought against a public body established by prerogative; *R v Barnet London Borough Council, ex p Nilish Shah*,[19] where it was used to quash a decision refusing a mandatory grant to a student; *R v Hull Prison Board of Visitors, ex p St Germain*,[20] where the decision of a Board of Visitors resulting in the loss of remission for prisoners was

11 *R v Cambridge Area Health Authority, ex p Child B* [1995] 1 All ER 129.

12 *Re Kirkpatrick's Application* [2004] NIJB 15, 23, para 36.

13 See, e.g., *R(Bibi) v Newham London Borough Council* [2002] 1 WLR 237 (declaration issued in case where the applicants had established that they had a legitimate expectation of permanent housing); and 15.4.

14 See, in England and Wales, Part 87 of the Civil Procedure Rules. On *habeas corpus* see *Rahmatullah v Secretary of State for Foreign and Commonwealth Affairs* [2012] UKSC 48, [2013] 1 AC 614.

15 *Boddington v British Transport Police* [1999] 2 AC 143, 154.

16 *M v Home Office* [1994] 1 AC 377.

17 *R v Electricity Commissioners, ex p London Electricity Joint Committee (1920)* [1924] 1 KB 171 and *Ridge v Baldwin* [1964] AC 40.

18 [1967] 2 QB 864.

19 [1983] AC 309.

20 [1979] QB 425.

quashed; *R v Hillingdon London Borough Council, ex p Royco Homes Ltd*,[21] where the court quashed conditions attached to a grant of planning permission that were considered to be *ultra vires*; *R v General Medical Council, ex p Gee*,[22] which concerned the exercise of the statutory powers of the disciplinary committee of the General Medical Council; and *R v Army Board of the Defence Council, ex p Anderson*,[23] where the remedy was granted to secure the procedural safeguards of a fair hearing after the Board's initial rejection of allegations of racial discrimination.

Quashing orders are not without difficulty, however, precisely because they render the decisions or other measures in respect of which they are made as having been without any legal effect. For instance, in some cases the challenged decision or other measure may not be wholly unlawful and it might be doubted whether it is necessary to quash the full decision/measure (an example here may be regulations made under primary legislation); and complex questions may also arise when the remedy is sought in circumstances in which other decisions or acts have since been taken on the basis of the impugned decision. In each of these instances there can be a tension between, on the one hand, the need to uphold the rule of law and, on the other, the need to safeguard the administration from the practical difficulties that may follow from quashing a partially lawful decision or quashing a measure that has formed the basis for a range of other decisions. In that sense, the courts may appear to be faced with something of a stark 'either/or' choice.

Inevitably, there is case law to support both the 'rule of law' and the 'flexibility' approaches. For instance, *R v Paddington Valuation Officer, ex p Peachey Property Corporation Ltd* is an authority for the proposition that a quashing order can issue even if this would result in far-reaching administrative consequences.[24] The facts here were that an order of *certiorari* was sought to invalidate a valuation list prepared by the local authority for an entire area. Although the remedy was not granted in this case, Salmon LJ was in no doubt that it would have issued had there been an illegal action:

> If the valuation officer acted illegally and thereby produced an unjust and invalid list, this would be . . . an abuse of power and one which the courts would certainly redress. It could be no answer that to do so would produce inconvenience and chaos for the rating authority—otherwise the law could be flouted and injustice perpetrated with impunity.[25]

On the other hand, the court may find it appropriate to exercise its discretion and not grant a quashing order while at the same time deciding to issue another remedy. The other principal remedy here would be likely to be a declaration, as this remedy does not invalidate a decision but identifies the source of illegality, thereby inviting the decision-maker to make the necessary modifications. In *R v Secretary of State for Social Services, ex p Association of Metropolitan Authorities*,[26] the court was thus prepared to grant a declaration to the effect that there had been inadequate consultation of the local authorities concerned before housing benefit regulations were formulated, but nevertheless an order of *certiorari* was not granted. Webster J stated that he had exercised his discretion here on the basis of the procedural

21 [1974] QB 720.
22 [1986] 1 WLR 226.
23 [1992] QB 169.
24 [1965] 2 All ER 836.
25 Ibid, 849.
26 [1986] 1 WLR 1.

nature of the challenge and because the regulations had already been put into effect nationally for several months.

A particularly important case—and one that prioritised the rule of law over executive convenience—is *HM Treasury v Ahmed*.[27] This was a complicated case involving the legality of subordinate legislation that enabled the UK government to freeze the assets of terror suspects who were identified by the UK government itself and/or whose names were on 'sanctions lists' produced by the UN.[28] Part of the challenge to the legislation centred on the lack of procedural protection for individuals who were named on sanctions lists, and the Supreme Court quashed the relevant provisions as contrary to the fundamental right of access to an effective judicial remedy. Given this, the Treasury asked the Court to suspend the effect of its ruling so that appropriate changes could be made to the law in the light of the ongoing threat of terror. However, while the Court acknowledged that it had a power to suspend the effect of its rulings, it held that it was important to be clear that the legislation in question should never have had the force of law. The Court therefore refused to suspend its order as that would 'obfuscate the effect of its judgment' by suggesting to third parties such as banks that the legislation was valid.[29] In the event, Parliament subsequently intervened to enact legislation that had the effect of overriding the Supreme Court ruling.[30]

Two further points should be made under this heading. The first concerns a complementary remedial power that is contained in section 31(5) of the Senior Courts Act 1981.[31] This provides that, where the High Court has quashed a decision it may, among other things, substitute its own decision for the decision in question. However, while this may appear as an important change to the law, it is to be noted that the power of substitution is available only where the decision in question was made by a court or a tribunal; where the decision has been quashed because of an error of law; and where, without the error, there would have been only one decision which the court or tribunal could have reached. Limited to these circumstances, this power is probably of only limited relevance in practice, and it certainly does not enable the courts to substitute their decisions for those taken by administrative and executive decision-makers (albeit that the section does allow the court to remit decisions to such authorities and to direct it to 'reconsider the matter and reach a decision in accordance with the findings of the High Court').[32]

The second point concerns 'void' decisions, *viz* decisions which, in law, are to be regarded as having never had legal effect. In short, it might be imagined that those affected by such a decision could simply ignore it. However, the fact that a decision is *potentially* void does not in itself prevent its full implementation until the moment when it is contested. This is called the presumption of validity and it is very important to the functioning of the administrative state because it allows

---

27 [2010] 2 AC 534. For commentary see C Forsyth, 'The Rock and the Sand: Jurisdiction and Remedial Discretion' [2013] 18 *Judicial Review* 360.

28 The legislation, which was made on the basis of the United Nations Act 1946, was the Terrorism (United Nations Measures) Order 2006 (SI 2006/2657) and the Al-Qaida and Taliban (United Nations Measures) Order 2006 (SI 2006/2952).

29 [2010] 2 AC 534, 690, para 8.

30 The Terrorist Asset-Freezing Act (Temporary Provisions) Act 2010 and the Terrorist Asset-Freezing Act 2010.

31 As substituted by the Tribunals, Courts and Enforcement Act 2007, s 141.

32 And compare, in Northern Ireland, the Judicature (Northern Ireland) Act 1978, s 25.

decisions to have immediate practical effects without having to wait for a time limit for challenging the decision to pass. Moreover, it should be noted that, if potentially void decisions are left unchallenged they will, after a lapse of time, be regarded as valid law. If one chooses to ignore a decision that has not been challenged, one therefore does so at one's own peril.

18.3.2 Prohibiting order (formerly *prohibition*)

Prohibiting orders have historically served to restrain public bodies from acting in a way that is, or would be, unlawful, for instance in circumstances where an individual knows in advance that an illegal decision is to be taken. Otherwise, the nature of the remedy is such that it may be requested in tandem with a quashing order as, to the extent that the quashing order renders the original decision void, prohibition can issue to prevent the respondent making the same decision in the future. The prohibiting order is now also regarded as indistinguishable from a mandatory order and an injunction,[33] as all three remedies can require a respondent to do, or not to do, anything in relation to the issues before the court. As with quashing orders, the remedy is coercive and a failure to observe it may be regarded as a contempt of court.[34]

Examples of cases in which the remedy has been granted include *R v Kent Police Authority, ex p Godden*.[35] Prohibition here issued against a police authority to stop a doctor determining a case of compulsory retirement because the doctor may already have formed a concluded view of the matter. In another well-known case, *R v Liverpool Corporation, ex p Liverpool Taxi Fleet Operators' Association*,[36] prohibition was issued when the city council went back on a public undertaking not to license any further taxi cabs. In the specific context of the case, the remedy was used to prevent the relevant committees and sub-committees from acting on the resolutions and issuing any further licences. The remedy also served to force the committees to consider the matter afresh and, in so doing, required them to recognise that they had given a binding undertaking that could be overridden only by some imperative public interest.

18.3.3 Mandatory order (formerly *mandamus*)

The mandatory order is also a coercive remedy and, as outlined above, it has the effect of requiring the decision-maker to perform a public—usually a statutory— duty. The coercive nature of the order again entails that a failure to comply with it may be a contempt of court and that the respondent may be punished by means of, for instance, a fine. In earlier case law, it was thought that the individual who wished to obtain the remedy should first have to demand that the authority perform the duty and that proceedings could follow only where the authority refused to do so.[37] However, the so-called 'demand and refusal' requirement has featured

---

33 *M v Home Office* [1994] 1 AC 377, 415, Lord Woolf.
34 Ibid.
35 [1971] 3 All ER 20.
36 [1972] 2 QB 299.
37 For a judicial survey see *The State (Modern Homes (Ireland) Ltd v Dublin Corp* [1953] IR 202, 213–16.

less prominently in the modern case law, and its relevance may for that reason be doubted.

Mandatory orders are granted infrequently in the case law and they tend to issue where there is only one course of action lawfully open to the decision-maker. Where a duty entails the exercise of discretion on the part of the decision-maker, the courts will therefore typically consider that a mandatory order would be inappropriate. Although the extent of any discretion is, at the same time, a matter for judicial interpretation of the relevant statute,[38] the courts consider that the existence of discretion militates against the mandatory order as a remedy. The corresponding rationale is of the need to observe the constitutional limits to the judicial role, as it is perceived that a mandatory order could result in the courts dictating how a particular choice should be made.[39] The judicial concern for restraint will thus be at its highest where proceedings relate to 'target duties' in respect of public services like policing, healthcare, housing, child protection, and road safety:[40] while the imposition of duties here reflects the social imperative of providing services to members of society, the courts are aware that decision-makers may have to make value judgements and that the courts should, for reasons of relative expertise, be slow to intervene in the decision-making process.[41]

Nevertheless, there are examples from the case law of mandatory orders being made. For instance, it will be recalled from chapter 11 that a mandatory order (then *mandamus*) was made in *Padfield v Minister of Agriculture* to compel the minister to exercise his discretion lawfully and without frustrating the policy of the statute.[42] Another example is *R v Camden London Borough Council, ex p Gillan*,[43] where the council was found to be in breach of its statutory duty under the Housing Act 1985 to deal with applications for homelessness. The homeless persons unit was open only from 9.30 to 12.30 on weekdays, and applications had to be made by telephone. Financial constraints caused by rate capping were not accepted as mitigating this failing, and *mandamus* was granted against the authority, together with a declaration.

18.3.4 **Injunctions**

An injunction is an order that requires a party to proceedings either to act or not to act in a particular way (it may thus be mandatory or prohibitory in form and, for that reason, is sometimes said to be indistinguishable from *mandamus* and *prohibition*). The remedy is coercive,[44] may issue at any time in proceedings, and may be interim or final.[45] Interim injunctions are granted in accordance with the 'balance

---

38 On 'duties' and 'discretion' see 8.4; and on the importance of statutory interpretation see 11.2.

39 See *R v Secretary of State for Employment, ex p Equal Opportunities Commission* [1992] 1 All ER 545, 560, Nolan LJ.

40 On which duties see 8.4 and 11.5.1.

41 See further, e.g., *R (McDonald) v Kensington and Chelsea RLBC* [2011] 4 All ER 881 and *R v Gloucestershire County Council, ex p Barry* [1997] AC 584, discussed at 11.5.1.

42 [1968] AC 997; and 11.4.1.

43 (1988) 21 HLR 114.

44 *M v Home Office* [1994] 1 AC 377.

45 See, e.g., *Bradbury v Enfield London Borough Council* [1967] 3 All ER 434, where the remedy was granted to local ratepayers to prevent the changeover from selective to comprehensive education, despite the fact that it was argued that this would cause administrative chaos in schools.

of convenience' test that is associated with private law[46] but which is applied in a modified form in public law proceedings to the extent that the courts take account of the public interest.[47] Final injunctions, in turn, issue only where the grounds for review have been made out and where the court considers in its discretion that the remedy should be granted. Once granted, a final injunction is definitive of the rights of the parties and a subsequent failure to act in accordance with it may be regarded as a contempt of court.[48] The contempt principle also applies where an injunction is granted against a Minister of the Crown.[49]

The position in relation to Ministers of the Crown deserves some further comment, as we have already mentioned in the introduction that it was previously thought that section 21 of the Crown Proceedings Act 1947 precluded the courts from granting such relief in 'civil proceedings'.[50] The matter was eventually resolved by a line of case law that began with the *Factortame* litigation and ended with the House of Lords ruling in *M v Home Office*.[51] It will be recalled that the *Factortame* case concerned the impact of the Merchant Shipping Act 1988, which imposed UK nationality requirements on the owners of vessels registered under the Act. A number of Spanish fishing boat operators contended that this provision was contrary to various provisions of EU law and they sought an interim injunction to prevent the Secretary of State for Transport enforcing the statute pending the outcome of the case. The House of Lords initially held that section 21(2) of the Crown Proceedings Act 1947 precluded the grant of interim relief and, moreover, that the granting of the remedy in this case would have the effect of suspending an Act of the sovereign Parliament.[52] However, it was further argued by the applicants that the denial of a remedy would amount to a failure to observe the supremacy of EU law and the corresponding requirement that individuals should enjoy effective protection of their EU law rights. Given the point, the House of Lords referred the matter to the Court of Justice of the European Union (CJEU), which held that EU law rights should enjoy effective protection and that any rule of national law that prevented such protection should be set aside.[53] In *R v Secretary of State for Transport, ex p Factortame Ltd (No 2)*[54] the House of Lords thus overruled its earlier decision and held that injunctive relief was available against the minister. An in-road into section 21—and the sovereignty of Parliament—had been made in a case falling under the European Communities Act 1972.

M v Home Office then extended the remedy into non-EU law cases.[55] In *M*, an asylum seeker was deported by the Home Office before the judicial process had been exhausted, notwithstanding an apparent assurance from counsel for the Home Office

---

46 *American Cyanamid Co v Ethicon Ltd* [1975] AC 396.

47 *R v Secretary of State for Transport, ex p Factortame Ltd* (No 2) [1991] AC 603, 672–3, Lord Goff. And see, e.g., *R v Ministry of Agriculture, Fisheries and Food, ex p Monsanto plc* [1999] 2 WLR 599.

48 *M v Home Office* [1994] 1 AC 377.

49 Ibid.

50 Section 21(2) reads: 'The court shall not in any civil proceedings grant any injunction or make any order against an officer of the Crown if the effect of granting the injunction or making the order would be to give any relief against the Crown which could not have been obtained in proceedings against the Crown.'

51 *M v Home Office* [1994] 1 AC 377.

52 *Factortame Ltd v Secretary of State for Transport* [1990] 2 AC 85.

53 Case C-213/89, *R v Secretary of State for Transport, ex p Factortame Ltd* [1990] ECR I-2433.

54 [1991] 1 AC 603.

55 [1994] 1 AC 377. On its extension to Scottish law see *Davidson v Scottish Ministers* (2006) SC (HL) 41.

that this would not happen. The assurance in question had been necessary because of the perceived effect of section 21 of the Crown Proceedings Act 1947 but, when the matter came before the House of Lords, it was held that injunctions could also be granted in non EU law cases. Some of the reasons for this finding have already been outlined above in the introduction—that is, judicial review proceedings are not 'civil proceedings' within the meaning of section 21—and Lord Woolf, giving the lead judgment of the House, also held that section 31 of the Supreme Court Act 1981 (now Senior Courts Act 1981) gave the courts necessary jurisdiction. This left the matter of contempt, where it was held that, if a minister acted in disregard of an injunction made against him in his official capacity, the court had the jurisdiction to make a finding of contempt of court. This could not be punitive, but an order of costs could be made to underline the significance of the contempt. However, Lord Woolf also stated that this jurisdiction should be exercised only in exceptional circumstances. In that sense, the judgment perhaps leaves the ultimate power of sanction with Parliament, while at the same time emphasising that ministers are subject to the rule of law administered by the courts. It also makes clear that the courts will seek to ensure equal protection of an individual's rights, whether those are found in EU law or domestic law.[56]

One last point about injunctions concerns the special role played by the Attorney General, who is sometimes described as the 'guardian of the public interest'.[57] In broad terms, the Attorney General acts in an *ex officio* and independent capacity to ensure the upholding of certain public rights and interests, including preventing public bodies from taking *ultra vires* action. For example, if a magazine were to be established for the purpose of promoting terrorism, the Attorney General might act on behalf of the public to enforce the law under the relevant legislation and to close it down. Likewise, this power to resort to injunctions may be exercised if a public authority commits an unlawful act, such as creating a public nuisance, which does no special damage to any private person. Moreover, the Attorney General can either act on his own initiative or, alternatively, he can authorise a private citizen to proceed in so-called 'relator proceedings', in which case the Attorney General remains only the nominal plaintiff.[58] In other instances, a power to initiate proceedings on much the same basis as might be done by the Attorney General is exercisable by local authorities acting in the interests of the 'inhabitants of their area'.[59]

18.3.5 **Declarations**

The declaration, deriving from the Court of Chancery and the common law Court of Exchequer, is a very wide-ranging remedy that has been developed in public law largely during the last 100 years or so.[60] In general terms, it has the effect of stating the law based on the facts before the court, thereby clarifying the legal position between the parties to the action. The remedy in that way sets out the respective rights

---

56 On the case see further 3.3.4.

57 *R v DPP, ex p Manning* [2001] QB 330, 343, Lord Bingham.

58 See, e.g., *Attorney General v Manchester Corporation* [1906] 1 Ch 643 and, most famously, *Gouriet v Union of Post Office Workers* [1978] AC 435 (in which the Attorney General did not give his consent for a relator action).

59 Local Government Act 1972, s 222 and, e.g., *Stoke-on-Trent City Council v B & Q (Retail) Ltd* [1984] AC 754.

60 For guidance on when it should issue see *R v DPP, ex p Camelot* (1998) 10 Admin LR 93 and *R v Medicines Control Agency, ex p Pharma Nord Ltd* [1998] COD 315.

of the parties without directly affecting those rights, and it is for that reason that the courts often prefer to grant a declaration rather than, for instance, a quashing order and/or a mandatory order. Moreover, in contrast to the other remedies, the declaration is non-coercive and a failure to act in accordance with it will not give rise to a question of contempt of court. However, a declaration to the effect that a decision-maker has acted or would act illegally should prompt the decision-maker to modify its position. In the event that the decision-maker continues to act contrary to the established legal position, a further coercive remedy may thus be sought.[61]

The courts generally adopt a flexible approach to the granting of declarations,[62] which can perform many different functions. For instance, they can be used to confirm that administrative orders and notices are invalid, or to clarify issues of taxation, or for determining matters of marital status and nationality. To take some well-known examples from the case law, a declaration was obtained in *Vine v National Dock Labour Board*[63] in relation to invalid dismissals; and in *Agricultural, Horticultural and Forestry Industry Training Board v Aylesbury Mushrooms*[64] a declaration stated that bye-laws were *ultra vires* and therefore not binding. The willingness of the courts to grant declarations instead of other remedies can also be seen in some other well-known cases. For instance, we have already observed in chapter 8 that the court in *R v Felixstowe Justices, ex p Leigh*[65] was prepared to grant a declaration in a situation where a quashing order/*certiorari* was refused, and in another well-known case, *R v Independent Broadcasting Authority, ex p Whitehouse*,[66] Mrs Whitehouse was given standing as a TV licence holder to seek a declaration in respect of the (now defunct) Independent Broadcasting Authority's performance of its statutory duty. Indeed, the flexibility of the judicial approach has been at its most marked in cases where it has not been deemed necessary to identify a particular decision of a public body that is challenged as *ultra vires*. Declarations have thus been granted in order to provide guidance in contentious areas of law, for example where there were concerns about the legal position of nurses who have participated in, or may participate in, the termination of pregnancies.[67] In another case, *Gillick v West Norfolk and Wisbech Area Health Authority*,[68] the applicant, who had teenage daughters, sought a declaration in respect of the validity of a circular about contraception that had been issued by the Department of Health and Social Security.

The courts are, however, concerned that they should not strain the separation of powers doctrine, and the terms of declarations will sometimes reflect that fact. For instance, in *Bibi*,[69] a legitimate expectation case that we discussed at 15.4, the Court of Appeal varied the terms of a declaration that had been made by the High Court for the reason that it came too close to dictating how choices about the allocation of housing resources should be made. The courts are also cautious about allowing the declaration to be used in a purely advisory way, that is, where there is no live issue between the parties (so-called 'advisory declarations'). Although

---

61 As in, e.g., *Webster v Southwark London Borough Council* [1983] QB 698.

62 *R v DPP, ex p Camelot* (1998) 10 Admin LR 93.

63 [1957] AC 488.

64 [1972] 1 All ER 280.

65 [1987] QB 582; and 8.10.1.

66 *The Times*, 4 April 1984.

67 *Royal College of Nursing v DHSS* [1981] AC 800.

68 [1986] AC 112.

69 *R(Bibi) v Newham London Borough Council* [2002] 1 WLR 237.

the courts will not decline to hear a case where it raises a point of broader public importance[70]—something that will often be true of appeals heard by the appellate courts—there can still be a reluctance to hear cases that raise solely academic questions or those that are hypothetical. This is simply because the courts do not wish to become a forum of convenience for parties who are interested in obtaining clarity about points of law that may never give rise to disputes in practice.[71]

18.3.6 Damages

We have already noted above that damages are available as a remedy in judicial review proceedings, albeit that they are rarely awarded by the courts.[72] The basic rule is that they will be granted only where the facts that give rise to the claim for judicial review would also sustain a cause of action in private law, for instance for negligence, trespass to the person, breach of statutory duty, and so on (claims may also be appended for damages under the European Communities Act 1972 and/or the Human Rights Act 1998). The legal principles applied within these causes of action are generally at one with those that apply in damages claims between two private parties, although there are some differences within the public authority case law and there is, moreover, one cause of action that can be taken solely against public bodies (the tort of misfeasance in public office). We examine the corresponding case law and legal principles in chapters 19 and 20.

However, one point that we would emphasise here is that damages claims will, in any event, often be taken outside of the judicial review procedure and that this will typically provide a much more effective means of gaining redress. This is because claims for damages will often be very fact-specific and require courts to reach their own conclusions on facts and to apply the law accordingly. As we know from chapter 12, this is not something to which the judicial review procedure lends itself, as the courts will often accept findings of fact made by other decision-makers when assessing the legality of their conclusions. When we state that damages are rarely available in judicial review proceedings, this should therefore not be taken to mean that the courts are opposed to the award of damages as a point of principle. The absence of damages is, instead, an outworking of the nature of the judicial review procedure and its emphasis on questions of legality rather than fact-finding.

18.4 Remedies and the European Communities Act 1972

It will be remembered from chapter 3 that section 3 of the European Communities Act 1972 requires UK courts to give effect to the remedies case law of the CJEU in cases that come under the Act.[73] That body of case law, which has been developed

---

70 *R v Secretary of State for the Home Department, ex p Salem* [1999] 1 AC 45.

71 *Vince v Chief Constable of Dorset Police* [1993] 1 WLR 415.

72 On the availability of the remedy see, e.g., in England and Wales, the Senior Courts Act 1981, s 31(4).

73 'For the purposes of all legal proceedings any question as to the meaning or effect of any of the Treaties, or as to the validity, meaning or effect of any Community instrument, shall be treated as a question of law (and, if not referred to the European Court, be for determination as such in accordance with the principles laid down by and any relevant decision of the European Court)'.

on the basis of the supremacy and direct effect doctrines,[74] imposes significant remedial obligations on national courts that are hearing disputes involving EU law rights. Although the CJEU has long emphasised that EU law rights are to be protected through national procedures and practices—subject to the requirement that the protection is effective and equivalent to that given to rights under national law[75]—it has since also introduced a number of specific remedies requirements that have sought to heighten the standards of protection that are given to individuals.[76] The most notable example in the context of UK law of course remains that of the *Factortame* case that we discussed above and which resulted with injunctions becoming available in proceedings involving Ministers of the Crown.[77]

Otherwise, there are two further points to note about EU law's remedies regime and judicial review. The first concerns the discretionary nature of the remedies, as discussed above. Until recently, influential judicial comments had suggested that the remedies could not be regarded as discretionary in EU law cases as to hold otherwise would undermine the essence of the doctrine of the supremacy of EU law.[78] However, the Supreme Court has since addressed the matter in the important case of *Walton v The Scottish Ministers* and held that relief need not always be granted, even in EU law cases.[79] As we have already explained in chapter 8, the case involved a (statutory) challenge to the lawfulness of ministerial approval for the construction of a road network outside Aberdeen, which was argued to have been granted in breach of consultation requirements imposed by EU law (specifically by the Strategic Environmental Assessment (SEA) Directive).[80] When the case came before the Supreme Court the main issues on appeal were: (i) whether the applicant had standing to bring the proceedings; (ii) whether the SEA Directive was of application in the case; and (iii) whether the applicant should be denied a remedy even if the SEA Directive did apply. Holding that the applicant did have standing but that the SEA Directive was not engaged on the facts, the Supreme Court made clear that remedies need not always be granted in EU law cases and that the courts can refuse relief where, for instance, an applicant has suffered no substantial prejudice as a result of a procedural error but where the broader public interest or some private interest would be disadvantaged by the grant of a remedy. In that circumstance, the Supreme Court was of the view that a remedy may be withheld in the discretion of the court and that this would be wholly consistent with EU law's emphasis on national procedural autonomy and the related principle of the 'effective' protection of EU law rights. As Lord Carnwath expressed the point:

---

74 Case 26/62, *Van Gend en Loos v Nederlandse Aministratie der Belastingen* [1963] ECR 1; Case 6/64, *Costa v ENEL* [1964] ECR 585; and Case 106/77, *Amministrazione delle Finanze dello Stato v Simmenthal SpA* [1978] ECR 629.

75 See, e.g., Case 33/76, *Rewe-Zentralfinanz eG and Rewe-Zentral AG v Landwirtschaftskammer für das Saarland* [1976] ECR 1989; Case 47/76, *Comet v Produktschap voor Siergewassen* [1976] ECR 2043; and Case 158/80, *Rewe Handelsgesellschaft Nord mbH v Hauptzollamt Kiel* [1981] ECR 1805.

76 See P Craig and G de Búrca, *EU Law: Text, Cases and Materials*, 6th edn (Oxford: Oxford University Press, 2015), ch 8.

77 Case C-213/89, *R v Secretary of State for Transport, ex p Factortame Ltd* [1990] ECR I-2433; *R v Secretary of State for Transport, ex p Factortame Ltd (No 2)* [1991] 1 AC 603.

78 Most notably in *Berkeley v Secretary of State for the Environment* [2001] 2 AC 603, 616, Lord Hoffmann.

79 [2012] UKSC 44, [2013] 1 CMLR 28; and 8.10.1.

80 Directive 2001/42/EC.

Where the court is satisfied that the applicant has been able in practice to enjoy the rights conferred by the European legislation, and where a procedural challenge would fail under domestic law because the breach has caused no substantial prejudice, I see nothing in principle or authority to require the courts to adopt a different approach merely because the procedural requirement arises from a European rather than a domestic source.[81]

The other point concerns damages. As we explained in chapter 3, it is possible to claim damages under the European Communities Act 1972 when the facts of a case satisfy the elements of the 'state liability' doctrine.[82] Little would be gained from considering the elements of that doctrine again in this chapter, and we would simply note that, where an individual wishes to claim damages, he or she will ordinarily do so through the tort of breach of statutory duty.[83] The elements of that tort are discussed in chapter 20.

18.5 Remedies and the Human Rights Act 1998

We turn, in this final section, to consider remedies under the Human Rights Act 1998. As we have already noted in chapter 4, the Act seeks to give domestic effect to most of the rights in the European Convention on Human Rights (ECHR) while leaving unsettled the UK constitution's emphasis on the sovereignty of Parliament.[84] In terms of remedies, the Act thus sub-divides between those provisions that enable the courts to grant binding relief to individuals who make out an argument of illegality in a particular case (sections 6–8) and those that do not permit of binding relief because of the absence of a domestically recognised illegality (principally section 4 and 'declarations of incompatibility').[85] In practice, a clear majority of cases will fall under sections 6–8, and the courts will decide whether there has been, or would be, an illegality and, if so, whether a remedy should issue. However, it is also possible for judicial review cases to raise issues under both sets of provisions, and the remedies granted by the court may therefore be a mixture of those with legal effect and those without.[86] Other cases may simply fall under the provisions that do not have binding legal effect where the legal position of the parties will remain unaffected unless and until Parliament changes any legislation at issue.

18.5.1 Binding remedies

The starting point in respect of binding remedies is section 6(1), which makes it unlawful for a public authority to act in a manner which is incompatible with the

---

81 [2012] UKSC 44, [2013] 1 CMLR 28, para 139. See further, e.g., *R (Champion) v North Norfolk DC* [2015] UKSC 52, [2015] 1 WLR 3710.

82 See, most famously, Cases C-46 and 48/93, *Brasserie du Pêcheur SA v Germany, R v Secretary of State for Transport, ex p Factortame Ltd* [1996] 1 ECR 1029.

83 *R v Secretary of State for Transport, ex p Factortame (No 7)* [2001] 1 CMLR 1191.

84 See, in particular, 4.4.

85 See, too, s 6(2).

86 See, e.g., *A v Secretary of State for the Home Department* [2005] AC 68—Anti-terrorism, Crime and Security Act 2001, s 23 declared incompatible with the ECHR, and the Human Rights Act 1998 (Derogation Order) 2001 quashed. See further 4.4.3 and 13.6.3.1.

ECHR rights contained in the Act.[87] Although we have suggested in chapters 4 and 9 that the term 'public authority' has been given an unduly narrow interpretation by the courts,[88] section 6 is intended to allow individuals to enforce their rights against the state and all of its manifestations (subject to the facts that give rise to any proceedings post-dating the Act's coming into force on 2 October 2000).[89] Section 7 on this basis provides that a person who claims that a public authority has acted or proposes to act in a way which is made unlawful by section 6(1) may rely upon the ECHR in proceedings so long as he or she is, or would be, a 'victim' of the unlawful act. Where those proceedings are in the form of a claim for judicial review, section 7(3) provides that the applicant is to be taken to have a 'sufficient interest' in relation to the unlawful act only if he or she is, or would be, a victim of the act.[90]

Section 8 is the key provision on the binding remedies and it provides that, 'In relation to any act (or proposed act) of a public authority which the court finds is (or would be) unlawful, it may grant such relief or remedy, or make such order, within its powers as it considers just and appropriate'. In the context of judicial review proceedings, this means that each of the remedies discussed above—quashing order, declarations, and so on—are at the disposal of the court in cases under the Human Rights Act 1998. However, while those remedies are traditionally regarded as discretionary, it is important to remember that any decision about whether to refuse relief under the Human Rights Act 1998 must be reached in the light of the case law of the European Court of Human Rights (ECtHR). This is because sections 2 and 8 of the 1998 Act require courts to 'take into account' all relevant ECHR case law in proceedings before them, including that on remedies. We would thus suggest that remedies might safely be refused in cases of illegality under sections 6–8 only where there is ECHR authority to support that conclusion. Any other outcome would surely run contrary to the ECtHR's understanding that the ECHR 'is intended to guarantee not rights that are theoretical or illusory but rights that are practical and effective'.[91]

We would lastly note that damages are also available under section 8, which requires a court to grant that remedy where it is satisfied that the award is necessary to afford 'just satisfaction' to the person in whose favour the award is to be made (the term 'just satisfaction' corresponds directly with the language of Article 41 of the ECHR that allows the ECtHR to award damages).[92] In determining the necessity of any award, the court must take account of all the circumstances of the case, including any other relief or remedy granted, as well as the principles that guide the Strasbourg Court when it is deciding whether to award damages.[93] We return to the corresponding case law of the courts in chapter 20.

---

87 In Sch 1.

88 As in *YL v Birmingham City Council* [2008] 1 AC 95.

89 Sections 7 and 22. But see *Re McCaughey* [2011] 2 WLR 1279 and *Keyu* [2015] 3 WLR 1665; and 4.4.6.

90 On the victim requirement and the corresponding concept of 'sufficient interest' see 8.10.3.

91 *Airey v Ireland* (1979) 2 EHRR 305, 316, para 26.

92 Article 41 ECHR reads: 'If the Court finds that there has been a violation of the Convention of the protocols thereto, and if the internal law of the High Contracting Party concerned allows only partial reparation to be made, the Court shall, if necessary, afford just satisfaction to the injured party.'

93 See further *R (Greenfield) v Home Secretary* [2005] 1 WLR 673 and, e.g., *R (Sturnham) v Parole Board* [2013] UKSC 23, [2013] 2 AC 254.

18.5.2 **Declarations of incompatibility**

The desire to leave the doctrine of parliamentary sovereignty unsettled by the reception of the ECHR is of course most evident in section 4, as read with the Act's section 3 interpretive obligation.[94] It will be recalled that the combined effect of these provisions is that a court should try 'so far as it is possible to do so' to interpret legislation that interferes with rights in a manner that is compliant with the ECHR but that, where such interpretation is not possible and the legislation is primary legislation, the court may make a declaration that the relevant provision or provisions of the legislation are incompatible with the ECHR (the courts that may make declarations are listed in section 4(5) and, for our purposes, are essentially the High Court, Court of Session, and above; it has been emphasised on several occasions that the courts have a discretion whether to grant a declaration of incompatibility).[95] That the doctrine of legislative supremacy is to remain unaffected by the Act is apparent from section 4(6), which provides that a declaration '(a) does not affect the validity, continuing operation or enforcement of the provision in respect of which it is given; and (b) is not binding on the parties to the proceedings in which it is made'. Primary legislation in that way remains sovereign and it is for Parliament to choose whether to repeal or amend the legislation or to leave it in force.

Sometimes, declarations of incompatibility may also be made in respect of subordinate legislation and, where they are made, this is a further outworking of the doctrine of legislative supremacy.[96] Although it is implicit in sections 3 and 4 of the Act that subordinate legislation that is incompatible with the ECHR may be struck-down as *ultra vires*, section 4(4) makes an exception where the legislation has been 'made in the exercise of a power by primary legislation' and 'the primary legislation concerned prevents removal of the incompatibility'. Under those circumstances, the courts may merely make a declaration that the subordinate legislation is incompatible with the ECHR and it is for Parliament to decide whether to repeal or amend the legislation or to leave it in force. The doctrine of legislative supremacy similarly underlies section 6(2) of the Act, which affords public authorities a defence where they were required to act in a particular way as a result of primary legislation.[97]

18.6 **Conclusion**

This chapter has described the remedies that are available at the end of a claim for judicial review and, given that they mark the terminus of proceedings, we can perhaps use the conclusion to this chapter to offer some reflective comments about judicial review as a whole. Certainly, it will be evident from the previous chapters

---

94 On which see 4.4.2 and 4.4.3.

95 See, e.g., *R (Chester) v Secretary of State for Justice* [2013] UKSC 63, [2014] AC 271, 303, para 39, Lord Mance, and *R (Nicklinson) v Ministry of Justice* [2014] UKSC 38, [2015] AC 657.

96 Primary and subordinate legislation are defined in s 21 of the Act.

97 For judicial analysis see *R (Hooper) v Secretary of State for Work and Pensions* [2006] 1 All ER 487 and *Manchester City Council v Pinnock (Nos 1 & 2)* [2011] 2 AC 104. See also *R (GC) v Metropolitan Police Commissioner* [2011] 1 WLR 1230, 1249–50, paras 67–8, Baroness Hale.

that judicial review has performed an increasingly important role since the 1960s and that it has helped to ensure more effective control of government at the local, devolved, and central levels. However, it will also be apparent that this is just one part of the story of judicial review and, indeed, that it is perhaps only a small part of that story. Another narrative would hold that access to judicial review in terms of obtaining a final, effective remedy is limited and that the procedure has much less impact than the seminal cases would suggest. To take some of the requirements that must be satisfied along the way: the claimant must be sure that judicial review is the appropriate procedure (the public–private divide and effective alternative remedies); he or she must have standing; he or she must be able to satisfy the court that one or other of the grounds for judicial review has been made out; and he or she must be able to convince the court, in its discretion, to grant one or more of the remedies that we have discussed above. Add to that the fact that a remedy may have only limited value—a decision-maker may return to the matter and make substantially the same decision again—and the story of judicial review becomes a very different one.

That said, it is always to be remembered that judicial review can be analysed not just from the perspective of the individual claimant but also from the perspective of the wider community. Although, on the face of it, a claim for judicial review will often affect only the claimant, the issues raised before the court may sometimes have implications for society as a whole or for large sections of it. In those circumstances, a decision in favour of an individual could well have consequences for other members of the community and may serve indirectly to deny them some benefit that they might otherwise have obtained. In that instance, the court must attempt to balance the interests of the individual with those of the community, while remaining aware of the constitutional limits to its supervisory role. It is perhaps for that reason that there is merit in retaining discretionary remedies in judicial review rather than having those that should issue as of right.

FURTHER READING

Bingham, Sir T [1991] 'Should Public Law Remedies be Discretionary' *Public Law* 64.

Cane, P (1997) 'The Constitutional Basis of Judicial Remedies in Public Law', in Leyland, P and Woods, T (eds), *Administrative Law Facing the Future: Old Constraints and New Horizons* (London: Blackstone Press).

Forsyth, C [2013] 'The Rock and the Sand: Jurisdiction and Remedial Discretion' 18 *Judicial Review* 360.

Horne, A [2007] 'The Substitutionary Remedy under CPR 54.19(3): A Final Word' 2007 *Judicial Review* 135–8.

Kolinsky, D [1999] 'Advisory Declarations: Recent Developments' *Judicial Review* 225.

19

··

Contracting and public bodies

19.1 Introduction

This chapter will consider the legal position in regard to the contracting powers of the Crown and other government bodies. It is an accepted constitutional principle that the government should be subjected to the ordinary law of contract. As was discussed in a previous chapter, the Crown is a generic term that is used to refer to persons or bodies exercising powers which historically were the monarch's personal powers.[1] Now it is applied to the executive branch of government.[2] Contracts are actually entered into by Crown servants as agents acting on behalf of the Crown itself. It has been established that officials responsible for negotiating contracts on behalf of a government department are not personally liable under contract because it is the principal (the department) and not the agent (the official) who is responsible. Even where the office of minister has been created under common law rather than statute, he or she appears not to have a separate contracting capacity. Rather, the minister will possess an equivalent power to the Crown and is capable of making valid contracts, indicating to the other party that any contract made by a minister in a public capacity binds the Crown. The decision in *Town Investments Ltd v Department of Environment*[3] established the principle that the Crown and ministers are non-divisible. This is because the minister as the head of a department, is responsible for all of the activities of his or her department.

Until 1947, a petition of right was required to recover damages from the Crown. This could be for the recovery of a debt or for a liquidated sum due under a contract and for damages for a breach of contract. However, a general right to sue the Crown under contract was provided by section 1 of the Crown Proceedings Act 1947:

Where any person has a claim against the Crown after the commencement of this Act, and if this Act had not been passed, the claim might have been enforced, subject to the grant of His Majesty's fiat, by petition of right . . . then, subject to the provisions of this Act, the claim may be enforced as of right, and without the fiat of His Majesty, by proceedings taken against the Crown for that purpose in accordance with the provisions of this Act.

---

1 See 5.1.1.

2 For an analysis of changes in the nature and conception of the Crown see M Freedland, 'The Crown and the Changing Nature of Government' in M Sunkin and S Payne (eds), *The Nature of the Crown* (Oxford: Oxford University Press, 1999).

3 [1978] AC 359. But compare *M v Home Office* [1994] 1 AC 377, which drew a distinction between the Crown and its officers in the context of the remedies available on application for judicial review. See further 18.3.4.

This provision removed the need to obtain the leave of the Attorney General to bring an action against the Crown, and thus it dispensed with the most irksome procedural obstacle to taking such actions. Today, therefore, in most respects the Crown is treated in the same way as any other defendant, that is, to initiate an action against the Crown a litigant sues the department concerned or the Attorney General. It should also be noted that the Unfair Contract Terms Act 1977 applies to the Crown and other public authorities. This legislation invalidates any contractual terms which exclude or restrict liability for negligence or for breach of contract. However, while acknowledging that the Crown is exposed to general proceedings in the courts, it should be emphasised that, in practice, it is rare for disputes involving government contracts to give rise to litigation (see 19.2.2 and 19.2.3).

19.2 Government power to contract

Modern governments possess extensive powers to enter into many different types of contractual arrangements, and these powers will be most important and sensitive when they concern the policy-making process.[4] In the course of their operations ministers and civil servants 'may make promises, conclude contracts, acquire and dispose of property, acquire and disseminate information, make and receive gifts, form companies, set up committees and agencies, and perform a wide variety of other functions within the policy process'.[5] In some instances, legislation may be piloted that directly imposes obligations in the pursuit of policy objectives. The Timeshare Act 1992 is a well-known example that introduced qualifications to the law of contract in order to prevent abuses affecting the public at large concerning the sale of holiday 'timeshare' apartments. Another example is the Tobacco Advertising and Promotion Act 2002, which banned the advertising of tobacco products. Pursuing a different approach, governments have also avoided the need to legislate to enforce their incomes policies by inserting pay control observance clauses in all government contracts. Yet another strategy is when ministers draw up voluntary agreements with industry to regulate certain forms of activity. An example here—dating from the nineteenth century—is fair wages agreements that were introduced to combat sweated labour.

Governments have also exercised their wide contracting powers in the public sector to achieve ulterior policy purposes. A noteworthy example of this was a scheme for a less economically developed region, where the award of contracts was turned into a device to combat high unemployment in a designated area. However, whatever the motive, this kind of approach may also amount to a non-accountable means of favouring one interest over others.[6] Indeed, contracts have been entered into by government which indirectly undermine the principle of 'parliamentary sovereignty'. The doctrine (as expounded by Dicey) suggests that Parliament is

---

4 For discussion of the powers of central government see 8.2.

5 T Daintith, 'The Techniques of Government' in J Jowell and D Oliver (eds), *The Changing Constitutiton*, 3rd edn (Oxford: Oxford University Press, 1994), 211.

6 e.g., the use of government contractual powers for 'collateral' purposes: see P Cane, *Administrative Law*, 5th edn (Oxford: Oxford University Press, 2011), 226ff.

incapable of binding its successors (subject to certain exceptions),[7] but in some areas contracts have been awarded which may, in effect, tie up the functioning of particular services/organisations for many years in the future. This makes it extremely difficult, if not impossible, for an incoming government of a different political complexion to extricate itself from the consequences by repealing legislation that included such provisions. The Labour Government elected in 1997 faced the serious ramifications that would be caused by breaking or renegotiating the contracts that were set in place by its predecessor. Rail privatisation serves as a useful example. The Office of Passenger Rail Franchising, established by the Conservative Government under the Railways Act 1993 to sell off the railway network to the private sector, awarded franchises lasting from seven to 15 years; and private companies bidding for franchises were required to commit considerable sums of money to upgrading the system in the expectation of future profitability. It should be noted that the Department of Transport has since taken over this function of the Strategic Rail Authority (which earlier took over franchising from the Office of Passenger Rail Franchising). The Department is now directly responsible for awarding rail franchises.[8] In addition, it is worth remembering that the Private Finance Initiative (PFI) is a form of public–private partnership which has been regarded by successive governments as an important method for improving the quality and cost-effectiveness of public services. It enlists the skills and expertise of the private sector in providing public services and facilities. For example, in the health sector this involves the private firms building hospitals and then leasing them back to the health service.[9]

19.2.1 **Standard form contracts**

It has been pointed out above that a general freedom to contract applies to government. But although a contract entered into by the government is recognised from the standpoint of enforceability in the same way as its private sector counterpart, large-scale contracts for the procurement of goods or services usually incorporate standard sets of conditions which have been developed specifically for government contracts. These conditions are useful in establishing a degree of uniformity between different departments. For example, there are distinct sets of terms that have been developed for contracts concerning construction and supply. The *laissez-faire* approach, which might be considered part of our Diceyan legacy, has resulted in no superior status for public law powers of contracting; but although these powers of the Crown (in reality the government) are the same as for other individuals, in practice the courts will often be reluctant to intervene in the substance of government contracts. This is overwhelmingly because procurement contracts are likely to raise policy issues which will be regarded as unsuitable for resolution by courts and also because the standard terms within government contracts usually make special provision for dispute resolution through arbitration procedures. As part of the 'Best Value' initiative,[10] central government in its National Procurement Strategy set local government key targets for e-procurement with the

---

7 See chs 2–4.
8 See the Railways Act 2005.
9 See 5.4.1.
10 See 5.6.2.5.

objective of achieving efficiencies in the procure-to-pay cycle, including reduction in cycle time and reduction in transaction costs. The government's aim was to free resources which were to be directed into front line public services. The Labour Government's Transforming Government Procurement 2007 initiative stated that:

Good procurement means getting value for money—that is, buying a product that is fit for purpose, taking account of the whole-life cost. A good procurement process should also be delivered efficiently, to limit the time and expense for the parties involved. Successful procurement is good for the public, good for the taxpayer, and good for businesses supplying the government.[11]

The objective was to establish a common framework for procurement across government, albeit that the levels of government spending has been greatly reduced in recent years.

19.2.2 EU law and government procurement

The UK public sector spent £242 billion on the procurement of goods and services in 2013/14 which comprised 33 per cent of all public sector spending.[12] Under EU economic law, which is intended to establish a single market and promote free and fair competition with respect to government contracting, there are strict rules that are applied to procurement contracts of public authorities above a certain value.[13] Ministers of the Crown, government departments, both Houses of Parliament, local authorities, and police and fire authorities are all designated contracting authorities to which public contracts regulations apply. To meet the criteria, these public authorities have to inform the EU authorities, who, in turn, have a role in advertising the contract, and resulting bids must be considered objectively by the authority concerned. Central to much of the procurement process, now, are the Public Contracts Regulations 2015 and the Utilities Contracts Regulations 2016 (these implement requirements of EU law as apply in the fields of public contracts and utilities contracts, respectively).[14] A novel feature of these regulations is the *competitive dialogue procedure*, which allows public authorities to enter into dialogue with bidders before seeking final tenders. Further clarification on social and environmental issues is among other key features of the EU's regulatory regime. The current regime also has modernising features that are intended to simplify procurement procedures and reduce the amount of red tape. The Public Contract Regulations 2015, mentioned above, implement many of these changes as part of UK domestic law,[15] while the Small Business, Enterprise and Employment Act 2015 places

---

11 <http://www.hm-treasury.gov.uk/d/government_procurement_pu147.pdf>.

12 HM Treasury, Public Spending Statistics: April 2015 release.

13 See L Booth, 'Public Procurement' Briefing Paper, No 6029, 3 July 2015, House of Commons Library. For examples of some of the earliest secondary legislation by which EU Directives have previously been implemented, see the (now repealed) Public Works Contracts Regulations 1991 and the Public Supply Contracts Regulations 1995.

14 The regulations are published as SI 2015/102 and SI 2016/274.

15 Directive 2014/24/EU of the European Parliament and of the Council of 26 February 2014 on public procurement and repealing Directive 2004/18/EC; Directive 2014/25/EU of the European Parliament and the Council of 26 February 2014 on procurement by entities operating in the water, energy, transport and postal services sectors repealing Directive 2004/17/EC; Directive 2014/23/EU of the European Parliament and of the Council of 26 February 2014 on the award of concession contracts.

duties on public sector contracting bodies in terms of how they conduct procurement with small businesses.

19.2.3 **Government and Parliament**

Powers to contract are ultimately subject to the consent of Parliament or limited by specific Acts of Parliament. Crown servants enter into contracts, provided they fall within the statutory authority, which will, in turn, be binding on the Crown. Any expenditure will be sanctioned by Parliament when the Appropriation Acts are passed. In general, the government does not need authority from Parliament to authorise specific payments to contractors. However, exceptionally, Parliament has affected the validity of a contract by intervening to refuse funding. This was the situation in *Churchward v R*,[16] which concerned the position when the government entered into a binding contract that was made subject to Parliament voting sufficient funds for the agreement to be honoured. The Admiralty had arranged for the carriage of mails by Churchward, but the continuation of the agreement depended on the availability of a sum of £18,000. After several years had passed, Churchward's services were no longer used by the Admiralty, but Parliament voted expressly not to pay over the outstanding sum. In effect, this was to renege on an agreement which still had seven years until its termination. The court held that, in circumstances where there was such a clause, the government was not bound by the agreement because the funds had not been made available by Parliament before the existence of the contract.

The *Churchward* decision focuses on the extent to which control might be exercised by Parliament over public finance. In a general sense, it is a fundamental principle that government procures money from Parliament through the Appropriation Acts for the public finances, but it should be emphasised that the appropriation of funds by Parliament is not a condition precedent for any contract involving the government. In *New South Wales v Bardolph*,[17] an Australian authority, it was indicated that even if the funds were not made available, a valid contract would have been formed in situations comparable to that in *Churchward*. However, it would also appear that such a contract might prove to be unenforceable as payment would be dependent on the availability of funds from Parliament. On the whole, the present position is that such funding is obtained on a general basis and amounts are not normally designated except under broad categories of expenditure. Government contractors therefore have no need to be overly concerned about government reneging on its contractual obligations. Indeed, litigation of the type that arose in *Churchward* is now extremely unusual.

19.3 **Fettering discretion**

How far can the government fetter its own future freedom of executive action by entering into a contract?

---

16 (1865) LR 1 QB 173.
17 (1934) 52 CLR 455.

19.3.1 **Public policy defence/the *Amphitrite* principle**

First, there may be exceptional circumstances where it is deemed in the public interest for the government to fail to honour its contractual obligations. This will depend on taking an assessment of the wider public interest. The important case of *Rederiaktiebolaget Amphitrite v The King*[18] established that the government cannot fetter its future executive action by any contract that it enters into when there are overriding public interest considerations at stake. The *Amphitrite* case arose out of a policy that had been adopted during the First World War. A Swedish company had been given an express undertaking that if its ship, *The Amphitrite*, landed a cargo of approved goods at a British port, it would be able to leave. This was despite the fact that the assurance amounted to an exception to a policy whereby neutral ships were prevented from sailing from British ports unless replaced by other ships of the same tonnage. In any event, *The Amphitrite* was detained for a long period and the ship eventually had to be sold to minimise losses by the company. The parent company then sought damages for breach of contract against the Crown. Rowlatt J reached the conclusion that in the circumstances there was no enforceable contract because the government could be bound only by a commercial contract and this amounted to an arrangement involving assurances in respect of future executive action. It was 'merely an expression of intention to act in a particular way in a certain event' ([1921] 3 KB 500, 503). Rowlatt J appeared to be making a distinction between contracts of a purely commercial kind that would be enforceable, and other contracts, involving the state, where there is some overriding state interest that may make the contract unenforceable. He held that the government could not fetter its discretion in respect of any future executive action and thereby hamper its freedom of action in matters concerning the welfare of the country.

How far does this rule of executive necessity elaborated in the *Amphitrite* case extend? The answer would appear to be not very far. For example, it certainly does not apply to ordinary commercial contracts. In fact, in *Robertson v Minister of Pensions*,[19] Denning J made it very clear that the *Amphitrite* doctrine would apply only when there was an implied term to this effect. It may therefore be that *Amphitrite* is best seen as a case that is almost limited to its facts—a war-time case in which it was self-evident that the national interest in executive freedom was engaged.

19.3.2 **Fettering discretion by contract**

It is unlawful for a public body to fetter a discretion conferred by statute by entering into a contract. Lord Birkenhead set out the basic principle in *Birkdale District Electricity Supply Co v Southport Corporation* when he stated 'that if a person or public body is entrusted by the legislature with certain powers and duties expressly or impliedly for public purposes those bodies or persons cannot divest themselves of these powers and duties. They cannot enter into a contract or take any action incompatible with the due exercise of their powers or duties'.[20] This means that a public body cannot enter into a contract where the terms of the contract conflict with the exercise of a power conferred by statute. It is quite possible that this

---

18 [1921] 3 KB 500.
19 [1949] 1 KB 227.
20 [1926] AC 355, 364.

would prevent a body from lawfully exercising a discretion in the way intended by Parliament and, at the same time, it may be contrary to the public interest. The same rule applies to bye-laws and grants of planning permission. Such a contract will be unlawful and held to be invalid.[21]

19.4 **Judicial accountability**

Despite the evident deficiencies in our system, it is important to recognise that there are circumstances in which the courts will intervene with regard to the new regime of contracting in the provision of public services. It has been pointed out that: 'If those powers were free of judicial review the zone of immunity surrounding the exercise of government powers would substantially increase.'[22] In common with other justiciable issues, this will primarily depend on whether the claimant has standing to seek a remedy, and upon which side of the public–private law divide a decision is deemed to fall.[23]

There is remaining uncertainty in this area, something that is well illustrated by *R v Lord Chancellor, ex p Hibbit & Sanders*.[24] Here a firm of shorthand writers, which had provided a service since 1907, challenged a decision by the Lord Chancellor's department to award a contract for the provision of court shorthand writers to another firm. This was following invitations to tender for the service. The court regarded the procedures adopted by the department as being unfair; however, it considered that there was an insufficient public law element at the tendering stage. It was observed that the department was not required to obtain statutory authority for its actions and the decision was not regarded as a matter of policy. Thus the matter was held to fall outside the scope of judicial review. In France, by contrast, the pre-contractual stage of government contracting is subject to strict procedural requirements and is not beyond the scope of review.[25] Under the common law, then, there is no established approach which allows the courts to oversee the process of competitive tendering, except when this falls within existing domestic or European legislation.[26]

19.5 **Void contracts**

The courts have intervened when public authorities have entered into contracts which result in them going beyond the limits of their statutory powers. In *Crédit Suisse v Allerdale Borough Council*,[27] it was held that an interest rate swap transaction

21 The case law on fettering discretion by contract is examined in more detail at 12.4.

22 S De Smith, H Woolf, and J Jowell, *Judicial Review of Administrative Action* (London: Sweet and Maxwell, 1995), 315.

23 The decision in *R v Panel on Takeovers and Mergers, ex p Datafin plc* [1987] 1 All ER 564 and the test for determining which side of the public–private divide an issue will fall is analysed at some length at 9.2.2.

24 [1993] COD 321.

25 See N Brown and J Bell, *French Administrative Law* (Oxford: Oxford University Press, 1998), 202ff.

26 As explained at 19.2.1 and 19.2.2.

27 [1996] 3 WLR 894.

was void and this therefore made the recovery of damages impossible.[28] The case concerned a local council which wished to provide a swimming pool amenity under section 19 of the Local Government (Miscellaneous Provisions) Act 1976, but which, in order to finance the scheme, needed a device to circumvent restrictions on local government borrowing set out in the Local Government Act 1972. With the object of sidestepping these controls, the council set up a company to develop the site. Furthermore, the building of a swimming pool was linked to the construction of 'timeshare' units which were designed as part of the same complex. The company obtained loan guarantees of up to £6 million from the bank. However, the project proved unsuccessful because the timeshare units failed to sell. As a result the company set up by the council went into liquidation and the bank sought to recover its money from the council.

It was held by the Court of Appeal, in a private law action for recovery of the monies, that the provision of timeshare units exceeded the powers of the council under section 19(1) (it was said that the council merely had the power to provide recreational facilities). The Court also held that the plan to set up the company was part of a composite scheme designed to circumvent Schedule 13 of the Local Government Act 1972 which comprehensively defined and limited the authority's powers of borrowing. Given these findings, it followed that one of the parties to the scheme (namely the council) had lacked capacity to enter into the contract; that the contract between the bank and the company was a nullity; and that the bank had no means of recovery against the council in respect of these loan guarantees. Hobhouse LJ declared that:

Private law issues must be decided in accordance with the rules of private law. The broader and less rigorous rules of administrative law should not without adjustment be applied to the resolution of private law disputes in civil proceedings . . . When the activities of a public body, or individual, are relevant to a private law dispute in civil proceedings, public law may in a similar way provide answers which are relevant to the resolution of the private law issue. But after taking into account the applicable public law, the civil proceedings have to be decided as a matter of private law. The issue does not become an administrative law issue; administrative law remedies are irrelevant.[29]

It is an established principle that the other party to an agreement which is a nullity has no right to recover damages under the law of contract. However, it is clearly unsatisfactory that the matter was treated simply as a private law question, entirely overlooking any public interest dimension. The implications are potentially far-reaching in several senses. In the first place, this might be considered against the background of the dilution of Lord Diplock's exclusivity principle in *O'Reilly v Mackman*.[30] The exceptions to the rules of procedural exclusivity have become wide, with the result that this matter ended up in the ordinary courts (rather than under the application for judicial review procedure). Thus the authority concerned escaped from any public law consequences of what had been regarded in the High Court to be *ultra vires* action by the authority.

It is apparent that public law principles of judicial review concentrate on controlling the unlawful exercise (or abuse) of power, while private law principles are

---

28 See also *Hazell v Hammersmith and Fulham London Borough Council* [1992] AC 1 and also the Local Government (Contracts) Act 1997.

29 [1996] 3 WLR 894, 938.

30 [1983] 2 AC 237. See 8.7.

directed at a narrow determination of the obligations and duties of the parties to an action. Nevertheless, it is difficult to justify an approach that divorced issues from their context by adopting a narrow legalistic analysis. In *Crédit Suisse* this, in effect, allowed the public authority to walk away from its obligations not only to the bank, but to the community as a whole, simply because the rights and duties were considered only in relation to a contract. However, this also created the unwelcome possibility that public authorities that were acting in good faith in the future might find that lenders would be reluctant to enter into contracts with them if they thought that the contract would be unenforceable. To guard against that, Parliament enacted the Local Government (Contracts) Act 1997, section 2 of which allows local authorities to enter into 'certified' contracts that will be legally binding even if the authority had acted *ultra vires* in a public law sense.

19.6 **Restitution and public authorities**

Restitution is a possible remedy that was applied, controversially, in *Hazell v Hammersmith and Fulham London Borough Council*,[31] when the contracts were declared invalid. A claim of restitution can be made when an applicant has paid money to a public authority either under demand but where the demand lacks legal authority, or where the contract has been held to be *ultra vires* and therefore void. Essentially, restitution applies in situations where, rather than attempting to obtain an award of damages, an individual or body is seeking the return of money that has been wrongly paid over to a public body.

In what circumstances will a remedy be available against a public authority when the authority has made some charge or rate that turns out to be *ultra vires*? How far should this question be treated under the principles of ordinary law? It is not unusual for public authorities to act voluntarily in repaying any disputed funds. However, *Woolwich Equitable Building Society v Inland Revenue Commissioners*[32] has been regarded as a 'revolutionary decision' that has removed some of the barriers to recovering damages against public authorities when unlawful demands have been made.[33] In addition, the case serves as an example of the intervention of the common law to enforce a remedy against a public authority that has made a demand without lawful authority. A new public law rule has been established. The facts of the *Woolwich* case were that the Woolwich Building Society paid designated sums of money 'without prejudice' to the Inland Revenue Commissioner (IRC) while disputing its tax liability. Judicial review proceedings were subsequently instituted to challenge the regulations under which the claim for tax had been paid and these were found by the court to have been *ultra vires*. The Revenue subsequently repaid the money, but with interest only from the time of the court order and not from when the money was originally paid. An action was then brought against the IRC for the lost interest of £6.7million. The court had to decide whether the IRC were right in maintaining that no interest was payable because the society had not been liable to pay the tax, that is, the money had been handed over voluntarily.

---

31 [1992] 2 AC 1.
32 [1993] AC 70.
33 W Wade and C Forsyth, *Administrative Law*, 11th edn (Oxford: Oxford University Press, 2013), 679.

The case ultimately hinged on the interpretation by the House of Lords of the principles of the law of restitution. On the one hand, if it can be established that money is paid over by duress or compulsion, it is recoverable. On the other hand, when funds are paid over by mistake of law no remedy is available. The error in this situation was not attributable to the building society but originated in the Revenue's demand. Lord Goff considered that the retention by the state of taxes that had been unlawfully levied was obnoxious and contrary to the principles established under the Bill of Rights of 1688 and 'as a matter of common justice . . . unsustainable' (see [1993] AC 70, 172).

The approach to restitution in the *Woolwich* case was extended by the House of Lords in *Kleinwort Benson Ltd v Lincoln City Council*,[34] which again concerned appeals arising from interest swap agreements that had been considered valid at the time, but were held on final appeal to be *ultra vires*, and therefore void. The bank appealed to the House of Lords to determine: (a) whether the mistake of law rule precluding a restitutionary claim for money paid under a mistake of law should be maintained; and (b) whether a change in a rule of settled law by judicial authority would allow recovery. The House of Lords decided by a majority of 3:2 to depart from established principle and held that the mistake of law rule was no longer part of the law of restitution. Their Lordships further held that money paid under a settled understanding of law was recoverable. For the majority Lord Goff of Chieveley cited German and French law, as well as New Zealand statutory provisions, when holding that 'the importance of this comparative material is to reveal that, in civil law systems, a blanket recovery of money paid under a mistake of law is not regarded as necessary' (see [1999] 2 AC 349, 375). The decision was controversial. It dispensed with a bad rule (unanimously criticised by their Lordships), but it did so without dealing with the far-reaching implications that this change would have, leading to much commercial uncertainty. Indeed, the dissenting judgments of Lords Browne-Wilkinson and Lloyd of Berwick argued that fundamental alterations in the law of this kind should be the subject of primary legislation.[35]

19.7 Conclusion

We have seen in this chapter that the government is able to enter into binding contracts in the normal way, subject to certain limited exceptions. Moreover, as part of the performance of its routine functions, government enters into many agreements for the supply of goods and services (e.g., procurement contracts). However, if we view this issue against the background of the evolving nature of the contemporary state discussed in chapter 5, it becomes apparent that contracts and contracting, in both formal and informal ways, have become a particularly important feature of the way government conducts its activities. For example, first, with the formation of Next Steps agencies, a type of non-enforceable contract, referred to as a framework agreement, was used to

---

34 [1999] 2 AC 349.

35 For related case law see *R v East Sussex County Council, ex p Ward* (2000) 3 CCLR 132 and *Deutsche Morgan Grenfell Group v Commissioners of the Inland Revenue* [2007] 1 AC 558.

reformulate the internal arrangements of government. This included setting out responsibilities for the carrying out of policy. Secondly, a central concern of public sector management has been to achieve continuous improvement in measurable efficiency, and at many levels types of contract have been used to set out the parameters and conditions of service delivery. Thirdly, many functions which used to be performed by government and local government are now undertaken by private sector companies. In this situation formal binding contracts are employed to determine the precise nature of the services that are provided. However, these developments raise an altogether broader question, namely, whether exposure to private law liability in the form of damages is appropriate when it comes to the provision of certain kinds of public services. Should public bodies be subject to liability, or should the process of contracting allow them to place certain activities beyond the reach of the routine mechanisms of accountability and control?

FURTHER READING

Arrowsmith, S (1992) *Civil Liability of Public Authorities* (London: Earlsgate Press).

Arrowsmith, S (1996) *The Law of Public and Utilities Procurement* (London: Sweet & Maxwell).

Arrowsmith, S (2012) 'The Purposes of the EU Procurement Directives: Ends, Means and the Implications for National Regulatory Space for Commercial and Horizontal Procurement Policies' *Cambridge Yearbook of European Legal Studies*, 14.

Boyron, S and Davies, A (2011) 'Accountability and Public Contracts' in Noguellou, R and Stelkens, U (eds), *Treatise on the Comparative Law of Public Contracts* (Brussels: Bruylant).

Burrows, A (2011) *The Law of Restitution*, 3rd edn (London: Sweet & Maxwell).

Daintith, T (1994) 'The Techniques of Government' in Jowell, J and Oliver, D (eds), *The Changing Constitution*, 3rd edn (Oxford: Oxford University Press).

Davies, A (2001) *Accountability: A Public Law Analysis of Government by Contract* (Oxford: Oxford University Press).

Davies, A (2008) *The Public Law of Government Contracts* (Oxford: Oxford University Press).

Freedland, M [1994] 'Government by Contract and Private Law' *Public Law* 86.

Freedland, M [1998] 'Public Law and Private Initiative—Placing the Private Finance Initiative in a Public Law Frame' *Public Law* 288.

Freedland, M (1999) 'The Crown and the Changing Nature of Government' in Sunkin, M and Payne, S, (eds), *The Nature of the Crown* (Oxford: Oxford University Press).

Halliday, P [2007] 'Restitution and Public Bodies: Overview and Update' *Judicial Review* 178.

Harden, I (1992) *The Contracting State* (Buckingham: Open University Press).

McCrudden, C (2007) *Buying Social Justice: Equality, Government Procurement and Legal Change* (Oxford: Oxford University Press).

Neill, J [2012] 'Procurement Challenges and the Scope of Judicial Review '*Judicial Review* 61.

Rawlings, R (2008) 'Poetic Justice: Public Contracting and the Case of the London Tube' in Pearson, L, Harlow, C, and Taggart, M (eds), *Administrative Justice in a Changing State* (Oxford: Hart Publishing).

Virgo, G [2006] 'Restitution from Public Authorities: Past Present and Future' *Judicial Review* 370.

20

Public authority liability in tort

20.1 Introduction

Public authorities are, *in general*, liable in tort in exactly the same way as any private individual. This means that public authorities can be sued in negligence, nuisance, trespass, etc, and also that they can bring proceedings in tort (the position in respect of the Crown was different but was aligned in large part by the Crown Proceedings Act 1947). This position follows from the historical fact that the Diceyan conception of the rule of law did not distinguish between 'public' and 'private', but preferred instead to subject all classes equally to the ordinary law of the land.[1] Where a claimant wishes to sue another party it should in theory therefore not matter whether the defendant is a public authority or private individual, as the same legal principles will govern the action. Claims for personal injury resulting from a road accident with a vehicle owned by a public authority provide an obvious such example.

   The advent of the modern administrative state and the corresponding emergence of the public–private divide have, however, complicated the issue of public authority liability in some areas.[2] This is particularly true where a public authority is given discretion under a statute to decide how to perform a public function. We will look much more closely at specific examples later, but decisions that would involve exercises of discretion typically include the provision of care services for abused children, the provision of special educational needs programmes, and the improvement of road safety. The issue of liability under such circumstances becomes complex because an individual who has suffered loss as a result of a decision cannot obtain damages as a public law remedy, but must rather make out an action in private law.[3] However, even within the framework of private law proceedings the courts have often reasoned in ways that reflect upon public law considerations and they have emphasised that the broader public interest is sometimes served better where public authorities performing public functions are not readily made liable in damages. The result is a body of case law that is doctrinally complex and unpredictable.[4]

---

1 On the rule of law see 2.7.

2 On the public–private divide see 8.7.

3 For proposed changes to the law—not yet acted upon—see the Law Commission paper, *Administrative Redress: Public Bodies and the Citizen*, critiqued in T Cornford, 'Administrative Redress: The Law Commission's Consultation Paper' [2009] *Public Law* 70.

4 See R Buckley, 'Negligence in the Public Sphere: Is Clarity Possible?' (2000) *Northern Ireland Legal Quarterly* 25.

The analysis in this chapter begins with an outline of some of the main torts that may affect public authorities that are performing public functions, and how public law concepts have been factored into judicial reasoning. It then focuses in more detail on case law on public authority liability in negligence. Negligence has been the area in which the courts have most frequently emphasised that there is a wider public interest in limiting liability, and this is something that has, at its most extreme, resulted in *de facto* immunity from liability for certain categories of decisions. While these lines of case law have since been moderated by common law developments and the European Convention on Human Rights (ECHR), the underlying judicial reasoning remains important. Courts hearing negligence actions are essentially faced with a number of questions about their own institutional role and the relationship between public law and private law concepts. For instance, how far should the courts seek to offer a remedy to an individual who has suffered loss as a result of a decision, and how far should they seek to protect public authorities—which have only finite resources and are financed by the taxpayer—from liability? (The fear here is that damages awards may have a negative impact on a public authority's service delivery by causing decision-makers to develop, as a priority, the need to avoid liability.) Moreover, where a decision is based on a statutory discretion and an award of damages is made, does this mean that the courts have thereby interfered with the exercise of a power that Parliament has given to an authority? Should damages never be awarded under such circumstances, or should they only be awarded where a decision is also *ultra vires* in a public law sense? Or is it possible for damages to be awarded for a decision that causes loss in a private law sense yet is at the same time lawful in public law terms (*intra vires*)?

There are, as we shall see, no easy answers to such questions and the courts continue to grapple with the need to balance the competing interests. One distinction that will be seen to be of importance in the context of negligence actions is that between 'policy' and 'operational' decisions. Although the distinction has been much criticised[5] and is no longer used by the courts in its original terms, the distinction reflects the understanding that there are certain types of choices that the courts should never enquire into; or, in the language of tort law, assess with a view to liability. We will thus see that the courts have historically emphasised that 'policy' decisions cannot give rise to liability, as such decisions are non-justiciable in the sense that they are not suited to the judicial process.[6] Policy decisions are typically associated with questions of resource allocation, for example, about how many new social workers a local authority should train and employ in a financial year. The reason for not allowing such decisions to give rise to possible liability is that judicial interference here—in the form of an award of damages—would create unforeseen difficulties for the process of local government. However, where a social worker employed by a local authority makes a negligent decision about the welfare of a child, this type of act will move much closer to what was formerly called the 'operational' side of the distinction. It is in this category of case that the challenge for the courts is at its most pronounced.

---

5 SH Bailey and MJ Bowman,'The Policy/Operational Dichotomy—A Cuckoo in the Nest' (1986) 45 *Cambridge Law Journal* 430.

6 There are overlaps here with judicial review case law on economic policy choices as at the very outer-reaches of judicial control: see ch 13 for discussion of super-*Wednesbury* review and, e.g., *R v Secretary of State for the Environment, ex p Nottinghamshire County Council* [1986] AC 240.

20.2 Public authority liability: the principal torts

20.2.1 Negligence

Negligence actions are taken where harm is caused to a person (or persons) by the acts or omissions of another party, whether the harm is in terms of personal injury (including psychiatric injury), damage to property, or economic loss.[7] To bring a successful action in negligence there are three elements that must be satisfied:

(1) that the defendant owed the claimant a common law duty of care;

(2) that the defendant breached the duty of care; and

(3) that the breach of the duty of care caused the loss complained of.

There are many reported cases where individuals have successfully sued public authorities for negligence and these accord with the Diceyan principle outlined above. Some examples include *Cassidy v Ministry of Health*[8] (where surgeons at a hospital under the control of the Ministry of Health treated a man's hand in such a way as to render it useless); *Hughes v Lord Advocate*[9] (where post office workers failed properly to cover a manhole, and a young child fell in and was burned by a lamp that exploded); and *Kent v Griffiths*[10] (where an ambulance was unjustifiably late in responding to an emergency call and a patient suffered severe complications as a result of the delay).

The elements of the action that have seen the 'grafting-on' of public law considerations when cases have concerned the exercise of statutory discretion are the 'duty of care' and 'breach' requirements. We will consider the case law in more detail below, but it is helpful at this stage to outline how the courts have approached the elements, in particular the duty of care. Common law duties of care are owed where:

(1) the defendant should foresee that his or her act or omission will harm the claimant;

(2) there is a sufficient relationship of proximity between the parties; and

(3) it is fair, just, and reasonable to impose a duty of care.[11]

Each of these requirements is malleable in the sense that courts must apply them in the light of the variable facts of individual cases, and it is this flexibility that has allowed the courts to factor in wider public law considerations. The leading example of such use of the requirements remains *X v Bedfordshire County Council*, albeit that the House of Lords ruling on some of the issues before it has since been distinguished.[12] This was a case that concerned, among other things, questions about a local authority's failure to take appropriate measures to protect young children from abuse, for instance by not initiating proceedings to take them into care

---

7 See C Witting, *Street on Torts*, 14th edn (Oxford: Oxford University Press, 2015), chs 2–6; although note that omissions are legally different from positive acts, on which see *Gorringe v Calderdale MBC* [2004] 1 WLR 1057.

8 [1951] 2 KB 343.

9 [1963] AC 837.

10 [2001] QB 36.

11 *Caparo Industries v Dickman* [1990] 2 AC 605.

12 [1995] 2 AC 633. But see also *Jain v Trent Strategic Health Authority* [2009] 1 AC 853.

(there were also conjoined claims in respect of education services). In finding that there could be no liability Lord Browne-Wilkinson reasoned that it would not be 'fair, just and reasonable' to impose a duty of care. This limitation was because decisions about child protection are governed by a complex statutory framework and that findings of liability 'would cut across the statutory system set up for the protection of children at risk', thereby further complicating an already 'extraordinarily delicate' task and potentially causing local authorities to 'adopt a more cautious and defensive approach to their duties'.[13] Moreover, his Lordship reasoned that decision-makers in such cases endeavour to provide a public good and that courts 'should proceed with great care before holding liable in negligence those who have been charged by Parliament with the task of protecting society from the wrongdoing of others'.[14]

The manner in which the breach element incorporates public law principles can be seen in the way some judges have alluded to *Wednesbury* unreasonableness as the standard that might be used when deciding whether an authority's decisions have been negligent. Courts, when assessing breach, typically consider whether the actions of the defendant fell below those standards that would have been expected of the reasonable person, if faced with the same circumstances.[15] While the 'reasonable person' test is meant to be of general application, the courts have recognised that certain types of cases—for instance medical negligence cases—require a modified test that is context sensitive (use is therefore made of what is in effect a 'reasonable practitioner' test in medical cases).[16] In *Barrett v Enfield London Borough Council*[17]—another case concerning alleged local authority failings *vis-à-vis* an abused child—Lord Hutton suggested that, where the issue is whether a public authority has acted reasonably in the exercise of its statutory discretion, courts should again display caution. Emphasising that there will be 'room for differences of opinion as to the best course to adopt in a difficult field and that the discretion is to be exercised by the authority and its social workers and not by the court', his Lordship concluded that a court 'must be satisfied that the conduct complained of went beyond mere errors of judgment in the exercise of a discretion and constituted conduct which can be regarded as negligent'.[18] This would appear to imply that, even where a duty of care is owed, final liability will depend on the authority's decision having approached something that is unreasonable in a public law sense (although note that *Wednesbury* exists on a sliding scale).[19]

However, an important case in which it was found that a public authority had breached its duty of care is *Connor v Surrey County Council*.[20] The claimant in this case had been employed by the Council as the head teacher of a multicultural school in which a majority of students were Muslim. In 2003, a newly elected parent governor began to complain that there were insufficient links between the school and the local community and that this was because the claimant was racist and Islamophobic. Relations between the claimant and the parent governor

---

13 [1995] 2 AC 633, 749–50.

14 [1995] 2 AC 633, 751.

15 *Blyth v Birmingham Waterworks Co* (1856) 11 Ex 781.

16 See *Bolam v Friern Hospital Management Committee* [1957] 1 WLR 582 and *Bolitho v Hackney Health Authority* [1997] 3 WLR 1151.

17 [2001] 2 AC 550.

18 Ibid, 591.

19 See 13.3.3.

20 [2011] QB 429.

became increasingly fraught and personalised, and this inevitably had a highly negative impact on the workings of the school's governing body, on staff morale, and on the health of the claimant. Through time, the claimant had to stop work because of ill-health caused by the allegations made against her, and she brought proceedings in which she argued that the Council should have used its statutory powers under the Schools Standards and Framework Act 1998 to replace the governing body and that, by failing to do so, it had breached its duty of care and caused the claimant psychiatric harm (the Council intervened in the governing body only after the claimant had left work). It was common ground in the case that the Council owed a duty of care given the employer–employee relationship, so the Council contended that the argued breach had involved the exercise of statutory discretion and that it was therefore non-justiciable. However, the Court of Appeal disagreed on the facts and held that the claimant was entitled to damages for the harm she had suffered. Noting the pre-existing duty of care, the Court held that, where the only or primary means of meeting a pre-existing duty of care was through the exercise of discretion, the Council could be required to exercise that discretion in appropriate circumstances so long as this did not create any inconsistency with the performance of other public law duties. On this basis, the Court held that the Council should have intervened at an earlier stage to replace the governing board and that there was no corresponding public law duty that could justify its failure to have done so. As a result it had breached its common law duty of care.

Connor is clearly a very important ruling, although we would make two cautionary comments about its significance. The first is that, as there was a pre-existing duty of care, the court was able to move directly to the question of breach. The case is, in that way, very different from most of the cases that we consider below, where the issue has been whether a common law duty of care has been owed within the framework of statute. The second point is that the Court of Appeal itself noted the unique facts of *Connor* and indicated that the judgment did not mark any fundamental shift in the law. The facts of the case truly were disturbing, as the claimant was subjected to an offensive, aggressive, and defamatory campaign of intimidation. As Laws LJ expressed it:

This is an unusual case, partly because of the council's lamentable capitulation to aggression . . . It is of first importance to recognise that the [findings of the court] are only justified by the specific place in the whole extraordinary history of events . . . I wish for my part, therefore, to stress that the result of this case offers nothing remotely resembling a vade mecum for others in the future to build private law claims out of what may be sensitive and difficult decisions, including policy decisions, of public authorities.[21]

20.2.2 **Breach of statutory duty**

An action for breach of statutory duty is similar in form to an action in negligence, although the duty owed to the individual originates from the statute rather than the common law (the claimant must again also demonstrate breach and causation). The answer to the question of whether a statutory duty is owed to a particular claimant, thereby founding a private law cause of action, depends upon

21 Ibid, 473.

judicial interpretation of the relevant legislation. In some instances, for example in the context of health and safety at work, the existence of a duty will be evident from a literal reading of the statute and the imposition of liability will be uncontroversial.[22]

The issue becomes more complex when an action is brought in respect of a duty under what may be termed social welfare legislation; that is, legislation that requires an authority to provide a service that can be associated with wider conceptions of the public interest (note that such duties often still entail an element of discretion and are sometimes called 'target' duties).[23] The leading authority is, again, *X v Bedfordshire County Council*,[24] where it was argued that the decisions of the local authorities were also in breach of a statutory duty owed to the plaintiffs under various pieces of legislation (the Children and Young Persons Act 1969, the Child Care Act 1980, and the Children Act 1989). In rejecting the claim, Lord Browne-Wilkinson considered that the duties owed under the legislation were to wider society rather than specific individuals, as the legislation had created an overarching regulatory structure. It followed that the action could not be sustained as there was nothing within the Act to suggest that it was intended to give rise to private law remedies.

Two other cases illustrate an apparent concern to limit the scope of the tort. In *O'Rourke v Camden London Borough Council*,[25] the issue for the House of Lords was whether a local authority could be liable for a breach of its duty to provide housing to a homeless person under the Housing Act 1985. The House of Lords overruled earlier decisions in holding that the authority was not liable. In doing so, it construed the legislation in question as being preclusive of private law causes of action. The claimant in this case had presented himself as homeless to the local authority but, after having initially been given accommodation, he was evicted and was not re-housed. On a claim for damages it was held that there could be no liability as the legislation was intended to create a general social welfare scheme that had a corresponding remedy in applications for judicial review. Private law causes of action were not envisaged as part of that framework.

The second case—*Cullen v Chief Constable of the Royal Ulster Constabulary*[26]—concerned the relationship between the breach and causation elements of the action. The facts were that the claimant had been arrested on suspicion of involvement with terrorism but he claimed that he had been denied access to his lawyer in breach of the duty to ensure access under section 15 of the Northern Ireland (Emergency Provisions) Act 1987. While Lords Bingham and Steyn considered that the breach should *per se* be actionable because the right of access to a lawyer is a fundamental constitutional right at common law, the majority of the House of Lords disagreed. Reaffirming the requirement that all elements of the tort need to be made out, their Lordships considered that damages should not be awarded both because there had been no concrete loss to the claimant and because other remedies had been available at the time of the denial (judicial review proceedings). By adopting this approach their Lordships appeared to be preventing the emergence

---

22 See Witting, n 7, ch 19.
23 See 8.4.2 and 11.5.1.
24 [1995] 2 AC 633.
25 [1998] AC 188.
26 [2003] 1 WLR 1763.

of common law 'constitutional' torts that would allow damages to be awarded without proof of harm.

One further point that should be made under this heading concerns damages claims for the breach of an individual's rights under EU law. As we have explained in chapter 3, it is possible to claim damages under the 'state liability' doctrine, albeit that the Court of Justice of the European Union (CJEU) has long emphasised that rights are to be protected through national procedures and remedies (subject to requirements of equivalence and effectiveness).[27] Although it was initially unclear how claims for breach of EU law should be brought within the framework of national law, it is now generally accepted that the claim should be presented as breach of statutory duty.[28] The corresponding statute is the European Communities Act 1972 that gives effect to EU law.

20.2.3 Nuisance

Nuisance, which here refers to private nuisance, is solely a property tort that offers a common law cause of action to those individuals whose property is affected by the activities of another (the test is whether there has been a substantial and unreasonable interference with the claimant's property or enjoyment of the same).[29] A nuisance can affect either the physical or amenity value of a property, for example flooding and noise pollution respectively. Public authorities involved in nuisance proceedings may, depending on the facts of a case, seek to rely upon statutory authorisation for an activity. The basic principle here is that a public authority cannot be liable in tort where the injury suffered is the inevitable consequence of what Parliament has authorised[30] (although note that the position can become more complicated if the Human Rights Act 1998 governs the case).[31] Judicial interpretation of statute is also of central importance in this area and the courts have sometimes accepted that legislation by 'necessary implication' permits an authority to carry out an activity that is a nuisance.[32] However, where an individual suffers from a nuisance caused by public works, he or she may be entitled to compensation under the Land Compensation Act 1973. It is also noteworthy that, if an authority has a choice of sites for the carrying on of an activity, the courts may consider that the authority is duty bound to choose the site that causes the least interference.[33] The proportionality principle would also require that the 'least interference' option be taken if rights under the ECHR are in issue.[34]

---

27 On state liability see, most famously, Cases C-46 and 48/93, *Brasserie du Pêcheur SA v Germany, R v Secretary of State for Transport, ex p Factortame Ltd* [1996] 1 ECR 1029. And on equivalence and effectiveness see, e.g., Case 33/76, *Rewe-Zentralfinanz eG and Rewe-Zentral AG v Landwirtschaftskammer für das Saarland* [1976] ECR 1989; Case 47/76, *Comet v Produktschap voor Siergewassen* [1976] ECR 2043; and Case 158/80, *Rewe Handelsgesellschaft Nord mbH v Hauptzollamt Kiel* [1981] ECR 1805.

28 *R v Secretary of State for Transport, ex p Factortame (No 6)* [2001] 1 WLR 942.

29 See *Coventry v Lawrence* [2014] UKSC 13, [2014] AC 882. See also Witting, n 7, chs 17–18 (which also examine public nuisance and the rule under *Rylands v Fletcher* (1868) LR 3 HL 330).

30 See, e.g., *Dormer v Newcastle upon Tyne Corporation* [1940] 2 KB 204.

31 See 4.4.2 and 4.4.3 for discussion of the s 3 interpretive obligation and s 4 declarations of incompatibility under the Human Rights Act 1998.

32 See *Allen v Gulf Oil Refinery Ltd* [1981] AC 1001. But for the limits of 'necessary implication' in the analogous context of trespass to land see *Manchester Ship Canal Co Ltd v United Utilities Water plc* [2014] UKSC 40, [2014] 1 WLR 2576.

33 See *Manchester Corporation v Farnworth* [1930] AC 171.

34 See generally ch 13.

The interplay between public law and private law principles in the context of nuisance proceedings—in particular as reflects upon judicial concern about the imposition of burdens affecting the efficiency of public service provision—can be seen in the House of Lords judgment in *Marcic v Thames Water Utility*.[35] Mr Marcic's property had on several occasions been flooded with effluent as a result of structural shortcomings in the local sewage system. Thames Water Utility—a privatised company—was responsible under the Water Industry Act 1991 for the maintenance and repair of the sewage system. Mr Marcic sued Thames Water in nuisance and under the Human Rights Act, claiming that there had been a violation of his home and property rights under Article 8 and Article 1 of Protocol 1 of the ECHR, respectively. The claim was successful in the Court of Appeal, but Thames Water's appeal to the House of Lords was allowed. The House of Lords reached this decision because it recognised that the relevant statutory scheme provided a regime of remedies with the provision of an industry regulator to oversee the activities of Thames Water. It was emphasised that, as Parliament had provided for this alternative remedy, Mr Marcic should have channelled his concerns through the regulator and not pursued the matter by way of private law proceedings.[36] The House also held that the statutory scheme was ECHR compliant, as it required the regulator to balance the competing interests of individuals and the wider public in the manner envisaged by ECHR case law.

It is important to identify the rationale that underlies judgments like *Marcic*. If a finding of liability in nuisance had been upheld it would have exposed Thames Water (and other comparable operators of utility services, etc) to an ever-increasing number of claims that would fundamentally affect the company's pricing policy and the overall provision of the service.[37] However, the denial of a private law remedy in this situation raises the problematic issue of how far private individuals such as Mr Marcic should be required to carry burdens in the public interest (Mr Marcic had invested heavily in trying to protect his property). Questions may also be asked about how far the courts should seek to safeguard the interests of privatised utilities that arguably place profit margins ahead of effective public service provision.

20.2.4 Misfeasance in public office

The tort of misfeasance in public office is one that is available only against public authorities and it is used where the authority, or its officers, has, or have, acted maliciously or in bad faith. Clearly, arguments of this kind will be difficult to substantiate, but, where the argument is made out, the courts will grant a remedy to the affected individual. The leading case on the elements of the tort is *Three Rivers District Council v Bank of England (No 3)*,[38] which was an action brought by 6,000 depositors of the Bank of Credit and Commerce (BCCI) who claimed £550 million in respect of losses incurred by the collapse of the bank. It was alleged by the

---

35 [2004] 2 AC 42.

36 See also, e.g., *Barratt Homes Ltd v Dwr Cymru Cyfyngedig (Welsh Water)* [2013] 1 WLR 3486 (contrary to the scheme of the Water Industry Act 1991 to allow a nuisance action to be brought in respect of a decision wrongfully to refuse connection to public sewers under s 106 of the Act).

37 See also Lord Millett's comments in *Southwark London Borough Council v Mills* [1999] 4 All ER 449, 470 regarding the importance of not dictating the resource allocation priorities of local authorities.

38 [2003] 2 AC 1. For earlier consideration see, e.g., *Calvely v Chief Constable of the Merseyside Police* [1989] 1 All ER 1025 and *Racz v Home Office* [1994] 2 AC 45.

claimants that the Bank of England had acted improperly by granting a licence to the BCCI, but, in order to succeed, they needed to overcome the Bank of England's immunity from actions under section 1(4) of the Banking Act 1987 and prove misfeasance. Refusing to strike out the claim, the House of Lords explained how the tort is actionable where (a) the public officer has, with malice, acted or failed to act in a way that has the object of injuring the plaintiff; or (b) the public officer has intentionally done or omitted to do something that he or she did not have the power to do or to omit to do and which he or she knew would probably injure the plaintiff.[39] The House of Lords emphasised that bad faith on the part of the officer inheres in both (a) and (b), and case law since *Three Rivers* has sought to ensure that such bad faith does not escape sanction.[40] The tort is therefore a little-used but very important part of the common law's safeguards against the abuse of power.[41]

Before leaving the tort we should make two further points about it, both of which concern damages. Damages are typically intended to compensate an individual by reflecting the extent that they have suffered harm and, so far as it is possible to do so, returning him or her to the position he or she was in before the harm was suffered. However, in some circumstances the courts are willing to award exemplary/punitive damages by way signalling their displeasure with the actions of defendants, notably where those actions have been 'oppressive, arbitrary or unconstitutional'.[42] The facts that give rise to claims for misfeasance in public office may often lend themselves to just such an award.

The second point is that an action for misfeasance in public office cannot succeed where a public officer has acted in bad faith but where the individual has suffered no special damage. This is the result of *Watkins v Home Office*,[43] where the House of Lords held that a prisoner could not succeed under the tort as he had suffered no special damage when prison guards had interfered with his correspondence with his lawyer. Although the Court of Appeal in England and Wales had held that bad faith *per se* was here sufficient as the officers had interfered with the prisoner's common law constitutional right of access to a court,[44] the House of Lords held that proof of special damage had been expressly or implicitly central to the cause of action for over 300 years. Such long-standing rules, it was held, should be disturbed only where there are compelling reasons to do so, and no such reasons were present in the instant case. The House of Lords also held that a reinvention of the tort in the light of common law constitutional rights was unnecessary as plaintiffs would in the future be able to make a claim for damages under the Human Rights Act 1998 (on which see below). *Watkins* can in that sense perhaps be said to correspond with the restrictive approach to 'constitutional torts' in *Cullen v Chief Constable of the Royal Ulster Constabulary*, above.[45]

---

39 And see, e g., *Bourgoin SA v Ministry of Agriculture, Fisheries and Food* [1986] QB 716.

40 See, e.g., *Karagozlu v Metropolitan Police Commissioner* [2007] 2 All ER 1055.

41 See further C Harlow, 'A Punitive Role for Tort Law? in L Pearson et al (eds), *Administrative Law in a Changing State: Essays in Honour of Mark Aronson* (Oxford: Hart Publishing, 2008).

42 *Rooke v Barnard* [1964] AC 1129S. See also *Kuddus v Chief Constable of Leicestershire Constabulary* [2001] 3 All ER 193.

43 [2006] 2 AC 395.

44 On common law rights see 4.2.

45 But compare *Karagozlu v Metropolitan Police Commissioner* [2007] 2 All ER 1055: Court of Appeal holding that special damage for the purposes of the tort can, as argued here, include the loss of liberty that follows from a prisoner being moved from open conditions to closed. And on case law post-*Watkins*, see CJS Knight, 'Constitutionality and Misfeasance in Public Office: Controlling the Tort' [2011] 16 *Judicial Review* 49.

20.2.5 **False imprisonment**

False imprisonment is perhaps the tort that is most commonly pleaded against public bodies (it is one of several torts that cluster under the more general heading of 'trespass to the person', where other torts include assault and battery).[46] The tort of false imprisonment is committed when there is a complete restriction of a person's liberty in circumstances where the public authority has acted *without lawful excuse or authorisation*. The words in italics are key to the question of whether a cause of action will be sustained, as there will be no tort if, for instance, an individual is imprisoned after having been convicted of a criminal offence. However, if the individual's liberty is restricted without lawful excuse, he or she can seek the remedy of *habeas corpus* and sue for damages even without proof of special loss (such as financial disadvantage). This is because the liberty of the individual is regarded as so important that any interference with it will not be tolerated. The cause of action is therefore actionable *per se* and open where, for instance, there is a wrongful continuation of an imprisonment that was originally lawful.

A highly important ruling on the tort was given by the Supreme Court in the case of *R (Lumba) v Home Secretary*.[47] This was a case brought by a number of foreign nationals who had been convicted of offences in the UK and who, having served their sentences, were detained pending decisions about deportation. It later transpired that they were being detained on the basis of an unpublished policy that favoured blanket detention of persons in their position and which was inconsistent with published policy that favoured detention only where that outcome could be justified. In a lengthy judgment, the Supreme Court held that the government had thereby acted unlawfully and that it was liable for false imprisonment. However, on the question of quantum, the majority of the Court also held that the claimants should receive only nominal damages rather than any larger 'exemplary' or 'vindicatory' sum, even though the actions of the Home Office were described as 'deplorable'. This was because it was inevitable, on the facts, that the claimants would still have been detained even if decisions about them had been taken in accordance with the published policy. The ruling thus limited the financial implications for government and, in that way, complemented case law under other headings that have sought to safeguard the public interest in restrictive approaches to liability.

20.3 **Negligence, public functions, and limiting the common law duty of care**

We turn now to examine more fully the approach of the courts to negligence actions in respect of discretionary choices that underlie the performance of public functions. An important point to be made at the outset is that a public authority may have discretion both as a result of a statutory *power* to do something and as a result of a statutory *duty*.[48] Although the word 'duty' would on its face suggest that

---

46 See generally Witting, n 7, ch 9.
47 [2011] UKSC 12, [2012] 1 AC 245.
48 On powers and duties see 8.4.

an authority must act in a particular way, duties of the kind specified in social welfare schemes tend to relate to more widely drawn objectives, and legislation will give the authority a corresponding discretion as to how the duty is to be discharged (these are sometimes called 'target' duties).[49] An example duty can be found in section 17 of the Children Act 1989.[50]

The starting point in terms of understanding common law duties of care and statutory powers/duties is *Anns v Merton London Borough Council*.[51] *Anns* arose at a time when the courts were more inclined to expand the boundaries of tort liability and the House of Lords delivered a judgment that envisaged the imposition of duties of care on local authorities in some—though by no means all—cases. The legislation in question was the Public Health Act 1936. Under the Act, local authorities were responsible for overseeing building work through, for instance, approving plans and monitoring work as it progressed. It was argued in the case that the authority had been negligent in failing properly to examine the foundations for a block of flats, something that had resulted in structural damage to a number of properties. In holding that local authorities could owe duties of care in such circumstances, Lord Wilberforce introduced the policy/operational dichotomy as a means to guide the courts when assessing whether duties of care are owed:

> Most, indeed probably all, statutes contain in them a large area of policy. The courts call this 'discretion', meaning that the decision is one for the authority or body to make, and not for the courts. Many statutes, also, prescribe or at least presuppose the practical execution of policy decisions: a convenient description of this is to say that in addition to the area of policy or discretion, there is an operational area. Although this distinction between the policy area and the operational area is convenient, and illuminating, it is probably a distinction of degree; and many 'operational' powers or duties have in them some element of 'discretion'. It can safely be said that the more 'operational' a power or duty may be, the easier it is to superimpose on it a common law duty of care.

This dichotomy—which essentially sought to safeguard key decisions about, for instance, resource allocation—came to be criticised at a number of levels. A first criticism was that the distinction is often difficult to make in practice. Lord Wilberforce himself partly conceded the point, and some other judges went so far as to describe the distinction as 'inadequate'.[52] However, we will see below that the distinction still assumed a prominent place in subsequent case law and that the term 'policy' can still arise in deliberation.[53]

A second criticism was that the distinction had the potential to increase liability, something that would, in turn, have a negative impact on public service provision (the point again being that the prospect of increased liability would cause decision-makers to have, as their first concern, the need to avoid proceedings). The courts therefore moderated their approach to the imposition of duties of care in a number of ways (*Anns* itself was subsequently overtaken on its facts by the House of Lords'

---

49 See *R v Inner London Education Authority, ex p Ali* (1990) 2 Admin LR 822, 828, Lord Woolf.

50 '(1) It shall be the general duty of every local authority . . . (a) to safeguard and promote the welfare of children within their area who are in need; and (b) so far as is consistent with that duty, to promote the upbringing of such children by their families, by providing a range and level of services appropriate to those children's needs.'

51 [1978] AC 728.

52 *Stovin v Wise* [1996] AC 923, 951, Lord Hoffmann.

53 See, e.g., *Barrett v Enfield London Borough Council* [2001] 2 AC 550, considered below.

ruling in *Murphy v Brentwood District Council*).[54] One means by which liability was limited was by classifying decisions as 'policy' and thereby non-justiciable.[55] And a further means was through the restrictive application of the legal requirements that predetermine the existence of duties of care. Duties of care, as outlined above, are imposed only where there is a sufficiently proximate relationship between the claimant and defendant, and this is a requirement that can be applied flexibly and in a manner that allows courts to give effect to their own value judgements. One of the most striking examples of a court using the proximity requirement in this way was *Hill v Chief Constable of West Yorkshire*.[56] This case arose when the family of one of the victims of a serial killer known as 'the Yorkshire Ripper' sued the police in respect of a number of errors that had been made during the course of the investigation into the Ripper's murderous activities. In finding that no duty was owed, the House of Lords emphasised, first, that there was insufficient proximity of relationship between the police and the individual as a member of the general public (the police had had no prior knowledge of who the victim would be), and their Lordships also emphasised that the prospect of liability in such cases would in any event lead to defensive policing and to a diversion of resources (a public policy argument). This decision thus drew attention not only to a more general concern about the efficiency of public service provision but it also established a forceful precedent by providing an influential line of judicial reasoning. Indeed, the precedent was so strong that the Court of Appeal later held in *Osman v Ferguson* that no duty arose even where there was an arguable proximity of relationship between the parties.[57] The facts, in this instance, were that the police had earlier spoken both to the eventual perpetrator of a crime and to the resulting victims of that crime. However, while the case could for that reason have been distinguished on the proximity point, the Court of Appeal followed the public policy point that had been emphasised in *Hill*. No duty was owed in the result.[58]

20.3.1 *X v Bedfordshire County Council*: statutory duties and the common law duty of care

It is against the backdrop of these judicial concerns that the judgment by the House of Lords in *X v Bedfordshire County Council*[59] can be examined. The case, as outlined above, concerned the exercise of discretion by a local authority in the context of decision-making about the welfare of abused children (the case was conjoined with a number of other 'abuse' appeals, as well as several concerned with decisions about the provision of education services). Each of the cases had been struck out at first instance on the ground that they disclosed no reasonable cause

---

54 [1991] 1 AC 398.

55 See, e.g., *Rowling v Takaro Properties Ltd* [1988] AC 473 and *Lonrho plc v Tebbit* [1992] 4 All ER 280: exercises of ministerial discretion were, on the facts, policy matters.

56 [1989] AC 53.

57 [1993] 4 All ER 344.

58 And for application of the *Hill* ruling in cases involving the police see, among others, *Brooks v Metropolitan Police Commissioner* [2005] 2 All ER 489, *Smith v Chief Constable of Sussex* [2009] 1 AC 225, and *Michael v Chief Constable of South Wales Police* [2015] UKSC 2, [2015] AC 1732. Compare *Swinney v Chief Constable of the Northumbria Police* [1997] QB 464: police owed a duty of care to an individual who had supplied them with information about a crime that they then lost and which resulted with the individual being threatened.

59 [1995] 2 AC 633.

of action, whether for breach of statutory duty or negligence. The negligence point arose when the claimants argued that they had a cause of action in respect of the careless performance of a statutory duty (in addition to an action for a straight-forward breach of statutory duty). In finding that it had been correct to strike out the actions, the House of Lords held that the mere assertion that there had been a careless exercise of a statutory power or duty was not sufficient in itself to give rise to a private law cause of action. The plaintiff instead had to show that the circumstances were such as to give rise to a duty of care at common law, and the House of Lords concluded that no such duty was owed.

Lord Browne-Wilkinson, who delivered the leading judgment, began by emphasising that duties of care could never be owed where a decision was in the form of 'policy'—such matters are non-justiciable and beyond the reach of the courts. It therefore followed that duties could be imposed only where the decision at hand was not a policy decision and, moreover, where the decision was *ultra vires* in the sense that it was *Wednesbury* unreasonable. This latter requirement was based upon classic public law orthodoxy and his Lordship drew heavily on separation of powers considerations when emphasising:

> It is clear both in principle and from the decided cases that the local authority cannot be liable in damages for doing that which Parliament has authorised. Therefore if the decisions complained of fall within the ambit of such statutory discretion they cannot be actionable in common law. However, if the decision complained of is so unreasonable that it falls outside the ambit of the discretion conferred upon the local authority, there is no *a priori* reason for excluding all common law liability.[60]

In order to make out a claim an individual would thus have to show that each of the above requirements was met, and he or she would thereafter have to demonstrate that it would be 'fair, just and reasonable' to impose a duty on the facts of the case. As we have already explained above, the House of Lords held that it would not be fair and reasonable to impose a duty given the complexity of the overarching statutory framework and the corresponding public good being pursued.

We will shortly return to *X v Bedfordshire* but there are two points that can be made at this stage. The first relates to the striking out of actions as seen in the case. Striking out is a procedural mechanism that enables courts to control their calendar by disposing of cases at a preliminary stage when the assumed facts do not disclose a reasonable cause of action (the case will not then go to a full hearing). One consequence of the restrictive criteria laid down in *X v Bedfordshire* was that it became highly unlikely that future cases of a similar kind would disclose a reasonable cause of action; that is, the proceedings would be struck out (this is what happened in the *Osman* case, as heard in the light of *Hill*). Such striking out on the basis of 'no duty' was to become synonymous with the argument that certain categories of decisions enjoyed 'immunity' from suit because pleadings did not proceed beyond the preliminary stage. We will see that judicial concern to disprove that argument was one reason for subsequent modification of the approach to the imposition of duties of care (albeit that the case law has since returned, once more, to a more restrictive approach).

---

60 Ibid, 736. For earlier House of Lords authority to like effect, see *Home Office v Dorset Yacht* [1970] 2 All ER 294.

The second point concerns vicarious liability. In *X v Bedfordshire*, the claim in all of the child abuse and education cases was primarily against the authorities as directly liable for the loss suffered. However, another argument advanced by the claimants was that the authority was in turn vicariously liable for the actions of its employees. It is important to note that, while the law has since changed,[61] the House of Lords rejected the argument that the authorities could be vicariously liable in the child abuse cases on the ground that duties here would again complicate an already difficult task (it thus held that, while the employees owed a duty of care to their employer, they did not owe duties of care to the recipients of the service). The House of Lords did, however, envisage that authorities could be vicariously liable in education cases, as parents would here be working in tandem with the authority and its employees to achieve the best results for the affected children. This is a distinction that was to be of considerable significance in later education cases where claimants were able successfully to sue authorities in negligence.[62]

20.3.2 *Stovin v Wise* and statutory powers

A restrictive approach to the imposition of duties of care also underpinned the House of Lords ruling in *Stovin v Wise and Norfolk County Council*,[63] where the issue was whether duties could be owed in respect of a failure to exercise a statutory power (the failure corresponding with 'nonfeasance' rather than a positive act, or 'misfeasance'). Under section 79 of the Highways Act 1980, highway authorities have the power to require landowners to modify a land obstruction that presents a danger to the highway. The case, as originally brought, was between two private parties where the claimant sued the defendant for injuries suffered in an accident at a junction that was obscured by part of the defendant's land. However, the defendant joined the local authority as third party to the proceedings and argued that it was liable for the injuries. The defendant contended in particular that, as the authority had failed to follow up on proposals it had made about how to improve visibility at the junction, its omission made it liable.

In rejecting the defendant's argument Lord Hoffmann—who delivered the judgment on behalf of the majority—drew a distinction between positive acts that cause harm and omissions that are argued to cause harm. The distinction was significant as: 'there are sound reasons why omissions require different treatment from positive conduct. It is one thing for the law to say that a person who undertakes some activity shall take reasonable care not to cause damage to others. It is another thing for the law to require that a person who is doing nothing in particular shall take steps to prevent another from suffering harm from the acts of third parties or natural causes'.[64] Moreover, where the omission related to the non-exercise of statutory powers the distinction had an added force, and his Lordship identified criteria that were similar to those laid down in *X v Bedfordshire*. For a duty to be imposed a court would thus have to be satisfied, first, that 'it would in the circumstances have been irrational not to have exercised the power, so that

---

61 *D v East Berkshire Community Health NHS Trust* [2005] 2 AC 373.

62 *Phelps v Hillingdon London Borough Council* [2001] 2 AC 619, discussed below.

63 [1996] AC 923.

64 Ibid, 943.

there was in effect a public law duty to act, and secondly, that there are exceptional grounds for holding that the policy of the statute requires compensation to be paid to persons who suffer loss because the power was not exercised'.[65] On these criteria, no duty was owed.

20.4 A change in direction

The subsequent departure by the courts from the restrictive approach of *X v Bedfordshire* and *Stovin* was prompted by the coalescence of a number of considerations. One was that cases such as *X*, in which there were often extreme stories of abuse, simply demanded a remedy for the affected parties (Lord Browne-Wilkinson touched on the point in *X v Bedfordshire* when he said: 'the consideration which has first claim on the loyalty of the law is that wrongs should be remedied').[66] The facts of *X* were subsequently heard on human rights grounds by the European Court of Human Rights (ECtHR), which found, among other things, that there had been a violation of Article 3 of the ECHR's prohibition of inhuman and degrading treatment.[67] It may therefore have been that courts in the UK were already becoming aware that the common law was falling behind accepted minimum standards even before the ECtHR made clear that this was so.

Another consideration was concern that the striking out of proceedings on the grounds of 'no duty' was contrary to Article 6 of the ECHR's guarantee of access to a court. In *Osman v United Kingdom*[68]—the case was brought in the light of *Osman v Ferguson*, above—the ECtHR held that the striking out of proceedings on the basis of the *Hill* precedent/immunity was a disproportionate interference with Article 6 ECHR procedural rights (the ECtHR essentially ruled that Article 6 of the ECHR requires that all cases should be looked at on their merits, but that immunities precluded such analysis and resulted instead in an automatic procedural barrier on full access to courts).[69] Although the ECtHR was subsequently to rule that striking out does not have the effect of violating Article 6 of the ECHR,[70] the UK courts had already referred to *Osman* when deciding that they should be more cautious about preventing cases going to a full hearing on the facts. Indeed, given the above point about the common law needing to ensure remedies in the face of extreme abuse, a rethink about the practice of striking out may have been inevitable, notwithstanding the uncertainty in the ECtHR's case law.

20.4.1 *Barrett v Enfield* and *Phelps*

The case that heralded the change was *Barrett v Enfield London Borough Council*,[71] which was an appeal against a striking-out order. The case, discussed above at 20.2.1, again concerned decisions about child welfare, although the facts were distinguishable

---

65 Ibid, 953.
66 [1995] 2 AC 633, 749.
67 *Z v United Kingdom* (2002) 34 EHRR 97.
68 (2000) 29 EHRR 245.
69 For commentary see C Gearty, 'Unravelling *Osman*' (2001) 64 *Modern Law Review* 159
70 See C Gearty, '*Osman* Unravels' (2002) 65 *Modern Law Review* 86.
71 [2001] 2 AC 550.

from those in *X v Bedfordshire* as the issue here was whether there could be liability for decisions in respect of a child who had been taken into care (it was argued in *Barrett* that the defendant had been negligent by, among other things, moving the claimant amongst foster carers and thereby causing psychiatric injury). In modifying the criteria laid down in *X v Bedfordshire*, the House of Lords started by reiterating that there could be no liability for policy decisions, as these remained non-justiciable. However, their Lordships thereafter added a number of important qualifications. The first was that it was no longer desirable to use public law concepts of reasonableness when assessing liability for non-policy decisions, and that the question should instead simply be whether it would be fair, just, and reasonable to impose liability. Moreover, it was held that the question of whether there was a duty owed/whether a decision was non-justiciable was one that could only really be answered in the light of the full legal and factual circumstances of a case; in other words, that striking out would frustrate the full assessment of the matter on a case-by-case basis (Lord Browne-Wilkinson, while critical of the ECtHR, was here influenced by *Osman v UK*). The result was an approach that placed less emphasis on a prior need to show that a decision was justiciable and unlawful in a public law sense, and placed more emphasis on having a full hearing for the purposes of deciding whether it would be fair, just, and reasonable to impose a common law duty in respect of justiciable matters.

The House of Lords developed this revised approach in a number of subsequent cases. For example, in *W v Essex County Council*,[72] it was held that it had been wrong to strike out proceedings whereby children who had been sexually abused by a foster child sued, together with their parents, for psychiatric harm (the family had specifically requested that any child placed with them should not have a history of sexual abuse; the child in this case had such a history). And in *Phelps v Hillingdon London Borough Council*,[73] Lord Slynn stated that he considered that the *Barrett* criteria might allow for local authorities to be directly liable in damages in education cases too. In an important passage his Lordship stated:

I do not rule out the possibility of a direct claim in all situations where the local authority is exercising its powers. If it exercises its discretion by deciding to set up a particular scheme pursuant to a policy which it has lawfully adopted, there is no, or at least there is unlikely to be any, common law duty of care. If, however, it then, for example, appoints to carry out the duties in regard to children with special educational needs a psychologist or other professionals who at the outset transparently are neither qualified nor competent to carry out the duties, the position is different. That may be an unlikely scenario, but if it happens, I do not see why as a matter of principle a claim at common law in negligence should never be possible. Over-use of the distinction between policy and operational matters so as respectively to limit or create liability has been criticised, but there is some validity in the distinction. Just as the individual social worker in *Barrett v Enfield London Borough Council* could be 'negligent' in an operational manner . . . so it seems to me that the local education authority could in some circumstances owe a duty of care and be negligent in the performance of it. The fact that . . . consultation and appeal procedures exist . . . does not seem to me to lead to the conclusion that a duty of care does not and should not exist.[74]

Phelps is of further interest as the claimants in the case argued successfully that they should be able to sue the local authority as vicariously liable for the actions

72 [2000] 3 WLR 776.
73 [2001] 2 AC 619.
74 Ibid, 658.

of its employees.[75] The first three claimants were suffering from severe educational difficulties and were referred by the local authority to an expert educational psychologist who failed to identify dyslexia. It was argued that in each case severe problems were caused by the misdiagnosis, ranging from lack of educational progress, to social deprivation and psychiatric injury. The fourth claimant, G, was in turn a boy with Duchenne muscular dystrophy who had been removed from a mainstream school and transferred to a school with facilities for specific disabilities. It was argued that he had not been provided with computer technology and suitable training to cope educationally and that he had thereby suffered from lack of educational progress, social deprivation, and psychiatric injury in the form clinical depression.

It was held by the House of Lords that a person exercising a particular skill or profession might owe a duty of care in its performance, and that this was so in education as in other fields. This duty of care did not depend upon a contract between the parties and it was not affected by the fact that the employee owed a duty of care to his or her employer. The duty depended instead on whether there was the necessary 'nexus' for a duty to arise, something that depended on relations between the claimant, the employee, and the authority. It followed that where, for example, an educational psychologist was specifically asked to advise as to the assessment of and future provision for a child and it was clear that the child's parents and teachers would follow that advice, a *prima facie* duty of care arose. Moreover, it was clear that the local education authority was vicariously liable for a breach of that duty, notwithstanding that the authority itself may not be directly liable in damages (but see also Lord Slynn's comments above). In turn, the same principles were applicable to teachers, where local authorities would again be vicariously liable where teachers failed to exercise the skill and care of reasonable teachers when providing education.

20.4.2 More or less liability?

Do we now have a system in which there is increased public authority liability? *Barrett*, *W v Essex*, and *Phelps* certainly suggested such a change, and there was also some case law on policing in which it appeared that duties of care might more readily be imposed.[76] Indeed, even more notable given the facts of *X v Bedfordshire* and *Barrett* was the judgment of the Court of Appeal in *D v East Berkshire Community Health Trust*.[77] This case raised a number of important issues, key among which was whether it would ever be legitimate—in the light of common law developments and the Human Rights Act—to deny that duties of care are owed to children when an authority is investigating allegations of abuse with a view to pursuing care proceedings. In holding that there is an assumption that duties of care are owed to children by local authorities in such cases, the Court of Appeal stated that *X v Bedfordshire* should be read as restricted to its facts; that is, it provides a precedent only where decisions about whether to take children into care are in issue. Outside

---

75 Ibid, 658. D Fairgrieve, 'Pushing Back the Boundaries of Public Authority Liability: Tort Law Enters the Classroom' [2002] *Public Law* 288.

76 See, e.g., *Darker v Chief Constable of the West Midlands* [2000] WLR 747; and *L (A Minor) and P (Father) v Reading Borough Council and Chief Constable of Thames Valley Police* [2001] 1 WLR 1575.

77 [2004] 2 WLR 58.

such cases, the Court of Appeal emphasised that there is a clear understanding that duties should be owed to children, as the interests of the child are paramount and trump prior concerns about liability having a negative impact on the quality of service provision. The Court of Appeal also emphasised that this approach would allow protection at common law to parallel that under the ECHR, as cases of this kind would be embraced by Articles 3 and 8 of the ECHR (the Human Rights Act did not govern *D* itself as the facts pre-dated the date of its coming into force).[78]

On the other hand, there have been some countervailing lines of reasoning that make clear that duties of care will not be owed in all categories of cases. For instance, when *D v East Berkshire* was heard on appeal in the House of Lords (reported as *JD*),[79] it was held that duties of care are not owed to parents who are erroneously accused by health officials of having abused their children. This was the central issue in the appeal and, while the House of Lords apparently accepted that duties of care are owed to children,[80] it held that duties are not owed to parents as 'the well-being of innumerable children up and down the land depends crucially upon doctors and social workers . . . being subjected by the law to but a single duty: that of safeguarding the child's own welfare'.[81] Moreover, in an important line of case law involving the police, it has been confirmed that the *Hill* precedent is still to be followed. While the courts have acknowledged that *Hill* can no longer be applied in an unquestioning manner, they have nevertheless held that its essential point about public policy remains sound. In *Brooks v Metropolitan Police Commissioner*,[82] the House of Lords thus held that no duty of care had been owed to a victim of a crime who considered that the police had treated him more as a suspect rather than a victim when investigating the crime; while in *Smith*, it was held that no duty of care had been owed to a man who had been seriously injured by his former partner in circumstances where the man had alerted the police to threats that were being made against him by his former partner.[83] Most recently, the Supreme Court in *Michael* held that no duty of care had been owed in a case of domestic violence that resulted in death where technological and human error had delayed the police response to an emergency call: while the victim had tried to make use of an emergency response system, that system had been set up for the benefit of the public at large and it would not be correct for the public to have to bear the additional cost of paying compensation for harms that are caused by a third party for whom the state had no responsibility.[84]

One last point to be made under this heading is that, even if duties of care are owed in a particular case, it is to be remembered that the claimant must also establish 'breach' and 'causation'. We have already seen above how public law conceptions of unreasonableness may guide the courts when assessing whether an exercise of

---

78 See 4.4.6 on the non-retrospective effect of the Act. For a further example of a case being allowed to proceed to trial see *Smith v Ministry of Defence* [2013] UKSC 41, [2014] AC 52 (Supreme Court refused to strike out a claim brought by the family of soldiers who alleged negligence in the context of preparation for military operations in Iraq).

79 [2005] 2 AC 373. But see also *MAK v UK* (2010) 51 EHRR 14, noted below.

80 The point was not made explicitly during the ruling but can be deduced from the judgment as read with the House of Lords ruling in *Lambeth London Borough Council v Kay* [2006] 2 AC 465.

81 [2005] 2 AC 373, 422, Lord Brown.

82 [2005] 2 All ER 489.

83 *Smith v Chief Constable of Sussex Police* [2009] 1 AC 225.

84 *Michael v Chief Constable of South Wales Police* [2015] UKSC 2, [2015] AC 1732. See too, in relation to other public authorities, *Mitchell v Glasgow City Council* [2009] 1 AC 874; *Jain v Trent Strategic Health Authority* [2009] 1 AC 853; and *Gorringe v Calderdale Metropolitan Borough Council* [2004] 1 WLR 1057.

discretion has breached a duty of care—but see, too, our discussion of *Connor v Surrey County Council*[85]—and proving causation can also be difficult. The point can be seen in relation to facts of the kind in *Phelps* (although note some of the claimants in *Phelps* had successfully made out a claim). Litigants who argue that an erroneous diagnosis of dyslexia has caused educational difficulties and psychiatric harm must prove that there is a causal link between the misdiagnosis and loss. This requires proof that the defendant's actions caused the loss as a matter of fact (factual causation) and also that it was 'reasonably foreseeable' that the claimant would have suffered the loss (legal causation). Reasonable foreseeability is, in turn, a malleable test and, given previous judicial willingness to use flexible standards to prioritise preferred value judgements, it may be that the causation element, too, could result in authorities avoiding liability (whether direct or vicarious).[86] The duty of care is thus only one part of the equation and liability can be limited in other ways too.

20.5 The Human Rights Act and liability in tort

We have already made several references in this chapter to the impact that the ECHR has had on the tort liability of public authorities. Bringing those references together here, it is perhaps best to conceive of that impact as both indirect and direct in form. The indirect has occurred when the courts have referred to the principle and practice of the ECHR in cases where the relevant facts have pre-dated the Human Rights Act 1998 but where the courts have considered that the common law should develop in the light of the UK's international obligations.[87] On the other hand, the direct impact has been felt in cases that have been heard under the Human Rights Act 1998, where section 2 of the Act requires the courts to take into account the case law of the ECtHR when determining claims against public authorities. According to section 7 of the Act, those claims may be made either with sole reference to the ECHR or by adding ECHR points onto a more general claim based upon a common law cause of action.[88]

Where a claim is brought under the Act, section 8(3) provides for awards of damages where the court is satisfied that this is necessary to afford 'just satisfaction' to the person in whose favour the award is to be made (note that the term 'just satisfaction' corresponds directly with the language of Article 41 of the ECHR). Although there were some initial indications that the courts would adopt a liberal approach to damages under the Act,[89] it is now established that the courts will be cautious before making awards (albeit that all will depend on context and on the nature of the rights involved). The leading authority on the point remains *R*

---

85 [2011] QB 429.

86 For some cases that have failed in the education context see *Bradford-Smart v West Sussex County Council* [2002] ELR 139; *Liennard v Slough Borough Council* [2002] ELR 527; *Smith v Havering Borough Council* [2004] ELR 629; and *Carty v Croydon London Borough Council* [2005] 2 All ER 517. And for some cases that were successful see *DN v Greenwich London Borough Council* [2005] ELR 133; and *Devon County Council v Clarke* [2005] ELR 375.

87 e.g., *Barrett v Enfield London Borough Council* [2001] 2 AC 550, considered above.

88 On the Act and its key provisions, see ch 4.

89 *Anufrijeva v Southwark London Borough Council* [2004] 2 WLR 603.

(Greenfield) v Home Secretary,[90] which concerned the question whether a prisoner whose rights under Article 6 of the ECHR had been violated by a prison disciplinary procedure should receive damages in addition to a declaration that the respondent had acted unlawfully. In holding that a declaration was sufficient in the context of the case, the House of Lords emphasised that the ECtHR itself frequently does not make awards of damages in Article 6 ECHR cases, and that it tends to do so only where it finds a causal connection between the violation of Article 6 of the ECHR and any non-pecuniary loss for which the individual claims compensation. The House of Lords also emphasised that the Human Rights Act 1998 should not, in any event, be regarded as a tort statute that automatically gives rise to a remedy in damages, as the Act's objectives of ensuring compliance with human rights standards can in many cases be met simply through the finding of a violation. The Act, it was said, is not intended to give individuals access to better remedies than they would have were they to go to Strasbourg, but rather to incorporate in domestic law the ECtHR's case-by-case approach and to require domestic courts to have regard to that approach. On the facts of the case as read with the Strasbourg jurisprudence, there were thus no special features that warranted an award of damages.

Another case that is indicative of a conservative approach to damages claims—this time on the question whether a right had been violated—is *Van Colle v Chief Constable of Hertfordshire.*[91] The proceedings in this case were brought by the family of a man who was threatened and then murdered by a former employee against whom the deceased was due to give evidence in a criminal trial. The High Court and Court of Appeal both held that there had been a violation of the Article 2 ECHR right to life because witnesses are a particular class of persons who might be at risk on account of their links to state agents and because, on the facts, the police should have known that there was a threat to the victim's life. However, in the corresponding appeal to the House of Lords, it was held that Article 2 of the ECHR had not been violated, as the evidence did not show that the police had been aware of a 'real and immediate risk' to the life of the individual. According to the settled case law of the ECtHR, it is only when such knowledge is present that the state comes under a positive obligation to protect the individual, for instance by installing alarms at the individual's home and/or by patrolling in the vicinity of their neighbourhood.[92] But in this case the House of Lords was unanimous when allowing the Chief Constable's appeal for the reason that there had not been any obligation that required police action. While the Lords noted some evidence of erratic behaviour on the part of the killer, they cautioned against the dangers of hindsight, and stated that the central question was whether the police, 'making a reasonable and informed judgment on the facts and in the circumstances known to [them] at the time [should] have appreciated' the risk.[93] Chronicling how the police had been aware of only non-threatening approaches to other witnesses and some sinister phone contact between the deceased and his killer, the Lords concluded that there was insufficient evidence to justify the finding of a violation of

---

90 [2005] 2 All ER 240; applied in, e.g., *R (Sturnham) v Parole Board* [2013] UKSC 23, [2013] 2 AC 254.

91 [2009] 1 AC 225.

92 *Osman v UK* (2000) 29 EHRR 245. See further G Anthony, 'Positive Obligations and Policing in the House of Lords' (2009) *European Human Rights Law Review* 538.

93 [2009] 1 AC 225, 258 at [36], Lord Bingham.

Article 2 of the ECHR. The ECtHR likewise held that there had been no violation of Article 2 of the ECHR when the case was subsequently argued before it.[94]

A less restrictive approach to liability was, however, adopted by the Supreme Court in *Rabone v Pennine Care NHS Trust*.[95] This was a case brought by the parents of a woman who had been a voluntary psychiatric patient with the Trust and who had committed suicide while on a home visit. Her parents had brought and settled a negligence action under the Law Reform (Miscellaneous Provisions) Act 1934, and the key issues on appeal concerned Article 2 of the ECHR and whether the claim was time-barred as outside the one-year time limit for initiating proceedings under section 7 of the Human Rights Act 1998.[96] A first question, which was answered in the affirmative, was whether the Trust had owed the deceased an operational duty under Article 2 of the ECHR given that she was a voluntary patient (the Court discussed in detail the nature of the relationship between the deceased and the Trust when finding that the state's positive obligations had been engaged). A second question, again answered in the affirmative, was whether her parents could bring an Article 2 ECHR claim in their own name as section 7 'victims' who had suffered from bereavement.[97] This answer, which broadened the scope of 'victims' in cases involving Article 2 of the ECHR, gave rise to a third question about whether the settlement of the negligence action meant that the parents had impliedly waived their right to sue under Article 2 of the ECHR. Holding that the settlement did not have that effect, the Supreme Court observed, among other things, that the parents' claim in negligence had been taken on behalf of their daughter's estate, and that it did not compensate the parents for their bereavement. The Court also noted that the sum awarded to the estate, while reasonable, was not unduly generous and could not be said to provide adequate redress for the claim under Article 2 of the ECHR. On the facts, it was thus considered appropriate to extend the time limit for the claim—the extension sought was less than four months—and the Court awarded each of the claimants £5,000.

It is lastly to be noted under this heading that individuals can, as in *Van Colle*, still petition the ECtHR should they be unable to obtain a remedy in the domestic courts. There are many more examples that could be used further to illustrate the point, but the one that we will use is the progression from *JD v East Berkshire*[98] through to *MAK v UK*.[99] As we explained above, the House of Lords in *JD* was of the view that parents who were wrongly suspected of abusing their children had no remedy under the common law as the relevant health officials did not owe them a duty of care (neither could the parents sue under the Human Rights Act, as the facts in the case pre-dated the Act's coming into force). However, when the case went to the ECtHR as *MAK v UK*, the ECtHR found that there had been a violation of the Article 8 ECHR right to private and family life, as decisions taken in the light of the suspicion of abuse—among others, to limit the father's access to his daughter—had not been taken in accordance with the law. The ECtHR also held that the decision to strike out the proceedings for the reason that no duty of care was owed

94 *Van Colle v United Kingdom* (2013) 56 EHRR 23.
95 [2012] 2 WLR 381.
96 On which see 4.4.6.
97 On the victim requirement see 4.4.5 and 8.10.3.
98 [2005] 2 AC 373.
99 (2010) 51 EHRR 14.

was contrary to the right to an effective remedy under Article 13 of the ECHR. For the ECtHR, there was an arguable case that should have been heard rather than dismissed at a preliminary stage.

20.6 **Conclusion**

This chapter commenced by referring to the Diceyan understanding that there should be no distinction between the rules that govern the tort liability of public bodies and private individuals. However, since the 1970s that understanding has, in some important areas of activity, been rendered as something of a fiction. Although the negligence case law has ebbed and flowed between the imposition of duties of care on public authorities performing public functions, one constant has been a judicial concern to reconcile the competing interests of private individuals and those of the wider public. While the original trend was very much towards shielding the decisions of public bodies from liability, the decisions in *Barrett v Enfield* and *Phelps* seemingly placed a greater emphasis on the interests of the individual, or, in Fairgrieve's words, took society closer to a more consumerist version of liability.[100] But such exposure to liability raised again the more basic question of the financial implications for public bodies that must meet damages claims on a regular basis, and it would appear that the more recent decision-making of the House of Lords and Supreme Court has slowed the move towards increased liability. In any event, we would suggest that there is a need to explore alternatives to litigation and that, where proceedings are initiated, there should be limits on the amount of damages that can be obtained from public bodies performing public functions. We would also suggest that it would be better in this domain for government to provide further schemes of statutory regulation and, where appropriate, to increase the numbers of alternative remedies (for instance, ombudsmen applicable to the relevant public bodies).[101] In the absence of government doing so, it of course falls to the courts to try to balance the many competing interests on a case-by-case basis, while at the same time providing an overarching framework for principled analysis. However, that is something that 'no single decision is capable of' doing.[102]

FURTHER READING

Anthony, G (2006) 'The Negligence Liability of Public Authorities: Was the Old Law the Right Law?' 57 *Northern Ireland Legal Quarterly* 409.

Anthony, G (2009) 'Positive Obligations and Policing in the House of Lords' *European Human Rights Law Review* 538.

Bailey, SH and Bowman, MJ (1986) 'The Policy/Operational Dichotomy—A Cuckoo in the Nest' 45 *Cambridge Law Journal* 430.

---

100 [2001] 2 AC 619, 658. D Fairgrieve, 'Pushing Back the Boundaries of Public Authority Liability: Tort Law Enters the Classroom' [2002] *Public Law* 288, 307.

101 For an example of a statutory scheme governing damages see the Criminal Justice Act 1988, s 133, considered in *R (Adams) v Secretary of State for Justice* [2011] UKSC 18, [2012] 1 AC 48.

102 *Gorringe v Calderdale Metropolitan Borough Council* [2004] 1 WLR 1057, 1059, Lord Steyn.

Buckley, RA (2000) 'Negligence in the Public Sphere: Is Clarity Possible?' *Northern Ireland Legal Quarterly* 25.

Cornford, T [2009] 'Administrative Redress: The Law Commission's Consultation Paper' *Public Law* 70.

Fairgrieve, D [2002] 'Pushing Back the Boundaries of Public Authority Liability: Tort Law Enters the Classroom' *Public Law* 288.

Gearty, C (2001) 'Unravelling *Osman*' *Modern Law Review* 159.

Gearty, C (2002) '*Osman* Unravels' *Modern Law Review* 86.

Knight, CJS [2011] 'Constitutionality and Misfeasance in Public Office: Controlling the Tort' 16 *Judicial Review* 49.

Markesinis, BS, Auby, J-B, Coester-Waltjen, D, and Deakin, SF (1999) *Tortious Liability of Statutory Bodies* (Oxford: Hart Publishing).

Witting, C (2015), *Street on Torts*, 14th edn (Oxford: Oxford University Press).

Wright, J (2001) *Tort Law and Human Rights* (Oxford: Hart Publishing).

21

....

Conclusion: administrative law facing the future

21.1 Introduction: is there now a system of administrative law?

In this final chapter we conclude our discussion both by mentioning the likely impact of recent reforms and by attempting to draw together some of the central themes of the book. Our aim is to provide the reader with a brief evaluation of the state of administrative law as part of the current legal system.

If we cast our minds back to the remarks made by judges of an earlier generation, we find that there was a preoccupation with the creation of a system of administrative law remedies. For example, Lord Reid in *Ridge v Baldwin* commented: 'We did not have a developed system of administrative law—perhaps because until fairly recently we did not need it',[1] while Lord Diplock stated in *R v IRC, ex p National Federation for the Self Employed*, that: '[T]he progress towards a comprehensive system of administrative law . . . I regard as having been the greatest achievement of the English courts in my judicial lifetime'.[2] Now that some decades have passed since these prescient remarks were made, how far can it be said that we now have a settled *system* of administrative law?

As the reader will have observed in successive chapters of the text, there is a variety of methods of accountability which have become accepted features of the modern administrative state. The Administrative Court is now at the pinnacle of the system with its supervisory jurisdiction, but the seat of that jurisdiction has changed from being based exclusively in London to having regional centres in Birmingham, Manchester, Leeds, and Cardiff (Scottish law and Northern Irish law have their centres in Edinburgh and Belfast, respectively). Moreover, there has been a strong trend towards the introduction of a much more uniform and coordinated system of administrative justice, most obviously through the revised Tribunal Service that was launched in 2006. It comprises a network of tribunals presided over by tribunal judges and operating under common procedural rules. Indeed, the second phase of these reforms resulted in individual tribunal jurisdictions doing similar work (with the exception of the Employment and the Employment Appeals Tribunal) being brought together into a greatly simplified two-tier tribunals system—consisting of a First Tier and Upper Tribunal (see chapter 7).

As a result, at an intermediate level in the grievance chain we now have this unified tribunal service which is capable of delivering a significant improvement in

1 [1964] AC 40, 72.
2 [1982] AC 617, 641.

institutional performance for the citizen. In addition, there is an ever-increasing cohort of ombudsmen able to investigate a wide range of institutions, from central and local government, to other public and private bodies. In a rather different context, a series of schemes of statutory regulation have been introduced following the privatisation of industries previously in the public sector. At the same time, at the lowest level there has been an increasing concern to channel disputes away from formal legal remedies. Not only has the idea, if not the language, of the Citizens Charter been continued, with the more customer-orientated treatment of users, but also informal methods have been encouraged in the form of proportionate dispute resolution, independent non-statutory grievance handlers, and alternative dispute resolution (ADR) initiatives.[3] Back in 2001 Lord Woolf had stressed the paramount importance of avoiding litigation by first exploring the possibility of ADR.[4] The introduction of online dispute resolution (ODR) appears to be the latest manifestation of a trend towards broadening access to justice and at the same time resolving disputes more easily, quickly, and cheaply.[5] Indeed, in the current economic climate citizens faced with the scale of government cuts, including substantial reductions to the legal aid budget, may be forced to accept alternative remedies even where judicial resolution might be considered appropriate. In effect, such a trend is leading to a further rationing of judicial remedies. In fact it has been pointed out that: 'The harsh reality . . . is that public funds are not available to provide legal representation or advice to tribunal appellants as a matter of course and so . . . the emphasis must be on facilitating effective direct participation in tribunal proceedings.'[6] A similar emphasis on self-representation with assistance from facilitators and/or adjudicators characterises many of the forms of ADR now available to the citizen.

At the highest remedial level in the public domain, the assertion of the rule of law through ongoing development of judicial review has been our central theme. The courts re-emerged, in a public law sense, during the latter part of the twentieth century as an increasingly important institution. As we have seen, they have consolidated their role by frequently—though not always—protecting citizens from the arbitrary actions of those in authority. That said, judicial review can be a very expensive remedy, and it should be noted that the rules of procedure have recently been modified by the Criminal Justice and Courts Act 2015, ostensibly to deter 'unmeritorious applications' whilst at the same time reducing the burden on the public purse. Although proposals to change the rules of standing were eventually dropped at the Bill stage, there is concern that changes to the way Public Costs Orders (PCOs) are awarded could significantly increase the financial exposure for claimants in judicial review cases. One critic concludes that: 'For the sake of promoting efficient public decision-making, judicial review has been weakened by the Criminal Justice and Courts Act 2015, and with it the protection of the rule of law'.[7]

3 PASC, *Citizen's Charter to Public Service Guarantees: Entitlement to Public Services*, HC411 (2007/8).

4 See *Cowl v Plymouth City Council* [2001] EWCA 1935.

5 See R Susskind, 'Online Dispute Resolution: For Low Value Civil Claims', February 2015: <https://www.judiciary.gov.uk/wp-content/uploads/2015/02/Online-Dispute-Resolution-Final-Web-Version1.pdf>.

6 M Elliott, 'Ombudsmen, Tribunals, Inquiries: Re-fashioning Accountability Beyond the Courts' in N Bamforth and P Leyland (eds), *Accountability in the Contemporary Constitution* (Oxford: Oxford University Press, 2013), 239. See also the discussion of *Unison* [2014] EWHC 4198 (Admin), [2015] EWCA Civ 935 at 7.41.

7 A Mills, 'Reforms to Judicial Review in the Criminal Justice and Courts Act 2015: Promoting Efficiency or Weakening the Rule of Law?' [2015] *Public Law* 583, 593–4.

21.2 **United Kingdom Supreme Court**

The introduction of a Supreme Court for the United Kingdom in 2009 in place of the Appellate Committee of the House of Lords as the highest domestic appellate court perhaps remains the most prominent reform of recent years. Apart from acquiring competence in relation to devolution issues—matters that were previously heard by the Judicial Committee of the Privy Council—the Supreme Court of 12 Justices has the same jurisdiction as the House of Lords. The Constitutional Reform Act 2005 formally recognises the constitutional importance of judicial independence and the rule of law.[8] Now the existence of the Supreme Court in its own building on one side of Parliament Square has become the physical embodiment of the principle, but the issue for some commentators is whether the Supreme Court should evolve into a US-style Supreme Court having the final word on constitutional issues, including the constitutionality of Acts of the Westminster Parliament. Already, the constitutional importance of some of its decisions is reflected in the fact that, in common with its predecessor, the Court often sits as a panel of nine or seven judges, rather than the traditional five.

Instead of remaining largely isolated from public debate, individual members of the judiciary can now be associated with high-profile decisions.[9] As with appointments to the United States Supreme Court, such exposure to political controversy could lead to judicial careers in the UK, particularly at the highest levels, becoming influenced by political rather than legal considerations. Given these additional pressures, it is crucial that the provisions of the Constitutional Reform Act 2005 relating to judicial appointments are successful in maintaining the independence of the judiciary from everyday politics. Indeed, it is vitally important that the Supreme Courts' political impartiality is maintained. Clearly, this will depend on the appointment process for Justices to the Supreme Court. The task is now undertaken by an *ad hoc* selection commission consisting of not less than five members including one non-legally qualified member, one member of the Court itself, together with representatives of the Judicial Appointments Commission for England and Wales and the equivalent bodies in Scotland and Northern Ireland.[10] The selection process is structured in such a way as to ensure that the Court will have knowledge and practical experience of the law of each part of the UK.[11] To date, the candidates who have been selected have been recognised as qualified for the task on merit. Supreme Court judges appointed following the abolition of the Appellate Committee of the House of Lords are still given the title 'Lord', but do not have the right to participate in the legislative proceedings of the House of Lords while serving as judges.

The senior judiciary is more exposed to public controversy than ever before, in part because, as we have observed in previous chapters, it increasingly finds itself being asked to determine matters with a strong political and moral content. For instance, some months after the 2010 general election, a decision by the Secretary of State for Education to cancel a national scheme for school building introduced

---

8 Section 3.

9 As in, e.g., *R v Bow Street Metropolitan Stipendiary Magistrates, ex p Pinochet Ugarte (No 2)* [1999] 1 AC 119, discussed at 17.4.2.2.

10 Constitutional Reform Act 2005, s 27.

11 Constitutional Reform Act 2005, s 27(8).

by the previous government was challenged in the courts.[12] The claim succeeded on procedural grounds and, while this is not insignificant, it is noteworthy that the High Court adopted a decidedly orthodox approach to arguments based upon irrationality and substantive legitimate expectation.[13] We return to that orthodoxy—and what it means for the judicial role more generally—below.

21.3 Freedom of information

The heightened transparency of public bodies in the way they operate is another important factor, especially since the Freedom of Information Act 2000 came fully into force on 1 January 2005. The legislation was subjected to strong criticism by academic commentators. In particular, adverse comment has concentrated on the formidable list of exempted categories of information set out in Part II of the Act and the inclusion of a mere test of 'prejudice' (rather than 'substantial prejudice') which is employed to establish whether information can be withheld by public bodies.[14] A further contentious issue, recently contested before the UK Supreme Court,[15] is the ministerial override in regard to decisions to order disclosure in accordance with the Act. Under section 53, the Justice Secretary and the Attorney General are granted the power to veto a finding that contested information should be disclosed. Several cases have arisen where government has invoked exemptions under the Act. In determining the issue, the Commissioner and Tribunal have not accepted that the status of information will automatically make it exempt. Professor Birkinshaw observes that they 'have not been easily impressed by official pleas of damage to civil service impartiality, neutrality or effectiveness in using the public interest override to disclose advice to ministers'.[16] In practice, the ministerial veto of disclosures ordered by the Commissioner and Tribunal has rarely been used. Moreover, the Supreme Court's decision in *Evans* sets limits on the exercise of the discretion of the executive under section 53. In upholding the Court of Appeal's ruling that quashed the Attorney General's decision to exercise the veto, the Supreme Court held that 'reasonable grounds' were necessary in order to issue a certificate overturning a *judicial* decision by the Upper Tribunal. 'Reasoned grounds' were therefore interpreted as requiring the clearest possible justification amounting to an even higher threshold. It was not enough for the minister to come to a radically different conclusion on the factual position; rather a full explanation would be required as to why the original tribunal was wrong in making its findings.

It can be concluded that the Freedom of Information Act has had an important effect on administrative law and administrative practice in several ways. First, it has given citizens a general 'right to know', which means not only that many types

---

12 *R (On the application of Luton et al) v Secretary of State for Education* [2011] EWHC 556 (Admin).

13 On these grounds for challenging decisions see chs 13 and 15, respectively.

14 S Palmer, 'Freedom of Information: A New Constitutional Landscape' in N Bamforth and P Leyland (eds), *Public Law in a Multi-Layered Constitution* (Oxford: Hart Publishing, 2003), 234ff.

15 *R (Evans) v Attorney General* [2015] UKSC 21, [2015] AC 1787.

16 P Birkinshaw, 'Regulating Information' in J Jowell, D Oliver, and O'Cinneide (eds), *The Changing Constitution*, 8th edn (Oxford: Oxford University Press, 2015), 399.

of information can now be demanded on request from thousands of public bodies, but also that much more information will routinely be made available. Secondly, under the Act many public bodies such as local authorities are required to adopt publication schemes covering wider categories of information. Indeed, both the above trends towards disclosure are further encouraged by the prevalence of e-government initiatives. Thirdly, the Information Commissioner has been granted an important role in policing the implementation of the Act, which encourages general compliance with its provisions. Fourthly, the right to know gives added impetus to the trend towards making reasons for decisions available right across the spectrum of administrative decision-making by public bodies. In turn, the availability of reasons facilitates challenges to decisions at all levels and makes obtaining a remedy more straightforward.

21.4 **Constitutional codification and the proposed reform of the Human Rights Act 1998**

In addition to the Constitutional Reform Act and the Freedom of Information Act, there have been a series of other far-reaching constitutional changes. The province of administrative law in the United Kingdom is now bounded by a battery of 'constitutional statutes', including the devolution legislation, the Human Rights Act 1998, the House of Lords Act 1999, the Constitutional Reform and Governance Act 2010, and the Fixed Term Parliament Act 2011 (there are earlier constitutional statutes too, notably the European Communities Act 1972).[17] This move towards progressively codifying key aspects of the constitution has redefined the relationship between Parliament, the executive, and the courts in a wide range of different contexts. It can be argued that the greater visibility of judicial review, allied to such recent constitutional changes, means that the modern judiciary have a new role and that this represents a silent shift in the balance of the constitution, and hence of administrative law, with the courts reacting over the last 40 years to the increase in the powers of government, to charges of elective dictatorship, and to failings in parliamentary accountability. This has led to a rediscovery of the kind of judicial assertiveness that is associated with historical rulings on, among other things, the right to hearing. For example, we have discussed in chapters 11 to 17 the development of the wide-ranging grounds for review that are structured around concepts such as 'abuse of power' and 'substantive fairness'. More recently, Parliament has surrendered some of its own powers to the courts in the shape of the Human Rights Act 1988,[18] leaving the courts with responsibility for making the final judgment on matters of an essentially political and moral nature by, among other things, using the proportionality standard of review.

The Human Rights Act itself was welcomed for achieving the 'reconciliation of the inevitable tension between the democratic right of the majority to exercise political power through the legislative process; and the democratic need of

---

17 On the nature of 'constitutional statutes' see 2.2 and 3.3.2.
18 See ch 4.

individuals and minorities to have their rights secured'.[19] Indeed, the government stated in debates on the Human Rights Bill in Parliament that the Act would be likely to lead the judges to develop new causes of action, for instance in relation to privacy.[20] The prospect of handing such potentially wide-ranging power over to the judiciary has led to concerns about judicial intrusions into politics, a matter we return to in the next section. In a different sense, critics have pointed out that a serious deficiency with the Human Rights Act regime is that the European Convention on Human Rights (ECHR) lacks democratic legitimacy and that the European Court of Human Rights (ECtHR) needs to be reformed.[21]

At a more general level, it might be doubted whether the Human Rights Act has actually caused the revolution in legal reasoning that some commentators had anticipated.[22] Rather, it might be said that the jurisprudence has been more notable for a general reluctance to go beyond traditional boundaries in order to provide a remedy. Indeed, it has been argued that there has been continuing judicial restraint (viewed historically such restraint can be regarded as a recurrent feature of judicial approaches during the course of the twentieth century), which was often at its most pronounced in the very areas where a more robust stance might have been expected for the protection of basic individual rights.[23] The courts have not only sometimes been reluctant to challenge policy decisions in the domain of national security and public safety, but they also failed in a number of instances to intervene decisively where an abuse of power by public authorities had occurred, resulting in substantial infringements of individual rights. While a case like *Bank Mellat* perhaps shows that the courts will sometimes constrain executive choices,[24] there are other rulings that have pointed towards ready restraint in the face of legislative and executive preferences.[25] Indeed, in some cases in which the UK courts have held that there has not been any violation of Convention rights, the ECtHR has subsequently found the UK to have been in breach of its international obligations.[26]

Nevertheless, since they are required to decide (compatibility with ECHR rights) all cases brought before them, the conferral of greater power on the courts by means of the Human Rights Act has become increasingly important in public law. The government itself had previously been accused of eroding individual rights by introducing the Anti-terrorism, Crime and Security Act 2001,[27] and the decision by a nine-panel Appellate Committee of the House of Lords in *A v Home Secretary*[28]

---

19 Lord Irvine <http://webarchive.nationalarchives.gov.uk/+/http://www.dca.gov.uk/speeches/1998/lc-const.htm>.

20 And see now *Campbell v Mirror Group Newspapers* [2004] 2 AC 457 and, e.g., *Weller v Associated Newspapers* [2015] EWCA Civ 1176.

21 See most notably the Brighton Declaration on ECHR reform 2012.

22 See T Campbell, K Ewing, and A Tomkins (eds), *The Legal Protection of Human Rights: Sceptical Essays* (Oxford: Oxford University Press, 2011), 1.

23 For an earlier account to this effect see K Ewing, 'The Futility of the Human Rights Act' [2004] *Public Law* 829.

24 *Bank Mellat v HM Treasury (No 2)* [2013] UKSC 38 & 39, [2014] AC 700, discussed at 12.7.1.

25 On the Act see further B Dickson, *Human Rights and the United Kingdom Supreme Court* (Oxford: Oxford University Press, 2013).

26 Compare and contrast *R (on the application of Gillan and Quinton) v Metropolitan Police Commissioner* [2006] 2 AC 307 and *Gillan v UK* (2010) EHRR 45.

27 A Tomkins, 'Legislating Against Terror: The Anti-terrorism, Crime and Security Act 2001' [2002] *Public Law* 205.

28 [2005] 2 AC 68.

to quash delegated legislation and issue a declaration of incompatibility in respect of the Act of 2001 remains one of the landmark decisions of the Human Rights Act era. During the course of his analysis of the respective roles of Parliament, the executive, and the judiciary, Lord Bingham decisively rejected a distinction that the Attorney General had attempted to draw between democratic institutions and the courts. He maintained:

> ... the function of independent judges charged to interpret and apply the law is universally recognised as a cardinal feature of the modern democratic state, a cornerstone of the rule of law itself. The Attorney General ... is wrong to stigmatise judicial decision-making as in some way undemocratic. It is particularly inappropriate in a case such as the present in which Parliament has expressly legislated in section 6 of the 1998 Act to render unlawful any act of a public authority, including a court, incompatible with a Convention right, has required courts (in section 2) to take account of relevant Strasbourg jurisprudence, has (in section 3) required courts, so far as possible, to give effect to Convention rights and has conferred a right of appeal on derogation issues.[29]

In relation to the impact on individual rights of what was regarded as flawed legislation, it was explained by Lord Hope that:

> The Secretary of State was, of course, entitled to discriminate between British nationals on the one hand and foreign nationals on the other for all the purposes of immigration control, subject to the limitations established by the *Chahal* case. What he was not entitled to do was to treat the right to liberty under article 5 of the Convention of foreign nationals who happen to be in this country for whatever reason as different in any respect from that enjoyed by British nationals ... Put another way, the margin of the discretionary judgment that the courts will accord to the executive and to Parliament where this right is in issue is narrower than will be appropriate in other contexts.[30]

Of course, the above has all occurred precisely because the Human Rights Act 1998 has been in force, and this is a state of affairs that may not be guaranteed. There is, at the time of writing, a growing hostility towards Europe among some political groupings in the UK, which is manifest in the question whether the UK should leave the EU ('Brexit') and also whether the Human Rights Act 1998 should be repealed.[31] On the issue of repeal of the Human Rights Act 1998, the Conservative Party pledged in its 2015 election manifesto to replace it with a 'British Bill of Rights and Responsibilities', but it may be that it would be difficult for the current government to achieve such an outcome.[32] As explained in chapter 4, in the absence of a constitutional charter of citizen rights, the Human Rights Act gives effect to the ECHR as part of our UK domestic law, which means that UK citizens can directly seek protection of their rights under the ECHR in domestic courts. Moreover, the courts, while not being bound by the ECHR, are required to take Strasbourg jurisprudence into account when applying the law. Repeal or reform of the Human Rights Act raises a series of complex and controversial challenges. To name but a few: first, and most obvious, is the question whether it would be possible to reach an agreement (let alone consensus) between and within political parties on

---

29 Ibid, 110.

30 Ibid, 134.

31 On Brexit see the European Union Referendum Act 2015; and 4.1.

32 S Dimelow and AL Young, *'Common Sense' or Confusion? The Human Rights Act and the Conservative Party* (London: The Constitution Society, 2015).

the text of a replacement, UK inspired alternative.[33] Secondly, there are critics of the Human Rights Act who regard reform as an opportunity to extricate the UK from the influence of Strasbourg, which raises the further question of whether any reformed version that dilutes the rights recognised by Strasbourg would be compatible with our international obligations under the ECHR (to go a stage further and withdraw from the ECHR would put the UK out of step with its European partners). Thirdly, the Human Rights Act applies to the UK as a whole, which means that consultation with the devolved governments in Edinburgh, Cardiff, and Belfast, with a view to reaching a general consensus, would be essential. For instance, there is no evidence of any backing for a UK Bill of Rights at the devolved level, and any attempt to proceed with reform without support in Scotland, Wales, and Northern Ireland would undermine both the letter and spirit of the devolution settlement (including the Good Friday Agreement negotiated with the government of the Republic of Ireland). In other words, repeal of the Human Rights Act could fatally threaten the integrity of the UK state against a backdrop of the current momentum for change generated by the referendum on Scottish independence. Fourthly, the Human Rights Act has gone some way towards establishing a culture of rights by allowing challenges to be brought to the decisions and policies of public authorities and by requiring the courts to identify minimum legal standards in the corresponding case law. Given the UK's common law tradition, it might be expected that, even if the Act itself were to be repealed, its legacy might remain, as the courts may well draw upon their experience with the Act when interpreting any UK Bill of Rights.[34] With the above considerations in mind, it is not surprising that at the time of writing (January 2016) there is no sign of the publication by the government of draft legislation for a UK Bill of Rights.

21.5 A balanced constitution?

As noted above, the launch of the UK Supreme Court in 2009 coincided with a continuing debate over the judicial role within a substantially reformed constitution. Despite extending the jurisdiction of the new court to cover devolution issues arising under the Scotland Act 1998, the Government of Wales Acts 1998 and 2006, and the Northern Ireland Act 1998, in implementing this change the government had no intention of creating a Constitutional Court. However, it has been argued in some quarters that the heavy-handed exercise of executive power should be redressed at a constitutional level, especially as parliamentary oversight of legislation and of the executive is very often ineffective under the Whitehall model, which usually sees the government predominate in Parliament.[35] Some judges and academics contemplate a shift towards a judicial constitution. For instance, in *R (Jackson) v Attorney General*,[36] where there was an unsuccessful challenge to the

---

33 Such disagreements exist within the main political parties, including the Conservative Party, as was vividly demonstrated by the inconclusive report of the Human Rights Commission set up under the Conservative–Liberal Coalition Government.

34 On the potential within the common law see, e.g., *Re Reilly* [2013] UKSC 61, [2014] AC 1115.

35 See 2.4.

36 [2006] 1 AC 262.

validity of primary legislation in the form of the Hunting Act 2004, three of the Law Lords made *obiter* statements which suggested that primary legislation might successfully be challenged in the courts. Lord Hope opined that: 'The Rule of Law enforced by the courts is the controlling principle upon which our constitution is based.'[37] Lord Steyn believed that: 'In exceptional circumstances involving an attempt to abolish judicial review or the authority of the courts, the courts may have to consider whether this is a constitutional fundamental which even a complaisant House of Commons cannot abolish.'[38] Baroness Hale stated that: 'The Courts will treat with particular suspicion (and might even reject) any attempt to subvert the rule of law by removing governmental action affecting the rights of the individual from all judicial powers.'[39]

On the other hand, there have always been objections to the judicial resolution of political, moral, and ethical disagreements at a constitutional level. Echoing the famous defence of the 'Political Constitution' by Professor Griffith, it could be argued that any change towards judicial supremacy would raise issues of legitimacy and could potentially undermine the political process. As Professor Waldron explains in a recent discussion of this issue:

By privileging majority voting among a small number of unelected and unaccountable judges, it disenfranchises ordinary citizens and brushes aside cherished principles of representation and political equality in the final resolution of issues about rights.

Secondly, Waldron considers that judicial resolution does not:

. . . provide a way for society to focus clearly on the real issues at stake when citizens disagree about rights; on the contrary, it distracts them with side-issues about precedent, texts and interpretation . . . By the time cases reach the high appellate levels we are mostly talking in our disputes about judicial review, almost all trace of the original flesh-and-blood right-holders has vanished, and argument such as it is revolves around the abstract issue of the right in dispute. Plaintiffs or petitioners [i.e. claimants] are selected by advocacy groups precisely in order to embody the abstract characteristics that the groups want to emphasize as part of a general public policy argument.

On this view, where issues of rights are in need of settlement, there need to be legitimate decision-making procedures which are part of the democratic process as a response to the problem of settling disagreement. In particular, 'legislatures are better placed to assess the importance of an individual case in relation to a general issue of rights which might affect millions . . .'[40]

Before summarising our thoughts on this issue it is worth noting that, in concluding his study of the British Constitution, Professor King observed that:

The judges have further augmented their role all by themselves. Having been sleeping partners in the British system, they have gradually over several decades become extremely active partners. They have ceased to be, in effect, the servants of the government of the day and have instead become its assertive and sometimes unruly tormentors. They still know their place, but their conception of their place has changed. They have effectively rewritten their brief so that it now encompasses not only procedural due process but substantive due

---

37 Ibid, 304.

38 Ibid, 303.

39 Ibid, 318.

40 J Waldron, 'The Core of the Case Against Judicial Review' (2006) 115 *The Yale Law Journal* 1346, 1353 and 1379–80.

process. Public Authorities not only have to take decisions following the proper procedure: their decisions have to be rational and defensible . . . [41]

This assessment summarises nicely a prevailing view which recognises the positive aspects of a higher judicial profile as a constitutional counterweight to what, under the Whitehall model, is regarded as a trend towards executive dominance. However, it is important to note the emphasis here on the judges 'knowing their place' in redefining the limits of their judicial power. In a much commented upon lecture, Jonathan Sumption QC, a high profile Justice of the Supreme Court, spoke of the need for judges to be wary of trespassing into areas in which political choices should be made, not judicial ones.[42] His comments were to draw something of a rebuke from a number of former judges, who are firmly of the view that the development of a more far-reaching judicial review jurisdiction was carefully tailored with separation of powers considerations in mind.[43] Whichever view is correct, we are left with an ongoing debate about the judicial role, where the really controversial issue is whether judges should have the power to subject primary legislation to some form of review within the framework of a written constitution. At the heart of all this is the need to maintain an appropriate balance between the executive, legislative, and judicial branches, and, if the judges become too activist, this might only provoke a backlash from the political classes. At that stage, the very idea of balance in the constitution might be lost. As Lord Bingham expressed it:

To substitute the sovereignty of a codified and entrenched constitution for the sovereignty of Parliament is . . . a major constitutional change. It is one which should be made only if the British people, properly informed, choose to make it.[44]

21.6 **Conclusion**

Returning to the specifically legal contribution to the grievance chain, we have seen the extension of the grounds of review to include proportionality and human rights principles, whether on the basis of the common law, EU law, and/or the Human Rights Act. The time-honoured principle of fairness has now been augmented by the doctrine of legitimate expectation, both procedural and substantive; and there is also a standard test of bias consistent with other Commonwealth jurisdictions. Further, the need for reasons for a decision has been recognised across a large and diverse range of public and private bodies. Standing has been generously defined to include not only individuals but also public interest actions by a wide variety of pressure groups (albeit that a more restrictive approach is required where cases are brought under section 7 of the Human Rights Act). Not least, the remedies have been standardised so as to provide a broad, flexible, and adaptive

---

41 A King, *The British Constitution* (Oxford: Oxford University Press, 2007), 346.

42 J Sumption, 'Judicial and Political Decision-making: The Uncertain Boundary' [2011] 16 *Judicial Review* 301.

43 e.g., Sir Stephen Sedley, 'Judicial Politics' [2012] 17 *Judicial Review* 95.

44 T Bingham, *The Rule of Law* (London: Allen Lane, 2010), 170. On options for a written constitution see R Gordon, *Repairing British Politics: A Blueprint for Constitutional Change* (Oxford: Hart Publishing, 2010).

set of solutions for grievances alleged by the citizen, provided by the courts at their discretion.

If we agree that there is now an identifiable system of administrative law, how democratic is it, and where might this lead in the future? Remembering the remarks of Lord Reid and Lord Diplock above, we appear to have travelled a long way towards the goal they outlined. However, there are a number of frequently reiterated criticisms. The first might be that the boundaries of the state, as defined 30 years ago, have now been modified, so that 'public law' finds itself in the position of applying to a shrunken concept of the 'public' as opposed to the 'private' sphere of social life.[45] Another view would emphasise that the development of administrative law has adverse implications for parliamentary democracy and citizen participation.[46] A third concerns the fact that public law has little real potency as a check on governmental action because only a small proportion of decisions of administrative bodies are ever challenged. In particular, judicial review remains at the margins of political, economic, and social issues of concern to the public at large, in that it is concentrated on a relatively small number of areas, for example, immigration and housing.[47]

More radically, the boundaries of the state can never be precisely predetermined because the margins of governmental and non-governmental institutions (and definitions of power) are constantly shifting.[48] The result of this basic ambiguity is that no sharp cut-off point can readily be discerned in correcting alleged abuses of power, whether nominally located in the 'public sector' or in the 'private sector'. It is argued from this perspective that a democratic public law should be applicable to corporations and to all discrete levels of economic activity, for example, concerning the workforce, healthcare, and safety at work. However, what are the limits of a democratic public law? For there is no neutral space within which law operates, since it is always contextualised by the political, economic, and social environment within which it has originated, and which gives it its meaning and purpose.

Perhaps the most important, if rarely discussed, element is the context within which administrative law operates, because this reveals the inextricable nature of constitutional and administrative law, and their connection to political, economic, and social theories, as well as the dominant policy issues of the day.[49] In particular, the range of conservative, liberal, social-democratic, and socialist thought (as well as more recent ideas of a 'green' politics or a 'third way') helps us to understand not only the origins and evolution of modern administrative law, but also the nature and utility of its central concepts as they change by way of meeting new social pressures and concerns. Further, it indicates that their meaning will inevitably vary, indeed be dependent upon, the framework provided by constitutions and their attendant political processes, for example, what has been termed the United States model and the European model of contemporary capitalist societies. Moreover, the rights accorded to citizen participation in the

45 I Holliday, 'Is the British State Hollowing Out?' (2000) *Political Quarterly* 166–77.

46 See generally, A Tomkins, *Our Republican Constitution* (Oxford: Hart Publishing, 2005).

47 M Sunkin and K Pick, 'The Changing Impact of Judicial Review: The Independent Review Service of the Social Fund' [2001] *Public Law* 736.

48 M Foucault, *Power/Knowledge* (C Gordon, ed), *Selected Interviews and Other Writings* 1972–1977 (Brighton: The Harvester Press, 1980).

49 C Harlow and R Rawlings, *Law and Administration*, 3rd edn (Cambridge: Cambridge University Press, 2009).

administrative system with respect to welfare rights for claimants, employment rights, or, more generally, access to justice will ultimately depend upon which variety of political theory is held by individuals and groups in society at any one time and, in particular, which of them is held by the élites. In turn, the balance prevalent among them will determine to a considerable extent how important issues come before the courts. This takes us a long way from what Dicey described in the late nineteenth century as a 'self correcting democracy'. If we have found a balance today, have we found the right one? Or is any such balance always going to be imperfect and contingent?

FURTHER READING

Allan, T (2013) 'Accountability to Law' in Bamforth, N and Leyland, P (eds), *Accountability in the Contemporary Constitution* (Oxford: Oxford University Press).

Allison, JWF (2007) 'Variation of View on English Legal Distinctions between Public and Private' *Cambridge Law Journal* 66(3) 698–711.

Bamforth, N and Leyland, P (2013) 'Introduction: Accountability in the Contemporary Constitution' in Bamforth, N and Leyland, P (eds), *Accountability in the Contemporary Constitution* (Oxford: Oxford University Press).

Bingham, T (2010) *The Rule of Law* (London: Allen Lane).

Craig, P (2015) *UK, EU and Global Administrative Law: Foundations and Challenges* (Cambridge: Cambridge University Press).

Dickson, B (2013) *Human Rights and the United Kingdom Supreme Court* (Oxford: Oxford University Press).

Fredman S (2013) 'Adjudication as Accountability: A Deliberative Approach' in Bamforth, N and Leyland, P (eds), *Accountability in the Contemporary Constitution* (Oxford: Oxford University Press).

Gearty, C (2002) 'Reconciling Parliamentary Democracy and Human Rights' 118 *Law Quarterly Review* 248.

Griffith, JAG (1997) *The Politics of the Judiciary*, 5th edn (London: Fontana Press).

Harlow, C and Rawlings, R (2009) *Law and Administration*, 3rd edn (Cambridge: Cambridge University Press).

King, J (2013) 'The Instrumental Value of Legal Accountability' in Bamforth, N and Leyland, P (eds), *Accountability in the Contemporary Constitution* (Oxford: Oxford University Press).

Le Sueur, A (2013) 'Parliamentary Accountability and the Judicial System' in Bamforth, N and Leyland, P (eds), *Accountability in the Contemporary Constitution* (Oxford: Oxford University Press).

Lever, A [2007] 'Is Judicial Review Undemocratic' *Public Law* 280.

Leyland, P (2016) *The Constitution of the United Kingdom: A Contextual Analysis*, 3rd edn (Oxford: Hart Publishing).

Loughlin, M (1992) *Public Law and Political Theory* (Oxford: Clarendon Press).

Loughlin, M (1999) *Sword and Scales: an Introduction to Law and Politics* (Oxford: Hart Publishing).

Loughlin, M (2010) *The Foundations of Public Law* (Oxford: Oxford University Press).

Mills, A [2015] 'Reforms to Judicial Review in the Criminal Justice and Courts Act 2015: Promoting Efficiency or Weakening the Rule of Law?' *Public Law* 583.

O'Cinneide, C (2013) 'Legal Accountability and Social Justice' in Bamforth, N and Leyland, P (eds), *Accountability in the Contemporary Constitution* (Oxford: Oxford University Press).

Poole, T (2005) 'Legitimacy, Rights and Judicial Review' 25(4) *OJLS*, 697–725.

Rawlings, R (2005) 'Review, Revenge and Retreat' 68 *Modern Law Review* 378–410.

Sedley, S (1999) *Freedom, Law and Justice* (London: Sweet & Maxwell).

Sedley, S (2012) 'Judicial Politics' *London Review of Books* 34(4): 23 February 2012.

Special Issue (2004) 'Constitutional Innovation: The Creation of a Supreme Court for the United Kingdom; Domestic, Comparative and International Reflections' 24(1) and (2) *Legal Studies*.

Sumption, J [2011] 'Judicial and Political Decision-making: The Uncertain Boundary' *Judicial Review* 301.

Taggart, M [1999] 'Reinvented Government, Traffic Lights and the Convergence of Public Law and Private Law' *Public Law* 124.

Tomkins, A (2005) *Our Republican Constitution* (Oxford: Hart Publishing).

Waldron, J (2006) 'The Core of the Case Against Judicial Review' 115 *The Yale Law Journal*, 1346–1406.

Windlesham, Lord [2006] 'The Constitutional Reform Act 2005: the Politics of Constitutional Reform' *Public Law* 35.

Young, AL (2013) 'Accountability, Human Rights Adjudication and the Human Rights Act 1998' in Bamforth, N and Leyland, P (eds), *Accountability in the Contemporary Constitution* (Oxford: Oxford University Press).

INDEX